# Scholarship and Nation Building

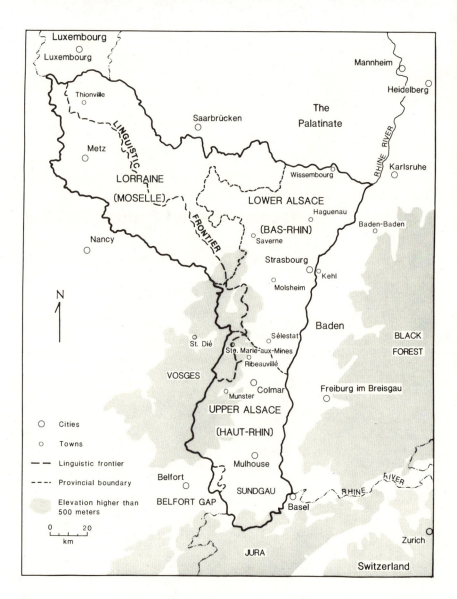

Alsace-Lorraine

# John E. Craig

# Scholarship and Nation Building

## The Universities of Strasbourg and Alsatian Society

## 1870–1939

The University of Chicago Press

Chicago and London

The University of Chicago Press, Chicago
60637
The University of Chicago Press, Ltd.,
London

**Library of Congress Cataloging in Publication Data**

Craig, John E.
  Scholarship and nation building.

  Bibliography: p. 435
  Includes index.
  1. Universities and colleges—France—Strasbourg—
History. 2. Universities and colleges—Germany—Alsace-
Lorraine—History. 3. Higher education and state—
France—History. 4. Higher education and state—Germany
—History. I. Title.
LA691.C8  1984        378.44′383        83-24341
ISBN 0-226-11670-0

John E. Craig earned his degrees in history
and is now associate professor of education
and director of the Comparative Education
Center at the University of Chicago.

# Contents

# List of Tables

# A Note to the Reader

The term "Alsatians," unless modified, refers to those indigenous to the territory ceded by France to Germany following the Franco-Prussian War, to those from the ceded portion of Lorraine as well as to those from Alsace. In accord with Alsatian traditions, the terms "old Germany" and "across the Rhine" refer to Germany excluding Alsace-Lorraine and the terms "from the interior" and "in the interior" refer to France excluding Alsace-Lorraine.

Unless noted, translations are the author's.

# Acknowledgments

It is a pleasure to acknowledge my indebtedness to the many who have contributed to the completion of this book.

My greatest debt is to Gordon A. Craig. (No, we are not related.) He supervised the dissertation that lies behind the first six chapters of this study, and he did so with just the right mix of curiosity, advice, and patience. While working on the dissertation I also received valuable counsel from the other members of my dissertation committee, Philip Dawson and Paul Robinson, and, at decisive junctures, from Fritz K. Ringer and Gordon Wright. I am grateful.

Of the archives and libraries visited there are several on which I made particularly heavy demands: the Archives départementales du Bas-Rhin, the Archives municipales, and the Bibliothèque nationale et universitaire in Strasbourg; the Archives nationales and the Bibliothèque nationale in Paris; the Bundesarchiv in Koblenz; the Bayerische Staatsbibliothek in Munich; the New York Public Library; the Library of Congress in Washington; and the libraries of the Freie Universität Berlin, the University of Chicago, Harvard University, Stanford University, and the University of Virginia. The staffs of these institutions, and of the several other archives and libraries visited for a day or two, were without exception hospitable and helpful and often went to unusual lengths to assist me. I am especially grateful to François-J. Himly, the director of the Archives départementales du Bas-Rhin, for giving me unlimited access to the as yet uncataloged archives of the University of Strasbourg established in 1919.

For authorization to consult manuscript collections not in the public domain I am indebted to Gerta Andreas-Marcks, André Benoit, Fernand Braudel, Philippe Dollinger, Helmut Goetz, François-J. Himly, Hélène Kiener, Georges Livet, Wolfgang Mommsen, R. Naudin, Victor de Pange, Hilah J. Thomas, Etienne Trocmé, Lothar Wickert, and Georgine Wittich. For advice on specific points and on sources I am grateful to C. Arnold Anderson, Mary Jean Bowman, Jean Fourquet, Christian Hallier, Etienne Juillard, J. L. Koszul, Guillaume Labadens, Roger Mehl, André Néher, Félix Ponteil, Albert Soboul, and all of the individuals interviewed (their names are listed in part 2 of the Bibliography).

Several have read all or part of the manuscript and shared their reactions with me: Bernhard vom Brocke, Robert Dreeben, Susan W. Friedman, Larry V. Hedges, Konrad H. Jarausch, Paul Leuilliot, Brenda F. Nelms, Paul Ricoeur, R. Steven Turner, and the two anonymous readers for the University of Chicago Press. I have profited. I have also profited from the comments of those interviewed on my general objectives and inter-pretations and on my impressions of individuals and incidents familiar to them. The notes suggest how much I owe to my informants.

For assistance in the preparation of the final draft I am grateful to Therese Chappell, Penelope Flores, and Joel Mambretti.

At various stages my research was supported by the Canada Council, the Deutscher Akademischer Austauschdienst, and the Spencer Foun-dation. I appreciate their confidence and generosity.

To acknowledge is not to implicate. The blunders that survive are my own.

# Introduction

Behind the emergence of the modern European university lay the pervasive influence of nationalism and its associate, the nation state. The most significant university reforms of the nineteenth and early twentieth centuries received much of their impetus from nationalistic considerations; as at other educational levels, a prime objective was to strengthen the nation state, not least by helping to construct and to define it. And trends within institutions and academic systems, including those attributable to professors' and students' evolving definitions of their roles, reinforced the pattern. This is not to deny the importance of changes in the demand for higher education or of events internal to the world of scholarship. Yet to the extent that these changes and events affected the development of Europe's universities, the rationales tended to emphasize statist or nationalistic considerations. Indeed the story of the transformation of the European university in the nineteenth and early twentieth centuries is essentially a story of how higher education came to be adapted to the requirements of emerging nation states—to their requirements for bureaucrats and teachers, for political socialization, for advanced technology, and for cultural identity and prestige.

Yet while national imperatives shaped the development of all European universities, they influenced some more directly and more profoundly than others. Among the most affected were those at the centers of their respective academic systems, such as Oxbridge and the Universities of Berlin, Leiden, Paris, and Vienna. Because of their contributions to the selection and formation of political elites and their stature as centers of scholarship, they tended to be considered national universities and, as such, to be treated more generously than their provincial rivals. But it was not only at the centers of academic systems that one found universities with clearly defined national identities and missions. In some countries, in fact, those with the strongest national associations and the most explicit national responsibilities were in the provinces, specifically in provinces of uncertain allegiance. These institutions, to employ some of the military metaphors popular at the time, were considered bastions or advance guards of the national culture dedicated either to shoring up a vulnerable flank or to pacifying occupied territory. Examples from the nineteenth century and the early decades of this century include the German-language uni-

1

versities in Chernovtsy (Czernowitz) and Prague, the Polish-language university in Lvov, the French-language university in Ghent, and the Russified universities of Kiev, Odessa, Tartu (Dorpat), and Warsaw.

Most studies of the development of European higher education emphasize the former group. They either restrict their attention to institutions at the center or view the evolution of national academic systems from the standpoint of the center. This work adopts a different approach. The focus is on two universities in the second group, two of those founded to advance the national cause in peripheral regions. One is the university established in Strasbourg following the Franco-Prussian War of 1870–71 and the resulting German annexation of Alsace-Lorraine. Its missions were to further the Germanization of the conquered territory and, more generally, to add to the growing renown of German higher education abroad and thereby to contribute to the extension of the nation's influence. The other is the university founded in Strasbourg following World War I, when France regained her lost provinces. Its missions were similar, if antithetical, to those of its German predecessor: to hasten France's assimilation of Alsace-Lorraine and to reinforce the country's efforts to regain cultural and scholarly hegemony in Europe.

On one level this study is an analysis of the relation of these two universities to the indigenous population of Alsace-Lorraine. Subjects explored include the professors' perceptions of their environment and their responsibilities, patterns of student recruitment, the values and activities of the Alsatian students and graduates, and the images of the universities among Alsatians generally. The objectives are twofold. On the one hand, the study seeks to assess the universities' contributions to the forging of national identities and loyalties—to what is known to political sociologists as nation building.[1] And on the other, it seeks to illuminate one of the more troublesome and poorly understood themes of modern European history, the Alsatian question, and in the process to indicate one of the advantages of the history of higher education as a field of study. It is now widely recognized that to understand why universities have evolved as they have it is essential to consider their social and cultural surroundings. What is less often noted is that because of their links to their environments universities can provide clear windows through which to observe social and cultural patterns. One objective of this study is to suggest the feasibility and utility of such an approach.

On another level the study is concerned less with Alsace-Lorraine than with the character of higher education in France and Germany and with the evolution of the modern European university. Of course it could hardly be argued that the particular institutions considered were representative of those in their respective academic systems. Their unique environment and special responsibilities distinguished them both from other provincial universities and from the institutions at the center, and so did their youth and their modernity. Yet precisely because of their unique characteristics the universities of Strasbourg offer unusually good vantage points for assessing more general developments in higher education. In this regard three related themes receive extensive treatment.

One of them concerns university reform. Both universities were new creations. Neither was burdened by inherited traditions and commitments or, a few Alsatians aside, by inherited faculty members. In addition the authorities promised strong budgetary support for these national undertakings. The combination meant that those planning and staffing the two institutions had opportunities for reform not often available elsewhere. And they also had incentives for reform. Their desire to impress Alsatian and foreign observers encouraged them to design thoroughly modern universities, and so did their desire to attain prominent positions for the institutions within their respective academic systems. In addition there were pressures from without. Each university was the first founded in its country in decades and as such attracted special attention from outsiders favoring reform. The result in each case was a wide-ranging debate, one in which participants discussed not only the merits of specific innovations but also the distinguishing features of their own and other academic systems, the likely directions of future developments, and the constraints on reform imposed by the practices of other universities and by institutionalized patterns of student recruitment and status attainment. The impetus may have come from the need to plan new universities for Strasbourg, but the issues debated and the fate of the innovations attempted have implications for our understanding of French and German education generally.

A second theme concerns the relation between higher education and the social and cultural order. This was a subject about which the professors and students at the two universities as well as Alsatian observers were unusually articulate. Because of their special missions the professors gave more attention than they would have elsewhere to assessing what a university could and could not do to further social and cultural change and to evaluating their own institution's progress. In the process they tended to become self-conscious and outspoken concerning the characteristics of higher education in their respective countries, both the good and the bad. Their Alsatian students and observers also had special cause to think about the interaction of higher education and society. The history and internal divisions of their homeland encouraged them to contrast what a German university could offer with what a French university could offer—and with what a genuinely Alsatian university might offer. Put differently, they were more conscious than students and outsiders generally are of the social and cultural significance of higher education and of the implications of replacing one sort of university with another. This, in turn, forced both the professors and government officials to be more explicit about their educational values and objectives than they would have been otherwise. As a result one can see in clearer focus how the professors and policymakers of Germany and France regarded the social and cultural roles of their universities: what they thought they should accomplish and what they thought they did accomplish.

The third general theme concerns the relations between higher education and the state, between the professors and the policymakers. Because of the environment and missions of Strasbourg's universities, there was greater potential for conflict with the authorities than at most German and French universities. The professors at both institutions had an unusually strong esprit de corps and a conviction that their special tasks entitled them to special treatment, and hence they were inclined to react quickly and resolutely to governmental provocations. And there were numerous provocations. In each case there were disputes over the government's failure to honor commitments allegedly made at the outset. In each case there were disputes over whether the university was living up to expectations as an instrument of nation building, over the appropriate criteria for evaluating its performance, and over the steps that might be taken to increase its effectiveness. And in each case there were disputes over the government's more general policies in Alsace-Lorraine, particularly those affecting the level of the region's autonomy. As a result of these and other confrontations the professors tended to be more than normally opinionated and assertive concerning their rights and obligations. Thus, once again, the unique features of Strasbourg's universities make them good vantage points for examining subjects of broader significance. Above all they permit us to see with unusual clarity the relation in theory and practice between professors' responsibilities as scholars and their responsibilities as servants of the state, between their commitment to scholarship and their commitment to nation building.

# 1

# Higher Education and Alsatian Society to 1870

Alsace is one of Europe's crossroads. Here the north-south route along the Rhine meets the route from Paris to Munich and Vienna as well as the route through the Belfort gap to the Rhone and the overland route from the British Isles and Belgium to Italy. This location has decisively shaped the province, exposing it to more than its share of cultural imports and covetous neighbors. It is essentially for this reason that the traditions of higher education in Alsace are at once distinguished and disharmonious.

Between the Reformation and the middle of this century Alsace hosted six institutions of university rank, and each bore a distinctive imprint from its location in a region marked by cultural diversity and conflict. Not one transcended the province's cultural differences and served the interests of all elements of the concerned population. This was impossible in the sixteenth, seventeenth, and eighteenth centuries, when Lutheranism and Catholicism dueled and each side found it necessary to sponsor its own university. It was just as impossible after the French Revolution, when a conflict between national cultures joined and in part replaced the older one between religions. At least in this respect the universities featured in this study, those founded in 1872 and in 1919, did no violence to local traditions.

· 1 ·

The Protestant Reformation provided the impetus for the province's first institution of higher education. The new faith actually triumphed in only a few Alsatian communities, but among them was the leading town of the region and of the whole valley of the upper Rhine, the imperial free city of Strasbourg. This community of perhaps 30,000 now began its long history of proximity to a major cultural frontier, albeit a frontier unlike that most associated with contemporary Strasbourg. The competing cultures were Protestant and Catholic, not French and German; the Catholic sphere of religious and political dominance extended almost to the gates of the town, but the eastern limits of French linguistic and cultural influence still lay far to the west.

In 1538 the humanist Johannes Sturm, after Melanchthon the most prominent educational reformer of the German Reformation, organized a

Gymnasium in Strasbourg and recruited a staff that included the theologians Martin Bucer, John Calvin, and Wolfgang Capito. The school thrived from the start, becoming a mecca for students from throughout Protestant Europe and a model for institutions in other German towns. Indicative of its renown was an imperial decree in 1566 transforming the upper classes into an academy with two faculties, theology and philosophy, and degree-granting powers. But because of a change in the political and religious climate, the next step, becoming a full university, had to wait. In the last third of the sixteenth century, only a few years after Calvin and others had made Strasbourg one of Europe's leading centers of theological debate, Lutheran orthodoxy emerged triumphant and the town became as inhospitable to Calvinists as it already was to Catholics and Jews. This development encouraged the academy's professors and friends, now threatened by rigid censorship, to campaign for the academy's conversion into a university, for this would bring special rights and immunities. But the municipal authorities, fearing the prospect of an independent corporate body within the city, successfully resisted until well into the seventeenth century. It was not until 1621 that the institution received its charter as the University of Strasbourg.[1]

For our purposes only two aspects of this university's development in the seventeenth century merit mention. First, it was now that the institution began to acquire a reputation as an international university. Attracting students from throughout Protestant Europe but few from predominantly Catholic Alsace, it was probably less regional in orientation than any other university in the German-speaking lands. Second, the institution retained its Protestant and German character even after the capitulation of 1681 brought French rule and initiated a reassertion of Catholic influence in Strasbourg. The document of capitulation expressly stated that there was to be no change in the status of the university.[2]

In the eighteenth century the university developed into one of Europe's major centers of learning. The French annexation and its effects on the city contributed to the institution's reputation as a "cavaliers' university," as a place where one could learn riding, dueling, and dancing while becoming familiar with a foreign language and a foreign intellectual tradition. At the same time the university gained renown as a center of medical and legal studies and as a "clearing house for enlightenment."[3] The result was the enrollment of large numbers from Germany, Switzerland, England, the Netherlands, Scandinavia, Russia, and, after mid-century, what Alsatians still refer to as the French interior. Indeed in the third quarter of the century the university had as international a student body and as cosmopolitan an ambience as any in Europe. These features were particularly striking in the Faculty of Law, the faculty that enrolled nearly all the students from the interior, among them Talleyrand, and most of those of foreign nationality, among them Goethe and Metternich.[4]

But despite the university's evident prosperity, threats to its traditions and stature were mounting. Some came from across the Rhine, specifically from the reform movement inaugurated at the University of Halle (founded in 1694) and developed at the University of Göttingen (founded in 1734). Halle rejected the religious orthodoxy and preoccupation with the classics so characteristic of seventeenth-century universities, and in their place stressed pietism and the rationalism of its most distinguished professor, Christian Wolff. It also introduced instruction in the vernacular and made room in its curriculum for the doctrine of natural law. Göttingen went further, giving special attention to the Faculty of Philosophy, traditionally subordinated to the three professional faculties, and replacing the pietism of Halle with an emphasis on liberal and universal education and on the advancement of knowledge. With its excellent library, its affiliated scientific society, its aggressive recruitment of renowned scholars, and its recognition of the new concept of academic freedom, it quickly became the leading center of learning in the German states and began to popularize the idea that a university should combine both teaching and research.[5]

The University of Strasbourg could not keep pace. Although there were some concessions to modernity, including the offering of the occasional course in German rather than Latin and a greater emphasis on scholarly productivity, the institution lacked the resources and freedom required to meet the challenge from across the Rhine. Its limited income—most of it from a secularized religious foundation, the Thomasstift—permitted the employment of only fourteen to nineteen ordinary (titular) professors, many at low salaries. (The few instructors of lower rank received no salaries, and hence depended on student fees, extracurricular employment, and family wealth.) In addition faculty members had to be both Protestant and, the monarchy insisted, natives of France, which effectively limited recruitment to Alsatians. The result was a faculty with close ties to local society, particularly to Strasbourg's Lutheran patriciate: more than 80 percent of the instructors were natives of the city, most of them from what amounted to an academic oligarchy. But as this suggests, it was also a faculty based less on scholarly distinction than on personal connections, family wealth, and a willingness to wait until chairs became vacant; that some members enjoyed wide reputations as scholars was almost an accident. There were efforts at reform, to be sure. In 1782, for instance, the jurist Christophe Guillaume Koch, the institution's most renowned professor, called for the establishment of several additional chairs, for a faculty for the historical and political sciences, for the appointment of foreign and particularly German professors, and for the introduction of salaries for extraordinary professors. But there was no noticeable improvement in the size or the quality of the faculty, and the number of students, particularly foreign students, tended to fall. By the last year before the Revolution there were only 182 students (a decade or two before there had usually been between 400 and 600) and only 9.7 percent of the new matriculants came from outside France (as compared to 48.9 percent at mid-century).[6]

The university also faced a challenge from Strasbourg's rapidly growing Catholic community. Actually the Catholics had their own university; in 1617 the Jesuits had established an academy in the nearby town of Molsheim, the refuge for many of the Catholic institutions driven from Strasbourg during the Reformation, and in 1702 this episcopal university, as it was now known, had moved to Strasbourg. But the institution lacked faculties of law and medicine and the prestige of the municipal university.[7] As a result more and more Catholics attended the latter and Catholics in high municipal positions took steps to transform the institution. On at least two occasions, for instance, the Catholic officials attempted to gain control over half the appointments to the faculty. The Protestants successfully stood their ground, but in view of the changing composition of the city's population—by the 1780s Catholics were in the majority—the university presumably would continue to face threats to its character as a bastion of Protestantism.[8]

Yet another challenge came from the French government and, more generally, from French culture. By the middle of the eighteenth century officials from the interior were becoming concerned about the university's German character and its almost complete lack of contact with the scholarly life of the rest of France. They considered various projects designed to diminish or counter the institution's influence. In the 1760s, for example, plans were prepared for a Royal Academy of Sciences and Arts to be established in Strasbourg as a French balance to the university, and there were rumors that the authorities intended to make the university more like those in the interior. Nothing came of these plans and rumors, to be sure, in part because the faculty put up stout resistance.[9] But there were more subtle forces at work. By the 1760s the pronounced cultural and social gap that had hitherto separated the immigrant "société française" from the indigenous elites was narrowing, and on the former's terms. Many local notables—like many throughout Europe, the German states included—were beginning to emulate Parisian styles of dress and behavior and to admire French furniture, architecture, and letters. The first to succumb were the relatively few Catholic notables, for they had less cause to respect or preserve local traditions. But they were soon joined by a large proportion of the Lutheran patriciate or, to use the immigrants' term, the H.S.P. (haute société protestante). Although some patrician families refused to abandon their solid and straitlaced traditions, others, led by their younger members, eagerly inhaled what one descendant described as "the wind from the west, the wind from France which comes . . . laden with freshness, with intoxicating perfumes, with unknown pleasures and new ideas."[10] And the municipal university, essentially an extension of the H.S.P., was not immune. Indeed by the last quarter of the century some professors regularly lectured and published in French. The university's character as a bulwark of German culture was under attack from within as well as without.[11]

With the coming of the Revolution the threats to the university became more pronounced and immediate. Strasbourg quickly lost the free city privileges it had jealously guarded since the annexation, thus undermining the university's legal foundations. The apparent determination of the revolutionary regime to reform French education along uniform and highly centralized lines jeopardized the institution's autonomy and traditions. And the regime's plan to confiscate all religious endowments imperiled the university's only significant source of income. The professors resisted, arguing in petitions and personal appeals that it was in France's interests to maintain a university with extensive liberties and close ties to German scholarly life. For a while they succeeded. The authorities did not interfere in the administration of the university, and in 1790 they agreed to omit its religious endowments from the list of those to be expropriated. But as the Revolution moved to the left, the university's situation—and that of its Catholic rival—became less tenable. In 1791 local officials disbanded the episcopal university when all but one of its professors refused to subscribe to the civil constitution of the clergy.[12] And with the founding of the French Republic and the beginning of war with Prussia and the Hapsburg Empire, the municipal university faced a similar fate. Leaders of the National Convention denounced the institution as a stronghold of reaction and a "hydra of Germanism," professors were hounded into exile or imprisoned, and potential students were kept away by the unfavorable political and military situation. But the university did not fare much worse than those in the interior—for the Convention all universities were politically unreliable—and its end came no sooner: like the others, it was suppressed by the Convention's law of 15 September 1793.[13]

When higher education returned to Alsace, it was organized along new and thoroughly French lines. The reforms of the revolutionary and Napoleonic years replaced the dismantled universities with a system of "special schools" or faculties, and these were to remain France's basic institutions of higher education for almost a century. Above the faculties stood the rectors, each of whom supervised public education at all levels in a district typically embracing about five of France's ninety-odd departments. The faculties of each district were usually located in a single city and known collectively as an academy, but they hardly constituted a university in the conventional sense. Their only formal links were through their rector, and his responsibilities were to Paris, not to the faculties. Reinforcing this tendency toward subordination to a central bureaucracy were the examinations for the various credentials recognized by the government. Officials of the educational ministry composed these examinations, and the obligation to prepare students to pass them shaped the teaching methods and the curriculum of every faculty in every academy.[14]

During the Napoleonic years higher education in Alsace was reorganized in accord with this highly centralized system. The Academy of Strasbourg—whose district comprised the two Alsatian departments, Bas-Rhin and Haut-Rhin—was distinguished structurally only by its size: after the addition of a Protestant theological faculty in 1818, it had five faculties as compared to four in the Academy of Paris and no more than three in any other academy. (There was one other Protestant theological faculty, in Montauban in southwestern France; there were a few Catholic theological faculties, but most bishops, including Strasbourg's, took advantage of their right to train their clergy at their own seminaries.) The language of instruction was French, and about half the professors were from the interior.[15]

As a center of learning the Academy of Strasbourg was the best in the provinces, and in some fields it rivaled the Academy of Paris. Each faculty could boast distinguished professors, particularly after 1830, and there was a commitment to scholarship not generally associated with the Napoleonic educational system. But why? Good fortune with appointments deserves much of the credit, but environmental factors were also important. Local notables took pride in their city's tradition as a center of scholarship and accorded more support and status to distinguished professors than could be found elsewhere in France.[16] Sectarian rivalries, reflected in frequent disputes over faculty appointments, probably strengthened professors' self-consciousness and dedication as scholars, particularly if they were Protestant (as many were, thanks in part to the lobbying of the H.S.P.).[17] And the city's frontier location together with a desire to popularize France and French culture caused the government to give the academy more favored treatment than those in the interior, the one in Paris excepted. Strasbourg's medical faculty was one of only three in the country, for instance, and in 1856 its resources and prestige were enhanced by the addition of France's only school for the training of military doctors.[18] All these factors helped to create an environment which was, by contemporary French standards, unusually conducive to scholarly productivity.

But despite these features and advantages, the Academy of Strasbourg never attained the renown of the municipal university it replaced or of the now flourishing German universities. Like the other provincial academies, it always suffered from the institutional and cultural forces—the official policies and popular attitudes—tending to concentrate French scholarly life in Paris. All its faculties were poorly funded, and as a result facilities for research were almost nonexistent: the few laboratories were miserably equipped, while the library lacked many standard works and had almost no funds for new acquisitions. While the overall enrollment was impressive by provincial French standards—in the 1850s and 1860s it fluctuated between about 320 and 544[19]—most students were careerist in the extreme; they cared little if they received a solid or up-to-date education, as long as they were adequately prepared for the all-important state examinations. Symptomatic was the unpopularity of the Faculties of Letters and the Sciences, the two most identified with learning for its own sake and the extension of knowledge. These faculties occasionally had professors of renown or great promise (notably Louis Pasteur, from 1848 to 1854, and Fustel de Coulanges, from 1860 to 1870), but they never attracted many students. The low point came in 1865–66, when the two faculties together enrolled only twelve.[20]

But one faculty, that of Protestant theology, was something of an exception. It was the only faculty to maintain consistently high standards of scholarship before 1870, largely because it was the only one in close contact with German academic life. This faculty was dominated by Alsatian scholars and, through them, linked to the city's Protestant Seminary, an autonomous institution organized in 1803 as the legal successor to the disbanded municipal university. After 1818 the seminary's five theologians occupied chairs in the faculty as well, typically teaching in German at the seminary and in French at the faculty (and typically to the same students, since most of the faculty's students were seminarians seeking diplomas). These connections help to explain why the theological faculty was more attuned than the others to the traditions of the old municipal university, including its orientation toward scholarly life across the Rhine. Most of the faculty's professors attended German scholarly congresses, corresponded with German professors, and saw it as their mission to mediate between French and German research or, more accurately, to introduce the French to the methods and results of German research.[21] And their students reflected this orientation. They were more likely than those in other faculties to spend a few semesters at German universities, and, at least before mid-century, they tended to organize their extracurricular activities on the German model: they looked to the German fraternities for their standards while the students in the secular faculties found theirs in the Parisian Latin Quarter.[22]

• 2 •

The Academy of Strasbourg may have been the best in the French provinces, but few of its professors took pride in this distinction. Particularly in the 1850s and 1860s the members of all faculties generally agreed that France's centralized and bureaucratized educational system operated to the disadvantage of higher learning. Admittedly, similar dissatisfaction could be found at other provincial academies and even in Paris, but nowhere was it more deeply and widely felt than in Strasbourg. The reasons, again, relate to Strasbourg's unique traditions and location. The Alsatian professors naturally made comparisons with the eighteenth-century municipal university, which in retrospect took on a luster it may never have had in reality. And all professors made comparisons, often at first hand, with the contemporary German universities. In both cases the results were far from flattering to their own institution or to French higher education. Before turning to their specific observations, however, we should consider the standard that most preoccupied them, the nineteenth-century German university.

The origins of the modern German university can be traced to the eighteenth century, particularly to the innovations introduced at Göttingen. But the decisive impetus came from reforms initiated early in the nineteenth century by a group of idealist philosophers and neohumanists, a group including Friedrich von Schelling, J. G. Fichte, Friedrich Schleiermacher, Henrik Steffens, and Wilhelm von Humboldt. Motivating these reforms was dissatisfaction both with the existing German universities, which were considered bastions of corruption and reaction, and with the utilitarian correctives advocated by others. As in revolutionary France there had been proposals in "enlightened" circles that the universities be replaced by specialized institutions more suited to their states' requirements for bureaucrats, professionals, and applied research.[23] But the universities' idealist and neohumanist critics favored a different remedy. They wanted to resuscitate the universities by transforming them into centers of cultivation (*Bildung*) and scholarship (*Wissenschaft*) pursued for their own sake. They rejected both the emphasis on professional training typical of the universities' "enlightened" critics and the utilitarian approach to scholarship associated with Göttingen. Career preparation and technical, or "realistic," scholarship, denigrated as "bread-and-butter studies," had no place in the university; all learning must stem from humanistic or idealistic concerns, with students seeking the full development of their capacities and their individuality and with professors dedicated to the search for the ultimate truth. Hence it was essential that academic freedoms be guaranteed. Professors must have the right to teach whatever they wish (*Lehrfreiheit*) and students the right to study whatever and wherever they wish (*Lernfreiheit*); neither state nor church should impose any restrictions on higher education. In addition, the faculty of philosophy must become the central and highest branch of the university, for it was the natural home of pure research and the unencumbered pursuit of the truth.[24]

The collapse of Prussia in 1806 facilitated the popularization and implementation of these ideas. In the aftermath of defeat several bureaucrats and intellectuals argued that it was no longer sufficient for the state to restrict its activities to the military and administrative spheres. If Prussia was ever to rise and cast off the French yoke, it must become what Fichte termed a *Kulturstaat;* the state must ally itself to cultural forces. According to this logic, with the appropriate cultural and educational policies—particularly policies fostering *Bildung* and *Wissenschaft*—the government could narrow the gap between rulers and ruled, strengthen German resistance to Napoleon's hegemony, and acquire a position of moral and intellectual leadership in central Europe. The national culture would also benefit from the alliance, for with the arrival of French troops and French ideas its ability to defend itself without government support seemed open to question.[25] This reasoning found expression in two institutions identified with Wilhelm von Humboldt and his brief tenure (1809–10) as director of the cultural section of Prussia's Ministry of the Interior: the upgraded Gymnasium and the new University of Berlin. The reformed Gymnasien were distinguished from other secondary schools by their more or less standardized curricula, their heavy emphasis on Latin and Greek, and, before long, their monopoly over access to higher education and to the educated bourgeoisie (*Bildungsbürgertum*).[26] As for the new university, it symbolized the alliance of power and learning, of *Macht* and *Geist,* that was the hallmark of the *Kulturstaat,* and it incorporated many of the innovations recently advocated by neohumanists and idealist philosophers. Thus Humboldt argued that while the state should support the institution and on a handsome scale, it must not expect any practical return. He insisted on complete academic freedom, fully aware that this was directed against the meddling of the state as well as that of the churches and other outside forces. It was in the untrammeled pursuit of truth and the development of the free man that the university was of political importance, for ultimately these were also the goals of the state.[27]

According to the traditional interpretation these ideas and their institutionalization in Berlin led directly to the modern German university—to the university that so impressed French and other foreign observers later in the century. It is an interpretation requiring qualification. Although Humboldt and his fellow reformers were certainly committed to making the universities centers of scholarship pursued as an end in itself, the foundation of the universities' later renown, they differed over what scholarship entailed. The basic conflict was between the philosophers and the philologists, or, on a more personal level, between the idealists, including Schelling and Fichte, and the neohumanists, including Humboldt and Friedrich August Wolf. The two groups were united in rejecting the utilitarian and encyclopedic approaches to scholarship characteristic of the eighteenth-century universities, but at odds over what to substitute. The philosophers' orientation was speculative and synthetic, with an emphasis on the organic unity of all knowledge and on the primacy of philosophy among the disciplines, while the philologists' was critical and analytic, stressing methodological rigor and the mastery of carefully and narrowly defined fields of study. Eventually the latter approach would prevail, but to understand why it does not suffice to invoke the ideology behind the university reforms, additional factors must be considered.[28]

Among these factors are the largely unintended consequences of certain innovations introduced at the reformed universities, notably the research seminar, the upgraded *Privatdozent,* and *Lernfreiheit.* Led by F. A. Wolf, first classical and Germanic philologists and then historians and other scholars began to transform their seminars, originally intended to train schoolteachers, into centers for advanced research and the preparation of specialists. By raising the requirements for appointment, the reformers changed the role of the *Privatdozent,* or unsalaried lecturer, from that of a private tutor to that of an apprentice professor. Henceforth the *Privat-dozenten,* taking advantage of their *Lehrfreiheit* and constrained by the professors' monopoly of the general courses that attracted most students, sought to make their mark by offering innovative and specialized courses, thus contributing to the modernization of the curriculum and, ultimately, to the triumph of the specialists over the generalists. At the same time, *Lernfreiheit,* the students' freedom to choose their courses and their universities, limited the professors' ability to abuse their privileges and their authority. In itself *Lernfreiheit* did not encourage specialization at the expense of broad syntheses, but once the former began to come into vogue it helped to speed the transition.[29]

Another factor relates not to innovations within individual universities but rather to the structure of the German academic system. There were over two dozen German-language universities scattered among more than a dozen states, each fully independent in educational matters. Combined with the diffusion of *Lernfreiheit,* this decentralization fostered competition among the universities for students, for professors, and for prestige. Such competition acted as a check on backward and oppressive tendencies within individual universities and individual states, encouraging them to adopt the values and innovations, including *Lehrfreiheit,* increasingly needed if they were to attract distinguished scholars and raise enrollments. To the extent that the eventual triumph of specialized, empirical research represented a revolt against the ideals of the reformers, and in part it did, the character of the system facilitated the revolt—just as it had earlier facilitated the diffusion of the reformers' ideals.[30]

This brings us to yet another important factor, the role of the state. In all cases it was the state that provided the essential wherewithal and bore ultimate responsibility for faculty appointments (*Privatdozenten* aside) and for the adoption of innovations. If the German states had been uniformly hostile, the reform movement would have had little impact. But with the partial exception of a few dominated by Lutheran orthodoxy, such as Mecklenburg-Schwerin, or by Catholicism, such as Austria and

Bavaria, the states tended to support the movement. The case of Prussia is of particular importance. Prussia's prominence among the German states and her large number of universities—between 1818 and 1866 there were six—meant that her educational policies strongly influenced those of the smaller states. To the degree that these states subscribed to the ideology of the *Kulturstaat,* they found it necessary to respond to the Prussian challenge by upgrading their own universities. And there continued to be a Prussian challenge, for in the three or four decades following the Humboldtian reforms, a period otherwise characterized by reaction, the government pursued policies conducive to university reform. Two of these policies merit special attention.

First, the educational ministry, established in 1817, refused to favor the new university in Berlin at the expense of those in the provinces—it refused to adopt a one-university strategy. Overall the University of Berlin was the most distinguished academic institution, but there were always fields in which it was outstripped by other Prussian universities, notably by two which, like Berlin, had been assigned special missions on behalf of Prussian and German culture: the University of Breslau, organized in 1811 and expected to defend the state and her culture in Silesia against a presumed Slavic challenge, and the University of Bonn, founded in 1818 with an eye to undoing the effects of almost two decades of French rule on the left bank of the Rhine. By giving strong support to these two institutions as well as to the older provincial universities (in Greifswald, Halle, and Königsberg), the ministry fostered competition not only between the Prussian universities and those of other states but also among the Prussian universities, thus accelerating the pace at which innovations were introduced and diffused.[31]

The second policy concerned responsibility for professorial appointments. The ministry insisted on controlling the selection of professors. Its motives, at least until the 1840s, were enlightened. Humboldt had argued that in making appointments the ministry would be more objective and less conservative than the faculties; the latter, if permitted, would naturally favor representatives of their own outlooks, which tended to be narrow and outdated.[32] Humboldt's successors agreed, and acted accordingly. But what did this mean in practice? There was a potential for abuse in ministerial control just as there was in the alternative, and it was not always avoided. In the 1820s, for instance, the ministry seems to have been unduly sympathetic to Hegelians. But on balance the result, initially unintended, was to hasten the triumph of specialized, empirical research. Unimpeded by the vested interests and preoccupation with collegiality and pedagogical skills that allegedly corrupted the faculties, the ministry moved almost by default to the other extreme; rejecting the traditional primacy of institutional or particularistic criteria, it relied on disciplinary or cosmopolitan standards. More specifically, the ministry, advised by a small group of experts, selected professors on the basis of their scholarly contributions, which in most cases meant their accomplishments as research specialists. And ambitious scholars adjusted to the new incentives, slighting their other responsibilities in order to establish their reputations as innovative and productive specialists. By the 1840s the transition was essentially complete, at least in Prussia. The ministry's policies and the response of scholars had institutionalized what has been called the research imperative—the principle that research and the dissemination of the results are basic to the professor's role and that academic positions should be defined and filled accordingly.[33]

This development undermined the justification for close ministerial supervision of appointments advanced by Humboldt and his reformist successors. Now that the new values had gained hegemony within the universities, the professors could presumably be given greater responsibility. And the ministry did make concessions. Beginning in the 1830s it permitted the faculties to propose three or four candidates for each vacancy, and during the revolution of 1848 it went further, expressly recognizing the right of faculties to select their new members. But after the revolution the ministry adopted a decidedly more conservative course. Through the 1850s and 1860s it regularly violated the faculties' right of nomination, made concessions to pressures from the Lutheran and Catholic churches, and in other ways infringed on what the professors had come to think of as their rights. Yet the government could hardly be expected to stand aside while the universities threatened the very foundations of the state, and in the eyes of Prussian conservatives they had been doing so for years.[34] This brings us to a final set of factors contributing to the triumph of the new scholarly values—and to the reputation the German universities came to enjoy abroad. It concerns the political and social role of the professors.

The conservatives' fears of the universities were well founded. Although most German professors were apolitical or conservative, a growing and increasingly vocal minority, composed largely of jurists and historians, sought fundamental changes in the political order. At the time, these "political" professors had no serious rivals for leadership of the movement seeking an end to arbitrary government and feudal privileges and the introduction of constitutional rule and national unification. In addition all professors, regardless of their political leanings or educational values, were now popularly identified with the campaign to limit access to coveted careers to those possessing talent and that emerging object of conspicuous consumption, *Bildung*. It was natural, then, that the professors enjoyed great influence with the social group that stood to gain the most from these reforms, the educated middle class. This relationship, manifest in the second quarter of the century, helps to account for the strong interest of the *Bildungsbürgertum* in academic affairs and the high status it conferred on professors. Indeed those reaching professorial rank enjoyed such prestige and influence that their relationship to the rest of the educated middle class has been described as that of a substitute nobility. The liberal and nationalist press reflected this respect for the professor and his activities: it published summaries and reviews of the most esoteric scholarship, and gave extensive coverage to professorial appointments, budget debates, and other matters relating to the welfare of the universities. It is thus easy to understand why cases involving violations of academic freedoms, such as the affair of the "Göttingen Seven" in 1837, could take on the overtones of major political events.[35]

The relationship between the professors and the educated middle class had implications not only for the liberal and nationalist movement but also for the universities' development as centers of learning. It reinforced the professors' commitment to the new scholarly values, for these were the values held in highest regard by their outside admirers. It encouraged governments to treat their universities generously, not least because this might lessen the pressures for less acceptable concessions elsewhere. And it made academic careers more desirable for middle-class youths of talent and ambition, thus increasing the number and improving the quality of those competing to enter the profession. The effect was to hasten the triumph of the research imperative and related innovations, and thereby to contribute to the universities' exalted position in the eyes of educated Germans and, increasingly, foreign observers.

It was in the 1830s that the victory of the specialists over the generalists, of the philologists over the philosophers, became definite. It was also in this decade, not coincidentally, that the reformed German universities began to gain wide recognition abroad as Europe's leading centers of advanced scholarship and as the appropriate standards for the evaluation and reform of higher education. By mid-century few doubts remained: foreign observers agreed that in virtually every scholarly field hegemony had passed or was passing to the German states—usually from France but in some cases from Great Britain or the Netherlands—and that the unique features of the German universities were somehow responsible.

But how should the challenge be met? In the case of France those who cared (few did, which was part of the problem) tended to focus on the resources available for higher education and research: most thought the remedy lay in increasing the number of professors and improving the quantity and quality of research facilities. Some also proposed concentrating resources in five or six favored cities (Strasbourg included) or establishing a special institution in Paris dedicated to advanced research. But few faulted the basic structure of the French educational system.[36] Even Victor Duruy, the minister most committed to meeting the German challenge, saw little need for fundamental changes. "The organization of our system of higher education," he assured Napoleon III in 1868, "does not require major reforms: the edifice is old, but its foundations are solid; we only need appropriations for new necessities."[37]

In Strasbourg, however, the pattern was different. Professors tended to be more dissatisfied with the existing system than their counterparts in the interior, more probing in their diagnoses, more radical in their proposed remedies. They agreed, of course, on the need for larger budgets. They complained as much as anyone about the inadequate laboratories and clinics, about the meager allotments for equipment and library purchases, about the lack of positions in many fields of scholarship, and about how the proliferation of faculties spread the available resources too thinly.[38] But they went further. They also criticized the organization of the system and the prevalent values concerning higher education. They contrasted the *Lehrfreiheit* recognized in Germany with the petty regulations, surveillance, and reprisals professors faced in France. They complained about the lack of institutional autonomy, again contrasting their situation with that in Germany. They lamented the almost complete absence of full-time students in the faculties of letters and the sciences and the resulting pressure on professors in these faculties to cater to students in other faculties and, worse yet, to the general public. And they criticized the attitudes of their auditors and of some professors and the resulting lack, even in Strasbourg, of an atmosphere conducive to scholarship. The historian Fustel de Coulanges characterized his faculty as "about three-fourths dead," and complained that he lacked colleagues with whom he could discuss his research and received no encouragement from others.[39] A rector, an unlikely critic of the system, insisted that academic institutions needed a special atmosphere in which to flourish, the kind found at Göttingen or Oxford but not in France.[40] And the Nordic philologist F. G. Bergmann, an Alsatian, complained that the prevalent values were hostile to research:

> The Frenchman has a natural and very pronounced disposition to be eloquent, and this is why when lecturing (if it is at all possible) he likes to play the part of an orator and to do what it takes to be accepted as such. Besides higher education has been overrun by men who are not always superior on the basis of their scholarship, but who are good enough speechmakers. What is more, the young, even they, believe that the good minds, the distinguished minds, are those who know how to develop received ideas, the ideas that are à la mode, in an amusing and ingenious way, while those pursuing knowledge for its own sake are only pedants, grammarians, philologists, etc.[41]

The research imperative might have been firmly established in Germany, but in France many professors still deferred to what might be termed the rhetorical imperative.

The remedies proposed by the Strasbourg critics, like the diagnoses, went beyond those advanced in the interior. Most called for major structural changes. Indeed several professors and officials, among them Fustel de Coulanges and one of the rectors, prepared memorandums recommending a thorough overhaul of the system.[42] Typical in tone was the analysis presented in a book published early in 1870 by Charles Schützenberger, an Alsatian member of the medical faculty. Like many of his colleagues Schützenberger used the German universities as his standard. "Of our students returning from tours of the universities across the Rhine," he noted, "there is not one who fails to point out, with a wounded sentiment of national pride, the relative inferiority of our institutions."[43] In elaboration, he furnished figures on faculty size and course offerings showing that the Academy of Strasbourg, reputedly the second-ranking in France, stood far behind the University of Marburg, one of the more modest German universities.[44] But what was the solution? The essential first step was the dismantling of the overly centralized and bureaucratized French academic system: "It is in administrative centralization . . . that one must seek and that one will find the causes of this enfeeblement, this inertia of higher education in France. Centralization has absorbed all, adapted all to its uniform mold, regulated all, bureaucratized all."[45] The only hope lay in granting extensive autonomy to each institution. Specifically Schützenberger called for the selection of rectors from lists submitted by the faculties, the election of deans by their faculties, the appointment of *Privatdozenten,* the institutionalization of *Lehrfreiheit* and *Lernfreiheit,* and—so that these freedoms would not be meaningless—the assured provision of resources on a lavish scale. The solution, in short, was to remodel French higher education along German lines.[46]

Such proposals had little impact. Although by the late 1860s the ministry recognized the need to respond to the German challenge, it lacked the resources and the inclination to take the steps favored by many in Strasbourg. Indeed from the perspective of the Strasbourg critics some of its efforts at reform actually aggravated the problem. Thus the establishment in 1868 of the Ecole pratique des hautes études, intended to foster advanced research and the training of research specialists, only contributed to the isolation of research from the faculties and to the concentration of resources in Paris.[47] Other proposals were less objectionable, but they remained just that, proposals. Meanwhile the German universities continued to flourish, the hegemony of German scholarship became more pronounced, and the dissatisfaction and pessimism of the Strasbourg critics deepened.

• 3 •

The failure to keep pace with the German universities was not the only cause for dissatisfaction within Strasbourg's academic community nor, for some, the most important. Among a significant minority of educated Alsatians, professors and students included, there was concern over the French government's pursuit of the linguistic and cultural assimilation of Alsace, and over the manifest and likely results.

With the French Revolution, the general indifference with which the authorities had hitherto regarded the language question in Alsace came to an end. The denunciation of Strasbourg's municipal university as a "hydra of Germanism" was symptomatic of the revolutionary regimes' association of language with nationhood and of their commitment, particularly between 1792 and 1795, to the linguistic assimilation of all territories not already assimilated, Alsace included. Admittedly little was accomplished in these years, for the revolutionary decrees concerning language tended to be unrealistic or unenforceable, and the resistance among Alsatians was strong. But the language policies of the 1790s did leave important legacies. They established French as the language of instruction in state-supported institutions of secondary and higher education. They set precedents for policies pursued more systematically by later regimes, particularly concerning primary schooling. And they politicized the question. Henceforth Alsatians who did not understand or habitually speak French would be regarded in certain circles, even in certain Alsatian circles, as either reactionary or of suspect loyalty.[48]

Compared to the revolutionary governments, the Napoleonic and Restoration regimes assigned low priority to the language question. During the first three decades of the nineteenth century there was nothing resembling the energetic promotion of linguistic assimilation that had marked the 1790s. But other developments in these years contributed indirectly to the Frenchification of Alsace. Three merit attention.

First, it was then that most Alsatians began to think of themselves as Frenchmen and to identify with their *grande patrie*. For this Napoleon and his accomplishments deserve much credit. By ending policies aimed at forcible Frenchification and by restoring religious peace, Napoleon removed the chief causes of the disaffection so prevalent in Alsace during the revolutionary years. And the prosperity and the glory associated with his rule as well as the prominent positions attained by many from Alsace, above all as generals, gave the regime a popularity far surpassing that of any previous French regime; for Alsatians the Napoleonic era was, at the time and in retrospect, *la belle époque*. This helps to explain why Alsatians would henceforth show a predilection for regimes offering strong authority, order, and glory, and would assign unusually high status to those distinguishing themselves in military careers—at the expense, in part, of those making their marks as scholars. It also had implications for the position of the French language. As the prestige of *la grande patrie* rose, so did the prestige of the national language and of those who habitually spoke it. Thanks largely to the popularity of the Napoleonic regime, the

French language began to become an important sign of social status in Alsace; to paraphrase a later German observer, French now began to take over as the Alsatians' *Hochdeutsch*.[49]

The second development, closely related, concerns the administrative and economic integration of Alsace. The revolutionary governments had taken the decisive steps, removing the distinctive institutions and obstacles to commerce in place before 1789, including the barriers to trade with the interior, and substituting the same leveling and centralizing reforms introduced everywhere else in France. But the Napoleonic regime carried the process further, and the Restoration rulers consolidated the inherited reforms. For Alsatians the results were similar to those of the conciliatory policies and military successes of Napoleon: integration strengthened their ties to and identification with the rest of the country, particularly the omnipotent Paris, and gave them new incentives to learn the national language. It should be noted, too, that the economic policies of the revolutionary and Napoleonic regimes redistributed wealth in ways that increased the size and status of the social group that was already most Francophile, the urban bourgeoisie. The landed nobility lost its place at the top of the Alsatian social order to a tight-knit and self-conscious elite of industrialists, bankers, merchants, and lawyers—bourgeois notables with a natural sympathy for the ideals of the Enlightenment and the Revolution and with special cause to favor strong centralized government over local traditions.[50]

The third development involved ideological trends across the Rhine. Early in the nineteenth century German reformers, seeking arguments conducive to German unification, began to rally to one of the central ideas of the French Revolution, the association of language and nationhood. The consequences for Alsace were profound. Suddenly the Alsatian language question, hitherto a domestic matter, took on an international aspect: some Germans now insisted that since language defined nationhood, Alsace should be included in a united Germany. For the French there were two obvious responses. It could be argued that language was but one of many possible determinants of nationhood, and not the most important. This would be the position of those who defended France's claims to Alsace during and after the Franco-Prussian War. Or, accepting the troublesome argument on its own terms, steps could be taken to undermine the German claims by completing the linguistic assimilation of Alsace. During the Napoleonic and Restoration years the latter response was not seriously considered, presumably because the revolutionary efforts at rapid Frenchification had discredited the policy. But the pattern soon changed.[51]

During the July Monarchy (1830–48) policymakers in Paris continued to show little interest in linguistic assimilation, but their subordinates in Alsace—the prefects, sub-prefects, rectors, school inspectors, and so on—

thought differently. Motivated largely by a desire to immunize Alsatians against German ideas (above all German nationalism, but also socialist and communist ideas), these functionaries attempted to accelerate the pace of Frenchification. They lobbied for projects likely to strengthen commercial and personal ties with the interior, notably the construction of a railway line between Paris and Strasbourg (authorized in 1844 and completed in 1851). And, exploiting the impetus and resources provided by the Guizot Law of 1833, they pursued assimilationist educational policies. They set up day-care centers (*salles d'asile*) under French-speaking supervisors, they increased the time allotted to French in the primary schools, and they stocked the schools with French readers. They also took steps to make the teachers more qualified and more fluent in French, expanding the normal school founded in Strasbourg in 1810 (as the first in France) and establishing another in Colmar. There were limits to what could be done, since schooling was not compulsory and most older teachers knew little if any French, but within these limits the accomplishments were impressive.[52]

The officials of the Second Republic (1848–51) and the Second Empire (1851–70) pursued similar objectives, but with stronger support from Paris and a greater sense of urgency. By now the growth of German nationalism had convinced many that full linguistic assimilation was a matter of national security: "This determination of a large province to remain German," warned the rector of the Academy of Strasbourg in 1859, "is the argument which is fueling the rash hopes in Prussia and in Austria. In fact Alsace will be fully won over to the French Empire only when it has adopted, without reservation, the language and the spirit of France."[53] Some also argued that linguistic assimilation would make it easier to administer the region and would raise the moral tone; there were assertions that the dialect-speaking communities of Alsace were unusually prone to antisocial behavior—to drunkenness, to fighting, to crime, to poor work habits, to the circulation of unfounded rumors. There was also the matter of equity. Until Alsatians knew French, some observed, they could not exploit the opportunities for self-improvement offered by the educational system or participate fully in the political and cultural life of the nation. Hence, whether they realized it or not, it was in the interests of all Alsatians to learn French.[54]

As befitted their concern with permanent and far-reaching results, the officials gave most attention to education. To attain their goal, the rector informed the ministry, "One cannot do too much to encourage and strengthen our institutions of public instruction: day-care centers, primary schools, collèges, lycées, faculties—true citadels from which France commands Alsace and is bringing about its transformation."[55] Officials greatly expanded the number of day-care centers, which they considered particularly important means to linguistic assimilation since the children enrolled were so young. (By the late 1860s there were more than 300 such centers in Alsace, one-sixth of the national total.) In addition, various directives and the cumulative effect of the normal schools strengthened the position of French in the primary schools. Indeed in 1853 French became the official language of instruction for all but the required classes in religion. This directive was often honored in the breach—many teachers used French only when the inspector visited, if then—but by 1870 French was the predominant language of instruction in most primary schools. As for the higher levels, the struggle was over. French had long been the language of instruction in the faculties, the two lycées (in Strasbourg and Colmar), and the Catholic seminaries, and by mid-century it had dislodged German in the communal collèges and the private secondary schools, including Strasbourg's Protestant Gymnasium. The only institution still teaching in German was the Protestant Seminary, and it did not hold out for long. Beginning in the 1840s its professors gave more and more of their instruction in French in response to pressure from, among others, their students. By the late 1860s all but two or three courses were taught in French, and the exceptions enrolled only a handful.[56]

In assessing the results of the campaign for linguistic assimilation, the appropriate perspective, as educational patterns suggest, is social rather than geographic, vertical rather than horizontal. The diffusion of French was not from west to east (there was no change in the location of the linguistic frontier). Rather it occurred from the top of the social order down.

For most of those in the emergent elite of Alsace, the urban haute bourgeoisie, the dialect and German gave way to French during the Restoration or the July Monarchy. Typically, generational differences appeared within families in the 1820s, with parents adhering to their inherited Germanic dialect and customs while their children, reflecting their schooling and the innovativeness of youth, spoke French and emulated the fashions popular in Paris. In the 1830s, as those exposed to French schooling began to reach positions of influence, French attained parity with German as a language of business transactions and of high culture and scholarship. In the following decade it took over. By mid-century, French was the language of discourse for most bourgeois families and Paris was the undisputed center of the cultural world. Symptomatic was the evolution of the theater. In the 1820s plays in German had predominated and troupes from across the Rhine had regularly included Alsatian towns on their itineraries. A generation later German troupes no longer found it profitable to visit Alsace, while performances by resident companies, even of plays by Goethe and Schiller, were almost always in French.[57]

By the 1850s French was also making inroads among those lower in the social order—government employees, technicians, shopkeepers, and so on. Exposure to the language at school contributed, and so did service in the army. Probably more important, however, were economic and social factors. As networks of communication and trade expanded and the local economy became more specialized and more integrated with that of the interior, the French language acquired a utility for many that it had not had before. Put succinctly, it was during the Second Empire that "the invention of the railway finally begins to make its full influence felt. Each new line is a route for the infiltration of French."[58] The social factors were related. For those in the lower middle class the development of the economy and the associated reforms increased the pace of social mobility and popularized the idea that one should emulate one's betters. And emulating one's betters in this context meant, above all, abandoning the dialect and German in favor of French. As one Alsatian observed on returning from a prolonged stay abroad, "People here who wish to lay claim to being cultured must, I believe, show contempt for the German language in order not to appear boorish."[59] By the 1850s, in short, the regular use of French and identification with Parisian styles and intellectual life had become important signs of social status and, as such, important elements of conspicuous consumption.

For most Alsatians, however, French continued to have little utility, either economic or social. The artisans, peasants, and urban workers— who, with their dependents, constituted four-fifths of the population— tended to dismiss French as "the language of the rich,"[60] as a foreign language linked to an alien culture. They were generally indifferent to the language question, seeing no conflict between their Germanic dialect and their French patriotism. And through most of the period they resisted official efforts to use the schools as agents of linguistic assimilation, putting pressure on the teachers to use the dialect and failing to reinforce their children's efforts to learn French. Yet French did make progress among the popular classes, particularly in the 1860s. By the end of this decade, one contemporary observed, children fortunate enough to have competent and dedicated teachers were leaving school with a good knowledge of both French and German. (Those with poor teachers learned neither.)[61] And among parents there was lessening resistance to instruction in French. Admittedly the campaign was far from over. Few in the popular classes over the age of twenty had a working knowledge of French, and those younger often forgot what they had learned for lack of practice; in the mid-1860s, official estimates suggest, less than 15 percent of the population to the east of the linguistic frontier could speak French, and many in this minority did not speak the language regularly or fluently. Yet there was optimism in government circles, for the most formidable obstacle to linguistic assimilation, the resistance of the popular classes, was giving way. The full assimilation of these classes would presumably take a generation or more, as it had for those higher in the social order, but the eventual success of the campaign no longer seemed in doubt.[62]

These trends and prospects had implications for the social structure and political culture of Alsace. Until the 1860s the diffusion of French had the effect of widening the gap between the region's elites, particularly the urban bourgeoisie, and the mass of the population. On one side was a small but self-confident and powerful group whose members were, if anything, more French than their counterparts in the interior, not least because in the Alsatian context French was identified with liberalism and progress. On the other side was a largely self-contained and tradition-bound society whose members saw no more reason to abandon their semifeudal practices and attitudes than to abandon their dialect. For those in the popular classes the rest of France might as well have been a foreign country; the centers of their cultural universe were their own towns or villages, not Paris; and their behavior and outlook were governed by what was traditional, not by what was chic.[63] As for their relationship to the local elites, the characteristic disposition—except for the marginal members who were upwardly mobile—was one not of emulation but of deference. Their readiness to defer to figures of authority was most evident in the political realm, which was monopolized by the region's French-speaking notables. Until mid-century, to be sure, this monopoly did not distinguish Alsace from the interior; throughout France traditions and voting restrictions tended to leave political power in the hands of the notables. But in the rest of France the introduction of universal suffrage in 1848 and the centralizing and hence leveling reforms of the Second Empire did much to undermine the position of the notables. In Alsace they did not. Profiting from the conservatism of the mass of the population and from their possession of a locally scarce resource, knowledge of the national language, the Alsatian notables were in a more secure position than their counterparts to the west of the Vosges.

Of course their favored position could be a transitional phenomenon. Largely the result of the partial diffusion of French in Alsace, it might well be eroded by the completion of the process. In fact this possibility helped to motivate the government's efforts in the 1860s to hasten assimilation; officials hoped that the French language would be a vehicle for extending the government's authority at the expense of the local elites.[64] Viewed from this perspective, full assimilation threatened the interests of French-speaking Alsatians. But did these Alsatians see it this way? Those in the commercial and entrepreneurial bourgeoisie did not, presumably because they felt secure in their status and associated assimilation with economic and intellectual progress. There were others, however, who had misgivings. Three important groups can be distinguished: the Catholic clergy, certain scholars and literary figures, and the majority of the Lutheran clergy.

The Catholic clergy were fluent in French and often preferred to speak French among themselves. But they rarely used the language in religious services or on other public occasions, and they stoutly resisted all efforts to promote linguistic assimilation. They advanced various reasons for their stand, but easily the most important concerned the faith of their parishioners. They believed that teaching children to abandon their native tongue, their *Muttersprache,* would weaken the authority of the parents and of the others who used the language of the home, including the clergy. And substituting French made it all the worse. Spokesmen for the church, reversing one of the assimilators' standard arguments, insisted that it was not the dialect that undermined morality and order in Alsace but rather French, the language of Voltaire. From their standpoint those preferring French were uprooted and status-conscious *arrivistes* with corrupt morals and a penchant for dangerous ideas, above all anticlericalism. The faithful must be protected, and this necessitated limiting the spread of the major carrier of the disease, French. Viewed more cynically, limiting the diffusion of French would help to preserve the clergy's great influence among Catholic Alsatians, particularly in the villages and smaller towns. In much of rural Alsace the priests had replaced the landed nobility as the local notables, as those to whom commoners looked for social and political leadership, and they feared they might lose this position once the faithful knew French.[65]

The second group opposing assimilation considered it the mission of Alsace to mediate between French culture and German culture. Many Strasbourg professors contributed to this mission, as we have seen, and mediation was a primary objective of several scholarly societies and periodicals. Thus the *Revue germanique* (1858–65), founded and edited by two Alsatians, dedicated itself to reporting on literary, artistic, and scientific developments across the Rhine and called for reforms that would further this end (such as replacing the Academy of Strasbourg with a bicultural university).[66] The Société littéraire de Strasbourg (1861–70) had similar aims; on taking office its first president, Louis Spach, expressed the hope "that the Society will become in a sense the center of the entire intellectual life of the Rhine valley, that it will make known all the various works of this half German and half French region."[67] But could Strasbourg and Alsace fulfill their mediating missions if they were fully assimilated into France? Many had doubts. In a speech at the Société littéraire Spach noted that "Strasbourg, considered as a center of learning, has always been, sometimes instinctively and sometimes by design, the mediator between the two nationalities that meet within its walls; it would foolishly break with its traditions and responsibilities if it were to throw itself exclusively into the arms of one or the other nation."[68] Such reasoning encouraged many French-speaking Alsatians to support organizations dedicated to keeping alive the Germanic cultural heritage of their province, notably the Société pour la conservation des monuments historiques d'Alsace (founded in 1855). It also encouraged many to oppose the government's language policies, to warn Alsatians against viewing German with disdain, and to do much of their own writing in German. In 1852, for instance, a professor in the Faculty of the Sciences argued—in a German-language weekly—that "we must not and should not let the German language disappear in Alsace, not out of political ambitions for a possible German regime in the future but rather for historic and literary reasons. . . . I am the first to step forward when it is a matter of manifesting French patriotism; but I disapprove when Alsatians are ashamed of the German language, just as I disapprove when people are ashamed of the gospel."[69]

The third group opposing assimilation was the Protestant clergy. More precisely, it consisted of most of the Lutheran pastors. The few Calvinist ministers adapted quickly and easily to French, which was natural enough considering their intellectual links to Geneva and to southern France and the social composition of the Calvinist community. (The Calvinists, perhaps 3 percent of the population of Alsace, came primarily from the French-speaking bourgeoisie of Mulhouse and other towns in southern Alsace.) Some Lutheran pastors also supported assimilation. A few even attempted to be more French than the French, attacking Alsace and the German states for their cultural backwardness and mastering the art of speaking German with a Parisian accent. But most Lutheran clergymen considered a policy of linguistic assimilation an attack on the interests of their church. They associated French either with irreligion, as the Catholic clergy did, or with Catholicism, and they thought of German as, above all, the language of their faith—of its Bible, its hymns, and its theological scholarship. Indeed many thought the very survival of Lutheranism in Alsace was at stake: if German was under siege, so was their church.[70]

The resistance of these groups, particularly the Catholic and Lutheran clergy, slowed the pace of assimilation, as government officials readily admitted. In 1859, for instance, the rector reported that "when the Alsatian people are left to themselves, they come spontaneously to us. They would have been won over to France long ago were it not for the efforts of the Germanophile castes."[71] But it was an uneven match. The government had greater resources, and, perhaps more important, most Alsatians either seemed indifferent or, increasingly, were becoming convinced of the utility of learning French, while bourgeois Alsatians generally welcomed assimilation. Even within the Lutheran clergy there were disturbing trends. It is true that some students of Protestant theology opposed the Frenchification of Alsace, notably those belonging to two fraternities founded in the 1850s, Argentina and Wilhelmitana. (The mission of Argentina, the more Germanophile of the two, was "to be a sanctuary of the German language and German customs in the midst of an environment thoroughly steeped in French culture.")[72] But these students could not reverse the trend. In 1861 a report to the governing council of the Lutheran churches of Alsace noted that "the antipathy to German among most students in the seminary is so great that, despite the recommendations of their professors, they rarely pick up a work by a German author."[73] And a few years later a young pastor, once a stout defender of German, attempted to convince a professor that there was no future for German in Alsace and that the clergy should cease trying to postpone the inevitable: "It is necessary to sacrifice a generation and to Frenchify as rapidly as possible, regardless of cost, if we Protestant pastors are not to remain behind in the wilderness."[74] Few pastors reached this conclusion, but by the late 1860s most agreed that they were fighting a lost cause. "It is all in vain," a professor of theology conceded a month before the start of the Franco-Prussian War; "another two years of this regime and Alsace will be irretrievably lost to Germany."[75]

# 2 The Making of a Modern University

In the early stages of the Franco-Prussian War the most outspoken proponents of annexing Alsace to Prussia or to a united Germany were members of the German intellectual community: poets, novelists, and professors. These men of letters and learning buttressed their case with arguments concerning the territory's cultural traditions. Their emphasis was not on the will of the people, military necessity, or economic gain, but rather on language, culture, and ethnicity. Annexation was desirable even if it violated the wishes of those involved, for objectively the Alsatians were more German than French.[1]

Bismarck, the man primarily responsible for the decision to annex, put little stock in the racial and cultural justification, dismissing it as a "professors' idea."[2] Nor is there reason to believe, as many did at the time, that in opting for annexation the Iron Chancellor bowed to popular pressures fueled by this argument. But he did not attempt to correct this misconception, presumably because, with reasons of his own for annexation, he recognized how effectively the "professors' idea" could mobilize the support of Germany's educated middle class.[3]

The argument that Alsace should be annexed because its inhabitants were at root German rested on the assumption that this latent Germanness could be brought to the surface. More specifically, the protagonists reasoned that the Alsatians would soon discover their true identity if only the proper cultural and educational policies were pursued.[4] It was a logic that assigned a key role to German intellectuals and educators. Indeed the whole outlook of the German professors on the Alsatian question may be seen as a product of a more general desire, now that *Realpolitik* had registered its most important successes, to turn attention back to the idea of the *Kulturstaat* and, with it, to the special responsibilities of the professors that this idea implied. Bismarck may have brought about German unification, but now the professors should return to the fore since they could make major contributions both to the consolidation of the new state and to the spread of its renown abroad.[5] This high opinion of the importance of education and of the educators was shared by those annexationists who, beginning in August 1870, advanced what amounted to another "professors' idea": establishing a German university in Strasbourg.

Two historians, Wilhelm Maurenbrecher of Königsberg and Heinrich von Treitschke of Heidelberg, were the first to call for a new University of Strasbourg. They did so late in August, a few days before the decisive Battle of Sedan (2 September) and a month before the capitulation of Strasbourg (28 September). Maurenbrecher advanced the idea in a pamphlet advocating Prussian annexation of the German-speaking sections of Alsace and Lorraine. Although conceding that Prussia would have difficulties integrating this territory, he argued that a properly designed university would facilitate the job: "What the University of Bonn has been for the Rhineland, the University of Strasbourg, expanded to the full richness of a German university, will be for Alsace: a center of intellectual life that fosters the most direct association with all sources and currents of intellectual activity in the entire fatherland."[6] Treitschke's remarks, which had much in common with Maurenbrecher's, appeared in an article on war aims in the influential *Preussische Jahrbücher*. In justifying the annexation of Alsace and Lorraine, Treitschke referred to the right of the sword and, in the case of the French-speaking regions of Lorraine, to militarily "natural" borders, but he put his main emphasis on racial and cultural arguments: "We wish to give them back, against their wishes, their true selves."[7] Following annexation, of course, efforts would have to be initiated to reconcile the Alsatians to their new rulers and to German culture. In this connection Treitschke turned his attention to the educational institutions of Strasbourg, and particularly to the proposed university: "Why should not Strasbourg's venerable university, restored after its disgraceful mutilation, work just as prosperously for German culture on the upper Rhine as Bonn has worked for the lower Rhine? Another *Rhenana* in the upper valley—surely a worthy outgrowth of this German war, this contest of ideas against material selfishness."[8]

During the autumn of 1870 other Germans publicly called for a university in Strasbourg, usually emphasizing, like Maurenbrecher and Treitschke, its potential contributions to the assimilation of the annexed territory.[9] And several discussed the subject privately in ways suggesting that the early establishment of a university was inevitable. Thus within days of the capitulation of Strasbourg a Berlin professor had made recommendations "in the appropriate place" concerning scholars to be called "to the new University of Strasbourg that is to be established."[10] And by the end of November a number of scholars, sensing an opportunity to further their careers, had informed friends or officials of their interest in positions at the proposed institution.[11] In sum, by late 1870 the belief that a new university would be organized in Alsace was widespread in Germany, particularly within the academic community.

But what was the thinking in government circles? This question can best be considered in the context of events in the captured provinces.

At the outbreak of the Franco-Prussian War the sympathies of virtually all Alsatians were with France. Even those who had led the resistance to Frenchification doubted that any good could come of a Prussian victory. While Strasbourg was under siege, for instance, the most Germanophile of the professors in the Protestant Seminary wrote to a German friend as follows:

> As we again look ahead to the future we are ready to shed tears of blood, those of us who count ourselves among the more cultured and elevated part of the local citizenry. The dreadful material destruction will be repaired after a number of years, yet with sadness we say: Strasbourg is done for! Nothing can bring back to our town its old literary reputation, nothing can connect it anymore with its beautiful past. . . . We have been wounded in our deepest feelings, we, the Protestant inhabitants.[12]

Another seminary professor would later comment that the period when the French cultural influence finally became dominant in Alsace, and particularly in its leading city, began not in 1789, 1830, or 1848, but rather on 24 August 1870, the first day of the German bombardment of Strasbourg.[13]

But if Alsatians were united in supporting France, behind the unity lay divisions along linguistic, religious, social, and geographic lines, divisions which became more pronounced as the prospects of a future under German rule grew. For some the very idea of such a future was intolerable, leaving emigration as the only alternative. For most, emigration was not an acceptable option, at least not until more was known about the new regime; undesirable as their new situation might be, they were resigned, at least for the time being, to living with it. But living with it would mean different things to different groups and be easier for some than for others. It could be assumed, for instance, that the new rulers would meet less resistance in Lower Alsace (Bas-Rhin) than in Upper Alsace (Haut-Rhin), and less in Alsace generally than in the annexed part of Lorraine. It was probable, too, that rural areas would pose fewer problems than the towns and cities, particularly since most of the countryside had not experienced the war at first hand while many towns and cities had come under bombardment. And in all likelihood the Lutherans would reconcile themselves to German rule more easily than the Calvinists or the Catholics or the Jews. In this regard the war itself had exacerbated religious and linguistic divisions, with those who were Catholic or French-speaking becoming increasingly suspicious of the loyalties of the Protestant and dialect-speaking minority, and the latter, in response, becoming increasingly worried about its prospects should Alsace-Lorraine remain under French rule.[14]

Yet, while such observations could be made with confidence, it would have been difficult to be more specific without knowing how the annexed territory would be governed. Would the new rulers be repressive, as the Prussian army officers seemed to favor being, or conciliatory? If the latter, what would this mean in practice? Which subgroups of the region's diverse population would the authorities seek to conciliate first, and at whose expense? The very uncertainty over these questions meant that Alsatians had to consider another: should they try to influence their new rulers? There might well be room to maneuver, with opportunities for those seizing the initiative to improve their positions at the expense of the new regime and of their traditional rivals within Alsace-Lorraine. But if seizing the initiative involved bargaining with the German authorities, it could entail heavy costs, for it would be widely regarded as a form of collaboration with the enemy. The resulting dilemma faced many Alsatians, including those concerned with higher education.

Following the capitulation of Strasbourg deep differences developed among the local academy's professors over what to do about the institution. Some simply avoided the problem by emigrating; by the time the German authorities arrived, the rector and many of the professors who were not Alsatian had moved to the interior of France. Another group—the majority, it seems—remained but showed no interest in returning to the classroom. Like most Strasbourgeois, they continued to hope that the war would somehow take a turn for the better and that French troops would oust the Germans. It would not be until late in the winter, after France's National Assembly voted to cede Alsace-Lorraine to the newly established German Empire, that they would seriously consider whether to teach under the new regime. Finally, there were a few professors who favored reopening the academy as soon as possible. Their leader was Johann Friedrich Bruch, the dean of the Faculty of Protestant Theology. Shortly after the fall of Strasbourg, Bruch convened the academy's deans to discuss the project. But he received little encouragement. One dean refused to attend the meeting, two others rejected Bruch's proposal outright, and the fourth expressed serious reservations. The only real support came from the other Protestant theologians, who with one exception agreed to teach at least through the winter. The necessary preparations were soon completed, and by the end of November the faculty was in session again, with about forty students.[15]

Bruch's motives are unclear. It is known that there was considerable suspicion among the Strasbourgeois. Some accused him of trying to exploit the confusion that followed the city's fall to usurp control of the academy. And in view of Bruch's reputation as a defender of German culture and scholarship in Alsace, many probably assumed he was trying to facilitate the consolidation of the new regime. Bruch himself insisted that his only objective was to defend the interests of the city and the academy.[16] Where the truth lies is uncertain, but there is probably something to be said for both Bruch and his critics. In this regard it should be noted that the academy's professors knew little if anything of the provisional government's intentions. Some seem to have assumed that if the region remained under German rule the establishment of a German university was inevitable.[17] But others had their doubts, among them Eduard Reuss, a Protestant theologian who, like Bruch, belonged to the academy's small minority of Germanophile professors. In a letter written in early November to a German theologian, Reuss expressed the hope that the war and its outcome, for all the suffering they had caused, would at least mean "that our ties to German scholarship, which we have always cultivated so conscientiously, will be closer and more productive." But, he added,

> is it not just as likely that we shall fare poorly even in this regard? Our university library, as well as the city library, is destroyed, and it is irreplaceable. Our lecture halls are sick bays, our students are scattered. The French are naturally not coming anymore; the Alsatians will prefer to attend German universities, and with reason. And considering Germany's abundance of such institutions, what government, especially with exhausted resources, will be disposed to establish one in Strasbourg merely because of the renown that our ancestors brought to the city?[18]

In light of these remarks it may be speculated that one of Bruch's objectives was to pressure the new regime. He may have hoped that by keeping alive Strasbourg's reputation as a center of higher education he would encourage the Germans to establish a university and to incorporate within it many of the academy's traditions and professors. Such an objective would have been consistent both with a desire to facilitate the consolidation of the new order and with a desire to defend the interests of the city and the academy.

Whatever Bruch's motives, the provisional government, intent on restoring stability and a sense of continuity to the annexed territory, supported his initiative. But at the same time, and apparently without the knowledge of Bruch or his colleagues, it took steps of its own. As early as September the possibility of organizing a German university in Strasbourg had been discussed in Berlin. By early November—when Reuss was expressing his concern about the new regime's intentions—it was assumed within the provisional government that there would be a university. Soon planning began. In December officials asked the Bonn historian Heinrich von Sybel for advice concerning the project and, guided by Sybel's detailed response, prepared a tentative budget.[19] In February

1871 the director of the provisional government's civilian branch recommended to Berlin that the former academy, "the glory of Alsace and
its gateway to advancement," be transformed into a German university.[20]
And in March, in the first public discussion of the new regime's intentions,
an article by an official of the provisional government argued that a completely new and thoroughly German university must be established in
Strasbourg. It would be a university with a special mission:

> The German university must become the central point from which
> German learning and culture, the German morality and point of view,
> are diffused through Alsace. . . . If there is anywhere that German
> learning has an opportunity and a motive to demonstrate its moral
> strength, it is here. . . . With respect for German learning and culture
> will be linked respect for the nation and the proud feeling of belonging
> to it.[21]

Such official pronouncements and the realization that France intended
to abandon Alsace-Lorraine stimulated interest in the project among Alsatians and caused many to speak out in the hope of shaping the government's as yet uncertain plans. In at least one case, that of the Lutheran
pastor and historian Julius Rathgeber, this meant encouraging the authorities to establish a thoroughly German university under Prussian control.[22] But most Alsatian lobbyists stressed the need for concessions. Thus
F. G. Bergmann, an earlier critic of the Napoleonic university, privately
urged the provisional government to offer attractive positions at the new
institution to the former academy's professors.[23] Louis Spach, a leading
proponent of Strasbourg's mediating mission, defended the academy against
the criticisms common in the German press and recommended that the
academy provide the foundation for the new university.[24] In mid-April an
assembly of ninety-one notables from Lower Alsace called the establishment of a university in Strasbourg "a matter of vital importance to our
town, which does not wish to descend from the heights of its splendid
past to the level of a mere garrison town," and suggested that the institution should be under Alsatian control and, perhaps, bilingual.[25] About
the same time an anonymous Alsatian contributor to Augsburg's influential *Allgemeine Zeitung* argued that the projected university should have
professors who would lecture in French, "so that a significant resource
will not be withdrawn from the province through the emigration of gifted
youths."[26] And at the end of April, Charles Schützenberger sent the authorities a twenty-seven page memorandum calling for extensive concessions. Schützenberger began by acknowledging the general excellence of
the German university system, as he had a year before in his critique of
the Napoleonic university, but he went on to argue that the proposed
institution should not be modeled on those in the rest of Germany: "An
exclusively German university erected on the ruins of our old institutions

would appear as something hostile in Alsace, as an institution destined to destroy the French language—which has become, in the past few generations, the scientific and literary language of the entire population—and all with a view to enslaving minds and smothering all autonomous development in our provinces."[27] The university should be under Alsatian control, and the German authorities should make a declaration to this effect so as to encourage the academy's Alsatian professors to remain. An exodus of these professors, he added, would result in a boycott of the new university by Alsatian students, which would not be in Germany's interests. In conclusion, Schützenberger insisted that the university would offer the most to all concerned "if the imperial German government decides to take more account of the intellectual needs of the people of Alsace and Lorraine than of the ultra-Germanic impatience of some of the university professors across the Rhine."[28]

Of course the authorities could dismiss such recommendations as merely the desperate proposals of Alsatians intent on obstructing the Germanization of their homeland. But the developing struggle over the character of the proposed university did not simply pit Francophile Alsatians against "ultra-Germanic" nationalists. This became clear in May, when Germany's newly constituted national assembly, the Reichstag, took up the matter.

During May and early June 1871 the Reichstag devoted much of its attention to enacting legislation designed to regularize the situation in Alsace-Lorraine, the territory having been formally ceded to Germany with the ratification on 10 May of the Treaty of Frankfurt. The key bill, introduced by Bismarck on 2 May and passed on 10 June, stated that the region would neither form an autonomous state within the German Empire nor be attached to any existing state. Rather, it would be an imperial territory, a *Reichsland,* directly administered by the imperial government. Eventually the provisions of the new German constitution were to be introduced, but during an interim period—it actually lasted through 1873—the emperor, advised by the Bundesrat, the assembly that represented the empire's constituent states, and by the chancellor, would have full authority. In practice this arrangement put effective control of Alsatian affairs in the hands of Bismarck and the Imperial Chancellery.[29]

Although the Reichstag's deliberations focused on constitutional and administrative questions, they provided an opportunity to consider other matters relating to Alsace-Lorraine. Among those matters was the future of higher education in the region. The stimulus came from two related resolutions. The first, cosponsored by Georg Thomas (National Liberal) and Hermann Köchly (Progressive), dealt in general terms with the cultural policies to be pursued in Alsace-Lorraine and recommended specifically that "the establishment of a German university in Strasbourg be brought about." This resolution was distinguished by its conciliatory tone; it suggested that the Alsatian educational system be reorganized "with every possible regard for existing conditions," and that the proposed "model German university" be designed "with the greatest possible retention of hitherto proven and prepared teachers and the necessary consideration of the peculiarities of that borderland."[30] The second resolution, sponsored by Wilhelm Wehrenpfennig (National Liberal), was offered as a substitute for the first. It dealt exclusively with the proposed university, simply stating that the Reichstag wished "to call upon the Imperial Chancellor to bring about the establishment of a German university in Strasbourg as soon as possible."[31]

A few participants in the debate opposed both resolutions. A spokesman for the Conservatives did so for constitutional reasons. Although in favor of a university, he thought the Reichstag should not limit the authority of the chancellor and his subordinates to proceed as they saw fit.[32] Another deputy, a Catholic clergyman, expressed the general opposition of his church and its political arm, the Center party, to the introduction of state-controlled education in Alsace-Lorraine. If this predominantly Catholic region was ever to be assimilated, he argued, it was essential that its Catholic clergy be appeased, and this could not be accomplished by the proposed university, which would doubtless be a bastion of anti-Catholicism.[33] A third critic, Heinrich Ewald, also distrusted state-controlled higher education, but for different reasons. Ewald was a retired biblical scholar long active in the defense of academic freedom against political and bureaucratic pressures. One of the "Göttingen Seven" of 1837, he had returned to Göttingen after the upheavals of 1848 only to be dismissed again in 1867 when he refused to declare his allegiance to Prussia following its annexation of Hanover. It was as a Hanoverian deputy—as an anti-Prussian protester—that he now attacked the proposed university as yet another attempt to subordinate higher education to political objectives: "As soon as one desires to use instruction as a means of naked coercion in order to gain political ends, as so often happens now, at this point I say, that is the most perverted and deplorable thing one can do."[34] Ewald went on to question the very idea of reorganizing the educational system of Alsace-Lorraine "according to the German style and in the German spirit." What, after all, was the basis of education? Was it to be assumed that only some people, perhaps only the Germans, had a monopoly on knowledge and truth? Rejecting this possibility, he proceeded to criticize the wisdom of establishing a "German university" in Strasbourg.[35]

In defending their resolution, Köchly and Thomas employed different approaches. Thomas stressed practical considerations. He agreed that the educational system of Alsace-Lorraine should be used to advance Germany's political objectives, but insisted that the best approach would be a conciliatory one. More specifically, while a university was of the utmost importance, it should not break completely with its French predecessor: "The main concern with the transformation of the University of Strasbourg will be to keep the teachers, the French teachers, insofar as they are capable and experienced—indeed it will be in our interests somewhat later even to hear French lectures in certain subjects."[36] Köchly went further. An academic with credentials as an educational reformer, he began by expressing the hope that Alsatians would be consulted before any decision was made. He then spelled out what he thought they would recommend. Regarding higher education he argued that Alsatians did desire a German university, in the sense of a university with full academic freedom and administrative autonomy. But what they really wanted was a university that combined the best of French and the best of German learning.

> There are certainly things that we can still learn from the French, and, Gentlemen, for that reason the idea of some kind of—do not be frightened by the term—some kind of "international university," at which a number of professorial chairs would be occupied jointly by distinguished German and distinguished French scholars, would surely not be a monster in theory, nor can Strasbourg be considered an unsuitable place for it.[37]

Köchly added that in the previous decade this ideal of a model university with courses taught in both French and German had been "the objective of the most enlightened Swiss statesmen."[38] It should be noted, too, that another German had recently made a similar proposal with reference to Strasbourg: late in 1870 a Prussian lawyer had recommended publicly that universities be established in Strasbourg and in Metz—the first and last proposal that there be two universities in the captured territory—and that these be "hotbeds both of German scholarly methods and of French stylistic grace."[39] But such ideas could expect little support from Germans in the aftermath of the Franco-Prussian War, a war widely regarded as having either confirmed or established Germany's cultural supremacy in Europe.[40]

The two major spokesmen for the second resolution, Robert Roemer and Wehrenpfennig, more accurately reflected prevailing sentiments. They put their emphasis not on cosmopolitanism or on the need to conciliate Alsatians but rather on the greatness of Germany's culture and the excellence of her educational traditions. This emphasis led them to reject the recommendation that the new institution retain ties to the old academy. Since the academy had not embodied the idealistic and neohumanistic precepts that had guided the development of the German universities, Wehrenpfennig argued, the only solution was to establish a totally new university, one patterned on those in Germany and staffed with "pioneers of the German intellect." He even suggested, by distorting the meaning of the petition prepared by the ninety-one notables from Lower Alsace, that this was also the objective of concerned Alsatians.[41] Roemer made essentially the same points, although with more emphasis on what the German universities represented and on what establishing one in Alsace-Lorraine would accomplish:

> The German universities, resting on the first principles of freedom, are so characteristic a German institution that no other people, even a kindred one, has been able to develop this institution, and for that very reason a German university is also one of the most powerful means of once again uniting and reconciling to their mother country comrades of the German race who have long been separated from it. If we establish a German university in the grand style in Strasbourg, we may be assured that it will work wonders toward the goal that we all seek.[42]

In support Roemer cited the example used by Maurenbrecher and Treitschke nine months before, the University of Bonn, insisting that it had contributed as much as all the military fortresses to Prussia's assimilation and defense of the Rhineland. A new university in Strasbourg would have a similar impact; indeed it would be "one of the most solid bastions" of the new Germany.[43]

The debate ended with two voice votes, one resulting in the defeat of the Köchly-Thomas resolution, despite strong support from liberals, and the other in the almost unanimous acceptance of Wehrenpfennig's substitute.[44] The first resolution lost both because of a widely shared reluctance to involve the Reichstag in the details of policymaking in Alsace-Lorraine, a reluctance encouraged by Bismarck, and because many opposed the particular policies proposed in the resolution and the supporting speeches.[45] To most deputies the substitute resolution appeared preferable since it only expressed the wishes of the Reichstag, restricted itself to higher education, and said nothing about specific policies. In other words, it passed largely because it was so innocuous.

The Reichstag's action had no noticeable effect on the policies of Bismarck or of the Imperial Chancellery or of the Reichsland's provisional government. But it did have an unforeseen impact in France. At the end of May a resolution was introduced in France's National Assembly in direct response to the Wehrenpfennig bill just passed by the Reichstag. Aimed at undercutting the projected German university, it called for the merger of the four secular faculties of Strasbourg's defunct academy with the three faculties (law, sciences, and letters) in Nancy, the largest town in the part of Lorraine still under French rule. The resulting University of Nancy—it was to be called a university, not an academy—must be as distinguished as the best German universities, for it would have an important national mission: "It will be . . . the living fount where the youth of Alsace and

Lorraine—the youth of the cities of Metz, Strasbourg, Colmar, Mulhouse—will come to reinvigorate its love for the French *patrie*. There is a political interest in this whose importance it is unnecessary to emphasize."[46] The resolution was referred to a committee without debate, but over the next few weeks the project received serious attention elsewhere. A delegation from French Lorraine petitioned the premier to transfer the former Strasbourg faculties to Nancy. The municipal council of Nancy, welcoming this opportunity to build up the local academy, made its sentiments known. And the French government's commission on higher education recommended the development in Nancy of "a scientific center of the first rank designed to assert on the new frontiers the intellectual authority and the scientific life of France."[47]

These proposals and petitions did what the Wehrenpfennig bill had failed to do: they convinced German officials that a university must be organized in Strasbourg as soon as possible. Thus early in July the Reichsland's provisional governor-general complained to the Imperial Chancellery about its continued silence concerning the Strasbourg project and argued that the French plan to attract Alsatian students to Nancy made it imperative that Strasbourg's university be organized quickly. The goal should be to begin courses in the more important subjects at the start of the next academic year, in October. To attain this goal, he continued, it was necessary that

> a distinguished individual who is completely familiar with the German university system, perhaps a statesman or scholar, be sent here immediately to make an authoritative judgment about the reorganization. It would be desirable that he not adhere to a fixed political philosophy, and such a man would perhaps most likely be found among the gentlemen of the law; also the former Baden minister Herr von Roggenbach has been suggested to me for the job because of his familiarity with local conditions.[48]

The Imperial Chancellery, persuaded of the need for haste, recommended to Bismarck that Roggenbach, the one candidate mentioned in the appeal from Strasbourg, be commissioned to organize the new university. The chancellor assented, and on receiving the emperor's authorization offered Roggenbach the position. Within days Roggenbach accepted the commission and informed Bismarck that he would orient himself and then request an audience to discuss his responsibilities.[49]

Baron Franz von Roggenbach was in many respects an obvious candidate for the commission. Since the early 1860s, when he was the leading minister of the state of Baden, he had been one of the most prominent south German supporters of German unification under Prussian leadership. He was familiar with conditions in Alsace and had been an early proponent of the region's annexation.[50] He was a Catholic, which would presumably make his appointment more acceptable in the Reichsland, but not an ultramontane, which would have made it unacceptable to most Germans.[51] And he had a strong interest in academic affairs and moved comfortably in professorial circles. In the early 1860s he had worked closely with the grand duke of Baden on a program of reform for the state's schools and universities, one embodying neohumanist ideals as they had evolved over the previous half century. He had also campaigned successfully for the appointment of Prussophile professors to the grand duchy's universities in Freiburg and Heidelberg, and was close to many prominent figures in German academic life, including Hermann Baumgarten, Wilhelm Dilthey, Robert von Mohl, and Theodor Mommsen.[52]

Yet despite these qualifications Roggenbach's selection was somewhat surprising, for his relations with Bismarck had long been characterized by conflict and mutual distrust. Since 1865, when he resigned from the ministry in Baden, Roggenbach had become closely associated with the queen and the crown prince of Prussia and had encouraged them in their liberal inclinations and their misgivings about the chancellor.[53] For his part, Bismarck never thought more highly of Roggenbach than he did of the others in the crown prince's entourage; as far as he was concerned, he remarked privately in 1870, Roggenbach "always was a fool." But if this was his opinion, why did he ask Roggenbach to organize the University of Strasbourg?[54] Perhaps he welcomed the opportunity to divert Roggenbach's time and energies from politics and Berlin. Or perhaps he hoped to appease those, led by the crown prince, lobbying for Roggenbach's appointment to an administrative post in Alsace-Lorraine. Earlier negotiations over such an appointment had foundered when Bismarck refused to offer Roggenbach more than a subordinate position and Roggenbach decided that he could not work comfortably under the chancellor's direction.[55] Bismarck may have reasoned that the commission to organize the Reichsland's university was the one job in the region on which both he and Roggenbach could agree.

After accepting the commission Roggenbach went to Strasbourg to study the situation and to prepare a tentative plan for the university. Early in September he presented his preliminary proposals to Bismarck in Gastein (Austria), where the chancellor was vacationing. Bismarck, impressed by what had been accomplished, now authorized Roggenbach to proceed on the basis of his tentative plan and accepted his recommendation that the university's inauguration be postponed until the following spring.[56] Roggenbach then returned to Strasbourg to continue his preliminary studies. In mid-October, having completed these studies and presented the results in two long memorandums, he went to Berlin, where he consulted various professors and politicians and wrote several short reports elaborating on his original proposals. By the beginning of December he had completed his plans, and, following Bismarck's instructions, he submitted his recommendations to the Imperial Chancellery for its approval.

## • 2 •

Roggenbach had two basic objectives as he prepared his plans. The most important was to design a university that would make the greatest possible contribution to the reconciliation of Alsatians to German rule. The second objective, considered compatible with the first, was to introduce several innovations. Roggenbach believed, with others, that the University of Strasbourg should be to the 1870s what the Universities of Göttingen and Berlin had been to the mid-eighteenth and early nineteenth centuries, respectively: the spearhead of an overdue movement for reform in German higher education.[57]

What kind of university would be most likely to succeed as an instrument of cultural assimilation? His proposals suggest that Roggenbach saw some merit both in the nationalistic arguments of Treitschke, Roemer, and others, and in the conciliatory approach advocated by Köchly, Thomas, and many Alsatians. He began one memorandum by noting that "there should be founded in Strasbourg a German university of the first rank, a respectable cultural home of the German intellect and guardian of the German scientific method."[58] And he was quite willing to employ the derogatory oversimplifications so popular with educated Germans when discussing the intellectual life of France. Thus he defended one proposal with the claim that its adoption was necessary at "a university which is to be newly founded as an outpost of German culture and German intellect in an originally German borderland harmed in many ways by Romance dilettantism and scientific superficiality."[59] He also believed, at least at first, that some professorships would contribute directly to Germanization. In one of his earlier memorandums, for instance, he argued that a chair of German history, an unprecedented position, was necessary "particularly in order to instruct the numerous prospective Protestant clergymen and secondary school teachers who will be educated [in Strasbourg] and will become the representatives of German nationalism in the province."[60] Yet Roggenbach was rather pessimistic about the missionary potential of German learning in isolation, and the more familiar he became with local conditions the more pessimistic he became. He doubted that a university that was exclusively "an outpost of German culture and German intellect" would have much impact on Alsatians not already sympathetic to the new regime, for he feared they would not respect or even attend an institution identified only with an alien culture. Accordingly he recommended concessions. Two received particular emphasis: offering chairs to the Alsatians who had taught at the academy or the Protestant Seminary, and *not* establishing a faculty of Catholic theology.

Roggenbach realized that the appointment of Alsatian scholars would enhance the university's appeal to prospective students from the Reichsland. But there were risks. Of the twenty-four professors of the academy or the Protestant Seminary still in Strasbourg only the seven Protestant theologians had reputations that extended across the Rhine, and some of the others were no longer active scholars. Thus reserving several chairs for Alsatians would adversely affect the new university's stature and hence its attractiveness to students from outside the Reichsland. In addition most Alsatian professors were strongly Francophile, so their appointment might limit the university's potential as an agent of assimilation. For these reasons some Germans argued that all Francophile scholars should be excluded from the university and encouraged to emigrate.[61] But Roggenbach, believing the risks justified, recommended that chairs be offered all those in question. His one qualification concerned the professors of medicine. To ensure that the new medical faculty would be of high stature and not a Francophile enclave within the university, Roggenbach proposed that Germans be named to all chairs. To accommodate the Alsatians willing to join them, the appropriate positions would be shared by two occupants.[62]

As his second major concession Roggenbach recommended that there be no Catholic theological faculty. Shortly after arriving in Strasbourg he had learned that the local bishop would recognize such a faculty only if given the authority to appoint its professors. This condition was consistent with the concordat of 1801, which still regulated Catholic affairs in Alsace-Lorraine, but at odds with the practice in Germany.[63] Roggenbach sought a compromise, but when the bishop proved obstinate he decided to abandon the project. He defended his recommendation with two arguments. First, he observed that recent developments within the Catholic church—he was referring to the debate over papal infallibility—made this a particularly inappropriate time to establish a Catholic theological faculty. Here Roggenbach, himself a Catholic, hinted at the idea, popular with German liberals, that Catholic scholarship was a contradiction in terms and had no place in a modern university. Second, and more significant, he emphasized that any attempt to establish a Catholic theological faculty without meeting the bishop's terms would antagonize the Reichsland's influential Catholic hierarchy. In principle a confrontation between the state and the church might be desirable, but the proper place for it was "in areas that have long been securely German," not in Alsace-Lorraine.[64] As with his recommendation concerning chairs for Alsatian scholars, Roggenbach reasoned that the university would defeat its purposes if it violated the wishes of influential segments of the local population.

Roggenbach felt obliged to set one objective above all others: the organization of a university that would make the greatest possible contribution to the assimilation of Alsace-Lorraine. But he considered this compatible with a second goal, that of institutionalizing reforms as yet uncommon in the German academic system. Since the 1850s Roggenbach had favored major changes in German education. In 1859 and again in 1862 he had advised the grand duke of Baden on reforms designed to establish a model system of education, a system he had hoped would soon be emulated throughout a united Germany. Because of strong opposition, particularly from religious interests, Roggenbach and the grand duke had accomplished little. But the commission to plan the first German university founded in over half a century provided Roggenbach with another chance, and he seized it: he set out to make the Alsatian institution the very model of a modern university.[65]

He had strong support within the German academic community. Despite the great renown of the German universities several professors had become convinced in recent years of the need for reform. Of course the German universities had changed in certain ways since the era of Schelling and Humboldt and Hegel. Most significantly, their scholarly climate had become increasingly empirical, a trend reflected in the establishment of numerous philological seminars beginning in the 1820s and of scientific laboratories and medical clinics after the middle of the century.[66] But the proponents of reform sought more than new facilities for research. Impressed by the industrial revolution and by the accomplishments of *Realpolitiker* like Bismarck, they thought the trends of the time necessitated adding new subjects to the curriculum and altering the structure of the university. As yet, however, they had made little headway. In only a few cases had they overcome the formidable opposition put up by defenders of vested interests and of the traditional academic order. This record explains why news of the plan to establish a university in Alsace aroused such interest among advocates of educational reform. As the historian Alfred Dove put it, "Unencumbered by the deadweight of medieval prejudices and statutes, the organization of the university can be changed to accord with the demands of the spirit of the age."[67]

But what were the demands of the spirit of the age, and how could the new university be adapted to them? Dove was but one of many who made known their views in the hope of shaping the university. These men advocated numerous reforms in their articles, memorandums, letters, and conversations, but two received by far the most attention: the division of the faculty of philosophy into two separate faculties and the elevation of the social sciences to higher academic status.

Central to the movement for university reform was the campaign to divide the faculty of philosophy into two faculties, one for the humanistic disciplines and the other for mathematics and the natural sciences. The prolonged debate over this reform revealed clearly the split between the traditionalists and the modernists within the German academic community.[68] The traditionalists, true to the teachings of Schelling, thought the faculty of philosophy should remain intact to symbolize the unity of all knowledge. They defended the medieval structure of the German university and complained that the movement to dismantle the faculty of philosophy reflected the lamentable trend toward the proliferation of specialized disciplines.[69] The modernists, on the other hand, argued that the faculty of philosophy no longer functioned efficiently as an administrative unit. Not only had the number of professors increased significantly but also, whatever the traditionalists might think, many disciplines had nothing in common. Since chemists and Greek philologists exhibited little understanding of each other's interests, how could they vote sensibly on them in faculty meetings? Before 1871 the modernists had prevailed at only one German university, in 1863 at Tübingen.[70] But they continued to lobby at every promising opportunity, and in 1871 they gained another victory: Roggenbach recommended that there be two separate faculties in Strasbourg rather than the traditional faculty of philosophy.[71]

The second major reform concerned what were coming to be known as the social sciences. In 1871 at least four professors argued that the German universities should give greater attention to such disciplines as economics and political science and that the University of Strasbourg would be a good place to begin.[72] The fullest discussion appeared in a short book written during the summer by Carl Dietzel, a political economist at Marburg. Dietzel began by insisting that German unification had given new importance to the social sciences. Recent events had demonstrated the irrelevance of idealistic theories about the state and society; what was now needed was a concern for the state as it really is. If the universities were to do their share to strengthen Germany, he continued, they must contribute more to the "dissemination of correct political thinking and learning."[73] A good way to start would be to make one German university a center for the study of politics and economics. Here a separate faculty of political science should be organized, with close ties to the faculty of law. But this reform would be impossible at any of the existing universities, since they were too tradition-bound. Hence it was particularly important to exploit the opportunity presented in Strasbourg "to create a model institution for the study of the political sciences."[74] Such an institution, Dietzel argued, would be a more effective instrument of Germanization and would also provide a stimulus for the reform of the other German universities.[75]

Roggenbach was as sympathetic to the social sciences as he was to the natural sciences. In one memorandum he argued that the recent expansion of knowledge in political economy and political science necessitated setting aside several chairs for these disciplines, and a little later he recommended appointing a total of ten professors in the social sciences. (Most German universities had no more than two or three.)[76] Roggenbach also proposed affiliating these professors not with the Faculty of Philosophy, as precedents would suggest, but with the Faculty of Law or, as he suggested naming it, the Faculty of Political Science and Law. This faculty was to have two sections, one corresponding to a traditional law faculty and the other to the kind of faculty advocated by Dietzel.[77]

The division of the Faculty of Philosophy and the upgrading of the social sciences were the most significant of the reforms proposed for the new university, and the most widely supported. But other innovations received consideration. Typically each was the pet project of a single person. Thus in the spring of 1871 the occupant of one of Germany's two university chairs of forestry proposed that a third chair be established in Strasbourg, a recommendation repeated by Roggenbach.[78] In October a Forty-Eighter who had recently returned to Germany, Friedrich Kapp, convinced Roggenbach to make room in his plans for an *Extraordinarius* (associate professor) in American history.[79] And in November someone persuaded Roggenbach to revise his proposals to include a chair of astrophysics, apparently Germany's first.[80] But with one exception such individual appeals sought only limited changes in Roggenbach's plans. The exception was a memorandum composed by the Breslau philosopher Wilhelm Dilthey.

On one level Dilthey's memorandum was a response to those proposing that the university give special emphasis either to the natural sciences or to the social sciences. Dilthey wanted reform, too, but he was a modernist with a difference. He favored separating the administration of mathematics and the natural sciences from that of the humanities, and he thought the study of law and political science should receive particular attention in Strasbourg. But his chief concern was with revivifying the human sciences (*Geisteswissenschaften*), with making relevant to an age of realism the disciplines most closely identified with traditionalism and idealism. Accordingly he recommended that the new university give special attention to these disciplines. For too long, he argued, German higher education had slighted the human sciences in favor, particularly, of the natural sciences; this tendency must be corrected, and the University of Strasbourg was the proper place to begin. But there was an additional reason for following his advice, one specific to the university's mission in the Reichsland:

> The natural sciences are not what raise the moral and political ideas of a suppressed people. Examination of the deterioration of France while her exact sciences were in their prime demonstrates this. The power to stimulate national sentiments and moral strength lies in the historical-philosophical sciences. At the same time these sciences are the distinctively German ones. Through them Alsatian culture will again be linked to a great past. Through them a direct influence will be exerted on the Alsatians' understanding of history and politics.[81]

Not content with generalizing about the virtues of the human sciences, Dilthey offered a detailed plan for the new university's Faculty of Philosophy (defined as excluding mathematics and the natural sciences). He listed eighteen chairs that should be established—no German university had more for the humanities, and only Berlin had as many—and recommended suitable candidates for half of them. That six of the positions had few if any German precedents suggests that Dilthey's preoccupation with the human sciences did not stem from traditionalist sympathies. These six were the chairs for the modern history of the Romance peoples, for the history of modern art, for finance, for politics, for a philosopher "thoroughly grounded in mathematics and physics" (who would be difficult to find "at present and perhaps for a long time to come"), and for a philosopher "thoroughly grounded in historical science." About the last of these chairs, Dilthey observed:

> One of the philosophers must also bear responsibility for the history of the intellectual movements of modern Europe: for only the philosopher possesses a sufficiently rigorous foundation for this most complicated division of the history of recent literature. A university at which the study of the peaceful interaction of France and Germany in the development of scholarship by all means needs strong representation must give particular attention to the treatment of the history of intellectual movements in modern Europe. Accordingly the third professorship of philosophy would probably best be filled in this sense.[82]

Although Dilthey recommended candidates for many of the positions he proposed, he nominated nobody for this chair, the one that evidently interested him most. Perhaps he assumed that no candidate was more qualified than himself.

Roggenbach shared Dilthey's desire to give new life to the human sciences, even if he did not follow many of Dilthey's specific recommendations. Like Dilthey he proposed that there be eighteen *Ordinarien* (full professors) in the Faculty of Philosophy (defined, again, as excluding mathematics and the natural sciences). And like Dilthey he allotted several chairs to subjects given little if any attention at other German universities. In addition to the chair in German history, already mentioned, Roggenbach recommended establishing the country's first chair for modern German literature, the first chair for Jewish studies, the second chair for art history, and the first chair for ethnography, anthropology, and paleontology. And although rejecting Dilthey's specific proposals concerning the positions in philosophy, he did think there should be two *Ordinarien* in this discipline "even today, despite the lack of interest which philosophical study has encountered owing to the spirit of the age."[83]

In defending their recommendations both Dietzel and Dilthey argued that it was to a university's advantage to specialize in a few areas.[84]

Roggenbach agreed, but with reservations. Concerned that the new university would have difficulty attracting students under the best of circumstances, he refused to let an emphasis on certain disciplines come at the expense of the standard fields of study. The solution was to have an unusually large number of professorships. In fact, his proposals called for a faculty larger than that of any other German university: Roggenbach recommended that there be 124 professors, 62 *Ordinarien* and 62 *Extraordinarien,* at a time when the two largest German universities, Leipzig and Berlin, each had only 102 professors.[85]

But size alone would not suffice. If the university were to attract many students—particularly students from "old Germany," to use the Alsatians' term for the rest of the country—its chairs must be occupied by scholars of distinction. This assumption touches on a complex of issues about which Roggenbach became increasingly concerned as his work progressed. His preliminary studies convinced him that it would be years at best before the university would attract many students from the Reichsland. Indeed in the early years only one faculty, that of Protestant theology, was likely to enroll more than a few Alsatians. Hence, if the university were to prosper or even to survive, it must draw large numbers from elsewhere. But how could this be done? Some German universities attracted students from outside their immediate hinterlands because of advantages their locations offered, but in Roggenbach's opinion Strasbourg as a location offered nothing but disadvantages: a war-torn environment, a hostile native population, bad weather, poor housing, and high living costs. The problem, then, was to overcome these obstacles. An innovative curriculum might help, which explains in part why Roggenbach was so interested in introducing reforms. (Thus he found Kapp's ideas about American studies particularly appealing because he wanted to make the university attractive to American students.)[86] Financial inducements also might help. This may explain in part why Roggenbach called for a sizable fund to support fellowships for advanced and "postgraduate" students, a project without precedent in Germany.[87] But the impact of innovations and fellowships was likely to be minor. If the university were to attract many students from outside Alsace-Lorraine, Roggenbach argued, what was needed above all was a distinguished faculty.[88]

How, though, were prominent scholars to be attracted to the new university? Presumably the location would be as unappealing to them as to students. And uncertainty about enrollments would make accepting a call to Strasbourg seem risky to scholars accustomed to large incomes from student fees. These considerations encouraged Roggenbach to take steps to ensure that the academic environment in Strasbourg would be attractive even if the larger environment was not. For instance he defended his proposed fellowship fund by arguing that advanced students selected solely on the basis of merit—he compared them to the fellows of Oxford and

Cambridge—would do more than anything else to raise the level of academic life in Strasbourg and to give it a distinctive character. In addition, he asked that a commitment be made to establish facilities for teaching and research—seminars, institutes, laboratories, observatories, clinics, and so on—that would be the envy of any university. In view of the increasingly specialized nature of scholarly research, these facilities would be necessary if prominent scholars were to be appointed.[89] Yet an attractive academic environment would not suffice. There also must be attractive salaries. Indeed Roggenbach recommended that Strasbourg professors receive salaries significantly higher than those at other German universities: the average annual salary for *Ordinarien* was to be 7,500 marks, as compared with 4,716 marks at Berlin and 3,990 marks at Göttingen. Handsome salaries alone would not attract scholars to Strasbourg, but they would make the move less risky and Roggenbach wanted all the help he could get.[90]

Considering the large faculty, lavish facilities, and high salaries that Roggenbach proposed, the university's budget would have to be sizable. In this regard officials in Berlin and Strasbourg, evidently influenced by Sybel's memorandum of late 1870, had expected the university to have an annual operating budget of between 600,000 and 660,000 marks.[91] But Roggenbach's proposals required even more: for the university's first year he requested an operating budget of more than one million marks. For the sake of comparison, in 1870 the University of Berlin had a budget of 774,000 marks for both operating and building expenses and in 1873 the University of Leipzig, at the time considered Germany's leading university, had an operating budget of 944,000 marks.[92]

Roggenbach's desire that the new university be funded on a handsome scale led him to propose yet another innovation. He realized that it would be a long time before the Alsatians could support a university of the size and character he projected, even if so inclined. But he had misgivings about the obvious alternative, making the institution heavily dependent on the generosity of the imperial government. He was particularly concerned about the Bundesrat. It was unreasonable to expect the delegates of other states to vote annually for a large allocation to the Reichsland's university, since doing so would force their own states to spend more to keep their universities competitive. And the problem would become more serious as time passed and enthusiasm over unification and the annexation of Alsace-Lorraine waned. The solution, Roggenbach argued, lay in having the imperial government establish a large endowment for the university. Although he did not specify a figure, he recommended an endowment at least large enough to cover the professors' salaries, which accounted for about three-fifths of the proposed operating budget. Only if the university's income was shielded in this way from the vagaries of public opinion could it attract distinguished scholars and, hence, a sizable number of students from outside Alsace-Lorraine. The alternative, Roggenbach warned, would be a faculty of second-rate scholars without reputations and without students, and if this were the case, "it can be confidently said in advance that the attempt to give new life to the University of Strasbourg will fail."[93]

When preparing his basic proposals, Roggenbach assumed that within the guidelines agreed upon with Bismarck he could organize the university as he wished. But he soon learned otherwise. Beginning in late October his recommendations met resistance in several influential quarters. Roggenbach successfully defended his proposals against most challenges, but not all. Only after extensive modifications did he receive official authorization to proceed with the organization of the university.

The first challenge came from Bismarck and Eduard von Möller, the Reichsland's recently appointed *Oberpräsident* (high president). Although generally satisfied with Roggenbach's work, they took exception to his recommendations concerning Catholic theology. In Möller's opinion the Faculty of Protestant Theology as planned by Roggenbach should be replaced by a nondenominational theological faculty, one with Catholic and Jewish as well as Lutheran and Calvinist professors. This proposal, while not entirely new, broke radically with German academic practices, and any attempt to realize it presumably would have met strong opposition from all sides. In any case, nothing was heard of Möller's suggestion after he submitted it to the Imperial Chancellery.[94] As for Bismarck, his opinions were more traditional but equally at odds with Roggenbach's. When asking Roggenbach to plan the university, he had recommended that there be a Catholic as well as a Protestant theological faculty,[95] and nothing subsequently done by Roggenbach had changed his mind. His reaction when informed that Roggenbach's negotiations with the bishop had failed was merely to decide that someone else should try. The person selected was Franz Xaver Kraus, a liberal priest and art historian from Trier. Only when it became clear that Kraus would have no more success with the bishop than Roggenbach did Bismarck drop the idea of teaching Catholic theology at the new university.[96]

A second challenge to Roggenbach's plans came from bureaucrats who felt that the facilities and salaries proposed for Strasbourg threatened the interests of other universities. The most outspoken expression of concern appeared in a letter from an official at the University of Bonn, Wilhelm Beseler, to the Prussian minister of culture, Heinrich von Mühler. Although recognizing the need for a university in the Reichsland, Beseler complained that "opinions have been expressed in the periodical press and in brochures that openly make the absurd contention that the University of Strasbourg must be founded as a German national or model institution . . . ; no robbing of other universities ought to be shunned, no financial sacrifice deemed too high, in order to establish such a high temple of German learning.'' Beseler then focused on why his own institution must not be sacrificed:

> From my numerous reports and also no doubt from other sources, Your Excellency knows how things stand with the intellectual life of the Rhineland—how seriously the University of Bonn still contends with the shallow, easygoing, utilitarian disposition of the Rhineland with its orientation toward prosperity and profits; with cosmopolitan superficiality; with the lack of German idealism; with the Jesuit spirit which permeates and retards the populace in a terrible manner; with the influence of bigoted Belgium. . . .
> . . . At this time the University of Bonn is still as important for the Germanization of the Rhineland as it was half a century ago, and it can be asserted without exaggeration that it has at least as much significance for the interests of the German Empire and the Prussian state as the University of Strasbourg.[97]

Mühler welcomed this appeal, with its overstatements and inconsistencies, as evidence he could use in trying to protect the Prussian universities from the challenge raised by Roggenbach. Late in November he sent Bismarck a copy of Beseler's letter and expressed his own concern about the potentially harmful effects of the new university in Strasbourg. He agreed that the institution should be founded and that some professors would have to be recruited from Prussian universities, but he hoped that those called would be younger scholars rather than established ones with distinguished reputations. He also wanted Bismarck to encourage Roggenbach to look to the non-Prussian universities for professors, particularly to Leipzig and Heidelberg. If establishing a university in Strasbourg required sacrifices by other German universities, Mühler suggested, the main burden should be borne not by Prussia's universities but by their leading rivals.[98]

The most serious challenge came from the Imperial Chancellery, the bureau to which Roggenbach was responsible. The misgivings here developed for two reasons. First, the ministry's director, Rudolf von Delbrück, objected to one of Roggenbach's specific proposals. As a committed free trader he viewed with concern the recommendation that the social sciences receive special attention, for he suspected, not without reason, that Roggenbach intended to fill the resulting chairs with advocates of state interventionist ideas. Delbrück did not want to approve the plans until assured that classical liberalism would also be represented.[99] The second reason for dissatisfaction was financial. Delbrück believed the projected expenditures went far beyond the available resources. It was primarily for this reason, it seems, that he delayed taking action on Roggenbach's proposals, the implication being that he would need more modest recommendations before giving his authorization to proceed.[100]

But Roggenbach defended his right to organize the university as he wished, insisting that nobody else could decide what chairs to establish or whom to appoint. And he defended his initial proposals concerning the number of chairs and professors' salaries, proposals already approved by Bismarck. His original recommendations must be accepted in their entirety, he argued, if the university were to be a success.[101] When these appeals had no noticeable effect, Roggenbach resorted to more extreme action: he made it known that the lack of support from Berlin gave him little choice but to resign his commission.[102]

This threat brought a quick response from the chancellor, who was determined to see the organization of the university completed on time and without crisis. Bismarck now intervened at the Imperial Chancellery, and the result was a long and generally conciliatory letter to Roggenbach signed by Bismarck as well as Delbrück. The letter began by thanking Roggenbach for his recommendations and expressing agreement with his general objectives. Delbrück and Bismarck shared Roggenbach's belief that the university must be staffed with excellent professors and that this necessitated a high salary scale and a full complement of institutes, laboratories, and other facilities for research. They agreed that Roggenbach would have full freedom in deciding which chairs to fill and which scholars to appoint; by implication he was to ignore the complaints of Beseler, Mühler, Delbrück, and others concerning prospective appointments. Indeed there was only one important issue on which Roggenbach could not have his way: the budget. The basic difficulty was that the government could not furnish the requested endowment. Such a fund had obvious advantages, and the proposal should be considered again in the future. But initially the university must depend on "whatever local funds are made available and whatever is to be granted as an annual contribution from imperial resources." And since the amount requested was not available from these sources, Roggenbach would have to revise his original proposals. It would be necessary, for instance, to postpone the introduction of the recommended fellowship fund. More serious, Roggenbach would have to leave several professorships vacant, since the government could only furnish about three-fifths of the amount requested for salaries. The question of which chairs to leave vacant was left to Roggenbach.[103]

Roggenbach accepted these terms, but not without bitterness. Bismarck and Delbrück had offered with one hand what they had taken away with the other; Roggenbach had received authorization to proceed with complete freedom, only to be informed that the available resources necessitated major revisions in his plans.[104] What this meant to his aspirations is evident from the revised list of professorships he submitted in mid-December. Roggenbach recommended that forty-six to forty-eight *Ordinarien* be appointed rather than the sixty-two originally proposed, and he implied that the number of *Extraordinarien* would be reduced from sixty-two to no more than twenty. The cuts would be distributed unevenly. Roggenbach refused to eliminate positions (such as those in the Faculties of Protestant Theology and Medicine) considered important to the university's reputation in the Reichsland. But the chairs associated most directly with his reform proposals, and the reforms themselves, fared less well. There now was to be just one professor of political economy rather than a large and semiautonomous "Section for Political Science." And since Roggenbach could now assign only four chairs to the natural sciences, it no longer made sense to divide the Faculty of Philosophy.[105] These changes together with the elimination of the fellowship fund and the endowment meant that the new university would be much less innovative than Roggenbach had hoped. The effect of the restrictions imposed by Bismarck and Delbrück was to make the university not only smaller in size but more conventional in form.

But there seemed reason for some optimism for the near future. Bismarck and Delbrück had suggested that the imperial government might in time establish a large endowment. If only this or some other financial support materialized, there would be a chance to expand and to reorganize the university in accord with the original plans. With this in mind Roggenbach added to his revised proposals both a list of chairs to be established as soon as more funds became available and a list of chairs to be added eventually. If he could not organize the university as he wished, Roggenbach at least wanted to provide guidelines for its future development. This procedure was acceptable to the Imperial Chancellery, as were the recommendations concerning the chairs to be filled immediately. On 22 December Delbrück informed Roggenbach that his revisions had been approved and that he should now begin negotiating with prospective appointees.[106]

· 3 ·

For this second phase of his commission, the staffing of the university, Roggenbach was well prepared. Since early October he had devoted much of his time to contacting potential candidates for chairs and people qualified to recommend candidates. By the end of October he was negotiating with a number of scholars, and by the end of November he had selected a first candidate for each of the positions proposed and second and third candidates for many of them.[107] Accordingly there was no need for further delay when Bismarck and Delbrück authorized him to staff the university. As soon as Roggenbach heard from them he began making formal offers.[108]

In selecting his candidates Roggenbach had proceeded with care as well as dispatch. He had repeatedly examined lists of those teaching at German-language universities and had solicited the advice of prominent scholars in virtually every discipline.[109] He had also taken advantage of the abundant unsolicited advice at hand. In this regard many had nominated themselves for positions at the new university; between October 1870 and September 1871 at least twenty-two German and Austrian scholars had informed officials of their availability, and during the summer of 1871 nearly all the German-born professors at the University of Zurich, where there had recently been anti-German agitation, applied for positions in Strasbourg.[110] Once Roggenbach's appointment became known others came forward, including Bismarck himself (who recommended the jurist Rudolf von Gneist of Berlin) and Delbrück (who recommended two laissez-faire economists).[111] In general, Roggenbach did not heed such unsolicited suggestions, but there were exceptions. The most important concerned advice received from Wilhelm Dilthey. In his memorandum on the new university Dilthey recommended candidates for ten of the positions he proposed. Roggenbach included eight of these positions in his own plans, and for all but one either his first choice or the man ultimately appointed was the scholar nominated by Dilthey. The exception was the chair in the history of philosophy, to which Roggenbach appointed an Alsatian rather than Dilthey's candidate (Eduard Zeller of Heidelberg).[112]

There was another, more general way in which Dilthey may have influenced Roggenbach. Dilthey argued that the best way to proceed when staffing a university was to make sure the first professor called to each faculty was a scholar of considerable distinction. Such scholars could propose good candidates for the remaining chairs, and their very presence would help to convince potential appointees that the institution had a promising future.[113] This was tactical advice which Roggenbach attempted to follow, with mixed success.

Staffing the Protestant theological faculty presented a particular problem. Roggenbach hoped Alsatians would fill most of the chairs, but persuading them did not promise to be an easy job, especially for a German. Accordingly he sought the assistance of Johann Friedrich Bruch, the man responsible for keeping the former faculty in operation after the academy's demise. Bruch was reluctant to accept a chair himself for reasons of age (he was well into his seventies), but eventually he agreed, prompted by the argument that the general public might regard a refusal as politically motivated. In the meantime he played a major role in staffing the rest of the faculty. He helped to persuade fellow Alsatians to take four chairs, and his advice was decisive when it became necessary to look beyond the Reichsland to fill the two remaining positions.[114]

The distinguished scholar selected as the nucleus of the medical faculty was Friedrich von Recklinghausen, the best of Rudolf Virchow's students and the heir to Virchow's reputation as Germany's leading pathologist. One of the first appointed to the new university, Recklinghausen had considerable influence over the selection of the other professors in his faculty. Indeed the university's medical faculty was as much Recklinghausen's handiwork as it was Roggenbach's.[115] This was not without an unfortunate consequence: until his retirement in 1906 Recklinghausen acted as though he were his faculty's unofficial leader, a presumption which irked his colleagues.[116]

In his memorandum Dilthey had suggested that Rudolf Ihering, a professor of Roman law at Vienna, would be an excellent nucleus for Strasbourg's Faculty of Law. Evidently Roggenbach agreed, for Ihering was one of the first scholars approached about moving to Strasbourg. Beginning in October 1871 the two men corresponded frequently and met at least once to discuss terms and the staffing of the rest of the faculty. Ultimately Ihering withdrew his own candidacy, apparently because a trip to Strasbourg to investigate living conditions had left a bad impression. But while not moving to Strasbourg himself, he had an influence over the staffing of the law faculty analogous to Recklinghausen's with the medical faculty.[117]

Before Roggenbach had a chance to consider what distinguished scholar might serve as a nucleus of the Faculty of Philosophy, he learned of the availability of one of the most distinguished of them all, the historian and classicist Theodor Mommsen. Motivated by dissatisfaction with his situation at the University of Berlin, by nationalist zeal, and perhaps by a touch of whimsy, Mommsen asked a friend early in October to inform Roggenbach of his candidacy: "You are acquainted with Roggenbach and a discreet man; write him that I am also among the countless men he can have for Strasbourg, if he wishes. . . . Here I am unhappy and so superfluous that what I do could easily be done in any other place; of course the situation there will also not be easy, but at least it will give one's life a great and precisely defined objective."[118] Roggenbach, elated to learn of Mommsen's interest in Strasbourg, did his best to attract him: he promised a salary double the average to be given *Ordinarien,* guaranteed funding for Mommsen's research projects, and offered the faculty's other positions in classical studies to men recommended by Mommsen. But his efforts proved unsuccessful. After a number of months Mommsen rejected Roggenbach's overtures, for two reasons:

> In the first place Strasbourg is so exorbitantly expensive that even with the high salary that was offered I feared I would have to live even more in harness there than I do here. And then, and most fundamentally, it soon became clear that all older men were declining and that in the end I would have found myself alone there with a number of disciples. In itself this would not bother me; on the contrary. But considering how Strasbourg is regarded, I would thereby acquire a responsibility before the eyes of the nation which I am in no way able to bear. For the blunders—and how are many and serious blunders to be avoided there?—I would be held responsible, and also for the failure that in the

short run is very possible. In short, as unhappy as I am here, I lack the courage.[119]

The withdrawal of Mommsen's candidacy left Roggenbach without a scholar of national prominence around whom to build the Faculty of Philosophy. As for the selection of those who were appointed, he received advice from various quarters. As noted above, Mommsen was responsible for the selection of some candidates. Others were proposed by Dilthey, by Sybel, and, particularly in the natural sciences, by academic patrons in Berlin.[120]

Although depending heavily on others to suggest suitable candidates, Roggenbach handled the negotiations himself. In doing so, he used two basic arguments. The first was a material one: he offered high salaries and impressive research facilities. But he realized that no matter how attractive the terms, they might not balance the uncertainties and disadvantages associated with Strasbourg. And his task was compounded since other universities, responding to the prosperity and optimism that marked the period following unification, were now attempting to upgrade their faculties. In particular, the University of Leipzig was taking steps to consolidate its recently acquired position at the head of Germany's universities, and the Prussian universities, after years of relative inaction, were beginning to make up for lost time. As a result the German academic marketplace was shifting to the advantage of the seller, and many scholars approached by Roggenbach—particularly, prominent ones such as Ihering and Mommsen—found themselves in strong bargaining positions.[121] Roggenbach did the best he could, and his rate of success was impressive. But when he succeeded, it was not only by offering better terms than the competition. He also relied on a second argument, one other universities found more difficult to counter.

The second argument was an appeal to candidates' idealism and patriotism, one stressing the new university's special mission. Some reacted skeptically, suspecting that Roggenbach was using nationalism to disguise the disadvantages of moving to Strasbourg. Thus Wilhelm Scherer, a professor of German literature in Vienna, complained that ''Roggenbach's letter of appointment was so utterly without concern for what I would relinquish here, and treated a position in Strasbourg so much as an honor and so little as a difficult duty, that I found it necessary to explain to him in detail how much my post in Vienna is worth to me.''[122] In general, though, the patriotic argument greatly facilitated recruitment. Scherer's testimony notwithstanding, Roggenbach knew well how to appeal to the ideals of the *Kulturstaat* and of the special national role of the professors prevalent in German academic circles. Where else, after all, could the value to Germany of learning and culture be better demonstrated than in the Reichsland? Where else could the importance of professors to the national welfare be made more evident than in Strasbourg? Only beliefs such as these can account for the readiness of many to accept Roggenbach's overtures. The art historian Anton Springer later recalled how most reacted when offered positions by Roggenbach: "A refusal was impossible. . . . To all of us the acceptance of the call seemed a patriotic duty. As a group we held the most splendid, almost extravagant notions of the strong bonds that the university would tie between the empire and the recovered province."[123] These professors considered it an honor to have been invited to the new university. Thus the legal historian Rudolf Sohm admitted to Roggenbach that "I feel it a high distinction that I should be permitted to represent German learning in the reconquered Reichsland."[124] The jurist Franz Bremer expressed similar sentiments: "Indeed I consider it a patriotic duty to live up to the confidence placed in me to the extent my abilities permit."[125] And the jurist Heinrich Brunner, who was leaving the embattled German university in Prague to take a chair in Strasbourg, explained his reasons as follows:

> The prospect of being able, immediately and with good conscience, to serve a cause to which my thoughts and endeavors have always been dedicated gives me great satisfaction. Employed until now at a university where the defense of German culture can expect few if any results in the immediate future, I consider it a gratifying turn of events to see my work displayed on a stage where progress is cheerfully expected.[126]

Patriotic commitment even motivated the relatively few who feared the new university would have difficulty fulfilling its mission. Thus shortly after accepting a call the historian Hermann Baumgarten privately expressed doubts about the university's potential, but added "and yet the work there must be done; as I suspect, a long, difficult, but necessary task."[127]

The staffing of the university, like the decision to establish it, can only be understood by emphasizing the optimism and nationalism prevalent in the German academic community immediately following the Franco-Prussian war. Roggenbach offered generous terms and promised that the university would be a leading center of learning, but in the end it was largely patriotic and missionary zeal that motivated those accepting calls. These scholars welcomed this opportunity to demonstrate to the Reichsland and the world the superiority of German learning and to reaffirm in their own country the idea of the *Kulturstaat* and the importance of the professorial estate. Roggenbach knew how popular this outlook was among German professors, and he openly and successfully appealed to it.

What kind of faculty resulted? Generalization is naturally difficult, but some observations can be made. In the first place, Roggenbach showed no preference for scholars particularly known for their oratory or their idealistic nationalism or their identification with *Bildung* as opposed to *Wissenschaft*. Thus for the chair in modern history he ignored Heinrich von Treitschke, who apparently wanted the position, and instead called Hermann Baumgarten, a respected scholar but not one noted for his appeal to students.[128] And for the chair of philosophy he turned not to Kuno Fischer, whose reputation as an orator and desire to move to Strasbourg were comparable to Treitschke's, but rather to Ernst Laas, a little-known *Gymnasium* teacher.[129] In the opinion of one contemporary, in staffing "those disciplines which traditionally have been considered the real bearers of German scholarship and the German spirit (as opposed to the only recently developed and in any case more international natural sciences)," Roggenbach was too willing to satisfy himself with second-raters.[130] This criticism may be unfair, but certainly the professors appointed in the cultural sciences were less distinguished overall than their colleagues in the natural sciences and in the law and medical faculties. Perhaps this was by design. Given his concern about the feelings of the Alsatians, Roggenbach may have thought it desirable to avoid highlighting disciplines or schools of thought closely associated with German nationalism.

Another characteristic of the faculty was its youth. Initially Roggenbach had hoped to fill several chairs with scholars of great distinction, and many of those considered, not surprisingly, were relatively old. Among his first choices, for instance, were at least five men in their fifties or sixties (Ihering, Mommsen, the historian Georg Waitz, the physicist Rudolf Clausius, and the theologian Albrecht Ritschl).[131] But his lack of success with such prominent figures forced him to choose between calling older men of lesser reputation and younger men of promise, and he favored the latter. Of the Germans accepting positions none was yet fifty and most were much younger. The average age of all *Ordinarien* called to Strasbourg in 1872, excluding the Alsatians, was between thirty-eight and thirty-nine, while the average age of *Ordinarien* at other German universities was fifty-three and at Berlin it was sixty-two.[132] Many a scholar brought to Strasbourg as an *Ordinarius* otherwise would have remained a *Privatdozent* or *Extraordinarius* for years before receiving a chair. It was enough to cause an older professor to comment on visiting the university after it opened, "It seems to me as though mere research assistants have been made *Ordinarien* here."[133]

Given the relative youth and high promise of those appointed, it was natural that they were at the forefront of new developments in their respective disciplines. The new university's professors were neither old enough nor conservative enough to feel bound by traditional concerns or methods, least of all those dating to the era when idealism and captivating rhetoric had been dominant features of German academic life. Rather, they were forward-looking scholars who in their own way were as committed as Roggenbach to the modernization of the German universities. In practice this meant that they tended to be dedicated to a positivistic or scientistic approach to scholarship, an approach still struggling for acceptance at Germany's other universities. A few examples will suffice. Among those appointed in 1872 was one of Germany's few positivist philosophers (Ernst Laas), a political economist more interested in empirical research than in theory (Gustav Schmoller), one of Germany's first and most prominent legal positivists (Paul Laband), the country's leading proponent of a positivistic approach to the study of German literature (Wilhelm Scherer), and a historian who compared the goals and procedures of his seminar to those of a scientific laboratory (Julius Weizsäcker).[134] It is unclear whether Roggenbach had wanted the faculty marked to the degree it was by positivism or scientism, but once the decision was made to favor younger candidates it was probably inevitable, given the scholarly trends of the times, that the faculty would have this character. In any event, Roggenbach assembled a faculty that immediately gave the new university a reputation as the most modern anywhere.

There was one group within the faculty, however, that contributed little to this reputation: the Alsatians. As already noted, Roggenbach was prepared to offer positions to all former professors at the French academy and the Protestant Seminary. Except for those who had been in the medical faculty the response was generally favorable. Five of the seven eligible theologians accepted positions, as did six of the seven offered positions in the Faculty of Philosophy; there were no candidates for the law faculty. But the case of the eleven eligible to join the medical faculty was different. Most had remained in Strasbourg in the hope that a separate Alsatian school of medicine might be permitted to operate, and plans for such a school were prepared under the direction of Charles Schützenberger. But by the time this Ecole libre de médecine opened, late in 1871, it was obvious the authorities would tolerate it for only a year or two—until the Alsatians whose medical education had been interrupted by the war had completed their studies. When the institution closed its doors for good in the autumn of 1872, only four of its professors elected to join the university's medical faculty. Of the remaining seven, two or three, including Schützenberger, stayed in Strasbourg as private physicians, while the others accepted calls to Nancy, where they formed the nucleus of the local academy's new Faculty of Medicine and Pharmacy. (This faculty aside, little came of the earlier proposals to reorganize and upgrade higher education in Nancy.)[135]

Roggenbach realized that his Alsatian appointees would do little to enhance the university's image beyond the Reichsland. In his opinion only four merited positions on the basis of their scholarly accomplishments, and their best work was behind them. (The average age of the four was sixty.) For the others, the only justification for appointment was political. Because of this, Roggenbach urged that their salaries be paid from funds set aside for political purposes rather than from the university's limited resources.[136] As for the motives of the Alsatians accepting positions, it would be wrong to regard their decisions as evidence of sympathy for the university's special mission. Two or three may have identified with this mission, but most hoped to contribute not to Germanization but rather to the defense of Alsatian particularism and the maintenance of ties to the intellectual life of France. They agreed with the opinions expressed by one of their number, the paleontologist Wilhelm-Philippe Schimper, in explaining his decision to a Parisian scholar: "I even believe that Alsatians have a duty not to forsake their homeland and not to abandon to their sad fate those who are absolutely unable to leave. Emigration provides space for the foreigner and favors Germanization, and this is indeed painful for those who remain."[137] Roggenbach knew of the prevalence of such opinions, but considered the risks justified by the need to legitimate the university in the eyes of Alsatians. Whether this calculation was correct was a question for the future.

Preoccupied with recruiting, Roggenbach could not look after many of the other matters requiring attention before the institution could open. Accordingly toward the end of 1871 the Reichsland's Oberpräsident, Möller, established a nine-man committee—three or four members were German bureaucrats and the others were Alsatians—to make the necessary local arrangements.[138] Within three months the committee's work was essentially complete, thanks largely to one member, a German official named Friedrich Althoff. It was Althoff who was primarily responsible for procuring the buildings and the instructional equipment needed if the university was to open on schedule. He also negotiated with representatives of the Protestant Seminary, the Ecole libre de médecine, and the municipal hospital concerning the relationships of these institutions to the university. These activities, incidentally, were of importance not only to the university but also to Althoff's career: they caused Roggenbach to reward him with a position as an *Extraordinarius* in the Faculty of Law, and they gave him experience on which he would draw when he later became the director of the higher education section of the Prussian Ministry of Culture.[139]

One matter about which neither Roggenbach nor Althoff had to worry was the university's library, for it already existed. During the German bombardment the city's municipal library, with an extremely valuable collection of manuscripts, had been destroyed (reportedly because the maps used by the German officers mislabeled the library "Rathaus").[140] When news of this disaster reached Karl Barack, the director of a private library in Swabia, he immediately dedicated himself to organizing a replacement. By mid-November 1870 he had acquired space for the projected library and the provisional German authorities had agreed to affiliate the library with the university if one were established. About the same time Barack issued an appeal for contributions bearing the signatures of forty-nine prominent German public figures, intellectuals, and publishers.[141] The response was immediate and enthusiastic. Within days thousands of books began arriving in Strasbourg. Three hundred publishing houses sent copies of every book in print, and some promised free copies of every book published in the future. The emperor donated 4,000 books from his private library, and contributions arrived from several foreign countries, particularly from the United States and Great Britain (including 650 volumes given by Oxford's Clarendon Press and others sent by the Foreign and Colonial Offices). When the library officially opened on 9 August 1871—the centennial of Goethe's graduation from the first University of Strasbourg—it already had 120,000 volumes.[142] A decade later it had over half a million volumes and was easily the largest university library in the world, a rank retained until World War I (when the honor passed to the library of Harvard University).[143]

Another matter to be resolved was the selection of the university's first rector. Roggenbach handled this himself. Seeking another symbol of continuity between the new institution and Alsatian traditions, he offered the position to Johann Friedrich Bruch. Bruch protested that he was unfit because of his age and his unfamiliarity with the workings of a German university, but when Roggenbach persisted he reluctantly agreed to serve during the university's first semester.[144]

In March 1872 Roggenbach turned his attention to the one major task which remained to be completed before the university could open: the composition of the founding charter. Early in April his draft charter and a suggested set of statutes were forwarded to Berlin.[145] They found a mixed reception. The resolution concerning the university passed by the Bundesrat late in April, which was to serve as the institution's charter, stated that the statutes were "to be proclaimed by the emperor after consulting representatives of the university"—that is, they were to be based not on Roggenbach's recommendations but on those of the university's professors. But on other matters the Bundesrat's resolution adhered closely to Roggenbach's memorandum. Among other things, it stated that the university was to have all the rights of a public institution including legal personality, that it was the legal heir of the Academy of Strasbourg and its faculties, that its *Ordinarien* would be officially appointed by the emperor, and that "for the maintenance of direct observation as well as the privileges of the university, and in particular the management of economic affairs and the treasury, a curator is to be appointed who carries out his duties as instructed by the imperial chancellor." The final section stated that the resolution went into effect when it was made public, which was on 28 April.[146] By this time students and visitors were already congregating in Strasbourg to attend the university's inaugural ceremonies, scheduled for 1 and 2 May.

• 4 •

In one of the last acts of his commission, Roggenbach had appointed a committee to plan an appropriate program for the university's inauguration. The committee prepared a crowded and varied agenda. There were speeches by various notables, including Möller, Roggenbach, the rector, and, in the featured address, Anton Springer, an art historian called to the new university from Bonn. Representatives of every German-language university and many universities of foreign tongue conveyed greetings and best wishes and in turn were offered a toast by a Germanophile Alsatian. On 2 May there was an excursion to Mont Sainte-Odile, a prominent hill in the Vosges, for another round of speeches and toasts and a concert of martial music. And in the evenings most celebrants, and particularly the many fraternity students from other German universities, marched in torch-lit processions through the narrow streets of Strasbourg singing patriotic songs and then went to the brasseries for serious beer-drinking.[147]

A few speeches were conciliatory in tone. Thus in his address Roggenbach called on the new university to heal the wounds opened by the war.[148] And the historian Georg Waitz of Göttingen, who spoke on behalf of the other German universities, expressed the hope that the institution would "not merely spread its influence over those of the German tongue, but also extend a hand in peace to the neighboring peoples with whom we are linked in a common commitment to culture and humanity."[149] But most speakers were less sensitive to local feelings. Typical was the keynote address by Anton Springer. After referring to the new university's "sacred cause" and asserting that "we feel right at home here," Springer traced the history of German culture in Alsace from the age of Siegfried, Gunther, and Hagen to that of Goethe. He went on to laud the distinctive characteristics of German universities and the close identification of German scholarship with the nation, before concluding with an openly patriotic appeal:

> May the activity that goes forth from this place result in the well-being of Alsace, the glory of the German Empire, and the happiness of the German people; may the spirit of truth, may the love of the fatherland never retreat from this place; may a school of free German culture grow strong here; may the new University of Strasbourg live, flourish, prosper, and grow within the circle of its sister institutions into the distant future!
> May God so grant.[150]

Such remarks and the general *Hurrapatriotismus* of the German visitors did little to conciliate the Alsatians present. To be sure, some Alsatians attended the ceremonies only to jeer and whistle, but even the more open-minded tended to be appalled by what went on; the chauvinism of most songs and speeches, the dress and arrogance of the fraternity members, and the heavy drinking of the celebrants hardly persuaded them of the high ideals of the university. At one point the tension erupted into the open: on the evening of 1 May a brawl began in a tavern between German students and soldiers and the Alsatian regulars, and there were injuries and arrests before peace was restored.[151] This was only the most violent of many incidents during the two days that manifested the lack of enthusiasm of most Strasbourgeois for the proceedings. The festivities, with their stress on the superiority of Germany and its culture and on the new university's "sacred cause," left most German observers with a heightened sense of their own importance, but they only increased the aversion of those Alsatians unsympathetic to the new regime.

A few Germans were deeply troubled by the chauvinism of their compatriots, considering it both distasteful and politically unwise. As dedicated as anyone to assimilating the Alsatians, they believed this goal could not be achieved in an atmosphere of extreme German nationalism. Only if the German administration and German learning were adapted to local traditions—which were in many respects French traditions—could success be expected. Thus a Bavarian publisher who attended the ceremonies observed afterward: "I missed only one thing at the festival, namely a conciliatory word about France, which would have reflected well not only on the conqueror but also on his learning."[152] Another visitor noted that he had witnessed great patriotic exuberance in Strasbourg, yet doubted that the university would be "a force of moral recovery" in Alsace-Lorraine. He added that a friend had commented during the celebration: "There is not much of distinction among us here."[153] Another who expressed such opinions—at greater length and with a greater sense of disillusionment—was Roggenbach.

For Roggenbach the events of the first two days of May only confirmed his private doubts about the new university's potential. At no point had Roggenbach shared the optimism voiced by professors such as Treitschke and Springer; he had never thought that "German" learning propounded at a typically German university would do much to reconcile Alsatians to their new rulers. Rather he had believed, like Charles Schützenberger, that the German institutions introduced in the Reichsland would remain ineffective unless modified to meet local needs.

But what modifications should be made? In the autumn of 1871 Roggenbach had proposed two: the omission of a Catholic theological faculty and the appointment of as many former members of the academy's faculty as would accept chairs. But early in 1872 he decided that these concessions would not suffice. One result was his decision to appoint Franz Xaver Kraus—the priest earlier brought into the negotiations concerning the Catholic theological faculty—as an *Extraordinarius* for Christian archeology. In justification Roggenbach emphasized the desirability of having a Catholic professor in the humanistic section of the Faculty of Philosophy to forestall charges of discrimination. He conceded that it was extremely difficult to find a Catholic who was both a reputable scholar and untainted by ultramontanism, but in his opinion, and in that of Sybel and other consultants, Kraus met these necessary conditions.[154]

Roggenbach lacked the time and the authority to make additional concessions before the university opened, but he hoped some would be introduced soon thereafter. To this end early in April he sent the Imperial Chancellery a memorandum entitled "The Conditions for the Success of the University of Strasbourg." In this report Roggenbach observed that most potential university students in the Reichsland would be from groups that were French in language and culture, and that these youths would boycott the university if it were characterized by "a far too hasty conversion to instruction exclusively according to German methods and in the German language."[155] For this reason, Roggenbach recommended that three conciliatory reforms be introduced as soon as possible.

The first proposed reform—the least significant of the three but remarkable in its own way—concerned an additional appointment. Roggenbach suggested that an attempt be made "to obtain a representative of the history of French literature, if feasible *a Frenchman sympathetic to German culture*." This would be in the interests of the university as a center of learning and would also demonstrate "that Germany pursues a higher political ambition and does not just seek linguistic Germanization."[156]

Second, Roggenbach proposed that the university's Alsatian professors be permitted to teach in French, at least during the university's early years:

> The more liberal the Imperial Chancellery will show itself in permitting the use of the reigning language of the region's educated classes, all the more readily and unopposed will the reception of German culture ensue—and be sought at the German university; the employment of the German language by no means signifies an assimilation of German culture, and the latter can be acquired very well without the exclusive use of the former.[157]

These remarks show that Roggenbach rejected the argument advanced by Treitschke among others that the Alsatians must be awakened to their true German identity even if it had to be done forcibly. A few Germans shared Roggenbach's belief that there should be instruction in French at the new university—the historian and journalist Alfred Dove, for example[158]—but the idea was unlikely to receive much support in academic and bureaucratic circles.

Roggenbach's third proposal was that institutes of technical education—in engineering, forestry, agriculture, and architecture—be established either as integral parts of the university or in close association with it. Roggenbach did not care about the precise arrangement as long as the institutes were founded and as long as their students were permitted and encouraged to take courses in the university's original faculties. This recommendation, like the other two, was motivated by a desire to enhance the university's appeal to Alsatians. Roggenbach had become convinced that few Alsatians would seek higher education out of a commitment to learning for its own sake; most wanted only the practical training needed to enter a professional or business career. But this meant that the university as organized in the spring of 1872 would have little attraction for Alsatian students not seeking a medical or theological education. There was a danger, Roggenbach argued, that "the most influential social classes of Alsace" would send their sons to Paris or to other towns in France or Switzerland for the technical training unavailable in Strasbourg. Under these circumstances it would be difficult to avoid the "atrophy of the new institution." If technical institutes were established in Strasbourg, however, Alsatian students would be lured in large numbers to the university community—where they presumably would come into contact with, and under the influence of, German scholars, German students, and German learning.[159]

The proposal that technical institutes be organized in association with the new university was the most radical of all the recommendations made by Roggenbach during his commission. It addressed a major problem that was to affect the university's relationship to Alsatian society throughout its history, the limited appeal of an institution dedicated to pure research in a region whose better educated residents were preoccupied with practical pursuits. The proposal also raised a question of fundamental importance for the future development of German higher education generally, that of the relationship between humanistic scholarship and technological training. When Roggenbach made his recommendation, Germany's universities were already erecting defenses against the claims of technological education for higher status. This conflict would become more pronounced in later years as practical and technological education became more relevant to the country's needs. But the problem was already serious in 1872, as Roggenbach knew; in his final plea for the association of technical education with the university Roggenbach admitted that this step had no precedents in Germany and would not be achieved easily in Strasbourg.[160]

When submitting these recommendations, Roggenbach still hoped that the proper reforms and a conciliatory attitude on the part of German professors and students would permit the new university to succeed in its mission. During the next few weeks, however, two developments combined to convince him that failure was all but inevitable. First, Berlin's rejection of his innovative statutes persuaded him that reforms necessary for the institution's success would never be introduced. And second, the events of the first two days of May indicated that the university would remain surrounded by an atmosphere repellent to Alsatians.[161]

Initially Roggenbach assumed that the Imperial Chancellery deserved the blame for rejecting his proposed statutes and substituting a temporary set of regulations modeled on those at other German universities. This is evident from a letter to the grand duke of Baden, his partner in an earlier campaign for educational reform:

> I greatly fear that the irreparable basic mistakes resulting from the whole manner in which this founding was carried out by the Imperial Chancellery have also laid the groundwork for the university's incurable ill health. Under these unfavorable circumstances none of the creative ideas of reform which German university life needs so badly could hope for any kind of realization. Still I am astonished at the extent to which the penny pinchers in the Imperial Chancellery have known how to eliminate every single trace of an improvement from the statutes sent back from Berlin on the eve of the inauguration.[161]

These observations reflected Roggenbach's resentment over the Imperial Chancellery's treatment of his proposals throughout his commission. But they did not represent his final allocation of blame. He later concluded that officials in Berlin were less at fault than the German university system itself. At least this is what he wrote Althoff in 1882 on learning that his former assistant had joined the Prussian Ministry of Culture. Roggenbach confided that he considered "the state of the German universities probably more corrupt than any other branch of public service." Innovation in higher education, he continued, was effectively prohibited by "the iron, unbending law of the persistence of the existing." Indeed it was impossible to establish a university that challenged the system:

> Strasbourg is a sad example of this. In the nineteenth century one would have thought it impossible to duplicate once again institutions which, in general and in particular, are so out of accord with common sense and what is appropriate. Worse was it to have had no choice whatsoever, as such a bad creation *must* be perpetuated because even Alsace-Lorraine must have a German university, and a German university can be nothing but a reproduction of all others if it wishes to find teachers and not do without students.[162]

Roggenbach had shifted the blame from the "penny pinchers" in the Imperial Chancellery to the general rigidity of the German academic system, but he still had the same basic complaint: he had been unable to organize a university that accorded with the "spirit of the age."

The events and the atmosphere of the opening ceremonies completed Roggenbach's conversion to unalloyed pessimism about the new university. He now concluded that the institution would be permanently identified with aggressive German nationalism and as a result would do more to alienate Alsatians than to assimilate them. Thus in his letter to the grand duke of Baden he complained of "the ominous retrogression that has befallen the German national character in general" since the military successes of 1870 and 1871, "but in particular the character and opinions of German scholars (so arrogant and touchy anyway)." Instead of remaining true to their contemplative calling, professors had become propagandists for German nationalism. They, like the youth of Germany, "seem in many cases to base their faith in the victory of the German cause in Alsace more on the right of the stronger than on that of the stronger culture." No doubt German learning was superior to that of Alsace, Roggenbach continued, but this would mean little as long as Germans behaved like conquerors:

> I cannot perceive how we are to have cultural success there, and hence I greatly doubt that the noisy fanfares of victory and rejoicing of the last few days will continue for long. Under these circumstances the entire unfinished work of the university is likely to fall victim only too soon to the bickering and immoderation which have always constituted the hereditary weakness of German scholars.[163]

These forebodings help to explain why Roggenbach hastened to sever his connections with the university. He had no desire to serve as the institution's first curator, a position many had assumed he would occupy, or even to accept responsibility for the university in the interim before a curator was appointed. On 10 May 1872 he informed the Imperial Chancellery that he considered his commission terminated as of three days hence.[164] Roggenbach was never again to have any official association with the university.

Roggenbach was not alone in his pessimism. Other German observers, as we have seen, were as appalled by the insensitivity manifested at the inaugural ceremonies. And all along there had been Germans, including the Protestant theologian Albrecht Ritschl, who considered the entire project premature if not mistaken.[165] In addition certain observers, less concerned with the university's national mission than with the deficiencies of German higher education, complained that a great opportunity had been missed to establish a thoroughly reformed university, a model for the transformation of German universities generally. (One of these critics, the political economist Robert von Mohl, put the blame on Roggenbach.)[166]

But among German observers the critics were unrepresentative. Most public comments had nothing but praise for Roggenbach's accomplishments and were as optimistic about the university's prospects as the initial proponents of the project. Government officials were pleased with the new institution, in some cases more pleased than they had expected to be. (In a report to the emperor, Bismarck praised Roggenbach for having proceeded "with prudence and skill" and for having completed his difficult mission "in a surprisingly favorable way.")[167] And the German professors and students joining the university were enthusiastic about the enterprise. As yet they knew little of the extent of the Alsatian's antipathy to things German and, with possibly one or two exceptions, nothing of Roggenbach's pessimistic predictions. It was with pride and confidence, not with doubt, that they manned their missionary outpost in the Reichsland.

# 3

# The German University and the World of Learning

For all their certainty, those at the inauguration, both the optimists and pessimists, could not foresee how the university would fare. Nobody could, for the university's fortunes would depend on the as yet unknown responses of groups and institutions over which it had little control, particularly the responses of its intended constituencies, its potential rivals, and its chief patron, the government. Who would enroll? How would other institutions react to the challenges posed by the new university? How much support would the university receive from the government? Of course the university's character and activities might affect these responses, but here, too, much remained unknown. How would the professors interact? How would they attempt to transform their missionary commitment into results? How would they complete the unfinished work left behind by Roggenbach?

During the university's first few years many of these questions were answered, and evidence accumulated suggesting answers to the rest. In these formative years patterns of behavior and attitude emerged and became institutionalized, giving the university a distinctive character that was to persist, at least in attenuated form, throughout its history. It is with these patterns that this and the next chapter are concerned. In this chapter the focus is on the position the university came to occupy within the German academic community and within the world of learning generally, while in the next it is on the institution's relationship to Alsatian society.

· 1 ·

Roggenbach did not complete the organization of the university. Shortage of time, uncertainty about the institution's budget, and disagreements with Berlin necessitated leaving many problems to be solved by others. As one professor observed shortly after the university opened, "There is an immense deal still to arrange, two Roggenbachs are hardly sufficient for all there is to do."[1] Among the items of unfinished business, four stood out: resolving the budgetary question, completing the staffing, drafting a set of statutes, and constructing buildings for teaching and research. During the 1870s the search for solutions occupied most sessions of the university's governing body, the academic senate, and much of the time of the university's first curator, Karl Ledderhose.

Roggenbach had planned the university without knowing how large its budget would be or even where its resources would originate. His one attempt to clarify the situation, the proposal that the imperial government establish a sizable endowment, met resistance in Berlin, with Bismarck and Delbrück arguing that further consideration of the idea would depend on how well France performed in paying the indemnity stipulated by the Treaty of Frankfurt. As it turned out, France's performance could not be faulted—the indemnity was paid in full by the autumn of 1873—but the Imperial Chancellery refused to honor its implied commitment to Roggenbach: it never reconsidered the proposed endowment.[2]

The failure to establish an endowment meant that the university, like every other German university, would receive most of its income from annual government allocations. But from which government, the Reichsland's or the empire's? Late in 1871 the chancellor and Delbrück decided that it should be financed by "whatever local funds are made available and whatever is to be granted as an annual contribution from imperial resources."[3] But there were to be no annual contributions from imperial resources, at least not initially. Except for small amounts from fees, gifts, and bequests—about 5 percent of that required—the university depended entirely on the Reichsland for its operating expenditures. And the sums involved were substantial. The university's annual operating budget of about 800,000 marks was exceeded only by those of the Universities of Berlin and Leipzig, and the Reichsland far surpassed other German states in the proportion of its public revenues set aside for higher education. (The proportion was about 3 percent as compared, for instance, with 1 percent in Prussia.)[4]

In the mid-1870s the pattern changed. The initiative came from Alsatians, specifically from those in the Reichsland's Landesausschuss, an indirectly elected assembly established in 1874 by Bismarck. During the assembly's first session its committee on judicial, religious, and educational affairs complained that the university put too great a burden on Alsatian revenues. "If the province is to provide all of the operating expenses for the university on its own," a spokesman reported, "then perhaps it would be more sensible to rebuild the institution on a narrower base." If, on the other hand, the university was to be maintained at its present level, "your commission is of the opinion that it would be fair if the empire supported a part of the burden, to the extent it exceeds 400,000 marks."[5] The full assembly seconded the proposal, and the Imperial Chancellery, seizing this opportunity to resolve the matter of the university's budget, responded quickly. Within weeks it recommended that the empire contribute 400,000 marks annually to the university's operating budget. Late in 1875 the Reichstag—after a debate concerned less with the merits of the subsidy than with the merits of German higher education and the *Kulturkampf*—approved the measure almost unanimously. Henceforth the empire would grant a large sum every year to what was now commonly termed Germany's imperial university (*Reichsuniversität*).[6] The arrangement satisfied the members of the Landesausschuss even though their own proposal—that the Reichsland's contribution, not the empire's, be fixed at 400,000 marks—had been rejected.[7]

The support the university received in its first half decade permitted the addition of several new professorships. When the university opened, there were forty-five *Ordinarien* and thirteen *Extraordinarien* and the faculty ranked ninth in size among the twenty German universities. Five years later there were fifty-eight *Ordinarien* and eighteen *Extraordinarien* and the faculty, while still smaller than Roggenbach had recommended, had advanced to sixth place.[8]

The new professors were selected in the conventional manner. For each vacancy the *Ordinarien* in the faculty concerned recommended to the curator three or four candidates, listing them in order of preference. After consulting the appropriate ministry or bureau—in the case of Strasbourg in the early and mid-1870s, the Imperial Chancellery—the curator generally selected one of the recommended scholars and pursued the necessary negotiations. He was not bound, however, by the faculty's list of candidates. In fact many professorial appointments in nineteenth-century Germany, perhaps one of every four or five, were made without or against the recommendations of the faculties concerned.[9] But the University of Strasbourg was atypical. Ledderhose, who remained curator until 1887, never appointed anyone not recommended by the appropriate faculty, and only rarely did budgetary constraints or pressure from the Imperial Chancellery or elsewhere cause him to deviate from the suggested order of preference.[10] The Strasbourg professors were more fortunate in this regard than the professors at most German universities; blessed with an able and sympathetic curator, they had only themselves to satisfy when recommending appointments.

In taking advantage of their good fortune, the professors tended to adhere to the guidelines established by Roggenbach. Their requests for new positions gave particular attention to what were known as luxury disciplines (*Luxuswissenschaften*), to esoteric or emerging fields of study with scant representation at other German universities.[11] And although they occasionally tried to attract illustrious older men to Strasbourg—in 1874, for instance, they sought unsuccessfully to recruit the Basel art historian Jakob Burckhardt[12]—they generally preferred younger scholars of great promise. Indeed the average age of the twenty-four *Ordinarien* called to Strasbourg between 1873 and 1882 was only thirty-seven.[13] Dutch-born Bernhard ten Brink was just thirty-two when he came to the university in 1873 to organize Germany's first seminar in English philology.

The medieval historian Paul Scheffer-Boichorst, a meticulous practitioner and skilled instructor of archival techniques, was thirty-one when he arrived in 1876. Georg Friedrich Knapp, one of the founders of the Verein für Sozialpolitik and the model of an empirical student of the social sciences, was thirty-three when he occupied Strasbourg's second chair in political economy in 1874, alongside his friend Gustav Schmoller. These and the other scholars called to the university during its first decade were as young, industrious, and innovative as those appointed by Roggenbach in 1872. With their emphasis on seminars rather than lecture courses, on the examination of the particular rather than speculation about the general, they enhanced the institution's reputation as a stronghold of modernity in the world of scholarship.[14]

The freshness of spirit characteristic of the Strasbourg professors manifested itself in the statutes they composed for the university. Completed and put into effect in 1875, these statutes introduced many reforms found at few if any universities elsewhere in Germany. To begin with, the faculty did not claim the policing and jurisdictional powers over students traditionally exercized by German universities. Students might be expelled or threatened with explusion by the academic senate, but the university would not act *in loco parentis* and there would be no student prison or *Karzer.* Instead, students were liable to punishment for their transgressions under civilian law and in the civilian courts.[15] The statutes also made unprecedented provisions for faculty retirement and pensions. Any professor could retire with full pay at the age of sixty-five, and the widows and children of deceased professors were to receive pensions if left without other support.[16]

A third major reform incorporated in the statutes, and the one which best symbolized the university's modernity, was the division of the Faculty of Philosophy. The provisional statutes issued in the spring of 1872 had not called for this change, and a few Strasbourg professors opposed the idea.[17] But most members of the unified Faculty of Philosophy, and all the scientists, favored division from the outset. They proposed the reform to the academic senate within a month of the opening of the university, and in July 1872 first the academic senate and then the Imperial Chancellery gave their approval. The change was immediately instituted unofficially, to be confirmed by the statutes approved in 1875.[18]

A reformist spirit was also evident in the statutes concerning how the university was to be governed. These gave the faculty full responsibility for administering the university, with this responsibility to be exercised through two bodies, the plenum and the senate. The plenum, composed of all *Ordinarien* and *Extraordinarien,* convened once a year to elect a professor to a one-year term as the university's rector. This assembly also had to approve all revisions in the statutes and could be called into session at any other time by the senate to consider matters of special importance.

The senate, a much smaller body, looked after the day-to-day administration of the university. It was composed of the rector, the prorector (the previous year's rector), the five deans, who were elected to one-year terms by their respective faculties, and one additional representative from each faculty, also elected annually. The Strasbourg professors preferred this type of academic senate to the most obvious alternative, one including all *Ordinarien,* because they believed it would limit the development of fixed traditions. Their goal was to rationalize the administration of the university without sacrificing the faculty's ultimate authority.[19]

Of the major items of unfinished business remaining when the university opened, the last to be resolved was the building question. In the mid-1870s the university was still housed in various old structures acquired during the winter of 1871–72, including a palace adjacent to the cathedral, the main building of the former academy, the Protestant Seminary, facilities in and near the municipal hospital, and several rented houses. But it had been recognized from the outset that these facilities were inadequate. For one thing, they furnished too little space. There was enough room for lecturing, but not for the many seminars, institutes, laboratories, clinics, and museums organized by the professors. Indeed, many professors in medicine and the natural sciences had accepted appointments only after receiving assurances that they would soon have the finest possible facilities. If they were to be retained, and if excellent scholars were to be attracted to Strasbourg in the future, the university would have to acquire new buildings.[20] In addition, the original facilities were widely separated. Both pedagogical and political considerations convinced the professors that their buildings should be contiguous. Treitschke reflected their opinions when he complained in the Reichstag that "as long as the university is scattered in four or five places in a large city, even with the best teachers it cannot become much more than it was in the French period, namely a collection of trade schools. But what especially matters to us in Germany is that there be a *universitas litterarum,* an active exchange of ideas among the different faculties."[21] The university's Germanizing mission also mattered, of course, but it too would benefit if the university's buildings were together. The professors pointed out, for instance, that the Alsatian students of Protestant theology, who accounted for a large share of the Alsatian enrollment in the early years, lived and studied at the Protestant Seminary and had virtually no contact with the Germans in the other faculties.[22] A single campus uniting all the university's buildings would foster closer personal relations between German and Alsatian students, just as it would promote the "active exchange of ideas among the different faculties."

But where should this campus be located? Clearly there was not enough space anywhere within the city's walls. The government intended to tear down the walls, however, thus making available large areas reasonably close to the center of the city. Particularly appealing was a site near the Fischer Gate on the northeastern side of the city, for it was an attractive location and could be prepared quickly and cheaply. But there was one drawback: the medical professors wanted their buildings adjacent to the municipal hospital, which was about a mile from the site by the Fischer Gate. Some consideration was given both to putting the entire university near the hospital and to replacing the hospital with a new one at the Fischer Gate, but neither option proved feasible. Accordingly it was decided, in 1874, to have two campuses rather than one; the Faculty of Medicine would occupy a cluster of new buildings next to the hospital, while the other four faculties would be housed by the Fischer Gate. With this issue resolved, the Imperial Chancellery invited a Prussian architect, Hermann Eggert, to prepare a master plan for the university. Eggert accepted this unprecedented opportunity—no other German university had had the benefit of a master plan—and late in 1875 he delivered his recommendations to Oberpräsident von Möller.[23]

Both Möller and his superiors in Berlin found Eggert's proposals generally acceptable, but the Landesausschuss reacted otherwise. After a heated debate the assembly decided not to appropriate any funds for the building program until learning how much the empire and the city of Strasbourg would contribute.[24] This response prompted the professors to appeal to the Reichstag. Specifically they wrote to various Progressive and National Liberal deputies requesting that the Reichstag, which had already made a large contribution to the university's building fund, appropriate the 2.3 million marks needed to construct the main building. As one put it, "Most certainly you will . . . not refuse an important grant for an institution which, if it fulfills its duty correctly, must contribute very significantly to the assimilation of Alsace-Lorraine with Germany and in this way to the removal of the seeds of discontent between France and Germany. It is a question here of a great and obvious German interest."[25] The Reichstag obliged. In April 1877 the suggested proposal was introduced, and a few days later the assembly gave its approval. The timing was excellent. On the day following the Reichstag's action, and in the presence of the emperor, the university celebrated its fifth anniversary and officially adopted a new name: the Kaiser-Wilhelms-Universität Strassburg.[26]

The Reichstag's action appeased the Landesausschuss. When the Alsatian assembly reconvened late in the year, it voted unanimously to appropriate 3 million marks for the projected laboratories, institutes, and clinics. This sum together with smaller contributions from the administrative region of Lower Alsace and the city of Strasbourg meant that Eggert's master plan could now be put into effect. The empire would be paying 71 percent of the total costs, while the Reichsland would provide 21 percent and Lower Alsace and the city of Strasbourg 4 percent each.[27]

With the necessary resources assured, construction proceeded rapidly. During the late 1870s and early 1880s the six buildings proposed for the medical faculty were erected as well as five of the six to be built at the Fischer Gate. Among those completed was the massive main building, which was to contain the university's administrative offices, the Aula (the great hall used on ceremonial occasions), and the lecture halls, seminar rooms, faculty offices, and exhibits of the Faculties of Law, Philosophy, and Protestant Theology. Since this was to be the largest and most conspicuous of the buildings, the government decided to make it the object of an architectural competition. Predictably the entries reflected the various schools and rivalries of late nineteenth-century eclecticism. It is noteworthy, however, that only 4 of the 101 entries were in the Gothic style, the style considered appropriate by certain politicians, including Bismarck. The first prize went to an architect from Karlsruhe who submitted a design in the style of the high Italian renaissance, "a cultural style which represented rather well the sentiments of the academic community in those days."[28] Construction began in August 1879, to be completed five years later.

On 27 October 1884 the university's professors and students gathered in the Aula to dedicate the main building and to celebrate the virtual completion of the building program prepared almost ten years before. They had cause for pride, for the institution now possessed buildings more integrated and more suitable for the requirements of modern scholarship than those of any other European university. For many observers, including many Frenchmen, these structures were tangible evidence of the excellence of German scholarship and higher education.[29] But others recognized that the new buildings were superior to those found at other German universities. In their opinion, if the main building and the many institutes and clinics symbolized anything, it was the modernity of the University of Strasbourg—a reputation already acquired for the institution by its professors and by its students.

· 2 ·

Basic to the *Lernfreiheit* enjoyed by German university students were the right to matriculate at any of the country's universities and the right to move to another institution after any semester. The result was a highly mobile student population, with its travels influenced by a variety of considerations. Distance was always a factor, although less so after the completion of the major railway lines; most students attended institutions relatively close to their homes. A university's surroundings could also be important, particularly for those who had just survived the *Abitur,* the rigorous examination qualifying students for matriculation. Thus students might be attracted to Heidelberg by its romantic reputation, to Rostock or Greifswald by the Baltic beaches, to Freiburg by its proximity to the Alps, or to Munich by the town's reputation for beer-drinking revelry and bohemianism.[30] Frequently economic considerations were influential. It is clear, for instance, that many Germans interested in studying in Strasbourg were deterred by the city's lack of inexpensive housing.[31] In some cases, also, political factors affected student mobility. For example, the political attitudes dominant in Bavaria in the late nineteenth century go far to explain why so few Bavarians attended Prussian universities. And patriotism attracted many German students to Strasbourg, especially in the 1870s. Reflecting on the university's first quarter century, the Strasbourg archeologist Adolf Michaelis recalled how, in the first few years, "patriotic fathers liked to send their not less patriotic sons to this place."[32]

But in choosing their universities German students did not respond solely to nonacademic influences. Those dedicated to their studies—especially older students who had put their dueling and heavy drinking behind them and were ready to work toward a doctorate or their leaving examinations—judged universities primarily on the basis of scholarly merit. They preferred institutions known to have excellent professors, fine facilities, and an atmosphere conducive to industrious study, the type of institution known in the jargon of German students as an *Arbeitsuniversität*. And prominent among the few universities in this category was the new one in Strasbourg. As Gustav Schmoller once put it, "Soon the word was out: anyone who wishes to learn must go to Strasbourg; in Strasbourg they are more industrious than elsewhere; there one finds institutes, there one learns something from the professors."[33]

The University of Strasbourg appealed in many ways to those serious about their studies. Some came because they considered it, in general, "the most modern of our universities."[34] Others enrolled because of the renown of an individual faculty; the Faculties of Medicine and Law, for example, were as highly regarded during the 1870s as any in Germany.[35] Still others came to work with specific professors. Thus Emil Fischer, who went on to win a Nobel Prize, transferred from Bonn to study chemistry with Adolf Baeyer, and Heinrich Braun, subsequently a prominent Socialist theorist, was attracted by the reputations of Georg Friedrich Knapp and Gustav Schmoller and of their seminar.[36] Like Fischer and Braun, many came to Strasbourg to pursue advanced research. During its first decade, in fact, the Alsatian institution probably had as high a ratio of doctoral candidates to freshmen (*Füchse*) as any university in Germany.[37]

Further testimony to its reputation as an *Arbeitsuniversität* was the number of students attracted from other parts of Germany. Admittedly the overall enrollment was not particularly impressive. It rose from 212 in the first semester to 654 in 1874–75, but then remained steady for several years. At the end of its first decade the university still had fewer than 800 students and only ranked eleventh in enrollment among the twenty German universities.[38] But these levels appear more remarkable when it is realized that the university, unlike its rivals, had few students from its own state. Thus a comparison of the enrollment of "old Germans" at the Reichsland's university in 1880–81 with that of out-of-state students at the other German universities reveals that only Leipzig surpassed Strasbourg in total number and no institution did in proportion of the total enrollment. More specifically, only Leipzig and Würzburg among the non-Prussian universities attracted more Prussian students than Strasbourg; only Leipzig among the non-Bavarian universities enrolled more Bavarians, while Strasbourg registered more than all Prussian universities combined; only Munich, Leipzig, and Württemberg's own university in Tübingen registered more Württembergers.[39] A patriotic desire to be identified with the university's Germanizing mission brought some of these students to Strasbourg, but relatively few compared with those attracted by a particular professor, a particular faculty, or the institution's general reputation as the most industrious and modern of Germany's universities.

It was also as a center of learning rather than as a bastion of German culture that the university appealed to foreign students, few of whom knew much about the political and cultural life of Alsace before arriving. Thus the American Bliss Perry, later a professor at Harvard, was "drawn to Strassburg by the fame of that great scholar and delightful teacher, Bernhard ten Brink."[40] And William H. Welch, who was to help organize the medical school of the Johns Hopkins University, could praise Strasbourg's professors and intellectual atmosphere without reference to the university's national mission:

> I find it to be pretty generally acknowledged that for scientific medicine Strassburg is much better than any other German university. On account of the number of patients in the great hospital in Vienna, that place is better fitted probably than any in the world for pursuing specialties and practical subjects. But what I want is just what I find here in Strassburg, laboratories for histology, pathology, physiological chemistry, superintended by the best teachers in Germany, viz., Waldeyer, von Recklinghausen and Hoppe-Seyler. Then the atmosphere of the town is well suited for study, for which that of Vienna is not. From all accounts a good deal more is done in Vienna than studying.[41]

Foreign students like Perry and Welch tended to seek the professors, facilities, and scholarly atmosphere best found at an *Arbeitsuniversität*. Hence a comparison of the number enrolled at the various German universities provides at least a rough indication of the relative stature of these institutions. And on this scale, the Reichsland's university ranked high. Although 1 of every 20 university students in Germany in the 1870s was foreign, at Strasbourg the proportion remained about 1 of 7 or 8 (see table

1, appendix B). Twenty-seven of the 212 students who registered in the first semester were foreign, and by the late 1870s there were more than 100 foreign students. By this yardstick the university ranked far ahead of all but four other German universities, and significantly behind only the great institutions in Leipzig and Berlin.[42]

The character of student life in Strasbourg was consistent with the institution's reputation as an *Arbeitsuniversität*. In contrast to most German universities the tone was set neither by fraternity members nor by *Brotstudenten* (bread-and-butter students) interested only in rapid preparation for specific professions. During the university's first decade ten fraternities were established, but they enlisted few and had little impact on student life. Some had no more than half a dozen members and had to devote an inordinate amount of time to recruiting, while one or two survived only with the aid of subsidies from affiliates at other universities. In short, fraternity life in Strasbourg was a pale reflection of that associated with most universities across the Rhine, particularly those in smaller towns like Bonn, Erlangen, Heidelberg, Marburg, and Tübingen.[43] Much more characteristic of student life were the numerous informal groups brought and held together by shared interests, more often than not scholarly interests. Typically the members ate together or met regularly in the evening at a brasserie or coffeehouse. Perhaps the largest group and certainly the most prominent was known as the *Strassburger Kreis* (Strasbourg circle). Organized in the late 1870s, it survived for at least a decade. Most members were advanced students who were, even by Strasbourg standards, unusually talented and industrious. The *Strassburger Kreis* was open only to students, but other groups included faculty members as well and some met regularly at professors' homes. These customs reflected another unique characteristic of Strasbourg's university community: social relations between students and faculty members were closer and more highly valued by both groups than at any other German university.[44]

· 3 ·

That the University of Strasbourg developed into an excellent center of learning was directly related to its nation-building mission. With a few exceptions the faculty members believed the university had to be of the first rank if it was to succeed as an instrument of Germanization. This had also been the opinion of some of the university's early proponents, of course, and no doubt most Strasbourg professors brought this opinion with them to the Reichsland. But the professors' strong convictions on this issue, and their near unanimity concerning what academic distinction entailed, largely resulted from the intense social interaction and pressures for conformity they found at the new university. It is appropriate, accordingly, to consider the social context before looking more closely at the professors' opinions concerning the university and its mission.

Members of Strasbourg's German community often described their situation as comparable to that in a colony, and it is easy to see why. Living alongside an inhospitable native population differentiated by language or dialect and by culture, they naturally felt like outsiders and banded together, much as they would have if they had been in Paris or Constantinople or Dar es Salaam. Thirty-five years after the annexation a prominent member of the immigrant community could still describe life in Strasbourg as "interesting, but not pleasant. One does not feel at home here; one always feels like part of a German colony in a foreign city. Whenever I return to Strasbourg from a trip, I never have the feeling: 'This is my city, my home,' but the same cool sensation as when I get to Paris: 'Here is a city in which I know my way around extremely well!'"[45]

The unpleasant, "homeless" character of life in Strasbourg and the immigrants' desire to emulate life in the "mother country" led to the emergence of social patterns and cultural institutions distinct from those of the Alsatians. This "old German" society supported theatrical and musical performances matching in number and quality those in any German city of comparable size. It organized art leagues, reading circles, hiking clubs, and the other types of associations characteristic of German bourgeois life in the late nineteenth century. It read its own newspapers, particularly the liberal *Strassburger Post*. It even organized imitations of such German institutions as the Cologne carnival and the Bavarian beer garden. The immigrants' desire to lead a life as familiar and German as possible was also reflected in their physical separation from the native population; most German families lived in the newer sections of Strasbourg, near the university but apart from the districts inhabited by Alsatians.[46]

But it would be wrong to assume, as did many Alsatians, that the immigrant community was completely united either socially or in its attitudes concerning the Reichsland. The community's five major component groups—bureaucrats, professors, teachers, businessmen, and army officers—were doubtless in closer contact than was usual in a German town, but there were still important divisions. The most obvious was that separating the army officers from the rest of the German colony. The officers, most of whom were Prussian, had the greatest distaste for life in the Reichsland and the least expectation of remaining long. Some became active in the life of the immigrant community, but most did not.[47] A second division, less pronounced but significant nonetheless, existed between the university community and the rest of the German colony. Bureaucrats in Strasbourg tended to attribute it to snobbery on the part of the faculty, and with some justification.[48] But the social exclusiveness of the academic community also reflected differences of opinion over

German policies in Alsace-Lorraine and particularly over policies affecting the university, differences examined below.

The tensions that characterized life in the Reichsland and the professors' common commitment to a special mission help to explain why the Strasbourg faculty was more cohesive and socially active than any other in Germany.[49] Not all professors welcomed this distinction. A few complained that the social life of the academic community was exhausting, others, that it was artificial, petty, and boring.[50] But professors from "old Germany" were more likely to consider the faculty's sociability one of the most attractive features of life in Strasbourg. Some thought it the only one.[51]

The chief focal points for the social life of the academic community were the *Stammtische,* or discussion circles instituted at various restaurants and beer halls in town, and the salons maintained by certain professors and their wives. As soon as the university opened, groups of professors began meeting at set intervals over beer or wine at a restaurant or, along with their wives, at a particular faculty home. These gatherings gave the professors an opportunity to discuss scholarly matters, political developments, and the general relationship of the university to German policy in the Reichsland. And at least in regard to questions of politics and the university, they fostered a remarkable homogeneity of opinion. A member of the faculty in the 1880s indicated the pattern when recalling the groups that met at two of the most popular brasseries, the Espérance and the Dicke Anna:

> At both places the events of the day in both the political and scholarly worlds would be discussed, and of course also all university matters. The two groups were in close touch with one another. They helped to bring about the agreement of the entire teaching staff on all important problems, especially if it was a question of opposition to government policy.[52]

Reaching agreement was all the easier since the German professors had similar opinions concerning their university's mission. They were most willing to express these opinions in the university's early years.[53] But their shared outlook persisted long after the 1870s and long after it became obvious that full success in the university's Germanizing mission, if it came at all, would come very slowly. Professors appointed in the first few years set the tone within the faculty into the early twentieth century, and they kept alive the ideals and the missionary zeal associated with the institution when it opened. Thus a philosopher who taught at the university in the 1890s later observed that "there certainly was still on hand much of the spirit in which the founding of the university had been completed; the consciousness of being at an exposed outpost and of having to accomplish pioneering work brought men together again and again despite any personal and disciplinary disagreements."[54] And a historian who joined the faculty in 1890 recalled:

> At the university, which was conscious of what was expected of it in the empire, there still prevailed . . . a fresh and lively spirit which was the legacy of the enthusiasm of the *Gründungszeit,* and there were the most delightful collegial and social relations within the faculty. One knew that one was observed with suspicion not only by the neighbors across the Vosges but also by the far too many foes of the German administration of the Reichsland, and one attached oneself all the more closely to the . . . [university] community.[55]

Put more abstractly, new faculty members encountered a fine example of what has been termed an organizational saga—a somewhat exalted definition of the university and its unique qualities that deeply affected individual identities and loyalties.[56]

Pride in the university and its mission—identification with its organizational saga—made it easier to tolerate many irritations that professors elsewhere were spared. The shortage of acceptable housing, the high cost of living, the inhospitable native population, and the small enrollments in several disciplines made life difficult for faculty members, as did, in the 1870s, the lack of facilities for research.[57] But for most, the satisfaction that came from identification with an important national mission was more than adequate compensation: living conditions at this colonial outpost may have been worse than in other German university towns, but the patriotic idealism and enthusiasm were greater.

Commitment to the university caused many professors to refuse even to consider calls from other institutions.[58] And others inclined to accept appointments elsewhere were persuaded to remain in Strasbourg through appeals to their patriotism. This was particularly true in the early years, when many argued that it would create a bad impression if professors departed so soon after the university opened. This position had the support of the Prussian Ministry of Culture, which until the late 1870s refused to consider Strasbourg professors for vacancies at Prussia's universities. It also had the support of the emperor, who once expressed the hope that the professors would turn down all calls elsewhere and remain at their outpost in the Reichsland.[59] With time the professors became rather cynical about such policies and appeals because the authorities seemed to use them as substitutes for matching the terms the professors might be offered elsewhere. Although most did not want to move, failure to be considered for chairs at other universities worsened their bargaining position in Strasbourg. Yet the professors were always willing to use patriotic appeals themselves when trying to persuade colleagues to remain in Strasbourg. They also relied heavily on such appeals when recruiting new professors, just as Roggenbach had when making the initial appointments.[60]

A desire to advance the university's special mission also affected how the professors approached their responsibilities as teachers and scholars. From the beginning they agreed that this mission necessitated, above all, a commitment to conscientious teaching and research of high quality. At least until the turn of the century most professors shared the outlook described by the daughter of the economist Georg Friedrich Knapp:

> The word *"germanisieren"* was not uttered at our home. . . . My father believed only in the effectiveness of indirect influences. He spoke the best German and taught German economic history and trained German men. He did not speak of *Deutschtum,* he lived it. . . .
> . . . Everything that was propagandistic was far from the thoughts of the scholars and the era. Unprejudiced scholarship was, avowed or inferred, the watchword.[61]

Only "unprejudiced scholarship" would be true to the best traditions of German higher education, and only it could win the respect of the Alsatians for the university and for German learning. It was as if the professors thought of their university as a work of art. Although certainly interested in recruiting and influencing Alsatian students, they did not think this was the only way or perhaps even the most important way in which the university would contribute to its mission. It would also contribute to the extent that its character as a center of learning caused Alsatians who were not students to admire and to take pride in the institution, much as they might admire and take pride in a monument such as the Strasbourg cathedral.

Attitudes like these appealed to the professors for reasons not directly related to their mission. Viewing the university as a work of art—or as a "bastion," "hothouse," or "showplace" of German learning, to mention some of the professors' own metaphors—provided a ready justification both for demanding that the institution's high stature be maintained regardless of cost and for insisting that no concessions be made to special interests. Of course this outlook also imposed responsibilities: if the university was to be a work of art, there must be a special commitment on the part of the faculty. But the professors were not derelict. All but a few took their obligations as teachers and scholars very seriously, and the exceptions faced strong incentives to conform, including the prospect of ostracism if they refused. It was an atmosphere perhaps best described by the economist Lujo Brentano, a professor in Strasbourg in the 1880s:

> It was considered self-evident that the instructors could not serve their fatherland better than by living above all for scholarship. . . . nowhere else at that time was there a university which could be compared with Strasbourg's as far as the zeal with which instructors and students

performed their duties was concerned. . . . Everyone was aware of the general importance of everyone doing his best. As a result there was only one standard there for judging colleagues, that of what each accomplished. One was inflexible in the demands one put on others, because one put them on oneself; whoever did not conform was relentlessly pushed to the wall; if a mistake had been made with an appointment, no thought was given to hindering the correction of the mistake by the appointment of someone better.[62]

As these remarks suggest, the University of Strasbourg was far from a typical university. Nor did its professors want it to be typical. In this regard it is useful to think of the German academic system as composed of a center and a periphery, with the institution(s) at the center establishing norms which the peripheral institutions, hoping to move closer to the center, find it in their interests to emulate.[63] Adopting this terminology, we can say that the Strasbourg professors thought of their university as belonging at the center in the sense that it approximated their ideal of a modern German university more closely than did any other institution. If anything this attitude grew stronger with time, as it became evident that the other universities were in certain respects moving away from this ideal. The Strasbourg professors failed to respond as they would have if they thought that the center had shifted and that the stature of their institution, now on the periphery, depended on its success in emulating the new center. Rather, they reacted as if they had taken on a second special mission, one involving not the Reichsland but the German academic community; at a time when the other universities were selling their souls, it was essential that their own institution remain a model of what a German university should be. This aspect of their organizational saga helps to explain the unusually high and uncompromising demands that Strasbourg professors put on themselves and their colleagues. It also goes far to explain why the faculty was unique in other ways deserving comment, notably in its attitudes toward anti-Semitism, toward honorific titles, and, to a lesser degree, toward Catholicism.

During the 1870s most Strasbourg professors generally approved of the cultural policies of the empire and its leading states. They particularly welcomed the *Kulturkampf,* a campaign against Roman Catholicism most closely identified with Prussia but also pursued in other German states, the Reichsland included. With few exceptions they were convinced that Roman Catholicism was incompatible with scholarly objectivity and that without governmental protection it soon would give way before the force of reason. In this spirit, they refused to consider the appointment of anyone suspected of being a believing Catholic. There were never more than a handful of Catholics on the university's faculty in its first decade, and most of them—the English philologist Bernhard ten Brink and the medieval historian Paul Scheffer-Boichorst, to cite two examples—no longer practiced their religion.[64] Apparently the only devout Catholic on the faculty in the 1870s was the *Extraordinarius* Franz Xaver Kraus, the priest appointed by Roggenbach as a gesture to Catholic Alsatians. And most Strasbourg professors never accepted Kraus as an equal; they refused to consider promoting him when a chair in his field became vacant and reacted with thinly disguised relief when, in 1878, he left to become an *Ordinarius* at Freiburg.[65] Only a few professors—notably the jurists Friedrich Althoff, Heinrich Geffcken, and Rudolf Sohm—were relatively free of prejudice against Roman Catholicism and against scholars who accepted its teachings.[66] For the rest, the only good Catholic was a lapsed Catholic.

Such attitudes were not peculiar to the University of Strasbourg; anti-Catholicism was strong throughout the German academic community. But the Strasbourg professors were more obsessed with the subject than their colleagues elsewhere, and more uncompromising. This became evident when, beginning in the late 1870s, the governments of Prussia and other states turned away from the liberal policies pursued since unification, the *Kulturkampf* included. Disturbing as this development was to the Strasbourg professors, it was made more so by the readiness with which professors at other German universities appeared to accept it. Thus late in 1878, within months of two attempts on the emperor's life and impressive conservative gains in elections to the Reichstag, the Strasbourg economist Gustav Schmoller observed:

> Only depressing news is heard from Berlin. [Hermann] Baumgarten just returned from there and has had all he can take of the miserable cowardice and quite idiotic reactionary atmosphere in those circles, above all in academic circles. He is of the opinion that for many of these people a coup d'état that did away with the constitution would not be too much. These people have the same point of view today as did [Friedrich von] Gentz and comrades in 1819. And these people still call themselves liberal![67]

As these remarks suggest, professors at universities east of the Rhine tended to react to the new political climate not with bitterness and a resolve to defend liberal values, but rather with an increased desire to identify themselves with the government. To mention but one symptom, they now wanted to be honorary *Geheimräte* (privy councillors) as well as professors.[68] It was not surprising, accordingly, that they became less assertively anti-Catholic than they had been in the heyday of the *Kulturkampf*.

The conservative trends evident by the end of the 1870s in Germany generally and at most German universities in particular found little support at the University of Strasbourg. The Strasbourg professors remained as hostile to Catholicism as they had been at the height of the *Kulturkampf*.

They also rejected the anti-Semitism which increasingly characterized German academic life. After 1880 the Reichsland's university was one of the few in Germany that provided a hospitable environment for Jewish students, and the only one, it seems, that did not discriminate against Jews when making faculty appointments.[69] In addition the professors differed from their colleagues elsewhere in their opposition to the wearing of academic robes and, perhaps most indicative of their liberal outlook, in their refusal to accept honorific titles. When poor health forced Heinrich Geffcken to resign his chair in 1882, the government awarded him the title of *Geheimrat*. It was the first time a member of the university's faculty had been honored in this way, and most professors agreed it should be the last. A widely publicized petition signed by all but two professors asked the government to end the practice; the professors were proud of their scholarly calling and did not want any additional distinction. This symbolic expression of the university's uniqueness displeased the authorities, but they honored its request and the University of Strasbourg, unlike its sister institutions, long remained *Geheimratfrei*.[70]

The Strasbourg faculty's position on such matters reflected a distinctive outlook concerning the proper relationship of universities to the state. In Germany generally the trend was toward a closer identification of higher education and the state. The completion of unification, the general satisfaction with the existing constitution and social order, the professionalization of politics, and the growing popularity of positivistic scholarship contributed to a decline in the involvement of professors in German political life. And those who were involved, unlike the political professors of the first two-thirds of the century, tended to be defenders of the status quo, not its critics.[71] But these trends were less evident in Strasbourg. The classical liberalism of an earlier era remained alive here long after it had faded elsewhere. In fact, it was still salient a generation after the founding of the university, as the historian Friedrich Meinecke later recalled: "Everyone who knew at first hand the University of Strasbourg of the period before the war knows of course that something completely unique had survived here, a last organic embodiment of the older liberal-humanistic culture."[72] This unique spirit had important implications for the way in which the Strasbourg professors interpreted both their own responsibilities to the state and those of their university.

Concerning the university's responsibilities, all but a few agreed with the assertion made long before by Wilhelm von Humboldt: "the state must . . . ask nothing of the universities that relates directly and plainly to itself, but rather should maintain the inner conviction that if they attain their own objective, they also, and indeed from a loftier viewpoint, satisfy the state's goals."[73] Late in 1881 the academic senate proposed that the phrase *Litteris et Patriae* be engraved above the entrance to the university's main building. Three years later, when the building was officially opened, Bismarck indicated that he would rather see the university's prominently displayed motto read *Patriae et Litteris*. But this phrasing would not have reflected the professors' opinions concerning the nature and goals of the institution.[74] It would be as a center of objective and distinguished scholarship, not as a source of patriotic propaganda, that the university would best contribute to the Germanization of the Reichsland. Learning could advance the interests of the nation, but only if learning came first.

This reasoning did not mean that the professors should be concerned with learning alone. In the tradition of the political professors of pre-unification Germany, most followed political developments with great interest; the apolitical professor may have become the norm in the rest of the German academic community, but he did not in Strasbourg. To be sure, not many became active politicians while on the Strasbourg faculty. Evidently the only one in the university's first decade who considered running for political office was the jurist Friedrich Althoff, perhaps the most eccentric of the professors. And in the 1880s and thereafter no more than a half dozen professors became active in national or Alsatian politics.[75] But participation might have been greater had not many professors believed that their hands were tied, that given the situation in the Reichsland the German colony must present a united front or at least the appearance of one.[76] In any event, the majority of Strasbourg professors had strong opinions about contemporary political events and trends, particularly those affecting Alsace-Lorraine. And for the most part these opinions were at odds with those of the government. Indeed through much of the period of German rule the Strasbourg faculty was a stronghold of opposition to the government's basic approach to ruling the Reichsland, just as was, for different reasons, the military. Since this division had important consequences for the development of the university and its position in the German academic community, it is a subject meriting close examination.

· 4 ·

Until 1879, when Eduard von Möller resigned as Oberpräsident, the university's German professors remained generally satisfied with the administration of Alsace-Lorraine. Their few complaints were concerned less with the policies pursued than with how they were executed. Some professors, for example, criticized the "irresponsible and very unnecessary chaos" that characterized the administration in its first few years.[77] And several complained that too many bureaucrats were from Prussia, for it was obvious that Prussians had a special talent for alienating Alsatians.[78] But the professors did not object to the bureaucratic centralism associated with Möller. They approved of Möller's efforts to win the trust of the

Alsatians through an administration that was both evenhanded and efficient and of his refusal to cater to the local notables or the Catholic clergy.
And they were naturally pleased that despite Möller's few contacts with
the faculty (Althoff was perhaps the only professor close to him) he could
be counted on to defend the university's interests.[79]

Yet, while the professors had few complaints, by the late 1870s there
was dissatisfaction in government circles. Bismarck and even Möller—
who had never been permitted much freedom of action by Berlin—were
among those now convinced that the regime introduced in 1871 should
be replaced. But what were the alternatives? Alsatians hoped at the very
least to see their homeland become an autonomous state within the empire. At the other extreme, many Germans favored Prussian annexation
of the territory.[80] But Bismarck's preference was for a third course whereby
Alsace-Lorraine would be ruled from Strasbourg but Germans would remain in control. And, as usual, he prevailed. Early in 1879 he met with
the leader of the Alsatian autonomists, and from this meeting emerged
constitutional changes put into effect later in the year. Henceforth there
would be an Alsatian government headed by a Statthalter (governor) responsible only to the emperor. The Statthalter was to have the authority
over the Reichsland previously exercised by the chancellor together with
the Oberpräsident. His policies would be carried out by the Ministry of
Alsace-Lorraine, an imperial ministry based in Strasbourg and directed
by a secretary of state appointed by the emperor. In addition the Landesausschuss would increase in size and receive the power to initiate
legislation. As for filling the office of Statthalter, the emperor was inclined
to appoint Möller but the chancellor favored Field Marshal Edwin von
Manteuffel—partly, it seems, because he wanted him far from Berlin—
and, once again, Bismarck had his way.[81]

Although seventy years old and reluctant to move to Strasbourg, Manteuffel accepted his appointment without complaint. A Prussian conservative in the tradition of Karl Ludwig von Haller and the Gerlach brothers,
he was ready to do whatever his emperor requested.[82] But the same
political philosophy that dictated obedience to his ruler also made Manteuffel an authoritarian in his relations with subordinates. As Statthalter
he was always prepared to bypass laws and bureaucratic chains of command whenever he thought his policies necessitated such action. And this
was often, for Manteuffel's policies differed dramatically from those pursued before 1879. His primary objective was to win over Alsatian notables,
the assumption being that if he succeeded the masses would follow. He
particularly catered to the Catholic clergy and the native industrialists. A
pious Lutheran committed to the alliance of church and state, he quickly
relaxed inherited policies directed against Catholicism and even appointed
Catholic clergymen to important posts in his administration.[83] By refusing
to introduce laws concerning business in force across the Rhine, he pro-

tected the interests of the Alsatian industrialists. He flattered French-speaking notables with requests for their counsel, with his willingness to converse in their language, and with his gracious comments about Alsace and its French heritage. And he won the admiration of natives of both religions and both languages for his efforts to curb the excesses of the military officers and the bureaucrats.[84]

Although Manteuffel's unorthodox methods and conciliatory policies pleased many Alsatians, they were unpopular in the German community. The bureaucrats tended to agree that the notables and the Catholics should be conciliated, but they disapproved of Manteuffel's methods. And the other immigrants, including the professors, were almost unanimous in their opposition to his basic policies.[85] The professors had little reason to complain about their own treatment; they were the only Germans whose company and respect Manteuffel seemed to desire, and he was more sympathetic to the university's interests than were many of his subordinates.[86] But as far as his general policies were concerned, the professors thought he carried conciliation too far and catered to the wrong elements of the native populace. Imbued with the spirit of the *Kulturkampf,* they naturally disapproved of Manteuffel's concessions to the Catholic clergy. And they complained that his attempts to appease the French-speaking notables undermined efforts to win the respect of Alsatians for Germany and German culture. To many the problem lay with Manteuffel's political philosophy. His romantic conservatism caused him to rule in the interests of the region's traditional elites, the clergy and the haute bourgeoisie. He did nothing to improve the lot of the dialect-speaking commoners, yet these were the only Alsatians, most professors believed, likely to repay concessions with sympathy for German rule.[87]

The professors did not keep their misgivings to themselves. Through private appeals to friends in "old Germany" and through resolutions and newspaper articles directed at the general public they campaigned against the "notables policy" throughout Manteuffel's tenure as Statthalter. In this campaign they had the support of the *Strassburger Post,* a newspaper founded in 1882. In fact this paper reflected their views so accurately and published so many articles by faculty members that it quickly became known locally as the *Professorenblatt* (professors' newspaper). And it was a valuable ally, for of all Alsatian publications it was the most widely read and quoted elsewhere in Germany and hence had the greatest influence on how other Germans regarded developments in Alsace-Lorraine. These were important considerations, for the professors had little hope of winning much support among Alsatians. If they were to influence the government's policies in the Reichsland, it would have to be indirectly, with the aid of public opinion across the Rhine.[88]

The professors' misgivings concerning Manteuffel's policies did not affect their personal relations with the Statthalter, but it did widen the gap between the faculty and the bureaucracy. During the so-called Manteuffel era the ministry's officials became increasingly convinced that the university's expenses and demands were excessive and that the professors were insufficiently loyal. In their eyes the university had become "a problem child of a hard-working bureaucracy."[89] For their part, the professors complained that the bureaucrats did not treat them with the proper respect, did not appreciate their contributions to the Germanization of the Reichsland, and were too willing to sacrifice the university's interests to appease the Landesausschuss.[90] In short, the sense of common purpose that had once united the bureaucracy and the university community now gave way to dissension and distrust.

The opposition of most professors to the "Manteuffel system" also conditioned their relations with the few professors who sympathized with the regime, particularly with the three who actively supported and advised the Statthalter, the jurists Heinrich Geffcken and Friedrich Althoff and the classical philologist Wilhelm Studemund. Geffcken sat on the council of state established when Manteuffel took office, while Althoff and Studemund served as advisers on educational and religious questions and other administrative matters. All three approved of Manteuffel's general objectives, and all three participated in negotiations aimed at appeasing the Reichsland's Catholic clergy.[91] Such attitudes and activities estranged them from most of their colleagues. One manifestation was the petition composed after Manteuffel awarded Geffcken the title of *Geheimrat*.[92] This petition attacked not only the practice of awarding honorific titles to professors but also, by implication, the idea that it was acceptable for professors to perform bureaucratic or advisory chores for the government. The few faculty members who thought such service proper found themselves isolated within the university community. Treated as outsiders by most colleagues, they avoided the cafés and brasseries where other professors discussed the issues of the day, meeting instead at the home of the philosopher Emil Heitz, an Alsatian professor who supported the university's Germanizing mission.[93] During the Manteuffel era social life within the faculty accurately reflected the division between the few who supported the government's policies and the majority who did not.

The death of Manteuffel in 1885 led to changes, but not as many as most Germans desired. The new Statthalter, Prince Chlodwig zu Hohenlohe-Schillingsfürst, relied heavily on his bureaucratic subordinates and treated these caste-conscious immigrants with the respect they wanted. He also differed from his predecessor in his insistence on the strict enforcement of all laws. And although exercising little control over the army officers, he gave them more prominence at court than they had enjoyed under Manteuffel.[94] But while Hohenlohe brought a new style, he did not bring new policies. Encouraged by the Alsatian notables and by Secretary of

State Karl von Hofmann, who had directed the ministry since 1880, he continued the major economic, social, and religious policies introduced by Manteuffel. This disillusioned many Germans. Thus the army officers, who tended to think of the Reichsland as an occupied territory, lobbied for more repressive measures. And while harsh policies shaped by the army did not appeal to most German civilians, more and more favored some kind of change.[95] By the end of Hohenlohe's first year in office several professors thought that the law of 1879 should be revised so Berlin might more effectively guide the policies and limit the excesses of the local officials. Only in 1887 did they learn that there might also be occasions when they would want the Statthalter to protect the Reichsland, and particularly its university, from the policies and excesses of Berlin.

On 14 January 1887 the Reichstag rejected an army bill supported by Bismarck, and the chancellor responded by calling an election. Bismarck then joined with the National Liberals and the two conservative parties— the so-called *Kartell*—to exploit the war scare stimulated by General Boulanger's activities in France, arguing that the French threat made approval of the army bill imperative. On the national level this strategy proved successful; the elections in late February gave an absolute majority to the *Kartell,* which quickly passed the controversial bill.[96] In the Reichsland, however, Bismarck's strategy failed completely: all fifteen of the deputies elected were anti-German "Protesters."[97]

This result caused consternation in Berlin and in Strasbourg's German community. The immediate reaction of most concerned Germans was that the returns demonstrated the bankruptcy of the conciliatory policies pursued since 1879; as one official put it, "This election was the receipt for the Manteuffel era."[98] The Alsatians had rewarded an extended period of rather mild rule by electing the most anti-German delegation yet sent to the Reichstag. For Germans in Berlin and Strasbourg the lesson was clear: there must be a more repressive administration.[99]

The first steps toward a harsher regime came within a few days of the election. One was the removal of Secretary of State Hofmann, an appointee of Manteuffel who symbolized the conciliatory policies of the early and mid-1880s.[100] Another was the intensified surveillance of suspect Alsatians and Alsatian organizations. Several natives were arrested as traitors on grounds that they belonged to the Ligue des patriotes, a French revanchist society. Decrees dissolved roughly 200 organizations—musical societies, hunting clubs, sporting clubs, and so on—regarded as strongholds of anti-German sentiment. And the police were instructed to watch the activities of other Alsatian organizations; they would also be dissolved if implicating evidence was found.

Almost without exception the German professors favored these steps. Indeed many believed that the best course would be for Prussia to annex the region.[101] And the professors' sentiments soon became widely known.

Aware that Berlin was now considering major changes in the Reichsland, several professors wrote to newspapers expressing opinions on the subject. Berlin's *National-Zeitung,* the first important paper to recommend, following the elections, that Prussia annex Alsace-Lorraine,[102] received one of these letters, and on 23 March used it as the basis for an article on the Alsatian question. Introducing the letter's author only as "one of the most renowned professors of the University of Strasbourg," the article quoted the following passages:

> The evil consists in the fact that the weak government we have had until now has been deprived of all its authority by the Landesausschuss. The government humiliates itself before the Landesausschuss. . . . What the officials provide in return for the assembly's cooperation . . . are the promotion of the protective association of Landesausschuss members and, above all, the lack of vigor with which they pursue the reform projects most important for the Germanization of Alsace. Our misfortune is the un-Prussian character of the administration here.[103]

This article attracted great interest both in the Reichsland, where it was reprinted in the *Strassburger Post,* and in Berlin. Particularly concerned was Hohenlohe, for he was attempting—successfully, as it turned out—to persuade the emperor and Bismarck *not* to make any major changes. Worried about the public image of his administration, Hohenlohe complained to his new secretary of state, Maximilian von Puttkamer, about the recent criticisms of his policies by "prominent professors" and apparently instructed him to find and reprimand the author of the letter quoted in the *National-Zeitung.*[104] A few days later, amid rumors that Hermann Baumgarten was responsible, Lujo Brentano informed Puttkamer that he had sent the letter. Puttkamer thereupon asked Brentano and his colleagues to cease commenting publicly on the situation in the Reichsland. This might have ended the matter had it not been for a fortuitous event: the publication of an incendiary dissertation by one of Brentano's students.[105]

Late in 1885 Heinrich Herkner, a Bohemian attracted to Strasbourg by the reputations of Brentano and Georg Friedrich Knapp, had accepted Brentano's suggestion that he write his dissertation on the textile industry of Upper Alsace and its workers. The condition of these workers had interested Brentano since his own arrival in Strasbourg three years before. For decades the industrialists of Mulhouse and nearby towns had been praised throughout Europe for their enlightened treatment of their employees. They had established savings banks, insurance plans, and old age homes for their workers, and the factory-owners of Mulhouse had built a well-publicized *cité ouvrière,* a suburb of small but pleasant houses sold to workers at cost on an installment plan.[106] But Brentano had misgivings about these projects. He believed that factory-owners and visitors had exaggerated the extent to which the workers benefited from this paternalism and that these projects increased the workers' subservience to their employers and thus strengthened the notables' position in the political life of Upper Alsace. Herkner's research supported his mentor's assumptions. In the summer of 1886 Herkner traveled through the region interviewing workers and inspecting their homes.[107] He found that conditions were almost unbearable for most working-class families; only four or five industrialists still seemed sincerely committed to making life more pleasant for their employees. Herkner also learned that there was considerable bitterness among the workers because the government had sought to conciliate the factory-owners by banning the legislation that protected workers in the rest of Germany. He concluded that "only when the empire convinces the Alsatian worker that protection is his right can it hope to compete successfully with the anti-German influence that the industrialist and the clergy exercise over the worker."[108] By the end of 1886 Herkner had completed his study and sent it to a publisher in Strasbourg. In February 1887 he successfully defended his dissertation, summa cum laude, and early in April the book appeared in print.[109]

The publication of Herkner's study could not have been more timely. Reviewed prominently and favorably in several major newspapers, including Berlin's *Deutsche Zeitung,* Munich's *Allgemeine Zeitung,* the *Frankfurter Zeitung,* and the *Strassburger Post,* the book quickly attracted the attention of those hoping to change the direction of German policy in the Reichsland. It attracted so much attention, in fact, that the Francophile notables mounted a publicity campaign designed to discredit it. In this campaign they had the support of Hohenlohe. Apparently hoping to pacify the notables, he asked a subordinate to look for errors of fact and judgment in Herkner's study. The search proved fruitless, not least because the official naively asked Brentano to advise him as he prepared his report.[110] But the failure to refute Herkner's arguments on scholarly grounds did not end the criticism; the book continued to be attacked for its political implications. This second wave of criticism originated not in the Reichsland, but in Berlin.

Government supporters in Berlin saw in Herkner's book not just an assault on the policies affecting Alsatian factory-workers but also a manifestation of the deep-seated opposition of Strasbourg's university community to the government's general policies in the Reichsland. They believed Germany could not achieve its objectives in Alsace-Lorraine unless all state officials, professors included, acted in unison; here, even more than elsewhere, the university should be the servant of the state, not its critic.[111] This opinion was implicit in an article on the university in *Die Post,* a Berlin newspaper with close ties to the government. The article strongly criticized the striving for political influence on the part of many professors who want most of all to be, in a sense, co-rulers. Because of this, considerable harm has already been done here. [These] men, who may of course be distinguished theorists in the realms of constitutional law, political economy, etc., hold . . . entirely different views than those not only of the native population but also of all the "old German" businessmen. . . . [Their] various highly critical opinions about what the province needs have recently received extensive publicity. Certainly theory and practice are here in open conflict.[112]

Similar opinions appeared in Gustav Schmoller's review of Herkner's book for the journal Schmoller edited. Never as willing as Brentano to criticize the government, Schmoller had become a strong supporter of Bismarck and his policies since called to Berlin five years before. His attack on the political overtones of Herkner's work reflected his growing differences with Brentano, his successor in Strasbourg:

The building up of the book into a weapon with which to attack the entire system of German rule established by Möller and Manteuffel could not help but arouse the suspicion that the book had been written for this purpose. . . . In this regard the author's dominant ideas are the conventional scuttlebutt (*fables convenues*) that circulates in discontented bureaucratic and professorial circles. For years these groups have longed for a strong administration instead of the so-called mild one, and in many cases, subscribing to radical and progressive ideals for their German homeland, have greatly desired a prefectural administration for Alsace which would be as bureaucratic and harsh as possible.[113]

Hohenlohe, who was in Berlin at the time, was shocked by some of the rumors he heard after the appearance of this review and of an article based on it in the pro-government *Norddeutsche Allgemeine Zeitung:* upon returning to the Reichsland he informed the university's rector that he had been warned that the Strasbourg professors were all republicans.[114]

Of course the professors were not republicans, and, doubtless, few in Berlin believed they were. But the events of the spring of 1887 demonstrated that the university was a center of stout opposition to the current administration of the Reichsland. And for many, including Bismarck, this was unacceptable. The Strasbourg professors must be punished, or at least prevented from causing further embarrassment. But how? The options available and the steps actually taken can best be understood if one is first familiar with certain recent developments affecting Germany's universities generally, specifically those identified with the "expert adviser for the universities" in Prussia's Ministry of Culture, Friedrich Althoff.

During his Strasbourg years, from 1872 to 1882, Althoff was the most obvious case of a professor who rejected the faculty's dominant ethos and paid the penalty, ostracism. Appointed by Roggenbach as a reward for his contributions to the organization of the university, Althoff had no scholarly accomplishments to his credit and never manifested much interest in acquiring any. He was a man of ability and ambition, but his talents were suited less to scholarship than to administration and politics. Thus he slighted his academic responsibilities in order to advise Möller and Manteuffel, both of whom valued his assistance. And he once informed an astonished colleague that he favored nothing less than the bureaucratization of Germany's universities.[115] In return most professors regarded him with thinly disguised disdain. In the opinion of one, Althoff was "the greatest ignoramus to occupy a professorial chair in recent times."[116] And when in 1882 Althoff was appointed Prussia's "expert adviser for universities"—a position for which his administrative experience in Strasbourg ostensibly qualified him—some remarked that there had not been a comparable scandal since Friedrich Wilhelm I gave the presidency of the Prussian Academy of Sciences to a court jester.[117]

Althoff brought to his new position a determination to end the relative freedom from state control that the Prussian universities had enjoyed in the previous decade. Like Bismarck, for whom he developed great admiration, Althoff did not respect the idea of a "republic of scholars" as interpreted by most professors.[118] He believed that since the universities were state institutions, the government should oversee their administration and influence the selection of their professors. In filling vacant chairs Althoff did not feel bound by the proposals of the faculties concerned. Nor did he regularly seek the advice or respect the authority of the curators. Their traditional chores, such as negotiating with candidates for vacant chairs, were now handled in Berlin. Even when Althoff sought the opinions of a particular university community, he tended to bypass the curator; he had at least one confidant in nearly every university community in Germany, and he valued their advice more than that of the titular officials.[119]

In defending his policies Althoff used an argument advanced long before by Wilhelm von Humboldt: state control reduced the likelihood that the development of individual faculties and institutions would be retarded by vested interests.[120] But Althoff also was willing to sacrifice the interests of one institution for those of another, or for those of the state. Thus he slighted lesser Prussian universities in order to build up Göttingen (hoping to reduce the Hanoverians' bitterness over their subjugation to Prussian rule) and Berlin (considering it politically desirable to have a university of the first rank, a *Weltuniversität,* in the Prussian capital).[121] His concern for the political implications of his actions also affected professorial appointments. For instance, when the *Kulturkämpfer* Wilhelm Maurenbrecher left Bonn for Leipzig, Althoff insisted that his replacement be someone the Rhineland's Catholics would not find offensive.[122]

All German universities felt Althoff's influence, not just those in Prussia. In part this was because the other German states tended to look to Prussia for guidance in cultural and educational matters. But Althoff was not a disinterested party. From the time he took office he attempted through pressure and persuasion to make the other states with universities bring their policies into accord with Prussia's.[123] Nowhere was this more evident, or more resented, than at the University of Strasbourg.

Althoff's concern with the administration of the Reichsland's university did not end when he left for Berlin. Perhaps the best indication is a secret agreement he negotiated with the government of Alsace-Lorraine shortly after his departure. The first part only confirmed what was common practice: no Strasbourg professor was to be called to a Prussian university without the permission of the Alsatian institution's curator. But the accord went beyond established practice in calling on the University of Strasbourg to make a comparable sacrifice in return: no professor was to be called from a Prussian university to Strasbourg without the prior agreement of Prussia's Ministry of Culture—in effect, without Althoff's consent.[124] By 1885 the Strasbourg professors to their dismay had learned of this agreement. They were angered both by the limits imposed on their freedom in selecting new colleagues and by evidence that Prussia was not honoring its side of the accord. The professors assumed, incorrectly, that Althoff had authorized a recent overture to the jurist Rudolf Sohm from Göttingen made against their wishes and their curator's.[125] To the Strasbourg faculty it seemed that far from protecting their university, the agreement was weakening it to the advantage of its Prussian rivals. Memories of Althoff's unpopular opinions and activities while in Strasbourg made it all the easier to believe that he cared little about preserving their university's honored position within the world of learning.[126]

How serious was the threat? Much would depend on the curator. As long as the university had a curator committed above all to the institution's welfare it should remain relatively immune. And Ledderhose was such a curator: he was consistently responsive to the faculty's wishes and vigorous and generally successful in defending the university's interests, Althoff's efforts notwithstanding.[127] But in 1887 Ledderhose left office. His dismissal from his other official position in the purge following the elections (for reasons unrelated to his handling of the university's affairs) promised to undermine his effectiveness as curator, and so early in April he took a leave of absence and four months later he resigned.[128] Hohenlohe named as his temporary replacement Heinrich Richter, the chairman of the Reichsland's advisory board for secondary schools.[129] This appointment caused consternation in the university community. The professors knew that Richter, unlike Ledderhose, fully shared the dissatisfaction with the university which was widespread within the Reichsland's bureaucracy. They also knew that of all those in the ministry, Richter was on the best terms with Althoff and most under his influence. In fact they suspected, with good reason, that he had been appointed at Althoff's insistence.[130]

Shortly after appointing Richter the Statthalter sent him to confer with Althoff. Hohenlohe's objective was an agreement that would bring the administration of the University of Strasbourg into closer accord with that of the Prussian universities. Why he sought such an agreement is unclear, but presumably he was following advice received when in Berlin a few weeks before. In any event, Richter's mission was successful. On 13 May Richter and Althoff approved a memorandum, prepared by Althoff, that obligated the two states to make available to each other their information concerning academic policies and individual professors, to consult before offering positions to professors from the other state, and to attempt to call professors the other state wanted removed for political reasons. The agreement also gave Althoff and Richter the authority to decide specific questions without first consulting their superiors.[131]

The Strasbourg professors apparently knew nothing of this agreement, but they soon concluded that something was afoot. By the early summer circumstantial evidence indicated that Richter was systematically attempting, as one observer put it, "to lower the imperial university to the level of a small provincial university."[132] This seemed the only possible explanation for his treatment of those offered chairs at other universities. When one distinguished professor informed him that he had been offered a chair elsewhere, Richter replied, "Surely you will accept the call." To another he commented, "When are you thinking of leaving?" And to a third his only response was "Congratulations."[133] Richter made no attempt to match the salaries that other universities offered, nor did he assure those receiving offers that their continued presence in Strasbourg would be appreciated. Treated in this manner, the scholars concerned saw little reason to remain. During the summer of 1887 three of the most popular members of the faculty decided to depart: August Kundt, a physicist, accepted a chair in Berlin; Rudolf Sohm was called to Leipzig; and the controversial Lujo Brentano decided to move to Vienna. And for a while it seemed that two more, the jurist Paul Laband and the biologist Anton de Bary, would join the exodus.[134]

Most professors were convinced that the ultimate responsibility for the crisis their university now faced lay in Berlin. The circumstances surrounding the departure and prospective departure of some of the faculty's most prominent members suggested that Berlin was punishing the university for its professors' recent criticisms of the Reichsland's administration. It was generally assumed that Althoff had instructed Richter not to resist the resignation of scholars offered chairs elsewhere, and that in at least one case, Brentano's, he even had encouraged a non-Prussian university to recruit a Strasbourg professor.[135] Evidently Berlin no longer considered it necessary to preserve the Alsatian institution's high rank among Germany's universities.

The professors responded with indignation and determined resistance. They publicly refuted the criticisms of the university and its faculty made in Schmoller's review of Herkner's book and in the article in Berlin's *Die Post*.[136] They appealed to the institutional and personal loyalties of the professors wooed by other universities. And, most important, they sought the aid of the one high official who shared their concern for the university's plight, Hohenlohe-Schillingsfürst.[137]

The Statthalter, like Bismarck, Althoff, and other officials in Berlin and Strasbourg, disapproved of the political pronouncements and activities of the university's professors.[138] But he did not favor retaliation. He had enough problems in 1887 without identifying himself with a politically motivated attack on the university. On the contrary, when informed by the university's rector that de Bary, Laband, and Sohm planned to leave, he immediately appealed to each to reconsider. It was too late to save Sohm—he had already committed himself to Leipzig—but Hohenlohe did convince de Bary and Laband to stay. And when the news prompted the students to organize a rally to express their gratitude to de Bary and Laband, Hohenlohe instructed the ministry's leading officials to attend. He was determined to dispel the rumors circulating among the professors and students "that one wishes to weaken the university."[139] To this end, he showed particular interest in persuading Brentano to reject his offer from Vienna, a development he knew nothing about until after his meetings with de Bary and Laband. Since Brentano was the faculty's most outspoken critic of the Alsatian government, strong efforts to keep him presumably would demonstrate that the university was not being purged for political reasons. Accordingly the Statthalter instructed Puttkamer to offer Brentano a substantial raise and to inform Berlin that this controversial political economist should be kept in Strasbourg.[140] But in this case Hohenlohe's intervention came too late; two days before receiving Puttkamer's letter Brentano had accepted the offer from Vienna. Hohenlohe also was unsuccessful in an attempt to dissuade Kundt from going to Berlin.[141] But despite these failures, the Statthalter's vigorous and obviously sincere efforts to stem the exodus had gone far toward conciliating the university community.

Hohenlohe also demonstrated his commitment to the university when, later in the year, it faced a serious threat on another front. Late in the fall the Bundesrat passed a resolution that seemed to jeopardize the university's annual subsidy from the imperial government. This was not the first time the Bundesrat had considered changing its contribution. In recent years the representatives of the south German states, the states with the universities that competed most directly with Strasbourg's for students, had voted regularly either to reduce or to eliminate the subsidy.

But they had never prevailed, chiefly because of Prussian opposition.[142] This time, however, the Prussian representatives supported a resolution to make the subsidy an extraordinary rather than a standing item in the budget, and it passed. The reaction in Strasbourg was one of surprise and concern. Why would such a change be made, asked the university's friends, unless Berlin no longer attached importance to maintaining the institution's high stature? Shortly before the decisive vote Hohenlohe telegraphed the chancellor that the university's decline "would be unavoidable without the continuation of the imperial subsidy granted up to now."[143] Bismarck's reply, communicated indirectly, was that while there were currently no plans to end the annual grants to the university, "how long this will be the case will depend entirely on the good conduct of the Alsatians."[144] But the Reichstag, which had ultimate control over the imperial budget, was more supportive. Early in 1888 its budget committee recommended that the annual grant to the Reichsland's university remain in the standing budget, and after a short and one-sided debate the full assembly, in what amounted to a vote of confidence for the university, agreed almost unanimously.[145] With this, the uncertainty provoked by the Bundesrat's resolution came to an end.

In his efforts to defend the university's imperial subsidy the Statthalter neither sought nor received assistance from Richter. By the autumn of 1887 Hohenlohe had concluded that the acting curator could not be counted on to represent the university and hence should be replaced. To the members of the academic senate it was clear who should replace him; they named Hohenlohe himself as their first choice. But Hohenlohe, while flattered, decided after some reflection that he lacked the necessary time and energy. Instead he appointed Heinrich Hoseus, an official in the ministry and the academic senate's third choice.[146] That Hohenlohe assumed that this choice would be criticized in Berlin is evident from comments he made to a friend there:

> Richter is unpopular at the university not because he has been too hard with the professors but rather because he has followed Althoff's directions instead of standing on his own feet. And this is the reason that I do not want to retain Richter. This Althoff who meddles in matters that are not his business, this intriguer behind the mask of an honest Westphalian peasant . . . who has in his pocket all of the high and higher officials in Berlin, this man naturally wishes to rule here as well, and hence he wants Richter to remain curator, and describes the situation as though it would be subversive and weakness before the university if Hoseus were named instead of Richter. . . . I have no desire to let anyone lecture me about my affairs, least of all Althoff, and I shall do what I consider correct.[147]

The professors greeted Richter's removal with relief.[148] In their opinion it ended the university's most serious crisis yet, and it did so without the institution having suffered serious damage. Three popular professors had left, but the special circumstances provoking their departure no longer existed. And although the Bundesrat had tampered with the imperial subsidy, the financial position of the university was unchanged. There was even one result of the crisis that gave the Strasbourg professors cause for pride: by the end of 1887 it was clear that the imperial government would extend to the Reichsland its regulations concerning business practices and the protection of workers, the reforms proposed by Herkner and Brentano earlier in the year.[149]

Yet the crisis of 1887 did mark a significant turning point, for it demonstrated that if the university were to act as a critic of society and the state it now ran the risk of retaliation. The effect was sobering. Henceforth the professors would be more reluctant to speak out on political questions and more inclined to judge the Reichsland's government not by its general policies but by how it treated the university.[150] It was as if they had reached an unwritten agreement with Hohenlohe and Hoseus: they would avoid complicating the government's work, and in return the Statthalter and the curator would protect the university.

The crisis of 1887 would have been serious enough had the university's critics confined their attention to the professors' political attitudes and activities. But many went on to attack the institution's performance as an instrument of Germanization. To be sure, there had long been dissatisfaction over the university's effectiveness among the Reichsland's German bureaucrats, with many complaining that the university's accomplishments did not justify the expensive facilities, the professors' high salaries, or the ministry's difficulties in getting the university's budgets through the Landesausschuss.[151] But heretofore the bureaucrats had kept their opinions to themselves. And nobody else, it seems, had claimed publicly that the university was not fulfilling expectations. In 1887, however, the situation changed. The assumption after the elections that the Germanization of the Reichsland had hardly begun led some to argue that the university deserved a share of the blame. This opinion was particularly prevalent after the dissolution in April of an Alsatian student club known as the Sundgovia, an event examined in the next chapter. In the absence of evidence to the contrary, many newspapers suggested that the club's members were both thoroughly Francophile and representative of all the university's Alsatian students. And at least one widely quoted article, the one in Berlin's *Die Post* that faulted the professors' "striving for political influence," went on to argue that the university permitted Alsatians to receive a higher education while remaining in contact with Francophile groups in the Reichsland and that Germanization would proceed more rapidly if Alsatians had to attend universities in "old Germany."[152] The conclusion seemed clear: as far as its special mission was concerned, the university had done more harm than good.

The professors considered such charges unfounded. They realized the criticisms were based on superficial and atypical evidence, not on underlying trends. And in any case, they thought it unfair to expect the university to complete in a decade and a half a mission that would take generations. Indeed the university's performance might never have become an issue, many professors believed, had not the local government been preoccupied with distracting attention from its own failings. In this regard, it was widely rumored within the faculty that the strongest attack on the university, the article in *Die Post,* had been planted by the Alsatian government's press bureau. It was a reassuring rumor, for it made it easy to dismiss the article as merely an attempt to blame others for the government's mistakes and as a reflection of the bureaucracy's jealousy of the university, "the only thing," to quote Lujo Brentano, "that had thus far succeeded for the Germans in Alsace."[153]

There were lessons in the experience. Most important, perhaps, the events of 1887 demonstrated that the professors should be more concerned with their university's public image. Rumors that the university was a stronghold of radicalism and that its Alsatian students were overwhelmingly Francophile, whether justified or not, could only hurt the institution in its efforts to attract students and professors from across the Rhine and the necessary funding from the government. From now on the professors should avoid actions likely to cause criticism in the German press or to provoke the imperial government into reconsidering its annual grant.[154] More specifically, the crisis of 1887 had demonstrated that emphasizing the university's Germanizing mission could cut two ways. Although critical of others for their unrealistic expectations concerning the university, the professors themselves had helped to raise these expectations. In the past they had been quick to stress their institution's special mission when trying to attract German students and professors or to justify their demands for expensive facilities. Henceforth the argument would have to be used more cautiously.

But these lessons did not affect the professors' own attitude concerning their mission or the chances for its success. On these subjects their opinions remained essentially unchanged. If the Germanization of the Reichsland was proceeding slowly, the blame must be borne by others, particularly by the bureaucracy and the military. Blinded by missionary enthusiasm, a commitment to the ideal of the *Kulturstaat,* and pride in their institution's stature in the world of learning, the professors could not believe that the university itself was at fault.

# 4

# The German University and Alsatian Society

As a center of learning the University of Strasbourg fulfilled the expectations of the most demanding. With its productive young professors, its industrious students, and its magnificent library and laboratories, it quickly gained a position among the world's most distinguished universities. Indeed, at a time when the prestige of German scholarship and German higher education was at its height, university reformers in other countries looked with particular awe and envy to the new institution in Strasbourg. Thus in 1872 a Belgian journal, after lamenting the current state of Belgium's universities, argued that the country would not be on the right course until it had a university like that just founded in Alsace-Lorraine.[1] In 1875 Daniel Coit Gilman, seeking European models for the university he had been commissioned to organize in Baltimore, The Johns Hopkins University, found himself more impressed by the University of Strasbourg than by any other.[2] And in 1884 an article on the Alsatian institution in the *Revue internationale de l'enseignement,* a publication dedicated to reforming French education at all levels, observed that "no city in Europe, not excepting the great capitals, . . . offers facilities for higher education so fine or with the different components so well designed and integrated."[3] Such tributes suggest that the university satisfied a primary objective of its sponsors: it demonstrated to the rest of the world the superiority of German learning. If judged by academic standards alone, its success could not be questioned.

But in this case another standard would also be applied. Since the university had been established to further the Germanization of the Reichsland, its success would depend largely on its contributions to this objective. Of course initially its ability to meet this standard had caused little concern. Most German observers—Roggenbach was an exception—had assumed that the university's success in its special mission would soon be significant and self-evident. But with time the optimism gave way to doubts, cynicism, and recriminations. Particularly after 1887 there was an intermittent and often bitter debate among Germans over the university and its accomplishments. This debate focused on three broad questions that proved, and still prove, inherently difficult to answer: How could the university best contribute to Germanization? How much could it be expected to contribute? And how should its achievements be measured?

These were questions of more than academic interest. As the events of 1887 demonstrated, the answers might jeopardize the government's commitment to the university and hence the university's honored position in the world of learning.

• 1 •

During the university's first decade its professors remained generally optimistic about the institution's nation-building potential. Even the small number of Alsatian students and the professors' lack of contact with indigenous elites failed to discourage them. Convinced of the worthiness of their cause, they regarded these developments as manifestations not of dissatisfaction with the university itself but rather of the Alsatians' bitterness over their fate, an understandable attitude which should soon wane. With time, they assumed, the university would win acceptance in the Reichsland comparable to that enjoyed by the other German universities in their respective states and regions.

Indeed it became evident during the 1870s that the university already had support among Alsatians. From the time it opened many natives respected the institution as a prestigious center of scholarship whose professors, in marked contrast to the army officers stationed in the Reichsland, carefully avoided all chauvinistic excesses. Of the few Alsatian students—in the first decade there were, on average, only ninety-six each semester—even the more skeptical admired the industrious scholarly activity characteristic of the institution and praised the freedoms basic to German higher education.[4] The university also received enthusiastic support in the Landesausschuss from the autonomists, the delegates ready to accept German rule if Alsace-Lorraine received the same rights as the empire's other constituent states. In 1877, for instance, a motion to reduce the Alsatian contribution to the university's budget provoked two autonomists to describe the university as "our pride and joy."[5] A third autonomist pointed out that "if we did not have this university, our province would be nothing but a military bastion."[6] And the group's leader observed that "if the university were to cost twice what is now assumed, I would vote for it. There is still something that is above purely material considerations. It is by fostering art and scholarship that a people shows it has truly noble sentiments."[7] These comments surprised and excited the professors. "It is the first time," Hermann Baumgarten observed, "that any German institution has been accepted with true warmth; as a rule everything is criticized."[8] Nine months later, when the Landesausschuss voted its large appropriation for the university's building expenses, Baumgarten confidently informed his brother-in-law that this vote "is highly gratifying to us. The university has become integrated into the life of the province."[9]

But Baumgarten was wrong. The university did not have the support of Alsatians in the sense that Tübingen's had the support of Württembergers or Bonn's that of Rhinelanders. The Strasbourg professors, always alert for evidence that they were succeeding, had been misled by the votes in the Landesausschuss and by the speeches of the autonomists, the assembly's most Germanophile members. For most concerned Alsatians the university was far from integrated into the life of the province. And it was not only because they associated the institution with the resented occupation of their homeland. Alsatians tended to identify the university with an alien type of learning and an alien way of life as well as with an alien ruler. There were three basic criticisms. They concerned the institution's Germanizing mission, the professors' attitudes toward religion, and the university's relevance to Alsatians' career aspirations and to the specific needs of the Reichsland's economy.

The strongest opposition to the university's Germanizing mission naturally came from those who spoke French. With little representation in the lower social strata except in parts of Lorraine, they constituted only one-fifth or one-sixth of the Reichsland's population. In nearly all of Alsace and much of Lorraine the linguistic pattern was essentially as Lujo Brentano once described it: "The broad mass of the populace in rural as well as urban areas was German; only the educated or those who passed themselves off as such thought and spoke in French."[10] But because of its social composition the French-speaking minority was an important group. To be sure, it had been weakened by the large migration of Alsatians to France following the war (about 8.5 percent of the population left), for most migrants spoke French.[11] Thousands of French-speaking businessmen and professionals remained, however, and as a result the Alsatian haute bourgeoisie was still predominantly French in language and culture. In fact, the Frenchification of the region's middle class actually progressed in the 1870s and 1880s, with conversing in French now an appealing means of defying the new and unwanted rulers as well as a mark of high social status.[12] This trend accorded with the argument used by French-speaking Alsatians to rationalize their decision not to emigrate: "We were told: Stay there," a member of a prominent Strasbourg family recalled. "Support France there, support the language there, the traditions and the ideal of your ancestors. Serve France on German soil."[13] After 1870 the French-speaking members of the Alsatian upper middle class, as the self-appointed guardians of French culture in the Reichsland, were as conscious of a special mission as the German professors.

It was the determination of these Alsatians to resist Germanization that governed their relationship to the immigrant colony and to the university. Thus personal and social contacts were kept to a minimum. Throughout the period of German rule, two upper-middle-class societies existed side-by-side in Strasbourg and the other major towns, with the native society adhering to the French language and style of life, frequenting its own shops, restaurants, salons, and evenings at the theater, and resisting all overtures, no matter how well intentioned, from members of the German community. As for the university, many French-speaking families eventually enrolled their sons and took advantage of the distinguished specialists in the medical faculty, but only because they believed the institution could never convince them or their children that German culture was superior to French culture or German rule preferable to French rule.[14] Otherwise, relations were almost nonexistent. Professors accustomed to the esteem and deference of middle-class society discovered that it was rare indeed for them to meet Alsatians socially, let alone visit their homes.[15] Even some of the Alsatians teaching at the university would have little to do with them. In many respects these Alsatian scholars constituted a foreign body within the faculty. They taught their classes but shunned involvement in the university's administrative and social life. Generally the motive was not personal dislike for the slighted professors, but rather opposition to German rule and solidarity with the social group from which most came, Strasbourg's French-speaking patriciate.[16]

There were, to be sure, highly educated Alsatians and some of considerable wealth who had never adopted the French language. In both Strasbourg and Colmar the local Germanic dialect continued to be the customary language for many professional families, particularly if Protestant. And in the villages and market towns of Alsace and much of Lorraine it was not often that a teacher, pastor, or landed proprietor could be found who habitually spoke French. But on social and cultural issues most of these middle-class Alsatians shared the values and opinions of their French-speaking counterparts. They associated France with intellectual refinement and good taste, and Germany, by contrast, with cultural backwardness and boorishness. Unlike most Germans, and particularly those settling in the Reichsland, they accorded higher status to businessmen and members of the free professions than to bureaucrats and military officers and men of learning. With specific reference to the university, they tended to regard the professors as either otherworldly or self-important and to find offensive the customs of the German students and the rhetoric and rituals through which the university presented itself to the public. (By German standards the professors and students from across the Rhine may have been unpretentious and sensitive to their surroundings, but to most Alsatian observers they were not.) Admittedly, to the extent that the university received strong backing from Alsatians in its first two or three decades, it came from within this group. In particular, many Lutherans from Lower Alsace—essentially the constituency of the autonomists— quickly rallied to the institution, regarding it as a defender of their traditional hegemony over Alsatian intellectual life against an emerging Catholic intelligentsia and against the Calvinist industrialists of Mulhouse. But they were in the minority. At least until the 1890s most members of the dialect-speaking middle class appear to have been as unsympathetic to the university and its Germanizing mission as those in the French-speaking elite.[17]

Left to consider are the dialect-speaking commoners, who accounted for the bulk of the population. What did they think of the university? The evidence, largely circumstantial, suggests that at least until the turn of the century those not indifferent tended to view it negatively; they were less likely to see the university as an impressive work of art or as an agent of upward mobility than as an alien and unnecessarily expensive imposition. No doubt, this was in part because they considered higher education a preserve of those higher in the social order or of those too lazy or weak to do real work, a sentiment hardly unique to commoners in the Reichsland. But antipathy to German rule and to German culture also contributed. It should be emphasized that these Alsatians, their dialect notwithstanding, did not share, respect, or even know much about the customs and opinions now prevalent in "old Germany." Separated from the rest of France by a language barrier and from the German states by a political frontier, the region's peasants, laborers, and artisans had hardly altered their attitudes and style of life since the seventeenth century. The result was a particularistic and rather primitive culture that was neither French nor German, but Alsatian. In 1870 many German proponents of annexation referred to these rustics as evidence of the true "Germanness" of the region, but they failed to persuade the Alsatians. The great majority of working-class and lower-middle-class natives opposed the German conquest of their homeland, and their natural inclination was to withhold their support from institutions identified with that conquest. They doubtless would have agreed with the Landesausschuss deputy who criticized the university's building program because he thought it unjust to ask peasants to pay taxes for this enterprise: "The agricultural class forms the core of our people," he commented, but "the members of this class are now the slaves of civilization."[18]

For many Alsatians, both commoners and those of higher status, the least attractive feature of the civilization associated with the university was its identification with free thought and, in particular, with anti-Catholicism. During its first three decades the university had a well-deserved reputation as a stronghold of irreligion, and this seriously limited its appeal to Alsatians, nearly all of whom were devout. For many Protestants, particularly orthodox Lutherans, the university was a dangerous center of rationalism. Even the Protestant theological faculty could not be trusted, for it was widely believed that its students found their religious convictions undermined "by the accursed critical theology of this faculty and by modern scholarly works in general," and that the faculty's professors were "heretics through and through."[19] The Reichsland's Catholics were even more critical. In churches, newspapers, and elected assemblies the university was repeatedly denounced as a "stronghold of Protestantism"—orthodox Protestants would hardly have agreed—and as a "bastion of the so-called 'Kulturkampf' in Alsace-Lorraine."[20] During Reichstag debates on the university's budget, for instance, the Reichsland's Catholic deputies, many of them clergymen, frequently complained that there were too few professors of their faith on the faculty and that the general atmosphere of the institution was hostile to religion in general and Catholicism in particular.[21] There were always liberal deputies and newspapers with ready replies to such charges, but they seem only to have increased the suspicions of Catholics. Certainly the Catholic clergy remained unpersuaded. Until after the turn of the century the Reichsland's bishops and priests were the university's most vehement and unrelenting critics. And since the Catholic clergy largely determined public opinion among Catholic Alsatians, particularly in the villages and smaller towns, the impact on the university's popular image was considerable. Indeed to the extent that Alsatian commoners had opinions about the university, these opinions probably reflected those circulated in the clerical press and from the pulpits.

The university's failure to win much support from Alsatians in its early years resulted chiefly from its identification with Germanization and with irreligion. But there was a third reason for the university's limited appeal. The institution embodied the ideal of learning for its own sake and the hostility to practical education that had become characteristic of German universities in the early and middle decades of the century. In some respects, in fact, the university was closer to these traditions than were other German universities. But these traditions, whatever their merits, were at odds with prevailing attitudes in the Reichsland. A few exceptions aside, middle-class Alsatians had been unaffected by the neo-humanistic and idealistic movements that had transformed the German universities and their relationship to society. Indeed the trends had been in the opposite direction. Since the beginning of the century the pursuit of learning had fallen in prestige among Alsatians relative to the pursuit of wealth. In the last few decades of French rule the disinterested scholar had not been an object of particular respect or deference for those in the middle class, as he had been across the Rhine. The wealthy industrialists and businessmen, not the men of learning, had set the standards emulated by most middle-class Alsatians. These included their standards concerning education. Alsatians tended to regard education as an investment that should yield a quick and profitable return. They considered the purpose of education to be to prepare students for careers as rapidly as possible, and they wanted their educational institutions to provide all the practical training for which there was a demand. But this, they complained, the University of Strasbourg did not do. Beginning in the late 1870s there were frequent proposals in the Landesausschuss and elsewhere that the university introduce programs in such career-oriented fields as agronomy, architecture, business, engineering, and forestry. As for the ideal of learning for its own sake, it tended to be dismissed as a *Schwowe-Ding* ("German thing"), as a peculiar notion with little relevance to the needs of Alsace-Lorraine.[22]

That Alsatians would initially regard the university as an alien institution came as no surprise to the professors. After all, the rationale for establishing the university had been to introduce Alsatians to a culture and type of learning that were unfamiliar. But the strength and duration of the resistance were surprising. Although most professors had come to Strasbourg with little sense of what they would find, they had assumed there would soon be tangible evidence that their mission was succeeding. But such evidence was hard to find. During the 1870s and 1880s the enrollment of Alsatians was low by any standard, and there was little to suggest that the few who did enroll became more Germanophile as a result. Thus there was reason to argue, as outsiders did in 1887, that as an instrument of Germanization the university had fallen short of expectations. It was an opinion the professors shared.[23]

Their disillusionment affected the professors in various ways. A few, including the jurist Heinrich Geffcken and the philosopher Paul Hensel, became convinced that the university was doing more harm than good and hence that its founding had been a mistake.[24] Others concluded that the institution was unlikely to have much influence one way or the other, that, as one professor complained privately in 1884, "the Germanizing mission, for which we are envied elsewhere, is a pure chimera."[25] But such opinions were atypical. Most professors, however disappointed, remained basically optimistic. Their response to charges that the university was failing in its mission was to counsel patience: they insisted that the university would have a healthy impact, but that it might be a generation or more before the evidence of that impact appeared. For some, the best course in the meantime was to devote one's full energies to disinterested scholarship and to avoid offending local sensibilities unnecessarily. Others, while equally committed to keeping politics out of the classroom, became involved in extracurricular activities designed to advance the Germanization of the Reichsland. As if to compensate for the university's alleged failings, they gave public lectures directed at Alsatian adults and helped to organize and administer such enterprises as a club sponsoring exhibits of German art, an association for popular education, and the local branch of the Allgemeine Deutsche Schulverein.[26]

But whatever the differences among the professors—whether pessimistic or optimistic, assertive or restrained—there was one potential response to their critics that they never seriously considered: changing the character of the university. The argument that the university would accomplish more if it were responsive to local opinion, advanced by Roggenbach and others even before the institution opened, found few adherents on the faculty. Thus the German professors showed virtually no interest in the conciliatory proposals made by Roggenbach shortly before resigning his commission. During the university's first quarter century they never considered instituting the programs in engineering, architecture, agricultural science, and forestry advocated by Roggenbach. Except in the Protestant theological faculty, the smallest and most Alsatian of the faculties, they made no efforts to seek or to favor Alsatian candidates for vacant chairs.[27] There was strong criticism when Ledderhose, following Roggenbach's advice, permitted the Alsatians joining the medical faculty to teach in French.[28] And the German professors manifested no interest in seeing their university become a bridge between the scholarly worlds of France and Germany, a possibility suggested by Köchly, Dilthey, and Roggenbach as well as by several Alsatians. The prevalent opinion on the faculty was that France in general and French scholarly life in particular were decadent and hence had nothing to offer.[29] In sum, the professors systematically resisted every change that might make their university more Alsatian or bicultural in character. They were, in the sociological sense of the terms, "cosmopolitans" rather than "locals" or "provincials"; their commitment was to the norms determining status in the world of scholarship, notably the disinterested and highly specialized pursuit of knowledge, not to their particular university's interests as defined by the Alsatians or by the government.[30]

But to conclude that the professors were unwilling to make sacrifices for the sake of their nation-building mission would be to misunderstand them. They simply saw no inconsistency. By their reasoning, the more distinguished the university—the more impressive the work of art—the greater would be its success in its mission. With a few exceptions the professors refused to believe that anything lessening their university's stature in the academic world could increase its effectiveness, and they responded accordingly to all demands for significant concessions. If there was to be an accommodation between the university and its local constituency it would be on their terms, not the Alsatians'.

## · 2 ·

The university's failure to make concessions presented its potential Alsatian constituents with a dilemma. Simply put, should they boycott the institution or accommodate themselves to it? In microcosm this dilemma reflected questions confronting most Alsatians after the Franco-Prussian War, the only exceptions being the few thoroughly Germanophile already. Given the reality of German rule, was it better to emigrate or to remain? If the decision was made to remain, was it better to have nothing to do with the new regime or to seek an accommodation? If the decision was made to seek an accommodation, how far should one go?

These questions would have been difficult enough had they involved only balancing cultural and political values with material interests. But there were more general considerations. First, it could be assumed that opportunities not exploited by Alsatians would be seized by German immigrants. To the extent that Alsatians boycotted German universities, for instance, positions in the Reichsland's bureaucracy and the professions would go by default to Germans. This prospect implied that whatever their material interests, it was consistent with the values of Francophile Alsatians to adapt to the new regime. By this reasoning, those collaborating and thus limiting the number of positions occupied by Germans exhibited a higher form of patriotism.

A second consideration related to the deep divisions among Alsatians themselves along religious, linguistic, social, and geographic lines. In determining how to respond to the new regime, many individuals and groups, however they may have rationalized their behavior, seem to have been less concerned with protecting the interests of Alsatians generally than with strengthening their own position within the indigenous social order. And once some were perceived as acting this way, others were encouraged to do likewise, if only to cut their losses; under the circumstances, opportunism proved contagious. But the question remained whether, as far as status and power in the indigenous social order were concerned, it was better to boycott the new regime or to collaborate. Consider, for instance, the case of the Catholics. Although the prevalent assumption within the Catholic hierarchy was that the church should have as little to do with the new regime as possible, some clergymen thought differently. Suspecting that a willingness to cooperate would be rewarded with concessions, they advocated cautious steps toward an accommodation. But the issue was more complicated. As critics within the church pointed out, what good would concessions be if the necessary bargaining alienated the faithful? And what would happen to the church if Alsace-Lorraine and France were reunited?[31] The problem, obviously, was one of balancing the potential gains from collaboration with the obvious risks, a calculation which necessitated considering the calculations of others. In one form or another this problem confronted Alsatians and Alsatian interest groups throughout the period of German rule.

These general considerations were particularly relevant to the responses of Alsatians to the university. Since higher education controlled access to a large and growing proportion of elite positions, its appeal to those with high aspirations for themselves or their sons was obvious, as was the danger of a general boycott. But against the benefits had to be weighed the alien character of the university and the possibility that attendance might affect students' values and friendships in undesired ways. Of course there was the option of studying elsewhere, either in "old Germany" or abroad. For most concerned Alsatians, however, the other German universities were even more alien and potentially more dangerous than Strasbourg's. And study abroad was something of a luxury unless one was planning to emigrate, for it provided little of the training and none of the credentials needed to enter most professions in the Reichsland. So what did potential students do? What choices did they and their families make? Although the evidence sheds little light on how Alsatians evaluated their options and formulated their strategies concerning higher education, many of the results are known. Matriculation records and other sources enable us to analyze the demand for higher education among Alsatians, how it changed over time, and how it was affected by socioeconomic, religious, linguistic, and geographic factors.

There remains the problem of assessing the extent to which the demand for higher education among Alsatians deviated from that expected under "normal" conditions. The approach adopted is to compare the patterns for Alsatians under German rule with those for the residents of three "old German" states, Baden, Prussia, and Württemberg. (Systematic comparisons with patterns in Alsace-Lorraine before 1871 and in France after 1871 are impossible, as the requisite data do not exist.) Unless noted, the Germans living in the Reichsland and the Alsatians living elsewhere are not considered. (For a fuller discussion of the sources and procedures used, see appendix A.)

Before the University of Strasbourg opened government officials assumed that it would soon enroll about 1,200 students.[32] They were too optimistic. During the 1870s the number never rose much above half this figure, and three decades after the university opened, with enrollment at all German universities having doubled in the interim, there were still fewer than 1,200 students. The main reason was clear: the university attracted few Alsatians. Although the number of students from outside the Reichsland dropped somewhat after the early 1880s—largely because other universities now had facilities and offerings once unique to Strasbourg—the university continued to attract more than its share. But judging by trends in Germany generally, it enrolled few from its own state.

It was not that Alsatians preferred other German universities. In a typical semester prior to 1900 more than four-fifths of the Alsatians attending German universities were in Strasbourg, a rate of loyalty to the local institution higher than that found in other parts of the country.[33] The problem, rather, lay with the low demand among Alsatians for higher education, or, to be more precise, for higher education in Germany. Through the 1870s the rate of attendance at German universities for Alsatians was less than one-quarter that for Germans generally. In the 1880s the gap began to narrow but the process was slow. At the end of the century (later trends are considered in chapter 6) the proportion was still only three-fifths that for Germany as a whole (see table 2, appendix B).

As indicators of how susceptible Alsatians were to the direct influence of a German higher education, these ratios may suffice. But for other purposes they are inadequate. This is particularly true when considering the social origins of the students. The emigrants of the early 1870s came disproportionately from those social groups most likely to seek a higher education, and so did the thousands who emigrated during the next two or three decades. Enrollment statistics for the French academies in 1887 suggest the impact. In this year there were 215 students born in Alsace-Lorraine enrolled at French faculties of law, medicine, and pharmacy (140 in Paris, 54 in Nancy, and 21 elsewhere), and probably close to 280 in all faculties. That is, there were about as many as at German universities, Strasbourg's included. It should be added that the great majority of those going to France to study prior to the turn of the century did not return to Alsace-Lorraine, at least not during the period of German rule. German sanctions against those escaping their military obligations were partly responsible: male Alsatians who left before reaching seventeen could not return until they were thirty-one, and those leaving between the ages of seventeen and twenty-five had to wait until they were fifty-five before coming back.[34]

The emigration of Alsatians to study in France did not particularly disturb the German authorities. Indeed it had the desirable effect of removing potential Francophile members of the indigenous elites, thus making Alsace-Lorraine "an intellectual desert" and hence more vulnerable to Germanization.[35] This reasoning was consistent with the approach to administering the Reichsland favored by the university's professors: rather than cater to the Francophile notables, who were considered irreconcilable, policies should favor the mass of the population. By extension, the Reichsland's schools and the university would be important not only as instruments of political socialization but also as agents of social and occupational mobility; they would give potentially Germanophile Alsatians of middle- and lower-class origins access to high positions open in part because of the emigration of Francophile Alsatians.

This logic assumed, of course, that Alsatian commoners would take advantage of the educational opportunities offered. But numerous incentives were provided. In the case of the university, two in particular deserve mention. First, it was made clear that Alsatians with a higher education and the correct attitudes would have no difficulty obtaining important positions in the bureaucracy. "Even if of very humble origins," a Francophile Alsatian later observed, "one could attain the highest positions in the region providing one was Alsatian by birth and made political concessions to the masters of the hour."[36] Second, financial aid was readily available for students from modest backgrounds. In 1896–97, for instance, almost one-third of the university's students—a high proportion by German standards—received stipends of some sort, with the average size (154.6 marks) large enough to cover about four-fifths of a typical student's annual fees (but only one-eighth of his total expenses). Not all of those supported were Alsatians, but the restrictions on many stipends suggest that Alsatians received a disproportionate share.[37]

The authorities' interest in attracting students from the popular classes is clear, but did they succeed? To what extent did the university act as an agent of upward mobility within Alsatian society rather than as a prop of the existing social order? Judging by comments made at the turn of the century by a Francophile critic, the institution's success in its early years was significant. "For a long time . . . "—he was thinking of the 1870s and 1880s—"the students tended to come from very inferior backgrounds, all the more so as the German administration strongly encouraged youths, even mediocre ones, to study. . . . The application of these students was unimportant; what was important was . . . to push them."[38] That a Francophile notable would regard such a development with misgivings is not surprising. But there is reason to question whether his depiction was accurate. Admittedly the proportion of Alsatian students who were of modest origins was greater than it had been at French faculties in the 1860s (see table 3, appendix B), and in all likelihood it was high by the standards of France in the mid- and late nineteenth century.[39] But by German standards the distribution of Alsatian students according to social origins was relatively selective or elitist, not relatively democratic. Controlling for differences in the composition of the relevant age cohorts only reinforces this conclusion.[40] At least until the turn of the century the overrepresentation of youths from higher in the social order was almost always greater among Alsatian students than it was among students from Baden, Prussia, and Württemberg. (These and the following observations are based on the students at all German universities, not just those at the universities of their respective states. The characteristics of the Alsatians at all German universities and of those at the University of Strasbourg were similar.)

The preceding comparisons are strongly affected by two occupational categories that accounted for most of the relevant cohorts but few of the students: the peasantry and the working class. How strongly becomes apparent when these groups are left out of account: access to universities was much more evenly distributed among the remaining groups than it was within the population as a whole and there was a pronounced tendency in some states for the distribution to become more representative with time. But the indices also show that the pattern for Alsatians was generally less open than it was for those from other German states (see table 4, appendix B). Thus the conclusion suggested by the initial comparisons requires no modification: the recruitment of Alsatian students was relatively selective or elitist by German standards, not relatively democratic.

But why? One factor was obvious. The recruitment of students in Baden, Prussia, and Württemberg would have been more selective socially were it not for the students of Catholic theology, most of whom had relatively humble backgrounds. There were no such students at the University of Strasbourg, however, and few Alsatians, never more than fifteen at a time, attended Catholic theological faculties at other German universities.[41] (If Alsatians preparing for the priesthood went beyond the local seminaries, it was usually to study abroad, notably at the Catholic university at Fribourg in Switzerland.)[42] Hence it seems appropriate to supplement the earlier comparisons with others made after excluding the students of Catholic theology. The new comparisons still indicate that the recruitment of Alsatian students was relatively elitist by German standards, but the differences are less pronounced (see table 4, appendix B).

Closer inspection reveals that the relatively select character of student recruitment in Alsace-Lorraine can largely be attributed to two groups, the Protestant clergy and, in the 1890s, French-speaking members of the free professions. The salience of the former is hardly surprising, for the Lutheran clergy had close ties to German culture and scholarship and many pastors had warmly welcomed the establishment of Strasbourg's university. But the reasons for the relative overrepresentation in the 1890s of the second group, those from French-speaking professional families, are less obvious. In this case it is necessary to look not to traditional affinities but rather to changes that had occurred since the German annexation.

In the 1870s and 1880s the Reichsland's French-speaking families had generally boycotted the local university. In many cases their sons moved to France on completing secondary school if not before, both to avoid German military service and, often, to receive a French higher education. Other youths studied in Belgium or Switzerland, while the rest, a few exceptions aside, entered careers for which a higher education was not required. But around 1890 a new pattern began to emerge. It reflected a general change in the political and cultural atmosphere. By this time support among Alsatians for uncompromising resistance to German rule and German culture was waning. The growth to maturity of a generation that did not remember the good old days under French rule contributed, and so did the strengthening of economic ties to the rest of Germany and the disillusionment fostered by recent developments in France—by the Panama scandal, by the Dreyfus affair, by the rise of anticlericalism, by the decline of revanchism. To be sure, French-speaking Alsatians did not become reconciled to their fate, but increasingly their stance was one of opportunism rather than of obstinate protest. One result was that it now became acceptable within the bourgeoisie for families to send sons to a

German university, and by the end of the century they were doing so in large numbers. What this meant for the University of Strasbourg and for its success in its special mission will be considered below. Here it need be noted only that the number of sons of Alsatian doctors, pharmacists, and lawyers attending German universities quadrupled between the mid-1880s and the late 1890s, and that by the latter date the enrollment rates for some of these groups and for the two highest occupational categories (consisting of high-level government employees and members of the free professions) were actually higher than the comparable rates for Prussia (see table 5, appendix B).

Of the occupations outside the highest category, five were responsible for disproportionately large numbers of Alsatian students by German standards: landed proprietors, rentiers, middle-level civil servants, teachers, and white-collar workers in private firms. Together these occupations accounted for a much larger share of the Alsatian students (30.9 percent in 1898) than of the students from Prussia (28.1 percent) and Württemberg (25.2 percent), and by the end of the century the rates for Alsatian youths with fathers in these occupations often compared favorably with those for their counterparts across the Rhine. By contrast, Alsatians in the remaining occupations tended to be poorly represented. The rates for the sons of industrialists, bankers, and merchants were far behind those in Prussia and Württemberg, and the pattern was similar for the sons of artisans, shopkeepers, peasants, and members of the working class.

In this connection it should be noted that the occupational distribution of Alsatians differed from that common across the Rhine. Because of the emigration of many bureaucratic and professional families since 1871, the proportion of Alsatian youths with fathers in the highest occupational category (.55 percent in 1895) was only about half as large as the comparable proportions in Baden (1.34 percent), Prussia (1.07 percent), and Württemberg (1.37 percent). The implications for the number of Alsatian students are significant. Although by German standards Alsatian students came disproportionately from the top of the social order, the Alsatian population was distributed disproportionately toward the bottom. A hypothetical example suggests the consequences: if the Alsatian population had been distributed among the occupations as was the Prussian population while the enrollment rate for each occupation remained constant, there would have been 588 Alsatians enrolled at German universities in 1898–99 rather than 436. Thus more than half the gap between the actual number and the number expected under "normal" conditions (731 if the Prussian rates are considered normal) can be attributed to the atypical occupational composition of the Alsatian population.

Sex and age aside, position in the social order was the strongest determinant of patterns of university enrollment among Alsatians. But, as elsewhere, there were additional determinants of significance. One of them, already discussed in general terms, was religion: Catholics were less likely to attend a university than Protestants, and Jews were more likely. This pattern was consistent with that found in the rest of Germany. But across the Rhine the disparities could be attributed largely to the disproportionately small number of Catholics and the disproportionately large number of Jews in the occupations exhibiting the greatest demand for higher education. Indeed by the late 1890s Catholics actually tended to be overrepresented at German universities after controlling for occupation. But in the case of the Alsatians, controlling for occupation does not have as striking an effect: in 1898 the enrollment rate for Catholics with occupation controlled was only 70 percent of that for Protestants.[43] Admittedly, comparisons may be more instructive if the students of Protestant and Catholic theology are left out of account. But even after making this adjustment it is clear that Catholics (and Jews) exhibited much lower enrollment rates relative to Protestants among Alsatians than they did across the Rhine (see table 6, appendix B). These differences take on added meaning when it is noted that of all the German states Alsace-Lorraine had the highest proportion of Catholics.

Also important were geographical factors. They were relevant on two levels. First, the characteristics of villages and towns affected the demand for higher education. In general, the larger the community the greater the demand, assuming occupation is controlled. And other things being equal, the demand for higher education was much higher in towns with a Gymnasium or an Oberrealschule, the schools preparing students for higher education, than in other towns. Although leaving home to board at a secondary school was common, youths with a Gymnasium or Oberrealschule in their hometown tended to have lower costs and hence stronger incentives to continue their education. There is, of course, no reason to believe that this pattern was unique to the Reichsland.

Second, there were pronounced differences in the demand for higher education among the regions of the Reichsland. In part these reflected linguistic divisions: the demand for a German higher education was lower in the parts of the Reichsland that were predominantly French-speaking—a few enclaves in Alsace and half of Lorraine—than it was elsewhere. (In the French-speaking regions the language of instruction was French in the primary schools but—beginning in 1883—German in the Gymnasien and Oberrealschulen, suggesting that to the extent that linguistic obstacles limited the demand for higher education the filtering occurred at the end of primary school rather than later.)[44] The regional differences also reflected, in part, religious differences. Although the numbers of Catholics in each of the Reichsland's administrative regions—Lower Alsace, Upper Alsace, and Lorraine—were comparable, about three-fourths of the Protestants lived in Lower Alsace, with the heaviest concentrations in Strasbourg and in the regions north and northwest of the city. This pattern together with the greater demand for higher education among Protestants help to explain why a disproportionately large number of the Alsatians who attended German universities came from Lower Alsace, Strasbourg excluded. (A disproportionately large number also came from Strasbourg, but in this case economic advantages—the lower indirect costs for those who could live at home—probably were an important factor.)

Yet, even after controlling for religion as well as father's occupation, large regional disparities remain. Thus in 1898–99 the enrollment rate for natives of Lower Alsace, Strasbourg excluded, was 1.65 times the rate for natives of Upper Alsace and 2.04 times that for natives of Lorraine (see table 7, appendix B). These differences suggest the need to consider another factor, namely distance, particularly cultural distance, from Strasbourg. Given the density of the railway network by the last quarter of the century, physical distance was not much of an obstacle to attending the university. But cultural distance was a different matter. In this regard, it is appropriate to begin with some general remarks about the cultural geography of the Reichsland.

Although outside observers tended to be impressed by what united Alsatians culturally and distinguished them from their neighbors, Alsatians themselves realized that it was misleading to talk of a single Alsatian culture. Religious and linguistic rivalries aside, there were significant cultural differences both within the Reichsland's three major subdivisions and among them. By way of example, consider the stereotypes associated by Alsatians with the inhabitants of Upper Alsace as opposed to those of Lower Alsace. In the opinion of a native of Upper Alsace who resided in Strasbourg, "The Upper Alsatian (drinker of wine, generally Catholic) is more imaginative, more impulsive, more enthusiastic, more expressive, more capable of impartiality and excitement over an idea; he makes decisions quickly and acts immediately. The Lower Alsatian (beer drinker) is more sluggish, more indifferent, more inscrutable, more matter-of-fact."[45] Another Alsatian, also Francophile but from Strasbourg, once observed that "under the German regime Upper Alsace and Lower Alsace were simply companions in misfortune, this is all that united them. . . . A Strasbourgeois—I do not exaggerate—feels more at home in Madrid, Rome, Budapest, and Paris than in the Sundgau [the southernmost region of Alsace], and a Mulhousien will gladly make a detour in order not to see the cathedral."[46] The differences, real and perceived, between Lorraine and both Upper and Lower Alsace were even more pronounced.[47]

How these regional rivalries affected the demand for higher education cannot be measured with precision, but some observations can be made. Generally the natives of Upper Alsace and Lorraine were more Francophile than the natives of Lower Alsace, even when controlling for religion and language. They went to greater lengths to avoid contact with Germans and their institutions, and they tended to look down on the residents of

Lower Alsace and particularly of Strasbourg for not being equally resolute.[48] By implication, they were more likely to regard as alien an institution known to be a bastion of "free German learning." These
considerations, together with their traditional resentment of the Strasbourgeois and their cultural pretensions, help to explain why natives of
Upper Alsace and Lorraine sent fewer students to Strasbourg than did
the natives of Lower Alsace—and more to universities in France and
Switzerland.[49]

## • 3 •

The success of the University of Strasbourg in its nation-building mission
cannot be judged only by the number of Alsatians enrolled. Also relevant
is the university's impact on its students' values. But before addressing
this question, some comments about its potential impact are in order. To
begin with, the values that students brought to the university must be
taken into account. Doing so presents difficulties, to be sure, for there is
little direct evidence concerning these values. But, as suggested above,
it is possible to infer certain patterns from what is known about the
students' social, religious, and regional origins.

In addition, the students' career objectives must be considered. Important here are the concepts of occupational socialization and anticipatory socialization. Concerning the former, one of the most important
ways in which educational institutions influence the values of students is
indirect, through their allocation of students into specific occupations.
This is so because occupations, particularly those requiring high levels
of education for entry, tend to have strong and continuing effects on the
norms and behavior of their incumbents.[50] Thus it can be argued that
whatever the direct contributions of the University of Strasbourg to Germanization, to the extent it trained Francophile students for careers offering environments and incentives conducive to Germanization it furthered
its nation-building mission.

As for anticipatory socialization, the very prospect of entering a certain
career—or a certain educational institution or program—can decisively
affect both individuals' values and their susceptibility to socialization
more conventionally defined.[51] The implications for the potential impact
of a school or a university depend largely on the students' social origins.
The children of professionals and others of high status, particularly those
planning to enter their fathers' occupations, can generally find role models
and informed advice about careers at home or among relatives and family
friends. But other students have few exemplars or sources of information
and guidance beyond those available at educational institutions. One implication is that the potential impact of the University of Strasbourg was
greatest with the students who were upwardly mobile. Of course the

results need not have been as intended. For instance, to the extent that the university recruited and prepared potentially Germanophile students of humble origins for careers in which advancement for Alsatians depended on being Francophile it may have defeated its purposes.

As these observations suggest, occupational socialization and anticipatory socialization for adult roles can have a political dimension. Put more abstractly, one's ethnic or national identity can be shaped or, in a sense, selected by one's actual or anticipated social situation. Thus it has been argued that individuals often acquire an array of alternative identities and sets of norms and that their choices among them depend on the specific situation.[52] Seen from this perspective, a university can affect its students' values in two important and distinct ways. It can introduce students to new models of behavior and standards of excellence, thus expanding or transforming their arrays of potential identities. And it can allocate its students among occupational and social positions that will, in turn, shape the choices that individuals make among their potential identities. Thus when evaluating a university's impact on values it is important to consider its impact on social status; how a university affects its students' identities cannot be understood without reference to the students' destinations and to the relationship between their destinations and their origins.

The destinations of the Alsatians enrolling at the University of Strasbourg tended to be precise and rather prosaic. The Alsatian students manifested little interest in learning as an end in itself or in entering careers that might require them to live outside the Reichsland. All that most sought were the training and credentials needed to attain secure and rewarding positions in their homeland. But what were the implications for the university's mission? The best evidence comes from the patterns of enrollment in the individual faculties.

By German standards the faculties least popular with Alsatian students, particularly in the 1870s, were those of philosophy and the sciences (see table 8, appendix B). In part, no doubt, this was due to these faculties' identification with that peculiar German notion, the ideal of learning for its own sake. But the greatest deterrent was their relationship to the job market. Most graduates of these faculties became secondary school teachers or, less commonly, university professors. Thus most entered careers obligating them either to serve the German cause in Alsace-Lorraine or to move to "old Germany." And prior to the 1890s few Alsatians aspired to such careers. As for the exceptions, they generally were of modest or humble origins—two-thirds were sons of schoolteachers, shopkeepers, artisans, peasants, clerks, or blue-collar workers—and had the most limited and practical of motives. The typical Alsatian student took the minimum number of courses required, shunned esoteric fields of study, and exhibited little sympathy for one of the distinguishing features of these faculties, their commitment to research. He saw his education as merely a prerequisite for a teaching position at a local Gymnasium or Realschule.[53]

In the 1890s the relative unpopularity of these two faculties with Alsatian students became less pronounced. Several factors contributed. Most important, probably, was the general change now occurring in the climate of opinion in the Reichsland, for it made potential students more willing to consider working for the German authorities. But the continued expansion of secondary schooling in the region and the government's interest in filling teaching positions with Alsatians provided strong incentives. Another incentive came from the opportunities now opening in the private sector for those with scientific training, particularly for chemists. In addition the worsening of job prospects in some of the free professions and in the more traditional sectors of the economy had an effect. Thus the Faculties of Philosophy and the Sciences doubtless would have attracted fewer Alsatians had there not been a developing surplus of candidates for posts as Lutheran clergymen.[54] Similarly the rapidly growing number of students from villages and small towns can be attributed in part to the chronic difficulties beginning to characterize the rural economy of the Reichsland.[55] In short, enrollment patterns increasingly responded to factors of the sort dominant in other German states and in other parts of Europe: the influence of the university's cultural and political associations was receding relative to that of perceived changes in the labor market, of the abilities and other resources of potential students, and of the status anxieties or mobility strategies of individual families.[56]

As the number of Alsatians enrolled in the Faculties of Philosophy and the Sciences grew, so did the proportions who were Catholic and Jewish and the proportions from Upper Alsace and Lorraine. But in other respects the characteristics of the students changed little. Except for the roughly 20 percent specializing in chemistry—half of them the sons of professionals, industrialists, or rentiers—the distribution according to father's occupation at the end of the century was essentially as it had been in the 1870s and 1880s. And the students' motives tended to remain practical in the extreme. Thus the philosopher Paul Hensel recounted his dismay on inquiring into the objectives of one of the rare Alsatians tempted to pursue a doctorate: the student expected to marry shortly and thought the title "Doctor" would increase the size of his dowry.[57] But if the Alsatian students fell short of the professors' ideal, if they failed to show the desired respect for *Bildung* or *Wissenschaft,* they were not alone. Indeed since the 1870s students of the humanities and sciences throughout Germany, not excluding those pursuing doctorates, had become increasingly careerist in outlook; the "bread-and-butter students" were in the ascendant everywhere.[58] Thus, once again, the differences between German students and Alsatian students were becoming less pronounced.

Of the remaining faculties, the one with enrollment patterns most like those in the Faculties of Philosophy and the Sciences was the Faculty of Law. Here, too, the share of all Alsatian students was low by German standards, particularly in the 1870s and 1880s. In this case a particular deterrent was the character of the students from across the Rhine: like law faculties everywhere in Germany, Strasbourg's attracted those least serious about academic work and most addicted to ritualistic beer-swilling, dueling, ostentatious uniforms, and other customs abhorrent to Alsatians. But more important, again, was the faculty's relationship to the job market. German law faculties, it has been observed, had a function analogous to that of the exclusive public schools of England and the grandes écoles of France: they trained the country's political and bureaucratic elite.[59] But Alsatians could not reasonably expect to enter the governing elite of Germany, and for a long time few aspired to high official positions in the Reichsland. Some studied law, to be sure, but until the 1890s the majority intended to become attorneys or to seek employment with an industrial or commercial firm. Put differently, they planned to enter careers identified locally with the French-speaking bourgeoisie, not with the German authorities.[60]

In the 1890s the pattern changed somewhat. As the number of Alsatians studying law grew, so did the proportion preparing for and later entering bureaucratic positions.[61] It should be noted, however, that almost half the Alsatian law students in this decade came from the French-speaking elite and that many of the rest—many of the sons of Catholic and Jewish shopkeepers, for instance—probably hoped to enter this elite. Thus it is likely that most Alsatians studying law still looked forward to careers in the private sector rather than with the government.

The faculty most popular with Alsatians by German standards, at least until the mid-1890s, was the Faculty of Protestant Theology. One reason is that it was the most Alsatian of the faculties: usually at least a third of the professors were of Alsatian origin, and before 1900 the Alsatian students always outnumbered those from across the Rhine. But also a factor was the faculty's particular constituency, for it was generally sympathetic to German institutions and German culture. The great majority of the students were the sons of pastors, of teachers or other public servants, of artisans, or of peasants, while the French-speaking bourgeoisie was hardly represented. And social origins aside, few would have enrolled in this faculty unless planning to enter the service of a church identified locally with German scholarship and with resistance against the extension of French influences. Typical in this and in other respects was Albert Schweitzer, who with his matriculation in 1893 began two decades of close association with the University of Strasbourg. Like about a third of the Alsatians studying Protestant theology, Schweitzer was the son of a pastor. Like many, he had been raised in a small and predominantly Protestant village. And like most, he arrived in Strasbourg with a high regard for the university and for the scholarly and cultural traditions with which it was identified.[62]

Left to consider are the Faculty of Medicine and the related program in pharmacy. Together these branches of the university usually accounted for about 40 percent of the Alsatian students, an impressive proportion by German standards. Contributing to this popularity was the less onerous military obligation facing medical students.[63] Also contributing was the relatively congenial environment the Faculty of Medicine offered those repelled by things German. Thanks to Roggenbach and Ledderhose this faculty had long had professors who not only were Alsatian and Francophile but actually taught their courses in French. (The last to teach in French retired in 1894.) And most officials and doctors of the municipal hospital, where medical students spent much of their time, were French-speaking Alsatians conscious of their responsibilities as role models and patrons.[64] But, as with the other branches of the university, career considerations dominated. In addition to being prestigious and financially rewarding, the professions of medicine and pharmacy offered relative freedom from state control and access to the region's French-speaking elite. Indeed, for the Alsatian seeking a secure place in this elite, no educational alternative held more promise than the study of medicine or pharmacy.

For these reasons one might assume that the programs in medicine and pharmacy appealed primarily to the sons of the well-to-do and to the few students from the western side of the linguistic frontier. And to an extent they did. Thus two-thirds of the students from French-speaking regions selected one of these programs, and so did almost half the sons of landed proprietors and rentiers and about 70 percent of the sons of doctors and pharmacists. Alternatively, medicine and pharmacy attracted barely a fifth of the students whose fathers were schoolteachers, clerks, peasants, or blue-collar workers. But something of an exception to this pattern was the appeal of these programs to those from the petty bourgeoisie: more than half the Alsatian students whose fathers were shopkeepers and almost 40 percent of those whose fathers were artisans studied medicine or pharmacy, rates much higher than those for their counterparts from "old Germany." The explanation probably lies in the *arrivisme* that tended to characterize these students and their families. Of course a preoccupation with upward mobility, with rising above one's origins and emulating one's betters, hardly distinguished the shopkeepers and artisans of Alsace-Lorraine from those elsewhere. But for Alsatians in the petty bourgeoisie, ascending socially had long been identified with mastering the French language and adopting the associated manners and values.[65] As a result some of the mobility routes popular with their counterparts across the Rhine and in France and with Alsatians of more humble origins—becoming a teacher in a secondary school, for instance, or entering the bureau-cracy—had relatively little appeal. In effect a process of elimination left medicine and pharmacy as the beneficiaries.

The background characteristics and the destinations of the Alsatian stu-dents put limits on the university's potential as an agent of nation building. But they did not condemn the university to impotence. Certainly most professors assumed that the institution would have a Germanizing effect on its students regardless of their origins and aspirations. And there were unsympathetic observers who shared this assumption. Consider, for in-stance, the assessment of the French novelist Maurice Barrès following a visit around the turn of the century: "I went from the cathedral to the university. Its vast buildings worried me as much as or more than the army barracks. German thought never ceases waging war. Could it not ruin what is left of France in our former departments? Are not the pro-fessors capable of shaping the outlooks of those on whom the arrogant army officers have not, I believe, had any effect?"[66]

That the university had the intended impact in individual cases is clear. Thanks typically to the influence of admired professors, some students came to think of themselves as German as well as Alsatian while at the university, or even as German rather than Alsatian. A good example was Georg Wolf, a student of Protestant theology. Invited to speak at a con-vocation in 1893, Wolf used the occasion to praise the university's ac-complishments and potential and to urge his fellow Alsatian students to join him in his commitment to Germany:

> We must have the strength to break with views that have been and will remain dear to our fathers, we must force ourselves to understand that their national ideas can no longer be ours. . . .
> In this contest of cultural influences you, the professors, are called upon more than others to be the real leaders of the educated youth of Alsace-Lorraine. As you introduce us to the intellectual life of the German people, you teach us to admire German scholarship, you fill us with enthusiasm for German art and poetry, you furnish us with the past that we lack. . . . The seed that you sow, if it still often falls on rocky and thorny ground, also finds fertile soil that permits its free growth and promises rich harvests.[67]

But how fertile was the ground? And how rich were the harvests? Lacking better evidence, contemporary observers gave particular attention to the character of student life. They assumed the Alsatian students would be influenced by their peers as well as their professors and by the university's social climate as well as its academic climate. Indeed this assumption helps to explain the continuing efforts to attract large numbers of German students to Strasbourg: the goals included making the atmosphere of the university community as German as possible and making it easier for Alsatians to develop friendships and share experiences with Germans.[68] By the same token, observers assumed that the extracurricular affiliations and activities of the Alsatian students reflected their political and cultural values and the ways, if any, in which the university shaped these values.

Judged by this gauge, the university's impact in its first quarter century was unimpressive. The Alsatian students fulfilled all their academic responsibilities—indeed their diligence impressed the professors—but their social contacts with students from across the Rhine were negligible. As a German who attended the university in the 1880s put it, "The Alsatians remained sulking in the corner."[69]

For many, this alone indicated that the university's contribution to Germanization was either insignificant or negative. But the situation was more complicated than they assumed. To begin with, there was the matter of the relationship between the university's Alsatian students and other Alsatians. Those expecting to remain in the Reichsland after leaving the university had reason to be concerned about how participation in the student life of the Germans would affect how they were labeled by fellow Alsatians and, perhaps, their career and marital prospects. A German later observed, referring to the 1880s, that "Alsatian students who openly identified themselves with German traditions did not have an easy time of it."[70]

It is also necessary to consider the character of German student life. On balance Alsatians' opinions about German student customs were more negative than their opinions about Germany generally. Like many across the Rhine and abroad, Alsatians tended to assume that the dueling fraternities—notably the Corps, the Burschenschaften, and the Landmannschaften—represented the mainstream of student life. And in their opinion these fraternities embodied in exaggerated form the worst features of the stereotypical upper-class Prussian: his caste consciousness, his militarism, his tastelessness and excesses in matters of dress, food, and drink.[71] The prevalence of such attitudes meant that joining a dueling fraternity was not an easy step for an Alsatian student even if Germanophile. Some did join, but the number was small: impressionistic evidence suggests that before 1900 no more than 10 or 15 percent of the university's Alsatian students ever belonged to dueling fraternities. The peak probably came in the early 1880s, when some Alsatians took the lead in establishing two dueling fraternities and others joined Corps and Burschenschaften founded earlier by Germans. From this time on the proportion seems to have declined more or less steadily, so that by the end of the century the membership of all dueling fraternities, including those founded by Alsatians, was overwhelmingly German. This change in composition brought a change in the outlook of the Alsatians who joined. In the 1880s many of the Alsatians in dueling fraternities had thought in terms of blending

German student traditions with local ones. But in later years there was none of this. The few Alsatians now joining Corps or Burschenschaften—most of them the sons of bureaucrats—did so with the zeal of converts. They tried to be more German than the Germans, as if to flaunt their desire to break all ties to Alsatian society and Alsatian traditions.[72]

Alsatians were not the only ones repelled by the dueling fraternities and what they represented. So were many Germans, including many professors and students. In the last three decades of the century there were increasingly frequent complaints within the German universities that the fraternities had outlived their usefulness, that the humanistic and national idealism identified with at least some of them earlier in the century had given way to degenerate behavior and reactionary attitudes.[73] Such opinions were particularly prevalent among the Germans at the University of Strasbourg, as might be expected given the faculty's progressive outlook and the institution's reputation as an *Arbeitsuniversität*. There were several Corps and Burschenschaften, to be sure, but they never had many members by German standards and, despite their determined efforts, never set the tone, even among the German students. If any groups represented the mainstream of German student life in Strasbourg, they were the various formal and informal organizations that had academic overtones, among them the Sozialwissenschaftliche Verein, the numerous *Seminarkneipe,* and the *Strassburger Kreis*. These appealed to students who were idealistic about scholarship and who tended, accordingly, to look down both on the *Waffenstudenten* (members of dueling fraternities) and the *Brotstudenten* (career-oriented students). But such groups held little attraction for Alsatian students, the majority of whom were, from the German standpoint, *Brotstudenten*. How many Alsatians participated cannot be determined, but the number doubtless was small. To give but one example, the *Strassburger Kreis,* which enlisted dozens of Germans in the decade or so of its existence, never had an Alsatian member.[74]

For some observers, the only assimilated Alsatian students were the few who joined organizations dominated by Germans. But others used a less tough and less unrealistic standard. In their opinion one should also count those affiliated with certain clubs or groups that were predominantly or exclusively Alsatian in membership. Although these students had few social contacts with Germans, their cultural affinities and organizational models were essentially German, and the net effect of their experience at the university was the desired one. Germanization, according to this view, did not mean that Alsatian students had to be indistinguishable from German students; it was also consistent with attitudes and behavior that were particularistic.[75]

The best examples of organizations that were predominantly Alsatian in membership but Germanophile in orientation were two confessional fraternities, Argentina and Wilhelmitana. Both dated from the 1850s, when they had been founded by students in the Protestant theological faculty. The differences between them were largely theological: Argentina attracted pietistic students while Wilhelmitana harbored theological liberals. But Argentina was more openly and self-consciously Germanophile, essentially because the pietists were the most Germanophile of Alsatian Protestants. Thus, while Wilhelmitana remained on the sidelines at the ceremonies opening the German university, members of Argentina marched at the head of all processions and in other ways demonstrated their support for the new regime. Henceforth there was no reason to question the loyalties of Argentina's members, even though they had few contacts with Germans. But for Wilhelmitana, reconciliation came more slowly. In the early years of German rule some members were basically Francophile, and the membership remained exclusively Alsatian for almost two decades. But the trend was clear. With time the club became more like the nondueling Protestant fraternities at universities across the Rhine. The reconciliation could be considered complete when, after the turn of the century, Wilhelmitana began recruiting German members, adopted colors (Argentina had been "color-bearing" all along), and joined a national association of Protestant fraternities. Symptomatic was the declaration of a former member at the ceremonies in 1905 marking the club's fiftieth anniversary: "Truthfulness forces us to say that with all our hearts we have thrown in our lots with the German fatherland."[76]

Before 1900 roughly 80 percent of Wilhelmitana's members came from the Protestant theological faculty, and the proportion was probably higher in Argentina. Of those joining Wilhelmitana about one-quarter were sons of pastors, another quarter were sons of teachers, and one in every nine or ten came from a peasant family. The social origins of Argentina's members are unknown, but given the club's orientation and the religious sociology of the Reichsland it is likely that there were proportionately more sons of peasants and village pastors than in Wilhelmitana. Together the two clubs appear to have averaged between twenty and thirty active Alsatian members during the university's first quarter century. In the 1870s one of every four or five Alsatian students probably belonged to one or the other, but in the late 1890s—when the total enrollment of Alsatians was much higher but the number studying Protestant theology was not— the rate seems to have been about one of every twenty.[77]

Argentina and Wilhelmitana were not the only confessional fraternities at the university. Two Catholic fraternities opened in 1875 and 1882, respectively, and a third appeared in 1898. But unlike their Protestant counterparts these fraternities were founded by and for German students, and their contributions to the university's mission before the turn of the century appear to have been negligible. Although the number of Alsatians who joined is unknown, it is unlikely that it exceeded a half dozen or so at any time before the late 1890s.[78]

The first organization of Catholic students that was essentially Alsatian in character and membership appeared in 1895. The initiative came from the clergy, specifically from some priests in Strasbourg who were, compared with most Alsatian priests, relatively Germanophile. Their objective was a club that would help both to immunize Catholic students to the dangerous ideas associated with the university (also a goal of the Catholic fraternities) and to groom a Catholic intelligentsia for the Reichsland. Now that the number of Alsatian Catholics at the university was growing rapidly—not least because many priests no longer advocated a boycott—there seemed a need for an organization that would channel these students' development in desirable directions. The result was a club known initially as the Cercle Ozanam, the name being that of a Catholic social reformer active in France in the 1830s and 1840s.[79]

The Cercle Ozanam can best be characterized as particularistic with bicultural overtones. Its members usually spoke French or the local dialect among themselves, and they shared a desire to preserve the French cultural heritage of the Reichsland. But their opinions about Germany and its culture were not entirely negative. Indeed a few members were of German origin, and the club's biweekly meetings occasionally featured speeches on such themes as the works of Sudermann and Hauptmann. As with most student organizations the number of Alsatian members is unknown, but it probably averaged about fifteen or twenty—about 10 percent of the Alsatian Catholics then attending the university. Most who can be identified studied medicine and came from villages or small towns in Lower Alsace, and several, bearing out the founders' desire to groom a Catholic intelligentsia, went on to distinguished careers in the arts, scholarship, journalism, or politics. But the life of the club was short. By 1902 it was no longer large enough to justify staging its annual ball, and a year or two later it disappeared for lack of members. The club was a victim, it seems, of the polarization evident among the Alsatian Catholics at the university after the turn of the century: it was insufficiently Germanophile for some and not Francophile enough for others.[80]

The Alsatian students considered thus far—those affiliated with the Corps or the Burschenschaften, with the Protestant or Catholic fraternities, or with the Cercle Ozanam—were basically either Germanophile or particularistic in outlook. But there were also students who were self-consciously Francophile and revanchist. According to some observers, in fact, these students were in the majority throughout the university's history; such was the opinion both of German chauvinists with inflexible ideas about what constituted loyalty and of French revanchists anxious to believe that most Alsatians agreed with them.[81] But were they correct? The answer is by no means obvious, for most students kept their national allegiances, such as they were, to themselves. What can be said is that student organizations that were clearly Francophile never came close to enlisting a majority of the Alsatian students. Although they attracted considerable attention both across the Rhine and in France—more than the other student organizations—this was because of their visibility and what they represented, not because of their size.

The first student club that was thoroughly Francophile appeared even before the university opened. Known as Alsatia, its mission was to provide a refuge for Francophile students choosing to remain in Strasbourg and to defend their customs and honor against the challenges expected from German students and fraternities. One of the club's first specific projects was a counterdemonstration complete with tricolors at the ceremonies inaugurating the university. At the time Alsatia had about forty members, many no doubt students in the Ecole libre de médecine rather than the university.[82] Beyond this little is known about the club, although the very absence of information suggests that it disappeared shortly after the university opened. One possibility is that many members and potential members decided in the autumn of 1872, when the Ecole libre de médecine closed, to move to France; dozens of Alsatian students emigrated in 1872, and they were the ones most likely to have supported Alsatia.[83]

Through the rest of the 1870s there were no student clubs in Strasbourg that were openly Francophile. But the hiatus ended in 1880 with the appearance of the Sundgovia, founded by law students from Upper Alsace. In the following year another group of students, mostly from Lower Alsace, organized a club known as the Erwinia (after Erwin von Steinbach, the fourteenth-century craftsman who designed the facade of the Strasbourg cathedral). Since their goals were similar and their memberships small, the two clubs soon merged. The result was known officially as the Sundgovia-Erwinia but commonly termed the Sundgovia. Of the various organizations of Francophile students founded before the turn of the century, this was easily the largest and the most important.[84]

The official goal of the club, set forth in the first article of its statutes, was the "promotion of good fellowship among students from Alsace-Lorraine."[85] But the real objective was to mobilize native students of revanchist sentiment. Although the statutes, which had to be filed with university officials, were in German, the only language used within the Sundgovia was French. Most meetings featured a speech on some subject followed by discussion, but the club also organized songfests, theatrical revues, and excursions into the Vosges. In addition it maintained a library, produced a journal in manuscript form, and staged an annual banquet, the so-called *Wurschtbankett,* to which all former members as well as the actives were invited. None of these activities was publicized outside the club, largely out of concern over how the authorities might react. But after the club's first few years the members grew more daring. The turning point came early in 1885, when they staged a procession of the sort known as a *monôme:* following the annual banquet members marched silently and in single file to the city's central square, there to pay their respects to the statue of Jean-Baptiste Kléber, a Strasbourg native who had been one of Napoleon's greatest generals. This *monôme,* a participant observed in the club's journal, was "the first sign of life that the students from Alsace-Lorraine have given since the annexation." The lessons, he added, were obvious:

> This first demonstration, Gentlemen, has been crowned by such success that it is to be desired that it not remain isolated, and that henceforth we assert ourselves energetically at every opportunity. Up to now abstention was the most dignified way in which we could have behaved. But today, now that we are numerous and now that, thanks to the *monôme,* the ties of close solidarity that unite us all have been made evident, today, Gentlemen, it is a patriotic duty for us to take the place in our homeland that is ours by right.[86]

It was advice the club attempted to follow.

The number of active members in the Sundgovia averaged about twenty-five. This made it the largest of the university's student organizations, the German fraternities included, but it accounted for only about one in every seven or eight Alsatian students. As for the members' origins and career plans, they differed, predictably, from those of most Alsatian students. Information concerning a sample of thirty-six members indicates that Catholic students were overrepresented in the club (36.1 percent as opposed to 23.6 percent of Alsatian students generally), and so were the sons of professionals and entrepreneurs (45.7 percent compared with 32.5 percent of all Alsatian students, and 40 percent compared with 17.1 percent if the sons of pastors are excluded). Alternatively the sons of landowners, peasants, and those in the working class were poorly represented (2.9 percent compared with 17.6 percent of all Alsatian students). Club members were much more likely than Alsatian students generally to be studying medicine or pharmacy (63.9 percent as opposed to 33.1 percent), about as likely to be studying law (19.4 percent compared with 18.6 percent), and less likely to be in the Faculties of Philosophy (8.3 percent compared with 13.6 percent), the Sciences (8.3 percent compared with 11.4 percent), or Protestant Theology (none compared with 23.3 percent). These differences reflect at least roughly the differential distribution of Francophile and revanchist sentiment among the university's Alsatian students.[87]

University and government officials left the Sundgovia alone during the Manteuffel era and the first period of Hohenlohe's tenure as Statthalter. But the elections of 1887 brought an end to toleration. Early in April the acting secretary of state, Maximilian von Puttkamer, complained about the club to the university's acting curator, Richter.[88] He also instructed the police to conduct an investigation. The police reported first, and with all the incriminating evidence that was needed: late in April Puttkamer ordered the club closed.[89]

The dissolution of the Sundgovia deprived the university's Francophile students of their only club, and the repressive climate that marked the next decade or so made it unrealistic to consider organizing a successor. But the Francophile students still made their presence and sentiments known. Indeed between 1887 and the end of the century these students were more conspicuous and assertive than when the Sundgovia was active, and more embarrassing to the university's defenders.

The reasons were largely demographic. As noted earlier, the number of Alsatians at the university began to grow rapidly in the early 1880s, and the trend continued to the end of the decade and beyond. At the same time the proportion of Alsatian students from entrepreneurial or professional families grew, and so did the proportion from west of the linguistic frontier. These trends suggest that the number who were basically Francophile when they entered the university increased even more rapidly than the overall number.

But other developments also contributed to the growing visibility and assertiveness of the Francophile students. Among them were the changes occurring in the political and cultural atmosphere of the Reichsland generally. The elections of 1890 and 1893 reflected the new climate. In 1887 the fifteen Alsatian delegates sent to the Reichstag had all been "protesters," but in 1890 only ten "protesters" were elected and in 1893, eight. The Social Democrats—in their own way influential agents of Germanization—won one seat in 1890 and two in 1893, while the remaining seats, four and five, respectively, went to men who generally supported German policies in the Reichsland.[90] These political trends and the social and cultural changes they mirrored deeply disturbed many Alsatian students. Coming from or aspiring to that segment of the Alsatian middle class that was French in language and cultural identity, they recognized that its size and influence were now in decline.[91] Thus they had an added incentive to articulate and to defend the spirit of the "protesters" and the French traditions of their homeland. Fearing that time might be against them, they attempted to establish at the university, founded as a bastion of German learning, their own bastion of French culture.

Despite the repressive climate after 1887 there were ways in which these students could manifest their sentiments without fear of reprisal. They could, for instance, remain aloof from the German students. After 1887 the gap between the university's Francophile students and those from east of the Rhine was as pronounced as before, and it was more obvious since more were involved. The Francophile students tended to emulate the bohemian life-style associated with the Parisian Latin Quarter, wore French clothes, had their hair and beards cut in French styles, spent much of their time at cafés and with girl friends, and in general did their best to violate the traditions of German student life. Like many Alsatian students who were basically particularistic, they frequented wine cellars and taverns considered off limits by the immigrants and during lectures sat in compact groups apart from the Germans. And if an opportunity arose to manifest their sentiments in more striking fashion, they were quick to seize it. Perhaps the best example dates from the spring of 1888. When a student assembly was convened to consider whether to send a delegation to the funeral of Wilhelm I, the university's namesake, Francophile students appeared en masse and, profiting from the low attendance of German students, voted down the proposal. Incensed German students immediately called a second meeting and reversed this decision. But the outcome aside, the incident represented a significant symbolic victory for the Francophile students, and one gained without the authorities taking reprisals.[92]

Although most activities of the Francophile students after 1887 were more or less spontaneous, there were two groups that provided some direction and coordination. One consisted of Alsatian students of pharmacy. In 1893 several of these students and some recent graduates established the Association des pharmaciens d'Alsace et de Lorraine. Technically it was not a student club and accordingly it was immune to the university's regulations, but students dominated the organization. Together with local artists—the ties between the university's Francophile students and Strasbourg's small colony of artists were close—these students produced a periodical known as $H_2S$, a suggestive title which became the popular name for the club as well. They also provided the initiative for many of the gatherings and protests of Alsatian students that occurred in the mid- and late 1890s.[93]

The second group consisted of the former members, the *anciens* or "Old Boys," of the Sundgovia. In this regard some additional comments concerning the Sundgovia are in order. In its short history this club had developed into what has been termed, in one taxonomy of student movements, a traditional socializing organization: one of its objectives was to prepare its members for status positions in the existing social order by inculcating traditional values. As with other student organizations of this sort—the German Corps, for instance—this mission meant that former members were active and influential in the club, both in supervising its affairs and "as living role images, exhibiting to the student the position to which he aspires and the behavior that goes with that position."[94] The involvement of the *anciens* in the club brought students into contact with the Francophile elite of Strasbourg and the Reichsland generally, with all that this implied in terms of career and marital opportunities. It also meant that the *anciens* remained in close contact with each other after leaving the university. By the time the Sundgovia was suppressed, the *anciens* constituted a network of young professionals that reached into all corners of the Reichsland, providing support and coordination for the campaign against Germanization.[95]

The dissolution of the Sundgovia and the fear that a successor would meet a similar fate changed the situation, but only slightly. The *anciens* simply adopted less formal and hence less vulnerable means of maintaining contact with one another and with students. One of them was the banquet of the *anciens*. Instituted in the fall of 1888, these banquets were held annually until World War I. Officially they were for all former students of Alsatian origin, but the ambience and activities of these banquets were decidedly revanchist—for instance, each banquet concluded with a *monôme* to the statue of Kléber—and only those in sympathy attended. But for sympathizers it was an occasion not to be missed. Particularly for former students living outside Strasbourg it provided an opportunity to reminisce, to establish contact with more recent graduates, and to receive assurances that their cause was not in vain. In short, the banquets helped to broaden and to strengthen the network of Francophile professionals that had its core among the *anciens* of the Sundgovia.[96]

Another institution that kept alive the traditions of Sundgovia was the Taverne alsacienne, a brasserie known throughout the period of German rule as a mecca for revanchist Alsatians. After 1887 the *anciens* of the Sundgovia residing in Strasbourg used the Taverne as their unofficial club-house. And so did Francophile students, not least because they associated the place with the legendary Sundgovia. Students and *anciens* met regularly at the Taverne to discuss the club's traditions, to sing its songs, and to plan for the future. The environment was different than that provided by the club and the activities less varied, but the results, in terms of establishing contacts and acquiring values and a sense of mission, were essentially the same.[97]

Both the *anciens* and the members of H₂S contributed to a significant strengthening in the 1890s of the group identification and solidarity of the Francophile students. Their central objective was to reduce the vulnerability of the Alsatian students to Germanization, and at least until the turn of the century they appeared to be succeeding. The best indication was the tense character of day-to-day life at the university. Fights and other confrontations between Alsatian and German students were now common, as were classroom disruptions by Alsatians indignant at comments made by their professors.[98] With the growth in their number, cohesiveness, and self-confidence, the Francophile students became more willing to protest against real or imagined slights. The culmination came late in 1896, when an incident led to the most serious crisis in the university's relations with the government and the German press since 1887.

The affair originated with an altercation involving two students in Rudolf Fittig's introductory chemistry course. Disruptions of this course were common occurrences. Because of its relevance for students of medicine and pharmacy, there were large enrollments of Germans and Alsatians, and the two groups took advantage of Fittig's inability to maintain control. Thus both Germanophile and Francophile students regularly responded with cheers or hisses to the nationality of the chemists mentioned and to the colors of the solutions mixed in Fittig's test tubes: combinations of red, white, and black won the acclaim of the Germans, while Alsatians reacted with foot stamping and applause to red, white, and blue. The particular incident in question was no more serious than many others. Provoked by a comment by Fittig, a medical student from Lorraine, Charles François, pounded and shook his desk. A German student named Martin demanded that François keep quiet. François responded by challenging Martin to meet him after the lecture, implicitly to fight. But Martin, on the advice of friends, ignored the invitation and instead took the step that permitted this squabble to become a cause célèbre: he reported the incident to the faculty's committee on student discipline.[99]

With Fittig's encouragement the faculty committee resolved to make an object lesson of the case, and the academic senate and the rector concurred. In mid-December the rector announced that François was to be suspended for an indefinite period and warned that the same fate awaited any other student convicted of disrupting lectures or other official university activities.[100] This pronouncement, far from restoring order, provoked a campaign of protest among the Alsatian students. The campaign was motivated in part by indignation over the sentence given François and in part, it seems, by a desire to exploit this opportunity to promote the solidarity of the native students and to widen the gap between them and the German students. After several evening meetings in cafés the leaders produced a petition criticizing the penalty given François and noting that in two recent cases Germans accused of similar offenses had received probationary sentences. The implication was that the faculty discriminated against Alsatians. Within a few days 144 Alsatian students, about half of those currently enrolled, signed the document. These signatures suggest the strength and distribution of anti-German sentiment among the Alsatian students. More than two-thirds of the natives studying medicine and pharmacy signed and about three-fifths of those studying law, but only one-fifth of the students in the Faculties of Philosophy and the Sciences and none of those studying Protestant theology.[101]

The faculty's reaction was quick and decisive. The rector referred the two who delivered the petition to the committee on student discipline, which immediately suspended them from the university.[102] But, again, the faculty's firmness only worsened the situation. The protesters had already decided to organize a boycott of classes if those delivering the petition were punished. This they now did, with the boycott beginning when the university reopened after the Christmas vacation. By this time the Cercle Ozanam was supporting the protest movement, which helps to explain why participation was greater than the support for the earlier petition; about 200 took part, roughly two-thirds of the university's Alsatian students.[103]

The organizers intended to continue the boycott until the faculty lifted its suspension of the students who had delivered the petition, but they soon realized that the faculty would stand firm unless the Alsatian students took the initiative. Accordingly they prepared another petition stressing "that it was far from their intention to accuse the academic authorities of partiality, and that they [were] sorry if the first petition . . . left room for this interpretation."[104] This document gave the professors an opportunity to reduce the tensions, and they exploited it: the academic senate ended the suspensions of the students who had delivered the first petition and fixed François's at one semester. The protesting students, having gained all they could reasonably expect, now ended their boycott.[105]

But the affair had not ended. The faculty may have appeased the Alsatian students, but it had not satisfied many of the outsiders now following the dispute. These critics fell into two distinct groups. The first included those covering the affair in the French press and in many Alsatian newspapers as well as the Alsatians who commented in the regional council of Lower Alsace and in the Landesausschuss. These observers questioned the Strasbourg faculty's impartiality. The *Express* of Mulhouse, for instance, asked whether the professors had behaved in a manner consistent with their supposed commitment to academic freedom. And *Der Elsässer,* the Reichsland's leading Catholic newspaper, accused the faculty of using disciplinary procedures one expected to find only in Prussian military barracks.[106] But many of these critics were not at all sorry the professors had left themselves open to these charges. Like the ringleaders of the student protest, they saw in the affair a means of rallying opposition to Germanization. Thus *Die Heimat,* a Protestant periodical, argued that the students' protest would encourage all Alsatians to be more assertive in resisting the German presence in their homeland.[107] The Strasbourg correspondent of a Parisian newspaper made a similar claim:

> Created twenty-five years ago with the openly acknowledged purpose of being a source of Germanization, the University of Strasbourg seems destined, on the contrary, to be for Alsace-Lorraine the school of our political emancipation. . . .
> . . . Without being a prophet one can foresee that the University of Strasbourg, while remaining a great center of German learning, will not in the slightest live up to its political purpose; on the contrary everything seems to indicate that the government will later have reg-

istered here one of the most complete defeats that Germanization will have experienced.[108]

This assessment would not have surprised the Germans who constituted the university's second group of critics. They had also concluded that the institution was doing more to retard than to advance Germanization. Representative was an article in Heidelberg's *Deutsche Zeitung,* a moderately conservative newspaper: "What can be learned from this whole affair? Simply that the founding of Strasbourg's Kaiser Wilhelm University in 1872 was a great blunder. One could not even have imagined that the majority of the natives studying in Strasbourg would seclude themselves from the old Germans as completely as in fact is unfortunately the case."[109] Another attack came in the Reichstag from Ernst Lieber, the leader of the Center party. Lieber demanded that the Strasbourg faculty make sure henceforth that it gave Alsatian students no incentives to organize protests or, more important perhaps, no pretexts for claiming to have triumphed over the German authorities. And he concluded with a warning reminiscent of one made implicitly by Bismarck a decade before: unless the university did more to advance Germany's interests, it would be impossible to justify its annual subsidy from the imperial government.[110]

These criticisms and threats did not go unanswered. The François-Martin affair, unlike the crisis of 1887, led to numerous statements of support for the university from newspapers, politicians, and government officials. Their basic theme was that the institution's critics had greatly exaggerated the significance of the recent confrontation. Thus in replying to Lieber's speech in the Reichstag a spokesman for the Alsatian ministry insisted that the François-Martin affair differed little from the disputes that occur on occasion at all universities.[111] The university's curator made a similar observation in the Landesausschuss: "Small political, confessional, and regional conflicts are to be found among students everywhere. . . . By adapting and exaggerating the difficulties that have appeared here in accord with political views . . . one gives greater significance to the doings of the students than is proper."[112]

But it did not suffice, the university's defenders believed, to note that the dispute's significance had been exaggerated. Ill-advised as they may have been, some Germans had concluded that the university was doing more harm than good, and these charges should not go unanswered. True, it was not the first time Germans had criticized the university to the point of suggesting that its establishment had been a mistake. Long before 1897 some had argued that assimilation would have advanced more rapidly without the university, that Alsatian students would gain greater respect for Germany if forced to cross the Rhine to receive a higher education. But prior to the François-Martin affair such observations had been made infrequently and, with few exceptions, privately. Even during the crisis of 1887 no German had claimed publicly that the university's establishment had been a mistake. It was in the winter of 1896–97 that this idea was first discussed widely in public—and first subjected to public criticism.[113]

Those defending the university employed two basic arguments. The first concerned the contention that Germanization would proceed more rapidly if Alsatians had to go to "old Germany" for a higher education. By 1897 evidence existed suggesting that the contention was unsound. There were about 150 Alsatians at other German universities, three or four times as many as a decade before.[114] But it would be wrong to assume that studying across the Rhine made them more sympathetic to Germany. This was a point made by Berlin's *National-Zeitung,* by Munich's *Allgemeine Zeitung,* and by Ernst Lieber in a second Reichstag speech. Lieber's comments are particularly noteworthy. Citing a report received on a recent trip to Strasbourg, he argued that the Alsatians who studied at "old German" universities tended to become more rather than less anti-German as a result. Far from constituting a corps of Germanophile professionals in the Reichsland, they returned strengthened in their conviction that Alsatians were second-class citizens and that the German way of life was not for them. Indeed Alsatians who had returned from other German universities had provided leadership and encouragement for the anti-German activities of students going no farther than Strasbourg.[115] Implicitly, whatever the faults of the Reichsland's university—and Lieber believed there were serious ones—it was not an obstacle to Germanization.

The second response to the critics was a modification of an argument used a quarter of a century before to justify establishing the institution: the university was an effective instrument of Germanization even though years might pass before its success became evident. Thus the *Münchener Neueste Nachrichten,* southern Germany's leading liberal newspaper, argued that "among the means contributing quietly and peacefully to the spiritual reunion of Alsace-Lorraine with its old estranged fatherland, the university obviously stands first."[116] An article by Gustav Schmoller in Munich's *Allgemeine Zeitung* predicted that the eventual assimilation of the Reichsland would be due in large part to the university, and called for continued support and patience: "He who plants vines should not expect to pick grapes in the following year; he who plants spiritual forces must be aware that generations will pass before they ripen."[117] And a front page article in Berlin's *National-Zeitung* argued that the university, whatever its impact on its Alsatian students, had had a healthy influence on how Alsatians in general regarded Germany and its culture. At the time of the annexation Alsatians had assumed that in the intellectual sphere Germany stood behind France, "so that culturally they were moving, so to speak, from the horse to the donkey." To correct this misperception it had been necessary to establish a well-endowed university. And in this aspect of its mission the institution had succeeded admirably: "The very magnificence of [its] buildings demonstrates even to the uneducated that a distinguished power reigns here. As for the richness of the collections and instruments and the erudition and skills of the professors, their impact on the broad sectors of the public . . . provides an invaluable counterweight to the logic of hatred and contempt into which the anger of the defeated so readily evolves."[118]

Such praise and optimism helped to offset the damage to the professors' morale caused by their university's critics. So did the lavish ceremonies in April and May 1897 marking the university's twenty-fifth anniversary. The professors now received messages of congratulation and support from, among others, the emperor, the chancellor (Hohenlohe, the former Statthalter), and the Prussian minister of culture.[119] And they heard numerous heartening speeches, notably one in which Hohenlohe's cousin and successor as Statthalter, Prince Hermann zu Hohenlohe-Langenburg, observed that "the university is exerting a beneficial influence on the populace" and promised that he would "strive to the best of my ability to look after the needs and the well-being of the university."[120] Absent from the speeches and messages was any mention of the François-Martin affair or any indication that there was dissatisfaction with the university in high places. The faculty's spokesman, the philosopher Wilhelm Windelband, responded in kind. He did comment briefly on how "all too frequently . . . we are endowed with an impossible mission so that it can be pointed out with regret that we are not reaching our objective."[121] But he indicated that he was not thinking of the government when he made these remarks. On the contrary, he had nothing but praise for how the university had been treated by the imperial and Alsatian governments, and he had plenty of that. It was as if he hoped through flattery to convince the authorities that the university was basically sound and on the right course.[122]

But if this was his intention, Windelband failed. In retrospect his speech and the ceremonies of 1897 can be seen as among the last serious attempts to recapture the enthusiasm and optimism that had marked the university's early years. The professors already sensed that the university's best years were in the past and that the future, notwithstanding their public optimism, would be difficult.[123] And their concern was justified. A new and, for the professors, much less pleasant period in the university's history was about to begin.

# 5

# The Government Intervenes

In the 1890s a striking change occurred in the political culture of Alsace-Lorraine. Developments both within the Reichsland and in France fostered a rapid decline in revanchist sentiment and in the nostalgia and wishful thinking that fueled it. By the turn of the century the region's political life was no longer dominated by irreconcilable "protesters," as in the 1870s and 1880s. Instead most political leaders and spokesmen favored a particularistic solution to the Alsatian question. They sought no more, they insisted, than local self-government within Germany; they would be content once Alsace-Lorraine became an autonomous state on a par with Baden, Bavaria, and the empire's other constituent states.[1]

Full autonomy was more than the German authorities were prepared to grant, but the decline of revanchism did cause them to govern in a more conciliatory manner. Beginning in the late 1890s they made a series of concessions long sought by Alsatians and took other steps to reinforce particularistic sentiment. This trend became especially pronounced after the appointment in 1901 of Ernst Matthias von Köller as secretary of state for Alsace-Lorraine. Given a free hand by Hohenlohe-Langenburg (who reputedly cared about little except hunting), Köller assured the Landes-ausschuss on taking office that he intended "to rule with the majority, even if it is clerical."[2] And he did. Throughout the so-called Köller era, which lasted until 1908, conciliating the Landesausschuss remained one of the ministry's highest priorities.

The implications for the university were far-reaching. As long as the "protesters" had dominated local politics the German authorities had treated the university generously; except during Richter's brief tenure as acting curator they had respected its autonomy and sought to preserve its high stature. But in the late 1890s they decided that the university should be made more compatible with Alsatian particularism. The problem, as they saw it, was that the institution was considered an alien imposition not only by Francophile Alsatians, as was to be expected, but also by many Alsatians who were potentially Germanophile. And since the faculty evidently would not make the necessary adjustments, the only solution was government intervention. The result was a series of challenges to the university's autonomy and to the character the institution had acquired in its formative years.

The professors resisted. They naturally regarded any challenge to their autonomy as unjustified, regardless of the objectives. They also opposed the specific changes the government promoted. Many wanted no changes at all. For them, the structure and character that the university had acquired in the 1870s were still those best suited to the institution's responsibilities. Others agreed that changes were needed, but not those favored by the government. Whether their desire for reform was sincere or whether they merely hoped to neutralize the government's efforts is unclear. But whatever their motives, they were as determined as those committed to the status quo to resist outside intervention.

The struggle proved one-sided. Determined as they were, the faculty could not prevent the government from doing as it wished. In the first few years of the new century the government succeeded in transforming the university. And it did so in ways that undermined the professors' self-confidence and commitment to their special mission. Whether the changes would have the desired impact on the institution's influence in the Reichsland would require time to assess. But the effect on the morale of the professors and on their pride in the university was evident from the start: judged by these criteria, the university's golden age was over.

· 1 ·

By the late 1890s concerned Germans agreed that as an instrument of nation building the University of Strasbourg had fallen short of expectations. They also tended to agree on the major reason. It was not the university or its professors that were primarily at fault, but the expectations themselves. Simply put, too much had been expected too soon. Inaccurate opinions about the situation in Alsace-Lorraine and unjustified assumptions about a university's capabilities had fostered unrealistic expectations.

But for some observers the unfounded expectations were not entirely to blame. Especially in government circles the university's relative ineffectiveness was believed to have resulted in part from its particular character; the initial claims may have been unrealistic, but a different institution would have accomplished more. Of special concern was the university's well-founded reputation as a bastion of anti-Catholicism. "What has been practiced at the University of Strasbourg:" Friedrich Althoff observed in 1897 to an Alsatian priest, "that is the *Kulturkampf.* . . . It is political shortsightedness without equal, and it is a crying shame, how Catholics are treated at the University of Strasbourg."[3] Althoff might have added that it was political shortsightedness which he would no longer tolerate, for he was about to take corrective action.

The project to which Althoff attached the highest priority was one proposed by Bismarck but vetoed by the bishop of Strasbourg back in

1871: adding a Catholic theological faculty to the university. Actually since the end of the *Kulturkampf* several officials had considered reviving this project. In the early 1880s Manteuffel had discussed the possibility with his advisors, in 1888 Hohenlohe had mentioned it to officials in Berlin, and in 1894 the German government had even submitted a formal proposal to the Vatican. Nothing had come of their initiatives, essentially because the Reichsland's Catholic clergy opposed the project altogether and the Vatican would only consider it if the local bishop could appoint all the faculty's professors. But these setbacks did not deter Althoff. Early in 1898 he recommended that the government launch a new effort. Hohenlohe, now the chancellor, concurred.[4]

Officials favored the project for two reasons. First, they hoped to end the university's reputation as a stronghold of anti-Catholicism. The addition of a Catholic theological faculty would have symbolic value; it would make the university less alien to Alsatian Catholics and allay the widespread belief that German culture and Catholicism were incompatible. Second, and at least as important, they wanted to promote the Germanization of the Reichsland's Catholic clergy. Since the annexation the Catholic clergy had been at the forefront of efforts to resist assimilation, and their influence, particularly in rural areas, had been considerable. But precisely because their authority was so great, it was desirable to turn it to Germany's advantage. Althoff and others were convinced that if only the priests were Germanophile they would prove to be valuable allies in the campaign to assimilate the Reichsland, and they assumed that a Catholic theological faculty would produce more Germanophile priests than did the seminaries in Strasbourg and Metz. At least in this case they had confidence in the university's potential.[5]

But clearly any attempt to establish such a faculty would meet stout resistance from the Reichsland's Catholic clergymen, politicians, and journalists. It is true that these individuals were no longer as united over the university as they had been in the 1870s and 1880s. A sharp division now existed between those wanting to transform it—to penetrate it and Catholicize it—and those favoring a boycott. The former group, which included several priests and journalists in Strasbourg and a few professors at the local seminary, called for the appointment of Catholic professors to the university's secular faculties, encouraged Catholic youths to attend the institution, and helped to found organizations like the Cercle Ozanam. It could be assumed that these relatively Germanophile Catholics would welcome the establishment of a Catholic theological faculty.[6]

But this group, although growing in size and assertiveness, still had less influence than the more Francophile Catholics who would have nothing to do with the university. When the latter attacked the university, they hoped not to transform it but rather to discredit it and to deter Catholic youths from attending. They feared that even if the institution became more attractive to Catholics, its net impact would be both Germanizing and secularizing; the university would always be a dangerous place for Francophile Catholics. And the consequences would be particularly unfortunate if there were a Catholic theological faculty. The result, one priest complained upon learning of the government's plans, would be that "we will soon have a young clergy both German and liberal. Alsace will be invaded by Protestantism."[7]

Aware of the prevalence of such opinions, Althoff decided to bypass the Alsatian clergy and, as in 1894, to appeal directly to the Vatican. To conduct the projected negotiations he commissioned the man who had presented the government's last proposal to the Vatican, Baron Georg von Hertling.[8] It was a good choice. A professor of philosophy at the University of Munich as well as a leader of the Center party, Hertling had a deep commitment to raising the standards of Catholic intellectual life. In fact, since its establishment in 1876 he had been president of the Görres-Gesellschaft, an organization dedicated to countering the influence of antimodernism and anti-intellectualism in Catholic circles, to encouraging and sponsoring scholarly research, and to lobbying for the appointment of Catholics to university chairs. In addition Hertling was on good terms with Althoff. The two shared an interest in overcoming the anti-Catholic bias characteristic of German academic life, and Althoff had frequently turned to Hertling for advice on the subject. Through these contacts each man had come to respect the other's opinions concerning the relationship of Catholicism and the German universities.[9]

Between late 1898 and the end of the following year Hertling made three trips to Rome in pursuit of his mission and spent a total of twelve weeks in the city. He accomplished little, however, other than persuading the Vatican to consider the project, and even this proved difficult. Two matters were particularly troublesome. First, the Vatican wanted the bishop of Strasbourg to have ultimate control over the selection of the proposed faculty's professors, a condition unacceptable to Hertling and to Berlin. Second, and equally objectionable, the Vatican wanted the bishop to have the right to dismiss any member of the faculty if the professor's personal behavior or theological views violated the precepts of the Catholic church.[10] But while these differences were serious, an accord might have been reached in the winter of 1899–1900 had the negotiations remained unaffected by political considerations. What made Hertling's efforts so frustrating was his well-founded suspicion that political pressures and objectives had convinced the Vatican and perhaps some German officials that an early resolution was undesirable.

Until late in 1899 Hertling's efforts to reach an accord remained an exercise in secret diplomacy.[11] But shortly after Hertling began his third series of talks in Rome the secrecy ended, apparently because of the calculated indiscretion of a Francophile official at the Vatican. In November 1899 newspapers in France, Germany, and Italy reported that Hertling had recently had an audience with Cardinal Mariano Rampolla, the papal secretary of state, and early in December the Parisian newspaper *Le Figaro* examined the background and objectives of Hertling's mission.[12] The Catholic clergy of the Reichsland, surprised and angered by these disclosures, reacted quickly. In the final weeks of 1899 Alsatian priests expressed their strong opposition to the Strasbourg project in addresses from the pulpit, in articles in the local Catholic press, and in direct appeals to the Vatican. Thus a Catholic weekly published in Strasbourg described the religious views of a scholar purportedly typical of those teaching Catholic theology at "old German" universities and then asked: "Do you wish to have priests who are trained in this image? Do you wish to pay for such education with your money?"[13] Another Catholic newspaper ridiculed Hertling's mission and confidently suggested that he would fail: "Rome remains justifiably suspicious. So does Catholic Alsace."[14] The bishop of Strasbourg warned Rampolla that the proposed faculty "could be an immense disaster for the church of Alsace"[15] And the cathedral chapters of Metz and Strasbourg insisted that the morale of Alsatian Catholics would be undermined if candidates for the priesthood were forced "to enter the university, to enter buildings that have on their pediments statues of Luther, Calvin, Zwingli, Melanchthon, Bucer, and other heroes of the so-called Reformation."[16]

The strongest critics were Catholics, but they were not alone. Predictably there were also misgivings among Alsatian Protestants and among the university's professors. The former, increasingly conscious of their vulnerability as a traditionally favored minority, feared the consequences of a university no longer alien to Catholics. They had benefited from the low demand for higher education among Alsatian Catholics and had no desire to see the situation changed. Admittedly a Catholic theological faculty by itself might not represent a serious threat. But to the extent its presence changed the image of the university and hence made other faculties more attractive to Catholic youths it would be dangerous. Alsatian Protestants were too alert to the growing control of higher education over access to power and status to want to see the Reichsland's university Catholicized.[17]

The professors' concerns were different. Their opposition to the project was rooted in a conviction that Catholicism and modern scholarship were incompatible. To Catholicize the university would be to violate the secularizing spirit of the age and to undermine the institution's character as a stronghold of "free German learning." The professors found it difficult to believe that "reason of state" could justify such a step. But they feared that these arguments would no longer suffice. In the aftermath of the François-Martin affair and the related criticism of the university the professors could not expect to prevail simply by insisting that the university be left as it was. This reasoning helps to explain why they now took the offensive. Rather than defending their university's existing character, they advanced their own proposals for change, proposals which, if instituted, would radically alter the university's relationship to Alsatian society and its position in the German academic community.

The professors' recommendations concerned technical education. Specifically, they called for the addition of a faculty offering programs in engineering, architecture, forestry, and agronomy. If adopted this would be a radical innovation, one without precedent in Germany or elsewhere in Europe. But the basic idea was not new. Before the university opened, it will be recalled, Roggenbach had suggested that programs in technical fields be established either within the university or in close association with it, on the grounds that they would increase the university's influence in the Reichsland. And beginning in the 1880s the idea had been discussed by various professors, notably the mathematician Felix Klein of Göttingen, with reference to the German universities generally. The objectives, in this case, were to adapt the universities to the needs of the modern world and to make higher technical education more scientific and respectable, thus raising the social status of those in the technical professions.[18] It is against this background that the recommendations of the Strasbourg professors should be seen. Like Roggenbach the professors seem to have been primarily motivated by considerations unique to their university and to the Reichsland. To justify their proposals, however, they relied heavily on arguments borrowed from Felix Klein and his allies.

Strasbourg professors first manifested a serious interest in adding a technical faculty shortly after learning of the negotiations at the Vatican. In December 1899 the philosopher Theobald Ziegler, currently the rector, and the mathematician Heinrich Weber, a former colleague of Felix Klein, composed a memorandum for the Statthalter describing and defending their project. The timing and the involvement of Ziegler, one of the faculty's most outspoken critics of Catholicism, suggest that concern about the government's interest in a Catholic theological faculty provided the stimulus. But whatever the stimulus, the memorandum observed that the project had been actively discussed at the university and that its authors were "in accord with a great number of their colleagues."[19]

The memorandum began with a discussion of the demand for higher technical education in the Reichsland. It emphasized both the growing need for scientists and engineers in industry and the growing importance of industry in the Alsatian economy. Given these trends, it continued, it was fair to question why Alsatians should have to go elsewhere to receive an advanced technical education and "why Alsace and Lorraine should not participate in the furtherance of technical scholarship, which is making such tremendous progress in all areas and exhibiting such brilliant successes."[20]

But the solution was not to establish a *Technische Hochschule,* as German precedents would suggest. Rather, there should be a technical faculty at the university. The advantages would be twofold. In the first place, it would be less expensive. Instruction in the basic sciences and the humanities could easily be handled by professors already at the university, and the existing laboratories and scientific institutes could meet some of the projected faculty's needs. There still would be substantial costs, both for salaries (the memorandum called for fifteen or sixteen new professors) and for physical facilities, but they would be even greater if a separate institution were established rather than a faculty.[21]

The second advantage was related to the movement led by Felix Klein. The memorandum noted that engineers and those in other technical professions were demanding that their disciplines and degrees be recognized as equal to those at the universities. The best way to resolve the dispute would be to add technical faculties to the universities: "The mutual stimulation resulting from the collegial relations of professors would promote and inspire collaborative work and scholarship; and likewise it is beyond question that the friendly interaction of students with fellow students from other faculties on the basis of a common humanistic education would do even more than the lectures . . . to promote mutual appreciation and a just respect for all scholarly endeavors." And there would be an added bonus for the Reichsland's government, for "it would step to the head of a cultural movement whose force in the future will be difficult to resist." In the original draft of the memorandum it was "our University of Strasbourg" that would step to the head of this movement, but the wording was changed for the version sent to the Statthalter, no doubt for tactical reasons.[22]

Ziegler and Weber assumed that the proposed faculty would be authorized only if it would contribute to the university's Germanizing mission, but they were confident it would. Their reasons were similar to those used three years before to defend the university against its German critics. Forcing Alsatians to go to "old Germany" for an advanced technical education was unwise since those who do go "associate exclusively with each other and in their homesickness find pleasure in sterile and spiteful criticism of the German surroundings in which they feel alien." In Strasbourg they were much more likely to have close relations with German students. In addition, a technical faculty in Strasbourg would attract many of the Alsatian youths—particularly numerous in Upper Alsace—who traditionally went to Switzerland or France to study engineering or architecture. As a result, "a great many young Alsatians who until now have not had the slightest contact with the German world would be introduced to it at the technical faculty in Strasbourg and eventually also

won over to it." In sum, there was no reason to fear the political consequences of the project; on the contrary, "here too there are factors
which favor its realization, indeed they actually make it seem politically
desirable and necessary."[23]

In attempting to justify their project, Ziegler and Weber concentrated
on the ways it would serve the Reichsland's economic interests and the
government's political interests. They said nothing about how it might
also serve the more specific interests of the university and its professors.
But there were several ways a technical faculty could advance the university's interests as defined by professors like Ziegler and Weber. To
begin with, it would bring more students to the university; the memorandum suggested that the new faculty would attract about 600 students,
while at that time there were only 1,105 in the entire university. The
increase would mean larger classes and higher incomes for many professors and would make the institution less vulnerable to complaints about
its expensive and underused facilities. In addition, because of its relevance
to the local economy, the proposed faculty would make the university
more popular with influential groups in the Reichsland generally and in
the Landesausschuss in particular, and hence might result in more generous support. The memorandum even mentioned the possibility of attracting gifts from private sources in the region, "where so much industry
and so much wealth are to be found, but also so much public spirit and
local patriotism."[24] As for the university's position in the academic world,
the addition of a technical faculty would reinforce its reputation as the
most modern in Germany, with healthy consequences for the faculty's
morale and sense of mission. And finally, the project would adversely
affect the government's recently publicized efforts to Catholicize the university. By making the institution even more modern and secular than it
already was, it might increase resistance at the Vatican and among Alsatian
Catholics to the proposed Catholic theological faculty. And if the latter
were added, the presence of a large technical faculty would help to limit
its visibility and its influence in the university's affairs. The memorandum
never mentioned the proposed Catholic theological faculty, but its implications for the project were clear.

And this may help to explain the government's reaction. Early in 1900
it became obvious that the government had no intention of establishing
a technical faculty in Strasbourg, at least not at this time. Their reasons
are unknown, but a few possibilities may be mentioned. There may have
been concern in Berlin about setting a precedent which was for some
reason considered undesirable. There may have been fear that a technical
faculty would attract large numbers of students from Francophile families,
with unfortunate consequences for the university and its influence in the
Reichsland. There may have been misgivings about the possibility of convincing the tightfisted Landesausschuss to provide adequate support. And,

of course, there may have been concern about the impact on the negotiations with the Vatican. Beyond this little can be said. All that is known is that the responsible officials did not proceed with the project. They were at least as interested as Ziegler and Weber in changing the university's character, but their plans involved making the university less modern and less secular, not more.

The protests during the winter of 1899–1900 over the proposed Catholic theological faculty failed to undermine the negotiations, but they did cause both sides to proceed more cautiously. Rampolla now argued that the sentiments of Alsatian Catholics made it essential that any accord incorporate his proposals concerning the appointment and dismissal of professors. At the urging of Hertling and the Statthalter (and over the objections of Althoff, who feared the consequences for Prussia's universities of precedents set in Strasbourg), Germany responded with some minor concessions in the hope that the Vatican would reciprocate.[25] The Vatican obliged, offering a few concessions when Hertling presented Germany's in April 1900 and a few more when he next visited a year later. But these modifications did not go far enough. Althoff insisted that the government have the right to nominate candidates for chairs as well as the right, already conceded by the Vatican, to veto the bishop's nominees. Otherwise, he argued, the faculty would be staffed by ultramontanists and would never be accepted by the other Strasbourg professors or by Germany's other faculties of Catholic theology. As if to verify these contentions, Althoff suggested that several German scholars be asked to assess whether the Vatican's terms were consistent with the traditions and objectives of German academic life.[26]

The foreign office saw merit in this suggestion. If the canvassed scholars expressed serious reservations about the Vatican's terms, as seemed likely, it would serve two useful purposes: it would strengthen the government's bargaining position, and it would make it easier for the government to defend itself against criticism from German Catholics if negotiations failed. Accordingly, in August 1901 it sent each of thirty-three academics (chosen from a list prepared by the Prussian Ministry of Culture in consultation with the Statthalter) a copy of the rules governing Prussia's Catholic theological faculties, a copy of the Vatican's terms for the proposed faculty, and a request to assess whether the latter were acceptable "from the standpoint of the German universities."[27] Among the Catholics canvassed were the historian Aloys Schulte and theologians Franz Xaver Heiner, Franz Xaver Kraus, and Hermann Schell. The Protestants included Hans Delbrück, Wilhelm Dilthey, Adolf Harnack, Friedrich Paulsen, Gustav Schmoller, and Rudolf Sohm.[28]

Hertling reacted to this venture with bitter disappointment. He complained to the foreign office that Althoff had lost interest in the proposed faculty and that he only sought an excuse for terminating the negotiations.[29] But Hertling was soon mollified by the so-called Spahn case, a dispute over a Catholic scholar that pitted Althoff and the Reichsland's government against the University of Strasbourg and, less directly, the rest of Germany's universities. This confrontation—the most serious involving the German academic community since the revolutions of 1848— made Hertling more tolerant of the government's determination to proceed cautiously in its negotiations with the Vatican. It also increased the likelihood that the Vatican would make the concessions needed if these prolonged negotiations were ever to succeed.

• 2 •

The events culminating in the Spahn case can be traced to a proposal first made in the mid-1890s by members of the Landesausschuss. Noting that some German universities had chairs of history and philosophy reserved for Catholics, clerical deputies repeatedly recommended that similar positions be established in Strasbourg.[30] In response the ministry's spokesmen pointed out that the only precedents were at universities with Catholic theological faculties and argued that the proposed chairs could not be justified unless there were such a faculty in Strasbourg.[31] But privately some officials came to think differently. Thus there are indications that by mid-1898 Althoff was considering reserving certain chairs in Strasbourg for Catholics even if the projected negotiations with the Vatican failed.[32] And in 1900 the Prussian minister of culture recommended such a step to the chancellor. If the Vatican refused to authorize a Catholic theological faculty, he observed,

> a significant measure still remains possible for which . . . the church's cooperation is not required: the establishment in the Faculty of Philosophy of a Catholic professorship of philosophy, one of history, and, I would like to add, one for religious studies. If men were chosen for these chairs who are qualified and acceptable to the church, the bishop of Strasbourg would not long be able to avoid sending his seminarians to their lectures. This would ensure a great improvement in the scholarly training and the Germanization of the theological students of the diocese of Strasbourg, and at the same time it would prepare the ground in an effective way for the establishment, should better days appear, of a Catholic theological faculty in Strasbourg.[33]

The matter was first pursued a year later, in the spring of 1901. The Statthalter, doubtless prodded by Althoff, now considered asking the Landesausschuss to fund two new chairs at the university, one for a Catholic philosopher and one for a Catholic historian.[34] He did not proceed with this plan, possibly out of concern over how the Strasbourg faculty might react. But later in the spring he and Althoff prepared another, one both more modest and more devious. It involved the chair of modern history occupied by Conrad Varrentrapp. Recently Marburg's Faculty of Philosophy, quite possibly at Althoff's urging, had nominated Varrentrapp as one of its candidates for a vacant professorship. Althoff and the Statthalter now agreed that they should convince Varrentrapp to move to Marburg, which should be easy since Althoff would handle the negotiations for the Prussian university and the Statthalter could instruct the curator of Strasbourg's not to match Althoff's terms. If Varrentrapp accepted the call, the government would replace him with a Catholic and at the same time establish a second chair of modern history for a Protestant. In insisting on the latter, the Statthalter observed that Strasbourg's Protestant theological faculty would object if the university's only professor of modern history were a Catholic, particularly since the occupant of the chair of medieval history, Harry Bresslau, was Jewish. Financing this new position, they agreed, should not be difficult. A special supplement to the Alsatian budget could be avoided providing the two appointed received relatively low salaries.[35]

The next stage in the plan began early in July, when Varrentrapp agreed to accept the call to Marburg. Althoff immediately notified the Statthalter's representative in Berlin and advised him to ask the Strasbourg faculty to proceed "with all possible speed" in selecting its candidates for the vacated chair. He continued:

> The faculty will probably then suggest Marcks (whose selection is out of the question), Hintze, and others. After the proposals have arrived two historians will be appointed, one Protestant and one Catholic. As for my more precise intentions in this regard, I wish to keep them to myself until you have informed me of the faculty's proposals. I hope you will not regard my remarks and instructions as unwarranted meddling. As you know, His Highness the Statthalter has been so kind as to discuss this plan with me, and I consider its completion to be integrally connected to the appointment of Varrentrapp.[36]

As Althoff had hoped, the Faculty of Philosophy proceeded quickly. By mid-July it had agreed on four candidates. The first and second choices, Erich Marcks and Dietrich Schaefer, were already historians of considerable distinction. "The appointment of either of these two scholars," the dean's report observed, "would be a great gain for our university, thus justifying the considerable outlay that would be required." The faculty's third and fourth choices, on the other hand, were scholars of less prominence without university chairs: Friedrich Meinecke, a *Privatdozent* in Berlin, and Felix Rachfahl, an *Extraordinarius* in Halle.[37] Rachfahl, nominally a Catholic, was on the list because the faculty members suspected the government might intend to call a Catholic historian, particularly if a Catholic theological faculty was about to be established. (They knew nothing of the current state of the negotiations with the Vatican.) If the chair were to go to a Catholic, they wanted one who, like Rachfahl, was nonpracticing and anticlerical.[38]

Shortly after receiving these nominations the university's curator—a bureaucrat named Julius Hamm in whom the faculty had little confidence, not least because he himself was Catholic—conferred with Althoff in Bonn. He seemed intent on deferring to Althoff, who was happy to oblige. Althoff insisted that only one of the four nominees deserved serious consideration. Marcks was unavailable since he had just gone to Heidelberg and it was against the government's policy to offer a scholar a new position so soon after he had taken another. Equally unacceptable was Rachfahl. As a nominal Catholic he could not be named to the chair reserved for a Protestant, while his religious views made him an inappropriate candidate for the other one. As for Schaefer, there was only a slight chance he would consider moving to Strasbourg, and he certainly would not move for the salary the government would offer. This left Friedrich Meinecke, a scholar Althoff held in high regard. All things considered, Althoff assured Hamm, Meinecke was easily the man best qualified for the chair reserved for a Protestant.[39]

Althoff also believed one historian had particularly strong qualifications for the other chair. He urged Hamm to offer it to Martin Spahn, a diligent young scholar—he was only twenty-six and had already published two books—who, thanks to Althoff, had recently become an *Extraordinarius* in Bonn. In defending this choice, he said nothing about Spahn's scholarly reputation or promise. Instead he praised Spahn's "good patriotic disposition" and his lack of ultramontane proclivities. Althoff admitted that conservative Catholics disagreed with Spahn's religious views and hence might have misgivings about his appointment. But he saw no reason to fear criticism from these quarters, if only because Spahn was the son of a leader of the Center party.[40] Hamm's account suggests that political rather than religious or scholarly considerations motivated the selection of Spahn; they chose him because he was sympathetic to the government and had ties to the Center party, not because he was a good Catholic or a good historian.[41]

The final matter discussed by Althoff and Hamm was that of procedure. How were their decisions to be put into effect, and how were they to be explained to the Faculty of Philosophy? They agreed that Hamm should make a perfunctory offer to Schaefer. As soon as Schaefer turned it down, Meinecke and Spahn would be offered positions. At this point Hamm would inform the faculty that after trying unsuccessfully to call Schaefer the government had decided to replace Varrentrapp with two younger historians. Althoff and Hamm were certain the faculty would raise no strong objections (in part, perhaps, because they intended to make the appointments in August, when most professors would be away on vacation).[42]

The Statthalter accepted all but one of these recommendations, that concerning Spahn. He refused to authorize Spahn's appointment before learning whether Aloys Schulte, the occupant of the Catholic chair in Breslau, was available, suggesting that he had doubts about Spahn's qualifications. But when Schulte demanded a salary (13,000 marks) much higher than the government was prepared to offer, the Statthalter reconciled himself to Spahn.[43] Hamm now asked Schaefer if he would move to Strasbourg, and upon receiving the expected reply he contacted Meinecke, Spahn, and Strasbourg's Faculty of Philosophy. He informed the faculty that the government intended to replace Varrentrapp with two historians rather than one and that the positions were being offered to Meinecke and Spahn, but he said nothing about the confessional considerations involved. In his letters to Meinecke and Spahn he simply stated that the government wished to fill two chairs of modern history in Strasbourg and offered each the modest salary of 4,500 marks. On 22 August Meinecke informed Hamm that he would accept the call, and Spahn responded in similar fashion two days later.[44]

But Althoff and Hamm had made one serious miscalculation. They had assumed that Strasbourg's Faculty of Philosophy would show "appropriate discretion" when informed of the creation of an additional chair and of Spahn's appointment.[45] Clearly they had not expected the outspoken criticism that was to come from the Strasbourg professors and, somewhat later, from the German academic community in general.

The first indication that the faculty might not react with "appropriate discretion" came in a letter sent to Hamm on 29 August by its dean, the oriental philologist Theodor Nöldeke. Although Nöldeke, like many of his colleagues, was not in Strasbourg, he had learned "from reliable sources" that the government had appointed Meinecke and another scholar. After praising Meinecke's selection "as Varrentrapp's replacement," he turned his attention to the second position. It was possible, he observed, that the government had decided "to impose a Catholic or even an ultramontane scholar on the faculty." But if this were the case,

> very unpleasant consequences would result. This would put an end to a principle that had endured since the founding of the university, that has developed through constant use into a customary right: a new position and a new professor will have been imposed on a faculty without its opinion even having been asked. And this on behalf of an outlook that is actually hostile to scholarship and to the interests of Germany. . . .
> That the faculty and the university as a whole would calmly submit to such an appointment is of course not to be expected.[46]

A few days later, upon learning of Spahn's appointment, Nöldeke returned to Strasbourg to summon a special meeting of his faculty. It now became clear that Nöldeke's colleagues shared his indignation, and for the same reasons: they wanted no chairs with confessional restrictions, and they wanted no professors appointed without their authorization. The second reason concerned a precedent that seemed particularly dangerous. The Strasbourg professors, it must be emphasized, still had a strong sense of their university's uniqueness. Admittedly many features that had once set apart the institution no longer did. Other German universities now had facilities as impressive and professors as innovative, and the consciousness of a special national mission was not as pronounced as in earlier years. But in one important respect the university had, if anything, become more unique. Through the 1880s and 1890s, decades marked by the progressive bureaucratization of higher education elsewhere in Germany, the Strasbourg professors had been generally successful in protecting their institution's autonomy. Except in 1887 they had had few confrontations with the authorities, and those that had occurred had been minor compared with trends across the Rhine. This record helped to perpetuate the highly developed esprit de corps and sense of superiority that had always characterized the Strasbourg faculty: in other respects their institution might no longer be the very model of a modern university, but when it came to the question of autonomy it still was. It is against this background that the professors' response to Spahn's appointment should be seen. In their opinion this unprecedented act might mark the beginning of the bureaucratization of the last relatively free German university and the end of one of the institution's few remaining claims to uniqueness.[47]

At their meeting the members of the Faculty of Philosophy, convinced that the circumstances justified extreme action, agreed on two measures. First, they instructed the dean to inform Spahn that he had been appointed without their authorization and against their wishes. Their intention was to convince him to reconsider his acceptance of the position. Second, they voted unanimously to send a petition to the man who officially appointed the university's *Ordinarien,* the emperor, requesting that he not authorize Spahn's appointment. The petition, composed by Harry Bresslau and Theobald Ziegler, did not mention the major reason for the faculty's concern, the precedent set by Spahn's appointment without faculty approval, for the emperor was unlikely to be sympathetic. Rather, it stressed the confessional character of the position and its political implications. It requested the emperor's intervention not because Spahn was unqualified, but rather because he had been called to a confessional chair. Since the faculty did not need a second chair of modern history, the position obviously had been established in response to "the repeatedly expressed demands of the ultramontane party." But such a position "can only be accounted for, if not justified, by the need to train Catholic priests"; adding one to a university without a Catholic theological faculty "would represent an innovation that is completely contrary to the prevailing conception of German learning." Even if political criteria were used the position could not be justified: a confessional professor would disseminate an "ultramontane conception of history" and thus seriously impede the campaign to teach Alsatians "religious toleration and nationalism." In sum, the petition argued that the emperor would act in the national interest as well as in the interests of learning if he vetoed Spahn's appointment.[48]

The emperor did not respond until mid-October, about five weeks after receiving the petition. In the meantime he solicited reports from the two officials most involved, the Statthalter and Althoff. Both naturally defended the decision to appoint Spahn, although the Statthalter did so with less conviction than Althoff. Hohenlohe-Langenburg conceded that the Strasbourg professors had made some legitimate complaints. He basically agreed, for instance, with their opposition to the use of religious criteria when selecting professors. But under the circumstances Spahn's appointment should be approved. Thus he noted the appointment's relationship to the negotiations with the Vatican and to the government's desire to make the university more attractive to Alsatian Catholics. And, he added, regardless of the merits of the initial decision to appoint Spahn, the government should not bow to pressure from the Strasbourg faculty: "If Professor Spahn is denied confirmation, it would give rise to unpleasant complaints in Center party circles and have an undesirable effect on the Alsatian government's relationship with the university."[49]

Althoff's report to the emperor, to judge from a memorandum he had just sent the Statthalter, attempted to refute each of the major contentions made in the professors' petition.[50] He insisted that Spahn had the experience and stature expected of an *Ordinarius*. He argued that Spahn would not disseminate "an ultramontane conception of history" and that the university did need an additional chair of history (in part because one of the existing chairs "is occupied by a scholar of the Jewish faith and of a distinctly Jewish intellectual orientation").[51] He noted that the position offered Spahn was technically not a confessional chair since it was not limited by statute to Catholics. And he asserted that Spahn had been appointed not in response to "the repeatedly expressed demands of the ultramontane party," as the faculty had contended, but as an act of justice. Currently there were only two Catholic *Ordinarien* at Strasbourg as compared, for instance, with nineteen in the secular faculties at Bonn and fourteen in the secular faculties at Breslau. Why were there so few in Strasbourg?

> To answer this question with references to the intellectual backwardness of Catholics, which doubtless exists, does not suffice. . . . Rather,

the chief reason is that in the last two decades the Strasbourg faculties have obtained for themselves, as a result of the government's unfortunate practice of always asking their views about the filling of professorships, a sort of unconditional right of proposal and presentation, and conscious of their independence from state control they have exercised the right in a biased manner and without any regard for the conditions of the region.[52]

Althoff concluded his memorandum with three recommendations. First, steps should soon be taken to establish a confessional chair of philosophy in Strasbourg. Second, the Reichsland's government henceforth should play an active role in the selection of all professors and should undertake to alter significantly the faculty's ratio of Catholics to Protestants. And third, the government should immediately authorize Spahn's appointment.

Everything that the Faculty of Philosophy in Strasbourg brings up in opposition to this is completely untenable. Indeed it hardly ever happens that a faculty presumes to bypass its appointed authorities with such an unfounded complaint. In addition the faculty has not even taken the precautions necessary to keep the matter secret. On the contrary, the news of the submission of the petition has been in all the papers, and articles on it have appeared . . . which could only originate with someone to whom the entire contents of the petition were known. If under such circumstances the faculty does not meet with a firm repulse, the authority of the government of Alsace-Lorraine will suffer a severe setback and discipline will be seriously endangered not only at the University of Strasbourg but at all other universities.[53]

Immediately after meeting with Althoff the emperor informed the Statthalter that he was authorizing Spahn's appointment. The Strasbourg professors learned of this the next day, 17 October, when the Alsatian government's official gazette published the text of the emperor's telegram. This message constituted the emperor's response to the professors' petition; he never sent a direct reply to the Faculty of Philosophy.[54]

The emperor's confirmation of Spahn's appointment did not end the dispute. On the contrary, it quickened the month-old debate in the German press, providing the impetus both for numerous articles defending Spahn's appointment, mostly in Catholic publications, and for countless articles opposing it, all but a few in liberal newspapers and journals.

The reaction of Germany's Catholic press to the initial reports of Spahn's nomination was favorable. Typical was the observation of the *Kölnische Volkszeitung,* the leading Catholic newspaper of the Rhineland, that if Spahn received a chair in Strasbourg "a legitimate demand of the Reichsland's Catholics . . . will have been met."[55] But late in September the liberal *Bonner Zeitung* disclosed that when Spahn was a *Privatdozent* in Berlin he had supported the anti-ultramontane campaign of Count Paul von Hoensbroech, a renegade Jesuit.[56] This allegation, which Hoens-

broech immediately confirmed, caused a sensation in Catholic circles.
Catholic newspapers both in the Reichsland and "old Germany" now
asserted that any scholar with ties to Hoensbroech was clearly unsuitable
for a position ostensibly reserved for devout Catholics. In the first half
of October no Catholic newspaper appears to have argued that the government had chosen wisely when it selected Spahn.[57]

But the emperor's telegram encouraged Catholics to adjust their stance
once again. Henceforth the Catholic press gave less attention to Spahn
and his views than to the government's blunt rejection of the Strasbourg
professors' petition. Newspapers that had recently suggested that Spahn's
appointment was an act of duplicity directed against Catholics now praised
the emperor for defending Catholicism against the biases of the academic
community. Thus Berlin's *Germania,* a leading organ of the Center party,
observed that as far as the emperor was concerned "in the naming of
professors, belief in the Catholic religion does not, as in certain circles,
constitute a stumbling block."[58] And the Reichsland's most influential
Catholic newspaper, *Der Elsässer,* criticized the "one-sidedness and lust
for power of the liberal professors' guild" and pointed out that the emperor, in contrast, "proceeds from the opinion that the university should
serve the common welfare and that hence in filling professorial chairs
proper regard should be taken for the needs and legitimate wishes of the
population."[59] Instead of castigating the government's policy in the Spahn
case, as it had a few days before,[60] *Der Elsässer* now defended it. And
so did virtually every other Catholic newspaper concerned with the dispute. Indeed it would have been surprising if the Catholic press had behaved otherwise in view of the attacks on the government's efforts to
foster Catholic scholarship now coming from the liberal press and from
the German academic community.[61]

The contributions of Germany's liberal press to the debate were, with
few exceptions, highly critical of the government.[62] Such influential publications as the *Frankfurter Zeitung,* the *Hamburger Nachrichten,* the
*Münchener Neueste Nachrichten,* Berlin's *National-Zeitung,* the *Preussische Jahrbücher,* and Stuttgart's *Schwäbischer Merkur* criticized the
appointment, as did innumerable newspapers and journals of lesser prominence.[63] Admittedly many liberal publications did little more than report
the latest news of the dispute in terms sympathetic to the Strasbourg
professors. But others viewed Spahn's appointment in a broader perspective, stressing the principles involved and the implications for the
future of German higher education. Of the articles in this category two
stood out. The first was by Theodor Mommsen, then an emeritus professor
in Berlin, and appeared on 15 November in the *Münchener Neueste Nachrichten.* The second was by Adolf Michaelis, a Strasbourg professor,
and appeared a week later in the Hamburg weekly *Der Lotse.*

Mommsen's intervention can be traced to a suggestion made by the editor of the *Münchener Neueste Nachrichten* to Lujo Brentano, the current rector of the University of Munich. The editor, G. Keyssner, argued that government officials would learn nothing from the Spahn case, as it had come to be called, unless it was clear that the Strasbourg professors had strong support in the rest of the German academic community. This support could best be demonstrated with "a thoroughly objective, concise, and intelligible manifesto that shows why the confessionalization of faculties of philosophy is incorrect logically and dangerous in practice." If enough professors signed, the manifesto might be sent to the Reichstag and to the assemblies and cultural ministries of the individual German states. And in any case copies should be released to the press. "Even if only seven sign," Keyssner observed, "then it will call to mind with all the more gratitude the other famous seven [the Göttingen Seven] of the year 1837."[64]

Brentano and most of his colleagues had, like Keyssner, followed the Spahn case with considerable apprehension, for they thought the outcome might have serious implications for their own university. In recent years Bavarian Catholics had been demanding the appointment of more Catholics to the Munich faculty, and the pressure doubtless would increase now that Spahn had been called to Strasbourg. These demands might be thwarted, however, if other professors publicly supported the stand of the Strasbourg faculty. But Brentano thought this support would be most effective if it originated at Berlin, Germany's most prestigious university. It was with this in mind that he wrote the venerable Mommsen requesting his assistance: "Nobody is better qualified than you to persuade your Berlin colleagues to associate themselves with such a manifesto. If you raise the standard of the protection of scholarship, everyone whose standard it is will follow."[65]

Mommsen shared Brentano's concern and his interest in organizing a public protest, but he had doubts about Brentano's specific proposal. In his reply he argued that in view of "the faintheartedness of the Germans in general and of the professors in particular" any attempt to obtain a large number of signatures would probably fail, and if it did fail the manifesto would do more harm than good. "Considering the pseudoconstitutional absolutism under which we live and with which our spineless people seem to have cordially come to terms, a very conspicuous reaction would probably have an effect similar to that of the Strasbourg protest, and I shudder to think of the outrages that might follow."[66] But Mommsen was willing to write a personal manifesto concerning the questions of principle involved. Brentano, finding this alternative acceptable, asked Mommsen to submit such a manifesto to Keyssner's newspaper. Mommsen obliged, and on 15 November his manifesto appeared in print.[67]

Mommsen's first few sentences succinctly summarized his theme:

The feeling of degradation is spreading through university circles. Our mainspring is unbiased research, the kind of research that does not discover . . . that which serves other practical objectives lying outside scholarship, but rather that which seems to the conscientious scholar to be logically and historically correct, in a word, the truth. It is on the truth that our self-respect depends, our professional honor, and our influence over the young. On it rests the German learning that has contributed its part to the greatness and the strength of the German people. Whoever interferes with it strikes the axe against the mighty tree in whose shadow we live, whose fruits nourish the world.

Such an axe-blow is every appointment of a university professor whose freedom of research is limited. Confessionalism is the mortal enemy of the university. To appoint a historian or a philosopher who must be Catholic or must be Protestant, and who should be of service to his confession, means nothing other than to oblige the appointee to set limits on his work when the results could be embarrassing to a confessional dogma.[68]

In the rest of the manifesto Mommsen did little more than elaborate on this theme.[69] He never mentioned the questions raised about Spahn's scholarly qualifications and religious views and about the rights of faculties in the selection of professors. Important as they may have been, Mommsen believed only one issue involved principles of great importance to German academic life generally: should universities have confessional chairs in their secular faculties? This issue received his full attention.

When Brentano saw Mommsen's manifesto, about a week before it was published, he decided it could be used to mobilize a general protest of the German academic community, Mommsen's intentions notwithstanding. The protest would be in the form of open letters thanking Mommsen for his resolute defense of "unbiased scholarship." Upon learning that Mommsen had no objections, Brentano asked friends at other universities to solicit their colleagues' support for such letters, and he coordinated the collection of signatures at his own university and at Munich's *Technische Hochschule*.[70] The campaign proved quite successful. During the last two weeks of November and the first week of December open letters to Mommsen were sent from three *Technische Hochschulen* (Karlsruhe, Munich, and Stuttgart), three Austrian universities (Graz, Innsbruck, and Vienna), and fifteen of the twenty German universities (Bonn, Breslau, Erlangen, Freiburg, Giessen, Göttingen, Heidelberg, Jena, Kiel, Königsberg, Leipzig, Marburg, Munich, Strasbourg, and Würzburg). At least thirteen of these letters contained more than thirty professors' signatures, and four had more than fifty.[71] Among those in the latter group was the one from Strasbourg: this well-publicized tribute to Mommsen was signed by all but two of the university's fifty-seven *Ordinarien,* the exceptions being Meinecke and Spahn.[72]

In evaluating the response of the German academic community to Mommsen's manifesto it is useful to distinguish the professors at Prussian universities from those elsewhere. The former proved much more reluctant to sign open letters; at Prussian universities only 37 percent of the *Ordinarien* in secular faculties signed, while at other German universities the rate was 73 percent.[73] But this disparity did not surprise Mommsen. He had predicted that the attempt to win the support of Prussian professors would be frustrated by the "prevalent cowardice" that characterized the Prussian academic community,[74] and in his opinion events proved him correct. He explained to Brentano that the reluctance of Prussian professors to offend their government, a phenomenon he termed the "Prussian nightmare," had been primarily responsible for their weak response.[75] In this regard many Prussian professors who signed did so in the belief that they were in fact supporting their government. The Marburg professors, for instance, hoped their letter and others would make it easier for the government to resist pressures from political parties when filling professorships.[76] The Protestant theologian Adolf Harnack, one of the few Berlin professors who approved of Mommsen's manifesto, argued similarly in a letter to a newspaper:

> With regard to our present situation I am of the opinion that the greatest threat to the autonomy of scholarship comes from the parliamentary parties, and that against them the governments are now, to the extent they can be, the caretakers and protectors of learning. For this reason I greeted Mommsen's grave remarks with joy and gratitude, and I hope that the great commotion they have caused will strengthen the governments in their efforts to protect the sanctuary of scholarship from the disturbing encroachment of confessional and related forces.[77]

As if to demonstrate his good faith, Harnack added that he had serious reservations about a recent article on the Spahn case that attacked the Prussian government in general and Friedrich Althoff in particular. He referred to the article by Adolf Michaelis.[78]

It was as a self-appointed spokesman for Strasbourg's Faculty of Philosophy that Michaelis wrote his article. He wished, he explained, to correct certain misconceptions concerning his faculty's opposition to Spahn's appointment and to draw public attention to some troubling implications of this appointment.[79] Most of what followed dealt with matters already discussed either in Mommsen's manifesto, which Michaelis did not see until after completing his article, or in the faculty's petition to the emperor. Michaelis argued, for instance, that his faculty did not need a second chair of modern history, that Spahn was unqualified, and that religious considerations should not influence appointments to secular faculties.[80] But Michaelis also made several points not previously expressed in the public debate over Spahn's appointment. The most significant concerned Althoff and the Prussian Ministry of Culture. Michaelis turned to the subject after noting that prior to Spahn's appointment the Alsatian government had never violated the Strasbourg faculty's wishes when calling professors:

> The sudden break with this good Strasbourg tradition is in accord with the practice in Prussia; indeed it apparently was done with the cooperation of the man who oversees university affairs in Prussia. . . . Outside academic circles there is only slight awareness of the destructive changes in the administration of the Prussian universities that have occurred in the past nineteen years [i.e., since Althoff went to Berlin]. The long-established right of the faculties to nominate their professors has become utterly illusory, their customary right to rule themselves has been completely revoked; in the place of the faculties . . . have appeared the bureaucrats, men who have almost unlimited control over the destiny of the Prussian universities. . . . At any German university one visits, indignant comments are heard about this unprecedented administration whose portrayal in days to come will fill the blackest page in the history of the Prussian universities. . . . One can hardly speak anymore of mutual trust between the universities and the educational administrators; bureaucratic might has replaced the once free and flourishing right of academic self-government.

Who could blame the Strasbourg professors, Michaelis asked, if they now feared that their university was also being subjected to bureaucratic control? Yet it was not surprising that their concerns had found little sympathy in Prussian academic circles:

> The older generation there has submitted to the inevitable, the younger one has never known anything else and consequently is in the habit of regarding grievances of this sort as normal. Therefore it is not considered at all strange when others do not fare any better. For one would surely do our Prussian colleagues an injustice if one believed all of them capable of the sentiments of the innkeeper who is glad that the other inns now also have bugs.[81]

"It seems to me," Mommsen wrote Brentano after reading these remarks, "that the contribution of Michaelis will not further our cause; he says much more than is correct and very much more than can be proved . . . ; I am afraid he does not understand exactly what he is doing."[82] His misgivings were justified. Although Michaelis reportedly received hundreds of personal letters thanking him for his attack on Althoff, the most significant effect of the article was the strong reaction it provoked, especially in Prussian academic circles.[83] Motivated in part by conviction, in part by personal indebtedness, and in part by self-interest, several Prussian professors publicly defended Althoff against the intemperate charges of Michaelis. Thus Harnack praised Althoff's policies and accomplishments in his letter to the *National-Zeitung*.[84] The Berlin astronomer Wilhelm Foerster and the Göttingen historian Paul Kehr defended Althoff in *Der Lotse,* the journal that had published the offending article.[85] And Gustav Schmoller organized a banquet in Althoff's honor. In his speech at this banquet, a speech reprinted in newspapers throughout Germany, Schmoller apologized for having been able "to assemble only a small collection of the devoted admirers and closest friends of Herr Althoff."[86]

The reaction to Michaelis's article in Prussia had two significant consequences. First, it complicated the already difficult task of soliciting signatures for open letters to Mommsen. Professors who might otherwise have signed such letters decided not to do so when they learned of the charges made by Michaelis, fearing that support for Mommsen might now be interpreted as support for Michaelis and hence as criticism of Althoff.[87] Second, the reaction strengthened Althoff's desire to remain in office. Between his arrival in 1882 and his eventual departure in 1907 Althoff seriously considered leaving the Ministry of Culture only once, when he came under attack in late 1901. That he chose to remain was largely due to the tributes he now received from men prominent in academic and government circles. Of these tributes the one that most impressed him was a Christmas gift from the emperor. The gift was a portrait of the emperor to which a brief inscription had been added: "The worst fruits are not the ones at which the wasps nibble."[88]

The Strasbourg professors had never expected to topple Althoff, desirable as this might be. In fact they had never expected to prevent Spahn's appointment. Their objective, rather, had been to prevent further violations of their autonomy; they had hoped a strong protest would insure that Spahn's appointment remained an isolated incident rather than the beginning of the bureaucratization of their university.

Viewed in these terms, did they succeed? The record is mixed. In at least one specific case the professors' willingness to speak out probably did serve their interests. Late in 1901 rumors circulated that the government was about to establish chairs in Strasbourg for a Catholic philosopher and for canon law, and that the former would go to Eugène Muller, an Alsatian priest on the faculty of the local seminary. Alarmed at this prospect, most professors decided, at least provisionally, that if the rumors were confirmed they would protest in the most dramatic way possible: they would resign. Whether this widely publicized threat actually deterred the government is unclear, for the government's prior intentions are unclear. It is known, however, that the chairs in question were not established and that the greatest fear in the Prussian cultural ministry at this time was that the Strasbourg professors would resign en masse. Perhaps there was a connection.[89]

But this victory, if this is what it was, may have been the only one the professors gained from the dispute. Certainly their position after the Spahn case was worse than it had been before. And although it is likely, given the government's policies, that it would have worsened anyway, the professors' recalcitrance seems to have accelerated the pace. In this regard two subjects merit particular attention: the projected Catholic theological faculty and the professors' efforts to strengthen their university.

•  3  •

Early in 1902, the national debate over Spahn's appointment having ended, Hertling went to Berlin to discuss the still unresolved negotiations with the Vatican. He learned that Althoff and other officials now wanted the negotiations resumed but on the basis of new and less conciliatory proposals. In insisting on stiffer conditions they were influenced by the scholars canvassed six months before. Actually seventeen of the thirty-one respondents had recommended accepting the Vatican's latest proposals, but all seventeen were practicing Catholics. The other fourteen, including one Catholic (Franz Xaver Kraus), thought the government should demand more favorable terms. Most scholars in the latter group enjoyed considerable distinction, a fact that led one official to comment that "in the event it accepts the Roman proposals the imperial government would find its strongest criticism and resistance coming from precisely the most renowned scholars."[90]

Hertling agreed to return to Rome providing the new German proposals were not significantly less conciliatory than the previous terms. The condition was met. The new proposals differed from the previous ones in two important respects: they called for ten chairs instead of six, the apparent objective being to reduce further the seminary's contribution to the training of priests, and they limited the bishop's supervisory rights over the faculty to those enjoyed by bishops in Prussia. The latter was essential, the explanatory remarks stated, if the faculty was to enjoy the respect of the professors in Strasbourg's other faculties and in Germany's other universities.[91]

To the surprise of Hertling and of officials in Berlin, the Vatican had no serious objections to the new proposals. In mid-June the Pope's advisory council decided that only a few minor revisions would be needed. This response suggests that the Vatican was now more interested in an accord than before. The change seems to have been related to the recent deterioration of the Vatican's relations with France, a trend reinforced by the Associations law of July 1901 and by the accession to the premiership in early June 1902 of a fanatic anticlericalist, Emile Combes. The policies of the French government along with indications that the German emperor was becoming more interested in defending Catholic interests—his confirmation of Spahn's appointment was one such indication—apparently convinced the Vatican that it should improve its relations with Germany, even if this required concessions earlier deemed unacceptable.[92]

The few substantive issues that still stood in the way were resolved in August. All that remained were two procedural questions, and by early November they too had been resolved: it was agreed that the final accord should be in the form of an exchange of identical notes between Germany and the Vatican, with Hertling and Rampolla signing for their governments, and that the specific provisions of the accord should be made public but not the accompanying *Note explicative,* which stated that Strasbourg's Faculty of Philosophy must have "one professor of history and one professor of philosophy who belong to the Catholic religion."[93] (Since the faculty already had a Catholic historian and had just appointed a Catholic philosopher—for reasons considered below—making this public seemed unnecessary.) On 5 December 1902, a little more than four years after the negotiations began, the exchange of documents took place signifying the formal conclusion of the accord.[94]

It did not take long to staff the new faculty. In mid-December the Statthalter informed Berlin that his deliberations with the local bishop had proceeded "without difficulty to a swift conclusion," and that negotiations were under way with the men selected.[95] Within the next few weeks eight scholars accepted calls—three Alsatians from the local seminary's faculty and five from Catholic theological faculties across the Rhine. The most distinguished appointee, and the most controversial, was Albert Ehrhard, a modernist theologian of Alsatian birth who came from Freiburg. Ehrhard had recently provoked considerable discussion with a book warning that Roman Catholicism was in danger of becoming a religion that appealed only to the weak and the uneducated. Among the others accepting calls were Eugène Muller, the government's rumored candidate the year before for a chair for a Catholic philosopher, and Michael Faulhaber, who later became the bishop of Munich.[96]

Before the end of 1902 the Statthalter concluded that the new faculty could open for the winter semester of 1903–4 providing the Landesausschuss granted the necessary funds. The assembly obliged, approving the faculty's budget with only one dissenting vote (from a Socialist). The university's sixth faculty opened on schedule, with the event marked by a special convocation at the university and a religious service at a nearby church. By the end of October, 177 students had registered in the new faculty, all but 8 of them from the Reichsland. No other faculty enrolled as many Alsatians.[97]

By this time, it should be added, most of the Reichsland's Catholic clergy had become reconciled to the new faculty. Since the outcry in the winter of 1899–1900 the clergy had become more sympathetic to Germany and to the idea of Catholicizing rather than boycotting the university (thanks largely to the anticlerical policies of the French government). And in any case there were not many priests willing to criticize a faculty established with the Vatican's approval. Some complained about the government's motives, to be sure, and the bishop of Metz, committed to his own seminary and to local traditions, sent few students from his diocese (contiguous with the annexed section of Lorraine). But no member of the Reichsland's clergy appears to have publicly criticized the accord, and a report prepared in 1904 by the new faculty's dean suggests that a large proportion actually welcomed it. This report estimated that 40 percent of the clergy of the diocese of Strasbourg (comprising Upper and Lower Alsace) could be considered friends of the faculty, another 40 percent were entirely satisfied with it, and only 20 percent either opposed it or continued to reserve judgment.[98]

The strongest opposition to the accord came not from Catholics who thought it made too few concessions to the church, but from liberals who thought it made too many. It is unlikely that Berlin and the Vatican could have concluded an agreement of any sort in 1902 that would have satisfied German liberals. Certainly this one did not. The public disclosure of the accord's terms confirmed what many liberals already suspected: Germany had paid too high a price. Even the claim that the new faculty would contribute to the Germanization of the Reichsland failed to impress many liberal critics. The *Frankfurter Zeitung,* for example, insisted that the faculty's proponents overrated its potential; it should be remembered, the newspaper argued, that many of the Alsatians who had studied law and medicine in Strasbourg over the last three decades had been as hostile to German rule and culture afterward as they had been before.[99] Equally pessimistic was Karl Schrader, one of three liberals who criticized the accord in the Reichstag. How could the new faculty bring students of theology into contact with German intellectual life, he asked, when the Catholic theological faculties at other German universities could not even do this?[100]

But the claim that the new faculty would contribute little if at all to Germanization was not one many Strasbourg professors would have made. Most of these professors apparently now recognized that a Catholic theological faculty made sense politically; they seem to have shared the government's assumptions about the likely impact of the faculty. Of course most did not think such a faculty made sense on academic grounds, at least not if set up according to the terms negotiated. But under the circumstances public criticism seemed imprudent. And the professors were not only thinking of the political objectives at stake. Remembering their disheartening campaign a year before against another fait accompli, they also suspected that public criticism would result in reprisals. That they kept their objections to themselves suggests how much they now distrusted the government and how concerned they were becoming over their university's character and prospects.[101]

· 4 ·

"The university," complained a professor in 1906, "is no longer able to maintain itself at the level that was projected for it."[102] He was correct. In recent years there had been a gradual but indisputable decline in the quality of the institution's faculty: by 1906 most *Ordinarien* called to Strasbourg in the 1870s and early 1880s had vacated their chairs, and the replacements had on balance been of lesser distinction. This, together with the improvement since the 1880s of the facilities and curricula of most other German universities, had caused the University of Strasbourg to lose the high stature enjoyed in its early years. Once one of the country's three or four most renowned universities, it was no more distinguished in 1906 than the better provincial universities; it was on a par not with Leipzig and Munich, as in the 1870s and 1880s, but rather with Freiburg, Halle, Marburg, and Tübingen.[103]

Symptomatic were the changes that had occurred in the pattern of student enrollment. The number of students had grown considerably, but youths from the Reichsland were almost entirely responsible. In 1906 the number from outside Alsace-Lorraine was about what it had been in the early 1880s, even though there had been a significant increase in the number of students at other German universities. Particularly striking was the decline in Strasbourg's attractiveness to foreign students. In the early 1880s the university had enrolled about 9 percent of all foreigners attending German universities, but a quarter of a century later it only attracted about 2.5 percent.

The university's failure to retain its earlier stature can be traced in part to changes in the opinions of Germans about the Alsatian question. As it became evident that the Germanization of the Reichsland would at best be a prolonged process and that the university was falling short of initial expectations, the patriotic argument for accepting calls to Strasbourg became less effective.[104] Here it is appropriate to refer again to the crises the university had weathered in 1887 and in 1896–97, for although the institution did not suffer serious immediate damage as a result of either, the adverse publicity doubtless had harmful effects. It is easy to imagine scholars otherwise impressed with the conditions in Strasbourg turning down calls due to misgivings about an institution thought of, to paraphrase Friedrich Meinecke, as a greenhouse in an alien climate.[105]

But to explain the university's difficulties it is also necessary to consider the policies of the Reichsland's government. Most significant was the government's response to the faculty's budgetary proposals. Until the late 1890s the professors were reasonably content with the university's annual appropriations, but henceforth the situation was different. Aware of the rapid advances being made by other German universities, they believed that special efforts were needed if theirs was to maintain its position. Yet their sense of urgency was shared neither by the Landesausschuss nor by the ministry. Although the assembly habitually granted the funds necessary for existing programs and facilities, it tended to respond unsympathetically to requests for additional appropriations. In 1900, for instance, it rejected a proposed allocation to finance a small raise in faculty salaries and another to construct a pharmacological institute.[106] As for the ministry, it seemed equally unconcerned about the university's failure to keep pace. Around the turn of the century the professors became convinced that their efforts to shore up their institution were being stymied by officials who, in the words of a member of the medical faculty, "started from the assumption that the university and the professors made excessive demands."[107]

That the Landesausschuss should show little interest in financing new programs and facilities is not surprising. Although most deputies apparently viewed the university with respect, they could not be expected to treat generously an institution still widely regarded as an alien imposition. But why did the ministry show so little concern for the university's welfare? One reason was that officials in Strasbourg, like many observers across the Rhine, were disappointed with the institution's accomplishments as an instrument of nation building. They may not have thought its establishment a mistake, but they doubted the importance of maintaining it as a showcase of German learning.[108]

In addition the Spahn case had an effect. Although the Strasbourg professors had hoped their protests over Spahn's appointment would cause the authorities to treat them with greater respect, the effect was the opposite. Embarrassed and angered by the professors' outspokenness and concerned about the precedent, the government was hardly inclined to make special sacrifices for the university. Indeed some officials, including Althoff, seemed intent on reprisals. A striking example was the forced departure of the classical philologist Eduard Schwartz, a distinguished and popular member of the Strasbourg faculty. In the midst of the dispute over Spahn's appointment Schwartz received a call to Göttingen. Schwartz had spent the happiest years of his scholarly life in Strasbourg and had no desire to leave, least of all for a Prussian university. But a letter from the Berlin classicist Ulrich von Wilamowitz-Möllendorff, a confidant of Althoff, left him with no choice: for his own sake and that of the University of Strasbourg, the Berlin professor warned, Schwartz must accept the Göttingen position without procrastinating and without any questions. Unwilling to jeopardize the future of the Reichsland's university, Schwartz complied with this ultimatum. Under the circumstances he and his colleagues had reason to attribute this forced departure to the government's desire to punish the faculty.[109]

Finally, the government was responding to the change in the Alsatian political climate that came around the turn of the century. As the ministry's interest in conciliating the local assembly grew, its readiness to back the university declined. Here it is appropriate to refer again to the confrontation over Spahn's appointment (which itself resulted, in part, from a desire to appease the Landesausschuss).[110] This confrontation demonstrated that at least in the Reichsland the government had less to gain from respecting the faculty's wishes than from defying them. Articles in the Alsatian press and speeches in the Landesausschuss praised the government for resisting those seeking to keep Catholics in a state of cultural isolation and backwardness, spoke of strengthened support for the regime among Alsatian Catholics, and forecast a new era of harmony between the region's clerical politicians and the ministry.[111] Thanks largely to the professors' protest, Spahn's appointment took on a symbolic importance that served the government's interests: the lesson seemed to be that much could be gained by defying and criticizing the faculty. That this was not lost on the authorities is evident from the warning to the professors—disdainfully referred to as civil servants—made by Secretary of State Köller in response to praise for the government in the Landesausschuss: "I would like to think that enough discipline and decorum exist among the civil servants of the Reichsland's administration so that they do not express publicly and before the ears of others their depression or their discontents over an undertaking that does not succeed. If I should hear this, the civil servants in question will very quickly lose all influence with me."[112]

The government's reprisals and threats convinced the professors that their protest over Spahn's appointment had only worsened the situation. "The whole movement has remedied nothing," one observed. "It is very depressing that the voices of learning have simply been treated with contempt by the authorities on high. This cannot be without destructive and poisonous consequences for the future."[113] An immediate consequence was that the professors, sensing themselves on the defensive, began to lose the courage of their convictions. Persuaded that the government would prevail if there were another confrontation and conscious of their vulnerability, they henceforth behaved with greater restraint. A good example was their failure to criticize the accord authorizing the Catholic theological faculty. Another came after Wilhelm Windelband, the man most responsible for Strasbourg's distinguished reputation in philosophy, decided in mid-1902 to accept a call to Heidelberg. Aware of the government's interest in bringing a Catholic philosopher to Strasbourg, the faculty reluctantly included one, Clemens Baeumker, among its nominees to replace Windelband. The government, with Althoff participating in the negotiations, made a handsome offer to Baeumker, and he accepted it. Windelband's reaction to these events was symptomatic of the change in the mood of the faculty evident since Spahn's appointment: "We now live in the world of the least evil—even Leibnizian optimism is being reduced to this."[114]

Contributing to the faculty's deepening malaise was Köller's decision late in 1902 to replace Hamm as the university's curator, adding the position's responsibilities to those he already had as director of the ministry. The professors had little respect for Hamm but even less for Köller, an authoritarian Junker seemingly intent on politicizing the university. And Köller did not surprise them. During his five-and-a-half years as curator his treatment of the university was, in the words of one member of the academic community, "decidedly bad."[115] One example will suffice. Late in 1905 the historian Friedrich Meinecke received an offer from Freiburg. Meinecke did not want to accept it—"I wished to live and die in Strasbourg," he later observed[116]—but he found that the ministry's reaction left him little choice. As he informed a friend, "the negotiations over the terms of my remaining were conducted by the government with such indifference and at the end so insultingly that I could do nothing but accept Freiburg."[117] Why the ministry treated Meinecke in this way is unclear, but he and his colleagues suspected that the motives were political. Perhaps Köller had decided that Meinecke, who was known for his anticlerical and antiparticularistic opinions, was a political liability. Or perhaps he was still intent on punishing the faculty for its stand when Spahn and Meinecke had been appointed four years before. But whatever the motives, Köller acted on this occasion, as on others, with scant regard for the faculty's wishes and morale.[118]

As it became evident that the university was losing ground and that the resources needed to reverse the trend could not be expected from the Reichsland, friends of the institution began to speculate about the possibility of receiving greater support from other sources, notably from the imperial government. In the winter of 1902–3, for instance, it was argued publicly, without success, that Berlin should increase its annual subsidy to cover some of the Catholic theological faculty's expenses.[119] And three years later there was discussion of a much more radical proposal: giving the imperial government full responsibility for the university. The idea was first considered publicly in an unsigned article in the *Strassburger Post,* the newspaper with the closest ties to the Strasbourg faculty. The article noted that the empire granted 400,000 marks annually because the university had been a national institution in conception and was still regarded as such. "Yet nobody will deny," it continued, "that the University of Strasbourg has not maintained the high level to be expected of an *imperial* university . . . but rather is in essence a *provincial* university." Only if full financial and administrative responsibility were given the imperial government, the article suggested, could the university "become what it should be: a national monument, the pride of the German Empire."[120]

Such a change would certainly have had the support of most professors, but it did not appeal to the government. Shortly after the *Strassburger Post* advanced its proposal, Berlin's semiofficial *Norddeutsche Allgemeine Zeitung* reported that "in authoritative circles" there were no plans to change how the university was funded or administered. Since the institution was obviously becoming an integral part of Alsatian life, the Berlin newspaper argued, it should receive its financial support, beyond that furnished by the empire's traditional subsidy, from the Reichsland.[121] This article effectively ended, at least for a while, all serious speculation about redefining the university's relationship to the imperial and Alsatian governments. Like it or not, the university's fortunes now depended on the policies of the Landesausschuss and the Alsatian ministry.

# Becoming Alsatian

Through the first few years of the new century the major challenges facing the University of Strasbourg came from the government. Officials in Berlin and Strasbourg repeatedly intervened for purposes relating to their more general policies in the Reichsland, above all the conciliation of the local clerical party. But around 1908 the pattern changed. Although the university continued to face serious challenges, they now came less from the government than from Francophile and particularistic Alsatians and from certain Germans in the university community. This change occurred for various reasons. Some related to developments in France, for instance, and some to Alsatian cultural movements. But of fundamental importance was a shift in the government's approach to the administration of the Reichsland.

· 1 ·

In 1908 Köller resigned as secretary of state, and dominance in the Reichsland's government passed to officials favoring much different policies—notably to Count Karl von Wedel, who had recently replaced the ineffectual Hohenlohe-Langenburg as Statthalter. Whereas the Köller era had been identified with the conciliation of indigenous elites, the period that now began, commonly known as the Wedel era, was to be marked by efforts to promote social and political democracy. Köller's conservative policies had been misguided, Wedel and his associates believed, because they had helped to perpetuate a social order dominated by the Catholic clergy and upper-middle-class notables, groups much more Francophile than Alsatians generally. What was needed, instead, was a concerted campaign directed at freeing the masses from their deference to Francophile elites. Like those in the 1880s who had criticized Manteuffel's policies—policies resembling Köller's—the officials who now came to the fore thought it in Germany's interests "to politicize and to mobilize" the middle classes [*Mittelstand*] and the lower classes, the segments of Alsatian society most susceptible to Germanization. To this end, the Wedel regime launched new policies in a number of areas.[1]

To begin with, Wedel concluded shortly after taking office that the Landesausschuss, an indirectly elected body dominated by clericals and notables, should be replaced by an assembly elected directly on the basis of full manhood suffrage. He encountered considerable opposition in Berlin, much of it provoked by fears that the democratization of the Alsatian assembly would make it more difficult to defend Prussia's three-class suffrage, but he gained the support of the chancellor, Theobald von Bethmann Hollweg, and together they prevailed. In 1911 the imperial government approved a new constitution for the Reichsland that granted essentially what Wedel and Bethmann Hollweg had recommended. Henceforth there was to be a bicameral Landtag, with a lower chamber of sixty deputies elected directly and secretly on the basis of full and equal manhood suffrage and an upper chamber composed in equal measure of appointees of the emperor and delegates from various Alsatian corporate entities, the university included.[2]

Second, Wedel favored extending greater autonomy to the Reichsland. It was still too early to give the region full equality with the other German states, he believed, but some movement toward an autonomist solution to the Alsatian question was needed to encourage the development of "a healthy and justified particularism."[3] Predictably this recommendation met stout resistance from the military and from organizations such as the Pan-German League, but the imperial government's reaction was, ultimately, favorable. Although the new constitution introduced in 1911 fell short of granting Alsace-Lorraine full autonomy—for example, it gave the emperor the right to veto the Landtag's legislation—it made significant steps in this direction and appears to have satisfied Wedel.[4]

Finally, as part of its campaign to promote a particularism that was "healthy," the Wedel regime strongly supported the Reichsland's educational system. "I am a warm friend of the teachers," Wedel once observed, "because their important role as the molders of our youth gives them a claim to special consideration and because in general they have proven to be strong disciples of German culture."[5] The Statthalter was apparently thinking of the teachers in the primary schools, but he also had a high regard for those at more advanced institutions, the university included. This does not mean that the Wedel regime invariably gave these "disciples of German culture" the moral and material support they sought. But on balance, and in marked contrast to the Köller regime, it treated them with respect and generosity.

The first direct indication that the university could now expect strong backing came in January 1908. At an assembly of the faculty summoned at his request, Wedel spoke at length of the importance he attached to the university's scholarly and national missions.[6] That this was more than rhetoric became evident when, a few weeks later, the ministry requested and received the assembly's authorization for a major improvement in the salary scale for Strasbourg professors, the first since the university opened.[7] During the remaining six years of Wedel's administration the ministry habitually reacted with sympathy to the faculty's requests for new outlays, and it usually succeeded in gaining the assembly's approval. The result was a substantial growth in the Alsatian government's annual contributions to the university. Indeed, with the exception of the Universities of Berlin and Leipzig and the possible exception of one or more of the Bavarian universities (for which the relevant figures are not available), no German university enjoyed a larger gain between 1908 and 1914 in its total income from government sources.[8]

Closely related to the improvement in the ministry's attitude toward the university was the faculty's considerable success just before the war in filling vacancies with scholars of high distinction. In contrast to the situation during the Köller era, the ministry under Wedel strongly backed the professors' efforts to strengthen the faculty. Worthy of special mention are the contributions of Otto Back, a civil servant whom Wedel appointed in 1910 as curator. It was largely because of Back's persistence and resourcefulness that the university succeeded between 1911 and 1914 in calling such prominent scholars as the historian Walter Goetz, the classical philologist Eduard Schwartz (the professor who had left Strasbourg against his will early in 1902), and the philosopher and sociologist Georg Simmel.[9]

Yet despite such appointments, and despite the rapid growth in the university's budget, most faculty members were even more pessimistic about their university's prospects on the eve of the war than they had been during the Köller era. For although the professors were generally satisfied with the treatment they now received from the ministry, they had become increasingly concerned about certain tendencies in Alsatian cultural and political life with implications for the university. Of these trends the most significant was the development in theory and practice of what was known as the double culture.

· 2 ·

The term double culture and the associated ideas first became popular around the turn of the century, thanks to the efforts of a small group of Alsatian writers and artists. Fearing that forces then at work might lead to their homeland's full integration into Germany linguistically and culturally, these intellectuals promoted Alsatian cultural particularism. They insisted that there was a distinctive culture indigenous to Alsace-Lorraine, a double culture that had evolved through centuries of contact with the national cultures of France and Germany, and that it was essential to the future well-being of Alsace-Lorraine that the region continue to feel the influence of both of these great national cultures. "Upon the unique blend of Germanic and Gallic traits," argued one spokesman, "depend the Alsatian's special character and strength. To preserve and to deepen this double culture, which has in the course of time developed within him into something strong and durable, is his duty."[10]

Most Alsatians with opinions like these, the claims of some German critics notwithstanding, were in no sense revanchist. Rather, to the extent they were politically conscious, they sympathized with the Reichsland's autonomist movement. They may not have valued Germany's national culture more highly than France's, but they realized that an autonomous Alsatian state within Germany would provide an environment more favorable to the double culture than would the reunion of Alsace-Lorraine with a highly centralized France.[11]

But this is not to suggest that revanchist Alsatians shunned the double culture. On the contrary, beginning in the late 1890s several Alsatians who would have welcomed French rule publicly identified themselves with the concept. They did so for reasons of expediency. On the defensive culturally as well as politically, they saw in the double culture a useful front for their efforts to bolster the cause of French culture. These tactics were personified by Pierre Bucher, a young Strasbourg pediatrician who was from the turn of the century until 1914 the most resourceful and effective Alsatian promoter of Francophile cultural enterprises.

Bucher argued that since the Reichsland's "official" culture—that disseminated by the schools, the university, the major theaters, and the other state-supported cultural institutions—was German, special efforts must be made by private citizens to keep alive the influence of French culture if the double culture were to survive. And Bucher himself did his best to foster such efforts. In 1898 he helped to establish the *Revue alsacienne illustrée,* a handsome magazine that carried articles in German and the local dialect as well as French but devoted most of its attention to Alsatian traditions that were unmistakably French in origin. Two years later Bucher and some friends established the Musée alsacienne, a museum in Strasbourg specializing in artifacts identified with the period of French rule in Alsace-Lorraine. In 1903 Bucher oversaw the founding of the Cercle des étudiants alsaciens-lorrains, an organization of Francophile students discussed below. And over the next decade he helped to develop such enterprises as the Cours populaires de langue française (courses designed to give Alsatian girls a thorough knowledge of French and an appreciation of Parisian styles), the Cercles des annales (meetings at which French literary works were discussed), the Conférences (a series of lectures by literary and political notables from Paris), and the Société dramatique de Strasbourg (a theatrical troupe dedicated to countering the Germanizing influence of Strasbourg's state theater).[12]

During the early years of the new century the impact of efforts to promote the double culture, either as an end in itself or as a front for the promotion of French culture and revanche, remained confined to artistic and literary circles and to the French-speaking middle class. Judging from the response of the press and the Landesausschuss, most Alsatians viewed the movement with indifference. But with the Moroccan crisis of 1905 and the related nationalist revival in France, the situation began to change.[13] During the last two or three years of the Köller era both Francophile sentiment and support for the idea of the double culture grew rapidly in the Reichsland. And the trend continued after Wedel took office. In fact, as it became clear that Wedel wished to promote the democratization of Alsatian society and the development of a "healthy" particularism, those most threatened by these policies, the Francophile clericals and notables, grew more aggressive in their efforts to advance the double culture. By equating the double culture with Alsatian cultural particularism, and by presenting themselves as the leading defenders of both, they evidently hoped to discredit the Alsatians favoring cooperation with the government and to frustrate Wedel's efforts "to politicize and to mobilize" the masses. And they had considerable success. During the first few years of the Wedel regime the Reichsland's major political parties, led by the clericals, became increasingly reluctant to cooperate with the ministry and vied with each other in promoting the double culture by transforming such institutions as the university.[14]

"There is much at our university," complained an Alsatian politician in 1913, "that is not as it should be, and the assembly will have to strive continually to insure that the university shall one day finally cease to be 'a foreign body' in our homeland and become what it ought to be—namely, the center of our intellectual and cultural life as this has evolved out of the entire past of our homeland, and not just out of the half of this past that has received the official stamp of approval."[15] This was more than a call to action; it was also an attempt to justify what the Alsatian assemblies, the Landesausschuss and the Landtag that replaced it in 1911, had been trying to do for several years. Beginning in 1907, deputies had used the annual debates on the university's budget to introduce proposals aimed at making the university more compatible with Alsatian particularism. Few successes had been registered, but not for lack of effort.

Among the proposals introduced, two received particular emphasis. The first concerned the university's curriculum. In 1908 it was suggested that the ministry establish a professorship for the history of Alsace-Lorraine, to be occupied by an Alsatian. The proposal was repeated frequently in the next few years, and once was the subject of a resolution that received the assembly's unanimous approval.[16] The second major proposal concerned the composition of the university's faculty. Alsatian publicists and politicians repeatedly insisted that steps be taken to increase the number of Alsatian professors. (In a representative semester in this period 23 of the 159 faculty members were Alsatian but only 4 of the 66 Ordinarien.)[17] Frequently these demands were coupled with the charge that the university systematically discriminated against Alsatians when filling vacancies. In 1911, for instance, a clerical deputy called for a large reduction in the annual appropriation for the university under consideration to punish the professors for their prejudice against Alsatian scholars:

> We must once and for all make clear to the university that the Landesausschuss of Alsace-Lorraine is not willing to put up with the way the university community has treated our legitimate political and cultural demands, and that we will have little sympathy for the university so long as the professors in the various faculties continue, as they have until now, to slight our native *Privatdozenten.* It is in our university that we find our strongest adversaries.[18]

Although strongly attacked by the ministry's spokesman and by two liberal deputies, the resolution passed. For the first time the Landesausschuss revised downward a budgetary request for the university approved by its committee on educational affairs.[19]

The university's faculty reacted quickly. Worried about the precedent set by the assembly, the academic senate publicly criticized "the attempts to represent our university as being hostile to the progress of Alsatian intellectual life and of native intellectuals." Particular attention was given the charge that Alsatian scholars were systematically slighted when vacancies were filled. This contention, it was argued,

> is based on a misunderstanding of the principles that have always been followed by *all* German universities when filling professorial chairs. . . .
>
> When making proposals for appointment the University of Strasbourg certainly must refuse to recommend promotions only because the individuals involved are natives. If it did otherwise, it would sink down to the level of a welfare institution for those university teachers who have been born in the Reichsland.[20]

These remarks did not entirely refute the resented charges. The assertion that the faculty must operate under no geographical restraints when appointing or promoting scholars provided an attractive front behind which the professors could easily discriminate against qualified Alsatians. And there is reason to believe they did discriminate. One promising Alsatian scholar, the Protestant theologian Guillaume Baldensperger, reportedly was informed by a senior professor on the day he joined the faculty as a *Privatdozent* that he should "abandon all illusions, abandon all hopes of ever obtaining a chair in the university."[21] And in the opinion of Robert Redslob, an Alsatian who was from 1908 until 1913 a *Privatdozent* in the Faculty of Law, the professors in his faculty would have considered offering a chair to an Alsatian only "on the strict condition that he had first spent time at universities across the Rhine to become familiar with things German."[22] But actually the few Alsatian scholars, Redslob among them, who met this condition in the hope that they would soon receive a call to Strasbourg may have been ill-advised. There seems to have been only one case in which a Strasbourg faculty attempted to appoint an Alsatian teaching at another university: in 1909 the Faculty of Philosophy tried without success to call the Romance philologist Heinrich Schneegans from Bonn.[23] And even this may have been nothing but a token gesture to appease the university's critics. This is not to suggest that the Strasbourg professors would reject an Alsatian if he were the most qualified candidate, or that they would give priority to a non-Alsatian over an Alsatian of comparable distinction. But this may have been the case, and in view of the political situation and the few natives on the faculty it is easy to see why Alsatian observers repeatedly charged that it was the case.

Although the main purpose of the academic senate's statement of May 1911 was to refute the charge that the faculty discriminated against Alsatians, the document also commented on the proposed chair for the history of Alsace-Lorraine. The statement did not categorically reject the idea, but its observations were hardly sympathetic. After stressing that the faculty should decide all curricular matters, the document noted that "except in Bavaria, where there is, in Munich, a chair of local history, in no federal state, especially not in Baden and Württemberg, are provisions made at the present time for special chairs for local history."[24] The implication was that a chair for Alsatian history would not be academically defensible.

But here, as in its resistance to demands that they increase the number of Alsatian professors, the academic senate may have been influenced by more than academic considerations. Faculty members, it should be noted, had not always doubted the merits of a chair of Alsatian history. Earlier in the century they had hoped to establish such a position—in part, it seems, to undercut Martin Spahn's influence—and to give it to Hermann Bloch, a promising Strasbourg *Extraordinarius* from across the Rhine whose specialty was the history of medieval Alsace. They had had no difficulty justifying the position, arguing that it was desirable that recent French works on the history of Alsace and Lorraine be countered with objective scholarship. But after Bloch accepted a call to Rostock in 1904 the Strasbourg professors lost interest in the project, apparently convinced that if there were such a chair "we would always have to fear that—the way things are—it would be occupied by an ultramontane Alsatian."[25] With time their concern only intensified. By 1911 the professors assumed that a chair of Alsatian history would have to go to a native and that the position and its occupant would become rallying points for Alsatian students opposed to the Germanization of their homeland.[26] These assumptions go far to explain why the faculty no longer favored such a chair.

The faculty's position was not fully shared at the ministry. Indeed the curators and their superiors took several steps designed to conciliate those wanting a university more "at home" in the Reichsland. In 1908, for instance, the ministry made an agreement with Fritz Kiener, a historian of Alsatian origin who was a *Privatdozent,* whereby Kiener would, in return for a special subsidy, teach a course every semester or two on the history of Alsace-Lorraine.[27] A year later the ministry urged the Faculty of Philosophy to seek an Alsatian for its vacant chair of Romance philology; although the sequence of events is unclear, pressure from the ministry may explain why the faculty nominated Heinrich Schneegans for the position.[28] In 1911 the curator, Otto Back, assured the Landesausschuss, in a statement perhaps also intended as a warning to the professors, that he would "oppose with the greatest determination all forces that in any way tend to slight the Alsatian members of our university faculty."[29] Two years later Back implied in a speech to the Landtag that a chair of Alsatian history would be established for Fritz Kiener as soon as Kiener had published enough to justify his promotion.[30] And in the same year he gave an encouraging response when asked by Robert Redslob, who was about to accept a chair at Rostock, if there was any chance of his ever receiving one in Strasbourg: "We shall call you back to Strasbourg in the not-too-distant future. This is in accord with our policy. We wish to have Alsatians at our university."[31]

Perhaps these concessions were made reluctantly and would not have been made at all without pressure from the Landesausschuss, the Landtag, and the Alsatian press. But this was probably not the case. Unlike many of their German critics, government officials favored Alsatian particularism; they believed, to quote Wedel, that "the more Alsace-Lorraine becomes conscious of its own individuality, the more it must detach itself morally and culturally from France . . . and gravitate to Germany, which defends its economic and political interests."[32] Accordingly they probably thought that making the university more "at home" in Alsace-Lorraine would contribute to the region's Germanization.

But motives aside, many of the ministry's policies accorded with the wishes of the university's Alsatian critics. And to the extent they did, they added to most professors' deepening concern over the pressures aimed at adapting the university to the double culture, pressures which, as we shall now see, were coming from within the university community as well as from without.

· 3 ·

On the eve of the war the distinguishing features of the university as a center of learning were essentially what they had been three or four decades before. The institution was still an *Arbeitsuniversität* and as such attracted more than its share of advanced and industrious students. It still had a faculty notable for its intellectual vitality, its accessibility to students, and its commitment to the positivistic approaches to scholarship in vogue in the late nineteenth century. And it was still renowned for the excellence of its library (in 1914 it was the world's only university library with more than a million volumes) and for the number and size of its laboratories and institutes. Although the university had declined in stature since the 1880s, this was less because of a failure to maintain standards than because of advances made by other institutions; it remained a university of considerable distinction.[33]

But if the university's defining features as a center of learning had changed little, continuity did not characterize the extracurricular realm. The first few years of the new century were particularly unstable and innovative: under the influence of events outside the university, previously established social and cultural and political commitments now eroded and several new movements and trends appeared. Of the new developments, three had profound implications for the university and its nation-building mission. First, efforts by Alsatian students to foster French culture and revanchist sentiment became increasingly determined and provocative, a development closely linked with an organization founded in 1903 by Pierre Bucher, the Cercle des étudiants alsaciens-lorrains. Second, there was a steady growth in the number of Germans at the university who viewed sympathetically the ideal of the double culture and the related notion that the university should abandon its Germanizing mission and become, instead, a cosmopolitan center of learning. And third, there was a development within the faculty, long one of the most liberal and self-confident in Germany, of pessimism about their university's prospects and of what can perhaps best be termed a siege mentality.

When the Cercle des étudiants alsaciens-lorrains was established, Francophile sentiment among the university's Alsatian students, as among Alsatians generally, was clearly losing ground to particularistic sentiment. Most students now manifested no more than passing interest in the literary and artistic life of France and had, at best, a poor command of French. Indeed in intellectual orientation, if not in political identity, they differed little from many of their German peers: they read the works of Nietzsche and the German naturalists, participated in the Wagnerian cult (highly developed in turn-of-the-century Strasbourg), and, if Catholic, often identified with the Görres-Gesellschaft and the reformist currents emanating from Cologne and Mönchen-Gladbach. Nor was the trend confined to those from dialect-speaking homes. As the case of René Schickele illustrates, there were also students who used French at home yet, as a result of their schooling, felt more comfortable expressing ideas in German and more in tune with intellectual currents across the Rhine than with those across the Vosges.[34]

Social patterns reflected these changes. Many Alsatian students now had no inhibitions about socializing with Germans or at least with the growing number of "young Alsatians," the more or less Alsatianized children of German immigrants to the Reichsland. One symptom was the rapid growth after the turn of the century in the number joining German fraternities (particularly clerical fraternities). Another was the steady decline in the proportion, and perhaps also in the number, involved in activities and clubs with revanchist overtones. To be sure, the events most closely identified with student revanchism, the annual *Wurschtbankett* and the midnight procession (*monôme*) to the statue of General Kléber that traditionally followed, still took place every spring. But these events no longer attracted as large a share of the native students as they had in the 1890s—in the early years of the century about 100 students, roughly one-fourth of the university's Alsatian students, participated—and a growing proportion of those taking part were particularistic rather than revanchist in sentiment. Here, too, trends were against those favoring cultural and political revanche.[35]

It is against this background that one should view the Cercle des étudiants alsaciens-lorrains. For like many of the organizations associated with Pierre Bucher, it was founded not in response to rising Francophile sentiment but rather in the hope that it would defend French culture at a time when its popularity was manifestly in decline. This helps to explain why the Cercle had relatively few members—in its early years it enlisted only about twenty of the roughly 500 Alsatian students at the university—and why it was so enterprising in its promotion of Francophile projects. The Cercle systematically attempted to make up in boldness and visibility for what it lacked in size. In 1906, for instance, members celebrated Mardi Gras by displaying the tricolor outside a regular meeting place, the Taverne alsacienne, by singing the Marseillaise, and by forcibly ejecting from the Taverne the German students who dared enter. In 1909 the Cercle sent a delegation to an international student congress in Nancy, one to which other German students had not been invited, and afterward it entertained 200 of the French delegates in Strasbourg. A few months later it took part in the dedication of a monument near the Alsatian town of Wissembourg that commemorated French losses at a battle in 1870. In 1910 the club organized a conference to which it invited all the university's Alsatian students and, as featured speakers, Pierre Bucher and others of like persuasion. And every year it sponsored a formal ball and took the lead in organizing the annual *Wurschtbankett* and *monôme*. Indeed so numerous and conspicuous were its activities that the Cercle soon gained a reputation as the most important revanchist organization in the Reichsland.[36]

Generally the Strasbourg faculty, reluctant to stimulate Francophile sentiment, treated the Cercle in a conciliatory manner. Thus its committee on student discipline took no action against the Cercle for participating in the dedication ceremonies near Wissembourg, despite evidence that the club had violated university regulations and despite demands for repressive measures from newspapers across the Rhine.[37] And on another occasion the rector, in an act severely criticized by the pan-German press, persuaded a fraternity to abandon its plans to send an open letter of support to students at the German university in Prague; the rector feared such a letter might cause Strasbourg's Francophile students to retaliate with a statement of support for the students at Prague's Czech university, thereby heightening tensions within the university community.[38] In both cases, and in many others, the faculty attempted to avoid the mistakes made during the François-Martin affair of 1896–97, when provocative acts by German students and harsh sentences handed down by the faculty had played into the hands of those seeking to promote anti-German sentiment.

But there were two notable exceptions to this pattern, cases in which the faculty, put on the defensive by professional German chauvinists across the Rhine, decided it could not leave provocations unpunished. The first was the so-called Taverne affair, the flag-waving incident on Mardi Gras in 1906. Unwilling to disappoint the many German newspapers demanding reprisals, the faculty expelled two of the students implicated and suspended the Cercle for four semesters. Francophile Alsatians immediately charged that these sentences were unwarranted, and they had reason on their side. It is open to question whether the faculty had taken sufficiently into account either the festive atmosphere in which the incident occurred or the provocative efforts of German students to enter the Taverne alsacienne, a brasserie known to be a stronghold of revanchism. And it is clear that although the expelled students were members of the Cercle they were not at one of its functions or following its policies when they displayed the tricolor and sang the Marseillaise. As it turned out, however, the Cercle's supporters had little reason to complain. The club gained many new friends as a result of its treatment, as became evident when the faculty, in a conciliatory gesture, decided late in 1906 to lift its suspension; the reactivated Cercle quickly enlisted more members than it had ever had before.[39]

The second major confrontation stemmed from an article that appeared in 1911 in the club's recently established newsletter, the *Echo du Cercle.* Written under the pseudonym "Polemicus Vosgemont," the article was antireligious, mildly pornographic, and openly revanchist. In perhaps its most provocative passage it asserted: "Alsace needs a new generation of young men, bold and undaunted, unruly and impatient. The struggle will last a long time, but already we can see the summit upon which we will raise the red and white flag of our homeland, and on the horizon we see the blue of hope. France is the land of generosity, of progress, and of great ideas! We must not despair, the day of justice and freedom will come."[40] The Cercle's members had intended that their newsletter circulate only within the club, but they failed to take the necessary precautions. Late in May 1911 Essen's pan-German *Rheinisch-Westfälische Zeitung* obtained a copy of the article and used it as the basis for a vehement attack on the Cercle and on the Strasbourg faculty's conciliatory treatment of the club. Soon other newspapers, notably the *Kölnische Zeitung* and the *Strassburger Post,* were speaking out in the same vein. Prodded by these attacks, and determined not to let such an embarrassing situation arise again, the academic senate examined the provocative article and decided that severe disciplinary measures were in order. In mid-June they were announced: "Polemicus Vosgemont," a student of philology named Etienne Munck, was expelled from the university for life and the Cercle was permanently disbanded.[41]

Although these measures pacified the university's chauvinistic critics, the price paid was high. To begin with, Etienne Munck proved as great a source of embarrassment to the university after his expulsion as he had been as a student. On learning of his sentence he went to Paris, to be met at the Gare de l'Est with a hero's reception. Two days later he was the featured guest at a protest rally at the Hôtel des Sociétés savantes that attracted 5,000 Parisian students and declarations of support from student groups at most French provincial universities. This rally and the others provoked by Munck's martyrdom—including one in Nancy attended by the novelist Maurice Barrès and the Alsatian humorists Hansi and Zislin—did more to hurt Germany's interests and gave more encouragement to revanchist Alsatians than anything Munck had done while a student.[42]

As for the dissolved Cercle, it was not long before two new clubs had been founded to keep alive its traditions and carry on its work. The first had its origins in late June 1911, when Pierre Bucher and a few friends publicly invited all university-educated Alsatians to join them in establishing an organization designed to defend the interests of Alsatian students. The response was impressive. Whereas roughly 100 alumni had been associated with the Cercle at the time of its dissolution, the new club, known as the Cercle des anciens étudiants alsaciens-lorrains, quickly enlisted over 300. In addition, several students regularly attended the meetings of the Cercle des anciens as its guests.[43] Late in 1911 these students, having received the necessary permission from the faculty in another of its occasional conciliatory gestures, set up the Club des étudiants alsaciens-lorrains. The Club soon had as many active members as the Cercle had had when dissolved—about fifty, roughly 7 percent of the university's Alsatian students—and it was as Francophile and as assertive as its predecessor. Like the Cercle it helped to organize the annual

*Wurschtbankett* and *monôme,* sponsored addresses by prominent revanchists from both France and Alsace-Lorraine, and established contact
with student groups at French universities. In addition, it was largely
responsible for the publication of the *Almanach pour les étudiants et pour
la jeunesse d'Alsace-Lorraine,* a handsomely produced yearbook that
numbered among its contributors the French historian Ernest Lavisse and
leaders of the Reichsland's most Francophile political organization, the
Union nationale. Admittedly no serious confrontations occurred between
the Club and the faculty before the war, but this was probably due less
to restraint on the Club's part than to the misgivings of the faculty; the
professors seem to have been persuaded by the events of 1911 that disciplinary action would only worsen what was already a disturbing
situation.[44]

The activities of the Cercle and the Club, like those of certain groups
before the turn of the century, caused many Germans to conclude that
the university was failing in its nation-building mission. Far from Germanizing its Alsatian students, they argued, the institution actually exposed them to French culture and brought them under its influence. By
extension it jeopardized the future development of the Reichsland, particularly now that the region seemed likely to receive greater autonomy.
Typical were remarks in the *Strassburger Post* following the dissolution
of the Cercle: "We are running a serious risk. . . . What should be the
outcome if someday people with such convictions, as doctors and clergymen, as lawyers and judges, as engineers and pharmacists, or even as
officials in our administration, should have cultural hegemony in our state
and should slowly push out German culture to install their own in its
place? This development is by no means unlikely."[45] Some went on to
argue that drastic changes were needed. Nobody seriously proposed closing the university, but in the three or four years before the war a few
suggested requiring Alsatian students to spend a number of semesters at
other German universities, and at least one newspaper recommended
ending the imperial government's annual subsidy unless the university's
performance improved. The underlying assumption was that the university was doing more harm than good.[46]

But was it? To what extent were the sentiments of those in the Cercle
and the Club shared by others enrolled at the university? For that matter,
to what extent were they shared by the few Alsatians on the university's
faculty? These questions cannot be answered with precision. Doing so
would be difficult under the best of circumstances, and in this case there
are a number of complicating factors: the uncertainty of many concerning
what was possible or desirable for Alsace-Lorraine, the tendency of those
strongly supporting or opposing German rule to keep their opinions to

themselves for careerist reasons, and the strong incentives for Alsatians after the war to insist that they had always been French patriots.

But despite the problems, some observations can be made. To begin with, those in the Cercle and the Club were not the only Alsatian students dedicated to protecting the French cultural heritage of Alsace-Lorraine. In fact Bucher and his co-conspirators had never intended that these organizations embrace all Francophile students. The goal, rather, had been to organize the most uncompromising and resolute in the hope that they would set the tone for the rest. And to a degree they did. Inspired by the Cercle and the Club—and by the post-1905 nationalist revival in France— many other students became openly and assertively Francophile in the decade before the war. Some founded clubs which, like the Cercle and its successor, limited membership to Alsatians and stressed their home-land's French traditions. A number participated in missionary undertak-ings such as the Université populaire, a student-run institution founded in 1909 that offered courses, many on how to speak and read French, to working-class adults. Many spent a year or two at the Sorbonne or a provincial French university before completing their studies in Stras-bourg. Large numbers considered it their "patriotic duty," as one put it, to take courses such as Kiener's on the history of Alsace under French rule, Redslob's on French political thought, and those on French literature taught by Hubert Gillot, a lecturer who was the only French citizen on the faculty. Many participated in the demonstrations provoked by certain professors' insensitive remarks or actions. (Among the targets were the jurist Paul Laband and two Romance philologists, Wilhelm Cloëtta and Oscar Schultz-Gora.) And dozens not belonging to the Cercle or the Club made a point of attending the annual *Wurschtbankett* and marching in the *monôme* that followed.[47]

But these students were not all as intransigent as those in the Cercle and its successor. Many manifested an interest in German as well as French culture and socialized with "young Alsatians" and other Germans. And many admitted that German rule had had good consequences in some areas—the economy, social services, municipal government—and that they would be satisfied once Alsace-Lorraine gained full autonomy within the German Empire. These Francophile particularists, to give them a label, tended to take seriously the ideal of the double culture; unlike Bucher and those in the Cercle and the Club, they saw it as an end in itself rather than as a means to promote Frenchification. Hence it could be argued that they were actually compatible with Wedel's efforts to develop a "healthy" particularism, the claims of German critics notwith-standing. Whether these moderates outnumbered the purists is unclear. But as a rough guide, it should be noted that a student club founded in 1909 that catered primarily to Francophile particularists, the Association des étudiants alsaciens-lorrains, had about as many members at its height as did the Cercle.[48]

As for the Alsatian members of the faculty, those from French-speaking families, perhaps half of the total of about two dozen, tended to sympathize with Bucher and his movement. Yet their professional positions brought them into close contact with Germans and with German culture, and their reactions were not entirely negative; they had a high regard for German scholarship and for the university and were on good terms with some of their German colleagues. A few participated in Bucher's movement, but they seem to have had few ties to the purists among the students. Unintentionally they may have served as role models for Francophile students or, like Kiener and Redslob, taught courses that attracted these students for symbolic reasons. But it would be wrong to conclude, as some Germans did, that these faculty members contributed significantly to the French cultural revival at the university.[49]

Even if one assumes that the Francophile particularists were obstacles to Germany's assimilation of the Reichsland, a questionable assumption, it does not follow that the university was doing more harm than good. For the Francophile students accounted for only a minority of the university's Alsatian students, a minority that seems to have been declining in size proportionately and perhaps even absolutely. The best indication is the level of participation in the *monôme* that followed the annual *Wurschtbankett*. For the Francophile student marching in this procession for the first time was an eagerly awaited experience, something akin to a rite of passage, while subsequent *monômes* would not be missed as long as one remained at the university. Yet from the time the Cercle was founded until 1912, the last year for which a reliable report is available, both the number and the proportion of Alsatian students participating declined. In 1905 approximately 150 marched in the *monôme* (about 29 percent of the university's Alsatian students), in 1908 roughly 120 participated (about 19 percent), and in 1912 only 100 or so did (about 14 percent).[50] These numbers and rates suggest that the Francophile students were neither representative of the Alsatian students nor successful in reversing the trend away from French culture evident since the turn of the century. Since the appearance of the Cercle they had certainly become more active and conspicuous, but they apparently had not become more numerous.

In some respects, in fact, the Francophile purists may actually have fostered the trends they sought to reverse. For one thing, both the Cercle and the Club were strongholds of anticlericalism. This is not surprising considering their members' determination to emulate the styles and opinions identified with contemporary student life in France. But it was hardly conducive to winning influence among the Alsatian students who were devout Protestants or Catholics, as most were.[51] In addition, both clubs were socially exclusive. They restricted membership to students whose Francophile sentiments were beyond question, which meant that virtually all who joined came from the Reichsland's French-speaking elite. In this regard the Cercle and its successor, like the Francophile student groups of the 1880s and 1890s, functioned as "traditional socializing organizations": socially their mission was to reproduce an existing elite, not to create a new one. Judged from this standpoint their success cannot be questioned. They contributed new blood and youthful enthusiasm and dedication to the French-speaking elite, helping to end the once prevalent fears that it could not perpetuate itself. The change could be noted at the annual banquets of the *anciens,* affairs that attracted Francophile university graduates from all corners of Alsace-Lorraine. After the 1907 banquet, for instance, one organizer reported to his Parisian brother: "We were more numerous than ever, more than 130. . . . Saw many old buddies, had wide-ranging conversations on the progress of Germanization—noted with pleasure that the older ones and many of the younger sense, like us, that 'We are again filling the elites—we are gaining ground.'"[52] But these remarks suggest the problem. The sense that Francophile Alsatians "are again filling the elites" and the assumption that this was an objective of the Cercle and the Club tended to discredit these organizations in the eyes of Alsatians who were not Francophile purists. With good reason they saw these organizations as instruments for protecting the position of the French-speaking notables and, hence, as obstacles to upward mobility for those of more humble origin or less uncompromising opinions. In a sense the very success of the Cercle and the Club as "traditional socializing organizations," by helping to identify French culture with the perpetuation of a social order dominated by a relatively closed elite, limited their ability to set the tone for Alsatian students generally. The results were similar to those once noted by Robert Redslob in discussing the isolation of Strasbourg's indigenous haute bourgeoisie, to which he, like many *anciens* of the Cercle and the Club, belonged:

> This isolation, justified by the objective it pursued [to save the language at all cost], had unfortunate consequences. It presented a barrier to the young men arriving from the countryside to study at the University of Strasbourg and to prepare themselves for the higher occupations. It also offended many of the representatives of the lower middle class who had the ambition, often justified by their merits, to ascend the social ladder. Now these men, who had no reason to repudiate France and would have been delighted to remain loyal to her, frequently felt discouraged by the difficulty they faced, even the impossibility, in being admitted to the consecrated bourgeoisie [*la bourgeoisie consacrée*]. When this happened a great temptation was presented them. Spiteful, they only had to take one step to find the best of receptions into German society.[53]

But the Francophile purists' social exclusiveness was not the only factor limiting their influence. There were more fundamental forces at work, forces relating to the composition of the student body and to the students' career plans. Specifically, since the turn of the century three significant and closely related changes had occurred: the Alsatian segment of the student body had become more Catholic, it had become more representative of the local social order, and it had become less committed to the free professions.

Between the turn of the century and the war the number of Alsatian students grew rapidly. Whereas there had been 341 in 1898–99, there were 635 in 1907–8 and 810 in 1913–14.[54] (These figures and the observations that follow concern the male students; beginning in 1909 women could matriculate in Strasbourg, but prior to the war the number of Alsatian women at the university never exceeded a dozen or so.) Contributing disproportionately to the increase were Catholics: between 1898–99 and 1913–14 the number of Catholics grew more than threefold while the numbers of Protestants and Jews grew only 76 percent and 40 percent, respectively. Admittedly the Catholic theological faculty accounted for much of this increase, but even if this faculty is not counted the enrollment of Catholic Alsatians grew by 119 percent. Part of this increase can presumably be traced to the organized Catholic efforts, beginning in the 1890s, to challenge the Protestants' traditional dominance of the professions.[55] It is likely, too, that the addition of a Catholic theological faculty and the appointments of Spahn and Baeumker helped, as intended, to make the university less alien to Catholics not planning to enter the priesthood, thus encouraging some to enroll who would not have otherwise.

The growth in the number of Catholic students was related to the democratization of the student body. In the late 1890s, it will be recalled, the social origins of the Alsatian students had been relatively elitist by the standards of the time, thanks largely to the recent "discovery" of the university by the Reichsland's Francophile haute bourgeoisie. But a decade later the reverse was the case; by German standards (and by earlier Alsatian standards) the recruitment of Alsatian students was relatively egalitarian (see tables 4, 5, 9, and 10, appendix B). In part this was a delayed and temporary consequence of the low number of Alsatians at the university in the 1870s and 1880s: between the turn of the century and the war there was a dip in the number of Alsatian professionals with sons in the age cohort accounting for virtually all the students. But the Catholicization of the university seems to have been a more important factor. In the years before the war, to judge by the patterns in 1907–8 and 1913–14, 35.9 percent of the Catholic Alsatians enrolled at the university were the sons of peasants or artisans and another 24.9 percent came from the working class or were the sons of teachers or petty bureaucrats. These students raised the proportion of all Alsatian students from these backgrounds to 49.5 percent, as compared to 33.6 percent in the 1890s (to judge by the patterns in 1892–93 and 1898–99). Looked at another way, on the eve of the war 24.9 percent of the Catholic students— the sons of free professionals, entrepreneurs, merchants, bankers, and rentiers, half the sons of shopkeepers, and those from predominantly French-speaking districts—came from families more likely than not to have habitually spoken French. Using the same criteria the proportion of all Alsatian students in this category was now 31.9 percent, as compared to 35.5 percent in the 1890s. This is a rough gauge, admittedly, but it does suggest one reason the Cercle and the Club did not have more success in setting the tone among the Alsatian students: the Catholicization and democratization of the student body reduced, at least proportionately, their potential constituency.

Another reason, one related to the changing social composition of the student body, was the declining proportion of Alsatian students preparing for the free professions. In the decade before the war, as earlier, the Francophile movement drew most of its support from students planning to become doctors, dentists, pharmacists, or lawyers. When the Cercle was dissolved, for instance, more than three-quarters of its 101 *anciens* were in these professions.[56] But the proportion of the Alsatian students preparing to enter the free professions was in decline. In the late 1890s more Alsatians enrolled in the medical faculty than in any other, and those studying medicine, dentistry, pharmacy, or chemistry, along with three-fifths of those studying law (an estimate of the proportion intending to enter private practice rather than government service), had accounted for 60.1 percent of the university's Alsatian students. In 1913–14, by contrast, the Faculties of Law and Philosophy both had more Alsatian students than the Faculty of Medicine, and those apparently intending to enter careers in the private sector (measured as above) accounted for 40.2 percent of the total. More and more Alsatian students seemed intent on becoming clergymen, Gymnasium teachers, or government officials. And these were not students likely to manifest much sympathy for the Francophile intransigents either at the university or later.

Of the Alsatian students who were not Francophile some were basically German nationalists. They supported the campaign to Germanize their homeland and doubted the wisdom of a particularistic solution to the Alsatian question. Some belonged to Argentina or Wilhelmitana, Protestant confessional fraternities which became thoroughly Germanophile in the years before the war. Others, as if to flaunt their national sentiments, joined one of the university's Corps or Burschenschaften. Considered together these fraternities apparently attracted about one Alsatian student in eight, a proportion somewhat higher than that in Francophile organizations like the Cercle and the Club. And doubtless a few students who never joined fraternities had similar sentiments. But the number of German nationalists, like the number of Francophile purists, was relatively small; it is unlikely that it exceeded one-fifth of the Alsatian students. As for the Alsatians on the faculty, none seem to have been German nationalists at heart, with the possible exceptions of the Protestant theologian Gustav Anrich and the Catholic theologian Albert Ehrhard.[57]

The remaining Alsatian members of the university community—on the eve of the war perhaps half those on the faculty and half the students—were what can best be termed Germanophile particularists. Unlike their Francophile counterparts they habitually spoke German or the Alsatian dialect and had few reservations about mixing socially with Germans. And many of the students in this group joined German fraternities; by 1910 about one-third of the university's Alsatian students were in fraternities, most of them Catholic particularists in confessional fraternities. (In Germany as a whole at this time roughly half the university students belonged to fraternities.)[58] In addition, many particularistic students and faculty members cooperated with Germans in other extracurricular enterprises: glee clubs, literary societies, tennis clubs, political organizations, adult education programs, and the like. To cite but one example, Albert Schweitzer, from 1902 to 1912 a *Privatdozent* in the Protestant theological faculty, belonged to an informal group of students and young faculty members, most of them "old German," who shared an interest in music, in bicycling, in skiing, and in the progressive ideas of Friedrich Naumann.[59]

Much of the "healthy" particularism of these members of the university community can be traced to their geographic and family backgrounds. Most came from small towns or villages and were the sons of dialect-speaking peasants, artisans, pastors, teachers, or petty bureaucrats. But, as with those who became German nationalists, they also were affected by their experiences at the university. Usually unimpeded by familiarity with French culture or ambitions to join the Francophile elite, they tended to develop a high regard for their professors and for German scholarship and to prove vulnerable to the university's informal or "hidden" curriculum.[60] It was a development little noted at the time, largely because the Francophile students were more assertive and conspicuous, but it should be remembered when evaluating the university's success in its mission: not all of the university's consequences were unintended ones.

In sum, at no time in the decade before the war did the Francophile sentiments identified with organizations like the Cercle have the support of more than a minority of the university community's Alsatian members. With the aid of external developments—the nationalist revival in France, the worsening of the international situation, the periodic causes célèbres provoked by the excesses of army officers and the pan-German press—these organizations may have moderated the trend away from French culture. But notwithstanding the opinions of many German and French observers, they succeeded neither in offsetting nor in reversing this trend.

• 4 •

Support within Strasbourg's university community for Alsatian particularism was not confined to Alsatians. There were also many German students and a few German faculty members who backed the autonomist movement and identified themselves with the ideal of the double culture. One need not look beyond the university to find confirmation of the novelist Romain Rolland's observation, made after a visit to Strasbourg in 1905, that "there are a number of Germans, and not insignificant ones, who are becoming Alsatianized (*qui s'alsacianisent*)."[61]

Most of the university's Alsatianized Germans subscribed to ideas first popularized by a literary and artistic movement known as Youngest Alsace (*Jüngste Elsass*). Launched in 1901 by about a dozen Strasbourg writers and artists, most of them students at the university, this movement was zealously modernist and cosmopolitan. Its members were "good Europeans" who, influenced by Nietzsche, disdained positivism, "bourgeois" liberalism, and anything that smacked of cultural traditionalism or provincialism (including Young Alsace, a movement dating from the mid-1890s that promoted the Alsatian dialect as a literary language). Although they proudly identified their movement with Alsace, this was not because they hoped to preserve the region's distinctive traditions but rather because they valued its potential as a meeting place for trends emanating from Berlin, Munich, Paris, and other centers of literary and artistic modernism. Since Alsace was on the frontiers of Germany and France, they reasoned, it stood in the heart of Europe and could become the home of a truly cosmopolitan culture.[62] Thus in 1902 René Schickele, the leader of Youngest Alsace, predicted that the movement would transform Alsace, at present "uncultivated land," into "the new kingdom in the realm of art" and "a republic of the spirit into which will enter all for whom the highest ideal is a free, united humanity."[63] And years later Hermann Wendel, one of the movement's "young Alsatian" members, recalled that a special objective had been "to turn the German face toward Europe."[64] As these comments suggest, it was not only cultural life in the Reichsland that concerned the members; they also believed Alsace had contributions to make to the cultural development of the rest of Germany and the rest of Europe.

As far as the political future of Alsace-Lorraine was concerned, the members of Youngest Alsace had little to say. But implicitly they wanted the region to remain under German rule, if only because this would make it easier "to turn the German face toward Europe." Their views were perhaps best summarized by the hero of a novel by Otto Flake, another of the movement's "young Alsatian" members. "There is no place I would rather be," Flake's German protagonist replied to two friends critical of life in Alsace, "no place over there across the Rhine and no place up in the north. It is fortunate that there is within Germany a region where the German is forced to see that one can still live one's life differently than he does."[65]

As a force in the cultural life of the Reichsland and of Europe, Youngest Alsace fell far short of expectations. Symptomatic was the fate of the publication most identified with the movement, a literary review called *Der Stürmer.* Launched with high hopes in the summer of 1902, it ceased publication after only nine issues, none of which attracted 100 buyers. In the spring of 1903 a second attempt to establish a viable literary review had even more discouraging results: after three issues the publication was suppressed by the government for lèse-majesté (Schickele having called the emperor a charlatan). In the months that followed most of the more talented and ambitious members of Youngest Alsace, convinced that Alsace would long remain "uncultivated land," moved to Berlin or Munich. With this exodus the brief career of Youngest Alsace came to an end.[66]

Yet although Youngest Alsace died at an early age, its cosmopolitan ideas about the mission of Alsace survived. Indeed in the decade before the war these ideas became increasingly popular both in the Reichsland generally and among the German members of the university community. Thus by 1914 several German faculty members had publicly manifested their high regard for modern French culture and their interest in mediating between France and Germany, and others, particularly among the *Privatdozenten,* privately shared these views.[67] In addition many German students were, in the words of a disapproving government official, "won over at Strasbourg's university to the ideas of a double culture and of the mediating role of the Reichsland." Like Flake's protagonist these self-consciously modern youths tended to revel in the idiosyncracies of prewar Strasbourg—the cultural ferment, the live-and-let-live atmosphere, the burghers in the cafés with their absinthe and their Parisian dailies. And, true to their cosmopolitan ideals, they tried to keep abreast of literary and philosophical trends in France. If liberated students across the Rhine gravitated to the youth movement or to Friedrich Naumann or to Stefan George, their counterparts in Strasbourg often turned instead, or as well, to André Gide's *Nouvelle revue française,* to Charles Péguy's *Cahiers de la quinzaine,* and to the works of Henri Bergson and Romain Rolland. A striking example is Ernst Robert Curtius, a "young Alsatian" who went on to become Germany's leading authority on modern French literature and an outspoken foe of cultural chauvinism.[68]

Within limits these "good Europeans" welcomed the efforts of the Alsatians endeavoring to strengthen French influences in the Reichsland. Some even became friends of Pierre Bucher and, hoping to build bridges,

spoke to groups or contributed to publications with which he was identified. A conspicuous example was Werner Wittich, an economic historian
who taught at the university from 1895 until the end of the war. In two
widely discussed articles in Bucher's *Revue alsacienne illustrée,* Wittich
praised the "mixed culture" of Alsace-Lorraine, called for full autonomy
for the region and an end to policies directed at its Germanization, and
expressed the hope that German culture would become more and more
like French culture.[69] A second German associated with Bucher was the
literary historian and expressionist poet Ernst Stadler, a "young Alsatian"
and veteran of Youngest Alsace who in 1909 joined the faculty as a *Privatdozent.* Stadler wrote articles on contemporary literature for the *Cahiers alsaciens,* a bilingual monthly founded in 1912 by Bucher, and also
contributed to the *Almanach pour les étudiants et pour la jeunesse d'Alsace-Lorraine,* another publication linked to Bucher.[70] Other Germans
who wrote for periodicals or lectured to groups organized by Bucher
included Ernst Polaczek, a *Privatdozent* of art history, Kurt Singer, a
student of economics who later taught at the University of Hamburg, and
Katharina Dehio and Elly Knapp, daughters of two of the university's
most distinguished professors.[71] And had it not been for the war Bucher
might well have recruited one of the most illustrious of the prewar ad-
ditions to the university's faculty, the philosopher and sociologist Georg
Simmel. Illuminating in this regard, and also suggestive of the optimism
now prevalent among Bucher's German associates, is a letter Stadler sent
just before the war to his friend René Schickele:

> All sorts of things are in the air in Strasbourg. In Simmel we have a
> valuable ally for our cause. He is eager for action, wants the university
> to have a greater impact on the city, is politically reasonable, and is
> sympathetic to things Alsatian. . . . A cause for some hesitation is the
> fact that Bucher is making a strong effort to win him over to his side,
> and with his truly ingenious skill he may eventually succeed. . . . But
> this is a thousand times better than having him allied with the other
> side.
> Bucher is once again full of plans, about which I will report in detail
> some other time: a new journal, . . . a free university alongside the
> state's, and so on—in short: Strasbourg is to become a cultural center
> by importing French and German luminaries, Bergson, Simmel, et cet-
> era. This is all rather fanciful and vague, but it really seems to me that
> the time is near when something can be done here.[72]

· 5 ·

Although the number of German faculty members won over to the ideas
of the double culture and the mediating mission of Alsace-Lorraine was
modest, it was large enough and growing rapidly enough to concern those

still committed to the university's nation-building mission—the "other side" to which Stadler referred in his letter. Wilhelm Kapp, a Germanophile Alsatian with many friends on the faculty, complained after the war that there had been in 1914 "an imminent danger that, because of the innate weakness of Germans for the language and culture of France, the consciousness within the university of a commitment to and responsibility for the German cultural mission in Alsace-Lorraine would weaken."[73] And Franz Schultz, a German philologist who joined the faculty in 1910, later observed that by the eve of the war "destructive forces of various kinds were eating away at [the university]. Even within the faculty the tradition of German nationalism confronted an attitude that showed little sympathy for the national mission. Who is able to say where this development would have led?"[74]

In the years just before the war most Strasbourg professors shared the concerns expressed by Kapp and Schultz. And compounding these concerns was their fear that an autonomist solution to the Alsatian question might be in the offing. The professors assumed, reasonably enough, that full autonomy would bring an end to the university's annual subsidy from the national government. And no doubt it would also bring intensified efforts to Alsatianize and Catholicize the university. Put differently, with autonomy for Alsace-Lorraine the university, already under attack from "destructive forces of various kinds," would rapidly become a mere provincial university. It was a prospect most professors found abhorrent.

But how should they respond? On this, they disagreed. During the university's first three decades there had been a high degree of consensus on the faculty about the institution's mission and how best to promote it. But as threats to the university mounted—and as more and more members of the "founding generation" retired—this consensus dissolved. In its place emerged two distinct groups of faculty members, groups labeled by one professor as the chauvinists and the moderates.[75]

On national and international issues the chauvinists tended, by German standards, to be rather restrained or liberal. Several favored political and social reforms within Germany, for instance, and some became active in the ill-fated peace movement and the associated Verband für internationale Verständigung. Alternatively, they manifested less interest than professors at other German universities in colonial expansion, the Pan-German League, the naval race, or the other pet causes of authentic German chauvinists.[76] When it came to the Alsatian question, however, they saw little room for conciliation and, increasingly, no reason for self-restraint. A few examples will suffice. Late in 1907 the jurist Paul Laband complained publicly about "the lack of German nationalism and German culture in large segments of the Alsatian populace," and argued that Germanization would have to advance much further before autonomy could be seriously considered.[77] In 1912 the jurist Hermann Rehm orga-

nized a political party that catered to those opposing an autonomist solution to the Alsatian question, a group composed almost entirely of German
immigrants.[78] And in 1911 the philosopher Theobald Ziegler publicly argued that the Alsatian autonomist movement was out of step with the
centralizing tendencies of German history, rejected as untenable the idea
of the double culture and suggestions that it was the mission of Alsace-
Lorraine to mediate between France and Germany, and insisted that most
Alsatians were at heart Francophile and that autonomy would be merely
a way station on the road to secession. Ziegler concluded that only one
solution to the Alsatian question accorded with Germany's national interests: Prussian annexation.[79] Whatever the merits of these opinions,
their public expression played into the hands of the university's many
Alsatian critics.

Also hurting the institution's reputation were professors' statements
and policies concerning the university itself. In this regard the suppression
of the Cercle and the faculty's reluctance to promote Alsatian scholars
or to establish a chair of Alsatian history may have caused the most
resentment, but other actions contributed. Worthy of special emphasis is
the faculty's reaction to the Catholicization of the university initiated in
the early years of the century. Many professors, perhaps most, never
reconciled themselves to this development, and they did not disguise their
feelings. They ostracized Martin Spahn, avoided contact with the members of the Catholic theological faculty, and complained about "the swell-
ing of the ultramontane flood" among the students and its most conspicuous
symptom, the growing number of confessional fraternities.[80] When it was
the Catholic theological faculty's turn to furnish the university's rector
for the first time, its candidate, who normally would have been elected
without opposition, was challenged and almost defeated.[81] And when, in
1912, the Catholic philosopher Clemens Baeumker accepted a call to
Munich and the ministry informed the faculty that his replacement would
have to be a Catholic, the faculty's anticlerical majority, hitherto unaware
of this part of the agreement with the Vatican, launched a protest reminiscent of that against Spahn's appointment eleven years before. Like the
earlier one it failed, but not before exacerbating tensions within the faculty
and bringing the university under attack both from Alsatian Catholics and
from Germans who thought the professors should subordinate their convictions to the success of their mission.[82]

The stout and principled opposition of most professors to the Alsatian-
ization and Catholicization of their university, harmful as it may have been
to the institution's local reputation, was consistent with its traditions and,
it could be argued, with its interests as a center of learning. In these cases
unpopularity in certain circles may have been a necessary price if the
university's integrity was to be defended. But the faculty compounded
the situation by essentially symbolic acts related less to scholarly than to

political considerations. With each year, for instance, the pomp at ceremonies marking occasions like the Kaiser's birthday seemed more elaborate and the professors' speeches more chauvinistic. Honorary degrees
went to such outspoken foes of Alsatian particularism as the composer
Hans Pfitzner (the director of the local opera and conservatory) and the
expatriate Alsatian poet Fritz Lienhard. And to fill the university's seat
in the Landtag's upper house the faculty elected Wilhelm Wiegand, a
Prussian-born historian identified with the chauvinists, over the economist
Georg Friedrich Knapp, an essentially apolitical moderate highly regarded
by Alsatians.[83]

Some of the chauvinists were long-time members of the faculty who
found it impossible to abandon the values identified with the university's
early years. Nostalgic for the good old days of the *Gründungsjahre* and
the *Kulturkampf*, they were too rigid and jaded to adjust to the university's
new challenges. But most chauvinists were relatively recent appointees.
Generally they were less likely than their predecessors to have been attracted to the university by appeals to their patriotism (the appeals were
still made) and less prepared to make special sacrifices for the university's
mission. Their almost instinctive response to the rise of Alsatian particularism was to accentuate their ties to the rest of Germany. They made
no attempt to develop social relations with Alsatians, although the opportunities were greater than they had been earlier. Nor did they take
special pride in the university's unique traditions, a fact reflected in the
increasingly formal character of the professors' social life and in the faculty's retreat shortly before the war from its long-standing opposition to
such symbols of status as academic robes and honorific titles. Unlike
those in the founding generation, they did their best to emulate the customs
of academic life across the Rhine; frustrated and threatened by pressures
aimed at making the university more Alsatian, they reacted by trying to
make it more German.[84]

The moderates reacted differently. Rejecting the fortress mentality of
the chauvinists, they favored a response to the university's challenges
that was offensive rather than defensive. They had a strong sense of
mission—in this regard they were closer to the professors called in the
1870s than to the chauvinists—but they believed that the university could
fulfill its potential only if the professors made special efforts to increase
its influence. They considered it important, for instance, that faculty members try to know their Alsatian students better, show an interest in Alsace-
Lorraine and its traditions, and avoid insensitive statements and actions
at all costs. And many went on to urge that systematic steps be taken to
narrow the gap between the university and Alsatian society generally.
Much like Bucher and his collaborators, they sensed that they were on
the defensive and concluded that the only course was to counterattack.

It was no longer enough for the university to merit admiration as a center of learning; it must extend its influence.[85]

Some of these moderates involved themselves in local political and social movements. Thus the controversial Martin Spahn attained a prominent position in the Alsatian affiliate of the Center party, representing it on Strasbourg's city council and advising its youth group. And several young faculty members were active in the local branch of the social reform movement headed by Friedrich Naumann, a movement very influential in prewar Strasbourg.[86] Others, equally committed to narrowing the gap between the university and Alsatian society, concentrated on educational and cultural activities. Some focused their research and that of their students on Alsatian topics—on the region's antiquities, its history, its literary and religious traditions, its geology, and so on. A few offered public courses that attracted large numbers of Alsatians (courses in art history were particularly popular). Separate groups established two organizations designed, in part, to bring independent Alsatian scholars into close contact with the university, the Wissenschaftliche Gesellschaft in Strassburg, founded in 1906, and the Gesellschaft für Elsässische Literatur, founded in 1912. Professors in the theological faculties occupied prominent positions in local religious associations and frequently visited Alsatian towns and villages to conduct church services. And in the spring of 1914 two or three *Privatdozenten* joined several students, some of them natives, in organizing the Strassburger studentische Wanderbühne, a theatrical troupe that visited Alsatian villages on weekends to present plays by Goethe, Kleist, Theodor Körner, and Hans Sachs.[87]

For a long while faculty participation in such activities, the scholarly societies excepted, was largely confined to peripheral members, particularly to *Privatdozenten* and to professors identified with the faculty's small and isolated "clerical party."[88] But in the year or two before the war the pattern changed. Encouraged by the curator, the faculty made a series of appointments that greatly strengthened the campaign to extend the university's influence. One was the appointment in 1913 of the historian Walter Goetz. From the outset Goetz did his best within the university to end the isolation of Alsatian scholars such as Fritz Kiener, seeing this "as the first step in establishing contact with the Alsatians." And outside the university he managed in the ten months between his arrival and the war to give numerous speeches to Alsatian audiences and to publish an article sympathetic to particularism.[89] Another professor committed to extending the university's influence was the classical philologist Eduard Schwartz. During his earlier stay in Strasbourg, from 1897 to 1902, Schwartz had shown little interest in improving the relations between the university and Alsatian society, but when he returned in the spring of 1914 his ideas about what was required and his sense of mission were similar to Goetz's.[90] A third in this group, and potentially the most significant, was Georg Simmel. In nominating Simmel, an *Extraordinarius* in Berlin who probably would have long since had an important chair had he not been of Jewish descent, the faculty emphasized that "Simmel is a very exciting teacher whose lectures are among the most popular at the university in Berlin." The assumption was that his appointment would make the university a more lively place, enhancing its appeal to the general public. And this was the result. In his first semester in Strasbourg—the last semester before the war—Simmel offered a public course on "Cultural Problems of the Modern Age" that proved very popular with the city's indigenous bourgeoisie, and he did his best to persuade his colleagues to join him in offering courses likely to appeal to the general public.[91]

What the impact of such appointments would have been had the war not come is impossible to say. But some general observations can be safely made. To begin with, it is unlikely that a major improvement in the university's relations to Alsatian society would have come quickly or easily. Within the faculty there were still chauvinists who effectively, if unintentionally, perpetuated the university's reputation as an alien imposition and thus undermined the efforts of the moderates. And among the latter there were often sharp differences, particularly between the "clerical party" and the anticlerical majority, over how best to extend the university's influence. In addition there were potential obstacles outside the university. Presumably any attempt to make the institution more "at home" in Alsace-Lorraine would have been resisted by Germany's influential pan-German press. More subtle but equally effective resistance might have come from Bucher and his collaborators, who did not stand to gain if the university's reputation with Alsatians improved. And, as always, there were the region's deep-rooted religious rivalries. It was often difficult to improve the university's relations with specific groups of Alsatians without offending others for sectarian reasons. The response to Simmel's appointment was symptomatic. Greeted warmly by Francophile and liberal Alsatians, the appointment came under strong attack from a Catholic deputy in the Landtag—and from the faculty's "clerical party"—on grounds that Simmel's religious and ethical views were "negative" rather than "positive."[92] Clearly efforts to improve the university's local popularity and influence would always be complicated by differences among Alsatians over what kind of university they wanted.

But despite the uncertainties, the university's reputation with Alsatians probably would have improved had the war not intervened. By 1914 the influence within the faculty of the moderates dedicated to this goal seems to have been dominant. An important catalyst was the acrimonious Saverne affair of late 1913, an incident provoked by an army lieutenant who insulted Alsatians and a commanding officer who responded to the resulting furor by imposing martial law. The officers' behavior and the mild reaction of the authorities in Berlin outraged the Reichsland's German

civilians as well as the Alsatians—for the first time many Germans identified with the Alsatians and their grievances—and reminded those who
still needed reminding of the virtues of moderation and self-restraint.[93]
The change in climate was soon evident at the university. In selecting
candidates for vacant chairs, for example, the faculty began to eliminate
from consideration scholars known to be outspoken chauvinists. And they
now viewed with favor the efforts of those intent on bridging the gap
between the university and Alsatian society. The case of Walter Goetz is
particularly instructive. In his two semesters at the university—his tenure
effectively ended when the war began and he joined the army—he demonstrated how much a moderate committed to the university's mission
could accomplish. He came to Strasbourg with an open mind concerning
the Alsatian question and a belief that the Alsatians had the right to expect
"that we accommodate ourselves to their interests and their existence.
Accordingly I attempted to familiarize myself as quickly as possible with
the history and culture of the region and with the spirit of the people, and
to seek out the numerous students who came from the region and to learn
from them."[94] It is a mark of the changing atmosphere within the faculty
that Goetz and his empathetic attitude proved popular not only with relative outsiders like Fritz Kiener ("Your activity in Strasbourg will never
be forgotten and will leave behind much that is good and lasting"), but
also with the faculty's majority; had he not been on leave early in 1915
Goetz apparently would have been elected to replace Wilhelm Wiegand
as the faculty's representative in the Landtag.[95]

All this suggests that the faculty members had profited from the challenges faced in recent years. In particular the French cultural revival
seems to have strengthened their sense of mission and given them a more
realistic outlook concerning the university's interests. From the outset
the prevalent opinion had been that no special concessions should be
made to local needs or pressures, for such concessions inevitably would
tarnish the university's integrity as a center of learning. But in the year
or two before the war this attitude changed. The professors remained
committed to upholding the university's stature, but they began to realize
that this might be consistent with taking steps to make the institution more
popular. In this regard it is noteworthy that the three leading moderates
appointed in this period—Goetz, Schwartz, and Simmel—were also among
the most distinguished scholars called to Strasbourg in recent years, and
that each apparently was attracted less by the university's stature than
by a desire to contribute to its mission by extending its influence. This
helps to explain why the faculty was now inclined, as one member later
observed, "to give up a certain national rigidity and to make some concessions to a more European mentality":[96] it had become evident that such
concessions not only could improve the university's relations with Alsatian society but also could strengthen its reputation as a center of learn-

ing. This change in outlook enhanced the moderates' position within the faculty and gave them reason to believe that a new and more successful period in the university's history was beginning. As a moderate later recalled, "one felt that now something was finally happening."[97] He was commenting on the atmosphere during the summer semester of 1914, a semester cut short, like the optimism, by the war.

# 7

# From *Universität*
# to *Université*

The coming of the war both disrupted the normal functioning of the university and transformed its prospects. Students were called up for military service, causing enrollments to plummet. University buildings became military hospitals. Younger professors enlisted and the rest turned much of their time and energy to war-related research, to special courses for injured and furloughed soldiers, to moonlighting as orderlies. In almost every respect the university became an extension of the war effort.

As for the future, obviously the university's fate would depend on the war's outcome. Yet even if Germany won, there doubtless would be major changes. By stimulating chauvinistic passions and strengthening misgivings among Germans about the Alsatians' loyalties, the war made it unlikely that the university would continue to become more Alsatian or more European. And if Germany lost the war and Alsace-Lorraine, the institution presumably would be replaced by an entirely different one. In either case, the war could be expected to result in a redefinition of the relationship between higher education and Alsatian society.

· 1 ·

"When the war broke out," a former Strasbourg professor observed years later, "Alsace stood almost unanimously on the German side."[1] He was basically correct. In the first few days of the war Alsatians generally believed that Germany's responsibility was no greater than that of the allied powers and expected and hoped that the German army would win a quick victory.[2] And these also seem to have been the sentiments of most of the Alsatians attending the university. Indeed one professor came away from a ceremony honoring those students joining the army (about two-thirds of the total) convinced that "complete national unity within the student body has been established."[3] He was overly optimistic (a common failing of German professors in the early days of the war), but probably no more than a small minority of the Alsatian students hoped from the outset for Germany's defeat.

It was not long, however, before sentiments changed. In the autumn of 1914 sympathy for the German cause among Alsatians began to wane, and the trend was to continue through the remainder of the war. The

195

turning point came with the Battle of the Marne. The news of France's success in this decisive battle activated in many Alsatians a pride in France hitherto latent and convinced others that it was in their interest—it now being apparent that Germany would not win the war quickly and might not win at all—to disassociate themselves from the German war effort.[4] These developments, in turn, made the Reichsland's military and civilian officials more nervous and more repressive. Censorship of the press and of private correspondence, introduced just before hostilities began, became more severe; politicians and priests suspected of Francophile sympathies came under close surveillance; Alsatian soldiers were treated by superiors in a discriminatory manner; and policies concerning the public use of French became harsher than any known before the war. Such measures alienated most Alsatians. Increasingly convinced that they could never be anything but second-class citizens within Germany, they became less and less sympathetic to the German cause. By February 1918 the situation had so deteriorated that the Statthalter had to warn Berlin that "Germany cannot take the risk of staging a referendum concerning the future of Alsace-Lorraine."[5] And by the eve of the armistice, a Germanophile observer estimated, 90 percent of the Alsatians wanted reunion with France.[6] As for the roughly 200 Alsatians now attending the university, no doubt they were as anxious for French rule as Alsatians generally.

With Alsatians increasingly hostile to all things German, the university could hardly survive unscathed. But it would have fared better had it not been for the wartime activities of its faculty. Particularly damaging were professors' contributions to the war effort as propagandists and certain decisions made concerning the university itself.

Although it would be going too far to say they welcomed the war, many Strasbourg professors, like many professors at other German universities, welcomed the opportunities the war gave them to serve as mentors to the German people and the German government. The result was an outpouring of propaganda, most of it chauvinistic and, accordingly, offensive to Alsatians. Early in the autumn of 1914, for instance, Albert Ehrhard, Paul Laband, and Martin Spahn signed the notorious "Manifesto of the Ninety-Three," a document addressed "to the civilized world" that referred to the "hard struggle for existence" forced on Germany, defended the German army against charges that it had violated Belgian neutrality and mistreated Belgian civilians, and insisted that "the German army and the German people are one."[7] A little later roughly three-quarters of the university's German professors supported a manifesto stating, in part, "it is our belief that the salvation of all of European culture is dependent upon the victory that German 'militarism' is going to win."[8] In addition faculty members delivered hundreds of public addresses on patriotic themes, often under the auspices of a government program that sent itinerant lecturers to Alsatian towns and villages to deliver "enlightening speeches."[9] And certain professors made chauvinistic contributions to the public debate over war aims. Martin Spahn, for instance, recommended in the autumn of 1914 that Germany annex Belgium and the French channel ports, and early in 1918 he called for the annexation of much of French Lorraine.[10] And in the last year and a half of the war at least four faculty members—Spahn, the philosopher Max Wundt, and the jurists Erich Jung and Hermann Rehm—publicly opposed the democratization of the Prussian and German constitutions.[11]

There were, to be sure, German professors who disapproved of such activities. Thus the economists Georg Friedrich Knapp and Werner Wittich refused to sign the patriotic manifestos that circulated at the university—to Knapp they bore "a strong similarity to the tribal chants of the Sioux Indians"—and apparently opposed the government's program of "enlightening speeches."[12] But under the circumstances it was difficult to publicize their opinions. Symptomatic was a controversy in 1915 involving Georg Simmel. The military officials who in effect now ruled the Reichsland were so incensed by remarks Simmel had made about Alsace-Lorraine and German attitudes toward France in two newspaper articles, one in the _Berliner Tageblatt_ and the other in Stockholm's _Svenska Dagbladet,_ that they tried to have him removed from his chair. The curator and the rector managed to persuade them that Simmel's intentions were not anti-German, and Simmel was let off with a warning that during the war Strasbourg professors should not publish articles such as his.[13] In this atmosphere it is not surprising that professors with moderate opinions on the Alsatian question or Germany's war aims tended to keep their silence. But their restraint made it all the easier to conclude, as many did, that the university had become a bastion of political reaction and pan-Germanism.[14]

Also damaging the university's reputation was the faculty's discrimination against Alsatian scholars who were not openly Germanophile. Such discrimination was not new, but it now became more pronounced. No longer, it seems, were serious attempts made to add to the number of Alsatian professors. In one case an Alsatian, assured earlier that he would soon receive a chair, was overlooked on two occasions when appropriate vacancies appeared.[15] And natives already on the faculty who were sympathetic to Alsatian particularism found themselves snubbed by many colleagues and effectively excluded from positions of responsibility. Revealing is a case involving the Catholic theologian Eugène Muller, an Alsatian and a strong critic of the repressive policies now pursued in the Reichsland. Early in 1917 the Catholic theological faculty, whose turn it was to furnish the next rector, nominated Muller. But when the professors from all faculties convened for the election—usually a mere formality—the majority, guided by political considerations, passed a resolution declaring Muller "not acceptable" and gave the post to a German in the Protestant theological faculty.[16] These acts, which could not be concealed from the public, provoked strong attacks on the university in the local press and in the Landtag. In fact, so indignant were the assembly's members at this affront to one of their compatriots that they twice rejected the bill funding the university for the next fiscal year, and on the third reading passed it by only a few votes.[17] Never before had the gulf between the university and Alsatian society been so wide or so visible.

The combination of the war and the growing disaffection of the Alsatians deepened the professors' concern over their university's future. Although most professors assumed almost to the end that Germany would win the war and retain Alsace-Lorraine, there was always the possibility of defeat. And even if Alsace-Lorraine did remain German, relations between Germans and Alsatians would be much worse than they had been before the war. Thus under the best of circumstances the university's position after the war would be very difficult.[18]

This prospect crippled efforts to maintain the faculty's quality. With the war the university's recent good fortune in filling vacant chairs came to an end. Efforts were still made to call distinguished scholars, but they invariably failed, largely because those sought were concerned, as one put it, about "the general uncertainty of the political development of Alsace and also, because of this, of the prosperity of the University of Strasbourg."[19] At the same time some Strasbourg professors successfully sought positions across the Rhine ("the rats are leaving the sinking ship," one Alsatian student remarked).[20] The effect was to worsen the malaise that already characterized the faculty.[21]

But many professors enjoyed one consolation. The worsening situation in Alsace-Lorraine made it easier to lobby for changes in the way the region was governed, changes giving greater protection to the university. Within months of the start of the war almost all the professors had concluded that the Reichsland as such could not continue to exist. And although censorship made it difficult to express their opinions publicly, they did an effective job of bringing them to the attention of Berlin: working primarily through private channels—letters, petitions, private audiences— several professors solicited official support for a solution to the Alsatian question consistent with their own interests and with their conception of Germany's.

Yet while the professors were almost unanimous in their desire for change, they did not agree on what changes should occur. There were three basic positions. First, some favored a plan whereby the Reichsland would be dismantled, Prussia would annex Lorraine, and Bavaria would incorporate Alsace. They argued that the ties between Alsace and the rest of Germany would become stronger if Alsace joined the "old German" state with which it had the most in common culturally and politically, Bavaria. As for Lorraine, military and economic considerations dictated assigning it to Prussia. The professor most prominently identified with these opinions was Albert Ehrhard. Early in the war he discussed his proposals in an audience at the Bavarian court (where interest in the annexation of Alsace was already strong), and late in 1916 he sent a memorandum on the subject to Chancellor Bethmann Hollweg and, subsequently, to the rulers of the various German states.[22] Other Strasbourg professors supporting this plan included the historian Georg Wolfram, the philosopher Arthur Schneider, the jurist Fritz van Calker, and, it seems, several of Ehrhard's colleagues in the Catholic theological faculty.[23]

A much larger group favored a Prussian solution to the Alsatian question. They also thought the best way to counter particularistic and revanchist sentiment in Alsace would be to attach the region to another German state, but for various reasons, anticlericalism prominent among them, they wanted the favored state to be Prussia. In the summer of 1915 this solution was recommended to the imperial government by the Elsass-Lothringische Vereinigung, an organization with close ties to the Strasbourg faculty.[24] And a few months later Lujo Brentano found during a visit to Strasbourg that almost every German with whom he spoke wanted Alsace joined to Prussia.[25] Among the professors known to have been sympathetic were the classical philologist Eduard Schwartz, who in 1916 defended the plan in a speech in Berlin and in a memorandum to the imperial government, the historian Harry Bresslau, the jurist Otto Lenel, the oriental philologist Theodor Nöldeke, and the romance philologist Oscar Schultz-Gora.[26]

Finally, a few professors wanted concessions to Alsatian particularism. Some, to be sure, were natives now privately convinced that the most desirable solution to the Alsatian question was a French one. In this group, it seems, were the historian Fritz Kiener, the Protestant theologian Paul Lobstein, and Eugène Muller.[27] But at least two German professors, Fritz van Calker and Werner Wittich, actively promoted a conciliatory approach. Van Calker did so beginning in 1917, after concluding that the Bavarian solution he had earlier favored was no longer feasible. In July 1917 he defended his new position at a meeting of the Reichstag's interparty committee (he had been elected to the Reichstag in 1912 as a National Liberal) and recommended, without success, that the peace resolution being prepared include a promise of autonomy for Alsace-Lorraine.[28] As for Wittich, he attempted on numerous occasions to convince government officials and others that the current regime was unnecessarily harsh and that it was in Germany's interests to make concessions to Alsatian particularism. He expected little—"I am preaching in the desert," he observed to an Alsatian friend[29]—but he did have an impact in some circles. Thus his revelations about the use and abuse of preventive detention in the Reichsland caused Lujo Brentano to complain to the chancellor, to resign from the chauvinistic Kulturbund deutscher Gelehrter und Künstler, and to recommend publicly that Alsace-Lorraine receive full autonomy.[30]

Until 1917 the debate within the government over the Alsatian question was dominated by supporters of the Bavarian and the Prussian approaches. But beginning in July 1917 the situation changed. For reasons related both to domestic political considerations, notably the reluctance of the other states to see Prussia or Bavaria strengthened, and to interest in a compromise peace, support for an autonomous Alsace-Lorraine now increased rapidly. By late summer this objective apparently had the backing of most Reichstag deputies, and it soon received support from the chancellor's office as well: as part of his agreement with the Reichstag upon becoming chancellor in October, Georg Hertling repudiated the Bavarian solution, which he had earlier promoted, and declared his qualified support for autonomy.[31]

These developments—and rumors concerning them—caused the professors to intensify their lobbying efforts. Thus in August 1917 a group sent the chancellor a strongly worded memorandum arguing that autonomy must be avoided at all costs.[32] At about the same time a few Strasbourg professors together with a few Freiburg professors began soliciting support in the German academic community for a petition declaring that the Reichstag's majority—with its commitment to a compromise peace and its growing interest in an autonomous Alsace-Lorraine—did not represent most Germans. When the petition was made public, in October, it bore the signatures of 906 professors.[33]

The events of 1917 also encouraged the Strasbourg faculty to undertake a new lobbying venture, one concerned not with the Reichsland generally but with the university. Until now the professors had assumed that their university's future would depend on decisions made concerning the government of Alsace-Lorraine. Indeed this assumption helps to explain why they had been so interested in the Prussian solution to the Alsatian question. As one professor observed privately, "best of all would be unification with Prussia; I believe . . . this would also be the best thing for the university; Strasbourg would certainly be treated by Berlin just as well as Bonn and Göttingen."[34] But in mid-1917 the professors turned their attention to another possibility, one that might be even better for the university. In July the academic senate unanimously agreed to seek a large increase in the annual imperial subsidy to the institution. Apparently the ultimate goal was to have the national government assume full responsibility for the university.[35]

The official response was encouraging. The Statthalter, Johann von Dallwitz, seconded the proposal: "This measure is necessary," he argued late in 1917, "to ensure that the youth of Alsace-Lorraine receive their academic training in the German way, and to keep the university in harmony with the intellectual currents dominant at the other German universities."[36] And the faculty also found support in Berlin. Although not promising to give the imperial government full responsibility for the university, high officials assured a faculty delegation early in 1918 that after the war their institution would be raised to the level of Germany's leading universities. Evidently the professors were not the only ones convinced, as one of their memorandums asserted, that "maintaining an eminent university in Strasbourg will be even more necessary after the war than it was before."[37]

During the eleven months of Hertling's tenure as chancellor the Alsatian question and the question of the future of the University of Strasbourg remained unresolved. Other than the pledge given to the faculty's delegation early in 1918, nothing was done about the university. Nor were any decisions made concerning who should rule Alsace-Lorraine, in part because the Supreme Command, which now dominated the government, would not accept an autonomist solution and in part because the major German states could not agree on any other.[38] (Although the Strasbourg professors' recommendations were frequently cited in government circles, their influence was at best secondary.)[39] But with Max von Baden's appointment as chancellor early in October 1918 and the related reassertion of the Reichstag's influence the situation changed abruptly. By appealing to Woodrow Wilson for peace negotiations on the basis of the Fourteen Points, the new chancellor as much as conceded that German rule in Alsace-Lorraine would not survive the war. (The news of this appeal, which reached the Reichsland on 6 October, ended the lingering optimism on this score hitherto shared by most Germans on the Strasbourg faculty.)[40] Yet although Max von Baden and his advisers were resigned to the loss of Alsace-Lorraine, they still hoped that the peace settlement might result not in a French solution to the Alsatian question but rather in the formation of an independent and neutral Alsatian state. And in any case the government now had nothing to lose by attempting to conciliate the region's natives. Accordingly the authorities, moving quickly, set out to remove the last vestiges of the Alsatians' second-class citizenship. On 18 October an Alsatian, Rudolf Schwander, was appointed Statthalter, and within the next few days a bill was framed extending full autonomy to Alsace-Lorraine within the German Empire—and, with it, full Alsatian control over the University of Strasbourg.[41]

But these measures impressed neither the allied powers, committed as they were to a revanchist solution to the Alsatian question, nor the majority of Alsatians, who for emotional and pragmatic reasons were no longer prepared to exhibit allegiance to Germany.[42] To expect under these circumstances that political initiatives could compensate for what was being lost on the battlefield was to expect too much. The fate of Alsace-Lorraine, and of its university, was now in the hands of the French.

• 2 •

France did not go to war over Alsace-Lorraine, but once hostilities began the lost provinces moved to the top of her list of war aims. Indeed it was the one war aim on which the French generally and consistently agreed throughout the war. Admittedly a few on the political left favored a plebiscite in the region, but only to show the world that France had nothing to fear; like the others, they were confident the Alsatians would welcome their return to *la mère patrie*.[43]

Yet while there was agreement that Alsace-Lorraine and France must be reunited, there was none concerning what should follow. Some assumed that reintegration would be simple; the rapid introduction of the laws and policies in force in the rest of France would suffice. But many disagreed, arguing that after four decades of German rule it was unreasonable to expect Alsatians to adjust easily to reunion. These concerns convinced government officials and others that the matter should be examined systematically. The result was the formation of several study groups and the commissioning of numerous reports. The recommendations that emerged were to lay the foundations for postwar policies in many areas, higher education included.

Of the sets of proposals concerned with higher education, three merit particular attention. The first came from the Conférence d'Alsace-Lorraine, a study group established in February 1915 by the Ministry of Foreign Affairs. On 22 March 1915 the Conférence unanimously approved a resolution calling for a new university in Strasbourg to replace the German one.[44] In most respects it was to be a typically French institution, but two breaks with French precedents seemed advisable. One concerned the language of instruction. Without debate the Conférence resolved that French must have primacy but that "it will be beneficial if certain courses are given in German, if only as a means of attracting to Strasbourg students from other French universities eager to perfect themselves in the German language."[45] The second concerned instruction in theology. The Conférence favored postponing the introduction in Alsace-Lorraine of the French legislation separating church and state, meaning that the new university could have theological faculties. Yet there would be strong opposition to such faculties within the French academic community, a bastion of anticlericalism. In addition some Catholic clergymen—notably Emile Wetterlé, an Alsatian refugee and a participant in the Conférence—did not want a republican and anticlerical government supervising the training of priests. Faced with these pressures, the Conférence proposed a compromise. In lieu of a Catholic theological faculty at the university it called for one or more "free" faculties to be subsidized by the government but beyond its control. As for Protestant theology, the Conférence favored maintaining a faculty at the university, but in the event of complications this faculty could also be "free."[46]

The second set of recommendations appeared a few months later in a twenty-one-page report prepared for an agency of the Ministry of War located in Belfort. There is reason to believe the author was Hubert Gillot, a French citizen who had been a lecturer at Strasbourg's German university from 1902 until the war.[47] In any case, the author clearly knew the German university at firsthand.

The first section of the report dealt with the German university, tracing its history and describing its features. After praising the university's facilities and the scholarly distinction and dedication of the first generation of professors, it emphasized that after the turn of the century—after "the heroic period of its history"—the university had gone into progressive decline. It was particularly critical of the Catholicization of the institution ("to be of Catholic birth counted in university circles as a certificate leading to a rapid and brilliant career"). The report neglected to note that this development had resulted from a desire to make the university more "at home" in the Reichsland and that it had been strongly resisted by most professors. As for the institution's influence in the region, it was judged insignificant: "with the exception of a small minority of students from the countryside . . . one can say that, because of lack of comprehension or ineptitude, the Germanizing activity of the Strasbourg professors only led to failure."[48]

The rest of the report consisted of recommendations concerning the projected French university. Of these the most basic was that the institution be one of considerable distinction: France must "spare neither money nor effort to assure the University of Strasbourg a brilliant rebirth and to permit the French institution to bear comparison physically, to its advantage, with its German predecessor."[49] A distinguished French university, the report continued, would be warmly received by the Alsatians. In this regard some had previously warned that the institution might have difficulty attracting students, particularly since there was a French university in nearby Nancy. But the report argued that there had been more than 1,000 Alsatians at the German university before the war—actually there had only been about 800 native Alsatians—and that a French institution would attract many more. How many more was not estimated, but the report predicted that the total enrollment would approach that in Nancy, where there had been about 2,250 students when the war began.[50]

Although confident that Alsatians would welcome the university in any case, the author recommended special steps to increase its popularity. He argued, for instance, that "it would be good politics to be very liberal when allocating scholarships." There should be courses in conversational

French for Alsatian students with an inadequate command of the language. Positions should be offered those Alsatians teaching at the German university who were basically Francophile. Special emphasis ought to be given to courses for the general public, an area in which the new university could have much greater success than its predecessor. And although "the region will welcome with joy the suppression of the Germanizing faculty of Catholic theology and the return to the status quo ante," there should be a Protestant theological faculty. Motivating all of these proposals was a desire to increase the institution's potential as an instrument of nation building.[51]

But contributing to the assimilation of Alsace-Lorraine would not be the university's only special mission. The report, foreshadowing later discussions, argued that the institution would also have a European mission. To be more precise, it would have two European missions. On the one hand, it should be a major center for the study of foreign cultures. The author showed no interest in the idea of a genuinely international university, one with professors from different countries and instruction in two or more languages, and he never mentioned the concept of the double culture. But he did recommend that several positions go to French scholars specializing in German studies, Italian studies, and comparative literature. The other European mission concerned not the study of foreign cultures but rather the influence of French culture abroad. The report asserted that "the French professors will find a marvelous site for propaganda" in Strasbourg and that the university would be "a center for the exportation and diffusion of French ideas." These remarks reflected a concern with the influence of French culture abroad currently widespread among French intellectuals. The hope was that victory in the war would permit France to increase her cultural influence in Europe at Germany's expense—much as Germany had increased hers at France's expense after the Franco-Prussian War—and that because of its location and distinction the new university would make a special contribution to this goal.[52]

The third and most comprehensive set of wartime proposals appeared late in 1917. The initiative came from the Service d'Alsace-Lorraine, a recently constituted bureau of the Ministry of War. In September 1917 the Service's committee on education formed a subcommittee for higher education consisting of seven Parisian professors, including four of Alsatian origin—the Germanists Charles Andler and Henri Lichtenberger, the physicist Paul Appell, and the historian Christian Pfister.[53] By the end of November this subcommittee had completed its deliberations and Pfister had summarized the results in a ninety-one-page report. Early in 1918 the Service forwarded this report to the reactivated Conférence d'Alsace-Lorraine, and on 7 October 1918 the Conférence considered and quickly approved each of its specific proposals.[54]

Pfister's report accepted most of the recommendations made earlier by the Conférence and by the report issued in Belfort, but it went much further. It began by urging that a university be organized in Strasbourg as soon as France regained Alsace-Lorraine and that it receive the resources needed "to permit it to establish itself from the start at a very high level." Like the Belfort report, Pfister's particularly stressed the need to outdo the Germans. Although insisting that the German institution had failed in its Germanizing mission and that Alsatians would warmly welcome its successor, the report argued that "the Alsatians must not be permitted to contrast the largesse of the German period to the economy of the new French period." Also of concern was France's reputation abroad: "Moreover do not forget that Germany wished to do great things in Strasbourg, and it is important that France, for her prestige in the world, not appear to yield in anything to her enemy."[55]

These considerations meant that many specific proposals were dictated, in effect, by what the Germans had done. Thus the new university was to have about as many professors as its predecessor. It was to maintain all the institutes and clinics established by the Germans, even though they far surpassed those at any other French provincial university. The library, which had many more volumes than any university library in France, would continue to receive subsidies as large as those received under German rule, and all French publishers would be asked to donate copies of their books. The endowments that had funded prizes and scholarships at the German university would be kept by the new institution—"which, by virtue of the laws of war, will have them at its disposal"—and used for the same purposes. And to attract and to retain distinguished professors, salaries should be relatively high by French standards (although not by German standards). In the French system all professors were in specific salary classes, with the salaries in each class identical at all institutions except the University of Paris, where they were higher. Pfister's specific proposal was that in Strasbourg there be a special class above the first class, with professors at this level receiving salaries equal to those of professors of the first class in Paris.[56]

In its facilities and stature the new institution was to be more like a German university than a French one. In other respects, however, it would be thoroughly French. Thus it was to be administered like other French universities, with its rector appointed by the government and both the rector and the deans serving indefinite terms. After a short transitional period the only language of instruction would be French. There were to be professors in all fields usually represented at French universities. And the curriculum, as elsewhere in France, would emphasize general courses and preparation for examinations. In this regard the director of the full committee, the physicist Lucien Poincaré, had earlier warned "against the idea that calls for establishing institutions in Alsace-Lorraine that would comply with ideas of reform that have currency in certain very qualified circles.''[57] The members of the subcommittee followed this advice. Although they proposed some innovations (among them France's first chair of sociology), they did not try to make the new university a model for the reform of French higher education.[58] Nor did they attempt to distinguish it from other French universities by giving it a cosmopolitan character. One member, Lichtenberger, had referred in 1915 to the possibility of a new university in Strasbourg becoming, ''in accord with a dream often cherished by intellects of a 'European' inclination, a sort of *world* university fostering exchanges among the rival civilizations that share the universe.''[59] But he never mentioned this possibility during the subcommittee's deliberations, nor did anyone else. The unquestioned assumption was that the university must be a bastion of French scholarship and culture.

But this objective did not prevent the subcommittee from proposing measures related to the university's special mission in Alsace-Lorraine. Thus some positions on the faculty were to go to Alsatians ''who offer sincere guarantees of French patriotism,'' even though they would lack the credentials—the *agrégation* or a French doctorate—normally required of French professors. For Alsatians wishing to matriculate the *Abitur* would be accepted as the equivalent of the *baccalauréat*. During a period not to exceed five years some courses would be offered in German, probably by Alsatians on the faculty, and students could write their examinations and theses in German.[60] Chairs would be set aside for the history and literature of Alsace-Lorraine. And there would be a Protestant theological faculty. On this subject the subcommittee was divided. Two members, Pfister and Lichtenberger, considered such a faculty desirable for political reasons, with Lichtenberger emphasizing that ''it is important to avoid having candidates for pastoral positions doing their studies of theology in Switzerland and Germany.'' But Andler and Auguste Souchon argued that the French parliament would never authorize such a violation of the separation of church and state. The subcommittee resolved the dispute by seconding the recommendation made earlier by the Conférence: there should be a Protestant theological faculty, but if this proved impossible a free faculty should be established. As for the possibility of a Catholic theological faculty, the subcommittee agreed that it deserved no consideration.[61]

After establishing these guidelines the subcommittee turned to the specific professorships to be authorized. Different members or consultants were asked to prepare plans for each faculty—Appell, for example, had responsibility for the Faculty of the Sciences—and the subcommittee approved the resulting proposals without significant revision. The subcommittee did not insist that all its proposals be instituted when the university was organized, but it did recommend that they be followed as closely as possible.[62]

As planned by the subcommittee, the faculty would be similar in composition to that of the German university, the theological faculties aside. The only major differences concerned the Faculties of Law and of Letters. The Faculty of Law, planned by Souchon, was to have more positions than its German counterpart, in part because law faculties in France normally had more and in part because of the particular situation that would exist in Alsace-Lorraine after the war. French officials had already decided that a transitional period would precede the full reintroduction of French law in the region, and some legislation introduced under the German regime might be kept permanently. Hence the faculty must offer courses in the public and private law of Germany and of Alsace-Lorraine in addition to those usually offered by French law faculties.[63]

The Faculty of Letters, planned by Pfister, would have about as many positions as its counterpart at the German university, but their distribution would differ. Most significantly, there would be less emphasis on the ancient and oriental languages (seven positions instead of thirteen) and more on the languages and literatures of modern Europe (sixteen instead of nine). For obvious reasons Pfister attached particular importance to French literature, to which he allotted three professorships, but he also wanted several chairs for foreign languages and literatures, including two for German literature. He justified the latter by arguing that "we shall always have an interest in understanding Germany, and whatever may have been said about it, the German literature of Goethe and Schiller has enriched all humanity and these poets are certainly not responsible for the crimes of the Prusso-Germans of today." The German university had given little attention to French literature, but Pfister did not want the new institution to reciprocate.[64]

The subcommittee did not nominate candidates for the positions proposed, but it offered advice on the procedure to be followed. The first professors in each faculty were to be appointed by the Ministry of Public Instruction on the advice of its advisory councils for the different faculties. (These councils were permanent bodies composed primarily of Parisian professors and responsible for advising on promotions and other matters concerning their respective faculties.)[65] If there was to be a Protestant theological faculty, the ministry would consult the Free Faculty of Protestant Theology in Paris, there being no appropriate advisory council. The few selected for each faculty according to this procedure—preferably "the instructors whose claims seem most serious"—would then convene, choose a dean from among their number, and nominate candidates for the remaining positions.[66]

The final subject discussed in Pfister's report was that of the university's motto. Pfister saw no reason to change the one the German professors had given their university, *Litteris et patriae.* Indeed he considered it more appropriate for the new institution than for its predecessor. The German university, he suggested, had subordinated scholarship to nationalism, but this would not be the case at the French university:

> The humanities and the sciences will be an end in themselves; nothing will divert those who have the honor of teaching at this university from always proclaiming the truth, and it is in this way that they will be true servants of the French *patrie.* The *patrie* of which the German professors made themselves the missionaries was a *patrie* alien to Alsace; for Alsace it was always the enemy. The new university will be dedicated to the French *patrie,* to this France which is loved by the Alsatians for its noble civilization, for its attachment to the great principles of liberty, justice, and truth; the French *patrie* is also the *patrie* of Alsace, and in the classrooms of the university Frenchmen from Alsace and Frenchmen from the interior will start out with the same loyalties.[67]

## • 3 •

The armistice of 11 November 1918, with its stipulation that all German troops be withdrawn from Alsace-Lorraine within fifteen days, convinced many professors at the German university that the institution should close immediately. But the officials of Germany's Armistice Commission, reluctant to concede anything before the peace talks, instructed the professors to remain at their posts indefinitely. Except for the few rumored to be on a French blacklist—among them Eduard Schwartz, Martin Spahn, and the Protestant theologian Gustav Anrich, an Alsatian—the professors obeyed. As a result the German university was still in session when, on 21 and 22 November, the last German troops left Strasbourg and the first French troops arrived.[68]

But the university did not survive much longer. Determined to complete the liberation of Alsace-Lorraine, the bureaucrats who accompanied the French troops hastened to close all institutions identified with German rule, the university included. On 27 November, the day he arrived in Strasbourg, the new French rector, Jules Coulet, ordered that courses at the university end within a week and that examinations be completed within ten days. The faculty had no choice but to comply, and on 7 December the Kaiser-Wilhelms-Universität Strassburg closed its doors forever.[69]

As for the professors, their treatment depended on their origins, their age, and their earlier political activities. All but two of the Alsatians received permission to remain—the exceptions were Anrich and Albert Ehrhard—and they took advantage of it. But the German professors were less fortunate. A few were expelled even before the university closed; at the beginning of December five professors received one day's notice and then were ushered to the bridge crossing the Rhine to Baden. Most of the rest (and Ehrhard) left later in December or were expelled in January, usually with two or three days' notice. A few older professors, among them Georg Friedrich Knapp and Theodor Nöldeke, were permitted to remain in Strasbourg somewhat longer. And one German professor, the economic historian Werner Wittich, had the option of remaining indefinitely since his wife was Alsatian. There was never any question about Wittich's decision: he took advantage of his good fortune and spent the rest of his life in Alsace.[70]

The decisions to close the German university quickly and to expel most German professors had the strong support of Alsatians. In nearly every part of Alsace-Lorraine—the only exceptions seem to have been a few predominantly Protestant villages and towns—Alsatians had enthusiastically welcomed the liberating French troops and were urging French officials to remove the most visible symbols of German rule, the German professors included. Indeed the first professors expelled found themselves accompanied on the long walk to the Rhine bridge by crowds of jeering Alsatians.[71]

German observers, noting that some of the most ardently Francophile Alsatians had earlier been among the most ardently Germanophile, found it comforting to argue that the Alsatians' enthusiasm over the arrival of the French was not genuine. And there is some truth in this. Inevitably there were Alsatians anxious to disguise or to compensate for past loyalties and Alsatians who hoped that outspoken support for French rule would improve their own lots or make the new regime more conciliatory. But opportunism was not the dominant factor. After more than four years of war and of subjugation to a repressive regime there was among Alsatians a pervasive hatred of Germany, a longing for peace and stability, and a desire not to be caught again between France and Germany. The desire for French rule may have resulted less from identification with France than from hostility to Germany, but it was genuine nonetheless.[72]

Even before the German university closed, France's Ministry of Public Instruction appointed a commission of seventeen scholars—including Charles Andler, Christian Pfister, and, as chairman, Paul Appell—to examine the institution's facilities and budget, to interview its Alsatian students and alumni, and to submit recommendations concerning its successor. In mid-December the members spent several days in Strasbourg discharging their responsibilities. The resulting report generally agreed with the earlier Pfister report, but there were refinements. For one thing, it suggested that the new university should be a model for the reform of French higher education, a possibility that the subcommittee of the Service had been instructed to ignore. Thus the report observed that the organization of the medical faculty "deserves a long and thorough study, and from this study perhaps could emerge ideas for the French universities; in this regard, we would appropriate the advice of Clemenceau: Alsace should be an example."[73] In a similar vein the law faculty, following the German precedent, should be, in effect, France's first faculty of the social and policy sciences. In defending this proposal an attached report by the economist Charles Rist recommended that the university become both a model for the reform of other French universities and "the intellectual center of an economic regionalism which all informed men today desire for the future of France."[74]

Other original proposals received their justification from the university's Alsatian mission. French should be the only language of instruction from the outset—there was to be no transitional period—although it might be advisable "to appoint lecturers capable of providing explanations in German to the students who need them."[75] Alsatian students preparing for teaching careers should be required to spend at least two years at universities in the interior to acquire a mastery of French.[76] And the chair for Alsatian literature should also have responsibility for the folklore and popular culture of Alsace. In this regard "it is advisable to give the Alsatian people the sense that we understand and like their uniqueness, their intellectual position in the common civilization of Europe. . . . The great geographic and folkloric discoveries initiated by the Germans offer our young scholars a field for exploration that must not be left to German learning, which derives tendentious interpretations from its observations."[77]

The Appell commission's report concluded by urging that the new university be organized as soon as possible. Specifically it recommended that instruction begin in January 1919 and that all professors be appointed and in residence no later than March. In justification it warned that unless the institution opened soon many Alsatians would enroll instead at the University of Paris, and that the exodus would be particularly large among those with the best command of French—that is, among those whose presence in Strasbourg was most desirable.[78]

The ministry considered the proposed March deadline unrealistic, but it did agree to institute a program of courses on a temporary basis. Within a few weeks it appointed a provisional administrator and a few instructors for each of the projected faculties. On 15 January 1919 the rector, Coulet, greeted this staff, and on the next day classes began.[79]

Within two weeks 800 Alsatians had enrolled, and by the end of the spring there were more than 1,000. Inevitably some of these students had difficulty adjusting: there were complaints about the equivalents assigned German examinations and degrees, and some could not keep up with courses taught in French, as most were. But on the whole the students adapted well. Many came from French-speaking families, of course, while most of the others had at least a basic knowledge of the language and a strong desire to master it and to work within the French system. And the professors were tolerant and eager to help. Some supplemented their lectures with tutorials for students who had difficulties with the language, for example, while others, among them the historian Marc Bloch, taught courses in introductory French in addition to their regular courses. In sum, there was goodwill and a readiness to compromise on both sides and little reason to believe the problems of adjustment would be long-lasting.[80]

But there were other problems. Most stemmed from the character of the provisional regime introduced in Alsace-Lorraine after the armistice. Paris had sent a high commissioner to Strasbourg, but he could do little without the authorization of the cabinet or the Service général d'Alsace-Lorraine, a Parisian bureau attached to the cabinet. And this authorization tended to be difficult to obtain, for there was indecision in Paris over what policies to pursue. Some favored the full and rapid introduction of the highly centralized French administrative system, while others wanted a transitional regime with concessions to Alsatian particularism. These differences together with the general inefficiency of the bureaucracy resulted in little being done. Although Parisian officials insisted on limiting the high commissioner's freedom of action, they seemed incapable of making decisions themselves.[81]

The situation angered both Alsatians, who soon began to compare the French administration unfavorably with the German, and those who had just come to the liberated provinces from the interior. Among the first to complain were the imported professors. They wanted to contribute to the planning of the new university, at which many of them hoped to teach. But Paris provided little support. Requests for more professors were ignored. Decisions concerning salaries were postponed. Recommendations relating to organizational matters went unanswered. And demoralizing rumors circulated, including one alleging that a high official at the ministry had asserted: "For the University of Strasbourg I foresee something small, I foresee something very small." Clearly there would be a university, but the professors were beginning to fear that it would not receive the special consideration it deserved; they had hoped "to put Strasbourg nearly at the same level as Paris," but their frustrating dealings with the ministry suggested that "one wishes to treat it like Grenoble or Clermont-Ferrand."[82]

Many Alsatians shared the professors' concern. Particularly worried were Pierre Bucher and other members of the reactivated Cercle des anciens and the members of the Cercle des étudiants de Strasbourg, an organization founded late in 1918 by veterans of the Club. There was no question of their loyalty to France, of course, but they feared that the enthusiasm of other Alsatians for French rule would decline rapidly unless the government did more for Alsace-Lorraine than the Germans had done. A case in point was the university. Bucher and his associates insisted not only that the institution be thoroughly French in character—they no longer referred to the double culture—but also that it be more distinguished than its predecessor. This was a matter of national prestige, they argued, and they were thinking of France's prestige in Alsace-Lorraine as well as abroad. But during the winter of 1918–19 they saw little evidence that Parisian officials agreed, and like the professors they began to fear that the new institution would be just another French provincial university and, as such, an inviting target for disaffected Alsatians.[83]

After a few months, however, the situation improved. Late in March the national government, persuaded that the initial system of administering Alsace-Lorraine was neither effective nor popular, replaced it with a decentralized one. Henceforth a commissioner general, based in Strasbourg and responsible only to the prime minister, would control the administration of the region. Appointed to the post was Alexandre Millerand, a prominent politician closely associated with the prime minister, Georges Clemenceau, and the president, Raymond Poincaré.[84] This reform and this appointment greatly improved the political climate in the recovered provinces, and so did Millerand's actions after taking office. Guided by his éminence grise, Pierre Bucher, Millerand quickly demonstrated a commitment to efficient government and moderated or undid many of the centralizing policies of his predecessors. As for the university, he went out of his way to reassure those most concerned: at separate meetings early in April he promised the professors that he would give high priority to the university and he promised the students that the new institution would be greater than the German one. As soon became clear, these were promises he intended to keep.[85]

One of the first problems addressed by Millerand concerned Catholic theology. Although the Conférence, the Service, and the Appell commission had agreed that the new university should not have a Catholic theological faculty, one of their underlying assumptions, that Alsatian Catholics shared this opinion, proved unfounded. To be sure, some prominent Alsatian Catholics supported this recommendation, among them the director of an institution certain to gain if there were no faculty, Strasbourg's grand seminary. And there was strong opposition among Catholics elsewhere. Thus the Vatican and France's ultramontane press criticized the idea of a faculty because they wanted to protect future priests from the corrupting influence of a French university, and the director of the Institut catholique in Paris criticized it because he feared the consequences of a state-supported rival in Strasbourg. But most educated Catholics in Alsace wanted a faculty. Support was particularly strong among those who had studied or taught theology at the German university, a group including most younger members of the Alsatian clergy. They appreciated the relative freedom enjoyed at the German university and valued the status that came from being university graduates. In addition there were political and symbolic reasons for maintaining a faculty. Obviously it was in the government's interests to oversee the education of the clergy. In addition, the regime's popularity with Alsatians would suffer if steps were taken toward the separation of church and state, and the substitution of a seminary for the faculty would be considered such a step. It would also suffer, as Bucher and others had argued elsewhere, if anything were done to reduce the university's importance in the eyes of Alsatians. Finally, it was in the government's interests to avoid a decision certain to be interpreted by many Alsatians as a concession to the Protestant minority at the expense of the Catholics.[86]

Following the armistice Eugène Muller had used these arguments to persuade the ministry to defer a final decision on the controversial faculty and to include courses in Catholic theology among those instituted on an interim basis. And in April 1919 Muller and others used them again to convince Millerand that a Catholic theological faculty was essential. Of course it was also necessary to gain the Vatican's approval, but presumably this would come once the Vatican was informed that France recognized the 1902 accord negotiated by Hertling and Rampolla and would regard a unilateral renunciation with extreme disfavor. Millerand entrusted the necessary negotiations to Louis Canet, a subordinate who was an authority on church law. Presumably Canet would complete his mission before the university's inauguration, now tentatively scheduled for the following November.[87]

Millerand left most other questions concerning the university to the rector and to the provisional deans and instructors. He assured them, however, that they could count on the freedom and the financial support needed to establish the institution on a grand scale. They were not even bound by the earlier proposals of the Service d'Alsace-Lorraine or the Appell commission. Thus encouraged, Coulet and the provisional faculty turned their attention to the most consequential of their responsibilities, planning the new university.

But how should they proceed? Many observers, developing a theme introduced by the Appell commission, wanted a thoroughly modern university, one providing a stimulus and a model for reforms in the interior. In this regard, the war and the promise of the peace had intensified a dissatisfaction with the state of French higher education that was already widespread. Beginning in 1917 there had been an outpouring of memorandums, manifestos, and articles urging that university reform receive high priority once hostilities ended.[88] To be sure, most assumed the needed changes must emanate from Paris. But after the war some lobbyists for reform, impressed by the opportunities available in Strasbourg and troubled by the ministry's failure to take the initiative, concluded that the most promising place to begin was the projected Alsatian university. The result was a series of memorandums and publications promoting particular innovations and insisting, to paraphrase Clemenceau, that Strasbourg should be an example.

Some of the most radical proposals came from the Cercle des anciens. In a memorandum prepared for Millerand in mid-May and in a thirty-nine-page pamphlet issued a little later, this society argued that the new university should have the resources, the autonomy, and the innovations that would permit it, quoting from the pamphlet, "to be what it ought to be: a model to follow or, perhaps still better, the lever for the reform of our system of higher education."[89] Thus while the institution should be of great distinction for reasons primarily relating to its special missions, the precedent would benefit France's other universities: "Let us aim high in Strasbourg so we can then aim high in the interior."[90] Of the specific innovations proposed, the most far-reaching concerned funding and governance. The university should receive as much as half its income from a regional government or from other local sources rather than from the national government, the body almost entirely responsible for funding France's other universities.[91] And it should be headed not by a rector appointed by the ministry, but rather by a president selected, ideally, by the faculty. The president and the deans would assume most of the powers now held by the ministry and all of those held by the rector, who would be concerned exclusively with education at lower levels. "Then, and only then, the University of Strasbourg would have real autonomy and would be shielded from the tyrannical influences of the ministry, of the director of higher education, and of the ministry's advisory committee."[92]

Another set of proposals came from Louis Canet, the official assigned special responsibility for the Catholic theological faculty. In a memorandum circulated in late May, Canet maintained that only a reformed university could have the desired impact on Alsatians' and foreigners' perceptions of France and of French higher education. Thus while the German university had had its faults, the solution was not "to turn everything upside down in order triumphantly to substitute preparation for the *licence* and the *agrégation*." Rather, the new institution should be true to the traditions of Strasbourg, "the only city in France that has known—thanks to Germany—a genuine organization for scholarly work, higher education in the authentic sense of the term." More specifically, the university should have the same facilities and level of funding and autonomy as its predecessor, and it should preserve such German precedents as the rank of *Privatdozent* and the division of the academic year into two semesters. But following this advice would necessitate circumventing the Ministry of Public Instruction, for the ministry, reluctant to innovate or to play favorites, seemed intent on organizing a university on the scale of, say, the one in Poitiers. To this end Canet recommended that the institution have as its rector not a functionary but rather a scholar who had studied the organization of education and science in France and abroad.

He considered two men particularly suitable, the medieval historian Ferdinand Lot and the Germanist Charles Andler.[93] Lot had long been an outspoken proponent of transforming the French universities along essentially German lines, while Andler was currently advancing yet another set of innovative ideas concerning the University of Strasbourg.[94]

Andler's boldest proposal was for an organizational reform: the new university should consist of several institutes rather than the traditional faculties. Andler argued that this reform would make it easier for the university to adjust to new developments in scholarship, would promote collegiality and research, and would be a corrective to the overemphasis of French universities on training for professional careers. A second, closely related proposal was that the university contain an institute of labor. It would offer courses to farmers and workers in such subjects as French literature, legal history, agronomy, hygiene, and physical education. Andler's underlying objectives, it seems, were to reduce the gap between the university and the mass of the population and, more generally, to undermine radical political movements by lessening class divisions and antagonisms.[95]

Another proposal relating to the university's internal organization came from the rector. In May Coulet suggested to the provisional deans and to Millerand that the founding charter, unlike the law of 1896 that governed universities in the interior, deny civil personality and budgetary autonomy to the individual faculties. The problem with the law of 1896, many reformers had complained, was that it gave the universities little power or identity beyond that vested in their constituent faculties; universities now existed in name, but they lacked the authority and other resources needed to control the faculties and to take major initiatives. Coulet echoed these criticisms and argued that his suggested reform would give the new university the strength and flexibility needed if it were to shape its future.[96]

Of all the reforms proposed for the university, this one provoked the strongest reaction from the provisional faculty. Within days of learning of Coulet's suggestion the four secular faculties unanimously passed resolutions rejecting it, and the six acting deans sent Millerand and Coulet a memorandum insisting that the founding charter be based on the law of 1896. Their reasons were concerned less with the prerogatives of the faculties than with the autonomy of the university: to give the university powers traditionally held by the faculties was to shift control from the professors to the ministry, since experience demonstrated that the heterogeneous university councils could easily be manipulated by their chairmen, the appointed rectors. The memorandum went on to associate Coulet's pernicious proposal with the idea, currently fashionable in certain circles, that the faculties be dismantled and replaced by institutes. By implication Andler's project, like Coulet's, would serve the interests of a ministry intent on curbing institutional autonomy. As if to confirm that the fundamental issue was autonomy, not the traditional rights of the faculties, the memorandum added that suppressing the civil personality and budgetary control of the faculties might be acceptable under one condition: if, as at German universities, the professors selected their rector.[97]

The faculty's campaign succeeded. Although Coulet took offense at the allegations concerning the role of the rectors and the motives of the ministry, he bowed to the pressure and recommended to Millerand that the founding charter be based on the law of 1896. At the same time he observed that the idea of an elected rector was unacceptable and that the concerns expressed about the substitution of institutes for faculties were unfounded, for there had never been any question of establishing a university of institutes in Strasbourg. Thus nothing came of the proposals for major organizational reforms advanced by Andler, by Coulet, and, in the case of the elected rector, by the Cercle des anciens.[98]

Nor did much come of the proposals for other reforms, at least not at this time. The plans prepared in the spring and summer of 1919 were not much more innovative than those earlier developed by the Service and the Appell commission. The institution would have better facilities and more professors than other provincial French universities, and for reasons that did not apply in the interior it would have two theological faculties. But this was about as far as those responsible were prepared to go. It was not that they lacked interest in reform. Rather, they considered it appropriate to leave many matters to be decided later, by the new institution's faculty. How distinctive and how modern the university became would be largely up to its professors.

Pfister's report of 1917 had recommended that the first professors be selected by the Ministry of Public Instruction on the advice of its advisory councils. And except for the theological faculties, for which there were no such councils, this was the procedure followed. Although all appointments had to receive Millerand's approval, the nominations came from committees of professors in Paris.[99]

But in making their nominations these committees relied heavily on the advice of others. In many cases they simply seconded the recommendations of those administering the provisional courses in Strasbourg. During the winter and spring of 1919 these acting deans spent much of their time in Paris interviewing candidates and proposing appointments, and although they faced many obstacles—particularly at first when the ministry would make few commitments concerning positions or salaries—their efforts often proved successful. Thus Christian Pfister, who administered the courses in the humanities, was largely responsible for selecting the other historians who joined the faculty (including Marc Bloch, Lucien Febvre, Fritz Kiener, and Georges Pariset). And Robert Beudant and

Georges Weiss deserved much of the credit for staffing the Faculties of Law and Medicine, respectively.[100]

Among those appointed on the recommendations of the acting deans were several Alsatians. Although Alsatian candidates lacked the degrees and the experience at lycées or other French institutions normally required of university professors in France, within limits the government and the acting deans favored concessions, fearing that otherwise there would be "an appearance of colonization."[101] As a result positions were offered most of the Alsatians who had taught at the German university in 1918 as well as to three Alsatians who had last taught at "old German" universities (Guillaume Baldensperger, Ernest Hoepffner, and Robert Redslob). In all about two dozen Alsatians received positions, most as professors rather than at lower ranks. There had been about as many on the German university's faculty in 1918, but only six had been *Ordinarien* and five of the *Ordinarien* were theologians.[102]

The acting deans were not the only outsiders who influenced the ministry's nominations. Also important were several prominent Parisians, most of them professors at the Sorbonne or at one of the grandes écoles. The pattern was consistent with the traditions of French academic life. Although in theory university appointments in France were based on universalistic criteria—one of the justifications advanced for the ministry's close supervision of the academic marketplace—in practice personal connections and political considerations often counted heavily. In particular for ambitious young scholars it was important to have a patron or two in Paris to look out for their interests and to promote their causes. And several professors and others had the stature, contacts, bargaining skills, and commitment required of successful academic patrons. Predictably many of them attempted to influence the staffing of the new university in Strasbourg either on their own initiative or at the request of clients.[103]

Two examples will suffice. The first concerns Gustave Cohen, a specialist in medieval French literature. Since 1912 Cohen had occupied the chair in French literature at the University of Amsterdam, but by the end of the war he wanted to return to France. He was particularly interested in the university planned for Strasbourg: "In this advanced bastion of Gallic thought I wanted to mount guard on the Rhine, as I had done [while in the French army during the war] in the Argonne."[104] To this end he wrote Gustave Lanson, one of his former professors and an influential patron, requesting his support. Lanson "kindly responded that I had all the qualifications, because of my military service in the war as well as my scholarly credentials, and that he would support me either for the position there or for Clermont or Montpellier."[105] During the next few months Lanson kept Cohen informed of his efforts on Cohen's behalf, emphasizing that much depended on the number of positions assigned French literature at the university in Strasbourg. By April he could report that Cohen's chances were improving, and two months later the ministry and Millerand authorized the appointment. Cohen assumed, no doubt correctly, that Lanson's support had been decisive.[106]

The second case was less typical, but it illustrates more vividly the methods and potential influence of the great patrons of Paris. The candidate was Prosper Alfaric, a historian of Christianity. Alfaric was a scholar of promise, but for many Parisian professors he had an important additional qualification: he was a defrocked priest who had become a zealous convert to anticlericalism. This odyssey no doubt explains why so many patrons took such an interest in promoting his academic career. Thus shortly after Alfaric defended his thesis for the *doctorat ès lettres,* late in 1918, two prominent patrons, the classical archaeologist Camille Jullian and the philosopher and ethnologist Lucien Lévy-Bruhl, encouraged the ministry to find a university position for Alfaric as soon as possible. A little later Jullian, possibly assured that success was likely, urged Alfaric to inform the ministry of his interest in Strasbourg. Alfaric did, and three days later he learned that his nomination was certain.[107]

But complications developed. On learning of the ministry's decision, officials in Strasbourg became concerned about how Alsatian Catholics and the university's theological faculties would react. Particularly worried was Millerand. Shortly after taking office he decided that Alfaric's nomination would have to be reconsidered.[108] But this resistance only strengthened the support for Alfaric's cause in Parisian academic circles. Many professors, it should be noted, were committed to freeing France from the influence of organized religion generally and Catholicism in particular and, partly for this reason, to protecting the centralized character of the government and the educational system. With the separation of church and state earlier in the century they had won a decisive victory, but they remained vigilant, for the enemy was still at large. This outlook helps to explain their concern about the situation in Alsace-Lorraine. As defenders of *la république une et indivisible,* they naturally wanted the region to enjoy the full benefits of French law, the separation of church and state included. They also feared, with good reason, that French regionalists and conservatives would welcome concessions made to the Alsatians and attempt to use them as precedents for the general decentralization of France. It is against this background that the Alfaric case should be seen. Alfaric's sponsors were not only interested in doing justice to a promising scholar or in finding a prominent position for an anticlerical historian of Christianity. They also had the Alsatian question in mind. Disturbed by the concessions being made to religious interests in Alsace-Lorraine, they attached special importance to winning what Alfaric himself termed "this new 'French victory.'"[109]

Of those rallying to the cause the most important was Lucien Herr, the librarian of the Ecole normale supérieure and a patron's patron. Like others supporting Alfaric's candidacy, including Lévy-Bruhl and Pfister, Herr was of Alsatian origin and belonged to the Ligue républicaine d'Alsace et de Lorraine, an organization dedicated to the full introduction of French legislation in the region. He had never met Alfaric, but he involved himself in the case after learning of it from a mutual friend. In particular he warmly recommended Alfaric to the historian Ernest Lavisse, the director of the Ecole normale supérieure and a member of one of the committees selecting professors for Strasbourg. This intervention proved important, for Lavisse, aided by his reputation for moderation, managed to convince the ministry to confirm Alfaric's nomination despite Millerand's objections.[110]

But the ministry's action did not end the matter. Although in every other case Millerand approved its nominees, in this one he did not; convinced that Alfaric's appointment was "politically impossible," he vetoed it. Pfister tried to dissuade him, pointing out that Jullian had even said he would nominate Alfaric for the chair in the history of religions at the Collège de France were it vacant. But Millerand was unimpressed: "One can call M. Alfaric to the Collège de France, to the Sorbonne, or wherever one wishes. His place is not in Strasbourg."[111]

Alfaric's numerous patrons urged Millerand to reconsider. Lévy-Bruhl, for example, insisted that the refusal to appoint Alfaric "for reasons that have nothing to do with the interests of scholarship" would be an inauspicious beginning for the university. "One would see in it an attack on the rights of free research which would be sadly reminiscent of the step taken by the Empire when [in 1862] it prevented Renan from taking his chair at the Collège de France."[112] By mid-July there were indications that Millerand might bow to this pressure, so Alfaric's supporters intensified their efforts. After a few more weeks Millerand gave way. Although still convinced that the appointment was undesirable for political reasons, he authorized it.[113]

The only other appointments causing serious problems concerned the two theological faculties. In the case of the Protestant faculty the difficulties resulted from the tendency of those in the interior to associate the Lutherans of Alsace with Germanophile opinions or, to use the term then popular in France, with *bochisme*. This attitude was shared by those asked to advise the ministry concerning the new faculty's professors, the members of the Free Faculty of Protestant Theology in Paris. At least this was the belief of some Protestant theologians in Strasbourg: in their opinion the Paris professors, concerned about the patriotism of Alsatian Lutherans and perhaps also about protecting their own institution, wanted the new faculty to be under their tutelage. Specifically they favored an institution that would be, like their own, more Calvinist in orientation than the theological traditions of Strasbourg, and they wanted many positions filled with scholars from the interior. The Strasbourg theologians, proud of their heritage and anxious to show they were not *bochistes,* resisted with determination and, on the whole, with success. Of the twelve scholars named to the faculty in 1919 only four came from the interior and only two, Jean Monnier and Paul Sabatier, seem to have sympathized with the objectives of the Paris faculty. The other appointees feared more challenges from Paris were to be expected, but at least initially they had prevailed.[114]

The problems faced in staffing the Catholic theological faculty stemmed from uncertainties over the Vatican's intentions. Would the Vatican adhere to the 1902 accord, or would it opt for suppressing the faculty and educating the Alsatian clergy at the grand seminary? Late in September its position became known: the Vatican had decided to recognize the faculty, but only to train those authorized by the local bishop to undertake advanced studies in theology; candidates for the priesthood must receive their basic training at the seminary.[115] Canet, Millerand's spokesman, reacted quickly and angrily, warning that the Vatican's decision jeopardized his government's readiness to pay the salaries of the Alsatian clergy and, by implication, to recognize the Napoleonic concordat as still valid in Alsace-Lorraine.[116] The Vatican yielded. Shortly before the university's inauguration the Vatican authorized the bishop of Strasbourg to send all Alsatian candidates for the clergy to the faculty providing he received certain guarantees concerning the curriculum, the selection of professors, and the protection of the theological students from alien influences. (Thus the bishop must "see to it that all contact between the seminarians and the other students who attend the university is avoided, so that, for example, the seminarians go directly to the places of instruction and return from them directly to the seminary without attending unauthorized courses and without pausing for conversations that could be dangerous.")[117] This reversal permitted the faculty to be established on terms acceptable to the French authorities. But the earlier uncertainties had impeded the staffing of this faculty. Although those primarily responsible, Eugène Muller and Canet, had persuaded some theologians to accept appointments if a faculty were established, they frequently had had to turn to their second or third choices. And for a few positions they had found nobody; when the university opened two or three chairs were still vacant.[118]

But this case was unique. Although the ministry's restrictions and indecisiveness complicated the task, the staffing of the other faculties was essentially complete by the end of July 1919. By this time 165 of the 176 allotted positions had been filled. (In 1914 the German university had had 166 faculty members—102 professors and 64 *Privatdozenten.*) Outside the Catholic theological faculty virtually no vacancies remained.[119]

Like their counterparts at the German university, those accepting positions in Strasbourg were motivated by patriotic as well as monetary and careerist considerations. A sense of mission particularly influenced the so-called *revenants,* those of Alsatian origin who returned from the interior. Some had so strong an attachment to Alsace-Lorraine and a commitment to its reintegration that they probably would have joined the new university regardless of the conditions. This helps to explain why most of the distinguished older scholars accepting chairs were of Alsatian origin. Thus the two who resigned professorships in Paris to take positions in Strasbourg, Georges Weiss of the medical faculty and Pfister, were *revenants,* and so were some prominent scholars who had taught in the provinces, notably the jurist Raymond Carré de Malberg, the historian Georges Pariset, and the physicist Edmond Rothé (all from the University of Nancy). One of these men, Carré de Malberg, had been so attached to Alsace-Lorraine that before the war he had requested a chair in Nancy to be nearby and had turned down a chance to move to Paris for the same reason. Another, Pfister, had declared his candidacy for a position in Strasbourg as soon as the war began. For them and for other *revenants* the opportunity to teach at a French university in Strasbourg was a dream fulfilled.[120]

It is more difficult to assess the influence of patriotism on the others accepting positions, but clearly it was significant. Indeed it could hardly have been otherwise, since a commitment to using education to promote national unity had long been prevalent in the French academic community and, as already noted, so had a commitment to extending the influence of French culture abroad. If anything the war had strengthened these attitudes, particularly among the younger scholars who served in the army. As a group the latter returned to civilian life determined to help their country exploit the victory. Those recruiting professors for Strasbourg appealed to this idealism, and with considerable success. More or less typical was the case of Lucien Febvre. After the war, in which he had served as an army officer, Febvre decided to apply for a chair in Strasbourg even though success would entail abandoning a good position at Dijon and, he suspected, his chances of soon being called to Paris. He explained why in a letter to a sponsor:

> I am very content in Dijon and close to my parents, who still live in Besançon. I like this region, which I know thoroughly. All of my ties are here. I do not have any in Strasbourg, and if I go there I shall be renouncing Paris, which otherwise will receive me in a few years. But what attracts me is the prospect of *serving.*[121]

But there was a limit to the sacrifices scholars could be expected to make in the name of patriotism. Those organizing the university realized they also must offer material and scholarly incentives to attract the men they wanted. Millerand did his best. Thus in May 1919 he promised that the salaries of faculty members from the interior (the case of the Alsatians was to be decided later) would be at least a third higher than the salaries at France's other provincial universities. In part this policy was designed to compensate for the higher cost of living in Alsace-Lorraine and for the loss of income from private consulting that many scholars moving to Strasbourg would experience. But it was also hoped that higher salaries would give greater prestige to the institution and facilitate competing with Paris. Whether the prospect of high salaries actually attracted scholars not available otherwise is unclear. It was easier to persuade candidates to make sacrifices in the name of patriotism, however, when these sacrifices did not involve their incomes.[122]

It was also easier when they did not involve their scholarship. Here, too, Millerand did his best to assist those organizing the university. Shortly after taking office he assured them that the funds needed to modernize and expand the university's facilities would be available. And during the spring and summer he met frequently with the acting deans and the rectors—Coulet resigned in June because of poor health and was replaced by Sebastien Charléty—to discuss what was required. In July they agreed to ask Paris for a special allocation of 28 million francs for Strasbourg (ten times the amount the government had set aside in 1919 for the facilities of all French universities).[123] This sum would be enough to cover the costs of the institution's facilities for a number of years, and it should reassure those with doubts about the university's prospects. "Such a grant," Charléty argued, "will demonstrate better than all statements the interest that the entire country has in the development of the University of Strasbourg and France's intention to make it the focus of a national effort."[124]

Millerand and Charléty persuaded the ministry's director of higher education, but they had less success with the prime minister, Clemenceau. Although he favored a special effort for the university, budgetary realities constrained him. Indeed all he could provide were grants totaling about 3 million francs for specific projects that could not wait. He held open the possibility that the university would eventually receive the full amount requested but made no commitments.[125]

There were, however, other potential sources of support. One possibility was to appeal to agencies of local government. There was, to be sure, no analogue to the former Landesausschuss and Landtag; the closest equivalent, the Conseil supérieur d'Alsace et Lorraine established by Millerand, was appointed rather than elected and had only advisory responsibilities.[126] But some consideration was given to seeking subventions from the Conseils généraux of the three departments that constituted Alsace-Lorraine. These assemblies, the successors of the Reichsland's three Bezirkstage, were directly elected and had the authority to collect taxes and make allocations. The Bezirkstage had given little support to the German university, however, and it was unlikely the Conseils généraux would be more generous with its French successor. And in any case those organizing the university did not want to become dependent on these assemblies for they considered them potential centers of clerical and particularistic sentiment. They were as reluctant as the German professors to let local assemblies influence their university's development.[127]

A more appealing option was to seek support from private sources. Admittedly the precedents were sobering: in the past philanthropists had contributed little to higher education either in France or in the Reichsland. But during the war some of those interested in the university projected for Strasbourg, perhaps influenced by American examples, concluded that a potentially significant source of income was there waiting to be tapped. Particularly optimistic was Pierre Bucher. Bucher wanted the projected university to be at the forefront of the French campaign to assimilate Alsace-Lorraine, but he feared that limited resources and the claims of other institutions would prevent the government from providing the necessary support. And in any case the university could never be too prosperous. He decided, accordingly, that there should be an organization dedicated to raising funds for the university from private sources.[128]

After the war Bucher had little difficulty interesting others, including Millerand, in the idea. By the summer of 1919 it was clear that a society would be founded, and specific projects it might undertake were already being discussed. The actual organization of the Société des amis de l'Université de Strasbourg, as it was known, came at the end of October. At a meeting of thirteen sponsors Bucher outlined his objectives, emphasizing that the society's mission would be "to contribute to making our university a grand center of French culture on the Rhine." The sponsors immediately set out to recruit additional members and to further their primary objective, fund-raising.[129]

On 15 October 1919 each of the new university's faculties and the school of pharmacy held its first meeting. After the members introduced themselves—many had just arrived in Strasbourg—they elected their deans and their other representatives to the university council, the institution's governing body. Over the next few weeks the professors determined what courses to offer and made the other preparations necessary before instruction could start. Early in November classes began, and later in the month a series of government decrees along with ceremonies in Strasbourg marked the official opening of the university. The festivities culminated on 22 November, the first anniversary of the arrival of French troops in Strasbourg.[130]

The inaugural ceremonies, like those in 1872 for the German university, were on a grand scale. They lasted three days and included banquets, concerts, excursions, the awarding of honorary degrees, and, as the featured event, a convocation with speeches by Poincaré, Bucher, and others. Everything proceeded according to plan—there were no public expressions of disapproval as in 1872—and left a memorable impression on those present. Pfister's and Millerand's reactions were typical: the former commented afterward on the "indescribable enthusiasm and joy" that marked the ceremonies, while the latter described them as "beautiful in every respect" and a "perfect demonstration of our talent and our taste."[131]

The tone, predictably, was one of patriotism and optimism. The speakers who mentioned the German university did so only to emphasize its failings. They argued that the institution had developed into a bastion of pan-Germanism and had had no success in its Germanizing mission; the impression conveyed was that all Alsatian students had been as hostile as those in the Cercle to German rule and culture.[132] As for the new university, the speakers predicted great success. In the featured address, for instance, Poincaré declared that it would be "the intellectual beacon of France on the eastern frontier" and that "from now on you can rely on all of France, with all of Alsace, to see to the greatness and prosperity of this magnificent institution."[133] One of the many foreign scholars present observed that "the advanced bastion of conquering pan-Germanism has again become a great center of French civilization and liberal ideas."[134] And Pfister, the only professor to give a speech, promised that the university,

> consistent with the wishes of the local population, will be above all a center of French high culture; it will disseminate, in Alsace and abroad, the language, literature, science, and art of our France. It will also mount guard on the Rhine. It will be the sower of the great ideas of justice, of the rights of man and the rights of nations which France had proclaimed and the entente has made triumphant.[135]

Considering the occasion, such optimism was to be expected. But was it justified? Many observers had their doubts. There was concern, for instance, over the general climate of opinion in Alsace-Lorraine and how it might affect the university. Recently autonomist and separatist movements had appeared, and disillusioned immigrants from the interior were beginning to talk of a *malaise alsacien*. Should the situation continue to worsen it would be difficult for the university to live up to expectations. And there were more specific reasons for concern. Most agreed that the university could not succeed unless it surpassed its predecessor as a center of learning, but it was still not certain that it would receive the necessary funding. In addition there were fears that the institution, regardless of its stature, would attract few students from the interior and from other countries. Some also had misgivings about its potential Alsatian constituency. Certain Alsatians whose own loyalty to France was beyond question thought the university would accomplish little unless thoroughly bilingual. Others, while committed to keeping the institution French, assumed that many Alsatian students would disapprove of its character or mission. Indeed even as the speakers at the inauguration were praising the patriotism of the Alsatian students, the vice-president of the Cercle was warning elsewhere that there was "a certain current of ideas among the university students which, considering the special situation of Alsace, seems dangerous to us."[136]

The professors shared some of these misgivings. They were concerned about how Paris would respond to the request for a large subsidy for the university's facilities, and some suspected that their special mission in Alsace-Lorraine might prove difficult. But on the whole the professors were optimistic. They had confidence in the goodwill of the government and of most Alsatians. And they had confidence in themselves. They approached their responsibilities with as much pride and enthusiasm as their German counterparts had approached theirs half a century before. They did not expect their university to be anything less than a great success. Disillusionment would have to wait.

# The French University and the World of Learning

The French university's professors believed their institution would fail in its missions unless it compared favorably with its predecessor. But they accepted the challenge. They knew their university would have better facilities and more professors than the German one, they had been assured it would enjoy greater autonomy, and they believed its faculty was of higher quality. In sum, they did not fear comparisons, they welcomed them; they welcomed the opportunity to show skeptics that a provincial French university could surpass a German one.

Of course, success would not come automatically. Special initiatives were necessary. For one thing, the faculty must broadcast the message; to correct the negative view of French higher education widespread in Alsace-Lorraine and abroad, efforts to extend the university's influence were essential. And obviously the university must remain a distinguished center of learning. Here the faculty's freedom of action was limited, for inevitably much would depend on the government's commitment to the institution and on the dynamics of French academic life generally. But the professors did what they could. They remained vigilant, insisting that the government honor its promises and give the university special treatment. They launched programs aimed at furthering their Alsatian and foreign missions and, in the process, at justifying their favored status. And most important, they attempted through a series of innovations to develop the university's full potential as a center of learning and to make it a model worthy of emulation. In so doing they were motivated not only by a general desire for reform but also by the specific interests of their university. They hoped both to enhance the institution's reputation and to foster changes in French academic life that would make it easier for an institution such as theirs, a well-endowed provincial university, to flourish.

• 1 •

The commitment of the Strasbourg faculty to university reform can be traced in part to the national debate over French education that had begun toward the end of the war. Few contributions to this debate referred directly to the University of Strasbourg, to be sure, and many specific proposals were unappealing to its professors. Yet the debate did much to discredit existing arrangements and thereby contributed both to the Strasbourg professors' interest in reform and to their optimism about the prospects for success.

But considerations unique to Strasbourg also contributed. The professors found facilities at the new university that provided opportunities for research unavailable elsewhere in France. In addition, no local traditions or vested interests obstructed efforts at reform. Nor were there many senior professors with fixed habits; the faculty was dominated by relatively young scholars, members of the "front generation" with most of their careers ahead of them. And the university's special missions provided incentive. The Strasbourg professors were particularly sensitive to the allegation made by many Alsatians and Germans after the war that France's provincial universities lacked distinction. They recognized that there was truth in the charge and that if their university was to succeed it must be much better than the typical French provincial university. They hoped, in fact, that it would be on a level approaching or surpassing that of the University of Paris and able to compete with that institution for professors and promising students.[1] But these ambitions were unlikely to be realized in an unreformed provincial university, regardless of its facilities or the quality of its faculty. This reasoning reinforced the professors' interest in reform: while certainly sympathetic to the general cause of reform, they also wanted to enhance their own university's visibility and prestige in France and abroad.

The professors agreed not only on the need for reform but also on the general direction reform should take. They had two basic objectives. First, they wanted to put more emphasis on research than was normal at French universities and less on preparing students for examinations and professional careers. Second, they wanted to counter what they considered the trend toward the compartmentalization of scholarship into increasingly narrow and isolated specialties. Their hope was that their university would become a major center both of scholarly research and, to use an expression current at the time, of "the spirit of synthesis."[2] They assumed, of course, that the two goals were compatible.

The Strasbourg professors were hardly the first to try to shift the emphasis of French higher education from preparation for examinations to advanced study and research. This had been a major objective of university reformers since the third quarter of the nineteenth century. Strongly influenced by German precedents, various ministries had greatly expanded the number of professorships, established seminars and laboratories, introduced degrees requiring original research, and in other ways attempted to alter the balance. They had also attempted to curb the institutions considered largely responsible for the relative lack of popular interest in scholarship and in university reform, the prestigious and intensely practical grandes écoles.[3] But their success had been limited. Even at the University of Paris, the chief beneficiary of their efforts, facilities continued to be inadequate and old practices and attitudes remained entrenched. Although most professors favored the reforms, they still devoted much of their time to preparing students for examinations, not least because their own advancement and status still depended largely on how their students performed. As for the students, most showed little sympathy for the reforms. The grandes écoles, their privileges and prestige essentially intact, continued to attract the brightest and most industrious. And most students at the universities remained preoccupied with examinations and committed to an ideal of higher education that stressed rhetorical flair, general culture, and the cultivation of individual genius, an ideal at odds with that of the reformers. The only serious students, one Sorbonne professor complained shortly before the war, were those from abroad, "foreigners who see very well that no French students are attracted to disinterested study—and who find this amusing."[4]

Aware of the limited success of these earlier efforts at reform, the Strasbourg professors believed they had an opportunity to put their university at the head of the movement. Their own commitment to reform was strong, and the environment was more favorable than in Paris or at the other provincial universities. The necessary facilities either existed or, they had been assured, were on the way. The relatively small number of students (1,510 in the first year) made an emphasis on work in seminars and laboratories more feasible than at the overcrowded Sorbonne. The professors did not have many of the responsibilities and distractions that consumed so much time in Paris. And the students and the general public were sympathetic: those who made their opinions known, including Bucher and the leaders of the Cercle, insisted that the new university outdo its predecessor as a center of advanced research. In Paris the criticisms of students and the general public—including the allegation that the reformers were Germanizing higher education—had done much to discredit and impede the reform movement. But in Strasbourg the pressures were in the opposite direction; the professors thought it necessary to demonstrate that, as one put it, "the instructors who have come 'from the interior' are not 'feuilletonists.'"[5]

The commitment to research was strong in every faculty. Indeed there was a spirit of healthy competition, with each faculty seeking the respect of the others through its promotion of scholarship. Each theological faculty, for example, established two research institutes, published a journal, and developed a curriculum that sought to reconcile theology with current scholarship in philosophy and the social sciences. The Faculty of Law gave more attention to economics and political science than any other in France and founded an institute of comparative law and a journal. The professors of medicine exhibited a greater commitment to research as opposed to practice, to the laboratory as opposed to the clinic, than their counterparts in the interior. The professors in the Faculty of the Sciences founded nine research institutes (the Faculty of the Sciences in Paris had four) and considered their primary mission to be not the traditional one, training teachers and prospective medical students, but rather advanced research. And the Faculty of Letters organized numerous seminars and institutes, published a series of monographs, and developed an innovative curriculum designed to introduce students to modern research methods.[6]

In shifting the emphasis from teaching to research, from the lecture hall to the laboratory and the institute, the professors went about as far as they could. Like it or not, they still had to prepare students for the examinations and *concours* governing entry to the professions and to higher positions in the bureaucracy. Their curricula, while innovative in many respects, took this into account. For instance the Faculty of Letters, like its counterparts in the interior, offered special courses for students preparing for the *agrégation,* the examination that led to teaching positions in the lycées. But the professors kept such responsibilities in perspective. As one admirer observed, "the proliferation of institutes here manifests the desire not to sacrifice everything—as in certain universities—to this consumer of intellectual energies that is the *agrégation.*"[7] There was, in short, a general atmosphere at the new university, an "environment for learning," that was conducive to productive scholarship. At least in this respect the institution matched its predecessor and, its professors agreed, surpassed every university in the interior, the University of Paris included.[8]

The professors' commitment to research was in the tradition of the prewar movement to modernize and "Germanize" the French universities. But their admiration for what this movement represented, and for what the German universities represented, was not absolute. Specifically the Strasbourg professors associated the reform movement and German higher education with the proliferation of increasingly narrow and isolated academic disciplines. And generally they opposed this trend. They approved of specialized research, of course, but they stressed the need to put the results in larger contexts and to make them intelligible to nonspecialists. Scholars should give less emphasis to analysis and more to synthesis.[9]

They were not alone in this belief. Before the war students and others had complained that efforts to modernize the French universities were leading to excessive specialization and the divorce of scholarship from the national culture and the real world. In 1918 a conspicuous group of young teachers and professors known as the Compagnons de l'université nouvelle had recommended that the Faculties of Letters give less attention to specialized scholarship and concentrate instead on providing general cultural training. And even in Germany, allegedly the source of the corruption, there was now much talk in academic circles of a developing crisis of learning and of the need to move from an age of positivism and pedantry to one of idealism and intuition.[10]

But these critics of specialized scholarship went much further than the Strasbourg professors. Either they wanted to de-emphasize research in favor of teaching or they wanted to base scholarship not on the cautious practices associated with the scientific method but rather on insights and ideologies. The Strasbourg professors rejected both options. Their goal was to transcend the barriers between disciplines and between specialized research and generalization, but without sacrificing recognized scholarly methods. If the more extreme critics influenced them at all, it was only to persuade them that anti-intellectualism was on the rise and that scholars now must give more attention to justifying themselves. And in any case, it would be wrong to stress ulterior motives. The professors were responding primarily to their own dissatisfaction with highly specialized scholarship, not to that of their critics.

The professors' "spirit of synthesis" manifested itself in numerous ways. Even if specific works of scholarship are ignored, many examples could be cited. Thus faculty members, breaking with the individualistic traditions of French academic life, often attended colleagues' courses. On occasion two professors taught a course together, a practice apparently without precedent in the interior. There was a strongly supported forum, the *réunions du samedi,* at which members of the various faculties reported on their current research and on recent developments in their respective fields. The many institutes fostered collaborative work and some of them—those, for example, for canon law, geography, and German studies—emphasized interdisciplinary research.[11] And on a more general level three *Centres d'études* coordinated research and instruction concerning, respectively, classical antiquity, the Middle Ages, and the modern world. These centers, which had no counterparts at other French universities, were "free federations of professors from the various faculties who have decided to collaborate fully, in accord with a program designed by them, in the preparation of young scholars in their specialties." The statement of purpose of one of these centers suggests the assumptions underlying all of them: a basic objective was

> to bring to consciousness and to develop this basic idea (the very one that inspired the organization of the center by professors of different callings, specialties and faculties): that one cannot study one of the aspects of a civilization without knowing, at least in summary, the others; that scholarship is a collective enterprise in every sense of the term: the cooperation and coordination of efforts that are distinct but convergent. Hence the center does not address itself to a certain category of specialists—historians, literary critics, philologists, jurists—

to the exclusion of others. It treats them all at once. It prepares specialists while giving them the resources to rise above their specialties.[12]

The commitment to collaborative and interdisciplinary research was strong throughout the university, but its most influential expression came from the Faculty of Letters. It was a journal, the *Annales d'histoire économique et sociale*. The *Annales,* founded in 1929 by Marc Bloch and Lucien Febvre, had a special mission: to revolutionize historical scholarship by opening it to the influence of other disciplines, particularly the social sciences. In formulating this program Bloch and Febvre had responded not only to their environment in Strasbourg. They had brought some of their ideas with them to the university and after arriving they were influenced by scholars elsewhere, notably the Belgian historian Henri Pirenne. But their experiences in Strasbourg were significant and perhaps decisive. They found an atmosphere conducive to innovation and professors in other fields who shared and stimulated their interest in interdisciplinary scholarship. Their indebtedness to this unique environment is suggested by a partial list of the Strasbourg colleagues who assisted them during the journal's early years: the geographer Henri Baulig, the psychologist Charles Blondel, the sociologist Maurice Halbwachs, the philologists Ernest Hoepffner and Ernest Lévy, the jurist Gabriel LeBras, and the archaeologists Albert Grenier and Paul Perdrizet.[13]

Clearly the new university was more closely identified with the "spirit of synthesis" than others in France. But why? In part the reasons were related to the age of the professors. Considered collectively they were quite young by French standards. The great majority were in their thirties or early forties when the university opened.[14] Thus most had come of age intellectually around or after the turn of the century, a period characterized in France as elsewhere by what has been called the revolt against positivism.[15] Admittedly few had become disciples of Bergson or other leaders of this revolt; the youths who did were not those most likely to become professors. But the new climate had helped to alert them to the disadvantages of highly specialized and compartmentalized scholarship. And in any case they were too young to have been at the forefront of the prewar movement to modernize the French universities. With less personal involvement in this movement than the preceding generation of scholars, they were in a better position to appreciate its weaknesses. In sum, the characteristic outlook of the Strasbourg professors seems to have been, in part, the manifestation of a generational revolt.[16] It would be natural for such a revolt to be particularly evident at the new university, for it was the first at which the new generation of scholars enjoyed a dominant position.

The physical environment in Strasbourg also contributed. The university's facilities were not only more extensive than those at other French universities but also better integrated. Thus the university's main building, rechristened the Palais universitaire, housed most of the professors in four faculties (Letters, Law, Roman Catholic Theology, Protestant Theology) and many of those in a fifth (the Sciences). Physical proximity did not guarantee close relations among disciplines and faculties, but it facilitated them. And the medical faculty, unlike those elsewhere in France, had all its laboratories together and in the same complex as the municipal hospital. This arrangement made it easier to advance the causes that came to distinguish this faculty: integrating scientific medicine with medical practice, promoting cooperation among the scientific disciplines, and, in general, moving away from narrow specialization in teaching and research.[17]

The social environment also had an effect. Relations among the Strasbourg professors were remarkably close and harmonious. In part this was because those from the interior had few ties to the indigenous society and felt isolated from it. Although the university's relations to Alsatian society will be examined later, it should be noted here that the sense of being in alien surroundings, of being members of a small colony, was as evident as it had been at the German university, and that the effects on the faculty's social life were similar. But the professors' involvement in the organization of their university had an impact as well. Their frequent meetings to decide curricular and other issues facilitated their getting to know each other and becoming acquainted with trends in their colleagues' disciplines. These relations together with their common sense of mission fostered a spirit of cooperation more pronounced than that found at other French universities. The contrast with the University of Paris was particularly striking. In Paris professors tended to have little contact with their colleagues. "Everyone works apart, in isolation, without knowing what his neighbor is doing, most often without even caring," a historian once complained about the Faculty of Letters. "We are a juxtaposition of personalities, celestial or modest; can one say that we are a faculty? For my part, I have never sensed . . . that I was one of a team."[18] This could not have been said about the Strasbourg professors. From the outset they shared a consciousness of belonging to a team, an esprit de corps, without counterpart at universities in the interior.

An additional consideration deserves mention, one relating to the university's special missions. Although the professors hoped their institution would compare favorably with its predecessor, they did not want it to be simply a French version, however distinguished, of a German university. Given their missions they considered it important to show that French scholarship was not only superior in quality to German scholarship but also different in character. But what made it different in character? Traditionally, most agreed, French scholarship had been distinguished by clarity of thought and expression, stylistic grace, and an interest in synthesis and generalization. But in recent decades reformist professors had tended to abandon these features and to emulate the German scholars' emphasis on thorough and highly specialized research.[19] The Strasbourg professors, it can be argued, sought to reconcile the best of both traditions: they approved of specialized research but thought it compatible with concerns they considered characteristically French. Viewed this way, their interest in moving from analysis to synthesis—from German strengths to French strengths—seems related to their desire to shift scholarly hegemony in Europe from Germany to France. But it also seems related to their desire to establish a special position for their university within France. Perhaps they hoped that by making the institution the first both to assimilate and to transcend what the German universities represented, they could put it at the head of a movement to de-Germanize French higher education.

### • 2 •

Between the wars Strasbourg professors often asserted that there were but two true universities in France, theirs and the one in Paris.[20] They may have gone too far, but clearly their university was the most distinguished in the provinces. And by design. The institution, it was generally agreed, had to be of high stature—it had to be an atypical provincial university—because it had two special missions. One of these, to be examined in the next chapter, was its mission in the recovered provinces. The other involved France's relations with foreign countries.

It is unclear which mission was judged more important. In their public statements, however, the university's supporters gave more attention to the foreign mission. It was not that they considered the Alsatian mission unimportant. To emphasize it, however, would have been at odds with the official French position that the Alsatians were already Francophile. In addition it could raise expectations and provoke demands incompatible with the university's interests as a center of learning. Focusing on the foreign mission entailed no such risks: success in this mission as commonly defined would obviously require a university of great distinction, a university that was a work of art.

Whatever their motives, the university's friends highlighted the foreign mission from the outset. Thus in the first speech to mention the university in the Chamber of Deputies, in June 1919, a Socialist argued that it would be through this institution "that we shall be able to assert the influence of Latin thought, or rather of the thought of Western Europe, over German thought. . . . One has spoken of a sort of crusade against the ideas of central Europe, against pan-Germanism."[21] At the inaugural ceremonies Millerand referred to the university as an "advanced citadel on the Rhine of the doctrines of civilization and of liberty."[22] In a speech a few months later the rector stressed the university's importance "to the development of French culture in the world" and predicted that it was "destined to counterbalance the efforts that the Germans are now making to retain the European clientele that formerly went to them for its scientific training."[23] And in 1921, to give but one more example, the deans composed a draft law concerning the university's finances that emphasized the foreign mission and never mentioned the Alsatian one: when the institution opened, the document began, "the opinion of all was that it ought to be a university without equal, capable of representing French scholarship with dignity in the eyes of the foreigner and of mounting the intellectual guard of France on the Rhine."[24]

In employing such rhetoric the university's friends were appealing to the growing concern in France over the reputation of French culture and scholarship abroad. Since the turn of the century French scholars and officials had become increasingly convinced that foreign cultural policy was a significant aspect of foreign policy generally. The reasons were many, but perhaps most important was the realization that Germany profited greatly from the reputation enjoyed abroad by her culture and particularly by her universities. Also important was the appearance of popular means of measuring the relative merits of nations as custodians of scholarship, notably the Nobel prizes and the exhibits and learned congresses at world's fairs.

The French government had responded by taking steps to promote the *rayonnement*—literally, the radiation—of French culture. In 1904, for instance, French officials lobbied to increase the number of French scholars invited to the international scholarly congresses at the St. Louis World's Fair, and in the next few years they made agreements to exchange professors with universities in the United States and elsewhere and opened several foreign *Instituts français*. Officials also became interested in attracting foreign students to France. They particularly wanted to bring them to Paris, the assumption being that a year or two in the Latin Quarter was more likely to make them thoroughly Francophile than a year or two in Lille or Rennes.[25]

The war provided new incentives and opportunities for the *rayonnement* of French culture, and they were exploited. Professors wrote numerous articles and books concerning French culture and higher education directed at foreign audiences and visited allied and neutral countries as semiofficial cultural ambassadors. Among those joining the Strasbourg faculty in 1919, for example, Fernand Baldensperger taught during the war at Columbia University and lectured in Scandinavia, Gustave Cohen taught at the University of Amsterdam, and Samuel Rocheblave lectured in the Netherlands and in Scandinavia. A basic objective of such activities was to take advantage of the hostilities to discredit German scholarship— a task made easier by the propagandistic efforts of German professors— and to increase the prestige of French scholarship abroad. But another goal may have been to enhance the reputation of higher education within France. Professors in France, like those in Germany, welcomed the opportunities the war offered to demonstrate their patriotism and their value as spokesmen for the nation. They did so in part, perhaps, because it served their interests as professors as well as the interests of their country: it improved the status of scholarship and scholars within France and the likelihood that the government would treat the universities more generously in the future than it had in the past.[26]

With the end of hostilities the French intensified their efforts at cultural propaganda. The war had given France hegemony on the continent, and it was hoped that cultural relations would help to consolidate this position and to perpetuate the alliance that had won the war. Once again special attention went to recruiting foreign students. Professors continued to travel abroad "on mission." New cultural institutes appeared in foreign cities; by 1924 there were nine. And, most important perhaps, determined efforts were made to exclude Germans from the international scholarly community. Late in 1918 two "Interallied Congresses of Academies of Sciences" were held, one in Paris and one in London, to lay the foundations for the postwar organization of this community. At these it had been agreed that for at least a dozen years German and Austrian scholars were to be excluded; they could not belong to international scholarly associations or participate in their congresses or other enterprises, and German would no longer be accepted as a standard language of scientific communication. To justify these policies it was argued that German scholars must be punished for their activities in support of the German war effort. But ulterior motives were obviously important. A thinly disguised desire on the part of many was to use the boycott to break the scholarly hegemony enjoyed by Germany before the war. Nowhere was this desire stronger than in the French academic community.[27]

It is against this background that the foreign mission of the new university in Strasbourg should be seen. The Strasbourg professors fully sympathized with the campaign to dislodge Germany from its prewar position in the world of scholarship. And they thought they could make a particularly important contribution. They assumed that as the successor of a German university their institution would be watched closely for evidence of the character and stature of French higher education. They also thought that the university's location would facilitate observing German scholarly developments and extending the influence of French learning in central and eastern Europe.

But how was this potential to be realized? It would not be enough, most agreed, to establish a university of high stature. If the university was to succeed in its foreign mission—and to justify the favored treatment sought because of this mission—special measures were necessary. The professors acted accordingly. Indeed here, as in the promotion of scholarship, there seems to have been a competitive atmosphere with each faculty doing its best to contribute to the university's *rayonnement*.

One way professors contributed was through speaking tours abroad. "It is necessary," the Minister of Public Instruction stated in 1920, "that one see our scholarly missionaries everywhere possible, as one saw and is again beginning to see German scholars."[28] The Strasbourg professors did their part. Every year the deans' annual reports proudly listed the numerous foreign missions undertaken by faculty members. Many trips were in response to invitations from abroad, but the initiative for others came from Strasbourg. In 1923, for instance, two Protestant theologians made a trip to Poland and Czechoslovakia (supported by a grant from the Foreign Ministry) to publicize their faculty. In 1922 a group of professors visited several Swiss institutions to acquaint local scholars with Strasbourg's university. And in 1924 Christian Pfister, the dean of the Faculty of Letters, led a mission to Italy and Yugoslavia with the same objective in mind.[29]

Another way the professors fostered their university's *rayonnement* was by inviting foreign scholars and dignitaries to the institution, either to speak or to participate in ceremonies. Thus faculty members invited many foreign acquaintances to the inaugural festivities in the hope that they would become unofficial ambassadors for the new university. Similar considerations influenced the selection of the recipients of honorary degrees, which, according to French law, could be awarded only to foreigners. Although the ostensible purpose was to honor the recipient, often the primary objective seems to have been to publicize the university in the recipient's country. An honorary degree was once awarded the grand duke of Luxembourg, for example, in the hope that it would result in more students from Luxembourg enrolling at the university.[30]

This illustration brings us to the most important way in which the faculty sought to extend the university's influence abroad: through attracting and impressing foreign students. Shortly after the university opened the professors introduced several programs intended to appeal to students from abroad. The Faculty of Letters offered summer courses in French and German for foreign students, for instance, while the Faculty of Law tailored a program to the needs of law students from Luxembourg, a country without a university.[31] In addition the faculty took steps to make foreign students feel welcome in Strasbourg: they provided meeting places, organized clubs, sponsored soirées and excursions, and so on. The university also reserved numerous fellowships for foreign students, most funded either by the Foreign Ministry or by the Société des amis. Finally, the professors gave considerable personal attention to recruiting students from abroad. When visiting foreign universities they often tried to persuade students to come to Strasbourg for a year or two; indeed many of their trips were primarily recruiting missions. They also resorted to less direct ways of publicizing their university and attracting foreign students. Thus some wrote acquaintances at foreign universities (particularly, it seems, American universities) to explain the importance of their institution and its missions and to urge that a student or two be sent. Professors also sent information to foreign newspapers and magazines in the hope, often realized, that sympathetic articles would be published.[32]

The results were mixed. By the end of its second year the university had 252 foreign students, more than the German university had ever had, and the number grew steadily through the 1920s, reaching 872 at the end of the decade. Admittedly the University of Paris usually enrolled about ten times as many, and in most years three or four provincial universities had more than Strasbourg. But this did not seriously concern the Strasbourg faculty, for these other institutions (notably the Universities of Paris and Grenoble) tended to attract foreign students with little interest in serious study. The professors were concerned, however, about the large proportion of students from eastern Europe. In 1921–22, for instance, 47 percent of the university's foreign students came from this area, and eight years later 72 percent did. By French standards these proportions were not particularly high; in 1921–22 and 1929–30 east Europeans accounted for 41 percent and 57 percent, respectively, of all foreign students at French universities.[33] And there had been much talk of Strasbourg's special mission to eastern Europe. But the professors had hoped to attract many students from the United States, from France's allies in western Europe, and from the countries of northern and central Europe that had been neutral during the war. In fact they seem to have given more attention to recruiting in these countries than in eastern Europe.[34] Yet with the exception of Luxembourg, which usually accounted for about fifty, these countries sent few students. The reasons are unclear, but one possible factor deserves mention. In the neutral countries and to a lesser degree in Great Britain and the United States, dissatisfaction was growing in the 1920s with French efforts to perpetuate her diplomatic and cultural hegemony on the continent. In view of this the identification of Strasbourg's university with the *rayonnement* of French culture may have made it less attractive, not more, to students from these countries interested in studying abroad.[35]

The university's foreign mission was not limited to France's allies and the neutral countries. Indeed it was generally agreed that the foreign country to which the institution should give the most attention was Germany. Because of its location, many argued, the university could make a unique and valuable contribution to France's relations with Germany. But what should this contribution be? Here there was disagreement.

Some expected the university to contribute to the *rayonnement* of French culture in Germany. The Belfort report of 1915, for instance, predicted

that the institution would be "a marvelous base for propaganda" directed
at Germany.[36] In the summer of 1919 a prominent Socialist, Albert Thomas,
spoke of the need for France to exercise "a sort of moral imperialism"
in Germany, and added that "for this it is necessary that the University
of Strasbourg have a vast program of propaganda and diffusion."[37] And
late in 1920 the novelist Maurice Barrès gave a series of lectures at the
university, subsequently published as *Le génie du Rhin,* that outlined a
related but more specific mission. In these lectures, described by Pierre
Bucher as "indicative of the orientation of our university," Barrès proposed that the institution play a leading role in popularizing French culture
in the Rhineland and, implicitly, in fostering separatist sentiment in the
region.[38]

But these ideas found little support among the professors. The reasons
were in part practical. Desirable as it might be to increase the popularity
of France and French culture in Germany, the university could do little.
The French boycott of German scholars and scholarship and the evident
determination of the Germans to respond in kind effectively eliminated
the possibility of close ties to the German academic community. And for
reasons relating to the university's Alsatian mission it seemed unwise to
encourage German students to come to Strasbourg. But the faculty was
also influenced by more general considerations involving differences over
the policies France should pursue in Germany and over the appropriate
public image for the university. Most opposed efforts to promote Rhenish
separatism, not least because such efforts might inspire regionalist movements in Alsace-Lorraine. Nor did they want their university identified
with a campaign to extend France's cultural influence in Germany. German observers, anxious to discredit the institution, were already arguing
that it was nothing but an instrument of French propaganda. The professors did not want to provide additional ammunition.[39]

It was not that the professors intended to ignore Germany. They agreed
that the university had a German mission. In their opinion, however, the
objective was not to disseminate French culture in Germany but rather
to make Germany better known to the French. The contrast with the
prewar German university is striking. With isolated exceptions the German professors, convinced that France was a nation in decline, had shown
no particular interest in French history, French literature, or contemporary events in France. But their French successors did not respond in
kind. On the contrary, their institution was from the start a major center
of German studies, the most important in France.[40]

Actually the university supported two distinct centers of German studies. One of them, the Centre d'études germaniques, was not in Strasbourg
but rather in the occupied Rhineland, at Mainz. This institution was founded
late in 1921 at the suggestion of Paul Tirard, the French high commissioner
in the region. The original purpose was to offer courses in the German

language and in German history to French officers stationed in the Rhineland. Within a year or two, however, the center began to admit others and added a new mission, the analysis of current events in Germany. Henceforth there were two sections: a literary one, offering courses in the language and literature of Germany, and a technical one, with courses on the contemporary German press, the geography of Germany, the German economy, and so on. The basic objective of both sections, but particularly the technical one, was to make Frenchmen—army officers, bureaucrats, journalists, and others—authorities on the German question. It was not, as some Germans insisted, to disseminate French cultural propaganda in the Rhineland.[41]

In many respects the center was a branch of the Faculty of Letters in Strasbourg. The literary section prepared students for Strasbourg diplomas. The resident director through most of the 1920s, Edouard Spenlé, was on the Strasbourg faculty. And many courses were taught by Strasbourg professors; every two weeks a small group—including, in some years, the sociologist Maurice Halbwachs and the historians Marc Bloch and Lucien Febvre—commuted from Strasbourg to hold their classes. The other courses were offered by specialists without university positions. Among them was the one German professor permitted to remain in Alsace after the war, Werner Wittich.[42]

In Strasbourg professors participated in several programs and projects concerning Germany. For a number of years, for instance, Edmond Vermeil edited a daily publication that reviewed the German press, an undertaking subsidized by the Foreign Ministry. And the Faculty of Law had an institute with a section devoted to German law.[43] But the major center of German studies was the Institut germanique in the Faculty of Letters.

The primary mission of the Institut germanique was to train future teachers of German. But this did not mean that its professors concerned themselves only with German philology and German literature. Influenced by Charles Andler and Henri Lichtenberger, the scholars most responsible for developing German studies in France before the war, and also by the interdisciplinary climate in Strasbourg, they considered it important to study German art, German philosophy, German politics, and all other aspects of German life, past and present. Their objective was to make their many students (the program enrolled more than any other in the faculty) authorities on Germany generally, not just on the German language or German literature. But they were not only thinking of the best way to train Germanists. They also believed that their approach served the national interest in a more general way. The institute's professors, one of them observed, "are defending in Strasbourg, with tenacity and unpretentiousness, a cause that is dear to them. They are doing their best to help their country better understand the ideas and the civilization of

Germany. And they believe, in doing this, that they are performing a mission extremely useful to France."[44]

The outlook that characterized the institute—and the other undertakings in Strasbourg and Mainz concerned with German studies—was not conciliatory. The tendency in assessing developments across the Rhine was to assume the worst. This is not surprising, perhaps, but it should be noted that some Germanists in France manifested a different approach. At the Ecole normale supérieure a group led by Henri Lichtenberger was conciliatory in its attitudes toward Germany and favored closer relations between the two countries. The Strasbourg professors, however, shared the more suspicious outlook associated with Charles Andler. Their basic position reflected an idea that can be traced back through French intellectual history to the Franco-Prussian War, the idea of the "two Germanies." They emphasized the need to distinguish sharply between the pastoral and peaceful Germany of the great poets and philosophers, the Germany of Goethe and Schiller and Kant, and the industrialized and militaristic Germany that emerged in the latter half of the nineteenth century, the Germany of Bismarck and the Kaiser and Ludendorff. The first Germany deserved admiration, but not the latter. As far as the study of postunification Germany was concerned, the prevailing attitude was comparable to that characterizing American programs of Russian studies at the height of the Cold War: it was an attitude of "know thy enemy."[45]

· 3 ·

The professors did what they could to make their university a distinguished and thoroughly modern institution, one comparing favorably with its predecessor. But they could not do the job alone; their success depended largely on the support received from others. And the professors soon concluded that this support was inadequate. They complained, in particular, that the government failed to provide the needed resources and that conservative attitudes and vested interests in the interior prevented the university from attaining the position it deserved.

The professors fought back. Beginning in the early 1920s they defended their cause in a series of confrontations with the government and, less directly, with the University of Paris. The results were mixed. But the net effect of these confrontations and of more subtle pressures—the expectations of students, the ambitions of professors—was to make the institution more conventional in character and to moderate the faculty's enthusiasm. Although the university remained the most modern in France and the best in the provinces through the interwar years, with time its distinctiveness became less pronounced. And the trend was clear to the professors. By the late 1920s they were already lamenting that as a center of learning their university's best years were in the past.

A major cause for dissatisfaction was the university's budget. Considering the fortunes of French higher education generally, the professors actually had little reason to complain. Compared to the support given universities in the interior, that in Paris excepted, their institution fared well: in most years its budget was about four times that of the typical French provincial university. It should be emphasized, however, that public funding of French higher education in these years was at a low level. The government, facing chronic economic difficulties and bent on retrenchment, tended to treat the universities as if they were wasteful enterprises meriting no special consideration.[46] And in any case the Strasbourg professors' expectations were based not on what other French universities received but rather on promises made in 1919 and on perceptions of how universities abroad were faring. By these standards they felt slighted.

The professors complained both about the university's budget for capital expenditures and about their salaries. Concerning the former, the commitments made in 1919 were not kept, at least not to the professors' satisfaction. Nothing ever came of Millerand's and Charléty's request for a special allocation of 28 million francs or of Clemenceau's proposed compromise, a grant of 17.5 million francs with another large one to come later if needed. Instead the university received relatively small amounts each year totaling, in its first decade, about 11 million francs. In the same period the university also received about 2 million francs for capital expenditures from private sources, in particular from the Marquise Arconati-Visconti, the Michelin brothers, John D. Rockefeller, and the Société des amis. But the total, especially if discounting for the rapid inflation of the 1920s, fell far short of the promises made before the university opened.[47]

The professors' dissatisfaction with their salaries can also be traced to commitments made or implied before the university opened. In May 1919 Millerand had promised the provisional professors that if they remained in Strasbourg they would receive large supplements to the salaries normally offered at France's provincial universities. But there were two problems. First, the government offered these supplements only to professors who came in 1919 from the interior. The Alsatians joining the faculty and those coming from the interior after 1919 were ineligible, as were laboratory assistants and other university employees not on the faculty. And second, no guarantee was given that the supplements would be permanent. The university had no statutes when it opened, and no law or decree stipulated that Strasbourg professors would always receive more than professors at other provincial universities.

At first the professors, while dissatisfied, accepted the situation. But in 1921 rumors that the government planned to introduce a law concerning state employees in Alsace-Lorraine, one eliminating or significantly reducing all salary supplements, caused them to speak out. In July the deans asked the government to exclude all university employees from the law under consideration and to introduce another guaranteeing that these employees, regardless of rank, place of birth, or date of appointment, would receive supplements amounting to one-third of their salaries.[48] In defending these proposals, which they did frequently in the months that followed, the professors gave some attention to purely economic considerations. They referred, for instance, to the high taxes in Alsace-Lorraine (required to fund the social programs inherited from the German regime) and to the lack of opportunities for outside income comparable to those in the interior. But their major arguments concerned the university's reputation and missions. They claimed, in particular, that the supplements were an important symbol of the university's unique character and responsibilities and that accordingly a reduction or termination of the supplements— whatever the effect on the professors' standard of living—would undermine the faculty's morale and lower the university's stature. One memorandum predicted an exodus "of all the scholars who provide the present strength of the faculties" and, as a result, "the complete downfall of the university."[49] Another appeal was equally emphatic. To approve the professors' proposed solution, it argued,

> is to guarantee for the future the greatness and the authority of the French university of the Rhine. To reject it is to make its recruitment difficult and to recreate in Strasbourg, after a short period, a university of beginners and apprentices. . . . One must choose. Either a special statute, with the advantages it involves, and the steady development of a great and strong university opposite its restless German rivals. Or a harsh return to the standard practice . . . and the progressive wasting away of a poor, small, provincial university. In that event it would not be a furnace that would have been ignited in Strasbourg in 1919, but a flash in the pan.[50]

Although they may not have agreed with these dire predictions, many politicians and government officials sympathized with the professors' cause. All the Alsatian deputies in the National Assembly supported it, and so did the commissioner general of Alsace-Lorraine and the Ministries of Justice and of Public Instruction. But the Ministry of Finance resisted for budgetary reasons, and it was strong enough to delay the resolution of the dispute for several years. To be sure, the professors' allies did succeed in excluding the faculty from the provisions of the law concerning state employees in Alsace-Lorraine passed in 1923.[51] But the matter was not settled until 1926, when a decree gave the professors most of what they had sought all along: all members of the Strasbourg faculty as well as all laboratory and clinical assistants and research associates, regardless of place of birth or date of appointment, would henceforth receive a supplement equal to one-fourth of their basic salaries.[52]

Although the professors welcomed this decree, soon they were complaining about a related matter. At issue was not their own supplements but rather those for professors in Paris. The decree of 1926 had given the Strasbourg professors salaries that were, on average, 8.5 percent higher than those in Paris. But in 1927 a thorough revision of all salary scales left Parisian professors with salaries, averaging the differences at each rank, that were 41.7 percent higher than those at most provincial universities and 13.3 percent higher than those in Strasbourg.[53] These disparities may have been justified by differences in the cost of living. Indeed members of the Strasbourg faculty admitted privately that they found it easier to make ends meet than they would at a comparable rank in Paris. But they protested nonetheless, emphasizing the symbolic significance of the favored treatment given the University of Paris. Both among themselves and in petitions to the government they complained about "the blow to the morale of the professors in the provinces" caused by the new salary scales and insisted that such large disparities were deserved "neither for the scientific works nor for the other merits of the professors of Paris."[54]

These complaints reflected a deeper sense of frustration that had been developing for a number of years. The professors believed that in many respects the university could hold its own with the one in Paris. Indeed one of them, Lucien Febvre, later described the institution as, in the 1920s, "the most brilliant of the French universities."[55] But the professors also thought their institution had failed to receive the recognition and support it deserved. For a while they had hoped that its facilities, innovative curriculum, and emphasis on research would enable it to compete with its Parisian rival for students, faculty, and status. But with time their optimism evaporated. Gradually they became convinced that they would always be constrained by the centralized character of the French academic system: for reasons beyond their control a provincial university, no matter how vibrant or brilliant, could not mount a serious challenge to the University of Paris.

Much of the blame, the professors believed, lay with the government. They had hoped the government would continue its prewar policy of promoting the decentralization of French higher education, but the government failed to oblige. Indeed in some respects the movement was in the opposite direction: during the early and mid-1920s the proportion of the state's expenditures for higher education going to institutions in Paris actually rose. The basic reason seems to have been the commitment to retrenchment. Because of the limited resources available and the authorities' interest in protecting the grandes écoles and the University of Paris—in part because of their supposed role in shaping foreign attitudes toward France—little could be done to improve the provincial universities. The only possible solution seriously considered was a radical one: closing some universities and some faculties at others so a few institutions might flourish. This idea appealed to several officials as well as to professors at the four or five provincial universities likely to be favored. Strasbourg professors, for instance, actively promoted the project. But nothing came of it; political obstacles and vested interests proved too strong.[56]

It was not only through the budget that the government favored the University of Paris. It also did so, in the eyes of Strasbourg professors, through its administrative policies. No significant steps were taken after the war toward increasing the universities' autonomy. Final decisions concerning appointments and the creation of new chairs continued to be made at the ministry, for instance, and on occasion scholars were given positions in Strasbourg without the ministry even consulting the faculty concerned.[57] Admittedly the ministry relied on advisory councils elected from within the academic community, but these councils were dominated by Parisian professors who often seemed more committed to protecting their own institution than to assisting those in the provinces. A dispute in 1924 exemplified the problem. An advisory council rejected the Strasbourg professors' unanimous choice for a vacant chair on grounds that the position should be offered to a member of the Strasbourg faculty, Gustave Cohen, who was then in his second year as a *suppléant* (a substitute lecturer) at the Sorbonne. Judging from the council's minutes, its members were particularly interested in having the position go to Cohen because they wanted to reward someone they hoped to retain at the Sorbonne as a *suppléant*:

> M. Brunot [Cohen's dean at the Sorbonne] pointed out that the faculty of Strasbourg does not wish to give a chair to M. Cohen because of the *suppléance* carried out by the latter in Paris. The appointment of this scholar who, even though a professor in Strasbourg, would continue to teach as a *chargé de cours* in Paris would indeed have the effect of obligating the faculty of Strasbourg to provide a portion of his salary without the possibility of profiting from his services. M. Brunot then pointed out that the systematic refusal of a provincial faculty to give a chair to one of its members on the pretext that he is teaching in Paris would have the most grave consequences. Indeed recruitment to the faculty in Paris is extremely difficult because the appointment of chaired professors at provincial faculties as *maîtres de conférences* in Paris does not offer any financial gain to those involved. Accepting the proposals of the faculty of Strasbourg would have the effect of further increasing the crisis of recruitment at the faculty of Paris.[58]

The Strasbourg professors, opposed to Cohen's promotion for the same reasons Brunot favored it, urged the advisory council to reconsider. The council did, and by a close vote—six to five with one abstention—accepted the Strasbourg faculty's recommendation. The vote probably would have gone the other way had not the council's members feared that a second rejection would cause the dean of Strasbourg's Faculty of Letters, the highly regarded Pfister, to resign.[59]

Government policies contributed to the centralization of French higher education, but they were not entirely responsible. Popular attitudes also had an effect. Of considerable importance, for instance, was the great appeal of Paris for students. The Parisian faculties had long enjoyed reputations as the best in France, and these reputations together with the delights of the Latin Quarter attracted large numbers of students from all parts of the country. In 1924, for example, 47.9 percent of the French university students not attending their respective local universities—those in the educational districts in which they lived—were in Paris. By contrast the University of Strasbourg enrolled 4.8 percent of these students. And while the students in Strasbourg were relatively talented and industrious, the very best and the most ambitious went to Paris. At both institutions, it should be added, most students were less interested in learning for its own sake than in preparing for professional careers. This orientation suggests another way prevailing attitudes worked to the disadvantage of Strasbourg. The Strasbourg professors had hoped their institution's special character would attract students from the interior, but they soon concluded that they could not be as innovative as they had intended without hurting the university's appeal. One consequence was that after a few years they reluctantly abandoned some of their curricular reforms in order to give more attention to courses preparing students for specific examinations and *concours*. The changes, it should be stressed, were not dramatic; the university continued to be distinguished by its emphasis on interdisciplinary study and research. But in response to unwelcome pressures, above all the expectations of students and potential students, the university was slowly becoming more like universities in the interior.[60]

Paris had a special appeal for professors as well as students. A widespread belief within the French academic community was that one's career was not a complete success unless it terminated in Paris, either at the university or at one of the grandes écoles. In part this was because of the social and cultural attractions of the capital. Provincial scholars usually had many close friends in Paris, often friends made during their own student days there at the university or the Ecole normale supérieure. For those with children the city offered the best schools. And of course many scholars—and many scholars' wives—liked the idea of being at the center of the country's literary, artistic, and musical life and of having easy access to the Louvre, the Opéra, and the bookstores of the Left Bank. But while the social and cultural attractions of Paris were strong, the professional attractions were stronger. For all but a few, positions in the capital meant better facilities for research and more stimulating colleagues and students. For those in esoteric fields the city provided constituencies that hardly existed in the provinces. And most important, perhaps, a chair in Paris meant prestige and power. It gave its occupant easy access to the scholarly journals, the national press, and the ministry. It made it possible to train the most promising students and to foster their careers. And, in general, it permitted exercising a strong influence over the development of one's discipline. Few qualified scholars could resist these opportunities.[61]

But what about the Strasbourg professors? Those who planned the university had worried about the attractions of Paris. They had tried to staff the new institution with the most promising scholars available, but doing so involved a calculated risk, for it meant many recruits would soon have opportunities to move to the capital. And no doubt a rapid exodus would jeopardize both the morale of those remaining and the institution's reputation in Alsace-Lorraine and abroad. In particular it would provide evidence for those predicting that the new university, however distinguished, would inevitably fall victim to the oppressive centralization of French academic life.[62] The organizers had hoped that higher salaries, better working conditions, and a sense of mission would immunize the professors to the appeals of Paris. But would they?

During the first few years there was little cause for concern. With two or three exceptions—including the philosopher Etienne Gilson, who went to the Sorbonne in 1921—the professors showed no interest in moving to Paris. In part this was because of a sense of obligation to their colleagues and to the new university. But there was also a prevalent belief that Strasbourg was a better place to work than Paris. Thus in explaining why he would not apply for a vacant chair in the capital, the archaeologist Albert Grenier observed that "the true reason is that I am well organized in Strasbourg to complete the project I have undertaken . . . , that I am convinced I could not have good conditions to complete it in Paris, and, in short, that the essential thing for us is not to be in Paris or elsewhere but to do good work. What I am telling you is perhaps a little . . . naive, but at root it is true."[63] The Romance philologist Ernest Hoepffner suggested another advantage of Strasbourg in a letter to a friend at the Sorbonne: "Don't you overwork yourself too much there? Really, I think I prefer my few dozen students to the hundreds there. Are you able to enter into direct contact with them?"[64]

But with time the appeal of Paris grew. Most professors, to be sure, either never had opportunities to move to the capital or ignored those that arose. This was true of all but a few of those in the two theological faculties and in the Faculties of Medicine and Pharmacy. (The School of Pharmacy had become the university's seventh faculty in 1920.) But in the other faculties, and particularly the Faculty of Letters, the pattern was different. Beginning in the mid-1920s more and more became convinced that their proper places were in Paris. Wanting to go to the capital was not enough, of course, but many professors also had the necessary opportunities, credentials, connections, and luck. In the university's first decade, in fact, twenty-three professors left Strasbourg for positions elsewhere, with all but a few going either to the Sorbonne or to the Collège de France.[65]

Some of them had always hoped to finish their careers in Paris. Others, however, had come to Strasbourg with the intention of remaining permanently, only to change their minds later. They changed their minds for various reasons. For example, some mentioned the harsh winters and the poor schools.[66] But the main reason seems to have been disappointment with the development of the university and of French higher education generally. With time the professors became convinced that their university's impact on French academic life would be smaller than anticipated, in part because the university failed to receive the promised support and in part because the system proved resistant to change, or at least to change not originating at the center. This disillusionment undermined the mystique and the esprit de corps that helped to define their university and to make it special, and thus lessened the attractiveness of Strasbourg relative to that of Paris. And once a few professors left, the incentives for others to leave increased. In this regard the close ties among members of the Strasbourg faculty proved a mixed blessing. They made life in Strasbourg's academic community unusually pleasant and stimulating, but they also resulted in friendships that caused those who did go to Paris to urge others to follow, and to do their best to smooth the way.[67]

The migration to Paris both reflected and fueled a decline in the morale of the Strasbourg faculty. In 1919 many had thought the special character and responsibilities of the new university would enable it to attract and retain professors worthy of positions in Paris. Indeed some claimed that the university would not be a success unless it did. With time, however, the restraints and incentives of the system, particularly the limited resources available and the careerism of the students, caused the university to become more conventional in character—and the professors to become more conventional in their ambitions. Even in Strasbourg, events proved, many professors could not think of their careers as successful unless they ended in Paris. This might have been predicted, perhaps, but the reality still hurt. The effect on those who remained was perhaps best suggested by Christian Pfister, the man most closely identified with the planning of the university and the dean of the faculty hardest hit by the migration to Paris. "This faculty, which had been so solidly organized, is going to be dismembered," he complained in 1925 to one of those leaving; "the best elements are deserting us. One must resign oneself: we shall have the glory of being the waiting room of the Sorbonne."[68]

Those loyal to Strasbourg, Pfister included, made the best of the situation. They proudly pointed to the number of colleagues who left for the Sorbonne or the Collège de France as evidence of the high stature of their own university. And by this standard and by others traditionally used when evaluating France's provincial universities, notably the success of students in various *concours*, they certainly had reason for pride.[69] But these were not the standards by which they had once wanted to be judged. Originally they had had different ambitions.

# 9

# The French University and Alsatian Society

To judge by their public statements the Strasbourg professors worried more about the new university's reputation in other countries and in the interior than about its impact in the recovered provinces. Compared to their German counterparts they said little about the institution's potential as an instrument of nation building, focusing instead on its likely contributions to the *rayonnement* of French culture. In part this was because of a reluctance to admit publicly that the Alsatians were not already thoroughly French. But also important was a belief that success in the university's Alsatian mission was assured. At least initially the faculty assumed that the Alsatians were already well-disposed and that as long as the university compared favorably with its predecessor it would win quick and general acceptance.

With time the professors became less sanguine. It soon became clear that their expectations concerning the university's relationship to Alsatian society, like those concerning its impact on French academic life, had been too optimistic. Among themselves the professors began to admit that the presence of goodwill on both sides might not be enough—and that among the Alsatians there might not be enough goodwill. Meanwhile outsiders, both disaffected Alsatians and foreign observers, began to complain about the institution. Some even insisted, as others had in attacking the German university, that it was a *Fremdkörper,* an alien imposition. Whatever the merits of this charge, it became evident that the new university did not enjoy the general popularity and relative immunity to criticism that many had initially taken for granted. The university's relationship to Alsatian society, like that of its predecessor, was proving problematic.

· 1 ·

The yardsticks most commonly used by contemporaries to measure the success of the French university were enrollment statistics. This emphasis is understandable. The goal was to convince others that the new university either had or had not outstripped its predecessor, and no other evidence provided so tangible a basis for comparison or seemed so likely to influence public opinion. But for those less interested in propaganda such evidence must be used with caution. For one thing, enrollment levels were influenced by general differences between the French and German academic systems. At French universities many registered who had not earned the *baccalauréat,* the French counterpart to the *Abitur,* and many registered who attended classes rarely if at all. Should they be counted? If so, should allowances also be made for the higher attrition rates at French universities or for the fewer years required to earn the basic diplomas of most faculties? And these differences aside, should changes over time in the general demand for higher education be taken into account? Put another way, should the comparisons be with the German university when it was at the same age, with the German university on the eve of the war, or with some projection of how the German university might have developed had there been no war? Even if these problems could be resolved, the question of the utility (propaganda aside) of such comparisons would remain. If the institution's success in its nation-building mission is at issue, a better gauge might be the extent to which its enrollment patterns approximated those elsewhere in its own country. And there is the more general question of whether levels of enrollment can ever be accurate measures of a university's stature or popularity or influence.

For these reasons the following discussion of enrollment patterns is limited in its objectives. Trends are examined and comparisons made, but not to judge whether the institution was a success. Such an evaluation must wait until more is known about other aspects of the university's development.

The official statistics indicate that except in its first year the French university always had more students than the German university had ever had. While the largest number enrolled at the earlier institution was 2,138 (in 1911–12), the interwar university once enrolled 3,627 students (in 1931–32), and after 1919–20 (when there were 1,510) never had fewer than 2,415 enrolled. In some respects the trend was similar to that at French universities generally. In both cases there was a more or less steady growth in enrollments through the 1920s and early 1930s, a decline in the mid-1930s reflecting the smaller cohorts born during World War I, and a modest recovery in the year or two preceding World War II. But viewed another way the Alsatian university reached the height of its popularity shortly after opening, in 1922–23: that year it enrolled 5.6 percent of all students at French universities and 5.65 percent of all those from France, but thereafter its share declined in almost every year, reaching lows of 3.59 and 3.42 percent, respectively, in the late 1930s.[1]

The growth in enrollments in the 1920s, both in Strasbourg and in the interior, resulted largely from increases in the number of foreign students. In 1920–21 foreign students already accounted for 10.4 percent of those enrolled in Strasbourg and 13 percent of those at French universities generally, but a decade later their respective shares were 29.4 percent and 22 percent. The proportions declined in the 1930s, in both cases to about 14 percent in 1938–39, but they were still as high as they had ever been at the German university in Strasbourg.[2]

Female students also contributed disproportionately to the growth in enrollments. In 1920 they accounted for about 12 percent of French students both in Strasbourg and in the interior, but their share rose steadily, reaching 27.3 percent in Strasbourg by 1930 and 26.1 percent at French universities generally.[3] By contrast, before the war female students had never accounted for more than 3.1 percent of those enrolled in Strasbourg, for more than 6.1 percent of those at German universities generally, or for more than 7.2 percent of the French students at French universities.[4] Thus if the comparisons are restricted to male students, the gap in enrollment levels between Strasbourg's German and French universities is much smaller. And it is smaller still if foreign students are not counted. In fact on average the number of French males studying at the interwar university was about the same as the number of German males studying in Strasbourg in the decade before World War I.

The patterns are different, however, if the analysis is limited to Alsatians. At the German university Alsatians had never accounted for more than half of the German students, but at its successor, judging from the fragmentary evidence available, Alsatians usually accounted for more than two-thirds of the French students. More precisely, in most years between the wars roughly 1,500 Alsatians and about 1,200 male Alsatians enrolled at the University of Strasbourg, while the German university had in no year attracted more than about 800 Alsatians (virtually all of them male).[5]

This difference cannot be attributed, even in part, to a greater propensity in the French period for Alsatian students to attend their local university rather than one elsewhere in the country. Computations based on the lists of students receiving diplomas at French universities in 1924 (the latest year for which complete lists are available) suggest that roughly 26 percent of the Alsatians at all French universities attended institutions in the interior.[6] The comparable rate in the German period—the proportion of all Alsatian students at German universities who attended "old German" institutions—never reached this level, and usually it was much lower.[7]

But these calculations rely heavily on official French enrollment statistics, and these sources can be misleading. Most serious is their failure to distinguish between the students who had earned the *baccalauréat*, and hence could seek university diplomas, and those who had not. Other evidence indicates that there were always many in the latter category. In 1923–24 and in 1933–34, for example, about a third of the French students in Strasbourg were not *bacheliers*.[8] Indeed there were probably few years between the wars in which the number of male *bacheliers* at the university exceeded the number of male students at the German university in 1914.

A related problem concerns the distinction between full-time and part-time students. A number of those who had not earned the *baccalauréat,* and a number of those who had, attended classes irregularly. Critics claimed that many enrolled only to enjoy the nonacademic benefits that came with student status, such as reduced prices at some shops and theaters and reduced railway fares. Others were schoolteachers who appeared only for the special classes offered for their benefit every second Thursday.[9] Part-time students were particularly prevalent in the Faculties of Letters and the Sciences. In the former no more than half those enrolled seem to have attended classes regularly, and in the latter the rate may have been still lower. (Cynics occasionally remarked that the Faculty of the Sciences appeared to have more professors than students.)[10]

If such problems are ignored, the average number of Alsatians at French universities between the wars clearly was much higher than the number at German universities at any time before 1914. But, to introduce a yard-stick that may be more relevant, was the number also impressive by contemporary French standards? Although information on the regional origins of French students in this period is not readily available, the lists of those receiving *licences* in 1924 (which record the birthplace of each *licencié*) indicate that the number of Alsatians was actually rather low. More precisely, the rate of attendance for Alsatians was 88.6 percent of that for France generally, if all students are considered, and 81.8 percent if the theology students are left out of account. And evidence from other official sources suggests that these disparities did not become smaller in subsequent years, at least not markedly. Thus in the late 1930s the esti-mated incidence of university attendance for Alsatians was still only 89.3 percent of that for France as a whole and 81.9 percent if the students of theology are not considered. These gaps were greater than the comparable gaps before World War I, those between the rates of attendance at German universities for Alsatians and the rates for all Germans (see table 2, ap-pendix B).

Left to consider are the students' background characteristics. Were the Alsatians at the interwar university similar in background to those at the German university? This is difficult to determine. The few matriculation records that survive are of limited use since matriculants were not asked to note their religions or their fathers' occupations. And with one excep-tion, considered below, officials never took other steps to gather infor-mation on such subjects. But there is another approach. From the lists of *licenciés* it is possible to estimate the number of students born in each commune and region of Alsace-Lorraine and then to analyze the distri-bution, taking into account both the characteristics of these places and the distribution according to birthplace of the Alsatians at the German university. This approach is risky for it rests on two major and untestable assumptions: that the ratio of *licenciés* to the total number of French students in each Strasbourg faculty also held for those from each area of Alsace-Lorraine, and that the characteristics of the students' birthplaces can shed light on the characteristics of the students. But considering the importance of the subject and the almost total absence of other quantifiable evidence, the risks seem justified.

Although the overall demand for higher education in Alsace-Lorraine was greater in 1924 than before the war, its distribution among the region's three departments and twenty-two *arrondissements* was similar. The proportion of Strasbourg students from Bas-Rhin was somewhat smaller (53.0 percent as compared with 56.7 percent), but this decline was consistent with a trend evident throughout the history of the German university. The increase in the proportion born in one of the four major Alsatian cities, from 26.8 percent to 37.4 percent, can largely be attributed to urbanization and to the female students enrolled in 1924, 62.2 percent of whom came from these cities as compared with 32.7 percent of the males. And the results of two tests suggest that little change occurred in the distribution of students according to religion. A slight decline was evident in the proportion born in predominantly Protestant towns or villages, from 15.2 percent of the total and 15.4 percent of the males in 1913–14 to 13.7 percent and 14.0 percent, respectively, in 1924. But the proportion of Protestant students in 1913–14 was much higher than the proportion born in predominantly Protestant communes. If this is taken into account—specifically, if it is assumed that for students born in each *arrondissement* (*Kreis*) the distribution according to religion was the same in both years—the results indicate that the proportion of the total who were Protestant in 1924 (41.6 percent) was slightly higher than it had been in 1913–14 (40.2 percent).

Different patterns emerge if the focus shifts to the Alsatians at universities in the interior. Proportionately these students were more likely to come from the reannexed part of Lorraine than from Bas-Rhin or Haut-Rhin, and, as this suggests, more likely to come from predominantly French-speaking areas and from predominantly Catholic towns or villages (see table 11, appendix B). In other words the Alsatians at the University of Strasbourg were not representative of the Alsatians at French universities. But, as one would expect given the large proportion of the total in Strasbourg, the differences were small. Hence it seems safe to extend to Alsatian students generally a conclusion suggested by those in Strasbourg: there were no major changes in the spatial distribution of the demand for higher education in Alsace-Lorraine that cannot be attributed to trends evident either in the region prior to the war or, as with the growth in the number of female students, in Europe generally after the war; neither the change of regimes nor the transformation of the university had much effect.

But what about the social origins of the students? The only direct evidence comes from the very end of the interwar period. Early in 1939 the Bureau universitaire de statistique, a government agency, instructed all rectors to collect information on the social origins of their universities' students, something not done in the past. The rectors' first reports concerned those enrolled during the 1938–39 academic year. Unfortunately these reports were not preserved, but a ministerial summary aggregating the results by institution and by faculty has survived. This summary provides the basis for much of the analysis that follows.[11] Other evidence, it should be noted, indicates that recruitment to French universities generally and to the University of Strasbourg became more democratic in the course of the 1930s; the following comparisons should be evaluated accordingly.[12]

A procedural problem remains. The rectors' reports did not distinguish among the students according to geographic origins. But other sources indicate that about one-quarter of the French students in Strasbourg in 1938–39 came either from families residing in the interior (17 percent)[13] or from families that had moved to Alsace-Lorraine since 1918 (about 8 percent).[14] If the distribution of these students according to social origin is assumed to match that of all French students at universities in the interior, the distribution of the Alsatian students in Strasbourg can be estimated. Since such an assumption seems reasonable, and since the Alsatian students accounted for an estimated 75 percent of the total, the resulting estimates are probably reliable.

The results suggest that the Alsatian students at French universities tended to come from higher in the social order than had those at German universities before the war. For example, an estimated 26.7 percent of those surveyed in 1939 had fathers who were professionals, high-level bureaucrats, or entrepreneurs, as compared with 19.6 percent in 1910. At the other extreme an estimated 15.9 percent of the Alsatian students in 1939 were the children of peasants, artisans, or members of the working class, as compared with 26.6 percent in the earlier year. The remainder, 53.8 percent in 1910 and an estimated 57.4 percent in 1939, had fathers who were shopkeepers, middle-level bureaucrats, teachers, white-collar workers in private firms, large landowners, or rentiers. (In both cases the small number for whom the fathers' occupations are unknown, 2.2 percent and an estimated 3.2 percent, respectively, have not been counted.)

Such comparisons can be misleading if viewed in isolation. It is also necessary to take secular trends into account. Two merit particular attention. The first is the growth in the number of female students. The 1939 survey did not distinguish between male and female students, but a survey conducted in 1948 revealed that female students both in Strasbourg and in France generally tended to come from somewhat higher in the social order than male students.[15] If this were also true between the wars it would account for part of the difference between the distributions of students by social origin in 1939 and in 1910. But in view of the slight variations between the sexes observed in 1948 and the small proportion of female students in 1939 (about 26 percent of the Alsatians studying at French universities),[16] it is unlikely that the impact was significant.

The second trend concerns shifts in the composition of the relevant age cohorts. Such shifts clearly affected the composition of the university's student body. Thus the rise in the proportion of students whose fathers were bureaucrats or white-collar employees reflected the growing importance of these occupational groups. And the pronounced decline in the proportion whose fathers were peasants, artisans, or small shopkeepers may have resulted in part from the decline in the share of the total population in these categories.[17] But do shifts in the occupational structure account for the more elitist character of the student body at the French university? Comparisons of selectivity indices and of indices of dissimilarity, which control for changes in the relative size of occupational categories, reveal that they do not. On the contrary, the overrepresentation of those of aristocratic or bourgeois origins (children of large landowners, rentiers, professionals, entrepreneurs, shopkeepers, bureaucrats, teachers, and other white-collar workers) and the underrepresentation of those from lower-middle-class and working-class backgrounds (the children of peasants, artisans, servants, and laborers) were greater in 1939 than in 1910; the ratio of the rates of enrollment for these two groups increased from 17.9:1 to 23.7:1 (and from 26.0:1 to 32.4:1 if the students of theology are excluded). These and other calculations indicate both that the French university's Alsatian constituency was much more elitist than that of its predecessor and that changes in the structure of the Alsatian economy and social order were only partly responsible.

But what else could have contributed? Two general hypotheses suggest themselves. The first concerns differences in the functioning of the French and German educational systems. A comparison of the social origins of French and German students in the 1930s (excluding those in theological faculties to control their biasing effect) shows that the French system as a whole was more elitist. The indices of dissimilarity were 68.4 and 63.5 in France and Germany, respectively, while the ratio of the enrollment rate for students of aristocratic or bourgeois origins to that for students from lower in the social order was much greater in France (31.3:1) than in Germany (19.1:1). These disparities suggest that something about the attributes of the two systems or about popular attitudes toward education made the French universities more socially selective. There are several possibilities. The meritocratic selection procedures and high attrition rates that distinguished the French system may have made the pursuit of secondary and higher education seem riskier to Frenchmen from lower-middle-class or working-class backgrounds than it did to their German counterparts. Counseling procedures and patterns of patronage may have had less egalitarian results in France. The individual costs of secondary and higher education, both the direct costs and the opportunity costs, may have been higher relative to perceived returns in France than they were in Germany. Or perhaps the cultural and political associations of France's lycées and universities—their associations with anticlericalism, with a centralizing bureaucracy, with a bourgeois life-style—were more alien to Frenchmen not already in the bourgeoisie than were the cultural associations of the German Gymnasien and universities to the comparable population. It could be argued, in sum, that the more elitist character of the French universities, including Strasbourg's, resulted not from differences in the distribution through the social order of a taste for higher education or a desire for upward mobility but rather from the incentives and constraints associated with the educational system itself.

The other hypothesis concerns conditions specific to Alsace-Lorraine. It is possible, for instance, that the differential distribution of French-speaking through the social order was largely responsible for the more elitist character of the French university. Of key importance is not the transition from secondary to higher education—for those reaching this level it is unlikely that language remained a serious problem—but rather the screening effect of primary schooling. Between the wars primary schooling, with its commitment to instruction from the outset in French (the "direct method"), represented a formidable hurdle for children from dialect- or German-speaking families—that is, for roughly 80 percent of Alsatian children. This forced teachers to devote more time to language instruction relative to other subjects than they would have at schools in the interior, with the result that even if pupils mastered French, and few did, they tended not to acquire the other skills or the motivation needed for success in secondary school. (This situation together with fears of having their children corrupted by dialect-speaking playmates caused many French-speaking parents—and some dialect-speaking parents—to send their children to schools in the interior or to the relatively exclusive and rigorous primary divisions of the lycées and collèges; in 1926, for example, the latter enrolled 2.5 percent of the cohort in Alsace-Lorraine, as compared to 1.2 percent in France generally.)[18] Put another way, for dialect-speaking families, linguistic and related problems raised the cost of investing in what economists term the option value: they increased the difficulty of completing the schooling required to have the option of going to a university. Since dialect-speaking families were concentrated disproportionately in the lower middle and working classes, the result would be to make the university's student body more elitist.

A related possibility, suggested by the experience of the German university, concerns popular attitudes toward the new regime. Linguistic problems aside, some who otherwise would have sought a secondary and higher education may have been deterred by the educational system's identification with a government and a nation-building mission to which their commitment was weak. Throughout the period, for reasons explored below, there was widespread dissatisfaction among Alsatians with the French regime and its policies, particularly in the lower middle class and the working class. This suggests that the cultural and political associations of the educational system did more to widen the gap in university attendance between the bourgeoisie and those of lower status than they had done in the German period—when the effect was probably in the opposite direction—or than they did in the rest of France.

The importance of these linguistic, cultural, and political factors is impossible to measure accurately, but there is reason to believe it was substantial. In 1910 the recruitment of Alsatians to German universities had been more democratic than the recruitment of Prussians; the respective indices of dissimilarity had been 60.1 and 66.1 for all students and 66.7 and 67.4 for those in secular faculties. But in 1939 the recruitment of Alsatians to French universities, excluding the theology students since there were none at universities in the interior, was less democratic than the recruitment of Frenchmen generally; the indices of dissimilarity were 69.6 and 68.4, respectively (see table 9, appendix B). Much of the increase in the indices for Alsatians probably can be traced to factors making the French system as a whole more elitist than the German. But the size of the change suggests that forces specific to Alsace-Lorraine were also important.

Before concluding this discussion a comment on the theology students is in order. One would expect these students to come from lower in the social order than those in other faculties, but at the French university the difference was pronounced. Thus 55.6 percent of the Alsatians in the theological faculties in 1939 came from lower-middle-class or working-class backgrounds, as compared with 12.2 percent of those in the secular faculties. (At the German university the rates in 1910 had been 52.5 percent and 20.4 percent, respectively.) Indeed if the theology students are counted, the university's student body was relatively egalitarian by French standards (the indices of dissimilarity were 65.9 and 68.3, respectively), although still not by German standards. In this regard it is worth recalling the debate during World War I over the merits of having theological faculties at the French university. Whatever their impact in other areas, these faculties did much to moderate the university's elitist character.

But there was room for improvement. By any yardstick the student body of the French university was more socially exclusive than that of its predecessor. This was not by design. No one in a position of authority

wanted the university to restrict its constituency to the region's predominantly French-speaking bourgeoisie. But this was the result, and it was
a result with important consequences both for Alsatian society and for
the development of the university. It meant that the institution's impact
on the Alsatian social order was essentially conservative; compared with
its predecessor the university did more to perpetuate traditional elites and
less to foster social mobility. It also meant that the students came disproportionately from the Alsatian groups most likely to be sympathetic
to French rule and to the university's Frenchifying mission. Whether this
was desirable in terms of this mission broadly defined—in terms of nation
building in Alsace-Lorraine generally—may be debatable. But as far as
the peaceful development of the university is concerned, the composition
of the student body could hardly have been more conducive to success.

· 2 ·

The professors came to Strasbourg committed to their nation-building
mission. But how was this commitment to be turned into results? What
special steps would be needed if the university were to fulfill expectations?
These matters the professors debated at length in their first few months
in Strasbourg, and the result, in effect, was two sets of policies: one
bearing on life within the university community and the other on relations
with the larger world. We shall consider each area in turn, examining both
the policies pursued and the reactions of the relevant constituencies. The
focus is on the first five or six years, the period when the basic patterns
took form.

Although all academic systems contribute to the selection and training of
elites, these functions are often obscured, particularly by professors, with
rhetoric emphasizing other missions. This was notably the case in nineteenth-century Germany, where professors' pronouncements concerning
the purposes of higher education tended to focus on learning for its own
sake and the advancement of knowledge while ignoring or belittling anything suggesting a preoccupation with status attainment. In France, however, the rhetoric was different. Central to the mission of the French
universities as understood by their professors and by others was the
formation of a national elite. There might be disputes over the extent to
which this elite should be selected on the basis of merit rather than birth
or wealth, or over the appropriate methods of training. But on the fundamental issue there was agreement: the universities were, above all,
agencies of elite formation.[19]
    This outlook affected how the Strasbourg professors approached their
more specific mission. At the German university the approach had been
essentially indirect; the emphasis had been on the symbolic value of a

university that embodied the best of German learning. But the professors at the French university stressed the importance of direct, personal influences. While hoping their scholarship would also have an impact, they assumed that it would be through the training of their Alsatian students— the future elite of the region and, in part, the nation—that they would contribute most to their special mission.[20]

There were two important consequences of this concern with elite formation. First, the professors sought to win the respect and confidence of their Alsatian students. Thus they took their teaching responsibilities seriously, including the responsibility to present their material with style and with an eye to the larger context. While anxious to disprove the allegations that French scholars were superficial *feuilletonists,* they did not sacrifice the concern for coherence and style that, in their opinion, distinguished the French approach to scholarship and teaching from the German. As one professor put it, they hoped to demonstrate that their methods were "no less rigorous, . . . more impartial, conducive to the purest truth, and, especially, more careful about the manner of presentation, more imbued with humanity and sensibility."[21] They intended to show that they could offer everything the German professors had offered, and more.

But impressing students from the lectern would not suffice. To have the desired impact, the professors believed, they must also establish close personal relations with the students. This assumption helps to explain their commitment to the university's numerous institutes, for they considered these not only central to their efforts to make the university a model of reform but also, since they fostered collaborative work and closer associations, important "from the point of view of the professor's impact on his students."[22] Similar reasoning encouraged professors to conduct seminars at their homes, to organize extracurricular organizations with academic overtones, to lead student excursions to various locations in Alsace, and to take an active interest in the social life of the students, a subject treated below.[23] Of course to some degree this professorial interest in close relations with students is present at all universities. But the evidence, including professors' and students' comparisons with their experiences elsewhere, suggests that by French standards the commitment of the Strasbourg faculty was unusually strong.

The second consequence of the faculty's interest in elite formation concerned the university's relationship to the French educational system generally. Although the professors hoped to distinguish their university from those in the interior, they also considered it "important above all to give the youth of the recovered provinces the means to serve the national community."[24] Hence it was essential that they prepare their students well for the national examinations governing entry to the bureaucracy and the major professions, and that their institution's diplomas be recognized as at least equal in value to those of other French universities. Whatever the professors may have thought of this preoccupation with examinations and diplomas—and of the impression it left on Alsatian and foreign observers—they must accommodate themselves if their students were to have access to elite positions in French society.

The professors' commitment to elite formation, predictable as it was, would have been less pronounced had it not been for the conditions they found in Alsace-Lorraine, both the conditions in the region as a whole and those at the university. Their observations of the more general environment quickly convinced them that full assimilation would not come automatically or easily, thus strengthening their belief in the need to recruit and train a Francophile elite. And their contacts with their Alsatian students also fueled their sense of mission, in part because they indicated that even with this select population much remained to be done and in part because they furnished encouraging evidence of progress. Two subjects received particular attention: the language problem and the difficulties many students had in adjusting to their professors' methods and expectations.

The dimensions of the language problem are difficult to assess. But in the first few years many Alsatian students, perhaps most, had difficulty understanding or expressing themselves in French. Most apparently spoke the dialect among themselves, suggesting that they came from families in which French was not the language of discourse. And the German regime, especially during the war, had assigned low priority to instruction in French as a second language. As a result many students had to choose between devoting time to learning French and leaving the university.[25]

But the difficulties, at least the more serious ones, were short-lived. From all reports the professors were sympathetic and supportive, taking pains to make themselves understood, helping students with their writing problems, and, in some cases, offering noncredit courses in the French language. In addition, during the first year or two students were permitted to write examinations and papers in German, and in the theological faculties some seminars were actually taught in German. For their part the students—those not giving up at the outset—did their best, with many registering for summer courses in French or visiting the interior to gain practice.[26] In the final analysis, however, the problem was resolved less by goodwill and determination than by the passage of time and changes in the composition of the student body. The proportion of Alsatian students from French-speaking families grew steadily, and increasingly those from dialect-speaking families who did reach the university arrived with a good working knowledge of French. Although there were occasional complaints that "many students still do not have a perfect understanding of the French language," after the first two or three years the problem was not one requiring special concessions or forbearance.[27]

The second object of concern for the professors involved the Alsatian students' opinions regarding their responsibilities and freedoms. Almost from the time classes began there was dissatisfaction with the policies of the university and its faculty. Students complained about the requirements for registration, about the emphasis on examinations, about the system of grading, and about the professors' policies of taking attendance, requiring excuses for absences, interrogating students in class, inspecting students' notebooks, and sending reports on students' performance to their parents. Often they went on to argue that while the German professors had respected their privileges as academic citizens, the French professors treated them as if they were still in secondary school. The only solution would be for the faculty to learn to respect their academic liberties and their *droits acquis,* their vested rights.[28]

Surprised and a little embarrassed by this controversy, the professors dismissed some of the students' charges as overblown and did their best to fend off the others. They insisted that the students must adapt to French customs and that the offensive policies were in the students' interests since the purpose was to ensure that students were adequately prepared for their examinations. Some professors even attempted to prevent those who complained from taking their examinations. As for the professors' classroom practices, there were no changes of note; this was not an area in which the professors were prepared to be conciliatory.[29]

The dissatisfaction never really ended. Whenever Alsatian students chose to criticize the university, the alleged deficiencies of French instructional methods tended to receive emphasis.[30] But as a subject of serious concern the issue did not survive the university's first three or four years. The professors' refusal to change their ways no doubt contributed, but probably more important were the decline in the number of students with firsthand knowledge of German practices and the worsening of students' job prospects. Later cohorts, lacking a standard of comparison, were more inclined to accept the professors' methods as those appropriate to higher education. And the careerism that increasingly characterized students in Alsace-Lorraine—as well as in the rest of France and, for that matter, in Germany—made them more sympathetic to the faculty's emphasis on careful preparation for examinations. Sacrificing traditional student freedoms for better career prospects seemed an acceptable exchange.

The matter of their *droits acquis* aside, the Alsatian students seemed generally satisfied with their professors and with the academic side of life at the university. Of course there were occasional gripes of the sort found at any university. Some students encountered professors they considered boring, pedantic, intimidating, or overly demanding.[31] And some lamented the lack of closer relations between students and faculty, the professors' efforts notwithstanding.[32] But overall the attitude was one of respect and confidence. Students, even the most Germanophile, were impressed by the scholarly authority of their professors and found most to be conscientious, tolerant, approachable, and generous with their time and advice. They discovered that the professors were neither *feuilletonists* nor disinterested in their students. In this respect there proved to be no reason to fear invidious comparisons with the German university.[33]

But if the students generally admired their professors, the latter did not reciprocate. Among themselves the professors complained that the Alsatian students were passive and unimaginative, that their ambitions were limited, and that they lacked the verbal and other skills needed to compete with students from the interior. Particularly frustrating was the Alsatians' general lack of interest in advanced degrees or the *concours* leading to high positions in the country's educational and governmental hierarchies.[34] With the aid of their university's unique resources and their curricular and organizational reforms the professors had hoped, as one put it, "to broaden the horizons of the students beyond the limits outlined by the different *licences*."[35] And by some standards they succeeded. Thus the Faculties of Letters and the Sciences awarded more doctorates between the wars than did those at any other provincial university, and in the one year for which figures are available (1929–30) they enrolled more candidates for the *agrégation*.[36] But the students preparing for advanced degrees or *concours* came disproportionately from the interior. In the mid-1920s, for instance, Alsatians accounted for about two-thirds of the university's French students but for less than one-third of those preparing for the *agrégation*.[37] But the students who came to Strasbourg from the interior—often supported by scholarships awarded on the basis of merit— were not typical French students. In fact the Alsatian students may have been no more prosaic in their tastes or restricted in their horizons than most students at France's other provincial universities. And if they were, the differences in their values and aspirations, like the language problem, presumably would diminish with time. Meanwhile the faculty could find consolation in knowing that their Alsatian students were, on the whole, well-disposed, industrious, and, in the words of one professor, "interested in discovering what these different methods were that we had to offer or to array against the methods of *Kultur*."[38]

In assessing the impact of higher education on students it is necessary to consider more than the formal curriculum and the character of faculty-student relations. The informal or "hidden" curriculum also has an impact; the general ambience of the institution and the dynamics of peer group relations leave imprints, just as do lectures and seminars and learned habits of study, thought, and expression. Indeed under certain conditions their lasting influence may be greater. This is often the case, for instance, with students living away from home, especially if reared in a culture at odds with that prevalent at the university.[39]

The importance of the informal curriculum was recognized by those who planned and staffed Strasbourg's French university. From the outset they assumed that the success of their efforts to mold a Francophile Alsatian elite would depend largely on the extracurricular subcultures to which the Alsatian students were exposed. And they proceeded accordingly. Convinced that student life was in this case too important to be left to the students, they sought to shape and control the extracurricular side of university life and to introduce their students to environments considered healthy.

For one thing, they encouraged Alsatian students to spend time at universities in the interior. They established special scholarships for those willing to attend other French universities, negotiated student exchanges, and offered students of Protestant theology full credit for up to two years of study at the free faculties of Montpellier and Paris.[40] They did so not because they considered institutions elsewhere in France superior academically but rather because the environments at institutions in the interior seemed more conducive to strengthening students' identification with *la patrie*. The reasoning was perhaps best expressed in an article on the Alsatian students in Paris that appeared in 1928:

> Exposed by themselves to French life, to its representatives, to its traditions, to its monuments, the Alsatian students—here we are referring especially to those for whom France was still an unknown entity—better appreciate its grandeur and gain a clearer sense of the reality. A stroll at Versailles, camaraderie in the French style at the Café d'Harcourt, the sight of the colonnade of the Louvre, the theater, the atmosphere of Paris have more of an impact than months of teaching, especially when a young man, temporarily freed from regional and familial influences, is alone to interpret these new impressions and to reconcile them with his view of the world.[41]

Did many Alsatians undergo such learning experiences? In 1924, the year for which the data are most reliable, about one-fourth of all university students born in Alsace-Lorraine were at institutions in the interior, with about two-fifths of them at the University of Paris. (These rates do not embrace those at the grandes écoles, a small group both absolutely and, it seems, relative to the numbers from other regions of France; in 1927–28 about forty Alsatians were enrolled at the grandes écoles, with about thirty of them at the Ecole des hautes études commerciales.)[42] In the case of the reannexed part of Lorraine, now known as the department of the Moselle, 40.6 percent of all students were in the interior, half of them in Nancy and most of the rest in Paris. Of the students born in Haut-Rhin, 26.9 percent were enrolled in the interior and 11.3 percent in Paris, while for Bas-Rhin the rates were 18 and 6.1 percent, respectively. The motives of these students differed. For some the incentives provided by the authorities were decisive. This seems particularly true for students in the Faculty of Letters, those for whom scholarships for study in the interior were most plentiful. Others were attracted by the charms of the Latin Quarter, by the prospect of academic requirements less rigorous than Strasbourg's, or, in the case of many from around Metz, by the proximity of Nancy. Still others were sent by dialect-speaking parents anxious to have their children master French. And some less than enthusiastic about French rule in Alsace-Lorraine went in the belief that they could expect fairer treatment from professors in the interior than they could find in Strasbourg.[43]

Closely related was the campaign to attract students from the interior to Strasbourg. The motives were in part similar to those for the recruitment of foreign students: to bolster the university's enrollment (all the more necessary if many Alsatian students attended other institutions) and to add to its stature in Alsace-Lorraine and beyond. But the authorities were also influenced by their desire to shape the student subculture. They wanted students from the interior because these students, to quote from a memorandum prepared by the Protestant theological faculty, "are in a position to spread the French spirit and a knowledge of the French language among the Alsatian students."[44]

This desire to attract students from the interior had several consequences. It contributed to the launching of a summer program offering instruction in German and courses on contemporary Germany.[45] It encouraged officials to take steps to improve the quality and lower the cost of student life. It led to attempts to persuade the ministry to assign more scholarship recipients from the interior to Strasbourg.[46] It was one motive for the student exchanges negotiated with other French universities. And, perhaps most important, it tempered the professors' zeal for curricular and pedagogical innovation: as it became clear that the university's appeal to students from the interior depended largely on its success in preparing candidates for national examinations and *concours*—on its success conventionally defined—the professors tended to adjust accordingly.[47]

Although the impact of these specific incentives cannot be measured, the overall pattern is evident. In the university's first year there were fewer than 200 students from the interior, but over the next decade the number rose significantly, in part because, as one observer noted, there were now university communities in the interior "where it is already à la mode to have 'studied a year in Strasbourg.'"[48] The peak was probably reached in the early 1930s, when in some years close to 600 students from the interior enrolled. Judging by figures from 1928–29 these students were most conspicuous in the Faculty of Pharmacy (natives of the interior, including those from families now living in Alsace-Lorraine, accounted for 53 percent of all French students) and, to a lesser degree, in the Faculties of the Sciences (39 percent) and Medicine (37 percent), and least evident in the Catholic theological faculty (5 percent). The rate in the Faculty of Law (31 percent) was close to that for the university as a whole (30 percent), while the rates for the Faculties of Letters (24 percent) and Protestant Theology (22 percent) were slightly below the overall mean.[49]

Another aspect of the efforts to shape the university's informal curriculum concerns students from Germany. Although the professors favored the recruitment of foreign students, they considered German students a special case for reasons relating to student life at the university. Thus the dean of the law faculty warned the rector late in 1919 that "the presence of Germans would risk poisoning the atmosphere of our faculty. . . . The presence of Germans would lead to two results: confrontations between Alsatians and Germans [and] a disastrous influence of the Germans on the Alsatians."[50] He repeated the warning two years later: "More than ever it seems to me that it would be a serious mistake to authorize the enrollment of Germans in the faculty. Although the faculty's students from Alsace and Lorraine satisfy us *completely, in every respect,* I believe that daily contact between them and the Germans could only have bad consequences."[51]

But while banning German students may have been consistent with the university's Alsatian mission, it was hardly compatible with certain aspects of its international mission. How could the university foster the *rayonnement* of French learning in Germany if it refused to admit German students? It was a question asked in one form or another by several professors. Those in the theological faculties were particularly insistent. Hoping to increase their relatively low enrollments, and perhaps also to raise their standing in the eyes of their secular colleagues, they had ambitions of competing with Bonn for youths from the Rhineland and the Saar planning to enter the clergy, and hence wanted to keep their options open.[52] But professors in other faculties had similar ambitions and similar arguments. Thus early in 1920 the dean of the Faculty of the Sciences took issue with a suggestion that potential students from the Rhineland, those interested in theology aside, be sent to Nancy: "It is reasonable to assume that the impact of our lay professors on the lay students would be just as significant from the standpoint of the *rayonnement* of France in this region; one can also note that such a solution *mortgages the future* and diverts from Strasbourg a sizable contingent of students, to the profit of our rival."[53] He and his allies conceded that it might be impolitic to admit German students immediately, but they assumed that after a year or so this would no longer be the case.

The dispute was resolved with a compromise. The faculty council decided to exclude all German students during the university's first year and subsequently to let the relevant dean decide each case on its merits.[54]

In practice this meant that after the first year Germans attended the university, but not many. Through the 1920s, when the number of Germans at French universities grew from 2 to 1,015, there never were more than 15 in Strasbourg.[55] Obviously the enrollment of Germans was too small to have an impact of consequence on student life in Strasbourg. It also called into question the earlier rhetoric concerning the university's potential impact abroad. If its German students were to be the agents, the institution's contribution to the *rayonnement* of French culture and scholarship in central Europe could not have been significant.

It was not only through shaping the composition of the student body that the authorities sought to influence the extracurricular life of the university. They also intervened in more direct ways. For instance they gave considerable attention to student housing, a subject traditionally neglected by French universities. The most tangible result—described by the rector as "one of our most important projects"[56]—was the acquisition in 1920 of a large and ugly building adjacent to the university, hitherto known as Germania, to serve as a dormitory and student center. Renamed Gallia, the building was redesigned to provide rooms for nearly 200 students as well as space for a student restaurant, meeting rooms, and offices. The objectives were to enhance the university's appeal to students from the interior and from abroad, to facilitate relations between these students and those from Alsace-Lorraine, and to provide a focal point and acceptable ambience for student life generally.[57]

The professors and officials also involved themselves in the actual orchestration of the students' extracurricular activities, both openly and covertly. As noted already, they arranged student excursions and supervised student clubs of an academic character, such as a Circulo italiano and a Cercle slave. They also staged soirées for students and directed political organizations catering primarily to students, such as the local branch of the Groupement universitaire pour la Société des nations.[58] And, most important, they worked behind the scenes to shape the clubs founded and administered by the students themselves. Exploiting their authority, their persuasive powers, and the funds budgeted by the ministry to foster student activities, they attempted to steer organized student life in directions considered healthy. As for the results, they can best be assessed after looking at the organizations in question and at the general character of student life in Strasbourg.

When the university opened, the largest and most conspicuous student organization was the Cercle des étudiants de Strasbourg. Essentially a reconstitution of the prewar Cercle and Club, it announced its formation on the eve of the arrival of the French troops with a ceremony at the Place Kléber followed by a procession to the Place de la République (formerly the Kaiser-Platz) and the toppling of the square's equestrian statue of the Kaiser. Activities such as these and its distinguished ancestry brought the group to the attention of officials and others from the interior and persuaded many that it represented all Alsatian students. And the Cercle exploited this favored position. It fêted and advised the members of the Appell commission. It helped to convince the authorities to close the German university immediately and joined Bucher and other *anciens* in lobbying for the establishment of the new university on a grand scale.[59] It affiliated itself with the Union nationale des associations d'étudiants de France (UNEF), whose officials apparently considered it an official organization representing all students in Strasbourg.[60] It sent a delegation to Paris (at the invitation of the Association des étudiants de Paris) to be honored at a series of receptions and banquets and praised for confirming the Parisians' "poetic image" of the Alsatian students.[61] It appealed to Clemenceau and Millerand to ban German students from the new university.[62] And at the university's inaugural ceremonies its dynamic president was the only spokesman for the Alsatian students and conveyed the impression, widespread already, that these students were united behind the Cercle's leadership.[63]

The Cercle did not represent all Alsatian students, however, nor did its members see this as their mission. It is true that some *anciens* argued that there was no longer a need for a counterpart to the earlier Cercle and Club, and that the new Cercle should transform itself into a general student association open to all.[64] But the active members rejected this option. Convinced that it was not yet possible to take for granted the cultural assimilation or allegiance of the university's Alsatian students, they argued that the Cercle should remain true to the traditions of its fabled ancestors. If it was to do justice to its motto, "Tout pour la France," it must remain small and select.[65]

In practice this meant that the Cercle enlisted about 1 of every 8 male Alsatian students. As with the earlier Cercle and Club, the great majority, 109 of 138, were students of medicine (80) or law (29). Viewed another way, roughly a third of the male Alsatians studying medicine belonged, about a tenth of those studying law, pharmacy, and the sciences, perhaps 1 of every 30 in the Faculty of Letters, and none of those in the theological faculties.[66] Considering this distribution and the Cercle's high fees and mission, most members presumably came from higher in the social order than Alsatian students generally.

Predictably many who did not belong resented the Cercle's exclusiveness, condescension, and influence. Late in 1918, for example, an anonymous group of students expressed "their most profound regret over the proclamations of the Cercle, which now is claiming leadership of the Alsatian students. We are sorry that the Cercle could ever come to be equated with the Alsatian students."[67] But, as this group's anonymity suggests, the political environment was not conducive to challenging the

Cercle. Nor, for that matter, were the economic and academic environments. Both the character of the French educational system and the careerist concerns that preoccupied students worked against the development of organized student life. The problem, one Alsatian student complained, was that "the student sees his fellow student as a rival, not as a comrade. An esprit de corps, so to speak, does not exist among today's university students."[68]

To be sure, the Cercle was not the only student club. In the year or so following the armistice several special interest organizations were reconstituted or founded, including H₂S, which remained restricted to students of pharmacy, a tennis club, an alpine club, and clubs for Socialist and Zionist students. In addition the two Protestant fraternities founded in the 1850s, Argentina and Wilhelmitana, reappeared, albeit without all the uniforms and other German trappings adopted before the war.[69] But with one exception these clubs and fraternities had few members and little impact on student life; none was a potential rival to the Cercle in size or prestige.

The exception was the Cercle Ozanam, an organization dedicated to furthering the interests and strengthening the religious convictions of the university's Catholic students. (Its objectives were similar to those of the Cercle Ozanam established at the German university in the 1890s, but there was no direct connection between the two clubs.) The founders, former members of the German university's Catholic fraternities, expected to attract more than 200 students. They also hoped to contribute to a revival of Catholicism among French students generally; this was one of the areas, they believed, in which Alsatians had something valuable to offer the interior. But they were only partially successful. The Cercle Ozanam did have an impact at the national level, notably as a catalyst for the founding, in 1922, of the Fédération des étudiants catholiques français, an organization which sought "to foster, more fully and more thoroughly than in the past, the recruitment and training of a Catholic elite."[70] But locally the club fell short of expectations. It never enrolled more than a few dozen and never had much influence in the university community.[71]

The picture of the Alsatian students that emerges is of a sharply divided group. But what did this mean from the standpoint of the university's Alsatian mission? Did any of the clubs or fraternities represent obstacles to this mission? And what about the many Alsatian students, probably a majority, who belonged to no extracurricular organization? Although the evidence is far from conclusive, some observations can be made. To begin with, in the first few years no student organization or movement could be considered revanchist; no Germanophile groups attempted to play a role analogous to that of the Cercle and the Club at the German university. But not all students were as ready as those in the Cercle to sacrifice "tout pour la France." Certainly the great majority welcomed French rule in the abstract and thought of themselves as patriotic, but when it came to the specifics of assimilation many were ambivalent or reserved judgment. This was the case, for instance, with the members of Argentina and Wilhelmitana, who habitually spoke the dialect, sponsored lectures in German, and favored a Franco-German rapprochement.[72] For them, and for others, much would depend on how systematically the new regime pursued the cultural integration of the recovered provinces, and this would only become clear with time.

This wait-and-see attitude found no favor with students whose commitment to France and to assimilation was unconditional. And their reactions only aggravated the situation. The Cercle's response and its effects have already been noted. But more significant was the response of another group counted on to contribute to the university's Alsatian mission, the students from the interior.

These students did not constitute a homogeneous group. They varied in their backgrounds and motives for coming to Strasbourg and in their expectations concerning what they would find. But most had little sympathy for the distinctive traditions of the recovered provinces or for the problems Alsatians faced in adapting to the new regime, and they had few inhibitions about manifesting their sentiments. They had confrontations with the many Alsatian students who had served in the German army, particularly those who had been officers. Through their general deportment and dress, including the wearing of berets, they flaunted their lack of identification with the region. They essentially appropriated the *monômes* and transformed these processions, once noted for their solemnity, into occasions for disrupting traffic and insulting Alsatian onlookers. And they organized forays directed either at "removing from liberated Strasbourg the last vestiges of Prussian tyranny,"[73] such as the statue of Germania and the painted insignia on the former headquarters of the Kriegerverein (veterans' association), or at demonstrating against newspapers critical of their efforts to purify the city.[74]

The many students involved in these activities (some demonstrations had close to 300 participants) were not all from the interior. Some foreign students took part, and so did a few Alsatians (motivated, according to one critic, by a fear of otherwise being labeled *boches*).[75] But the great majority of the Alsatian students abstained; although they often had friendly relations with students from the interior—indeed some sought them out as *copains* ("buddies")[76]—they disapproved of demonstrations likely to offend local sensibilities. The position of the Cercle was particularly noteworthy, for its commitment to assimilation was beyond question. On occasion the president and other members tried to convince students from the interior to refrain from activities offensive to Alsatians. And in 1921, following an unusually tumultuous incident, the Cercle issued a statement disassociating itself from the participants and warning the public to be on guard against student activities not authorized by established organizations. Its members obviously suspected that the patriotic demonstrations orchestrated by students from the interior were doing more harm than good.[77]

Others, similarly concerned, reacted differently. The gap between Alsatian students and those from the interior, together with the differences among the Alsatian students, convinced many of the need for a comprehensive student association, one that could unite and represent—and help to control—all students. Since the Cercle had renounced this role, and since no other extant club was an acceptable candidate, a new organization would be necessary.

It was easier to recognize the need than to satisfy it. The university's early years witnessed a number of well-intentioned efforts that foundered due to general indifference, to the opposition of the Cercle and other organizations, or to the demands of some that others be banned from membership. One project collapsed, for instance, because students from the interior insisted on excluding all former officers in the German army (a demand which did much to widen differences and heighten tensions among the students).[78] In the university's fourth year, however, there were encouraging developments. Some faculties established *amicales,* clubs uniting all students within a faculty for the purpose of organizing excursions and soirées as well as an annual banquet and ball. And early in 1923 a special assembly of students decided, by a close vote, to establish an Association générale des étudiants. The declared objectives were to give official representation to the university's students and to further their interests. The organization was to remain neutral on all questions of politics and religion.[79]

In its first two years the Association générale was active in several areas. It published a student newspaper, administered a student restaurant at the Gallia as well as a bar and a café, organized the *monôme* that followed the university's annual convocation, and sponsored lectures, dances, a photography club, and sports teams. It also gained recognition by the UNEF as one of the two "official" student organizations in Strasbourg, alongside the Cercle. But despite these accomplishments the Association had difficulty building or even maintaining its support among the students. In each of its first two years only about 500 students, a fifth of the total, paid membership fees, and in the third year the number was smaller. The problem was that students tended to identify less with the Association than with their respective *amicales.* In effect the Association and the *amicales* competed for the support of the same constituency, and the *amicales* were prevailing. Indeed by the end of 1925 the president of the Association had resigned in frustration and the organization hardly existed except in name.[80]

The university's professors and administrators followed these developments with concern. Over the years they had done much themselves to foster both the *amicales* and a general student association. Disappointed that the Cercle had resisted broadening its constituency, they gave it no more than nominal support from the university's funds for student activities and used the rest to refurbish the Gallia and, beginning in 1923, to support the Association générale.[81] A few days after this organization appeared the faculty council, "very eager to manifest its sympathy to the Association," approved its request for control over certain student services.[82] A little later the rector backed its application for affiliation with the UNEF, insisting that "this young association is certain to perform the greatest services for the students of Strasbourg and it seems to me to offer all the guarantees one could desire."[83] In their annual reports the deans expressed satisfaction over the appearance of the Association and the *amicales*.[84] And professors urged their students to involve themselves in these organizations. "In matters of cooperative life," one reported to his dean, "you know . . . how I have personally urged our students, albeit without seeking to decide for them, not to confine themselves to confessional associations, which are legacies of the German period and divide rather than unite, and to develop the *amicale* of the students in the Faculty of Letters, in which serious work and good fellowship are united."[85]

Some professors might have been just as sympathetic to organizations like the Association générale and the *amicales* had they been at other French universities. Certainly many in the interior believed that student life should be more organized, if only, as Durkheim once put it, to counter "this distressing impression of loneliness which too frequently dampens the enthusiasm of the French student."[86] What motivated most Strasbourg professors, however, was less a concern about French student life generally than a desire to further their Alsatian mission. Troubled by the divisions among their students and by the lack of a truly French ambience outside the university, the professors rallied to the idea of comprehensive organizations which, like the Association générale, seemed to offer "all the guarantees one could desire" and to promise "a prosperous life pursued in close contact with the university."[87] In short, they welcomed and supported the Association générale and the *amicales* because they considered them trustworthy and potentially valuable instruments of the university's informal curriculum.

· 3 ·

It was not only through their students, through the molding of an assimilated elite, that the professors hoped to advance their Alsatian mission. They also wanted to extend their influence beyond the university community. To this end they developed what amounted to a curriculum for

Alsace-Lorraine generally, with different programs tailored to different segments of Alsatian society.

But in doing so they faced serious obstacles, more serious than expected. These obstacles were related to what the professors and others termed, rather euphemistically, the *malaise alsacien*—the widespread disillusionment and disaffection that developed among Alsatians under the new regime. Since this malaise had a profound influence on the outlook of the professors and on the university's relations with Alsatian society, it merits closer attention.

Evidence of the developing *malaise alsacien* appeared almost as soon as the French authorities detrained. The enthusiasm with which most Alsatians greeted the arrival of French troops and the postarmistice visits of Clemenceau and Poincaré quickly gave way to disenchantment and sullen resistance. The dimensions and rapidity of the change were striking. Three weeks before the end of the war a German official had estimated that in a plebiscite 80 percent of the Alsatians would vote for France, 10 percent for independence and neutrality, and 10 percent for Germany.[88] But four months after the armistice an Alsatian priest whose own attachment to France was beyond question insisted that if given a choice the great majority would opt for independence and neutrality.[89] And over the next few years the situation did not improve, at least not markedly. A journalist from the interior who toured the region in 1920 concluded that "if one staged a plebiscite now there would not be a majority for France. In fifty years the Germans did not succeed in making themselves liked, but in less than twenty months the French have caused themselves to be hated."[90] Two years later a group of Alsatians told an American visitor that in a plebiscite 85 percent would vote for independence.[91]

At the root of the problem were the unrealistic expectations both Alsatians and those in the interior brought to their reunion. The enthusiasm with which Alsatians welcomed the French late in 1918 resulted less from identification with contemporary France than from hatred of Germany and a desire for peace. Most Alsatians knew little about France, and what they knew was based more on nostalgia for the period prior to 1870 than on familiarity with the France of the Third Republic. For their part, many in the interior, influenced by their schooling and the prewar nationalist revival, believed the Alsatians were French not only in allegiance but also in language and culture. And even those who knew better, such as the *revenants*, tended to assume that since the Alsatians were reputedly so patriotic they must want full and rapid integration into France. It was as if they expected a quick restoration of the relationship that had existed prior to the Franco-Prussian War. They seemed unaware of how much had changed since then in Alsace-Lorraine—and in France.[92]

Of the specific obstacles to assimilation, the most obvious was language. There had been linguistic problems before 1870, with the authorities attempting to use the schools to Frenchify the region over Alsatian opposition. But the situation had worsened in the interim, for the French language had lost ground in Alsace-Lorraine while the rest of France had moved closer to linguistic unity and, in the process, to the association of French patriotism with use of the French language. One result was that many officials from the interior fell easily into the habit of regarding Alsatians who spoke French as patriots while dismissing the rest, the great majority, as *boches* or *bochophiles*. In addition countless practical problems resulted from the inability of most Alsatians to communicate with officials or to understand court proceedings or official documents and from the government's insistence that French be the language of instruction in the schools. Undoubtedly most Alsatians wished they knew French and wanted their children to learn the language. But they did not want French taught to the exclusion of German for fear that this would create a barrier between parents and children and result in the latter learning nothing except French, if that. It was not long before Alsatians began to complain that an educational crisis was developing, with the primary schools, the only ones most children attended, producing a generation that did not know correct German and yet did not really understand French and had learned little of other subjects.[93]

Also causing discontent was the religious question, a question both constitutional and cultural. Under German rule church-state relations had been regulated by the legislation in effect in 1870, including the Napoleonic concordat (1801) and the Falloux law (1850), meaning that the government paid the clergy and supported confessional schools. But in the same period France had moved toward the total separation of church and state, a process completed in 1905. Hence full assimilation would necessitate abrogating the legislation concerning religious affairs honored by the Germans. Such a step would clearly damage the new regime's popularity, so the authorities decided to postpone it and to maintain the earlier laws in the interim. But this decision found little support. Alsatians who were anticlerical—a small group but one generally bourgeois and French-speaking and hence very influential in government circles—considered it an unjustified concession to obscurantism. And the clergy and their spokesmen, a few Protestants excepted, viewed the prospect of separation with alarm, seeing it as a threat to their material interests and to the influence of religion in the region. These concerns explain why the clergy quickly moved to the forefront of those demanding recognition of the Alsatians' *droits acquis,* that is, the preservation of the legislation and privileges recognized by the previous regime. This demand was basic to the program both of the Union populaire et républicaine d'Alsace (UPR), a clerical party organized more or less on the model of the German Center Party, and of the region's influential Catholic press.[94]

It was not just the prospect of separation that troubled and mobilized the clergy. The government's administrative and language policies also contributed. The clergy feared these policies would undermine what was, for most Alsatians, the language of the Bible and of religious services, replacing it with a language identified with free thinking (and, often, one the priests and pastors could not speak). They complained, too, that these policies resulted in the region being overrun by bureaucrats from the interior, most of them Jews or Protestants or Freemasons. They were particularly concerned about the teachers from other parts of France (about one-sixth of the total in the early 1920s),[95] whom they considered dedicated proponents of separation and serious threats to the clergy's traditional position of leadership. The situation had much in common with that found in the more devout regions of France in the late nineteenth century, when the lay school teacher, indoctrinated by the école normale, had begun to compete with the priest for dominance in the village. But there was an important difference: in Alsace-Lorraine the clergy could present themselves as defenders not only of their parishioners' faith but also of their language and, by extension, of their cultural identities. It was a formidable combination.[96]

Opposition to the government's linguistic and religious policies was primarily responsible for the *malaise alsacien,* but there were other sources. Among them was the economic situation. Although in some respects there was little reason to complain—Alsatians were spared the rapid inflation besetting Germany and the problems of reconstruction facing northeastern France—the need to reorient production to different markets caused difficulties, and the resulting discontent reinforced that developing for other reasons. In addition there were fears, particularly among urban workers, that assimilation would entail the dismantling of the insurance and welfare programs established by the German regime. One result was that the unions and the local branches of the Socialist and Communist parties joined forces with clerical interests in seeking recognition of the region's *droits acquis.*[97]

Also important was dissatisfaction, evident even among those supporting the government's policies, with how the region was administered. There were complaints about the incompetence of officials from the interior, about the slowness with which decisions were made, about waste, about high taxes, about the state of the railways, and, in general, about the new regime's inability to administer Alsace-Lorraine in an efficient and orderly manner. Compounding the problem was a belief, largely justified, that the bureaucrats from the interior did not like the region or most of its natives—those dismissed as *boches*—and that they had come only because of the salary bonuses and opportunities for rapid promotion associated with service in this "colonial" outpost.[98]

Closely related were the problems posed by the "sacrificed generation," by the Alsatians, often graduates of the German university, who had advanced to responsible positions in the government or certain professions under the previous regime. They would have had difficulty adjusting under the best of circumstances, for their training differed from that required for comparable positions in France and they often lacked fluency in French. But complicating the situation were the government's policies and the often vindictive attitudes and behavior of the region's French-speaking elite. After investigating their past activities the government dismissed some officials who had attained middling or high positions under German rule, demoted others, and sent others to the interior for retraining. In addition it did not pay Alsatian bureaucrats the handsome bonuses given those from elsewhere in France and made it clear that Alsatians should not aspire to high positions in the local administration. The predictable result was widespread resentment and complaints that the authorities treated Alsatians like second-class citizens. As for those in the free professions, their fate largely depended on whether they identified with the French-speaking bourgeoisie. Those who did—most doctors and pharmacists, for instance—had few problems. But the others were distrusted and spurned by the region's French-speaking elite and denied the stature enjoyed under German rule. One result was that many in this group— probably a majority of the poets and novelists who used German, about a third of the Lutheran pastors, and so on—resettled in Germany. Most members of the "sacrificed generation" remained, however, providing a reservoir of bitterness and leadership for the forces resisting assimilation.[99]

The unexpected strength of these forces convinced the authorities to modify their policies. The results included the decision to assign full administrative responsibility to a commissioner general based in Strasbourg and to give the position to Alexandre Millerand, a politician with regionalist proclivities. These steps and the concessions introduced by Millerand and his successor (Millerand left office after less than a year to replace Clemenceau as premier) led to some improvement in the situation, and so did the passage of time. By 1921 mounting evidence indicated that the *malaise alsacien* was abating. Letters sent home by Alsatians visiting the interior, regularly inspected by the police, were becoming less critical of the people and customs they encountered. Improvements in the economy, particularly for the peasants, strengthened identification with the rest of France, as did symbolically significant steps such as the appointment of a few Alsatian army officers. And political trends were encouraging. By the end of 1919 the neutralist movement, recently a cause of considerable concern, had been nipped in the bud. There was no visible support for the revanchist groups surfacing across the Rhine. The one party favoring full political and cultural autonomy experienced a crushing defeat in the cantonal elections of 1922, the first it contested, and was of little importance thereafter. And the programs of the more popular parties were evolving in desirable directions. At the end of 1921, for instance, control of the party with the most support, the clerical UPR, passed from its "regionalists" to its "nationalists."[100]

Problems remained, of course, and embarrassing incidents and talk of the *malaise alsacien* continued. But the situation appeared to be improving steadily. Indeed, the prospects were encouraging enough to permit the government to rescind some earlier concessions. Thus by the end of 1922 control over certain branches of the administration—justice, the postal service, bridges and roads, and so on—had moved back to Paris, and a few months later it was announced that the General Commissariat itself would be suppressed.[101] Obviously the authorities assumed that the worst difficulties were in the past and that it was now possible to proceed more directly toward full assimilation.

The reaction of the professors to these developments, to the *malaise alsacien* and to the government's responses, was far from uniform. There was a pattern to the differences, however, one which reflected a pattern prevalent at other French universities. Indeed when it came to politics, little distinguished the Strasbourg professors from professors in the interior: the level of activity and the distribution of opinions were essentially the same.[102] This is hardly surprising, for the politics of all French professors of this generation had been decisively shaped by a common set of formative experiences, notably the Dreyfus affair, the subsequent separation of church and state, the prewar nationalist revival, and the war. In short, most Strasbourg professors brought their political identities and their political differences with them from the interior, and these largely determined how they reacted to local developments.

Generally speaking the professors fell into three distinct groups. Of these perhaps the largest and certainly the most conspicuous consisted of the Jacobins, to use a label popular with their Alsatian critics. Typically the Jacobins had come of age politically during the Dreyfus affair—often while students at that bastion of support for Dreyfus, the Ecole normale supérieure—and they manifested the political idealism and the self-righteousness that had characterized the committed Dreyfusards. On the national level this meant remaining vigilant against the forces of reaction, as represented above all by the Catholic church and the military. To this end these *hommes de gauche* commonly identified with the Radicals or the Socialists and with organizations such as the Ligue des droits de l'homme and the Ligue de l'enseignement. On matters of foreign policy they were relatively cosmopolitan and conciliatory, supporting the League of Nations and the affiliated International Labor Office (which employed many *normaliens*) and favoring rapprochement with Germany. As for the Alsatian question, the Jacobins desired quick and total assimilation. Committed to the ideal of *la république une et indivisible,* they saw no reason to recognize the Alsatians' *droits acquis.* Indeed they believed concessions only strengthened the hands and stiffened the backs of those deemed responsible for the *malaise,* particularly the Catholic and Lutheran clergy. They assumed that full administrative and legal integration, including the separation of church and state, would undermine the power and the corrosive influence of the priests and pastors and thereby speed assimilation.[103]

In Strasbourg, as in the interior, most professors in the Faculties of Letters and the Sciences seem to have been Jacobins.[104] In the remaining faculties, however, another group was prevalent, the conservative nationalists. Generally the professors in these faculties came from more privileged backgrounds and, because of their opportunities for private practice and consulting, had higher incomes. This helps to explain why they remained somewhat aloof from their colleagues in Letters and the Sciences—a status distinction evident in Strasbourg, albeit less pronounced than at universities in the interior—and why they tended to be more conservative politically. The typical member of this group had been at best a lukewarm supporter of Dreyfus and the separation of church and state, did not share the Jacobins' interest in seeing France ruled by its mandarins, and identified on the national level with a right-of-center party or faction and with the assertive foreign policy of Poincaré. He was concerned less with the threat to republicanism posed by Catholicism or the military than with the threat to France posed by a resurgent Germany; if the Jacobin's rallying cry was "Vive la république!," the conservative nationalist's was "Vive la France!" When it came to the Alsatian question, he was as committed as any Jacobin to assimilation, but his motives had more to do with the strength of France's eastern frontier than with the sanctity of republican principles. In this regard his views were close to those of Strasbourg's *Journal d'Alsace et de Lorraine* and the Parti républicain démocratique, both of which appealed to constituencies that were predominantly bourgeois, conservative on social questions, and no more than moderately anticlerical.[105]

The third group consisted of the regionalists. Defined broadly this group overlapped the one just considered; some conservative nationalists, among them Fernand Baldensperger and a few jurists, wanted France restructured along regional lines and hoped, like Millerand, that Alsace-Lorraine would be a catalyst for such a reform.[106] But these professors did not think Alsace-Lorraine should be a special case, and for our purposes it is more useful to restrict the term "regionalists" to those who did—to those who believed the region should enjoy a degree of autonomy and other *droits acquis* regardless of the situation elsewhere. Defined this way it was a small group. It included some Alsatian professors but few if any of those from the interior.[107]

Some in each group were active politically. The Jacobins dominated the local branch of the Ligue des droits de l'homme and on occasion gave political advice to local Socialist leaders.[108] Conservative nationalists contributed articles on the Alsatian question to the local and the national press and helped to organize and direct the Parti républicain démocratique (its president was the jurist Frédéric Eccard), the Comité républicain national (its founders included Charles Staehling and Marcel Nast, professors of chemistry and law, respectively), the local branches of the reactionary Cercle Fustel de Coulanges and Union nationale des membres de l'enseignement public (both led by the historian of philosophy Henri Carteron), and the campaign to abolish legalized prostitution in Strasbourg (led by Paul Gemaehling, a political economist).[109] The regionalists included a member of the Conseil général of Bas-Rhin (Fritz Kiener) and the president of the region's strongest political party, the clerical UPR (Eugène Muller).[110]

But the activists were in the minority. Most professors did not think their political responsibilities went beyond reading *Le Temps* every evening and voting; they refrained from speaking out on public issues or involving themselves in political organizations. In this, as in their opinions, they were like most professors at other French universities. Since the war the French academic community had largely withdrawn from the political arena it had entered so decisively during the Dreyfus affair. To be sure, many professors, particularly conservative nationalists, had always shunned this arena, considering it a corrupt realm beneath their dignity. But now those formerly active, the Jacobins included, were moving to the sidelines. For some the struggles that counted had been resolved. But there was also a resigned sense that professorial involvement in politics was not worth the effort either because it had little impact or because, as in the decade before the war, it provoked an anti-intellectual backlash. As a result the typical professor was now more inclined to think of his university as an ivory tower, as an institution to be kept isolated from partisan conflicts.[111]

In Strasbourg the situation was different in that many important political and administrative questions remained unresolved and the professors had an unusually strong sense of mission. But while local conditions encouraged some to become politically active, they deterred others. Correctly sensing that political activity on the part of assimilationist professors would further alienate the Alsatians, and optimistic about what they could accomplish in other ways, most professors either avoided political activity altogether or kept their involvement behind the scenes. Their reasoning was similar to that employed by one of the deans when asked if he would publicly support a specific position on the Alsatian question:

> Let me emphasize at the outset that I consider it a duty to keep com-
> pletely aloof from all political struggles concerning Alsace. As dean of
> my faculty . . . I would lessen my credit in the eyes of both my col-
> leagues and our students if I were to involve myself in political disputes.
> If I were only a professor I would still be inclined to hold the same
> position; in my opinion French education appears more than ever to
> be the great instrument of Frenchification in the recovered provinces.
> I believe that those who have the honor to be involved in this under-
> taking have nothing better to do than devote themselves to it, and I
> am convinced that participation in political struggles could only reduce
> their credit, their "effectiveness." Accordingly do not count on my
> support for any campaign to be conducted.[112]

It was not that these professors intended to confine themselves to the
university. They wanted to extend their influence, but in their capacity
as educators. Troubled by the *malaise alsacien* and convinced that French
education was "the great instrument of Frenchification," they valued their
credit and effectiveness not only with their students but with the world
beyond the university.

Central to the program that resulted—central to the university's curriculum for Alsatians generally—were the *cours publics,* courses taught
at the university but largely designed for the general public. All French
universities offered such courses but the Strasbourg professors gave them
greater emphasis, at least by the standard of the time. Since the late
nineteenth century *cours publics* had been declining in popularity at French
universities, for reasons relating to the growing number of regular students, particularly in Letters and the Sciences, and to the progressive
differentiation and professionalization of the academic disciplines. The
professors, increasingly evaluated on the basis of their scholarship and
their students' success rather than on their ability to attract large general
audiences, assigned them lower priority, and, as if in response, so did the
general public.[113] In Strasbourg, however, the professors had reasons for
resisting the trend, and they did. In the first year they offered eighteen
*cours publics,* all taught late in the afternoon or in the evening, and in
each succeeding year they offered a similar number. In addition they
opened many of their regular courses to the general public.[114]

Another program provided for visits to other Alsatian towns to deliver
lectures. In stressing its importance Pfister expressed the hope that there
would develop "a true circuit of professors, thus creating a sort of traveling university."[115] The results fell short of this goal, but they were still
impressive. During the winter of 1919–20 the faculty agreed on the details,
which called for coherent sequences of lectures in selected towns, and
made the necessary arrangements with committees constituted in the fa-

vored communities.[116] The program began in February 1920, and between then and the end of the academic year 46 lectures were given in twelve towns. In the next year there were almost 100 lectures in seventeen towns, not counting the many given under other auspices, and in the years that followed the numbers remained at about this level.[117]

The faculty's interest in extending its influence beyond the university also manifested itself in other ways. Some professors became active in local scholarly organizations.[118] Some lectured at other educational institutions, notably at Strasbourg's Institut d'enseignement commercial supérieur and Ecole de formation sociale and Mulhouse's Ecole supérieure de chimie.[119] Some addressed professional or business organizations and contributed to such publications as *L'Alsace française,* a weekly established in 1920 by Pierre Bucher. The theologians conducted services in Strasbourg and towns nearby and helped to administer local religious institutions. And many professors, as well as many professors' wives, supported the various organizations founded by Bucher and his associates to make adult Alsatians more familiar with French and with France. For several years Adolphe Terracher, a historian of the French language, directed the Cours populaires de langue française, taking particular responsibility, with his wife, for the affiliated theatrical troupe.[120] Gabriel Maugain, a professor of Italian literature, arranged the numerous speeches given each week under the auspices of the Cours populaires.[121] Paul Perdrizet, an archaeologist, was involved in Livre français, an enterprise dedicated to acquiring French books for the libraries of Alsatian villages. ("It is the duty of everyone," Perdrizet once explained, "to support such a good enterprise. If I were able to be of service, I was only doing what I should.")[122] Other professors, as well as some students, were associated with the Université populaire de Strasbourg, an institution designed to bring intellectuals and working-class Alsatians together through such activities as free courses on subjects likely to be of broad interest.[123]

Obviously the professors' commitment to university extension was strong, stronger than that normally found at French universities, and stronger than that evident at the German university. But what was accomplished? Were the professors' efforts justified by the results? These questions, like those concerning the professors' impact on their students, cannot be answered with precision. We must content ourselves with impressionistic generalizations.

Judging by the size of their audiences, the *cours publics* offered in Strasbourg and the lectures given elsewhere were, at best, moderately successful. Some of the *cours publics* attracted large numbers, among them those taught by Pfister, by Jean Pommier, an authority on French literature, by the historian Georges Lefebvre, by the geophysicist Edmond Rothé, and, particularly, by the art historian Samuel Rocheblave.[124] But most were poorly attended, largely because the professors made few concessions to their special audiences and hence tended to be considered pedantic and boring. As one observer put it, "No, not even during those hours, worldly charm does not enliven this university."[125] Doubtless most professors would not have had it otherwise, but the price paid was limited interest in their offerings.

Outside Strasbourg the situation was more favorable since the appearance of a professor, whatever his speciality or his style, tended to be considered a special event deserving a special show of support. Indeed in many towns the half-dozen or so lectures given each winter or spring ranked among the major events of the social season. But there also were towns in which planning was poor, and towns in which professors had to be entertainers, preferably with slides, to attract an audience. And whatever the circumstances, those attending, like those attending the *cours publics,* came almost exclusively from the French-speaking bourgeoisie. Outside Strasbourg the audiences basically consisted of local lawyers, doctors, and industrialists, immigrant lycée teachers, government officials, and their wives. The pattern was similar for the more popular *cours publics,* such as Rocheblave's, while the less popular relied heavily on the academic community itself: on other professors, on professors' wives, and on regularly enrolled students. Neither program found much support outside the educated and entrepreneurial elites.[126]

Admittedly similar efforts in the interior would doubtless have attracted similar audiences. But because of the linguistic divisions in Alsace-Lorraine and the university's Alsatian mission this pattern of support took on special significance. It meant that the professors, initially motivated by a desire to contribute to nation building, not only found themselves preaching to the converted but also, by associating themselves with the French-speaking minority, may actually have widened the gap separating the university from the rest of Alsatian society. This helps to explain why the professors soon developed a rather jaundiced view of their itinerant lecturing and the *cours publics.* The prevalent attitude, once the initial enthusiasm dissipated, was that while these programs must be continued—abandoning them would convey the wrong message—they did little to advance the university's Alsatian mission.[127]

The professors' other extension activities were no more successful. Of particular interest are two projects specifically designed to narrow the gap between the university and the lower middle and working classes. One of them, the Université populaire organized late in 1919, never amounted to much. Although several professors offered their support, including some of Alsatian origin prepared to lecture in the dialect, the institution was moribund after its first year, presumably because of a lack of demand for its services.[128] The second project, the institute of labor authorized by the government at the urging of Charles Andler, had even less impact. Through the winter of 1919–20 a committee composed of several professors and François Simiand, an economist employed by the General Commissariat, considered the proposal. The members discussed possible models, including Ruskin College at Oxford, the London School of Economics, and the Université du travail in Charleroi, Belgium.[129] They also studied a memorandum by Andler stressing the need to link the university and the working class, in part to counter the anti-intellectualism and the outdated ideology (read revolutionary Marxism) of the latter: the institute, Andler argued, should be a "Sorbonne of the trades" offering practical courses to foremen, union organizers, and other working-class leaders, and thus permitting the university "to become relevant to the popular classes."[130] But nothing came of these deliberations. For reasons that are unclear the project was shelved in the spring of 1920.[131]

Had they survived, these projects might have made a difference, at least symbolically. But as it was the only professors who had much contact with the popular classes were the theologians, particularly those of Alsatian origin. They generally could communicate easily with the region's peasants, artisans, and workers (for most other professors the language barrier was formidable), they had more exposure to students from humble backgrounds, and they often came from such backgrounds themselves. In addition their academic positions gave them greater access to the popular classes both directly, through conducting religious services, and indirectly, through involvement in administering the churches and their contacts with the parish clergy. As a result the theologians had a much better understanding of the university's Alsatian environment than most other professors, and much closer relations with nonbourgeois Alsatian society.

But these relations were not always harmonious. Given local religious divisions this was to be expected, but the situation was complicated by pressures from other directions. Some came from those involved in staffing the theological faculties, notably the Catholic bishop of Strasbourg, Charles Ruch, and the members of the free Protestant faculty in Paris. These outsiders insisted that the faculties be thoroughly French in character. This they considered particularly important, for they recognized that the local clergy had great influence over the political and cultural life of the region and suspected that it had been more contaminated than other elites by exposure to German scholarship and to Germany's political culture. But the result was that they helped to give the faculties theological orientations offensive to much of the local clergy and to many of the faithful. In the Catholic faculty, chairs were given to "priests who are notorious modernists,"[132] bringing sharp complaints from the local clergy, while in the Protestant faculty a disproportionate number of chairs went to Calvinists from the interior while (as at the German university) the interests of the orthodox wing of the Lutherans were slighted.[133]

Additional pressures came from within the university community. Many professors in other faculties believed theology should not be taught at a truly French university and hoped the two theological faculties would be nothing more than temporary concessions to local traditions. Indeed early in 1923 the faculty council appointed a committee to consider whether the two faculties should be discontinued. The recommendation was that both be retained, largely because "their disappearance would be considered, in Alsace and abroad, as entailing a diminution and weakening of the University of Strasbourg."[134] That the question received such serious consideration, however, suggests the pressures on the theologians, both subtle and overt, to justify their continued presence at the university and to gain acceptance as more than marginal. There were also the influences resulting from the theologians' personal contacts with professors in other faculties, contacts facilitated by the housing of both theological faculties in the Palais universitaire. These environmental factors contributed to the theological liberalism and incipient ecumenicism that characterized both faculties between the wars and to their emphasis on pure scholarship at the expense of pastoral theology. And these were orientations which, like those encouraged by certain religious authorities, tended to isolate the theological faculties from the popular classes and hence to attenuate the university's only significant links to much of Alsatian society.[135]

As the case of the theological faculties demonstrates, contact with the larger society did not necessarily lead to popularity. Conversely it need not be assumed that the almost complete isolation of the other faculties from the popular classes adversely affected their university's image—that lack of familiarity breeds contempt. It might even be argued that a more aggressive extension campaign, one reaching all segments of the social order, would have helped to demystify the institution and in so doing undermined one of the props, perhaps the central one, of whatever prestige it enjoyed. But there were also potential disadvantages that came with isolation. Obviously the more isolated the university the less it could contribute directly—as distinct from indirectly, through its prestige—to its Alsatian mission. Isolation might also mean that the university, like its predecessor, would come to be widely regarded as an alien imposition, as a *Fremdkörper*. Or it might mean that the institution's popular image, to the extent that it had one, would depend largely on attitudes toward institutions and social groups with which it was commonly associated— toward the regime generally, toward the primary and secondary schools, toward the French-speaking bourgeoisie, and so on.

Of these possibilities, which was the most important? What did those in the popular classes think of the university? The evidence from the first few years, the period that concerns us here, indicates that these Alsatians, or at least their spokesmen, were neither indifferent nor satisfied. There were complaints about the chauvinistic antics of the students and warnings that they might cause Alsatians to have as little respect for French student life as they had had for German student life.[136] Catholic politicians and newspapers attacked the appointment of Alfaric ("a veritable insult to the devout portion of the population")[137] and the pervasive anti-Catholicism which, they claimed, characterized the Faculty of Letters. ("An outlook is dominant there whose very distinctive character is similar to a certain sectarian orientation, one which seems to be a leftover from earlier times.")[138] Some argued that the university should incorporate features of the German university system not found in France, such as the rank of *Privatdozent*[139] and the elected rector.[140] Some insisted that the faculty was too large and the costs too high.[141] Others claimed that the university was insufficiently distinguished, that despite official claims it had neither surpassed nor equaled the German university.[142]

And, most important, many found fault with the university's definition of its mission, for reasons reminiscent of those advanced earlier by critics of the German institution. The new university, they argued, should be more Alsatian in character, or more European, or both. They wanted more Alsatians on the faculty, with a few arguing that the French were less generous in this regard than the Germans had been.[143] And they complained—this was the criticism advanced most frequently and emphatically—about the lack of instruction in German. Most conceded, at least implicitly, that the university should be predominantly French in spirit and character. They agreed that it must represent French scholarship and considered it essential that its diplomas be recognized as equivalent to those offered in the interior. But these considerations did not mean that all instruction had to be in French. Indeed some critics insisted that if the university were bilingual and hence more accessible to Alsatians its effectiveness in its nation-building mission would be enhanced. "After all it should not be forgotten," one argued, "that we are situated on the Rhine and that our university must adapt itself to the surroundings in which it lives, both the larger and the immediate surroundings. Of course it must think and feel French, and teach to think and to feel French, yet without dispensing with the means which the *bilingualism of the province* puts at its command."[144]

Such observations were most numerous in the year or two following the war, for obvious reasons. It was then that the number of students who had difficulties with French was largest, and it was then, while the university was taking shape, that the possibility of influencing policies seemed greatest. But this does not mean that the university gained greater acceptance with time. It did, no doubt, with some. But others simply resigned themselves to defeat, concluding that the university was basically an extension of the French-speaking bourgeoisie and hence unresponsive to the needs of most Alsatians.

Of course the situation was similar in the interior: to the extent that any French university had contact with the larger society, it was almost exclusively with the social groups which in Alsace-Lorraine constituted the French-speaking bourgeoisie.[145] But there were circumstances peculiar to the Alsatian context that reinforced this pattern. Because of their expectations concerning what they would find in the region and the inability of all but a few to converse in the dialect, the professors tended to limit their contacts to those who habitually spoke French. At the same time the latter, anxious to reassert their hegemony over the local social and cultural order, manifested a particular interest in identifying themselves with the university and its faculty. For those in the French-speaking bourgeoisie the university meant more than other French universities did to comparable groups in the interior, precisely because its language and cultural orientation were identified with a specific sector of Alsatian society, their own. It was natural, accordingly, that they should rally to the institution and jealously seek to shield it from the influence of those lower in the social order.

Their basic objectives for the university were similar to those of its planners, with one addition. Judging by their public statements, they wanted an institution that would contribute to the Frenchification of Alsace-Lorraine, to the eclipse of German by French scholarship in Europe and beyond, and—this was the addition—to the economic vitality of the region in general and Strasbourg in particular. In the case of Strasbourg they hoped the university would attract students and hence business to a city which had lost its former importance as a major provincial capital.[146] And more generally they wanted the university to foster the economic development of the region. Thus they proposed such innovations as a special faculty to train businessmen, a proposal essentially met by Strasbourg's Institut d'enseignement commercial supérieur, and an institute of advanced technology closely related to the university, a proposal seriously considered but never realized.[147]

Obviously those in the French-speaking bourgeoisie wanted the university to make certain adjustments to local conditions and needs. But they did not favor adjustments that might threaten its character as a purely French institution. This put them at odds not only with other Alsatians but also with certain observers in the interior, including a few of Alsatian origin. Of particular note are remarks made in mid-1919 by Henri Albert, a Parisian journalist with roots in the French-speaking bourgeoisie of Alsace: "Do you wish to know how [the university] is to be helped? If it opens its doors wide! If courses are also taught in German! The University of Strasbourg must be international or it will not survive!"[148] The phrasing and the occasion, the opening ceremonies of an exhibition in Strasbourg, suggest that Albert directed these remarks to the local French-speaking bourgeoisie. But if this were so, the impact was negligible. It could be argued, of course, that Albert's proposals were unrealistic since Paris would never accept them. But this objection aside, French-speaking Alsatians could hardly be expected to favor the kind of institution sought by Albert. Although an international and bilingual university might have been a goal worth promoting under German rule, they now wanted a thoroughly French institution, and for the same reason: they were committed to enhancing the influence of French culture in Alsace-Lorraine—and, with it, the influence of the French-speaking.

Of the two distinct conceptions of the university advanced by Alsatians following the war, one identified with the popular classes and the other with the French-speaking bourgeoisie, the second was closer to that of the professors. But the fit was not perfect. Nor could it be, for there were differences among the professors themselves over the character the university should have and over how to respond to their Alsatian critics. The range extended from those who questioned the effectiveness of a university that was thoroughly French to those who regarded the Société des amis de l'université, essentially an agency of the French-speaking bourgeoisie, as a stronghold of particularism.

The professors at the more cosmopolitan extreme, most of them Alsatian, believed a university that made more concessions to local conditions, particularly on the language question, would have greater influence in the region. They also believed, like Henri Albert, that a bilingual university would have more influence abroad, with all that this implied for the welfare of the city and the prestige of France. Perhaps the fullest expression of these views came from Eugène Kohler, an Alsatian who specialized in Italian and Spanish literature. In an article appearing in 1922 in one of Strasbourg's German-language newspapers, Kohler criticized French higher education as overly centralized and bureaucratized and called for "an autonomy as complete as possible for the universities." He then focused on the local university, giving particular attention to the language question. After referring to Benedetto Croce's recent charge that the university was "denationalizing" Alsatian youth, he insisted that "all foreigners who come to Strasbourg, without exception, are astonished that no professors teach in German; they shake their heads and say with amazement: 'Strasbourg, a European university!'" Kohler added that the university should recruit German students in order to expose them to "our point of view and our ideas." But this could not he done, he implied, unless they were taught in their own language. Obviously he believed that the university's policies, at least on the language question, were at odds with its mission.[149]

When asked by the rector to comment on this article, Pfister, Kohler's dean, observed that it "contains interesting observations and Kohler has not exceeded his rights." He made clear, however, that except in two special cases—courses for those specializing in German studies and courses for foreign students "who come to Strasbourg to learn both French and German at the same time"—all instruction must be in French.[150] Most professors were no more conciliatory. Representative was the opinion of one who was otherwise among the more cosmopolitan, the Germanist Edmond Vermeil. Responding in 1922 to recent criticisms of the university in the Alsatian and German press (Kohler's among them), Vermeil insisted that "the French University of Strasbourg knows what it is worth and what it is doing. Neither the unjustified attacks of a regionalist press that is often poorly informed nor those of the German press, inevitably spiteful and full of hatred, will impede its progress on the road it is traveling."[151]

On other issues the professors tended to be more accommodating. As noted already, they took steps to limit chauvinistic demonstrations by the students and, after some indecision, agreed to retain the two theological faculties. In addition the deans and the rector, continuing a policy initiated in 1919, looked favorably on Alsatian candidates for faculty appointments and promotions. Late in 1920, for instance, the dean of the Faculty of Medicine recommended a promotion for the anatomist André Forster at least in part because he was an Alsatian,[152] while Pfister justified a proposed promotion for Fritz Kiener with the observation that "the Alsatians often complain of being sacrificed and it is necessary to make a concession to them."[153]

But many professors opposed such concessions. Some insisted that Alsatian candidates for chairs should not be regarded any differently than those from the interior, while others manifested a bias against Alsatian scholars, particularly those less than fluent in French, arguing that there were too many on the faculty already or that their political views were suspect.[154] And there continued to be opposition to the two theological faculties. None of this implies a lack of concern for the university's Alsatian mission or an unwillingness to make sacrifices. It was just that many professors thought all sacrifices should contribute directly to the prestige or dissemination of French scholarship. They did not believe concessions likely to make the university less French or to lower its stature could be compatible with their mission.[155]

Some even had misgivings about the Société des amis de l'université. This organization had great success in its primary objective, raising money for the university. Within a few months of its founding it had enrolled over 1,000 members and received several sizable contributions from individuals and firms in Alsace-Lorraine, in the interior, and in the United States. The proceeds supported such projects as the university's summer courses in French and German, the special courses for law students from Luxembourg, the construction of an institute of geophysics, soirées that brought students into contact with local French-speaking families, and student exchanges with universities in the interior.[156] Yet some professors reacted with ambivalence. While appreciating the society's generosity, they questioned its motives; they considered the organization "a threatening citadel of particularism" likely to favor projects incompatible with their conception of the university.[157] And there was some justification for these suspicions. The Alsatians in the society, Bucher included, tended to be moderately particularistic in outlook. Although committed to linguistic assimilation and to enhancing the prestige of the university, many remained attached to certain local traditions and *droits acquis* (the religious legislation, for instance) while others feared that full assimilation, desirable in principle, would intensify the *malaise alsacien*. In addition some members from the interior openly favored the restructuring of France along regionalist lines and looked to Alsace-Lorraine and its university for leadership. They included two of the society's cofounders and vice-presidents, André Hallays and Jean de Pange, and one of the most prominent members of its governing committee, the novelist and politician Maurice Barrès.[158]

A few months after the university opened the professors' concerns came into the open. The provocation was a request by Barrès for permission to offer a *cours libre*—a series of lectures authorized by the university but given by an outsider—on the cultural history of the Rhineland and the policies France should pursue in the area. The request came with the strong support of Raymond Poincaré, the recently appointed president of the Société des amis, and of Fernand Baldensperger, the faculty's liaison with the organization. But it provoked a heated debate within the Faculty of Letters, to which the request was addressed. On one side were those convinced that the lectures would be political in character and hence an embarrassment to the university. Thus Etienne Gilson argued that the lectures would convey a misleading impression of the university and undermine the campaign launched during the war to convince foreigners that France's universities, unlike Germany's, did not subordinate scholarship to nationalism: "We are assuredly an instrument at the service of French influence," he acknowledged, "but this instrument will be so much the more effective the less it gives the appearance of being such." Others argued that *cours libres* should be offered only by those with the appropriate scholarly credentials (Charles Blondel), that this was a particularly bad time to be discussing France's mission in the Rhineland (Edmond Vermeil), that the proposed course would set a precedent leading to equally controversial requests in the future (Lucien Febvre), and that, as a possible compromise, Barrès should be asked to give his lectures without the faculty's imprimatur, perhaps under the patronage of the Société des amis (Febvre and Maurice Halbwachs). Their opponents attempted to be reassuring. They insisted that Barrès enjoyed a good reputation abroad (Baldensperger and Samuel Rocheblave), that he had given assurances that the lectures would not be political in character (Baldensperger and

Pfister), and that because of his special relationship to Alsace-Lorraine his course need not set a precedent (Gustave Cohen). In addition Pfister observed that since Barrès had always been ready to come to the university's defense it would be unseemly if the faculty refused his request.[159] These arguments, together with a reluctance to embarrass Pfister and Poincaré, carried the day: by a vote of sixteen to eleven the faculty approved Barrès's request.[160]

On one level the visit of Barrès later in the year proved a great success. His five lectures, collectively titled "Le génie du Rhin," attracted large and distinguished audiences, including many literary and political figures from Paris, and they responded enthusiastically. In addition there were warm receptions for Barrès organized by the Cercle and the Société des amis.[161] But elsewhere the reaction was far from sympathetic. A basic theme of the course, that there should be an interpenetration of the cultures of France and the Rhineland and that Alsatians and the University of Strasbourg had a special responsibility to foster this, impressed most professors as misguided and dangerous.[162] Many outside the academic community reacted similarly. With one notable exception, the *Journal d'Alsace et de Lorraine,* the local press sharply criticized the lectures. And German observers exploited this opportunity to dismiss the university as nothing but a bastion of French chauvinism. As many professors had feared, the lectures conveyed an image of the university sharply at odds with the one the faculty had sought to establish.[163]

The dispute over the Barrès lectures was not the last of this sort. There continued to be concern on the faculty that outsiders, and particularly the Société des amis, were attempting to use the university for purposes incompatible with the institution's integrity and missions.[164] The officers of the Société des amis tried to adjust—"it is necessary to take care not to offend the professors of the university"[165]—but they thought the faculty should be more appreciative and accommodating: "If there is some grumbling at the university," Hallays observed in 1922, "from now on we shall give *all* our lectures elsewhere. . . . Ah! One could not say that the university is friendly to its friends!"[166]

As this suggests, the relations between the faculty and the local French-speaking bourgeoisie were not as harmonious as other Alsatians often assumed. Although the university had stronger ties to this social group than to any other, a gap remained. There were several reasons. The only segment of the Alsatian bourgeoisie to which the professors might have been expected to establish close personal relations, Strasbourg's Protestant patriciate, was an austere and close-knit group not readily accessible to outsiders. There were various issues in addition to those involving the Société des amis over which the professors and members of this patriciate were periodically at odds, including the relationship of the municipal hospital to the medical faculty and the administration of the Lutheran church.[167] There were the distinctive residential patterns that characterized the two groups, with most professors living in the area north and east of the university developed under German rule while the indigenous bourgeoisie remained in the older section of the city. There were also the distancing factors associated with the evolution of the modern university and with life in large cities; both the size of the faculty and the size of the local French-speaking elite meant that each could be self-sufficient socially and hence that special efforts would be required to bridge the gap.[168]

Many professors did make special efforts, considering this an essential part of their mission. Thus some professors acted as advisers to local politicians, and some joined Alsatian notables in discussion groups such as one that convened weekly at the Café Bauzin.[169] There were also professors who established ties to local scholarly organizations, professors who planned dinner parties with an eye to narrowing the gap between the two communities, and professors who worked alongside Alsatians in the propagandistic enterprises spawned by Bucher or in supporting local cultural institutions such as the municipal theater and the symphony orchestra.[170]

With time, however, the commitment to closing the gap waned. This was natural enough. Regardless of the circumstances one could hardly have expected the professors' readiness to make sacrifices for their Alsatian mission to remain at its initial level. But also a factor was the intensity that characterized social life *within* the university community. Compared with universities in the interior, social relationships both within and among the various faculties were unusually close and the obligations unusually heavy.[171] The professors considered this one of the appealing features of their university, and it is easy to see why. For one thing the intense social life reinforced, as it reflected, the pronounced esprit de corps that distinguished the faculty. But it also exhausted time and energy that might otherwise have gone to involvement in the world beyond the university. And by sensitizing the professors to each other, it tended to desensitize them to outsiders. This helped to perpetuate the gap dividing the faculty from local elites and to strengthen the professors' sense, shared with their German predecessors, that life in Strasbourg was much like life in a foreign colony.[172]

# 10                     On the Defensive

In the academic year 1922–23, the faculty council's vice-president boasted in his annual report, the university "completed a new stage in its progressive flowering." More precisely, it had continued "to manifest its firm resolve steadily to increase its activity with respect both to the intensity of its work and to the extension of its influence."[1] His colleagues shared this pride and optimism. To be sure, they had encountered difficulties and disappointments. They had faced not only the problems that normally accompany institution building but also those imposed by their special missions and by the government's efforts at retrenchment, and they had done so in an environment that was in some respects alien. But they had responded with resolve and, on the whole, with success. Their university was the most innovative in France and the most distinguished in the provinces. And there were signs it was succeeding in its Alsatian mission. There were already more Alsatian students than there had ever been at the German university, and now that most veterans and youths with language difficulties had left the students seemed overwhelmingly Francophile in sentiment. There was also an impressive program of university extension which presumably would become more influential with time. In short, by the fourth or fifth year the professors could assume that the most difficult period was behind them and that the university's future would be peaceful and prosperous.

This confidence proved short-lived. Beginning in the mid-1920s a series of challenges both less expected and more intractable than those faced earlier undermined the professors' optimism. By the end of the decade the once prevalent conviction that time was an ally had given way to a belief that the university's best years were in the past. And the trends and challenges of the 1930s only reinforced this assessment. Throughout this decade the basic mood within the faculty was one of anxiety tempered by pessimism and despair. The professors, once so confident and expansive, were now on the defensive.

$\cdot$    1    $\cdot$

The change in the faculty's outlook can be traced to a dramatic change in the character of the Alsatian question. In the mid-1920s the *malaise alsacien,* hitherto diffuse and apparently abating, developed into a full-fledged and strong autonomist movement. It was a process which did not culminate until late in the decade, but it had its origins in 1924 with the national elections of that year and the announcement of the new government's intentions regarding the recovered provinces.

The elections of 1924 brought to power the so-called Cartel des gauches, a moderately left-wing coalition headed by Edouard Herriot. Considering its anticlerical and Jacobin character, this coalition could be expected to pursue the integration of Alsace-Lorraine more vigorously than the previous regime, and Herriot quickly indicated that it would: he announced that his government would suppress the General Commissariat—a process started in piecemeal fashion by the previous regime—and introduce measures "which, while respecting existing conditions and treating with consideration the moral and material interests of the population, will permit the introduction in Alsace and Lorraine of all of the republican legislation."[2]

Many Alsatians would welcome these pledges. As for the rest, Herriot assumed they would accept their fate quietly. In this he was encouraged by the low level of disaffection recently evident in Alsace-Lorraine and by assurances given by Alsatian *revenants* and by the two Socialist deputies just elected in the region. But he miscalculated. On the day following Herriot's pronouncement a spokesman for twenty-one of the twenty-four Alsatian deputies warned that "to pursue the realization of such a program . . . would be to provoke serious agitation in our region for which we decline all responsibility."[3] The clerical press of Alsace-Lorraine responded similarly. And over the next few months a series of protests gave substance to the warnings. The government was attacked at public rallies, including one in Strasbourg attended by about 50,000. The region's departmental councils issued strongly worded statements, as did almost 1,000 of the roughly 1,700 Alsatian communes. Catholic newspapers and journals referred to an impending religious civil war, spread horrible rumors about the fate awaiting monks and nuns, and discussed the possibility of appealing to the League of Nations. The bishop of Strasbourg castigated the government, issued a decree prohibiting the faithful from reading anticlerical newspapers, ordered daily prayers against the church's persecutors, and organized a one-day school strike and a referendum on the desirability of confessional schools (both supported by about two-thirds of the Catholics in his diocese). The Protestant press and the president of the Lutheran consistory also protested, albeit less vehemently, and so did the grand rabbi of Strasbourg.[4]

This unexpected agitation caused the government to modify its plans. Herriot did suppress the General Commissariat, replacing it with a bureau in Paris directly subordinate to the premier. But he stopped short of tampering with the religious legislation of Alsace-Lorraine, using as his pretext a decision of the Conseil d'état declaring the Napoleonic concordat legally valid in the region. And his successor as premier—Herriot resigned in April 1925 for reasons unrelated to the Alsatian question—sought to restore calm by assuring Alsatians that "legislative assimilation would be pursued only . . . in consultation with all qualified advisors, showing respect for the *droits acquis* and concern for general good feeling and for national unity."[5] He was conceding, in effect, that the protests had slowed the pace of assimilation.[6]

But this retreat did not end the agitation. Herriot's policies had convinced many Alsatians that the government could not be trusted to honor its promises, making constant vigilance essential. In addition the vehement protests of 1924 and early 1925, particularly in the Catholic press, had done much to legitimize open attacks on French policies, and there were many in the wings ready to exploit this development. Noteworthy were those associated with *Die Zukunft,* a weekly launched in May 1925. The sponsors and contributors shared a determination to protect their homeland's Germanic cultural heritage and a conviction that since time was against them they must take the offensive.[7] It was to this end that they founded *Die Zukunft.* The journal reflected the bitterness, the alienation, and the cultural pessimism widespread among educated Alsatians, particularly those of the "sacrificed generation." It idealized the years of German rule, for instance, while depicting the period since the war as one of economic and social dislocation and cultural decadence. As for the future, it wanted Alsace-Lorraine to become a cultural bridge between western and central Europe—a theme stressed a generation before by Youngest Alsace—and in 1926 it added a monthly supplement, *Die Brücke,* designed to further this mission.[8] (There was talk of inviting René Schickele, then living in Baden, to edit this supplement, but nothing came of this.)[9]

The journal's impact was impressive. Within a year the circulation reached 35,000, a remarkable figure considering the size of the region's population, and the journal became the leading symbol of the self-consciousness and aspirations of disaffected Alsatians. It also furnished the inspiration and basic program for a new political organization, the Elsass-Lothringische Heimatbund. In its founding manifesto the Heimatbund called for stout resistance to the "assimilationist fanatics" and announced that its objective was "complete autonomy within the framework of France."[10]

*Die Zukunft* and the Heimatbund transformed the political climate. By focusing attention on autonomy they forced the region's political parties to take a stand on the issue. In two cases, the Socialists and the Democrats, this meant becoming more assimilationist than before. But the other parties moved in the opposite direction; either they became thoroughly autonomist (the Communists) or they split into two distinct factions with the autonomists in the majority (the clericalist UPR and the Radicals) or at least more salient than before (the Lothringischer Volkspartei, a cousin of the UPR). These developments reinforced the trends fostered by *Die Zukunft* and the Heimatbund—and, inadvertently, by Herriot. The issues of autonomy and cultural particularism now moved to the center of Alsatian political life, pushing aside such traditional concerns as social reform and the separation of church and state. And as this happened the autonomists—some with financial assistance from Germany—became increasingly bold. Thus by the end of 1927 four parties had called for self-determination for Alsace-Lorraine, two had appealed to the League of Nations, Catholic members of the Heimatbund had defended the autonomist cause in a memorandum sent to the Pope, and the recently founded Landespartei had established contact with Breton, Corsican, and Flemish autonomists and announced that its ultimate goal was an independent state.[11]

At first the government reacted cautiously. Concerned about foreign opinion and confident that time was on its side, it largely confined itself to trying to avoid further provocations.[12] But as the autonomists became less restrained so did the government. It wielded the carrot and the stick. Officials reiterated earlier assurances concerning the concordat and other *droits acquis,* gave rhetorical support to the ideal of a bilingual Alsace-Lorraine mediating between France and Germany, and made a few substantive concessions, notably concerning the study of German in primary schools. At the same time the government took repressive action. It suspended some of the government employees who signed the manifesto of the Heimatbund and fired the rest. It organized counterdemonstrations against the autonomists, apparently including the one provoking the tumultuous "Bloody Sunday of Colmar" (22 August 1926). It used informants and agents provocateurs to implicate autonomist leaders suspected of separatist sentiments. And it made liberal use of its judicial powers. The culmination came in the winter of 1927–28. Prodded by the activities of the new Landespartei, the government now suppressed several publications, including *Die Zukunft,* searched more than 100 residences for incriminating evidence, and arrested over two dozen autonomists on charges ranging from espionage to endangering the security or the credit of the state.[13]

This flurry of activity and the trials and convictions that followed—in May 1928 in Colmar—intensified the developing crisis. Disaffection with the government and with France was now deeper than at any previous time. Indeed late in 1928 an Alsatian who had warmly greeted French rule ten years before estimated that at least two-thirds of the Alsatians would now choose Germany over France, and more than 90 percent would prefer independence to France.[14] With time, and with the granting of amnesty to those convicted at the Colmar trials, the tension abated. On both sides there developed a desire to avoid open confrontations and a better understanding of the limits this entailed, and the result was a period of relative calm, one lasting until the mid-1930s.[15] But through these years the autonomists remained active and strong. The crisis had not ended.

· 2 ·

The rise of the autonomist movement affected the university in many ways. To begin with, it ended the relative immunity from public criticism that the university had recently enjoyed. Various publications now revived charges advanced when the university was being organized, and added new ones. Until its suppression *Die Zukunft* led the campaign. With arguments reminiscent of some earlier ones directed at the German university, it chastized the authorities for not making the institution a bridge between French and German culture, for discriminating against Alsatian scholars, and for slighting subjects of particular relevance to Alsace-Lorraine. It criticized the limitation on students' freedom to visit other universities—read German universities—and the devious tactics used by university officials to impede particularistic students from organizing. And it attacked the emphasis of French higher education on obligatory lectures and frequent examinations, arguing that while it produced some excellent specialists it also turned students into grinds and careerists who regarded their peers as rivals rather than compatriots.[16]

Some of the autonomist parties and politicians were as critical, and their proposed remedies as radical. Thus at a general assembly late in 1925 the UPR adopted a resolution calling for bilingual instruction at all educational levels.[17] A little later a prominent member of the party argued that the university must be bilingual both "to enable each student to preserve and develop the linguistic and cultural traditions of our homeland" and to permit it to contribute to "the world mission to which in my opinion we must henceforth be dedicated."[18] The manifesto of the Heimatbund insisted that the region's complete educational system "should . . . be developed not according to the dictates of the central administration in Paris, but rather in conformity with the individuality and cultural richness of the people of Alsace-Lorraine."[19] The leader of the autonomist wing of the Radicals wanted the university to become a clearinghouse for French and German scholarship, and added that "in the system of international intellectual cooperation, for which France has just put an institute in Paris at the disposal of the League of Nations"—he was referring to the controversial forerunner of UNESCO—"Alsace and the University of Strasbourg ought to claim a special place."[20] In a similar vein the program of the Landespartei argued that *"Our university should become a center of world culture* at which the elites of [France and Germany] can come together." It also proposed, more prosaically, that the institution be expanded "to offer the facilities for research in technology and in agriculture that we still lack."[21]

Of course none of these reforms was likely to be introduced, at least not unless Alsace-Lorraine actually received autonomy. But in some areas it was possible to resort to substitutes, and the autonomists did. In the mid- and late 1920s they founded several scholarly institutions and publications intended to fill, in part, the vacuum left by the university's alleged neglect of its Alsatian and cosmopolitan missions. Of particular note are the Gesellschaft für Elsässische Kirchengeschichte (1926) and the Elsass-Lothringische Wissenschaftliche Gesellschaft (1927). The former, directed by a leading autonomist, promoted research on local religious history and related fields, much of it appearing in the society's series of monographs, its biographical series, or its annual *Archiv für Elsässische Kirchengeschichte*. Virtually all of its publications were in German.[22] The latter sponsored research in all areas of scholarship, but with particular emphasis on Alsatian subjects. It published the results in a yearbook and five series of monographs, with one series set aside for works in French. Its flourishing activities and its very existence challenged the university's claims to be the center of research on Alsatian questions and thus made the latter institution appear more one-sided and alien. It is not surprising, accordingly, that French authorities tried to impede the society's development, albeit without noticeable success.[23]

The rise of the autonomist movement also affected events within the university. Most important, it fostered a growth of particularistic sentiment among the Alsatian students. This trend was best reflected in the evolution of the university's fraternities.

During the university's first few years its fraternities—Argentina and Wilhelmitana, both reconstituted in 1919, and Nideck, founded early in 1922—had gradually abandoned their Germanophile orientation. The trend was particularly apparent after their initial cohorts, composed largely of veterans of the German officer corps and former students of the German university, gave way to a new generation. By 1923 the fraternities obviously were becoming more open to French influences. Argentina began to admit students from the interior, for instance, while Wilhelmitana changed the language of its journal from German to French and dropped the *Kneipen* (stylized drinking parties), songfests, and costumes so central to German fraternity life in favor of debates and other activities of the sort associated with French *cercles*.[24]

But with the emergence of the autonomist movement this trend ended. Although the older fraternities avoided overt political activity—it would have jeopardized their existence—they now redefined their missions along more particularistic lines and put greater emphasis on the trappings and practices of German fraternities. Thus the members of Argentina began to celebrate their *Kneipen* and wear their uniforms more openly, and in the more circumspect Wilhelmitana singing and *Kneipen* and strict discipline returned to vogue, as did the displaying of colors.[25] In addition two new fraternities appeared—Alsatia (1926) and Wasgo-Lotharingia (1928)—and they manifested a similar commitment to traditional forms and cultural particularism. Both were Catholic fraternities, with the more important, Alsatia, linked closely if unofficially to the autonomist branch of the UPR. Among its honorary *Alte Herren* (old boys) were many of the most prominent Catholic autonomists, including Eugène Muller, Xavier Haegy (director of the region's leading network of newspapers), and the directors of the Gesellschaft für Elsässische Kirchengeschichte and the Elsass-Lothringische Wissenschaftliche Gesellschaft.[26]

Despite differences along confessional and other lines these fraternities, like the autonomist political parties and factions, collaborated in what amounted to a united front. Discussions in 1926 led to the formation of this front, the declared objective being "a slow reconquest of the powerful position which students at one time occupied at the university and which, with the armistice, was lost to them."[27] The front first manifested itself early in 1927 when the members of the associated fraternities attended a reception sponsored by Nideck for visitors from a fraternity in Basel.[28]

The number of students in these fraternities was small. In the late 1920s it averaged about 80, or roughly 7 percent of the male Alsatians at the university.[29] Thus the fraternities enlisted about as many students proportionately as had the Cercle and the Club before the war. But there were additional students in sympathy with the fraternities' cause, as there had been with the Cercle's and the Club's. How many is impossible to determine, but estimates at the time suggest that about 300 students—a fifth of the Alsatians at the university—supported the autonomist movement and that another 200 had autonomist leanings.[30] These students came from all faculties, but they were most evident in the two theological faculties (where most Alsatian students seem to have been proautonomist) and least evident in the Faculties of Law, Medicine, and Pharmacy.[31] As for their origins, the members of Alsatia, as described by one of them, were doubtless typical: "If we take a somewhat closer look at the origins of our active members we find that they are almost exclusively of rural or lower-middle-class origins. Representatives of the so-called bourgeoisie in the usual pejorative sense are not found among us."[32]

While some students reacted sympathetically to the emerging autonomist movement, others moved in the opposite direction, becoming more chauvinistic. Provoked both by local developments and by trends in the interior, where rightist ideologies dominated student life, many attached themselves to royalist or fascist leagues such as the Camelots du roi, a branch of the Action française, and the Jeunesses patriotes. But the majority of these students—80 percent according to one estimate—came from the interior.[33] Although some Alsatian students had earlier been attracted to the leagues by their attacks on the anticlerical and economic policies of the Cartel des gauches or by the federalist program of the Action française, a number now switched their allegiance to the autonomist movement.[34] This reinforced the changes occurring in the role of the leagues. Once known above all for their hostility to the Third Republic, they increasingly were distinguished by their commitment to defending France against the autonomist threat. This trend together with the ways they expressed themselves—their pranks and demonstrations, their insults and head-knocking—did much to widen the division within the student body between particularistic Alsatians and those committed to full assimilation.[35]

Most members of the university community lamented these developments. They identified neither with the autonomists nor with the leagues, and they feared that these groups' activities jeopardized the institution's reputation and its potential as an agent of assimilation. But what could be done to improve the situation? Of remedies specific to the university, that most widely discussed was the formation of a new student organization, one designed to counter both the corrupting influence of the fraternities and, at least indirectly, that of the royalist and fascist leagues.

Two projects received particular attention. The first was identified with Jules-Albert Jaeger, the editor of a conservative daily and the director of several enterprises inspired by Pierre Bucher (who had died in 1921). Beginning in 1925 Jaeger called for the formation of a society to be known as Jeune Alsace. Its basic objective would be to reverse the spread of the *Zukunft* movement within the university community by uniting the Alsatian students "in French surroundings." Beyond this little is known of Jaeger's intentions, although he seems to have envisioned a student union under the tutelage of the Société des amis de l'université.[36]

The second project originated about the same time with a group of students from the Faculties of Letters and Law. Essentially it involved a reconstitution along federal lines of the moribund Association générale. There was to be an *amicale* for each faculty—some existed already—and delegates from these *amicales* would administer the more general organization, to be known as the Association fédérative générale des étudiants de Strasbourg (AFGES). Officially the new society, formally constituted early in 1926, was to be concerned primarily with furthering students' material interests while remaining free of political ties. Yet unofficially it had an important political mission, as its officers emphasized when appealing to university and government officials for support. In their organization, they argued, "the Alsatian students will be able . . . to establish relations with their comrades from the interior; the latter will learn to understand better the mentality of the region, and will become more respectful of certain susceptibilities. Above all the possibility of gaining material advantages will give the students a good idea of what a determined French government can accomplish.''[37]

The organization's potential, its founders insisted, was much greater than that of its rival for official support, Jaeger's Jeune Alsace. The latter ''will actually group only the relatively few who, because of the character of their family traditions, have no need to be grouped.''[38] This minority ''is in full accord with the students from the interior'' but, and this was the key, not with their fellow Alsatian students: ''Their contact with the majority is at a minimum and their influence is very limited. They are proponents of energetic political action directed at the supposedly autonomist forces, that is at those who are not French in culture and tradition. They do not seem to have understood certain realities.''[39] Accordingly Jeune Alsace could serve no useful purpose; ''we even maintain that it could only *accentuate the schism.''* And they added a more general warning, by way of highlighting the utility of their own approach:

> If one does not want to experience complete defeat entailing the greatest international consequences, it is necessary to forget about the purely sentimental and verbal manifestations that no longer have any effect on popular opinion, to put into effect certain indispensable reforms in justice and administration, and to make France known objectively by her accomplishments. It is necessary that as soon as a young student has difficulties making ends meet he can turn to a well-constituted French organization if one does not want him to be thinking always about the past.
>
> The students will group themselves around their restaurant and around their flourishing student association; you will always find them at their student union without ever having exposed them to any moral pressure.[40]

These arguments proved persuasive. The professors welcomed the students' initiative and promised financial assistance, and key government officials—notably Poincaré, who returned as premier in June 1926—were equally supportive. In addition the UNEF quickly recognized the new society as the only ''official'' representative of the university's students. (The Cercle, long inactive, withdrew its claim when AFGES was constituted.) This combination of support effectively ended the threat from Jeune Alsace, which proved stillborn, and permitted the officers of AFGES to proceed with their plans.[41]

These plans, many inspired by foreign models, went beyond those of the earlier Association générale and of any other French student organization. In its first year AFGES opened a housing office, sponsored a tour of eastern Europe, organized a theatrical troupe, persuaded many local stores to offer student discounts, and established France's first compulsory student medical plan. Early in 1927 it opened a student restaurant, one objective being ''to provide a neutral place where students of all

religions, of all ideologies, will come together, will get to know each other
. . . at a time when there is reason to fear that a gulf is developing between
the various groups of students."[42] In 1928 it organized a sports club and
set up a vacation colony in Corsica. And over the next few years it
established a student newspaper, a tutoring service, and a placement
office. (The primary purpose of the placement office was to make it easier
for Alsatians to find jobs in the interior or in the colonial service.)[43]

In addition the officers commissioned plans and sought funding for a
*cité universitaire* to include, initially, two dormitories of 250 rooms each,
a gymnasium, a stadium, and other sports facilities. In defending the
project they argued that more students would come from the interior and
from abroad once it was known "that students can find in Strasbourg
facilities equivalent to those of foreign universities, such as the American
universities."[44] They noted, too, that the proposed complex, and particularly the athletic facilities, would make it easier to overcome divisions
within the student body. They emphasized both "the moral détente, *particularly necessary,* that sports will produce among the students,"[45] and
the potential of physical exercise and competition as substitutes for less
desirable forms of extracurricular activity: "We believe that an interest
in sports will easily take the place of the political and sentimental preoc-
cupations, of the sullen, gloomy, and sterile complaining in which students
often seem to delight."[46] These arguments persuaded the rector and Poincaré, and at their urging the government authorized the project. But the
needed funds did not materialize, and the depression soon ended hopes
that they would come soon. As a result the *cité universitaire,* the most
ambitious undertaking of AFGES, never moved beyond the planning
stage.[47]

Even so the record of AFGES was impressive. From the outset it was
France's most innovative and dynamic student organization, one looked
to as a model by its counterparts in the interior. It also had one of the
largest memberships. By 1928 about three-quarters of the Strasbourg students belonged, and the proportion remained near this level over the next
several years. This support together with dedicated leadership—the officers exhibited a sense of national mission rivaling that of the professors—
permitted AFGES, unlike its predecessor, to remain active and relatively
healthy.[48]

But there were crises and setbacks, some serious. By mid-1929 the
restaurant had developed such a deficit that AFGES had to be rescued
by a specially constituted group of patrons, the Société des amis des
étudiants.[49] This embarrassment as well as the various services AFGES
performed for the faculty and the government—including, some alleged,
sending the police lists of students suspected of autonomist sympathies—
convinced many that the organization was more an instrument of the
authorities than a genuine student union. For this and other reasons,

including the demands of their course work, students gave AFGES little support beyond their membership fees. Most who joined did so only for the material benefit and did not participate in the election of officers or the social events of the *amicales*. The number willing to devote much time to managing AFGES and its projects probably never exceeded a dozen or so. It was not an organization for which many made sacrifices.[50]

Nor did AFGES do much to heal the divisions within the student body. This would have been difficult under the best of circumstances, and the obstacles were formidable. In the first place the fraternities, despite attacks in the press and resistance within, were becoming increasingly Germanophile and assertive. Symptomatic was the so-called *Meiselocker* affair late in 1929. At the dedication of a statue of a *Meiselocker* ("titmouse caller") donated to Strasbourg by the city of Munich, delegates of the five fraternities appeared in their formal regalia. The resulting scandal— it was the first time since the war that Strasbourg students had worn full colors in public—had two important consequences. It caused the fraternities to boycott AFGES, the latter having denounced the demonstration at the *Meiselocker* and dismissed an officer who had participated. This boycott further isolated the autonomist students from the rest and, in the eyes of many, contributed to the politicization of AFGES. The scandal also aggravated the developing crises within the individual fraternities over their respective missions and rituals, crises leading to the resignation of many of their more moderate members. This exodus left the fraternities even greater strongholds of autonomist sentiment than before.[51]

Reflecting these developments was the changing attitude of the fraternity members toward relations with Germany. Hitherto Strasbourg students had had virtually no contact with Germans. In the mid-1920s, however, a new pattern emerged. Autonomist students began to cross the Rhine to buy German newspapers and to visit the Palatinate on camping trips. They also established ties to German fraternities. Late in 1931, for example, delegates from Alsatia and from Catholic fraternities in Freiburg and Basel convened in Freiburg for the first of what were to become regular meetings, and in 1932 Alsatia hosted a group of 123 students from Heidelberg while members of Argentina and Wilhelmitana visited Frankfurt as the guests of local fraternities.[52] In addition autonomist students welcomed the support of German benefactors, receiving gifts of scholarly books and, in a few cases, stipends for study at German universities.[53] Although such contacts need not imply separatism, these students were becoming more committed to the idea of a *Kulturgemeinschaft* uniting Alsace-Lorraine and Germany and were doing more to develop this community.

For some this commitment meant improving ties not only to German students and scholarship but also to Alsatian commoners. If the German heritage of their homeland was to survive, they reasoned, the intellectual vanguard must foster the cultural self-consciousness of the broad mass of the population, particularly the younger generation. Like their professors, albeit for different reasons, these students sought to narrow the gap between the university and Alsatian society. To this end some, especially Protestant students, participated in the hikes and songfests and folk dances of the Bund Erwin von Steinbach, a replica of the German Wandervogel established in 1926 by a student of Protestant theology.[54] In 1931 a group led by another student of Protestant theology founded *Der Wanderfalke,* a bimonthly literary magazine directed at Alsatian youth.[55] Students also provided valuable support for the radical Elsass-Lothringische Jungmannschaft. Organized in 1931 by a recent graduate of Strasbourg's law faculty, the Jungmannschaft based its program and tactics on those of German *völkisch* groups, particularly the Nazis. According to its characteristically vague manifesto, the movement "represents the band of youths who sense and know that in Alsace-Lorraine, as everywhere, a new era is beginning. . . . In the Jungmannschaft the student walks beside the young worker, the young farmer beside the young office worker. . . . We will reconquer the homeland that has been taken from us. Its destiny lies in our young, strong hands."[56] The Jungmannschaft eventually developed a following throughout the region, but its initial support came largely from the university community. In fact, according to its founder, it "would not have been conceivable without the fraternities."[57]

Yet this support was confined to a small minority of the students, while most of the rest were hostile. This apathy and hostility troubled those in the Germanophile minority, for despite their populist rhetoric they recognized the value of having the region's future elites on their side. How could they attain this goal? They tried various tactics. Germanophile students publicly criticized the disruptive *monômes* of the "béret students," terming them "incompatible with the dignity of students."[58] They tried to transform student demonstrations over such issues as compulsory military service and the recruitment of clinicians into protests against assimilation. They sought to infiltrate the *amicales*—a tactic facilitated by the low turnout for elections—and to disrupt AFGES.[59] And with their allies in the press they made more open appeals, reminding Alsatian students of their cultural heritage and their responsibilities to the masses. Early in 1931, for example, an article in Strasbourg's autonomist daily argued that while Alsatians had to attend the university to prepare for certain careers "we must be on guard so that it does not have an impact on us culturally." The article also warned the students against resigning themselves to impotence; like the Flemish students at the University of Ghent, it observed, they could transform their university if only they tried.[60] A similar message appeared on an anonymous flyer (the work of

the Jungmannschaft) addressed "To the Students from Alsace-Lorraine!"
and distributed late in 1931:

> You are students! As such you have a mission to serve later as models
> and leaders for your people. . . .
> Look at the world around you, look at the kindred Flemish, how
> they are proudly restoring to its rightful position their long suppressed
> language. Must we be the only servile ones who, in the Europe of the
> twentieth century, cast off their language for another, like a dirty shirt?
> . . .
> Think about all this on your own and discuss it with each other. And
> then reject what is Gallic [*das Welsche*]. Speak German, preserve as
> honorable men the authentic spirit of your people.[61]

Such appeals did little to broaden support for the cause and much to
discredit it. By associating Alsatian particularism so closely with German
culture, they made it less attractive not only to students who were completely Francophile but also to the many sympathetic to the ideals of the
double culture and of the region's European mission. In addition they
threatened more practical interests, for transforming the university along
the lines proposed, assuming that were possible, was likely to limit students' career opportunities. Respecting the traditions of one's ancestors
and homeland loses much of its intrinsic appeal when it endangers one's
prospects, and this was the choice offered. At least it was unless Alsace-
Lorraine were to rejoin Germany, a prospect appealing to a few students,
no doubt, but not to the overwhelming majority.[62]

Yet while the Germanophile activists evidently failed to expand their
following, they did register successes in other areas. At a time when
autonomist sentiment was apparently declining among the students, they
restored a sense of dynamism to the movement and kept its ideas in the
air. In fact their very extremism, like that of the prewar Cercle, may have
strengthened the appeal of a more moderate form of particularism and in
so doing slowed assimilation. In addition their provocations undermined
the stability and harmony so prized by the authorities. They helped to
polarize the student body, strengthening support for the royalist and fascist
leagues and thus weakening the unity of the nationalist camp. And, perhaps most important, they kept the university in the news. Incidents such
as the *Meiselocker* affair and that provoked by the tracts distributed late
in 1931 received extensive coverage in the Alsatian press. The accounts
varied widely, but the general impression conveyed was of a highly politicized university in which autonomist sentiment was more prevalent
than it was in fact. This reaction should be considered a success for the
Germanophile activists, for it contributed to the legitimacy and popularity

of their cause in the region generally and complicated the already complicated mission of their most resolute foes, the professors.

• 3 •

The professors reacted to the emergence of the autonomist movement
with shock and dismay. Until the mid-1920s they had been basically optimistic about trends in the recovered provinces. They had even adapted
to the *malaise alsacien,* convincing themselves that it was merely the
product of transitional problems soon to dissipate. But the autonomist
movement forced them to revise their opinions. The movement's program
and obvious popularity called into question their earlier assumption that
time was on their side. The more despondent now began to wonder whether
France might have been mistaken about the Alsatians' desire for reunion,
and even the most sanguine conceded that reintegration would be a much
more difficult and prolonged process than anticipated, one requiring greater
dedication and more sacrifices from France's servants. It was not an easy
adjustment.

Adding to the professors' disillusionment were more specific developments directly traceable to the autonomist movement. There were the
attacks on the university in the autonomist press and the indications that
autonomist sentiment might be gaining among the students. Because of
the disarray in official circles fostered by the autonomist challenge there
were often long delays before recommendations on matters such as appointments received approval.[63] After the autonomists gained control of
Strasbourg's city council in 1929 there were tense relations between the
medical faculty and the municipal hospital.[64] And there were disturbing
changes in the prevailing climate in Strasbourg and in the character of
the city's cultural life. The municipal theater, for instance, presented more
and more plays in German, often by troupes from Freiburg or Karlsruhe.
(Before 1926 the theater had offered no plays in German.) And the city's
natives, its patriciate aside, seemed increasingly hostile to anything or
anyone identified with the interior. Parisian authorities evidently did not
realize, one professor complained in 1928, that "for several years the
atmosphere has been becoming unbearable for French Alsatians [*les Alsaciens français*] and for the French from the interior, that it is sometimes
dangerous to express oneself in French, that in certain circles wearing
the Légion d'honneur or the Croix de guerre is considered a blemish and
is a cause for suspicion."[65]

The professors were unanimous in deploring these developments. But
the consensus went no further. There were differences within the faculty,
as elsewhere, over who was to blame: some focused on the vested interests
of the Catholic clergy; some, on the machinations of German revanchists;
some, on blunders by the government; and some, on the Germanophile

cultural orientation of graduates of the German university (an inherently appealing argument since it suggested that higher education could contribute significantly to nation building).[66] There were also differences over the seriousness of the autonomist threat, with the pessimists convinced that assimilation had suffered a decisive setback and the optimists maintaining that time was still with them.[67] There were differences, too, over how the government should respond to the threat, and over how they themselves should respond. Some favored a hard line, including repressive treatment of the autonomists and new assimilationist initiatives, while others preferred a more conciliatory approach.

On the matter of how to respond the most conspicuous were the hardliners. The autonomist movement encouraged many professors to become more involved in public affairs, and most showed little predilection or capacity for conciliation. They attacked suspected autonomists without restraint, charging, for instance, that the region's Catholic clergy indulged in pagan practices and that the mayor of Strasbourg was a *Schwob,* the local pejorative term for a German.[68] They stressed the similarity between the rhetoric of *Die Zukunft* and that of *völkisch* movements across the Rhine.[69] And they involved themselves in the various assimilationist organizations that appeared in response to the autonomist challenge. Thus the conservative nationalists provided support and leadership for the Ligue contre la ''Kultur'' et les menées allemandes en Alsace et en Lorraine, a short-lived counter to the *Zukunft* movement founded in 1925, and for the local branch of the technocratic Redressement français, established in 1926.[70] And the Jacobins, convinced that Herriot and the Cartel des gauches had been on the right track, did likewise for the Cercle Jean Macé, a branch of the anticlerical Ligue de l'enseignement organized at the end of 1926. In this case the faculty was in control, providing many of the most active members as well as the first two presidents, the geophysicist Edmond Rothé and the church historian Prosper Alfaric, and one of the first vice-presidents, the mathematician Georges Cerf.

Perhaps the best demonstration of the strength and resolve of the faculty's hard-liners came in 1928. The immediate provocation was a deposition at the Colmar trials in which Jean de Pange, a vice-president of the Société des amis de l'université, sided with the autonomists.[71] Three days later *Le Temps* printed an open letter from a professor in Strasbourg's law faculty announcing that because of de Pange's deposition he would resign from the Société des amis. ''On this question of autonomy,'' he remarked, ''one must be on one side of the barricade or the other. This is why I cannot remain a member of an organization whose vice-president has publicly supported the claims of the Heimatbund.''[72] The secretary general of the Société des amis received similar threats from other professors, including one announcing that every member of the medical faculty would leave the society and make public his reasons unless de Pange resigned within a week.[73] De Pange obliged, explaining that he did not want "to find myself in conflict with one of the professors of the university that we represent." He added that when he had helped Bucher and others establish the society in 1919, "I hoped to see our university return to its old traditions, becoming simultaneously the exponent of our regional as- pirations and the intermediary between two great cultures. I see neither in this nor in what I said before the superior court anything that could raise doubts about my sentiments concerning France."[74] As for the larger meaning of the incident, de Pange gave his opinion a few days later to an equally cosmopolitan and idealistic German friend: "I see starting again the mistakes for which we reproached the pan-Germans during the Ger- man period. I cannot tell you how depressed this makes me."[75]

There were also moderates on the faculty, particularly among the Al- satian members, but under the circumstances they could do little. The polarization of Alsatian society over the autonomist question made it difficult for moderates to convince those on either side of their good intentions, and the climate within the faculty tended to discourage them from even making the attempt. The fate of Fritz Kiener, the one who tried hardest, is instructive.

In the aftermath of the Colmar trial the normally timid Kiener, de- spondent over recent developments, decided to speak out in support of conciliatory initiatives. Using the good offices of de Pange, he traveled to Paris and presented his case in audiences with politicians, including Poincaré, and in a two-hour address to the Union pour la vérité, a forum for the discussion of contemporary affairs. He also outlined his views in an article in a Parisian journal, the *Revue des vivants*. His diagnosis was severe and his proposed remedy radical. Recent events, Kiener argued, had split Alsatians into two camps, "bourgeois Alsace, which is Fran- cophile, and populist Alsace, which is proving to be ill-disposed toward France."[76] Much of the responsibility lay with politicians and intellectuals in the interior, for they too readily assumed that the few Francophile Alsatians with whom they had contact were representative and hence underestimated the region's uniqueness and the seriousness of the crisis. This encouraged them to dismiss the autonomist movement as little more than a separatist conspiracy orchestrated from across the Rhine, although in fact its sources were primarily local. The only solution would be the introduction of a semiautonomous administration of the sort associated with Millerand; there must be a General Commissariat based in Strasbourg and headed by "a courageous and honorable man to whom France will assign its responsibilities and in whom Alsace will have confidence."[77] The candidate he had in mind was Marshal Hubert Lyautey, a national hero best known for his pacification of Morocco.

Other Alsatians on the faculty basically agreed with Kiener's criticisms and proposals, as did at least one professor from the interior, the jurist

Carré de Malberg.[78] But Kiener was reluctant to implicate them for fear of jeopardizing their relations with their colleagues and, perhaps, their careers. As he explained to de Pange just before embarking on his Parisian mission, "there is prevalent among us a spirit of denunciation which is frightening."[79] Possibly he exaggerated, but Kiener's own fate suggests otherwise. His defense of Alsatian particularism came under harsh attack in the local assimilationist press and caused him to be spurned by many colleagues. Although his ideas and his courage made him something of a hero to particularistic Alsatians, they isolated him within the university: the authorities and his colleagues withheld publicity from his courses and support from his institute and did not even involve him in ceremonies prompted by episodes in Alsatian history, his field of expertise. "Like you," he wrote de Pange, "I am treated like a heretic and excluded from all official ceremonies."[80]

In this respect the situation was like that found before the war at the German university. In each case the development of autonomist sentiment in Alsace-Lorraine fostered a "spirit of denunciation" manifested both in public criticism of the autonomists and in the ostracism of professors suspected of autonomist sympathies (including, in each case, Fritz Kiener). And this is not the only similarity. In each case the autonomist challenge also caused the faculty to modify earlier practices in the hope of shielding the university and enhancing its influence. The similarities even extended to the modifications introduced, as will become evident as we consider this aspect of the French university's response to the autonomists.

Central to this response was a desire to avoid unnecessary provocations. Most professors had recognized all along that impolitic statements or actions could hurt the university's reputation. But the emergence of the autonomist movement and the success with which its press exploited the assimilationists' gaffes made them even more sensitive and cautious, and more determined to rein in those less restrained. With the aid of AFGES the professors attempted to curb the rambunctiousness of the royalist and fascist students, particularly their disruptions of the university's annual convocations and their efforts, often successful, to transform the *monômes* into excuses for blocking traffic, taunting bystanders, and demonstrating against Strasbourg's autonomist mayor.[81] At the same time they treated the autonomist students rather leniently. Although they occasionally threatened to withdraw the scholarships of the most conspicuous, and in at least one case did, they took no action against the fraternities and resisted suggestions from Paris that they expel specific ringleaders. "I doubt that the council can find sufficient proof to apply this penalty," the rector responded to one such suggestion. "Moreover such a serious sentence would greatly arouse public opinion and would be exploited by various parties at the time of the elections."[82] Using similar logic, the rector once rescheduled a patriotic ceremony, the dedication of a statue commemorating French romanticism, to reduce the probability of an autonomist demonstration.[83] And the professors became more circumspect about their own public statements and activities. Like their German predecessors they were learning that the free expression of their opinions was a luxury their university could not always afford.

The professors were not entirely successful in avoiding provocations, but the failures only increased their determination. A case in point was the Bellocq-Merklen affair, the most tumultuous of the many incidents that disrupted the university in the late 1920s and early 1930s. The affair had its origins in the medical faculty's practice of occasionally filling clinical positions with candidates from other French universities. This practice angered the Strasbourg students since the other universities did not reciprocate: they reserved all their clinical positions for their own graduates. The discontent came to a head early in 1933 when the faculty appointed yet another clinician from the interior and a professor, Philippe Bellocq, publicly justified the appointment by contending that there were not enough qualified candidates from Strasbourg. "For a long time," Bellocq argued, "the students from Strasbourg have not had a taste for *concours*. . . . Positions are much too numerous and there are not enough candidates of high quality."[84] These ill-considered remarks and the appointment inspiring them—for which the dean, Prosper Merklen, was held responsible—provoked a series of protests. The students, believing their honor at stake, issued manifestos, staged a *monôme,* and so disrupted Bellocq's next two lectures that the rector canceled Bellocq's classes for two weeks. These events received extensive coverage in the press, particularly the autonomist press. That the incident had little to do with the autonomist movement (students from the interior and thoroughly Francophile Alsatians also protested) did not prevent autonomist newspapers from depicting it as a struggle between exploited Alsatians and French colonizers and as evidence that their cause was gaining at the university.[85] As for the authorities, they publicly stood behind Bellocq and Merklen but privately were critical. Thus the rector complained to Paris about Merklen, "who is often lacking in discretion and levelheadedness," and recommended that he be replaced as dean after a suitable delay. ("For now," he added, "it would be inopportune to hasten his departure, which would be considered a victory in autonomist circles." Merklen was replaced later in the year.)[86] The rector also noted that Bellocq "lacked the prudence that is so necessary here,"[87] and during a meeting with him emphasized "how regrettable these press polemics are."[88] But at least Bellocq recognized that he had been "imprudent and naive" and "learned at his own expense . . . how discretion is essential."[89] Of course Bellocq's colleagues also learned from the experience.

Yet while such incidents made the professors more circumspect, they did not make them more conciliatory. On the contrary, they stiffened their resistance to pressures aimed at making the university more Alsatian and reinforced their commitment to assimilation. About the only concessions not made under duress were strictly rhetorical and designed, it seems, to obscure the reality. Thus in a speech early in 1927 Poincaré asserted that the university was and would always remain purely Alsatian.[90] The facts hardly justified such claims. The professors, a few exceptions aside, showed no particular interest in Alsatian studies either in their own research and teaching or more generally. They resisted Kiener's efforts to promote the study of Alsatian history and ignored proposals by outsiders that they establish chairs for related subjects, notably for the history of Alsatian literature.[91] They also seem to have been less willing than before to favor Alsatians when filling vacancies, and in some cases insisted on conditions that effectively eliminated most Alsatian candidates. The controversial Merklen, for instance, argued that Alsatians should not teach at the university unless they had first studied or taught in Paris.[92] And the professors were no more generous when it came to essentially symbolic decisions such as the selection of representatives for official ceremonies. Thus when an Alsatian professor proposed that his faculty choose an Alsatian as its spokesman at the university's next convocation—in part because "the Faculty is watched by Alsatians who are autonomists or of autonomist leanings"—his colleagues dismissed the idea, arguing that they should recognize no distinction between Alsatian professors and those from the interior.[93]

When facing decisions of this sort, the opponents of concessions usually emphasized academic rather than political considerations, and there is little reason to doubt their sincerity. It would be difficult to maintain, to cite but one specific case, that the Faculty of Letters should have replaced the deceased Georges Pariset with Frédéric Braesch, the one Alsatian candidate, rather than Georges Lefebvre, another candidate and one of the country's most distinguished historians.[94] But in cases in which academic considerations might point in the other direction, toward policies more consistent with the distinctive traditions and potential of Alsace-Lorraine, the professors often resorted to political arguments. This was particularly true whenever the question arose of scholarly exchanges with Germany.

Among the manifestations of the spirit of Locarno—of the improvement in Franco-German relations that followed the Locarno talks of 1925—were a proliferation of student exchange programs and a dramatic growth in the level of participation. The most striking index is the number of Germans studying at French universities: it increased from 18 in 1924 (the highest level since the war) to 222 in 1926 and 1,015 in 1929.[95] But this was a development to which the University of Strasbourg hardly contributed, and the reasons were essentially political. They were summarized early in 1928 by Pfister, Charléty's recently appointed successor as rector, in response to a ministerial circular concerning a specific exchange program:

> The language question and the question of relations with Germany have provoked such debates and such passion in the liberated departments that it is perhaps advisable to avoid all questions likely to stir up the embers, especially at a time when the parties will be able to seize on the issue and turn it to their purposes. And the Ministry of Public Instruction would also run the risk of being charged with imprudence for having facilitated exchanges which, in the eyes of some, could seem likely to foster suspicious relations with Germany or at least to weaken the sentiments and the loyalty of Alsatians toward France.[96]

Pfister's recommendation, seconded by Poincaré, was that student exchange programs involving Germany be restricted to institutions in the interior. The ministry agreed, with predictable results. The number of German students in Strasbourg grew at a much slower rate than did the number at French universities generally—from fifteen in 1924 (88.3 percent of the total in France) to a peak of thirty-six in 1932 (4.4 percent of the total).[97] And the number of Alsatians studying in Germany remained small, despite the financial incentives offered by certain revanchist organizations. Between 1927 and 1930 there were, on average, only five Alsatians at German universities each semester and four at Technische Hochschulen.[98] (The numbers at Switzerland's German-language universities and polytechnical institute were probably somewhat higher.)[99] No doubt the migration would have been greater had foreign diplomas been recognized in France, but this was not the only factor. Most Alsatian students had no desire to study in Germany or even to visit the country, and the rest had cause for concern about the "spirit of denunciation" prevalent in their homeland. Indeed except for those who were openly autonomist in sentiment few ever crossed the Rhine, and the exceptions usually did their best to disguise the fact.[100]

The university also contributed less than its share to professorial exchanges with Germany. To be sure, many Strasbourg professors, particularly among the Jacobins, approved of the Franco-German détente (and of the abandonment of French ambitions in the Rhineland that it presupposed) and some took steps to further this objective. Thus Edmond Vermeil and the jurist Marcel Prélot involved themselves in the work of the Comité franco-allemand d'information, an organization promoting détente, and Charles Blondel and Maurice Halbwachs lectured at the Cours internationaux of Davos, a forum bringing together French and German scholars for a few days each spring.[101] But when it came to modifying their university's policies, to making them more compatible with the spirit of Locarno, the professors attempted little and accomplished less. Indicative was their reaction to a ministerial circular of November 1928 encouraging them to invite German professors to visit for a year. Six of the seven faculties rejected the idea outright, citing the unacceptable risks, while the exception, the Faculty of Letters, agreed to participate only if it could select its visitors and restrict their public lectures to invited guests.[102] As it turned out there would be no visiting professors from Germany even in this faculty, in part, perhaps, because the university's greatest patron, Poincaré, strongly opposed the idea.[103] Nor did any Strasbourg professor ever hold a visiting appointment at a German university.

Admittedly the university made concessions to the spirit of détente, concessions unthinkable in the early 1920s. Occasionally German scholars were invited to give lectures. (The first, Philipp Witkop of Freiburg, appeared in May 1928 at the invitation of Vermeil; the audience received him warmly, but outside there was a counterdemonstration organized by the Camelots du roi.)[104] And in the early 1930s the Centre d'études germaniques, which had moved from Mainz to Strasbourg in 1930, employed a German as a language instructor (who, as if to spite the faculty's liberalism, soon rallied to the Nazis, provoking a scandal that resulted in his dismissal).[105] But such initiatives tended to be motivated by political rather than scholarly considerations and by nationalism rather than cosmopolitanism. In supporting the idea of inviting German professors as visitors, for example, Lucien Febvre and the geographer Henri Baulig argued that the faculty should not give Germans or Alsatians cause to claim that the Strasbourg professors had something to hide, that they feared comparison with German scholars. In the same debate Vermeil stressed "the need to take in hand, in order to control, an enterprise that otherwise could be undertaken by others in a totally different spirit."[106] Similar logic helped to convince the faculty to commemorate the anniversary of Goethe's death: it was feared that unless the faculty took the initiative the autonomists might exploit the occasion.[107] At no time, it seems, did any professor resort to the justification that many outsiders found most compelling, the argument that the university should become a bridge linking the French and German scholarly communities.

The aspects of the professors' response to the autonomist movement considered so far were essentially defensive in character. The underlying objective was to protect the university's integrity while avoiding statements and disguising policies that might play into the hands of the autonomists. But there was, as well, an offensive side to this response: the autonomist challenge also intensified the faculty's efforts to advance their university's Alsatian mission.

The change was largely a matter of attitude and commitment. Thus the professors became more convinced of the importance of the university's informal curriculum and did more to involve themselves in the lives of their students. There was now talk at faculty meetings of how professors should attend the annual balls of the *amicales* and should foster "their relations of trust and tutelage with the students" in order to determine the causes of the students' discontents and "to ward off demonstrations."[108] Similarly the professors approached the university's extension programs—the *cours publics,* the lecturing in Alsatian towns, and so on—with an enhanced sense of urgency and spirit of sacrifice. In 1930 Jean Pommier, a professor of French literature, described the difference to a former colleague, one who had left Strasbourg for the Sorbonne just as the autonomist movement was emerging: "There is a kind of blackmail here which is very honorable but which after a time makes one a bit of a dupe. Whatever one asks of you, it is to fight autonomism. How can one resist? And this is why I have just returned from Ribeauvillé, why I am now departing for Haguenau and then for Colmar to spread the good (literary) word."[109]

But it was not just a matter of greater support for existing programs. There were also new programs, some directed at the students and some at Alsatians generally. Thus in 1928—at its first meeting since the Colmar trial—the Faculty of Letters unanimously approved two proposals by Marc Bloch designed to put the faculty's Alsatian students "in a position better to understand our country in all its rich diversity." One would require those entering the teaching profession to spend a few years at schools elsewhere in France before taking positions in Alsace-Lorraine, while the other would reward the best Alsatian students with grants for a summer of travel in the interior.[110] Both met with the approval of the rector and the premier, and in the latter case the government and private donors furnished generous support, enough to permit about twenty students to travel in the interior each summer.[111] Other steps taken included the reinstitution of noncredit courses in French grammar and pronunciation, the establishment of scholarships for Alsatians wishing to spend a year or two at other French universities, and, on a more symbolic level, the introduction of an annual ball for the students hosted by the prefect of Bas-Rhin.[112] Among initiatives directed at the world beyond the university were the occasional broadcasting of lectures over Strasbourg's new radio station (intended to counter propaganda now coming from radio stations across the Rhine)[113] and, most important, the founding of a new institution of adult education, the Université populaire de Strasbourg.

Like other initiatives the Université populaire had its origins in the autonomist crisis of early 1928. At the time of the Colmar trial the mayor of Strasbourg, a Socialist committed to assimilation, proposed that the university and the municipal government collaborate in founding a Université populaire, the purpose being to coordinate the city's adult education programs and to introduce new ones directed at the working class.[114]

The name he suggested brought to mind the short-lived Université populaire founded in 1919 and those organized in many French cities following the Dreyfus affair, and so did the mission: the objective was to bridge the gap between the academic community and the lower classes and, in the process, to convince the latter of the professors' altruism and of the merits of their cultural and political ideals. Under more normal circumstances such associations might have been a drawback, for these earlier efforts had fallen far short of expectations—most had lasted only a few years and had never had much contact with the popular classes.[115] But the professors, shocked by the disaffection now manifest among Alsatians, overcame their misgivings and endorsed the proposal. In July an organizing committee was constituted, and over the next few months it completed the necessary arrangements. The basic plan was to have a few professors offer courses on subjects of general interest, each course to meet one evening a week at the university and to be free and open to all, regardless of prior education.[116] The first courses began at the start of the 1928–29 academic year, with the inaugural ceremonies highlighted by a lecture on the French Revolution by Georges Lefebvre, a professor of relatively humble origins who was, according to the rector, "one of our best propagandists of the French idea in Alsace."[117]

The response was greater than predicted, causing the organizers to plan the following years on a more ambitious scale. In the second year, for example, they doubled the number of lectures and introduced courses by lycée teachers and courses in German, including one on the cultural history of France "for less advanced auditors."[118] (Henceforth about one-fifth of the courses would be taught in German.) They also added new activities, including visits to local industrial establishments and summer excursions to destinations in the interior.[119] The result was a program of impressive dimensions. In 1932–33, a typical year, thirty-one professors and a few outsiders gave a total of 84 lectures, while the overall registration was 1,817 and each registrant attended an average of 7.5 lectures, meaning that the average attendance at each lecture was 162. In addition the various tours and excursions enlisted roughly 1,000.[120]

Yet the registrants came overwhelmingly from the middle class. In 1931–32, for example, 43 percent were bureaucrats or white-collar workers in private firms, 10.2 percent owned businesses or were in the professions, 4.4 percent were teachers, and 4.2 percent were technicians. Another 11.9 percent were full-time students, while 23.3 percent listed no occupation (the great majority of them were housewives). The remainder, a mere 3.1 percent of the total and 4.9 percent of those listing occupations, came from the working class.[121] This pattern naturally troubled the organizers, since a prime objective had been to reach the working class. They should not have been surprised, however, for the social composition of their constituency differed little from that of similar ventures elsewhere, including the Dreyfusard *universités populaires*.[122] This suggests that the causes were rooted less in specific features of the Strasbourg program than in the general nature of the enterprise—its stress on self-improvement, its associations with high culture, its appeal to the middle class— and in the characteristics of working-class culture. Hence it is unlikely that the remedies frequently discussed, such as making the lectures simpler or offering more courses in German, would have had much effect, except perhaps to keep away some now attracted.[123]

Although the Université populaire did not develop as planned, it still made an important contribution to the university's relations with the larger society. It brought many Alsatians to the university who had hitherto never been exposed to higher education, German or French. This alone probably caused them to identify more closely with the institution, whether or not they were basically Francophile already. In addition, the very existence of the Université populaire left an impression on many who never attended. It is significant in this regard that the institution continued to have the strong backing of the municipal government even after 1929, when control passed to the autonomists, and that it received extensive and overwhelmingly favorable coverage in the local press. Even the autonomist daily praised it, noting in 1933 that it "has in the last few years . . . shown such progress that it is now an important factor in the city's program of popular education; it has proven its right to exist, indeed its necessity, and one can no longer think of the intellectual life of Strasbourg without it."[124] Praise from this source, coupled as it was with a call for more courses in German, may have given pause to the professors. Yet it does suggest that the Université populaire had developed a broad base of support. And this presumably benefited the university itself, causing it to appear less alien and defusing pressures aimed at making it more relevant to local needs. For these reasons, as well as for its more direct impact, the Université populaire must be judged a success.

• 4 •

In the mid-1930s Alsace-Lorraine entered a new period in its history, one dominated not by the government's efforts at assimilation, as in the 1920s and early 1930s, but rather by three more general developments. One was the depression. Although relatively slow in coming—as late as 1931 the Alsatian economy seemed healthy—once it arrived the downturn was pronounced in all sectors, and there was no real recovery before the end of the decade. The second development was the Nazi seizure and consolidation of power in Germany. This had important consequences both for Franco-German relations and for the images that particularistic Alsatians had of Germany and, accordingly, of France. It also impeded economic recovery since uncertainty about German intentions discouraged new investment in Alsace-Lorraine.[125] The third development was the intensification of the chronic instability and unpopularity of the French government, a trend accelerated by the Parisian riots of 6 February 1934 and by the policies of the Popular Front regime of 1936–38. This trend affected not only the character and effectiveness of the government's Alsatian policies but also, again, the images Alsatians had of their country and, accordingly, of Germany.

Initially these developments tended to favor assimilation. Of particular importance was the impact of the rise of the Nazis in Germany. The most extreme of the autonomists, those best represented by the Landespartei and the affiliated Jungmannschaft, responded by becoming even more extreme. Although stopping short of openly advocating separation, they adopted much of the rhetoric and ideology of the Nazis, including their anti-Semitism, and their press began to print admiring accounts of trends across the Rhine and to contrast the dynamism of Germany with the alleged decadence of France. But most particularistic Alsatians reacted differently. Repelled by the ideas and methods of the Nazis, and particularly by their religious policies and presumed interest in Alsace-Lorraine, they identified more closely with France. Most striking was the change in clerical circles, hitherto the main base of autonomist support. Certain clerical leaders, reversing their earlier emphasis, now argued that Alsatians should adapt to France. For the first time the clerical press gave extensive coverage to events in the interior. And in Strasbourg's mayoral elections of 1935 the clericals tipped the balance to the nationalist candidate, ending six years of autonomist rule. A similar pattern was evident among the liberals and the communists, groups with as much cause as the clericals to deplore events in Germany. The result was that by the mid-1930s the autonomist coalition forged in the late 1920s was in disarray and autonomist sentiment was as its lowest ebb since 1923.[126]

But with the national elections of 1936 the tide turned. Fearing that the victorious Popular Front would extend the separation of church and state to Alsace-Lorraine—the coalition's dominant partner, the Socialists, had advocated this step since 1919—Alsatian Catholics mobilized a preemptive campaign that included warnings in the press and massive demonstrations in Strasbourg and Mulhouse. This campaign may have persuaded the government to shelve the idea of separation, but it did not deter it from another blunder. In October 1936 a ministerial decree added a year to compulsory schooling in Alsace-Lorraine, the purpose being to improve pupils' knowledge of French. Alsatians, already suspicious of the government's intentions, reacted much as they had in 1924, condemning the decree as an illegal challenge to their *droits acquis*. The premier, Léon Blum, responded by offering a choice between the decree's terms and full integration into the French educational system, which would mean an end to all religious instruction and to all teaching in German. This attempt at blackmail, as Alsatians saw it, only intensified the crisis. With clerical forces in the lead there was a sharp escalation of the protest campaign, a development reflected in numerous petitions and manifestos, in an unofficial plebiscite in which 72 percent of the region's registered voters rejected Blum's decree, and in an assembly of Alsatian politicians which condemned the government's handling of the situation. The protests caused Blum's successor to refer the objectionable decree to the Conseil d'état, where it was modified in a way acceptable to Alsatians. But, as in 1924, the government paid a heavy price for its provocation. The crisis greatly enhanced the legitimacy of autonomist ideas, thus making it easier for Alsatians to blame their economic and other difficulties on their lack of autonomy and to conclude that their homeland was an island of stability and sanity in a corrupt and disoriented France. The crisis also contributed—as had German films and radio broadcasts, which now enjoyed great popularity in the region—to a rapid growth of overt anti-Semitism. (Blum and other leaders of the Popular Front were Jewish.) Combined with the worsening economic situation and the manifest dynamism of Germany, these developments resulted in growing support for the extremist Landespartei and Jungmannschaft.[127]

But soon the mood changed again, this time under the influence of the evolving international crisis. After the Austro-German Anschluss of March 1938 the fear of war increasingly preoccupied Alsatians. In one respect this fear united them, for there was overwhelming support for the government's efforts to appease Germany; Alsatians were even less willing than those in the interior to go to war over Austria or Czechoslovakia. But in other respects it widened the gap between the pro-Nazi groups and the other autonomists and regionalists. The former, taking heart from the successes of their counterparts in Austria and the Sudetenland, became more radical in the hope that Hitler and the appeasers would soon turn their attention to the Alsatian question. But the others remained or became openly loyal to France, and in the interests of national unity—and of not whetting Hitler's appetite—toned down their criticisms and demands. The change was evident at the Bastille Day fêtes of 1939: the turnout was the largest and most enthusiastic in years.[128]

These developments and the larger forces that lay behind them transformed the university's student subculture. Particularly significant—it conditioned all of the changes—was the impact of the depression. As at universities in the interior the growing fear of un- or underemployment, of entering an intellectual proletariat, intensified the careerism that already characterized the students. One result was a shift in enrollment patterns, with students avoiding fields such as law in which jobs were scarce (the adage "law leads to everything" no longer applied)[129] and turning instead to those offering relatively good prospects, notably medicine and pharmacy.[130] Another was a lessening of involvement in extracurricular activities. Anxious about their futures and preoccupied with earning credentials, with *bachotage* ("cramming"), students had even less time and inclination than before for nonacademic pursuits. Symptoms included the demise of various student organizations, a decline in the frequency and exuberance of the *monômes,* and a sharp drop in the numbers voting in the *amicales* elections.[131]

The depression affected not only the level of involvement in extracurricular activities but also the character of these activities. Above all student life in Strasbourg, as in the interior, became highly politicized.[132] In the 1920s the most popular organized diversions had been festive or social—banquets and balls and *monômes*—but in the 1930s such events declined in importance relative to more overtly political activities, to demonstrations and strikes and the like. This shift sharpened divisions within the student body, thus frustrating the fence-mending efforts of the ostensibly neutral *amicales* and AFGES. About all that now united the students were their disdain for the government and its efforts to alleviate the depression and their predilection for extreme solutions. Beyond this the tendencies were centrifugal, with the activists clustering into three distinct and, on the whole, increasingly radical groups: the Communists and their allies, the fascistic Right, and the autonomists.

The first group embraced those in a number of overlapping organizations, among them the local branch of the Union fédérale des étudiants (founded in 1928), the Société des étudiants pauvres (1931), and the Front universitaire antifasciste de Strasbourg (1934). Claiming to represent students' real interests—they dismissed AFGES as a tool of the authorities—these groups offered cheap meals, published newspapers, sponsored lectures, and called for the unionization of the students and for their representation on the faculty council and on the juries for all relevant *concours.* They also took stands on local, national, and international issues. They demanded the resignation of both principals in the Bellocq-Merklen affair, they staged antiwar demonstrations, and they took the lead in protesting both the Chéron decree of 1933, which limited new hiring by the government and thus worsened students' job prospects, and the law of 15 March 1935, which increased compulsory military service to two years.[133] Yet despite their dynamism and the popularity of some of their causes these organizations enlisted relatively few. Thus while they assigned high priority to gaining control of the *amicales,* they succeeded in only one case, the Faculty of Law, and then only because of the indifference of many students, a boycott by those on the extreme right, and their own informal alliance with the autonomists.[134] It is unlikely that overall membership in these organizations ever exceeded 100, a figure approached in 1932 and again in 1935, although specific rallies or demonstrations attracted more.

Perhaps the greatest show of strength came early in 1937, when more than 200 students convened to protest a rightist provocation.[135]

The second group consisted of the students associated with the royalist and fascist leagues. These leagues had been much in evidence in the 1920s—more, certainly, than the organizations on the left—but in the 1930s they became even more active and uninhibited and had a more pervasive impact on the student subculture. Beginning in 1932 they appealed to students' growing insecurity with a xenophobic campaign against the university's foreign students, charging that they were threats both to French students' job prospects and to the social order. (Many foreign students, particularly those from eastern Europe, belonged to left-wing organizations.) They orchestrated demonstrations against German culture and skirmishes with the pro-Nazi autonomists, including one at the municipal theater that forced the cancellation of a performance by a visiting German troupe.[136] And at public meetings and in their monthly, founded in 1933, they verbally assaulted Jews, Marxists, anticlericals, and anyone else contaminated by identification with the left. The attacks became particularly vicious after the Popular Front election of 1936 and the dissolution in the same year of the right-wing leagues. A striking manifestation of the trend came in February 1937, on the occasion of a speech at the university by Mme Léon Brunschvicg, a Jewish member of Blum's cabinet. Following a script prepared a day or so before over café tables, about 200 students greeted the speaker with whistling, firecrackers, the *Marseillaise,* and chants of "A Moscou!," "La France aux français!," "A bas les juifs!," and "Vous n'aurez pas l'Alsace et la Lorraine!" (The last was an all-purpose slogan, having been used earlier against the German theater troupe and the autonomists.) After a tumultuous twenty minutes Mme Brunschvicg and the official party, which included the prefect and the rector, gave up and withdrew.[137]

The royalist and fascist organizations may not have enlisted more members than those on the left, but their diffuse support was greater. The success of a two-day student strike in 1935 directed against foreign students indicates that on this issue, which pitted the leagues against the Communists and most professors, the groups on the right better reflected student opinion.[138] And judging from the response of the officers of AFGES a large proportion of the students even regarded the attacks on Mme Brunschvicg with indulgence: by margins of fourteen to nine the officers rejected a motion by the president expressing the association's regret over the incident, rejected another stating that partisan politics had no place within the university, and then defeated the president in a vote of confidence, forcing his resignation.[139]

The third student group consisted of the autonomists. In this case there were two basic trends, both reflecting trends evident among Alsatian autonomists generally. The first was a decline in overt support for the cause. As late as 1933 autonomists were optimistic about their prospects at the university, claiming on one occasion that the French authorities had always had doubts about the students in theology and letters and that "now the pillars of the 'Latin future' on the Rhine are beginning to waver: the medical students and the law students."[140] But developments over the next few years belied this optimism. Two fraternities (Nideck and Wasgo-Lotharingia) disbanded while membership in the remaining three appears to have declined. In the late 1930s the fraternities probably enrolled no more than fifty students, as compared with around eighty earlier in the decade.[141] The trend is all the more striking since after years of decline the proportion of Alsatian students who habitually spoke the dialect was now rising. This suggests that while the fraternities' traditional constituency, students of rural or lower-middle-class origins, was growing, it was also becoming less autonomist in outlook, or at least less openly so.[142]

The second trend was a widening of the gap dividing the extremists and the moderates. The extremists found their spiritual homes in Fritz Spieser's Bund Erwin von Steinbach and in Hermann Bickler's increasingly Nazified and separatist Jungmannschaft. They attended rallies across the Rhine and at Spieser's autonomist mecca near Saverne, the Hünenburg, and they involved themselves in the campaign to disseminate Nazi ideas in the region, particularly among the peasants. But the number of students involved was small, probably no more than a dozen at any time.[143] As for the other students in the autonomist camp, they disassociated themselves from the extremists and showed signs of becoming more open to French influences. In the mid-1930s, for example, Argentina expelled a member implicated in the propagandistic activities of the Jungmannschaft, while Alsatia joined the Fédération française des étudiants catholiques and received official recognition from the local bishop, no friend of the autonomist movement.[144] By 1938 the dean of the Protestant theological faculty, in the past the university's greatest bastion of autonomist sentiment, could even claim that there was no reason "to suspect our current students of being animated by autonomist and anti-French sentiments, even though some of them are interested in what is happening among German youth."[145] In short, both the number of openly autonomist students and the hostility of most of these students to things French were in decline.

But why? The extremists tended to blame the more repressive policies now followed by the faculty (including the occasional expulsion of compromised students), and no doubt these policies had an effect.[146] There were other factors, however, and collectively they were probably more important. To begin with, there was the impact on the attitudes that students brought to the university of years of exposure to French schooling and to French cultural and political life. By the mid-1930s even students of relatively humble backgrounds, those who had attended collèges in small towns and spoke the dialect among themselves, regularly read Parisian journals and tended to regard Germany as a foreign country and Paris as the center of their cultural universe; whatever their opinions of the government, they were learning to think of themselves as French as well as Alsatian.[147] The depression intensified this development, for not only did it make students more careerist, and in that sense more French, but it also raised the costs of remaining provincial in outlook and aspirations. Students now had an added incentive to speak French and to identify themselves with France—to invest in their own assimilation—for with jobs scarce this opened broader prospects for the future.[148]

Political developments in both France and Germany were also significant. In the case of France the mounting national crisis actually may have contributed to assimilation in that it helped to unite Alsatians with other Frenchmen—there was now a *malaise français* as well as a *malaise alsacien*—and it fostered the growth of other outlets for the discontents formerly channeled into the autonomist movement. In this regard the Communist student organizations openly appealed to particularistic students with their antimilitarism, their sponsorship of occasional lectures in German, and their emphasis on closing the gap between the educated elite and the masses.[149] Similarly the right-wing leagues drew support from students who in different circumstances might have gravitated to the fraternities. Even greater, however, was the impact of developments across the Rhine. For all but a handful of students the German threat discredited what was left of the radical autonomist movement and the idea of the double culture, tainted as they now were with Nazi and separatist associations. In compensation these students tended both to identify more closely with France, putting their hopes in national revival rather than in Alsatian particularism, and to devote more of their energies to essentially personal concerns, above all their studies.

The professors were no more immune to the larger forces at work in the mid- and late 1930s, no more isolated in an ivory tower, than the students. They could not be, for these forces resulted in a series of challenges to their university's distinctiveness and stature and, in the professors' opinion, potential as an agent of nation building. The faculty fought back, but with little success. Only toward the end of the decade was there a turn for the better, and by then it hardly mattered for the university would soon fall victim to events far beyond its professors' control.

This long period of crisis, which is what it was for the faculty, can be dated from the appearance of the government's budget for 1933. In addition to sharp cuts in general expenditures for higher education, the budget lowered the supplement paid Strasbourg professors from 25 percent of their basic salaries to 16 percent.[150] For the professors this decree represented a betrayal of a commitment, a violation of their *droits acquis*. It also had disturbing symbolic implications. Since it required the Strasbourg professors to make greater sacrifices than professors in the interior, it suggested that the ministry attached less importance than before to maintaining their university at a high level and, by extension, that the ministry was either losing interest in the institution's special missions or losing confidence in its ability to further these missions.

The professors reacted vigorously. In numerous memorandums and resolutions, including one passed unanimously by the faculty council, they insisted that their full supplements represented fair compensation for the unique disadvantages associated with Strasbourg. They mentioned not only the high cost of living, stressed in earlier debates over the supplement, but also the slow rate of promotion for junior members of the faculty, the distance from Paris, the weather, and the local environment, "eccentric by comparison to all of the other regions of France" and "situated on the most dangerous frontier."[151] Because of these conditions any reduction in the supplement would undermine the university. Professors now in Strasbourg, freed of all moral commitments to remain, would seek positions elsewhere, and it would be impossible to recruit comparable replacements: "Except for those with ties to Alsace the only ones who will come are those who cannot find positions elsewhere; and for them Strasbourg will only be a stepping-stone—they will never exercise the influence that comes with the authority acquired in the course of a long scholarly and professional career."[152] The result would be the rapid decline of the university. As one petitioner put it, "I really fear that the death knell has sounded for the 'great French university on the banks of the Rhine.' Soon a provincial university without luster and dependent on uncertain recruitment will take its place."[153]

The consequences would be of national significance, the professors argued. For one thing, "many foreign intellectuals judge France by the size of the effort it makes to maintain at Strasbourg a major center of international culture."[154] And of course any evidence of the university's decline would be eagerly exploited by France's enemies in Alsace-Lorraine and abroad: "Nobody will be more delighted . . . than the few in Alsace who remain hostile to French thought and the Germans who have always insisted that France does not have true claims to this province and that it would not succeed for long in maintaining a university there of the first rank."[155] Thus the university's decline would seriously limit its nation-building potential. Such reasoning implied that this potential was now significant, but on this the professors were emphatic. They argued in part by analogy, stressing the accomplishments of the earlier German university to suggest how much a distinguished university could achieve:

Before 1914 Germany appreciated the importance for the assimilation of the Reichsland of a strong German university in Strasbourg. Its perseverance was not in vain, and those that it succeeded in marking with its imprint are today among the foes of the French idea in Alsace. The same perseverance is necessary to carry through successfully the entirely different and more delicate task of reconciliation and intellectual merger undertaken by France. The University of Strasbourg must be either the second or the last in the country. If, gradually deserted by those coming from the interior, it becomes a small provincial university tending to function on the margins of French life, which is what academic and political circles in Germany hope, one could consider the attempt to reassimilate the recovered provinces permanently compromised.[156]

The campaign succeeded. The ministry backed down, leaving the supplements at the level agreed upon in 1926. But the victory proved temporary, for in 1934 and 1935 decrees lowered the supplements to 18 percent and then to 12 percent of the professors' salaries. Again the professors fought back, employing both their earlier arguments—often without changing a word—and new ones, including the contention that the professors deserved compensation for "the complexity of relations with student groups."[157] All they accomplished was to get the rate raised (in 1936) to 15 percent of their salaries, the implication being that this was where it would remain.[158]

The question of the supplements was but one of many issues over which the faculty and the government clashed in these years. Some of the others also resulted from efforts to economize. There were disputes, for instance, over the ministry's reluctance to fill certain vacancies, over its attempts to reduce the number of professorships, and over budgetary cuts that forced the university to use its discretionary funds to meet salary commitments, an unprecedented step.[159] While ready to bear their share of the burden imposed by the economic crisis, the professors argued, the government was repeatedly forcing them to make sacrifices not required of universities in the interior. In its defense the ministry noted that Strasbourg received more than three times as much for personnel costs as the average provincial university in the interior (and 43 percent of the amount allotted the University of Paris), but this rejoinder hardly consoled the faculty.[160]

In addition there were, as in the 1920s, disputes over such administrative matters as the changing of the designation of chairs, the appointment of *suppléants* (temporary replacements), and the delays in decision making resulting, the professors thought, from bureaucratic ineptitude or indifference. Among the specific provocations were two disputes over appointments, both without precedent: late in 1936 the ministry forced the Faculty of Letters to reopen its deliberations concerning a *suppléance* so a new candidate could be considered, one favored by the government, and a few months later it rejected the same faculty's nomination for a

vacant professorship.[161] Admittedly in such matters the university probably fared no worse than any other in France, but this was not the issue.
When it came to institutional autonomy or to the budget the Strasbourg
professors had always believed that they deserved special treatment. What
disturbed them was evidence that the government no longer agreed.

Adding to the professors' malaise were the changes occurring in their
more immediate environment. From the faculty's perspective the climate
of opinion in Alsace-Lorraine worsened steadily in the mid- and late 1930s.
Under the influence of Nazi and autonomist propaganda, commoners
seemed increasingly surly and disaffected and there was a startling rise
in overt anti-Semitism. The autonomist press repeatedly attacked the
university for its lack of ties to Alsatian society and its failure to serve
as a bridge between the French and German scholarly communities.
Meanwhile German cultural products—plays, music, books, periodicals,
and so on—were growing in popularity, thanks in part to the indulgence
of the French authorities. Indeed to a professor who came to the university
in 1938 it appeared that "to be in tune it is necessary to be Germanophile."[162] And, of more direct concern, there was declining support for
the professors' main institutional link to local society, the Université
populaire. Between 1935–36 (the peak year) and 1938–39 the overall
enrollment fell from 3,022 to 2,588 while the average number of lectures
attended by each registrant dropped from 6.5 to 5.6. Too, interest among
those from the lower ranks of the social order was even less than it had
been in the institution's first few years: in 1938–39 only 12 of the men
enrolled (0.9 percent of the total) and 29 of the women (2.2 percent) were
in the working class.[163]

Trends among the students were also disturbing. For the first time since
1919 the proportion who spoke the dialect when with friends appeared to
be growing, suggesting to many professors—erroneously it seems—that
Germanophile sentiment was growing.[164] Among the students generally
there was increasing anti-Semitism and xenophobia and a rising propensity
for slander and violence, all of which poisoned the atmosphere. And the
one student organization in which the professors had had some confidence, AFGES, was proving a disappointment. Although it still provided
important material services, few students were committed to its success
and it was not having the desired impact on the moral climate. Indeed
after the Brunschvicg affair there were even misgivings about the opinions
of its officers.[165]

In addition trends within the faculty itself caused concern. Their origins
were basically political. As among the students and among the French
generally the domestic crises of the 1930s polarized opinion within the
faculty. One manifestation was the growing assertiveness of those on the
left. In the mid-1930s the Jacobins founded and dominated two organizations closely linked to the Popular Front: the Rassemblement populaire

du Bas-Rhin (Edmond Rothé was president, aided by Georges Cerf and Prosper Alfaric) and the local branch of the Comité de vigilance des intellectuels antifascistes (Rothé was again president, flanked by René Capitant, a jurist, and Henri Maresquelle, a botanist). In addition they continued to control the anticlerical Cercle Jean Macé (Alfaric was president in the 1930s) and the local branch of the Ligue des droits de l'homme (Cerf was president from 1931 on) and to advise and encourage the university's leftist and pacifist students.[166] Meanwhile the debility of the Third Republic and the fears aroused by the Popular Front pushed other professors, particularly in the Faculties of Law and Medicine, far to the right.[167] And both developments—but particularly the former, for the Jacobins were more active and further removed from prevailing opinion in the region—added to the frustrations of a third group, the professors who, regardless of political opinion, remained alert to local sensitivities. To give a specific example, the Vatican's excommunication of Alfaric in 1933 may have been considered a great victory by the local clergy, who engineered it, and a great honor by Alfaric, who proudly noted the fact on his calling cards, but it could not have pleased the professors preoccupied with their university's reputation among Alsatians.[168]

These trends, the polarization of left and right and the polarization of activists and nonactivists, threatened to erode one of the university's most attractive features, the close relations among its professors. It appeared that political differences might jeopardize the unity of the faculty, just as they were jeopardizing the unity of the country (and, it might be added, worsening the chronically strained relations between much of the faculty and the Société des amis de l'université, a bastion of hostility to the Popular Front).[169] Symptomatic of the decline in collegiality were the faculty council's deliberations early in 1939 over promotion to the *classe exceptionnelle,* a step extending the legal retirement age from sixty-seven to seventy. Specifically concerned with the twelve professors reaching sixty-seven within the next three years, the council overwhelmingly approved the promotion of eleven but voted against the one candidate closely identified with political activism and the Popular Front, Edmond Rothé. The Faculty of the Sciences issued a bitter protest, suggesting with good reason that the council had ignored Rothé's impressive scholarly achievements and that its motives had been political.[170] But it did no good. Rothé would have to retire at sixty-seven, the victim, as his fellow activist Georges Cerf put it, of an act of cheap vengeance for his political opinions and activities.[171]

But of all the trends affecting the faculty's morale, easily the most discouraging concerned the international situation. After Germany's remilitarization of the Rhineland early in 1936 the professors began to fear another war was on the way. This fear, which was of course shared by others, took on added dimensions because of their exposed position: the professors assumed that Strasbourg would be one of the first German targets, thus jeopardizing their lives and possessions, and that the annexation of Alsace-Lorraine would be high on the list of German war aims, thus jeopardizing their university.[172] Yet they also worried about the consequences of continued peace, for any peace based on concessions to Germany—seemingly their government's objective—might also result in the loss of Alsace-Lorraine. Accordingly, while the professors hardly wanted a war, they were, on the whole, stout foes of appeasement. The clearest expression was an open letter sent early in 1939 to France's president, Albert Lebrun. Although the handiwork of a relatively small group—including the philosopher Martial Guéroult, who proposed the idea, and four Jacobin activists, Cerf, Maresquelle, Rothé, and the physicist Charles Sadron—it bore the names of 128 members of the faculty, more than two-thirds of the total. The text, published in *Le Temps* and elsewhere, stated that the signers were "profoundly disturbed" by recent international developments and urged the president to use his influence to bolster France's alliances, to maintain her liberal traditions, and to obstruct "not only all territorial concessions—this goes without saying— but also every measure that might lead to our expropriation or compromise the security of our frontiers and our communications."[173]

The most visible manifestation of the professors' growing uneasiness— and another of its causes—was the high rate of departures for other institutions. Although there also had been departures in the 1920s, the number was greater in the 1930s and so was the impact on the university's stature and on the morale of those who remained. Particularly affected, as earlier, was the Faculty of Letters. Between 1933 and 1937, for instance, it lost a dozen of its most distinguished members, including the historians Marc Bloch, Lucien Febvre, Georges Lefebvre, and Charles-Edmond Perrin, the psychologist Charles Blondel, the archaeologist Albert Grenier, the sociologist Maurice Halbwachs, and the Germanist Edmond Vermeil. Of course some had long been seeking a gate through which to enter Paris, as Halbwachs put it, and would have left regardless of the conditions in Strasbourg.[174] But with time the push factors were growing in significance. In 1931 Jean Pommier, a historian of French literature, noted that "after having been rather indifferent (except for reasons of friendship) to a return to Paris, we now yearn for it shamelessly. Winters here are harsh, and the moral climate is not much better."[175] By 1934 Georges Lefebvre, who had arrived with the intention of finishing his career in Strasbourg, was so uncomfortable that he considered applying for a vacancy in Toulouse.[176] And in 1938 the Protestant theologian Oscar Cullmann, a native of Strasbourg, accepted a call from the University of Basel, in part, he told his Strasbourg colleagues, because of the advantages in the event of war.[177] The last two cases exemplified another disturbing development: for the first time professors in significant numbers were willing to leave for institutions other than those in Paris.[178] Until now the Strasbourg professors had found consolation for their losses in knowing that their university, to use Pfister's metaphor, was the waiting room of the Sorbonne and the Collège de France. But Toulouse?

Through the mid-1930s the university succeeded in replacing most of those departing with scholars of comparable prominence or great promise. In a few areas it actually attained heights in the 1930s not approached in the previous decade, most notably, perhaps, in mathematics and physics. (Henri Cartan and André Weil, central figures in the Bourbaki group responsible for transforming modern mathematics, arrived in 1931 and 1933, respectively, and Louis Néel, co-winner of the 1970 Nobel Prize in physics, joined the faculty in 1934.) Although the university's national missions no longer had the appeal for potential candidates that they had had for the founding generation, its reputation as an excellent place for research helped to compensate, and so did its reputation as a springboard to Paris. Toward the end of the decade, however, the pattern changed. Because of the worsening international situation the university now had difficulty finding worthy candidates for its growing number of vacancies. As a result there was cause to take more seriously the dire predictions some professors had been making almost from the start: the university may have survived its earlier challenges, including the autonomist challenge, with its reputation more or less intact, but under the influence of the German threat it seemed to be entering a period of decline.[179]

Could the trend be halted? In the last year before the war there was, finally, some cause for optimism, thanks largely to the efforts of a new rector. When Joseph Dresch, who had replaced Pfister as rector in 1931, announced his intention to resign in 1938, the professors seized the opportunity to bring their concerns to the attention of the authorities and to stress the need to select Dresch's successor with special care. What was required, they argued, was someone who was experienced, industrious, cold-blooded, familiar with Alsace-Lorraine, and, above all, dedicated to strengthening the university.[180] They had reason to be satisfied with the results. The new rector, Adolphe Terracher, met the professors' stipulations, and in his first months in office his initiatives and successes were impressive.

One of Terracher's first accomplishments was to have the professors' supplements raised to 25 percent of their salaries, the rate sought by the faculty.[181] This resolved a long-standing grievance and indicated that Terracher and the government now attached particular importance to shoring up the university and its faculty's morale. And this was not the only encouraging sign. Toward the end of 1938 the ministry broke precedent and permitted René Leriche, the most distinguished member of the Faculty of Medicine, to teach an additional year in Strasbourg before occupying the position he had recently accepted at the Collège de France. (In urging this dispensation Terracher stressed that "in view of the anxieties created by recent events it is very desirable for reasons of morale to keep in Strasbourg a professor with the scholarly and professional distinction of Dr. Leriche.")[182] At the annual convocation in November 1938 Terracher abandoned convention and devoted his remarks to an analysis of the university's prospects, focusing on what could and would be done to enhance its stature.[183] And both at the convocation and at a later press conference the cabinet member with particular responsibility for Alsatian questions stressed the government's commitment to putting the institution on a more solid footing.[184]

Terracher also intended to improve the university's ties to Alsatian society. Although seemingly content with the professors' contributions to university extension conventionally defined—the *cours publics*, the lectures in other Alsatian towns, the Université populaire, and so on—he wanted more attention given to research on themes of special relevance to the region. Actually there had recently been a movement in this direction. Some recent migrants to Paris had been replaced by scholars who, while perhaps less distinguished, had more interest in fostering research on Alsatian subjects and in publishing the results in local periodicals (notably the historians Gaston Zeller and Félix Ponteil, who succeeded Lucien Febvre and Georges Lefebvre).[185] But in his inaugural address Terracher referred to complaints that "the University of Strasbourg has not sunk its roots deep enough into the dense and fertile soil of Alsace" and indicated that he agreed.[186] Specifically he proposed that the university establish an Institut des hautes études alsaciennes. This institute would foster and publish not only professors' and students' research on local questions but also that of well-intentioned private scholars. In the process, he might have added, it would contribute in important ways to the university's nation-building mission. As the "symbol and center of our regional activities," it should make the university seem less alien to particularistic Alsatians, less of a *Fremdkörper*.[187] It might also eclipse the two scholarly societies identified with the autonomists, the Gesellschaft für Elsässische Kirchengeschichte and the Elsass-Lothringische Wissenschaftliche Gesellschaft. And it would be a counter, symbolic and otherwise, to what had long been the most active and troubling center of research on Alsatian questions, Frankfurt's Wissenschaftliches Institut der Elsass-Lothringer im Reich. This was all the more urgent since in recent years the Frankfurt institute had established closer ties to Alsatian scholars and it now was negotiating its first cooperative agreement with an Alsatian scholarly society.[188]

The faculty, as alert as Terracher to the advantages of the proposed institute, responded favorably. In March 1939 the council unanimously approved the project and tentatively decided to establish a journal to further the institute's objectives, and three months later the university acquired a building to house the enterprise. The intention, apparently, was to inaugurate the institute sometime in the next academic year.[189]

Terracher's initiatives opened what promised to be a period of transition for the university. But transition to what? Would Terracher and the government succeed in their evidently sincere campaign to restore the beleaguered institution to its original stature? Would the Institut des hautes études alsaciennes gain the public acceptance required if it were to contribute much to its overt and covert missions? Could the university simultaneously become both more Alsatian and more distinguished, both more provincial and more cosmopolitan? These were among the pressing questions left unresolved when the war began.

# Postscript

On 2 September 1939, the day before declaring war on Germany, the government ordered the nonmobilized residents of Strasbourg and many other Alsatian communities to move immediately to the interior, in most cases to southwestern France. For those in the university community the destination was the university town of Clermont-Ferrand.[1] The evacuation occurred as planned. In September the professors not reporting for military service established themselves in Clermont and early in November the relocated university opened, sharing the facilities of the local institution but retaining its autonomy. The enrollment was small—about 1,000, or a third that of the previous year—but it was enough to justify keeping the university functioning, the professors' primary objective.[2]

The fall of France in June 1940 led to the university's reintegration of most of its mobilized professors and students. But it also resulted in Germany's de facto annexation of Alsace-Lorraine and in the return to the region of the great majority of the roughly 850,000 Alsatians evacuated the year before.[3] These developments added to the symbolic importance of keeping the university open—it was now the most conspicuous reminder of *l'Alsace française*—but they also complicated the task, for they isolated the university from most Alsatians and isolated many students from their families. They also made the institution's very existence an embarrassment to the Germans and hence to the collaborationist Vichy regime since, as soon became clear, the Germans intended to make permanent their annexation of Alsace-Lorraine and to establish their own University of Strasbourg.

Shortly after occupying Alsace-Lorraine the German authorities invited Ernst Anrich, a son of Gustav Anrich and a professor at the University of Hamburg, to plan their projected university. Anrich approached the assignment with enthusiasm, guided by two related objectives: to design the "most modern university of the Reich," meaning the one that best embodied the principles of National Socialism, and to make it a bulwark of German culture in the West, one resulting in the "dethroning of the Sorbonne."[4] The plan that emerged called for an institution distinguished by its many professors (129), by the prominence of its programs in German studies, and by the absence of theological faculties. Officials in Berlin proved less ambitious than Anrich, however, or at least less willing to make the recommended expenditures. Hence when the university opened late in 1941 it was on a much smaller scale than projected—it had only half the chairs proposed by Anrich—and was more conventional in character. The only major difference between it and the other medium-sized universities of Nazi Germany was the lack of theological faculties.[5]

The German university attracted few Alsatian students, probably no more than 500 in any semester. The small enrollment resulted in part from the absence of theological faculties, which forced many to study across the Rhine and did much to discredit the new institution in the eyes of Alsatians.[6] More important, though, was the refusal of most of the Alsatian students in Clermont to return to Strasbourg. To this refusal German authorities reacted with ambivalence. They considered it a matter of prestige that many return and did their best to bring this about, even sending delegations of students' parents to Clermont to plead with their children. Yet they did not want those thoroughly Francophile and hence decided against resorting to compulsion.[7] The choice was thus left to the students, and for most the choice was to remain in Clermont. As one asserted to a German emissary, "We would rather be Frenchmen and defeated than Germans and victorious."[8] A minority did move back, however, perhaps as many as 40 percent of the roughly 1,230 Alsatian students in Clermont in the summer of 1940. (In the autumn of 1940 about 570 Alsatians sought authorization to attend German universities or *Fachhochschulen,* while some 940 Alsatians registered at the relocated French university.)[9] Some of those returning welcomed the new German regime, at least initially, but for most familial and economic considerations and a belief that the war was over outweighed ideological motives. It should be noted, too, that the returnees were partly offset by the students, perhaps 200 or 300, who fled Alsace-Lorraine after the German occupation and found refuge in Clermont.[10]

With the founding of their University of Strasbourg the Germans intensified their pressure on the Vichy regime to do something about the French one, and with some success. The Vichy authorities returned the library collections and laboratory equipment evacuated from Strasbourg in 1939–40, and they refused to permit the relocated university to fill its vacant professorships.[11] They also kept the institution under close surveillance, particularly after resistance activities began in earnest early in 1942, and they arrested some of the many professors and students involved in these activities. (For obvious reasons the institution in Clermont was one of the most important centers of the resistance in the unoccupied territory.)[12] But Vichy stopped short of closing the university or, as the Germans also urged, of revoking its authority to grant diplomas or to use its name. Much of the credit should go to the rector, Terracher, for he vigorously defended his university's interests at every turn. He even decided, after considerable soul-searching, to accept a high position in the Vichy regime's education ministry in the conviction, apparently well-founded, that this step would facilitate protecting the university. (It was a decision, predictably, over which the faculty was sharply divided.)[13]

The German occupation of France's southern zone in November 1942 made the university's position even more precarious. Almost immediately the surveillance increased and arrests and other reprisals became more frequent. Early in 1943, for instance, the historian Gaston Zeller was prohibited from teaching because of an offhand remark in a lecture interpreted by an informant as critical of the status quo. A few months later German troops raided a dormitory and arrested the thirty-nine students on the premises, all of whom were deported to Germany. In November 1943 the Gestapo assaulted the university, apparently expecting to uncover an arsenal; no arms were found, but before they were through the Germans had killed one professor (Paul Collomp, a papyrologist), seriously wounded another, arrested about 350 members of the university community, and deported more than 100, including eight professors, to concentration camps. Over the next few months—with more and more students now leaving the university to join the *maquis*—there were additional raids, arrests, and deportations. And early in July 1944 it was learned that Vichy had decided to take the ultimate step: it would dismantle the university before the next academic year.[14] But by now Vichy's plans caused little concern, for liberation seemed imminent. It came to Clermont on 27 August and to Strasbourg three months later, on 23 November.

The professors had hoped to return to Strasbourg as soon as the city was liberated, but the military situation and the dictates of the academic calendar made this impossible. Not until March 1945 was it considered safe to return to the city, and by then a move would have jeopardized preparation for the next round of *concours*. It was decided, accordingly, to send a few professors to Strasbourg to offer extension courses, for which there was a huge demand, while keeping the rest in Clermont until the end of the academic year. On 30 June the professors had their last ceremonial convocation in Clermont—made particularly memorable by the presence of the embodiment of the resistance, Charles de Gaulle—and over the next few weeks they and their students returned to Strasbourg. The repatriated university opened in November 1945.[15]

If most professors had had their way, the postwar university would have been essentially a replica of that of the 1930s or, better yet, that of the 1920s. Their objectives were conservative; all they wanted were the resources and autonomy required to restore the features that had distinguished the institution between the wars. But some younger faculty members thought differently, and so did two former professors now in key government posts, René Capitant, the education minister in de Gaulle's provisional government of 1944–45, and his friend Marcel Prélot, Ter-racher's successor as rector. For the most part veterans of the resistance and fervent Gaullists, these scholars and officials reflected the self-confidence and passion for reform so prevalent in these circles following the liberation. And they saw much room for reform at the university. For one thing they believed that the interwar university, however distinguished, had contributed less than it should have to its special missions, particularly its Alsatian mission. They also recognized that the institution's environment and its options had changed greatly in the interim. Prélot, intent on preparing the faculty for major changes, even claimed that "in the general development of the world and in the evolution of our province there is a greater difference between 1919 and 1945 than between 1871 and 1919."[16]

But what changes were needed? Although the reformers differed on the particulars their general objectives, variations on familiar themes, were clear. Above all they wanted to narrow what they considered the wide gap between the university and Alsatian society. In their opinion this required more than the *cours publics* and the Université populaire and the other extension activities initiated between the wars, and more than the Institut des hautes études alsaciennes soon to be inaugurated. There must also be a change in the basic spirit of the university: the ivory tower of the 1920s and 1930s must give way to an institution more practical in orientation, which in effect meant more provincial. The reformers wanted more courses and research that related to social and economic questions. They favored the appointment of Alsatian businessmen to advisory and policymaking positions. And they wanted the professors to identify more closely with the region and to dedicate themselves to reconciling the Alsatians who had weathered the Nazi occupation with the new generation of *revenants*. Special sacrifices would be required, Prélot warned, and only those prepared should return: "Alsace is a combat post which can use only enthusiastic volunteers."[17] Among other things this meant that the professors must show greater loyalty to the university. The reformers put particular emphasis on reducing the high rate of migration to Paris evident between the wars, for in addition to causing instability and lowered morale it had tended to give professors less incentive to familiarize themselves with their Alsatian surroundings and to attract professors with little interest in doing so. One remedy might be to raise the salary supplements to the level enjoyed by Parisian professors, and Capitant attempted to do so, albeit without success. (In fact in 1945 the supplements were removed entirely.) Another would be to fill vacancies with scholars likely to remain in Strasbourg several years or permanently. Prélot promoted this policy, calling for the appointment not of those seeking a waiting room for the Sorbonne but rather of relatively young and unproven scholars with a preference for those of Alsatian origin.[18]

A second objective was to make the university more cosmopolitan. Like others subscribing to the ideology of the resistance, the reformers looked forward to the overcoming of national rivalries and the reconstruction of Europe on new and more solid foundations. And they believed that geography and history destined the University of Strasbourg to make a special contribution. There was even talk of transforming it into a genuinely European university, with courses in German as well as French and with chairs in such fields as the history of the Rhineland.[19] But was this plan realistic? In the immediate aftermath of the war it was not; public opinion in Alsace-Lorraine and in France generally was hardly ready for such a conciliatory venture. With time, however, the climate improved, and as it did the project began to be discussed more seriously. This was particularly true after the British Foreign Office proposed in January 1949 that a Council of Europe be established with its headquarters in Strasbourg. Thus in March 1949 the Nouvelle ligue franco-allemande issued a manifesto proposing, among other things, "the metamorphosis of the University of Strasbourg into a citadel of Franco-German culture at which the Germans will learn French, the Frenchmen will learn German, and the literature and scholarly disciplines of the two nations will be cultivated."[20] A few weeks later the first congress of the Union fédéraliste interuniversitaire, held in Strasbourg, included in its program a discussion of the organization of a European university.[21] And, most significant, there were indications that the French Foreign Ministry—headed by Robert Schuman, a Lorrainer and an alumnus of Strasbourg's German university—was considering founding an international university in Strasbourg, either by transforming the existing institution or by establishing another alongside it.[22]

Most Strasbourg professors had misgivings about these proposals, both those aimed at making their university more provincial and those aimed at making it more European. Committed to what the reformers considered an outdated and rigid conception of the university, they once again found themselves on the defensive. And they responded accordingly, doing what they could to impede the new challenges. They attempted to convince the ministry that their university still deserved special treatment. They passed resolutions objecting both to innovations specific to their institution, such as the chair of Rhenish history, and to general reforms likely to make the university more provincial, such as the ministry's efforts to limit the mobility of students. In speeches and articles they stressed the continuing importance of the university's missions as originally defined. And on occasion they proposed innovations of their own in the hope of forestalling more thoroughgoing changes.[23]

The professors' most concerted campaign came in response to the suggestions that their university be transformed into or joined by a European university. When these possibilities were first discussed openly, early in

1949, the faculty reacted quickly and strongly, hoping to undercut the ideas before they gained momentum and to influence the as yet uncertain positions of their government and the nascent Council of Europe. On 6 April the council of the Faculty of Letters unanimously rejected the idea of establishing a European university in Strasbourg.[24] Three days later the five professors attending a meeting to plan a local Comité du mouvement européen withdrew and publicly protested upon learning that a colleague thought to favor a European university for Strasbourg was to be named to this Comité.[25] And later in the month a group of professors interrupted the conference of the Union fédéraliste interuniversitaire to read a statement on the subject:

> The choice of Strasbourg as the seat of the European union could provoke proposals seeking the establishment of a European university in this city. We know that the project already exists.
>
> Now there can be no question of paralleling or replacing the University of Strasbourg with an international university. In particular we cannot allow, as has sometimes been suggested, a Franco-German and bilingual university.
>
> The only possible formula is that in existence now, that is, a university that is very open to students from other countries. Should the occasion arise the University of Strasbourg, where the study of foreign languages and civilizations has always had a prominent place, will be able to call upon non-French professors whom it approves. Any other solution would infringe on its dignity and its *rayonnement*.[26]

These protests may have influenced the conference—it recommended that the European university be in a town currently without a university[27]—but they did not end the threat. In May the Ministry of National Education indicated that it wanted the University of Strasbourg to become more international in character, and in September the recently convened Council of Europe voted to consider the subject of a European university at its 1950 session.[28] The Faculty of Letters responded by appointing a committee to prepare appropriate proposals. In January 1950 this committee, which was dominated by relatively young and reformist professors, recommended that the university be transformed into a "university with a European mission." More specific proposals included adding courses on subjects relating to general European questions, creating diplomas to be recognized in all European countries, establishing professorships reserved for visiting foreign scholars, soliciting financial support from other countries and from the Council of Europe, and appointing foreigners, including a representative of the Council of Europe, to as many as two-fifths of the positions on the council administering the institution.[29] But these proposals went too far for most members of the faculty. There was particular resistance to seeking the patronage of foreign countries and the Council of Europe, for it was feared it would result in German professors and students descending on the university in large numbers. The resolution, reached after prolonged negotiations among the faculties and indications that the Council of Europe was losing interest in the idea of a European university, was the adoption of a more modest program. There were to be two basic innovations: the addition of a few chairs for foreign scholars and the establishment of a center for research on European questions. Arrangements for financing and administering the university would remain unchanged.[30]

In the debates of 1945–50 over the proper character and mission of the University of Strasbourg it was the conservatives, those hoping to recreate the university of the interwar years, who prevailed. The few concessions to those seeking a university that was at once more Alsatian and more European did not fundamentally alter the structure or ambience of the institution. Yet while the conservatives succeeded in minimizing the impact of specific efforts at reform, more general challenges remained. There were those resulting from the rapidly expanding demand for higher education and from the government's efforts to meet this demand. How would these affect the close relations between professors and students and among the seven faculties that had earlier distinguished the university? And how would the activities of the Centre national de la recherche scientifique (CNRS), established in 1945, and the improvement of research facilities at other French universities and abroad affect the university's stature? There were also challenges relating to the changed situation in Germany. With Germany no longer the threat it had been between the wars, and the German universities no longer as distinguished, how important was the university's mission on the Rhine? Could its faculty continue to justify special efforts to maintain the institution as a showcase of French scholarship and an agent of France's *rayonnement* abroad? And, finally, there were challenges resulting from changes within Alsace-Lorraine. The German occupation of 1940–44 and the German defeat of 1945 had effectively terminated the Alsatian question. Problems of adjustment remained, of course, not least at the university: as in 1919 it was necessary to determine equivalences for German credentials and to make special arrangements for students with a weak grounding in French.[31] But there was no longer any doubt about the attachment of Alsatians generally to France or about the desire of Alsatian students to participate fully in national life; the Nazis and the war had resolved the problem of nation building in Alsace-Lorraine. But what were the implications for the university? With Alsace-Lorraine seemingly ready to become just another province of France, would the institution now become just another provincial university?[32]

In the immediate aftermath of the war the answers were far from obvious. Yet two predictions could have been made with confidence. It was likely that the Strasbourg professors would remain on the defensive, much as they had been almost from the time their university opened. And it was likely that they would have little success with the argument most often advanced in the past when defending the university: that in trying to preserve the unique character and high stature given the university when it opened they were also furthering the interests of France.

# Conclusion

The two universities featured in this study had clearly defined missions. Each was founded in the expectation that it would both contribute to its nation's integration of Alsace-Lorraine and advance its nation's claims to cultural and scholarly hegemony in Europe and beyond. And, unlike the original missions of many universities, these twin objectives remained central throughout each institution's history. Accordingly, it is by their contributions to these missions that the success of the universities must ultimately be evaluated.

Yet the need is more apparent than the solution. It is impossible to measure with any precision how the two universities affected their countries' reputations and influence abroad. It is also impossible to measure their direct and indirect impacts on Alsatians outside the university community or, in the absence of survey data, their net effect on the values and behavior of their Alsatian students. The most that can be offered are self-evident truths and impressionistic observations.

Both before and after the demise of the German university many observers, German as well as French, argued that as far as Germany's interests were concerned the institution had done more harm than good. As an instrument of Germanization it had not only fallen short of the high expectations of its initial proponents—no one could dispute this—but had actually proved counterproductive. Impressed by the activities of the Cercle and kindred organizations, French journalists and politicians proudly insisted that exposure to German learning and to German students and professors had only reinforced the Alsatian students' respect for French culture and longing for *revanche*. And many German observers agreed. Beginning in the 1890s several Germans concluded that founding a university in Strasbourg had been a mistake. The existence of this institution, they complained, had made it possible for Alsatians to receive a higher education without crossing the Rhine and hence without coming into direct contact with "the great stream of German life."[1] In addition, it had given Francophile students opportunities to establish social and cultural institutions that excluded Germans and, together with alumni such as Pierre Bucher, to proselytize among Alsatian students who might otherwise have become fully reconciled to German rule and culture. In short the University of Strasbourg, founded in the expectation that it would contribute significantly to the assimilation of Alsace-Lorraine, had turned out to be a major obstacle to Germanization.

But were they correct? Had the university, on balance, retarded nation building in Alsace-Lorraine? In attempting to answer these questions a number of points deserve emphasis. To begin with, the Alsatians who studied at the university did not constitute a homogeneous group. Many who viewed the institution from afar assumed that all or almost all its Alsatian students identified with organizations like the Cercle, but this was hardly the case. Certainly for some, as a Germanophile Alsatian admitted in the 1920s, the university "had, indirectly, a Frenchifying impact."[2] But for many more, it seems, attendance at the university had the opposite effect. "This whole generation," a particularistic Alsatian later observed concerning the Alsatians at the university shortly before the war, "had absorbed German culture, had accepted German methods and the German language, and had in the process gained in seriousness, in depth, in self-respect, and in consciousness of status. In general the basics of German culture had advanced strongly, and Alsatian individuality was no longer hostile to the German way of life but rather had developed a cordial relationship to it."[3]

It is impossible to determine the degree to which a particular institution was responsible, of course, but in all likelihood the university deserves much of the credit. Thus the professors, building on the accomplishments of the primary schools and the Gymnasien, helped to familiarize Alsatian students with German ways of thinking and acting and, as admired role models, made it easier for many to identify with Germany. At least after the turn of the century extracurricular activities and relationships apparently had similar effects. And its direct contributions to socialization aside, the university furthered its nation-building mission in its capacity as an institution that necessarily selects and allocates. It provided access to positions of status and influence to Alsatians of humble origins who were essentially Germanophile already and, because of its character and associations, encouraged many Francophile youths with high aspirations to emigrate. In addition it prepared students of all persuasions for careers likely to foster an identification with Germany. Thus through its relationship to the job market (and through the logic of anticipatory socialization) the university gave many Alsatian students incentives to become more German in outlook and identity—it gave them a stake in their own Germanization.

Between the wars, it should be added, graduates of the German university provided much of the leadership and support for the political parties and cultural organizations identified with the autonomist movement. Indeed French observers frequently noted that it was among the university's alumni that the new regime and its efforts at nation building met the stoutest resistance.[4] And while the frustrations that came with membership in the "sacrificed generation" certainly contributed, these observers assigned particular responsibility to the respect for German culture and for Germanic values and practices developed while at the university. At least in private they conceded that the German university had had considerable success in its nation-building mission.

Perhaps the impact would have been greater if Alsatians had had to cross the Rhine to receive a German higher education, but this seems unlikely. Many Alsatians who studied in Strasbourg would have been unable for economic reasons or unwilling for cultural reasons to attend other universities. This is particularly true of those of relatively humble origins—that is, of those potentially most sympathetic to German culture and German rule. It may be assumed, too, that many of those who did study elsewhere in Germany would have selected institutions with sizable colonies of Alsatian students and hence found it almost as easy as it was in Strasbourg to avoid close association with Germans. It is also possible that direct exposure to "the great stream of German life" would have caused many Alsatians to become more conscious and proud of the French components of their heritage. In sum, the likely effect of forcing Alsatians to study across the Rhine would have been to make the Reichsland's indigenous educated elite more Francophile, not less.

In addition a decision not to establish a university in Strasbourg would have had adverse consequences for Germany's reputation abroad. It would have denied the country the credit received for establishing what was long one of the world's most modern and distinguished universities. It would have given ammunition to those inclined to argue that Germany treated the Alsatians like second-class citizens. And it would have deprived Germany of one of the most striking symbols of the alleged Germanness of the annexed territory. For many in other countries the university was the only institution in Alsace-Lorraine with which they were at all familiar. Because of this, and because of its stature and thoroughly German character, the university probably did much to legitimize Germany's annexation of Alsace-Lorraine in the eyes of foreign observers, particularly those in academic circles.

There is yet another consideration, one relating not to the university's impact on its students or to its influence abroad but rather to its reputation among Alsatians generally. Lujo Brentano once insisted that "the university was the only institution established by the Germans that the Alsatians appreciated."[5] Although he may have overstated his case, at least until the war the university did enjoy considerable respect among Alsatians, even among those who complained about its curriculum or about the composition of its faculty. In this regard the professors believed all along that the institution's success in the Reichsland, as abroad, depended not only on its impact on its students—and on its students' impact on others—but also on its remaining an object worthy of admiration in its own right, on its remaining, in effect, a work of art. It was a defensible argument. Many Alsatians did admire the university in its role as a center of learning and take pride in the reflected attention and prestige it brought to their homeland. True, the institution never attained the popularity that other German universities enjoyed in their respective states and regions, but it would be wrong to conclude, as many French critics did, that it was a bastion of pan-Germanism with virtually no support among Alsatians. On balance the existence of the university almost certainly made German rule more acceptable to Alsatians than it would have been otherwise. For this reason, and for those discussed above, the contention that the university did its country more harm than good is unconvincing.

Nobody argued that the decision to establish a new university after World War I was ill-conceived. It was generally conceded that the German precedent left the French with no choice; it was essential to demonstrate both to Alsatians and to foreign observers that France would do as much for Alsace-Lorraine as Germany had done. Yet while the decision to found a university may have been immune to criticism, the institution that resulted was less fortunate. Almost from the time it opened observers on both sides of the Rhine predicted that it would fall far short of the expectations that justified its existence. For some this was because neither the government nor the faculty was likely to remain sufficiently committed; once the initial enthusiasm waned the university would go into decline. For others it was because the university as constituted was poorly suited to its special missions, either because it was insufficiently cosmopolitan or because it was insufficiently Alsatian. Thus Alsatian and German critics attacked the university for offering no instruction in German, for discriminating against Alsatian scholars when making appointments, for slighting research on matters of local interest, for being more overtly nationalistic than the German university had been. In short they considered the institution what others had considered its predecessor: an alien body within Alsace-Lorraine, a *Fremdkörper*.

In evaluating these allegations it is again useful to distinguish between the university's impact on its students and its impact on those outside the university community. As far as the students were concerned, even the most Germanophile conceded that the university had considerable success.[6] The students may have been sharply divided on political issues but, a small minority aside, their allegiance to France and their respect for French culture were beyond question. Of course all the credit should not go to the university. Many students came from the thoroughly Francophile elite of Alsace-Lorraine. Primary and secondary schooling had made important contributions. And many of the students from dialect-speaking families systematically invested in their own Frenchification; motivated by a combination of patriotism, careerism, and a conviction that "c'est chic de parler français," they sought out friends among the students from the interior, kept up with trends in French literature and the arts, seized opportunities to visit Paris, and did whatever else they could to polish their French and to acquire the tastes and dispositions identified with France's educated bourgeoisie. But the university did make an independent contribution. It exposed the students to some of the country's most distinguished and conscientious professors, and it deepened their familiarity with French history and literature, with French contributions to scholarship, and with French modes of thought and expression. It provided opportunities and time for the students to pursue their efforts at self-Frenchification. And it prepared its students—those overcoming the hurdles—to enter professional and bureaucratic careers likely to reinforce their efforts to participate fully in French life. All in all, the net contribution of the university may have been as great as that of the German university in its most successful years, the two decades preceding World War I.

But might not the impact have been greater had the Alsatian students spent more time at institutions in the interior? Many thought so, for reasons similar to those advanced by their German counterparts: assimilation would be facilitated if the Alsatian students were exposed to a thoroughly French environment. In this case the reasoning is more persuasive, for the students were more interested in becoming fully assimilated and in participating in national life than were the students under German rule. Yet there were drawbacks. Except for the few admitted to the grandes écoles it was difficult to find professors, facilities, or programs in the interior as good as those in Strasbourg. And for many who did go, exposure to a thoroughly French environment had the opposite of the desired effect; faced with unfamiliar surroundings and, often, discrimination against those less than fluent in French, they rediscovered their identity as Alsatians and spent much of their time with other Alsatians, conversing in the dialect. It is at least arguable that for youths from dialect-speaking families the University of Strasbourg offered conditions more conducive to Frenchification than did the universities in the interior. It is likely, too, that it attracted many Alsatians who would not have gone to the interior to study had this been the only option.

The university's impact on Alsatians outside the university community was less direct, less obvious, and, it seems, less significant. It is not that the professors were indifferent or negligent. Compared with those at the German university—or with those at other French universities—their commitment to extending their influence and the variety and scale of their extension programs were impressive. But the results were not. For the most part the professors found themselves preaching to the converted; although they established ties to the Francophone bourgeoisie of Alsace-

Lorraine, their direct influence hardly extended any further. As for the university's general reputation among dialect-speaking Alsatians, this was conditioned by its association with an unfamiliar language, with an unpopular government, and with a Francophone elite seemingly intent on disassociating itself from the "bochophile" masses. For those who cared, the activities and reputed stature of the university and its graduates probably helped to counter the widespread belief that the French could not compete with the Germans when it came to scholarship. But otherwise the situation was close to that described in 1937 by one of the university's deans: "I simply cannot get through to the Alsatians. They consider us foreigners who are coming to colonize them."[7]

Of course the university, like its predecessor, should not be judged only by its impact on Alsatians. It had a foreign mission as well. It was expected to contribute to the prestige of French scholarship in the world generally, to strengthen French influence in central and eastern Europe, and to symbolize the integral links between Alsace-Lorraine and the rest of France. For obvious reasons the extent to which it succeeded cannot be measured. It should be noted, however, that the professors expressed disappointment over the small number of students attracted from Switzerland, from northern Europe, from the British Isles, and from North America, and that political factors and personal biases effectively prevented them from establishing close ties to Germany. It should be noted, too, that there were no striking accomplishments abroad that could be cited when defending the university against its critics. Beyond this all that can be said is that the university had some impact on foreigners' perceptions of French scholarship and of the legitimacy of France's policies in Alsace-Lorraine and that presumably this influence was in the desired direction.

Neither university fulfilled the expectations voiced at its inauguration. On this the principals could agree. But why? Were the universities and their professors at fault? Were the governments on which they depended responsible? Or had the expectations been unrealistic? And the distribution of blame aside, were their remedies? Here there were sharp differences among those concerned. At the most general level the differences were over a single issue: would the universities come closer to success if more provincial in character?

In the case of the German university, government officials concluded around the turn of the century that, within limits, the institution should be adapted to its local environment. Concerned over the damage done by its reputation as a stronghold of anti-Catholicism and of opposition to Alsatian particularism, they systematically attempted to make the university more at home in Alsace-Lorraine. Thus they took steps to increase the number of Alsatian professors, they arranged to have courses in Alsatian history taught by a native, they set aside a chair for a Catholic historian and another for a Catholic philosopher, and, most important by far, they established a Catholic theological faculty. The results, particularly the results of the new faculty, were impressive. It would be going too far to suggest, as one Alsatian did in 1913, that with this faculty's appearance the university suddenly became popular in Alsace-Lorraine.[8] But in its brief history the Catholic theological faculty did succeed in winning the confidence of the bulk of the Reichsland's Catholic clergy, in attracting to the university hundreds of Alsatian students who would not have enrolled otherwise, and in instilling in these students a respect for the theological scholarship and religious traditions of Catholic Germany. Considering the prominence of the Catholic clergy in the cultural and political life of Alsace-Lorraine, these were significant accomplishments indeed. As for the other changes in the character of the university introduced by the government or at its insistence, they were, at the least, important symbolically. While it is unlikely that the courses of the Catholic philosopher Clemens Baeumker or the Alsatian historian Fritz Kiener contributed much to Germanization directly, such innovations made the university less alien in the eyes of Catholic and particularistic Alsatians and added weight to the government's claims that Alsatian interests were compatible with German rule.

The French authorities pursued similar policies, and for similar reasons. At the outset they established two theological faculties, the only two at French universities, and appointed several Alsatians to professorships. And later they attempted to increase the professors' commitment to research on subjects of special interest to Alsatians, to introduce courses and programs of particular relevance to the local economy, and to involve Alsatian businessmen in setting priorities for the university. In addition the authorities, like their German counterparts, withheld the resources that many considered essential if the university were to remain more than provincial in character and stature. Commitments for capital expenditures made before the institution opened were not honored and the professors' salary supplements, intended to facilitate the maintenance of a distinguished faculty, were periodically adjusted downward. Admittedly the government's options were limited by budgetary constraints, by the lobbying of other institutions, and by the imperatives of a highly centralized educational system. But whatever the forces at work, the university seemed destined to become more and more like the other provincial universities of France: an institution of relatively modest dimensions and stature that was incapable of competing with the University of Paris or of adding much luster to the image of French scholarship abroad.

If the governments' policies regarding the two universities were broadly similar, so were the professors' reactions. Both the German and the French professors resisted virtually all policies likely to make their universities more provincial in character. They were committed to their missions, of course, and in certain respects their spirit of sacrifice was pronounced. At both institutions professors made special efforts to impress their Alsatian students, to extend their influence beyond the university community, and to curtail political and other activities that might offend Alsatian sensitivities. But when it came to the structure and image of their universities they saw little room for compromise. They failed to initiate any significant concessions to their Alsatian critics, they strongly opposed most of those initiated by others, they resisted all constitutional reforms threatening to give more control over their universities to Alsatians, and they did their best to hold the authorities to the extensive commitments made at the outset. With few exceptions the professors adhered to the assumptions that had motivated the founding of their universities. Convinced that nation building in Alsace-Lorraine was far from complete, they could not see how making their institutions more Alsatian in character or permitting them to decline in stature could possibly serve the national interest. The universities could succeed in their special missions, they believed, but only if they retained the distinction as centers of learning they had had initially, only if they remained impressive works of art.

This logic was not without self-serving implications. It could be used, and was used, to justify requests for greater autonomy, for better facilities, and for other resources likely to improve the professors' working conditions and status. In addition it gave legitimacy to institutionalized attitudes and patterns of behavior: it helped to shield the professors from demands that they change their ways or abandon their *droits acquis* or modify their organizational sagas. But such implications do not mean the logic was wrong. Relevant here are observations made by Lucien Febvre five years after taking a chair in Strasbourg. For a people to abandon one language for another—or, to generalize, one identity for another—"the complicity of sentiment is necessary. The dominated must sense and be willing to acknowledge the prestige of the dominant. Or rather, renouncing every irreducible particularism, national or religious, they must aspire to distinguish themselves no longer from the dominant, to merge with them and into them more and more completely, to participate in their admittedly superior civilization, in their moral, scientific, literary, artistic, and religious culture, regarded as enviable and attractive."[9] By extension, an institution that represented the best a nation could offer, one embodying its "admittedly superior culture," would accomplish more than one tailored to local traditions. Adaptation would be necessary, of course, but the onus should be on the dominated, not the dominant—on the Alsatians, not the professors.

But however compelling the logic, there were major obstacles to its realization. For one thing, it was impossible to measure the returns to investments in prestige. Assessments of an institution's stature and symbolic significance and of their impact allow considerable leeway for self-deception and exaggeration on the part of the institution's friends—and for cynicism and debunking on the part of its critics. One person's work of art can be another's Potemkin village.[10] And the evaluation of the benefits aside, the costs implicit in the professors' logic were high. Universities of the sort desired by the Strasbourg professors could not be maintained without large commitments of resources, commitments likely both to strain public revenues and to threaten the particular interests of the responsible ministries and of other universities. In this regard the less costly policies actually pursued, whatever their impact in Alsace-Lorraine, at least made it easier to humor tightfisted legislatures and finance ministers and to forestall demands for more equitable treatment from other institutions.

The professors also had to contend with another, more insidious obstacle. Popular sentiment concerning the Alsatian question and concerning higher education was moving in unfavorable directions. In both the German and the French cases the national enthusiasm over the annexation of Alsace-Lorraine dissipated with time, and so did the readiness to make sacrifices to impress the Alsatians. At the same time public support for higher education and the willingness of others to defer to the opinions of professors were in decline. In this connection each of the universities featured in this study appeared toward the end of a period in which professors enjoyed great prestige and extensive influence over public opinion—the period of national unification and the *Kulturkampf* in the case of Germany and the period of the Dreyfus affair and the separation of church and state in the case of France. This timing goes far to explain the optimistic rhetoric that justified founding the two institutions and the pride and zeal with which the initial professors undertook their national missions. But in both cases the general climate of opinion soon changed for the worse. The professionalization of politics and other challenges to the educated middle class, economic difficulties, the growing careerism of students, the appearance of new yardsticks of national strength and prestige, the success of other instruments of national integration—these and other developments made it increasingly difficult to justify special treatment for higher education or to maintain the aura of sacredness with which professors like to surround their institutions and their activities. Thus it is not surprising that Strasbourg's universities failed to maintain the heights reached in their euphoric early years. Nor is it surprising that the policymakers tended to react skeptically to the Strasbourg professors' standard argument when seeking favors or protesting maltreatment: the argument that in defending their own interests they were defending their country's, that the promotion of scholarship was an efficient means of nation building.

# Abbreviations

**AACVS** Archives administratives et contemporaines de la ville de Strasbourg. (Archives municipales, Strasbourg)

**ADBR** Archives départementales du Bas-Rhin, Strasbourg.

**AFDP** Archives de la famille de Pange. (M. Victor de Pange, Strasbourg)

**AN** Archives nationales, Paris.

**BAK** Bundesarchiv, Koblenz.

**BCV** Briefe aus dem Nachlass des Professors Dr. Conrad Varrentrapp. (Preussischer Kulturbesitz, Geheimes Staatsarchiv, Berlin [W.])

**BFT** Bibliothèque des Facultés de théologie, Strasbourg.

**BN** Bibliothèque nationale, Paris.

**BNUS** Bibliothèque nationale et universitaire, Strasbourg.

**BTN** Briefwechsel Theodor Nöldekes. (Universitätsbibliothek, Tübingen)

**CFK** Collection of Correspondence of Friedrich Kapp, 1842–84. (Library of Congress, Washington, D. C.)

**FAT** Fonds Albert Thomas. (Archives nationales, Paris)

**FFD** Fonds Ferdinand Dollinger. (Archives municipales, Strasbourg)

**FHH** Fonds Hugo Haug. (Archives municipales, Strasbourg)

**FM** Fonds Millerand. (Bibliothèque nationale, Paris)

**GSP** Georg Simmel Papers. (Leo Baeck Institute, New York City)

**GST** Gustav von Schmoller: Teilnachlass. (Universitätsbibiothek, Tübingen)

**HEHC** Herman Eduard von Holst Collection. (University of Chicago Library, Chicago)

**HMP** Hugo Münsterberg Papers. (Boston Public Library, Boston)

**LJT** Lettres adressées à Johannes Tielrooy. (Bibliothèque nationale, Paris)

**MAE** Ministère des affaires etrangères, Paris.

**NAE** Nachlass Albert Ehrhard. (Byzantinisches Institut, Scheyern)

**NES** Nachlass von Eduard Schwartz. (Bayerische Staatsbibliothek, Munich)

**NFB** Nachlass von Franz Boll. (Universitätsbibliothek, Heidelberg)

**NFK** Nachlass von Felix Klein. (Niedersächsische Staats- und Universitätsbibliothek, Göttingen)

**NFM** Nachlass Friedrich Meinecke. (Preussischer Kulturbesitz, Geheimes Staatsarchiv, Berlin [W.])

**NHB** Nachlass Harry Bresslau. (Staatsbibliothek Preussischer Kultur-besitz, früher Preussische Staatsbibliothek, Berlin [W.])
**NHP** Nachlass von Hermann Paul. (Universitätsbibliothek, Munich)
**NJH** Nachlass Johannes Haller. (Bundesarchiv, Koblenz)
**NKA** Nachlass von Karl von Amira. (Bayerische Staatsbibliothek, Munich)
**NKF** Nachlass von Kuno Fischer. (Universitätsbibliothek, Heidelberg)
**NLB** Nachlass Lujo Brentano. (Bundesarchiv, Koblenz)
**NMH** Nachlass Maximilian Harden. (Bundesarchiv, Koblenz)
**NOH** Nachlass Otto Hartwig. (Hessische Landesbibliothek, Wiesbaden)
**NPG** Nachlass von Paul von Groth. (Bayerische Staatsbibliothek, Munich)
**NPN** Nachlass von Paul Natorp. (Universitäts-Bibliothek, Marburg)
**NPSB** Nachlass Paul Scheffer-Boichorst. (Staatsbibliothek Preussischer Kulturbesitz, früher Preussische Staatsbibliothek, Berlin [W.])
**NRS** Nachlass von René Schickele. (Deutsches Literaturarchiv, Marbach am Neckar)
**NWD** Nachlass Wilhelm Dilthey. (Niedersächsische Staats- und Universitätsbibliothek, Göttingen)
**NWG** Nachlass Walter Goetz. (Bundesarchiv, Koblenz)
**NWK** Nachlass von Wilhelm Kapp. (Universitätsbibliothek, Freiburg im Breisgau)
**PAH** Papiers d'Albert Houtin. (Bibliothèque nationale, Paris)
**PAL** Papiers d'Alfred Loisy. (Bibliothèque nationale, Paris)
**PEL** Papiers Ernest Lavisse. (Bibliothèque nationale, Paris)
**PFS** Papiers de François Simiand. (Archives nationales, Paris)
**PGC** Papiers Gustave Cohen. (Archives nationales, Paris)
**PHP** Papers of Henri Pirenne. (Pirenne chateau, Hierges)
**PRP** Papiers Raymond Poincaré. (Bibliothèque nationale, Paris)
**PWW** Papers of Werner Wittich. (Mlle Georgine Wittich, Bergheim)
**RMP** Richard von Mises Papers. (Harvard University Archives, Cambridge, Mass.)
**TFA** Teilnachlass Friedrich Althoff. (Deutsche Staatsbibliothek, Berlin [E.])

# Statistical Sources and Methods

The tables in appendix B and the discussion of enrollment patterns in the text are based on sources, samples, assumptions, and estimating procedures that require elaboration. These sources and methods can best be considered under three general headings: those relating to the characteristics of students, those relating to the characteristics of the populations at risk, and those relating to the indices used in presenting and comparing the observed patterns.

## 1. Students and Their Characteristics

The data concerning the number of students at each German university according to faculty and sex are from Prussia, *Preussische Statistik,* vol. 236, and Germany, *Statistisches Jahrbuch für das Deutsche Reich,* vols. 30–59. Those concerning the number according to geographic origins are based on figures for selected semesters and periods in Alsace-Lorraine, *Statistisches Handbuch;* Alsace-Lorraine, *Statistisches Jahrbuch,* vols. 1–6; Conrad, *Das Universitätsstudium in Deutschland;* Laspeyres, "Die deutschen Universitäten"; Prussia, *Preussische Statistik,* vols. 102, 106, 112, 116, 125, 136, 150, 167, 193, 204, 223, 236; Rienhardt, "Das Universitätsstudium der Württemberger"; and Riese, *Die Hochschule auf dem Wege zum wissenschaftlichen Grossbetrieb.* Evidence concerning the number of students at each French university according to faculty, sex, and geographic origin (French or foreign) is from France, *Annuaire statistique de la France,* vols. 6–56.

The basic data concerning the social, religious, and regional origins of the Alsatian students in the German period come from the matriculation registers of the University of Strasbourg (ADBR: AL 103, nos. 1–9). These registers record each student's name, faculty, date and place of birth, hometown, religion, father's occupation, and last secondary school, as well as the universities previously attended, if any. Since there were systematic differences in the number of semesters that students enrolled, selecting a sample directly from the matriculation registers would convey a misleading impression of the composition of the student body at specific times. Yet information concerning the composition at specific times is necessary both to calculate attendance rates and to make unbiased comparisons with patterns at other times and in other places. Accordingly an indirect approach was adopted. For selected semesters the names of all students from Alsace-Lorraine were determined from the lists of students and hometowns published each semester (University of Strasbourg, *Amtliches Verzeichniss des Personals und der Studenten der Universität Strassburg,* 1872–75; *Amtliches Verzeichniss des Personals und der Studenten der Kaiser-Wilhelms-Universität Strassburg,* 1875–1912; *Kaiser-Wilhelms-Universität Strassburg: Personalverzeichnis,* 1912–18), and the desired information concerning these students was then sought in the matriculation registers. The semesters selected were every tenth semester from the winter semester of 1872–73 to the winter semester of 1892–93 and the winter semesters of 1898–99 (for which valuable supporting data are available), 1907–8, and 1913–14. For all but the last two semesters considered, information was collected for all Strasbourg students whose families lived in Alsace-Lorraine, both natives and immigrants. For 1907–8 and 1913–14 a 20 percent stratified sample of the students from the Reichsland was used. Where there may be significant distortions attributable to this sampling decision, the results for these two semesters have been averaged and presented as the results for 1910–11.

Distinguishing native Alsatian students from "old German" students with homes in the Reichsland presents no problems for the 1870s and 1880s, since in this period one's birthplace is a sufficient indicator. But after 1890 many of the students born in the Reichsland were from families that had come from across the Rhine since 1871. To determine which of the students were natives in these years, various methods have been used. Some can be easily identified; all Cercle members were obviously natives, for instance, and so were those prominent in Alsatian political or intellectual life after 1918. For the others, assessments have been based on the results of an official survey conducted in the winter semester of 1898–99 that distinguishes native Alsatians from "old Germans" (see Alsace-Lorraine, *Statistisches Handbuch,* pp. 468–69), on extrapolations of earlier trends for specific groups (for instance, Catholic students of pharmacy from villages in Upper Alsace), on students' names, and on common sense. To give but two examples, it may be safely assumed that a student of Catholic theology named Constant Ortlieb whose father was a peasant in Hilsenheim was a native Alsatian and that a Protestant law student named Fritz Scheuermann, the son of a privy councillor in Strasbourg, was not. Most cases are less clear-cut and mistakes have doubtless been made, but it is likely that the aggregate figures for the subgroups of interest are good estimates.

When calculating attendance rates and for certain other purposes it is desirable to consider all Alsatians attending German universities, not just those studying in Strasbourg. The total number (including those of "old

German'' origin) can be determined for most semesters from the published sources noted above, but the distribution of those not studying in Strasbourg according to social, religious, and geographic origins can only be estimated. The estimates used rest on two assumptions: that in each of the selected semesters the distribution of the Alsatians at "old German" universities, the few studying Catholic theology excepted, was the same as the distribution of the Alsatians at the University of Strasbourg who had previously attended "old German" universities; and that the distribution of those studying Catholic theology was similar to the distribution of the Alsatians studying Catholic theology in Strasbourg in 1907–8 or 1913–14.

Comparable evidence concerning the social and religious origins of students prior to 1914 is readily accessible for three "old German" states, Baden, Prussia, and Württemberg. The evidence for Baden (from Cron, "Der Zugang der Badener zu den badischen Universitäten und zur Technische Hochschule Karlsruhe") and, except for one year (1909), for Württemberg (from Rienhardt, "Das Universitätsstudium der Württemberger") concerns the students from each state who matriculated within the state. Since in each case virtually all students no doubt spent at least one semester at a university in their native state, these data presumably reflect the characteristics of the students from Baden and Württemberg at all German universities. As for the numbers involved, the totals can be determined from sources noted above and it has been assumed that in each case the distribution according to social origins and other characteristics reflected that of those matriculating in the previous four (for Württemberg) or five (for Baden) years. (For the winter semester of 1909–10 there is direct evidence concerning the social and religious origins of all students from Württemberg enrolled at German universities, distinguished by faculty and sex; see Rienhardt, "Das Universitätsstudium der Württemberger," pp. 238–39, 280–81.)

The evidence for Prussia (from Prussia, *Preussische Statistik,* vols. 102, 106, 112, 116, 125, 136, 150, 167, 193, 204, 223, 236) concerns the German students enrolled at Prussian universities in selected semesters, with the Prussians distinguished from the rest. In this case it has been assumed that for each faculty (1) the distribution according to social origins of the Prussians at non-Prussian universities was similar to the distribution of the non-Prussians at Prussian universities, and (2) the distribution according to religion of the Prussians at non-Prussian universities was similar to the distribution of the Prussians at Prussian universities. Since in all cases the great majority of students were enrolled in their respective states, any biases resulting from these estimating procedures are unlikely to distort the overall estimates in significant ways.

In table 3 in appendix B evidence is presented concerning the social origins of Alsatian students enrolled at French faculties in the 1860s. This evidence is based on the results of an official survey conducted at public secondary schools. More specifically, it is based on the information collected concerning the fathers' occupations of graduates currently enrolled at French faculties and of the current students expecting to enroll in a faculty. Included are the results for all responding schools in the region subsequently annexed by Germany. (The responses to the questionnaire for this region are in AN: F[17] 6847, 6849.)

As noted in the text, the only direct evidence concerning the social origins of French students in the interwar years comes from an official survey conducted early in 1939. The results of that survey are aggregated by university and, for all universities, by faculty. (See the file headed STA* 13: Origine sociale, located in a closet in the office of the director of the Département de la documentation of the Ministère de l'éducation, Vanves [Hauts-de-Seine].) To estimate the distribution according to social origins of the Alsatians at the University of Strasbourg, it has been assumed that (1) for each faculty the distribution of Strasbourg students from the interior (their numbers having been determined from another 1939 survey as reported in Adolphe Terracher to Bureau universitaire de statistique, 26 April 1939, ADBR: UStr) was similar to that of all French students at French universities; (2) the enrollment rates according to father's occupation of those aged 20–23 who had moved to Alsace-Lorraine from the interior since 1918 was as in France generally (the number at risk and their distribution according to father's occupation having been estimated from census data and other evidence); and (3) the number of immigrant Alsatians enrolled at the University of Strasbourg was half the number from families currently living in the interior (for justification, see chap. 9, note 14). To estimate the distribution according to social origins of all native Alsatians attending French universities, it has been assumed that (1) as in the 1920s, 28.2 percent of those in secular faculties were at universities in the interior, and (2) their distribution according to social origins was similar to that of the native Alsatians enrolled in Strasbourg's secular faculties. The latter distribution can be determined through subtraction, since the distribution of France's students of theology, all of whom were in Strasbourg, is known.

## 2. The Populations at Risk

Information about the characteristics of students is useful in isolation, for it sheds light on the dynamics of student subcultures and of recruitment into certain professions and occupations. But to assess patterns of selectivity—to assess the likelihood that those with particular characteristics will attend a university—it is essential to consider the populations at risk; denominators are needed as well as numerators.

For present purposes determining the populations at risk entails estimating the numbers in the appropriate age cohort according to father's current occupation and, in some cases, according to sex, religion, and place of residence. But proceeding necessitates certain assumptions. To begin with, it is assumed that the appropriate cohort is that aged 20–23. This assumption rests on evidence indicating that in Germany the typical student enrolled for about four years and that the age-specific enrollment rates tended to be highest for those aged 20–23. Since there were variations over time and among groups in the average number of years that students enrolled, adhering to a fixed definition of the cohort at risk provides no more than a rough gauge of the proportions of groups matriculating. But, in compensation, it does provide reliable and comparable measures of the commitment of time to university study or, put differently, of rates of matriculation controlling for the length of time enrolled. The sizes of the male and female cohorts aged 20–23 in the relevant years have been determined or interpolated from the results of the German censuses of 1871 through 1939 (see Germany, *Statistik des Deutschen Reichs,* passim, and Germany, *Statistisches Jahrbuch für das Deutsche Reich,* passim) and of the French censuses of 1891 through 1936 (see France, *Annuaire statistique de la France,* passim).

The estimated distributions of the cohorts aged 20–23 according to father's occupation are based on the German occupational censuses of 1882, 1895, 1907, and 1925 (see Germany, *Statistik des Deutschen Reichs,* n. s., vols. 2–4, 102–10, 202–10, 402), and on the French censuses of 1921, 1926, and 1936 (see France, *Résultats statistiques du recensement général de la population effectué le 6 mars 1921;* France, *Résultats statistiques du recensement général de la population effectué le 7 mars 1926;* France, *Statistique des familles en 1926;* and France, *Résultats statistiques du recensement général de la population effectué le 8 mars 1936).* More specifically, they rest on data concerning the males in each occupational sector in particular age cohorts (30–39, 40–49, 50–59) and the number of children under 14 with fathers in each occupational sector. These data have been used to estimate for each relevant occupational category the number of children under 14 per male aged 33–46 on the assumption (supported by other evidence) that the typical father of a typical child under 14 was about 40 years old. The results were then multiplied by the estimated number of males in the same category aged 53–56 fifteen years later, when the typical child would be aged 20–23. The procedure is designed to control both for the career mobility of fathers between the median ages of 40 and 55 and for variations in fertility among occupational groups and over time. Interpolations and extrapolations are, where appropriate, logarithmic. In all cases the results have been adjusted so that they are consistent with the actual numbers aged 20–23 as determined from the population censuses.

The analysis is restricted to the occupational categories used in the available surveys of the social origins of German and French students.

In most cases these categories are broader than the most specific used in the occupational censuses. In the remaining cases multipliers based on other sources have been used in combination with data from the occupational censuses to estimate the populations at risk. The distinction between the children of university-trained teachers and those of other teachers is based on the number of male teachers employed in institutions of various types (see Alsace-Lorraine, *Statistisches Handbuch;* Alsace-Lorraine, *Statistisches Jahrbuch,* passim; Baden, *Statistisches Jahrbuch für das Grossherzogtum Baden,* passim; Prussia, *Statistisches Handbuch* passim; Prussia, *Statistisches Jahrbuch,* passim; Württemberg, *Statistisches Handbuch,* passim; and Württemberg, *Württembergische Jahrbücher,* passim) and on age-specific data for Germany as a whole in 1907 and 1925 (see Germany, *Statistik des Deutschen Reichs,* n.s., vols. 203, 402). The proportion of male landowners with holdings of fifty hectares or more is the multiplier used to estimate the proportion of the children of farmers whose fathers were estate owners (*Gutsbesitzer*) rather than peasants (see Germany, *Statistik des Deutschen Reichs,* n. s., vols. 5, 112, 212, 409; and France, *Recensement général de la population effectué le 10 mars 1946,* vol. 7). And the proportions of independent males in manufacturing and commerce owning firms employing more than five are the multipliers used to distinguish the children of entrepreneurs from those of artisans and the children of merchants and bankers from those of shopkeepers (see Germany, *Statistik des Deutschen Reichs,* 1st ser., vols. 34, 35; n. s., vols. 6, 7, 113–18, 213–19, 413; France, *Résultats statistiques du recensement général de la population effectué le 6 mars 1921;* France, *Résultats statistiques du recensement général de la population effectué le 7 mars 1926;* and France, *Résultats statistiques du recensement général de la population effectué le 8 mars 1936*). Although these procedures are somewhat arbitrary, experimentation with other multipliers yielded enrollment rates that seem less plausible and trends essentially the same as those that emerge using the multipliers selected.

In the case of France it has been assumed that for each occupational category the ratio of children under 14 to males in the labor force was the same in 1924 (that is, fifteen years before 1939) as in 1926, the only year in the period for which the relevant data are available. For the three departments constituting Alsace-Lorraine, data are available concerning the ratio of children under 14 to males in the labor force for broad social strata—owners, employees, workers, self-employed, unemployed—but not for occupations or occupational sectors. Accordingly it has been assumed that within each stratum the ratios of the occupation-specific ratios of children to adult males were as in 1907, the year of the last German census in the region.

The resulting figures do not distinguish between native Alsatians and those from immigrant families. Accordingly the numbers and distributions of the latter have been estimated using data on the Alsatian population according to place of birth collected in population censuses, the German occupational census of 1907 (the only one in the period with data for Alsace-Lorraine on occupation according to place of birth), and fragmentary evidence from other sources concerning the geographic origins of those in specific occupations.

To estimate the number and distribution according to social origins of the Alsatians aged 20–23 in Strasbourg, in the rest of Lower Alsace, in Upper Alsace, and in Lorraine, necessary for the analysis of regional disparities within Alsace-Lorraine in the German period, similar procedures have been employed. To estimate the number aged 20–23 according to religion, necessary for the analysis of religious disparities in the German period, it has been assumed that for each state considered the religious distribution of children in each occupational category was the same as that of all employed males in the category, with the latter determined from the occupational censuses. Here, as in all cases, the figures for the years of interest have been interpolated or extrapolated from those determined or estimated for census years.

The primary objectives throughout have been to take full advantage of the published census data and to maintain consistency. If systematic biases remain, the use of consistent methods across units and across time suggests that these biases are more or less constant and hence do not seriously undermine the utility for comparative purposes of the rates and indices that have been calculated.

### 3. Indices

Of the types of measures used in the tables and in the text to describe and to compare enrollment patterns, three deserve elaboration: the selectivity index, the index of dissimilarity, and the indices of religious and regional inequality.

The selectivity index measures, for specific groups such as occupational categories, the disparity between the number enrolled and the expected number if there were no differences among groups in enrollment rates. It can be calculated in two ways: by dividing a particular group's proportion of all those enrolled by that group's proportion of the total population, or by dividing the enrollment rate for a particular group by the rate for all groups. The tables do not present selectivity indices, but since they do give both rates for particular occupational groups and the overall rates, the relevant selectivity indices can easily be calculated.

The index of dissimilarity provides a single, overall measure of representativeness or equity. It can be defined as the percent of students who would have to be from other groups if the enrollment rates for all groups were to be the same. The simplest way to calculate the index is to determine for each overrepresented group (or for each underrepresented group) the absolute difference between the percent of students from the group and the percent of the population at risk in the group, and then to sum these differences. The limits of the index are 0 and 100, with 0 indicating complete equity. The number and character of the groups considered can affect the index, so comparisons are only legitimate when the groups considered are defined consistently. For each of the tables presenting indices of dissimilarity, tables 4 and 9, this condition is met. But since there are differences between the tables in the number of groups considered—the numbers are, respectively, 18 and 8—comparisons between these tables should not be made.

The indices of religious and regional inequality measure the disparity between the actual distributions of students and the distributions if religion or region had no effect. They use arbitrary standards as their bases—the rates, respectively, for Protestants and for Alsace-Lorraine as a whole—and assign each standard a value of 100. An index of 200 would mean that the enrollment rate for the group in question was twice the rate used as the standard.

Since the relationships among religion, region, and social status were not random, it is desirable to use appropriate controls. The controls employed are based on simulations, with a similar procedure used in each case. For instance, to control for social status when considering religious identification, it was first assumed that the students within each occupational category were distributed among the religions as if religion made no difference (that is, distributed like the population at risk). The results of this simulation were then summed according to religion and divided by the actual number of students of each religion. The final step involved dividing the fractions for the Catholics and Jews by the fraction for the Protestants and multiplying the results by 100. Similar procedures were used when introducing two controls. Thus to control for region and social status when considering the degree of religious inequality in Alsatian enrollment rates, it was first assumed that within each region the students within each occupational category were distributed among the religions as if religion made no difference. The results for each religion—both the simulated denominators and the known numerators—were then summed across regions and the resulting fractions compared, again using the Protestant fraction as the standard.

# Tables

**TABLE 1**  Enrollment at the Universities of Strasbourg

| Category | 1872 | 1882 | 1892 | 1898 | 1907 | 1913 | 1917 | 1919 | 1928 | 1938 |
|---|---|---|---|---|---|---|---|---|---|---|
| Geog. Origins | | | | | | | | | | |
| Alsace-Lorraine | | | | | | | | | | |
|   Native | 111 | 144 | 256 | 343 | 640 | 815 | } 453 | 1013 | 1460 | 1828 |
|   Immigrant | 3 | 95 | 164 | 294 | 347 | 332 | | 120 | 205 | 213 |
| Germany ex. A-L | 227 | 493 | 472 | 356 | 624 | 730 | 159 | — | — | — |
| France ex. A-L | — | — | — | — | — | — | — | 256 | 435 | 425 |
| Foreign | 49 | 105 | 77 | 82 | 98 | 215 | 4 | 116 | 776 | 409 |
| Sex | | | | | | | | | | |
|   Male | 390 | 837 | 969 | 1075 | 1709 | 2034 | 518 | 1357 | 2238 | 2116 |
|   Female | — | — | — | — | — | 58 | 98 | 148 | 638 | 759 |
| Religion | | | | | | | | | | |
|   Catholic | — | — | — | 359 | 797 | 948 | — | — | — | — |
|   Protestant | — | — | — | 605 | 787 | 919 | — | — | — | — |
|   Jewish | — | — | — | 94 | 95 | 200 | — | — | — | — |
|   Other, none | — | — | — | 17 | 30 | 25 | — | — | — | — |
| Faculty | | | | | | | | | | |
|   Cath. theology | — | — | — | — | 162 | 171 | 73 | 151 | 210 | 214 |
|   Prot. theology | 49 | 75 | 119 | 72 | 79 | 101 | 14 | 28 | 91 | 78 |
|   Law | 116 | 204 | 245 | 330 | 369 | 430 | 126 | 344 | 534 | 363 |
|   Medicine | 113 | 213 | 327 | 335 | 255 | 616 | 230 | 347 | 646 | 711 |
|   Pharmacy | 23 | 22 | 38 | 53 | 73 | 67 | } 173 | 57 | 207 | 380 |
|   Phil./Letters | 66 | 162 | 119 | 141 | 492 | 450 | | 332 | 625 | 684 |
|   Sciences | 23 | 161 | 121 | 144 | 279 | 257 | | 246 | 563 | 445 |
| Total | 390 | 837 | 969 | 1075 | 1709 | 2092 | 616 | 1505 | 2876 | 2875 |

*Sources:* See appendix A.

**TABLE 2**  Enrollment Rates (per 100 aged 20–23)

| Category | 1872 | 1882 | 1892 | 1898 | 1907 | 1913 | 1919 | 1928 | 1938 |
|---|---|---|---|---|---|---|---|---|---|
| Germany | | | | | | | | | |
|   Male | 1.021 | 1.460 | 1.432 | 1.499 | 1.850 | 2.207 | 3.953[b] | 2.753 | 2.212 |
|   Female | — | — | — | — | 0.013 | 0.143 | 0.322[b] | 0.460 | 0.385 |
| France | | | | | | | | | |
|   Male | — | — | 1.717[a] | 2.027 | 2.740 | 2.941 | 3.110 | 2.925 | 3.966 |
|   Female | — | — | 0.024[a] | 0.041 | 0.131 | 0.205 | 0.386 | 0.939 | 1.825 |
| A-L (natives) | | | | | | | | | |
|   Male | 0.241 | 0.344 | 0.668 | 0.852 | 1.559 | 2.140 | 2.732 | 2.782 | 3.738 |
|   Female | — | — | — | — | — | 0.021 | 0.249 | 0.790 | 1.434 |

*Sources:* See appendix A.
[a]Extrapolated from 1893 and 1898.
[b]Assuming foreign students as a proportion of the total is equal to one-third that in 1928.

TABLE 3     Characteristics of Alsatian Students (percentages)

| Category | 1860s | 1872 | 1882 | 1892 | 1898 | 1910 | 1924 | 1938 |
|---|---|---|---|---|---|---|---|---|
| Sex | | | | | | | | |
| Male | — | 100.0 | 100.0 | 100.0 | 100.0 | 99.5 | 84.1 | 74.5 |
| Female | — | — | — | — | — | 0.5 | 15.9 | 25.5 |
| Religion | | | | | | | | |
| Catholic | — | 14.5 | 24.4 | 34.5 | 48.1 | 64.1 | — | — |
| Protestant | — | 84.6 | 73.3 | 58.7 | 42.8 | 29.5 | — | — |
| Jewish | — | 0.9 | 2.3 | 6.8 | 9.2 | 6.5 | — | — |
| Region | | | | | | | | |
| Strasbourg | — | 25.9 | 29.2 | 34.4 | 27.6 | 21.1 | 17.1 | — |
| Lower Alsace, except Strasbourg | — | 57.9 | 45.0 | 41.1 | 39.4 | 34.0 | 30.7 | — |
| Upper Alsace | — | 13.8 | 18.9 | 13.4 | 18.4 | 25.2 | 27.5 | — |
| Lorraine | — | 2.4 | 7.0 | 11.1 | 14.6 | 19.8 | 24.7 | — |
| Father's occupation | | | | | | | | |
| Free professions | 21.8 | 31.4 | 21.1 | 18.9 | 17.2 | 5.1 | — | 13.2 |
| Bureaucracy: high | 21.1 | 3.8 | 9.9 | 10.2 | 10.6 | 7.5 | — | 28.4 |
| Bureaucracy: middle | 17.0 | 23.0 | 17.6 | 16.8 | 17.3 | 18.6 | — | |
| Entrepreneurs | 4.1 | 3.8 | 5.3 | 7.6 | 8.9 | 7.0 | — | 20.0 |
| Shopkeepers | 8.2 | 7.6 | 13.4 | 13.2 | 18.2 | 16.1 | — | |
| Artisans | 9.5 | 13.1 | 7.1 | 9.1 | 5.7 | 9.2 | — | 5.6 |
| White-collar workers | 3.4 | 0.0 | 2.9 | 3.5 | 4.1 | 7.0 | — | 18.7 |
| Landed gentry, rentiers | 6.8 | 5.0 | 7.5 | 9.2 | 9.5 | 12.1 | — | 3.9 |
| Peasantry | 6.8 | 8.6 | 14.5 | 10.5 | 7.2 | 14.9 | — | 6.1 |
| Working class | 1.4 | 3.8 | 0.6 | 1.0 | 1.4 | 2.5 | — | 4.2 |
| Institution | | | | | | | | |
| U. of Strasbourg | — | 91.0 | 83.5 | 79.5 | 78.7 | 79.4 | 74.0 | — |
| Other | — | 9.0 | 16.5 | 20.5 | 21.3 | 20.6 | 26.0 | — |
| N | — | 123 | 172 | 322 | 436 | 919 | 2024 | 2461 |

Sources: See Appendix A.

TABLE 4     Selectivity by Social Status: Germany (Indices of Dissimilarity[a])

| Category | 1872 | 1877 | 1882 | 1887 | 1892 | 1898 | 1910[b] |
|---|---|---|---|---|---|---|---|
| Overall | | | | | | | |
| All faculties | | | | | | | |
| Alsace-Lorraine (natives) | 62.5 | 68.9 | 64.4 | 67.6 | 66.9 | 72.8 | 60.6 |
| Baden | 57.5 | 60.8 | 66.9 | 59.4 | 53.9 | — | — |
| Prussia | — | — | — | 61.6 | 63.7 | 65.0 | 66.6 |
| Württemberg | 59.7 | 58.6 | 62.7 | 63.7 | 64.9 | 66.6 | 63.2 |
| All but Cath. theol. faculties | | | | | | | |
| Alsace-Lorraine (natives) | 62.5 | 68.9 | 64.7 | 68.1 | 68.1 | 74.2 | 66.3 |
| Baden | 68.0 | 66.9 | 70.8 | 64.4 | 59.4 | — | — |
| Prussia | — | — | — | 62.8 | 65.3 | 67.0 | 67.8 |
| Württemberg | 70.7 | 69.6 | 68.6 | 69.8 | 71.9 | 73.3 | 68.3 |
| Omitting peasantry and working class | | | | | | | |
| All faculties | | | | | | | |
| Alsace-Lorraine (natives) | 63.4 | 67.1 | 56.6 | 50.9 | 51.2 | 45.6 | 35.0 |
| Baden | 58.2 | 59.0 | 51.0 | 46.8 | 38.2 | — | — |
| Prussia | — | — | — | 40.0 | 39.3 | 39.5 | 42.2 |
| Württemberg | 61.3 | 62.7 | 56.8 | 54.1 | 53.4 | 52.1 | 47.6 |
| All but Cath. theol. faculties | | | | | | | |
| Alsace-Lorraine (natives) | 63.4 | 67.1 | 56.6 | 50.9 | 51.3 | 45.6 | 35.6 |
| Baden | 65.6 | 61.8 | 53.1 | 49.2 | 41.0 | — | — |
| Prussia | — | — | — | 40.6 | 40.3 | 40.4 | 42.7 |
| Württemberg | 68.0 | 68.1 | 60.3 | 57.2 | 56.8 | 54.9 | 48.7 |

Sources: See appendix A.
[a]See appendix A.
[b]1909 for Württemberg

**TABLE 5    Social Origins of Students, 1872–1898: Rates (per 100 males aged 20–23)**

| Father's Occupation | Alsace-Lorraine (natives) | | | Baden | | Prussia | | Württemberg | | |
|---|---|---|---|---|---|---|---|---|---|---|
| | 1872 | 1887 | 1898 | 1872 | 1887 | 1887 | 1898 | 1872 | 1887 | 1898 |
| **All faculties** | | | | | | | | | | |
| Free professions | 10.16 | 24.65 | 37.58 | 22.62 | 39.72 | 29.66 | 27.81 | 43.88 | 63.41 | 68.85 |
| Bureaucracy: high | 2.80 | 17.14 | 37.07 | 23.98 | 31.53 | 30.74 | 28.56 | 21.83 | 30.78 | 30.93 |
| Bureaucracy: middle | 3.51 | 5.49 | 9.20 | 7.54 | 15.69 | 10.77 | 10.33 | 7.53 | 19.27 | 17.69 |
| Entrepreneurs | 0.91 | 2.58 | 4.40 | 3.11 | 11.80 | 10.20 | 7.69 | 3.38 | 13.79 | 7.18 |
| Shopkeepers | 0.22 | 1.27 | 2.77 | 1.27 | 4.49 | 4.34 | 4.52 | 1.24 | 4.08 | 4.51 |
| Artisans | 0.16 | 0.31 | 0.44 | 0.47 | 1.53 | 1.15 | 0.80 | 0.59 | 1.13 | 0.90 |
| White-collar workers | 0.00 | 1.91 | 2.14 | 0.00 | 4.19 | 2.36 | 1.41 | 0.00 | 4.71 | 4.07 |
| Landed gentry, rentiers | 0.83 | 3.64 | 4.72 | 3.60 | 6.84 | 3.91 | 3.73 | 0.88 | 5.15 | 4.07 |
| Peasantry | 0.05 | 0.12 | 0.12 | 0.28 | 0.34 | 0.40 | 0.30 | 0.23 | 0.34 | 0.25 |
| Working class | 0.03 | 0.04 | 0.05 | 0.16 | 0.52 | 0.17 | 0.17 | 0.16 | 0.46 | 0.50 |
| All | 0.24 | 0.55 | 0.85 | 0.88 | 1.90 | 1.57 | 1.43 | 1.10 | 2.03 | 1.82 |
| **All but Cath. theol. faculties** | | | | | | | | | | |
| Free professions | 10.16 | 24.62 | 37.47 | 22.23 | 38.52 | 29.45 | 27.61 | 43.51 | 62.10 | 68.61 |
| Bureaucracy: high | 2.80 | 16.95 | 36.52 | 23.98 | 30.40 | 30.41 | 28.25 | 21.83 | 29.56 | 30.63 |
| Bureaucracy: middle | 3.51 | 5.36 | 8.81 | 6.77 | 13.85 | 10.42 | 9.85 | 6.48 | 17.06 | 15.78 |
| Entrepreneurs | 0.91 | 2.57 | 4.37 | 3.11 | 11.80 | 10.09 | 7.56 | 3.38 | 13.79 | 7.18 |
| Shopkeepers | 0.22 | 1.26 | 2.76 | 1.05 | 4.27 | 4.22 | 4.34 | 0.98 | 3.81 | 3.95 |
| Artisans | 0.16 | 0.30 | 0.41 | 0.20 | 1.14 | 1.06 | 0.69 | 0.33 | 0.75 | 0.56 |
| White-collar workers | 0.00 | 1.90 | 2.11 | 0.00 | 3.51 | 2.21 | 1.28 | 0.00 | 3.99 | 3.79 |
| Landed gentry, rentiers | 0.83 | 3.62 | 4.64 | 3.44 | 6.84 | 3.83 | 3.62 | 0.71 | 5.15 | 3.91 |
| Peasantry | 0.05 | 0.11 | 0.10 | 0.15 | 0.21 | 0.35 | 0.24 | 0.05 | 0.18 | 0.09 |
| Working class | 0.03 | 0.04 | 0.04 | 0.12 | 0.40 | 0.15 | 0.15 | 0.11 | 0.31 | 0.34 |
| All | 0.24 | 0.55 | 0.83 | 0.72 | 1.67 | 1.51 | 1.35 | 0.89 | 1.77 | 1.58 |

*Sources:* See appendix A.

**TABLE 6** Religious Disparities in Enrollment Rates (Indices of Religious Inequality;[a] Protestants = 100)

| State | Catholics | | | | Jews | | | |
|---|---|---|---|---|---|---|---|---|
| | 1877 | 1887 | 1898 | 1910[b] | 1877 | 1887 | 1898 | 1910[b] |
| **Without Controls** | | | | | | | | |
| All faculties | | | | | | | | |
| A-L (natives) | 4.7 | 9.6 | 25.2 | 43.5 | 27.0 | 90.5 | 192.7 | 222.1 |
| Baden | 81.3 | 71.5 | — | — | 244.1 | 373.8 | — | — |
| Prussia | — | 58.0 | 74.3 | 81.3 | — | 596.7 | 648.6 | 551.7 |
| Württemberg | — | — | — | 111.0 | — | — | — | 645.7 |
| Secular faculties | | | | | | | | |
| A-L (natives) | 6.8 | 14.7 | 33.0 | 35.8 | 38.6 | 146.0 | 270.0 | 248.2 |
| Baden | 75.2 | 72.5 | — | — | 289.1 | 492.7 | — | — |
| Prussia | — | 62.3 | 67.5 | 77.6 | — | 794.6 | 738.5 | 598.1 |
| Württemberg | — | — | — | 89.8 | — | — | — | 765.4 |
| **Controlling for Social Status** | | | | | | | | |
| All faculties | | | | | | | | |
| A-L (natives) | 14.1 | 21.5 | 45.2 | 66.9 | 17.0 | 38.8 | 66.6 | 81.0 |
| Baden | 106.5 | 98.4 | — | — | 93.5 | 125.0 | — | — |
| Prussia | — | 82.6 | 111.2 | 115.7 | — | 218.7 | 227.3 | 205.0 |
| Württemberg | — | — | — | 144.2 | — | — | — | 248.6 |
| Secular faculties | | | | | | | | |
| A-L (natives) | 16.9 | 27.6 | 53.6 | 62.3 | 26.1 | 56.7 | 88.9 | 88.8 |
| Baden | 101.0 | 101.9 | — | — | 108.1 | 173.4 | — | — |
| Prussia | — | 86.7 | 99.9 | 110.5 | — | 265.0 | 246.1 | 214.5 |
| Württemberg | — | — | — | 114.7 | — | — | — | 272.9 |
| **Controlling for Social Status and Region** | | | | | | | | |
| All faculties | | | | | | | | |
| A-L (natives) | 24.2 | 33.7 | 70.0 | 79.4 | 21.5 | 56.4 | 88.7 | 93.0 |
| Secular faculties | | | | | | | | |
| A-L (natives) | 30.4 | 44.2 | 84.5 | 69.0 | 36.0 | 79.4 | 121.3 | 98.5 |

*Sources:* See Appendix A.

[a]See Appendix A.

[b]1909 for Württemberg.

TABLE 7     Regional Disparities in Enrollment Rates for Native Alsatians (Indices of Regional Inequality;[a] Rate for Alsace-Lorraine [natives] = 100)

| Region | 1877 | 1887 | 1898 | 1910 | 1924[b] |
|---|---|---|---|---|---|
| | Without Controls | | | | |
| All faculties | | | | | |
| Strasbourg | 815.5 | 914.7 | 769.2 | 485.0 | 353.3 |
| Lower Alsace except Strasbourg | 131.4 | 101.9 | 100.7 | 90.6 | 84.9 |
| Upper Alsace | 34.0 | 59.1 | 65.0 | 89.9 | 97.4 |
| Lorraine | 28.1 | 37.4 | 50.4 | 66.4 | 80.6 |
| Secular faculties | | | | | |
| Strasbourg | 842.9 | 973.2 | 793.7 | 548.7 | 361.9 |
| Lower Alsace except Strasbourg | 130.2 | 91.2 | 95.4 | 78.7 | 81.1 |
| Upper Alsace | 39.6 | 57.6 | 67.5 | 76.9 | 94.5 |
| Lorraine | 20.2 | 46.8 | 52.1 | 79.6 | 85.4 |
| | Controlling for Religion and Social Status | | | | |
| All faculties | | | | | |
| Strasbourg | 221.4 | 268.1 | 223.6 | 167.6 | — |
| Lower Alsace except Strasbourg | 107.1 | 88.0 | 113.7 | 108.9 | — |
| Upper Alsace | 44.3 | 71.4 | 68.8 | 92.8 | — |
| Lorraine | 49.9 | 57.4 | 55.6 | 69.8 | — |
| Secular faculties | | | | | |
| Strasbourg | 214.5 | 296.8 | 220.8 | 181.3 | — |
| Lower Alsace except Strasbourg | 113.4 | 85.3 | 115.4 | 98.5 | — |
| Upper Alsace | 49.8 | 65.8 | 67.7 | 80.7 | — |
| Lorraine | 33.1 | 62.8 | 53.8 | 87.4 | — |

Sources: See appendix A.

[a]See appendix A.

[b]Assuming regional distribution of Alsatians aged 20–23 is as in 1913.

**TABLE 8**    Students by Faculty[a] (percentages)

| Faculty | 1877[c] | 1887 | 1898 | 1913 | 1919 | 1928 | 1938 |
|---|---|---|---|---|---|---|---|
| **All German students[b]** | | | | | | | |
| Catholic theology | 3.9 | 4.2 | 5.1 | 3.0 | 2.4 | 2.3 | 7.9 |
| Protestant theology | 9.1 | 16.9 | 8.0 | 7.3 | 4.1 | 4.2 | 3.0 |
| Law | 31.6 | 24.4 | 33.1 | 23.2 | 33.1 | 36.5 | 17.6 |
| Medicine | 18.2 | 29.8 | 25.7 | 27.2 | 29.0 | 19.4 | 43.5 |
| Pharmacy | 4.5 | 3.7 | 4.1 | 1.9 | 1.4 | 0.9 | 3.4 |
| Philosophy | 21.3 | 12.3 | 12.0 | 24.1 | 17.2 | 23.0 | 12.3 |
| Sciences | 11.3 | 8.8 | 12.1 | 13.4 | 12.8 | 13.7 | 12.4 |
| **All French students** | | | | | | | |
| Catholic theology | — | — | — | — | 0.4 | 0.3 | 0.3 |
| Protestant theology | 0.5 | 0.4 | 0.5 | — | 0.1 | 0.1 | 0.1 |
| Law | 50.7 | 51.4 | 33.2 | 40.0 | 31.3 | 28.1 | 30.2 |
| Medicine | 30.3 | 26.4 | 31.0 | 24.1 | 26.9 | 21.8 | 20.2 |
| Pharmacy | 12.9 | 14.6 | 12.0 | 4.3 | 5.3 | 9.1 | 8.5 |
| Letters | 2.7 | 3.3 | 11.2 | 16.0 | 12.9 | 20.3 | 25.7 |
| Sciences | 2.8 | 4.0 | 12.1 | 15.6 | 23.2 | 20.2 | 15.1 |
| **Native Alsatian students** | | | | | | | |
| Catholic theology | 0.0 | 1.4 | 3.1 | 13.3 | 10.1 | 7.9 | 7.4 |
| Protestant theology | 25.5 | 24.7 | 12.2 | 3.2 | 1.8 | 2.2 | 2.0 |
| Law | 23.3 | 20.3 | 28.0 | 30.1 | 25.6 | 23.1 | 15.0 |
| Medicine | 24.1 | 28.8 | 29.4 | 19.7 | 20.9 | 18.6 | 23.1 |
| Pharmacy | 14.1 | 6.5 | 9.3 | 1.9 | 3.0 | 3.7 | 9.8 |
| Philosophy/Letters | 4.3 | 10.2 | 9.2 | 23.8 | 24.6 | 29.7 | 30.0 |
| Sciences | 8.7 | 8.0 | 8.8 | 8.0 | 14.0 | 14.8 | 12.7 |

*Sources:* See appendix A.
[a]Excluding those studying abroad.
[b]For 1919, all students (foreign included) at German universities.
[c]1880 for French students.

**TABLE 9**    Selectivity by Social Status: Germany and France (Indices of Dissimilarity[a])

| | All Faculties | | | Secular Faculties | | |
|---|---|---|---|---|---|---|
| Country or State | 1910[b] | 1931 | 1939 | 1910[b] | 1931 | 1939 |
| **Overall** | | | | | | |
| Alsace-Lorraine (natives) | 60.1 | — | 65.9 | 66.7 | — | 69.6 |
| Prussia | 66.1 | — | — | 67.4 | — | — |
| Württemberg | 62.3 | — | — | 67.1 | — | — |
| Germany | — | 62.3 | — | — | 63.5 | — |
| France | — | — | 68.3 | — | — | 68.4 |
| **Omitting peasantry and working class** | | | | | | |
| Alsace-Lorraine (natives) | 33.8 | — | 35.5 | 32.0 | — | 35.5 |
| Prussia | 41.9 | — | — | 42.1 | — | — |
| Württemberg | 46.4 | — | — | 47.2 | — | — |
| Germany | — | 39.8 | — | — | 39.5 | — |
| France | — | — | 37.4 | — | — | 37.4 |

*Sources:* See appendix A.
[a]See appendix A.
[b]1909 for Württemberg.

**TABLE 10    Social Origins of Students, 1909–1939: Rates (per 100 aged 20–23)**

| Father's Occupation | A-L (natives) | | Prussia | Württ. | Germany | France |
|---|---|---|---|---|---|---|
| | 1910 | 1939 | 1910 | 1909 | 1931 | 1939 |
| **All faculties** | | | | | | |
| Free professions | 13.68 | 43.21 | 19.15 | 38.30 | 20.22 | 45.67 |
| Bureaucracy | 12.08 | 26.74 | 11.46 | 13.06 | 15.67 | 19.44 |
| Entrepreneurs, | | | | | | |
| shopkeepers | 3.20 | 6.10 | 3.67 | 4.46 | 5.12 | 6.28 |
| Artisans | 0.98 | 1.64 | 0.53 | 0.84 | 1.26 | 1.36 |
| White-collar workers | 2.56 | 8.73 | 0.84 | 1.17 | 1.61 | 7.30 |
| Landed gentry, rentiers | 6.35 | 14.08 | 2.33 | 3.25 | 5.90 | 15.09 |
| Peasantry | 0.29 | 0.60 | 0.20 | 0.25 | 0.38 | 0.36 |
| Working class | 0.08 | 0.23 | 0.11 | 0.27 | 0.21 | 0.22 |
| All | 0.93 | 2.59 | 0.98 | 1.23 | 2.03 | 2.90 |
| **Secular faculties** | | | | | | |
| Free professions | 12.95 | 40.95 | 16.30 | 28.47 | 19.58 | 45.61 |
| Bureaucracy | 9.06 | 25.42 | 9.87 | 10.88 | 14.26 | 19.45 |
| Entrepreneurs, | | | | | | |
| shopkeepers | 3.00 | 5.94 | 3.39 | 4.14 | 4.87 | 6.27 |
| Artisans | 0.72 | 1.38 | 0.47 | 0.64 | 1.12 | 1.35 |
| White-collar workers | 2.46 | 8.29 | 0.76 | 0.80 | 1.44 | 7.28 |
| Landed gentry, rentiers | 5.92 | 13.24 | 2.22 | 3.12 | 5.65 | 15.08 |
| Peasantry | 0.14 | 0.31 | 0.16 | 0.13 | 0.32 | 0.35 |
| Working class | 0.07 | 0.18 | 0.09 | 0.19 | 0.17 | 0.22 |
| All | 0.74 | 2.37 | 0.90 | 0.99 | 1.85 | 2.89 |

*Sources:* See appendix A.

**TABLE 11     Alsatian Students at French Universities, 1924 (estimates)**

| Student characteristics | N | University (%) | | | |
|---|---|---|---|---|---|
| | | Strasb. | Paris | Nancy | Other |
| Geographic origins | | | | | |
| Alsace-Lorraine | 2,024 | 74.0 | 10.0 | 7.3 | 8.7 |
| Strasbourg | 346 | 89.3 | 4.6 | 0.0 | 6.1 |
| Lower Alsace ex. Strasbourg | 621 | 78.0 | 6.9 | 2.3 | 12.7 |
| Upper Alsace | 557 | 73.1 | 11.3 | 5.7 | 9.9 |
| Lorraine | 500 | 59.4 | 16.1 | 20.3 | 4.2 |
| Catholic communes[a] | 1,754 | 73.7 | 9.0 | 8.4 | 9.0 |
| Protestant communes[a] | 270 | 75.9 | 17.0 | 0.0 | 7.0 |
| Dialect-speaking cantons | 1,754 | 77.1 | 10.7 | 4.2 | 8.0 |
| French-speaking cantons[b] | 270 | 53.7 | 5.9 | 27.0 | 13.3 |
| Sex | | | | | |
| Male | 1,703 | 74.3 | 10.1 | 6.8 | 8.8 |
| Female | 321 | 72.0 | 9.7 | 10.0 | 8.4 |
| Faculty | | | | | |
| Catholic theology | 124 | 100.0 | 0.0 | 0.0 | 0.0 |
| Protestant theology | 28 | 100.0 | 0.0 | 0.0 | 0.0 |
| Law | 555 | 72.8 | 16.0 | 7.7 | 3.4 |
| Medicine | 406 | 71.9 | 7.4 | 4.4 | 16.3 |
| Pharmacy | 51 | 62.7 | 9.8 | 27.5 | 0.0 |
| Letters | 650 | 69.7 | 10.2 | 5.7 | 14.5 |
| Sciences | 210 | 78.1 | 5.2 | 11.4 | 5.2 |

*Sources:* Based on the "répertoires des diplômes" for the various faculties in AN: F[17]* 3399, 3420, 3442, 3470, 3472; and, for the characteristics of the communes of Alsace-Lorraine about the time these students were born, Alsace-Lorraine, *Statistisches Handbuch,* pp. 3–55, 137–39.

[a]Defined as communes with Catholic or Protestant pluralities.

[b]Defined as predominantly French-speaking cantons as of 1910 plus the cantons of Metz-Ville and Ste. Marie-aux-Mines, both of which would probably have been in this category had the census counted only native Alsatians.

# Notes

## Introduction

1. See Almond and Powell, *Comparative Politics*, pp. 35–36, 314–22; and Rokkan, "Dimensions of State Formation and Nation-Building."

## Chapter 1

1. Schindling, *Humanistische Hochschule*.

2. See Gustav Anrich, "Die Universität Strassburg," pp. 188–91; Rodolphe Reuss, *Histoire de Strasbourg*, pp. 296–98; and Arthur Schulze, *Die örtliche und soziale Herkunft*.

3. From a manuscript at the Archives Municipales, Strasbourg, quoted in Ford, *Strasbourg in Transition*, p. 196. Also see Châtellier, Vogler, and Thomann, "Cultures, religions, société," pp. 421–34; and Klein, "La Faculté de médecine de Strasbourg au temps de Goethe."

4. Gustav Anrich, "Die Universität Strassburg," pp. 191–94; Ludwig, *Strassburg vor hundert Jahren*, pp. 118–19; Rodolphe Reuss, *Histoire de Strasbourg*, pp. 329–31; Arthur Schulze, *Die örtliche und soziale Herkunft*; Voss, *Universität, Geschichtswissenschaft und Diplomatie*, pp. 108–38.

5. Hammerstein, *Jus und Historie*, pp. 148–68, 309–31; Paulsen, *Geschichte des gelehrten Unterrichts*, 1:511–50, 2:9–14; Turner, "University Reformers," pp. 503–5.

6. Gustav Anrich, "Die Universität Strassburg," pp. 191–96; Dreyfus, "L'Université protestante de Strasbourg," pp. 87–97; Eulenburg, "Die Frequenz der deutschen Universitäten," pp. 294–99; Frijhoff, "Surplus ou déficit?" pp. 186–213; Ludwig, *Strassburg vor hundert Jahren*, pp. 111–12, 116–21; Rodolphe Reuss, *Histoire de Strasbourg*, pp. 329–30.

7. Metz, "La Faculté de théologie," pp. 201–4; Ludwig, *Strassburg vor hundert Jahren*, pp. 114–15; Rodolphe Reuss, *Histoire de Strasbourg*, pp. 31–32.

8. Gustav Anrich, "Die Universität Strassburg," p. 191; Châtellier, *Tradition chrétienne et renouveau catholique*, pp. 356–57, 467–68; Ford, *Strasbourg in Transition*, p. 115; Streitberger, *Der königliche Prätor*, pp. 215–16, 231.

9. Gustav Anrich, "Die Universität Strassburg," pp. 195–96; Dreyfus, "L'Université protestante de Strasbourg," p. 94; Lefftz, *Die gelehrten und literarischen Gesellschaften*, pp. 81–85.

10. Spach, "La ville et l'université de Strasbourg," p. 424.

11. Ford, *Strasbourg in Transition*, pp. 186–206; Spach, "La ville et l'université de Strasbourg," pp. 421–46; Streitberger, *Der königliche Prätor*, pp. 210, 224–45, 248–49.

12. Metz, "La Faculté de théologie," p. 223.

13. Dreyfus, "L'Université protestante de Strasbourg," pp. 196–97; Varrentrapp, "Die Strassburger Universität," pp. 448–72.

14. Aulard, *Napoléon $I^{er}$ et le monopole universitaire*; Liard, *L'enseignement supérieur*, 2:65–124.

15. Gustav Anrich, "Die Universität Strassburg," pp. 200–205; Leuilliot, *L'Alsace au début du XIX$^e$ siècle*, 3:263–80; L'Huillier, *Recherches sur l'Alsace napoléonienne*, pp. 634–43.

16. Foessel, "La vie quotidienne à Strasbourg," pp. 15–16, 26–28; Pfister, "Fustel de Coulanges," pp. 204–6; Wrotnowska, "Pasteur, professeur à Strasbourg," pp. 135–44.

17. Laurent Delcasso to the Ministry of Public Instruction, 8 July 1858, 7 Nov. 1858, and 4 Jan. 1859, AN: F$^{17}$ 2649; Foessel and Oberlé, "Le règne des notables," pp. 153–58; Genevray, "Professeurs protestants," pp. 288–304; Leuilliot, *L'Alsace au début du XIX$^e$ siècle*, 3:278–79; Pfister, "Un épisode," pp. 334–55.

18. See Klein, "La Faculté de médecine de Strasbourg sous le Second Empire," pp. 73–96; and Wieger, *Geschichte der Medizin*, pp. 127–66.

19. Hausmann, *Die Kaiser-Wilhelms-Universität Strassburg*, p. 19; Yves Laissus, "L'Université de Strasbourg," p. 181; Otto Mayer, *Die Kaiser-Wilhelms-Universität*, p. 12.

20. Gustav Anrich, "Die Universität Strassburg," pp. 204–l4; Hausmann, *Die Kaiser-Wilhelms-Universität Strassburg*, p. 19; Schützenberger, *De la réforme*, pp. 45–47; [Emil Alfred Weber], *Von der Schulbank zum Lehrstuhl*, p. 44.

21. Gustav Anrich, "Die Universität Strassburg," pp. 213–20; Baum, *Johann Wilhelm Baum*, pp. 110–12; Gérold, *La Faculté de théologie*, pp. 167–72; 228–30; 235–65; Lévy, *Histoire linguistique*, 2:121–24, 183–85, 301–6.

22. On Alsatian students at German universities, see Bopp, *Die evangelischen Geistlichen und Theologen;* and Jaffé, ed., *Elsässische Studenten.* On student life in Strasbourg, see M. B., "Zur Geschichte der elsässischen Studentenwesens," pp. 211–14; Bopp, "Strassburger Studentenleben bis 1850," pp. 172–259; and Bordmann and Imgart, "Strassburger Studentenleben," pp. 232–57.

23. See Bleek, *Von der Kameralausbildung zum Juristenprivileg*, pp. 65–101; König, *Vom Wesen der deutschen Universität*, pp. 22–34; McClelland, *State, Society, and University*, pp. 63–79; Turner, "University Reformers," pp. 495–531; and Wunder, *Privilegierung und Disziplinierung*, pp. 97–104, 198–201.

24. The classic pronouncements on university reform by Schelling (1802), Fichte (1807), Schleiermacher (1808), Steffens (1808–9), and Humboldt (1810) are collected in Ernst Anrich, ed., *Die Idee der deutschen Universität.* Also see König, *Vom Wesen der deutschen Universität*, pp. 65–197; McClelland, *State, Society, and University*, pp. 101–22; and Schelsky, *Einsamkeit und Freiheit*, pp. 41–122.

25. Holborn, "Der deutsche Idealismus," p. 367; Schelsky, *Einsamkeit und Freiheit*, pp. 102–15; Schnabel, *Deutsche Geschichte*, 1:296, 410–42 passim, 2:364, 3:13, 321–23; Vossler, "Humboldts Idee," p. 258.

26. See Jeismann, *Das preussische Gymnasium*, pp. 216–398; and Menze, *Die Bildungsreform Wilhelm von Humboldts*, pp. 232–79.

27. McClelland, *State, Society, and University*, pp. 122–45; Menze, *Die Bildungsreform Wilhelm von Humboldts*, pp. 304–27; Vossler, "Humboldts Idee," pp. 257–68.

28. Ben-David, *The Scientist's Role*, pp. 114–18; Turner, "Professorial Research," pp. 147–54, 172.

29. Ben-David, *The Scientist's Role*, pp. 117–18, 121–22; Alexander Busch, *Privatdozenten*, pp. 21–53; Turner, "Professorial Research," pp. 138, 144–46, 180–81.

30. Ben-David, *The Scientist's Role*, pp. 118, 123–25; and, for a particular case, Dickerhof, "Bildung und Ausbildung," pp. 147–69.

31. Turner, "Professorial Research," p. 145.

32. See Humboldt, "Über die innere und äussere Organisation," p. 259.

33. Andernach, *Der Einfluss der Parteien*, pp. 8–54; McClelland, *State, Society, and University*, pp. 162–81; Turner, "Professorial Research," pp. 158–82; Turner, "Prussian Universities."

34. Bezold, *Geschichte der Rheinischen Friedrich-Wilhelms-Universität*, 1:462–63, 499; Fritz Fischer, "Der deutsche Protestantismus," p. 492; Holborn, "Der deutsche Idealismus," p. 367; Max Lenz, *Geschichte der königlichen Friedrich-Wilhelms-Universität*, vol.

2, part 2, pp. 280, 322, 337, 381; McClelland, *State, Society, and University,* pp. 181–89; Schnabel, *Deutsche Geschichte,* 1:52, 450–51, 2:363–64, 3:140–41.

35. Elias, "Die Bedeutung der Universitäten," pp. 147–70; Holborn, "Der deutsche Idealismus," pp. 361, 365, 379; Krieger, *The German Idea of Freedom,* pp. 294–96, 440–41, 463–64; Lees, *Revolution and Reflection,* pp. 7–29; O'Boyle, "Klassische Bildung," pp. 590–99, 606–8; Ringer, *German Mandarins,* pp. 12–13, 44–46, 124–26; Sieber, "Der politische Professor," pp. 285–306; Turner, "*Bildungsbürgertum,*" pp. 124–29; Vierhaus, "Bildung," pp. 525–26, 531–46.

36. For exceptions, see Canivez, *Jules Lagneau,* 1:228–41; Fox and Weisz, "The Institutional Basis of French Science," pp. 8–17; and Weisz, "Reform and Conflict in French Medical Education," pp. 61–69.

37. Quoted in Liard, *L'enseignement supérieur,* 2:287–88. Also see ibid., pp. 179–99, 283; Geiger, "Prelude to Reform," pp. 338–39, 355–61; Shinn, "The French Science Faculty System," pp. 291–302; and Weisz, *The Emergence of Modern Universities in France,* pp. 29–81.

38. Millardet to Duruy, 11 Dec. 1867, BN: FNA 25171 (2); Yves Laissus, "L'Université de Strasbourg," pp. 181–82; Pasteur to Honoré Chapuis, July 1850, Pasteur, *Correspondance,* 1:165; Schützenberger, *De la réforme,* pp. 45–47.

39. Quoted and paraphrased in Guiraud, "Fustel de Coulanges," pp. 140–42.

40. Quoted in Liard, *L'enseignement supérieur,* 2:284.

41. Bergmann to Ernest Renan, 27 Feb. 1862, quoted in Pommier, *Renan et Strasbourg,* pp. 28–29. Also see Eduard Reuss to Renan, 15 Feb. 1860, quoted in ibid., pp. 171–72; Millardet to Victor Duruy, 11 Dec. 1867, BN: FNA 25171 (2); Johann Friedrich Bruch, *Johann Friedrich Bruch,* p. 46; Gerbod, *La condition universitaire,* pp. 61–62; Yves Laissus, "L'Université de Strasbourg," pp. 180–81; Lavisse, "Université de Bonn et facultés de Strasbourg"; and, for the pattern at another provincial academy, Daigle, *La culture en partage,* pp. 110–17.

42. L'Huillier, "L'enseignement primaire en Alsace," p. 43; Liard, *L'enseignement supérieur,* 2:283–85.

43. Schützenberger, *De la réforme,* p. 73.

44. Ibid., pp. 51–56. Also see Lavisse, "Université de Bonn et facultés de Strasbourg."

45. Schützenberger, *De la réforme,* pp. 56–57.

46. Ibid., pp. 82–115.

47. Liard, *L'enseignement supérieur,* 2:294.

48. Lévy, *Histoire linguistique,* 2:1–73; Gaston May, *La lutte pour le français,* pp. 45–63.

49. Lévy, *Histoire linguistique,* 2:80–96, 108–19. The remark paraphrased was made by Karl Barack, the first director of the library of the German university opened in 1872; see Baldensperger, "Quarante mois après," p. 391.

50. Leuilliot, *L'Alsace au début du XIX^e siècle,* 3:318–29; Lévy, *Histoire linguistique,* 2:96, 133–34; Marx, *La révolution et les classes sociales en Basse-Alsace,* pp. 433–45, 505–24.

51. Lévy, *Histoire linguistique,* 2:73, 134. On German expressions of interest in including Alsace in a united Germany, see G. Barthelmé, "Etudiants alsaciens et étudiants allemands," pp. 1021–24; Buchner, "Die elsässische Frage," pp. 80–91; and Fenske, "Das Elsass in der deutschen öffentlichen Meinung," pp. 233–80.

52. Lévy, *Histoire linguistique,* 2:135–95; Oberlé, *L'enseignement à Mulhouse,* pp. 33–47, 95–104, 113–21.

53. Laurent Delcasso to the Ministry of Public Instruction, 5 Jan. 1859, AN: F^17 2649.

54. Lévy, *Histoire linguistique,* 2:223–24.

55. Laurent Delcasso to the Ministry of Public Instruction, 5 Jan 1859, AN: F^17 2649.

56. Lévy, *Histoire linguistique,* 2:182–83, 266–301; L'Huillier, "L'enseignement primaire en Alsace," pp. 50–56; Gaston May, *La lutte pour le français,* pp. 131–58; Oberlé, *L'enseignement à Mulhouse,* pp. 51–54, 130–67; and the responses of the headmasters of the lycées and collèges communaux in Alsace and Lorraine to a ministerial inquiry of 1864, AN: F$^{17}$ 6847 and 6849.

57. Brunschwig, "L'assimilation d'une famille mulhousienne," p. 1106; Lévy, *Histoire linguistique,* 2:80, 96, 133–36, 142–47, 195–97.

58. Lévy, *Histoire linguistique,* 2:220. Also see Foessel and Oberlé, "Le règne des notables," pp. 61–62.

59. Lévy, *Histoire linguistique,* 2:142.

60. Ibid., p. 159.

61. Ibid., p. 293.

62. Ibid., pp. 207–19, 289–97; Gaston May, *La lutte pour le français,* pp. 159–205.

63. Lévy, *Histoire linguistique,* 2:158–60.

64. Ibid., pp. 223–24.

65. Ibid., pp. 106–7, 148, 160–63, 224–25, 249–66; Joseph Guerber to Carl Marbach, 9 Nov. 1859 and 3 Jan. 1860, [Guerber], "Briefe," pp. 394–95; Hauviller, "Un prélat germanisateur," pp. 98–121.

66. Hallays, "L'Université de Strasbourg," p. 268.

67. Quoted in Lefftz, *Die gelehrten und literarischen Gesellschaften,* p. 225.

68. Quoted in ibid., p. 66.

69. Quoted in Lévy, *Histoire linguistique,* 2:251. Also see ibid., pp. 183–85, 301–6; and Pariset, "La Revue germanique," 1:628–30, 2:32.

70. Gustav Anrich, "Die Universität Strassburg," p. 217; Lévy, *Histoire linguistique,* 2:162–63, 258–60; Karl Heinrich Graf to Eduard Reuss, 12 Mar. 1840, and Reuss to Graf, 22 May 1856, Eduard Reuss, *Briefwechsel,* pp. 92, 403–4.

71. Laurent Delcasso to the Ministry of Public Instruction, 5 Oct. 1859, AN: F$^{17}$ 2649. Also see Delcasso to the Ministry of Public Instruction, 9 July 1859 and 7 Jan. 1861, F$^{17}$ 2650.

72. From a fraternity report of 1865, quoted in Lienhard, *Jugendjahre,* p. 116. Also see Bronner, *1870/71 Elsass-Lothringen,* 2:363–64.

73. Quoted in Will, "Les églises protestantes de Strasbourg," p. 70n.

74. Quoted in Baum, *Johann Wilhelm Baum,* p. 161.

75. Quoted in ibid., p. 122.

## Chapter 2

1. See Bronner, *1870/71 Elsass-Lothringen,* 1:40–123, 143–65; and Faber, *Die national-politische Publizistik Deutschlands,* 2:587–602.

2. Moritz Busch, *Tagebuchblätter,* 1:172.

3. Bismarck's reasons for favoring annexation and his reactions to public opinion on the subject have recently been the subjects of debate among German historians. For a concise review of the literature and issues involved, see Wahl, "La question des courants annexionnistes," pp. 185–210.

4. For early expressions of these views (all date from August 1870), see Maurenbrecher, *Elsass—eine deutsche Provinz,* p. 22; Treitschke, "Was fordern wir von Frankreich?" p. 371; and Weizsäcker, "Eine Denkschrift," pp. 285–86.

5. On the impact of the Franco-Prussian War on German intellectuals and their sense of mission, see Höfele, "Sendungsglaube und Epochenbewusstsein," pp. 270–75.

6. Maurenbrecher, *Elsass—eine deutsche Provinz,* p. 22.

7. Treitschke, "Was fordern wir von Frankreich?" p. 371.

8. Ibid., p. 407.

9. See, for example, Dahn, "Die deutsche Provinz 'Elsass-Lothringen'"; Gustav Lenz, *Die alten Reichslande*, p. 51, as quoted in Bronner *1870/71 Elsass-Lothringen*, 1:54; and Volger, *Elsass, Lothringen und unsere Friedensbedingungen*, summarized in Faber, *Die nationalpolitische Publizistik Deutschlands*, 2:581.

10. Müllenhoff to Scherer, 3 Oct. 1870, Müllenhoff and Scherer, *Briefwechsel*, p. 403.

11. J. Hirschfeld to ?, 23 Nov. 1870, W. Rossmann to Bismarck, 25 Nov. 1870, and Louis Janke to the General Government of Alsace, 28 Nov. 1870, ADBR: AL 12, paq. 3; Scherer to Müllenhoff, 31 Oct. 1870, Müllenhoff and Scherer, *Briefwechsel*, p. 406; Treitschke to Salomon Hirzel, 1 Sept. 1870, Treitschke, *Briefe*, 3:284–85.

12. Quoted in Baum, *Johann Wilhelm Baum*, pp. 126–27.

13. [Emil Alfred Weber], *Aegri Somnia*, p. 75.

14. For contemporary observations and predictions, see the reports of Civil Commissioner Friedrich von Kühlwetter, 31 Aug. 1870–1 Jan. 1871, quoted in Igersheim, "L'occupation allemande," pp. 289–90, 294, 345–46, 350–51, 357; Auerbach, *Wieder unser*, pp. 191–94; and Löher, *Aus Natur und Geschichte*, pp. 97–98, 100, 199–200.

15. Johann Friedrich Bruch, *Johann Friedrich Bruch*, pp. 78–81; Burger, "Vor sechzig Jahren," pp. 244–45; Edouard Reuss to Paul Lobstein, 25 Feb. 1871, quoted in El. Lobstein and Ed. Lobstein, *Paul Lobstein*, p. 43.

16. Johann Friedrich Bruch, *Johann Friedrich Bruch*, pp. 79–80. On the acrimonious atmosphere in Strasbourg in the autumn of 1870 and the widespread suspicions concerning the loyalties of those who were Lutheran and German-speaking, see Baum, *Johann Wilhelm Baum*, p. 145; and August Schneegans, *Memoiren*, pp. 42–68.

17. Ficker, "Eine elsässische Denkschrift," p. 305.

18. Edouard Ruess to Ritschl, 1 Nov. 1870, quoted in Ritschl, *Albrecht Ritschls Leben*, 2:96.

19. Heinrich von Sybel to [Kühlwetter], 14 and 16 Dec. 1870, ADBR: AL 12, paq. 6; Gustav Anrich, "Die Universität Strassburg," p. 221; Igersheim, "L'occupation allemande," pp. 294, 338.

20. Report of Civil Commissioner Kühlwetter, 1 Feb. 1871, quoted in Igersheim, "L'occupation allemande," p. 338.

21. [Loening], "Die Neuschöpfung der Strassburger Universität," p. 395. Also see Ficker, "Eine elsässische Denkschrift," p. 306n.

22. Ehrismann, "Julius (Friedrich Emil) Rathgeber," p. 134.

23. Bergmann to Freidrich von Bismarck-Bohlen (?), 29 Mar. 1871, ADBR: AL 12, paq. 6.

24. "Die Universität Strassburg in neuer Zeit"; and "Ludw. Spach und die künftige oberrheinische Universität," p. 363.

25. Ernsthausen, *Erinnerungen*, pp. 304–5, 331–35. For the quotation, see ibid., p. 305.

26. "Elsässische Wünsche."

27. Schützenberger, "De la réorganisation," quoted in Ficker, "Eine elsässische Denkschrift," p. 309. The original memorandum is in ADBR: AL 12, paq. 7.

28. Schützenberger, "De la réorganisation," quoted in Ficker, "Eine elsässische Denkschrift," p. 314.

29. For a concise summary, see Silverman, *Reluctant Union*, pp. 36–39. On the origins of the decision to make the annexed territory a *Reichsland*, see Wentzcke, "Zur Entstehungsgeschichte des Reichslandes Elsass-Lothringen," pp. 607–26.

30. Germany, Reichstag, *Stenographische Berichte*, 1st leg. period, 1st sess., 3 (1871): appendix no. 144.

31. Ibid., appendix no. 155.

32. Hermann Wagener in Reichstag, ibid., 2 (1871): 906–8.

33. Christoph Moufang in Reichstag, ibid., pp. 902–4.

34. Ibid., p. 899. For biographical information, see Dillmann, "Ewald," pp. 438–42.

35. Germany, Reichstag, *Stenographische Berichte,* 1st leg. period, 1st sess., 2 (1871): 900.

36. Ibid., p. 895.

37. Ibid., p. 910. On Köchly's earlier activities as an educational reformer, see Boeckel, *Hermann Köchly,* pp. 49–70, 91–108, 191–95, 276–94.

38. Germany, Reichstag, *Stenographische Berichte,* 1st leg. period, 1st sess., 2 (1871): 910. In fact the idea of founding a Swiss university with teaching in both French and German (and perhaps Italian as well) dated from the Enlightenment and was a subject of active debate from the 1830s to the 1870s. Its proponents argued that a country the size of Switzerland could only afford a single university, since the small cantonal universities could never be outfitted on the scale of those in Germany or France or compete with them for students and faculty. But after 1870 this idea began to lose support, largely because the Universities of Basel, Bern, and Zurich could not agree on a suitable location for a federal university. See Boeckel, *Hermann Köchly,* pp. 169, 208–9, 219; and Koprio, *Basel und die eidgenössische Universität.*

39. Gustav Lenz, *Die alten Reichslande,* p. 51, quoted in Bronner, *1870/71 Elsass-Lothringen,* 1:54.

40. See "Für die deutsche Universität zu Strassburg"; and Höfele, "Sendungsglaube und Epochenbewusstsein," pp. 272–75.

41. Germany, Reichstag, *Stenographische Berichte,* 1st leg. period, 1st sess., 2 (1871): 898.

42. Ibid., p. 901.

43. Ibid., pp. 900–901. Roemer, like Maurenbrecher and Treitschke, seems to have been overly optimistic in his assessment of the impact of the University of Bonn. As recently as 1861 the university's curator had observed that in no sense could the institution be considered to have fulfilled its Germanizing mission. See Bezold, *Geschichte der Rheinischen Friedrich-Wilhelms-Universität,* 1:488.

44. Germany, Reichstag, *Stenographische Berichte,* 1st leg. period, 1st sess., 2 (1871): 911; "Aus dem deutschen Reichstag."

45. On 2 May the chancellor had asked the Reichstag to give him *carte blanche* in Alsace-Lorraine rather than legislate what it considered to be desirable policies; see Germany, Reichstag, *Stenographische Berichte,* 1st leg. period, 1st sess., 1 (1871): 520. On attitudes in the Reichstag to the two resolutions, see the speech by Wehrenpfennig, ibid., 2 (1871): 896–97, and Boeckel, *Hermann Köchly,* p. 349.

46. France, Assemblée nationale, *Annales,* 1st series, 3 (1871): 197.

47. Report of Commission d'enseignement supérieur, as quoted in Gain, "L'enseignement supérieur à Nancy," 2:77. Also see ibid., 2:76–78.

48. Bismarck-Bohlen to the Imperial Chancellery, 1 July 1871, ADBR: AL 12, paq. 7.

49. Eck to Bismarck, 15 July 1871, Bismarck to Eck, 19 July 1871, Roon to Lettow, 23 July 1871, Bismarck to Roggenbach, 25 July 1871, and Roggenbach to Bismarck, 30 July 1871, ADBR: AL 12, paq. 7.

50. On Roggenbach and Alsace before and during the Franco-Prussian War, see Josef Becker, "Baden, Bismarck und die Annexion von Elsass und Lothringen," pp. 172–73, 188–89; Friedrich III, *Kriegstagebuch,* pp. 431–44; and Gall, *Der Liberalismus als regierende Partei,* pp. 485–92.

51. On Roggenbach's religious attitudes, see Gall, *Der Liberalismus als regierende Partei,* pp. 195, 282–83; Gall, "Die partei- und sozialgeschichtliche Problematik des badischen Kulturkampfes," pp. 172–73, 188; and Samwer, *Zur Erinnerung,* pp. 35–36.

52. Treitschke to his father, 27 Dec. 1862, Treitschke, *Briefe,* 2:218–19; Ernst Anrich, "Geschichte der deutschen Universität Strassburg," p. 118; Dorpalen, *Heinrich von Treitschke,* pp. 79–80; Gall, *Der Liberalismus als regierende Partei,* pp. 193–94, 205, 255, 434; Wentzcke and Heyderhoff, eds., *Deutscher Liberalismus,* 1:10.

53. Gall, *Der Liberalismus als regierende Partei*, pp. 242–43, 311–28; Heyderhoff, ed., *Im Ring der Gegner Bismarcks*, pp. 13–14, 22–23; Samwer, *Zur Erinnerung*, p. 64.

54. Moritz Busch, *Tagebuchblätter*, 3:244. Also see Bamberger, *Bismarcks grosses Spiel*, pp. 45, 47, 61–62; Holstein, *The Holstein Papers*, 2:121; and Oncken, "Freiherr von Roggenbach," pp. 269, 272.

55. Friedrich I of Baden, *Grossherzog Friedrich I. von Baden und die deutsche Politik*, 2:249–50, 336, 367; Friedrich III, *Kriegstagebuch*, pp. 350, 414; Samwer, *Zur Erinnerung,* p. 129.

56. Roggenbach arrived in Gastein on 3 Sept. 1871 and remained at least four days; see Heinrich Gelzer to Grand Duke Friedrich, 7 Sept. 1871, Friedrich I of Baden, *Grossherzog Friedrich I. von Baden und die Reichspolitik*, p. 37. There is a copy of Roggenbach's tentative plan dated 4 Sept. 1871 in ADBR: AL 12, paq. 7. Prior to their meeting Bismarck had had misgivings about whether Roggenbach was the best man for the commission and had even considered replacing him, but Roggenbach's report in Gastein persuaded the chancellor that a replacement was unnecessary; see Bismarck to Delbrück, 31 Aug. 1871, ADBR: AL 12, paq. 7; and Gustav Anrich, "Die Universität Strassburg," pp. 222–23.

57. See Dilthey, "Entwurf zu einem Gutachten," p. 81; Friedrich Kapp to Ernst Kapp, 28 Oct. 1871, CFK; and Roggenbach to Althoff, 17 Nov. 1882, quoted in Sachse, *Friedrich Althoff*, p. 42.

58. Roggenbach, "Bericht die Reorganisation der Universität in Strassburg betreffend," 30 Sept. 1871, ADBR: AL 12, paq. 7 (hereafter cited as "Bericht").

59. Roggenbach, "Bericht."

60. Ibid. This position was not recommended in the revised proposals Roggenbach prepared two months later, and it was not established. In fact, no German university would have a chair of German history until the 1930s. See Roggenbach to the Imperial Chancellery, 1 Dec. 1871, ADBR: AL 103, no. 258; and Engel, "Die deutschen Universitäten und die Geschichtswissenschaft," p. 327.

61. See, for instance, Heinrich von Sybel to Kühlwetter, 14 and 16 Dec. 1870, ADBR: AL 12, paq. 6; and Löher, *Aus Natur und Geschichte*, pp. 214–17.

62. Roggenbach, "Bericht."

63. For a fuller discussion, see Craig, "A Mission for German Learning," pp. 149–51.

64. Roggenbach, "Bericht." Also see Loening, "Die katholische Kirche im Elsass und in Preussen," pp. 725–27.

65. Friedrich Kapp to Ernst Kapp, 28 Oct. 1871, CFK; Gall, *Der Liberalismus als regierende Partei*, pp. 192–99.

66. On the introduction of seminars and laboratories, see Borscheid, *Naturwissenschaft, Staat und Industrie in Baden*, pp. 33–82; Alexander Busch, *Privatdozenten*, pp. 69–75; and Riese, *Die Hochschule auf dem Wege zum wissenschaftlichen Grossbetrieb*, pp. 193–209, 215–19, 226–30.

67. Dove, "Der Strassburger Hochschule zum Grusse," p. 678. Also see Dietzel, *Strassburg als deutsche Reichsuniversität*, pp. 34–35.

68. The fullest discussion of the early stages of this controversy is Hofmann, *Die Frage der Theilung*. Also see, with particular reference to the University of Strasbourg, Alexander Busch, *Privatdozenten*, pp. 81–82.

69. It was common for those who shared this opinion to oppose the growing number of students at the universities, the opening of new universities, and other academic concessions to modern, industrial society; see, for instance, Wilamowitz-Möllendorff, *Erinnerungen*, pp. 294–95, 299–300.

70. For the preceding debate and relevant documents, see Engelhardt and Decker-Hauff, eds., *Quellen zur Gründungsgeschichte*. This reform had also been instituted before 1871 at the German-language universities in Dorpat and Zurich; see "Die deutschen Universitäten

und die neue Universität in Strassburg," p. 605; and Riese, *Die Hochschule auf dem Wege zum wissenschaftlichen Grossbetrieb*, pp. 82–87.

71. Roggenbach, "Bericht." For proposals that there be two faculties instead of a single Faculty of Philosophy in Strasbourg, see "Die deutschen Universitäten und die neue Universität in Strassburg," pp. 604–5; Dietzel, *Strassburg als deutsche Reichsuniversität*, pp. 66, 144; and [Loening], "Die Neuschöpfung der Strassburger Universität," p. 399.

72. "Die deutschen Universitäten und die neue Universität in Strassburg," p. 605; Dietzel, *Strassburg als deutsche Reichsuniversität;* Dilthey, "Entwurf zu einem Gutachten," pp. 82–83; [Loening], "Die Neuschöpfung der Strassburger Universität," pp. 399–400.

73. Dietzel, *Strassburg als deutsche Reichsuniversität*, p. 32.

74. Ibid., pp. 54–55.

75. Ibid., pp. 28–31, 34–35, 68.

76. See *Deutscher Universitäts-Kalender*, 1 (1872); and Christian von Ferber, *Die Entwicklung des Lehrkörpers*, pp. 198–99.

77. Roggenbach, "Bericht"; Roggenbach to Möller, 8 Oct. 1871, ADBR: AL 12, paq. 7. Also see Riese, *Die Hochschule auf dem Wege zum wissenschaftlichen Grossbetrieb*, pp. 87–89.

78. Hess, "Zur forstlichen Unterrichtsfrage"; undated memorandum by R. Hess, Giessen, ADBR: AL 12, paq. 7; Roggenbach to the Imperial Chancellery, 1 Dec. 1871, ADBR: AL 103, no. 258.

79. Actually Kapp was more ambitious: he advocated what amounted to a program in American studies, with chairs for American history, American geography, and American constitutional law. Roggenbach might have responded more sympathetically had he not doubted that suitable professors could be found. See Friedrich Kapp to Ernst Kapp, 28 Oct. 1871, CFK; Friedrich Kapp to Hermann von Holst, 31 Oct. 1871, HEHC: 12; and Roggenbach to the Imperial Chancellery, 1 Dec. 1871, ADBR: AL 103, no. 258. On a similar but unsuccessful proposal in England, see Ged Martin, "The Cambridge Lectureship of 1866," pp. 17–29.

80. Roggenbach to the Imperial Chancellery, 30 Nov. 1871, ADBR: AL 12, paq. 7.

81. Dilthey, "Entwurf zu einem Gutachten," p. 82. There is a slightly different version of this memorandum in NWD (W. Dilthey 6/3). On the evolution of Dilthey's ideas concerning the human sciences, see Ermarth, *Wilhelm Dilthey;* and Herrmann, *Die Pädagogik Wilhelm Diltheys.*

82. Dilthey, "Entwurf zu einem Gutachten," pp. 84–85.

83. Roggenbach, "Bericht."

84. See Dietzel, *Strassburg als deutsche Reichsuniversität*, pp. 52, 54–55; and Dilthey, "Entwurf zu einem Gutachten," p. 81.

85. Roggenbach, "Bericht"; Roggenbach to Möller, 8 Oct. 1871, ADBR: AL 12, paq. 7. For the number of professors at the Universities of Berlin (presumably in the summer semester of 1871) and Leipzig (winter semester of 1872–73), see, respectively, Roggenbach, "Budgetentwurf der Universität Strassburg," 4 Sept. 1871, ADBR: AL 12, paq. 7 (hereafter cited as "Budgetentwurf"); and Hart, *German Universities*, pp. 362–71. For a comparison by faculty and with the Universities of Bonn and Göttingen, see Craig, "A Mission for German Learning," p. 178.

86. Friedrich Kapp to Ernst Kapp, 28 Oct. 1871, CFK; Friedrich Kapp to Hermann von Holst, 31 Oct. 1871, HEHC: 12.

87. Roggenbach, "Bericht." For the number of chairs in the various disciplines at German universities, see Christian von Ferber, *Die Entwicklung des Lehrkörpers*, pp. 195–208; and Lexis, ed., *Die deutschen Universitäten.*

88. Roggenbach to the Imperial Chancellery, 30 Nov. 1871, ADBR: AL 12, paq. 6.

89. Roggenbach, "Bericht."

90. Roggenbach to Möller, 8 Oct. 1871, ADBR: AL 12, paq. 7; Roggenbach to the Imperial Chancellery, 30 Nov. 1871, ibid., paq. 6. The averages for the Universities of Berlin and Göttingen have been computed from data presented in Roggenbach, "Budgetentwurf." Even at universities with large enrollments most professors received less than a third of their incomes from student fees; see Hart, *German Universities*, p. 377.

91. Heinrich von Sybel to Kühlwetter, 14 and 16 Dec. 1870, ADBR: AL 12, paq. 6; Igersheim, "L'occupation allemande," p. 338; [Loening], "Die Neuschöpfung der Strassburger Universität," p. 400; "Die Universitäts- und die Festungsfrage."

92. Roggenbach to Möller, 8 Oct. 1871, ADBR: AL 12, paq. 7. For the budgets of the Universities of Berlin and Leipzig, see, respectively, Max Lenz, *Geschichte der königlichen Friedrich-Wilhelms-Universität*, 3:529; and Hart, *German Universities*, pp. 375–76. On the stature of the University of Leipzig, see Hart, *German Universities*, pp. 373–75; and Holtzendorff, "Der Rückgang der berliner Universität," part 1, pp. 1–3.

93. Roggenbach to the Imperial Chancellery, 30 Nov. 1871, ADBR: AL 12, paq. 6. The only German university with a sizable endowment when Roggenbach made this proposal was the University of Leipzig, and this endowment was large enough to support only about a tenth of the institution's operating budget; see Hart, *German Universities*, pp. 375–77.

94. Möller to the Imperial Chancellery, 29 Oct. 1871, ADBR: AL 12, paq. 7.

95. Bismarck to Roggenbach, 25 July 1871, ibid.

96. Hauviller, *Franz Xaver Kraus*, pp. 60–61; Kraus, *Tagebücher*, p. 300; Sachse, *Friedrich Althoff*, pp. 130–31.

97. Wilhelm Beseler to Heinrich von Mühler, 9 Nov. 1871, ADBR: AL 12, paq. 7.

98. Mühler to Bismarck, 22 Nov. 1871, ibid.

99. Wittrock, *Die Kathedersozialisten*, p. 151.

100. See Friedrich Kapp to Ernst Kapp, 28 Oct. 1871, CFK; Friedrich Kapp to Hermann von Holst, 31 Oct. 1871, HEHC: 12; and Delbrück to Möller, 11 Dec. 1871, ADBR: AL 12, paq. 6.

101. Roggenbach to the Imperial Chancellery, 30 Nov. 1871, ADBR: AL 12, paq. 6.

102. Theodor Mommsen to Gustav Freytag, 9 Dec. 1871, quoted in Wickert, *Theodor Mommsen*, 4:86; Friedrich Kapp to Hermann von Holst, 12 Dec. 1871, HEHC: 12; Delbrück to Bismarck, 11 Dec. 1871, ADBR: AL 12, paq. 7; Gustav Anrich, "Die Universität Strassburg," p. 223.

103. Delbrück and Bismarck to Roggenbach, 11 Dec. 1871, ADBR: AL 12, paq. 7.

104. For evidence that Roggenbach thought he had been betrayed by the Imperial Chancellery, see Friedrich Kapp to Hermann von Holst, 19 Nov. 1871, HEHC: 12; Roggenbach to Grand Duke Friedrich I of Baden, 3 May 1872, quoted in Schieder, *Das deutsche Kaiserreich von 1871 als Nationalstaat*, p. 93; and Roggenbach to Althoff, 17 Nov. 1882, quoted in Sachse, *Friedrich Althoff*, p. 42.

105. Roggenbach to the Imperial Chancellery, 18 Dec. 1871, ADBR: AL 12, paq. 7.

106. Ibid.; the Imperial Chancellery to Roggenbach, 22 Dec. 1871, ADBR: AL 12, paq. 7.

107. See, for example, Roggenbach to the Imperial Chancellery, 1 Dec. 1871, ADBR: AL 103, no. 258; Berthold Auerbach to Jakob Auerbach, 3 Oct. 1871, Auerbach, *Briefe*, 2:79; and Ihering to Oskar Bülow, 28 Oct. 1871, Ihering, *Rudolf von Ihering in Briefen*, pp. 266–67.

108. See, for example, Hermann Baumgarten to Roggenbach, 27 Dec. 1871, ADBR: AL 103, no. 302; Anton Springer to Roggenbach, 26 Dec. 1871, ibid., no. 690; and Laband, *Lebenserinnerungen*, p. 68.

109. Roggenbach to Ernst Traumann, 22 July 1904, Roggenbach, "Zwei Briefe," pp. 318–19.

110. Delbrück to Roggenbach, 24 Sept. 1871, ADBR: AL 12, paq. 3; "Die Universität Strassburg," *Allgemeine Zeitung* (Augsburg), 13 Sept. 1871.

111. Bismarck to Roggenbach, 25 July 1871, and Bismarck to Roggenbach, 12 Sept. 1871, ADBR: AL 12, paq. 7; Wittrock, *Die Kathedersozialisten,* p. 151.

112. Dilthey, "Entwurf zu einem Gutachten," pp. 84–85.

113. Ibid., p. 85.

114. Bruch, *Johann Friedrich Bruch,* pp. 81–85. Also see Richter to Möller, 16 Feb. 1872, ADBR: AL 103, no. 258; and Roggenbach to Albrecht‚Ritschl, 30 Jan. 1872, quoted in Ritschl, *Albrecht Ritschls Leben,* 2:118–19.

115. See Recklinghausen to Roggenbach, 29 Dec. 1871 and 13, 16, 17, 22, and 26 Jan. 1872, ADBR: AL 103, no. 658; Leyden, *Lebenserinnerungen,* p. 125; and Waldeyer-Hartz, *Lebenserinnerungen,* pp. 141, 150.

116. Hoche, *Jahresringe,* pp. 117–18; Naunyn, *Erinnerungen,* p. 430; Stein, "Aus der Geschichte der Strassburger Medizin," p. 203.

117. Roggenbach to the Imperial Chancellery, 1 Dec. 1871, ADBR: AL 103, no. 258; Roggenbach to the Imperial Chancellery, 20 Dec. 1871, ADBR: AL 12, paq. 7; Gustav Anrich, "Die Universität Strassburg," p. 226; Ihering to Oskar Bülow, 28 Oct. 1871, Ihering, *Rudolf von Ihering in Briefen,* pp. 266–67.

118. Mommsen to Jacob Bernays, quoted in Wickert, *Theodor Mommsen,* 4:10. Also see Mommsen to Wilhelm Henzen, 15 Aug. 1871, quoted in ibid., p. 9.

119. Mommsen to Wilhelm Henzen, 13 Jan. 1872, quoted in ibid., p. 11. Also see ibid., pp. 10–13; Roggenbach to the Imperial Chancellery, 20 Dec. 1871, ADBR: AL 12, paq. 7; and Delbrück to Roggenbach, 4 Apr. 1872, ADBR: AL 103, no. 241.

120. See Roggenbach to the Imperial Chancellery, 27 Feb. 1872, ADBR: AL 103, no. 241; Groth, "Lebenserinnerungen," pp. 113–19; Scherer to Müllenhoff, 23 Jan. 1872, Müllenhoff and Scherer, *Briefwechsel,* p. 460; "Zwanglose Briefe."

121. See Mühler to Bismarck, 22 Nov. 1871, and Roggenbach to the Imperial Chancellery, 20 Dec. 1871, ADBR: AL 12, paq. 7; and Roggenbach to the Imperial Chancellery, 1 Dec. 1871, ADBR: AL 103, no. 258.

122. Scherer to Müllenhoff, 8 Jan. 1872, Müllenhoff and Scherer, *Briefwechsel,* p. 456.

123. Springer, *Aus meinem Leben,* p. 288. Also see Springer to Roggenbach, 26 Dec. 1871, ADBR: AL 103, no. 691.

124. Sohm to Roggenbach, 15 Mar. 1872, ADBR: AL 103, no. 668.

125. Bremer to Roggenbach, 30 Dec. 1871, ibid., no. 331.

126. Brunner to Roggenbach, 26 Dec. 1871, ibid., no. 325.

127. Baumgarten to Rudolf Haym, 22 Feb. 1872, quoted in Marcks, "Biographische Einleitung," p. lxxxix. Also see Baumgarten to Roggenbach, 27 Dec. 1871, ADBR: AL 103, no. 302; and Gustav Schönberg to Friedrich Nietzsche, 1 Feb. 1872, Nietzsche, *Briefwechsel,* part 2, 2:531.

128. Dilthey, "Entwurf zu einem Gutachten," p. 85; Treitschke to Salomon Hirzel, 1 Sept. 1870, and Treitschke to his wife, 26 Mar. 1871, Treitschke, *Briefe,* 3:284–85, 314–15; Wehrenpfennig to Treitschke, 23 Sept. 1871, Wentzcke and Heyderhoff, eds., *Deutscher Liberalismus,* 2:26.

129. Roggenbach, "Zwei Briefe," pp. 316–17; Strauss to Eduard Zeller, 22 Feb. 1872, Strauss, *Ausgewählte Briefe,* p. 534.

130. "Zwanglose Briefe." Also see Scherer to Müllenhoff, 17 Jan. 1872, and Müllenhoff to Scherer, 20 Jan. 1872, Müllenhoff and Scherer, *Briefwechsel,* pp. 456–58.

131. For Roggenbach's first choices, see Roggenbach to the Imperial Chancellery, 1 Dec. 1871, ADBR: AL 103, no. 258.

132. Adolf Michaelis, "Die Kaiser Wilhelms-Universität Strassburg."

133. An unidentified "medizinische Grösse" quoted in Otto Mayer, *Die Kaiser-Wilhelms-Universität,* p. 82.

134. For a fuller discussion, see Craig, "A Mission for German Learning," pp. 226–43. For the remark by Weizsäcker, see Hübinger, *Das historische Seminar,* p. 97.

135. See *Création d'une université à Nancy*, pp. 5–8, 11, 18; Febvre, "L'Université de Nancy," pp. 177–78; and Wieger, *Geschichte der Medicin*, pp. 166–68. On 2 Oct. 1872 the French government decreed that the Faculty of Medicine and the School of Pharmacy of the Academy of Strasbourg were transferred to Nancy; see France, *Journal officiel*, 4 (1872): 6305–6. The two Protestant theologians who did not join the German university's faculty, Frédéric Lichtenberger and Auguste Sabatier, moved to Paris where, in 1873, they founded the Ecole des sciences religieuses (after 1877 known as the Faculté de théologie protestante à Paris). The Ministry of Public Instruction supported this project and regarded the new institution as the direct successor of the Protestant theological faculty of the Academy of Strasbourg. See Gérold, *La Faculté de théologie*, p. 289n; Frédéric Lichtenberger, "La Faculté de théologie de Strasbourg," p. 24; and Scheidhauer, "La création de la Faculté de théologie protestante de Paris," pp. 291–325.

136. Roggenbach to the Imperial Chancellery, 6 Feb. 1872, ADBR: AL 103, no. 258. The four Alsatians singled out as reputable scholars by German standards were Edouard Reuss and Charles Schmidt, both Protestant theologians, Emil Heitz, a classical philologist, and Wilhelm-Philippe Schimper, a paleontologist.

137. Schimper to Adolphe Brongniart, 7 Sept. 1872, quoted in Joseph Laissus, "Wilhelm-Philippe Schimper," pp. 200–201. Also see F. W. Bergmann to [Kühlwetter?], 29 Mar. 1871, ADBR: AL 12, paq. 6; and Charles Schützenberger to Karl Ledderhose, 19 June 1871, ADBR: AL 103, no. 241.

138. "Universitätscommission."

139. Althoff, *Aus Friedrich Althoffs Strassburger Zeit*, pp. 23–24, 59–61, 73–74; Brentano, *Elsässer Erinnerungen*, pp. 57–58; Sachse, *Friedrich Althoff*, pp. 15–17.

140. Hoche, *Strassburg und seine Universität*, p. 50.

141. Gustav Anrich, "Die Universität Strassburg," p. 221; Ernst Martin, *Karl August Barack*, pp. 228–29.

142. Althoff, *Aus Friedrich Althoffs Strassburger Zeit*, p. 7; Th. Lindenlaub, "Université de Strasbourg," pp. 457–58; Wolfram, "Die Bibliotheken," pp. 32–36.

143. Ficker, *Die Kaiser-Wilhelms-Universität Strassburg*, p. 43; *Minerva*, 2 (1893), 23 (1914).

144. Johann Friedrich Bruch, *Johann Friedrich Bruch*, p. 85.

145. Althoff, *Aus Friedrich Althoffs Strassburger Zeit*, p. 60.

146. Germany, Bundesrath, *Protokolle*, 1872 sess., 5th meeting (25 Apr. 1872), copy in ADBR: AL 12, paq. 7; Otto Mayer, *Die Kaiser-Wilhelms-Universität*, p. 24.

147. Berthold Auerbach to Jakob Auerbach, 1, 2, and 3 May 1872, Auerbach, *Briefe*, 2:110–13; Ernsthausen, *Erinnerungen*, pp. 306–8; "Die Eröffnung der Universität Strassburg"; Leyden, *Lebenserinnerungen*, pp. 142–43; Tönnies, "Lebenserinnerungen," p. 210; Wiegand, "Elsässische Lebens-Erinnerungen," p. 89. For the various speeches and tributes, see University of Strasbourg, *Die Einweihung der Strassburger Universität*.

148. Diary of Heinrich Gelzer, 2 May 1872, Friedrich I of Baden, *Grossherzog Friedrich I. von Baden und die Reichspolitik*, p. 73.

149. University of Strasbourg, *Die Einweihung der Strassburger Universität*, p. 30.

150. Ibid., p. 28.

151. "Die Betheiligung der Elsässer"; Burger, "Vor sechzig Jahren," pp. 260–61; Ernsthausen, *Erinnerungen*, pp. 305–6; Moerlen and Bechelen, *La lutte de la jeunesse estudiantine*, pp. 7–8; "Die Strassburger Festtage"; Taufflieb, *Souvenirs d'un enfant de l'Alsace*, pp. 83–85; Wiegand, "Elsässische Lebens-Erinnerungen," p. 89.

152. Ernst Rohmer to Heinrich Marquardsen, 18 May 1872, Wentzcke and Heyderhoff, eds., *Deutscher Liberalismus*, 2:53.

153. Diary of Heinrich Gelzer, 30 Apr.–2 May 1872, Friedrich I of Baden, *Grossherzog Friedrich I. von Baden und die Reichspolitik*, pp. 72–73. Also see "Ein Nachwort zu den Universitätsfesten dieses Jahres," pp. 196–97; and the diary of Hans von Aufsess, 1 May

1872, quoted in Jeanne Régamey and Frédéric Régamey, *L'Alsace au lendemain de la conquête,* pp. 308–10.

154. Roggenbach to the Imperial Chancellery, 27 Feb. 1872, ADBR: AL 103, no. 241.

155. Roggenbach, "Die Bedingungen des Gedeihens der Universität Strassburg," ADBR: AL 12, paq. 7 (hereafter cited as "Die Bedingungen").

156. Ibid.; the emphasis is Roggenbach's.

157. Ibid.

158. Dove, "Der Strassburger Hochschule zum Grusse," p. 678.

159. Roggenbach, "Die Bedingungen."

160. Ibid.

161. Roggenbach to Grand Duke Friedrich I of Baden, 3 May 1872, quoted in Schieder, *Das deutsche Kaiserreich von 1871 als Nationalstaat,* p. 93.

162. Roggenbach to Althoff, 17 Nov. 1882, quoted in Sachse, *Friedrich Althoff,* p. 42.; the emphasis is Roggenbach's.

163. Roggenbach to Grand Duke Friedrich I of Baden, 3 May 1872, quoted in Schieder, *Das deutsche Kaiserreich von 1871 als Nationalstaat,* pp. 93–94. Also see Roggenbach to Jakob Bernays, 7 Dec. 1872, Bernays, *Ein Lebensbild in Briefen,* pp. 145–46.

164. Roggenbach to the Imperial Chancellery, 10 May 1872, ADBR: AL 12, paq. 7. Also see Roggenbach to Bruch, 11 May 1872, ADBR: AL 103, no. 48.

165. Ritschl, *Albrecht Ritschls Leben,* 2:120.

166. Mohl, *Lebenserinnerungen,* 2:136–37.

167. Quoted in Gustav Anrich, "Die Universität Strassburg," p. 228.

## Chapter 3

1. Müller to Jakob Bernays, 31 May 1872, Friedrich Max Müller, *Life and Letters,* 1:458.

2. Althoff to Ludwig von Cuny, 19 Apr. 1877, Althoff, *Aus Friedrich Althoffs Strassburger Zeit,* pp. 66–68.

3. Bismarck and Delbrück to Roggenbach, 11 Dec. 1871, ADBR: AL 12, paq. 7.

4. Alsace-Lorraine, Landesausschuss, *Verhandlungen,* 1st sess. (1875), 1:179–82; Germany, Reichstag, *Stenographische Berichte,* 2d leg. period, 2d sess., 2 (1874): 831–32; Gustav Anrich, "Die Universität Strassburg," p. 225; Pfetsch, *Wissenschaftspolitik in Deutschland,* pp. 71–80.

5. Alsace-Lorraine, Landesausschuss, *Verhandlungen,* 1st sess. (1875), 2:156–57.

6. Germany, Reichstag, *Stenographische Berichte,* 2d leg. period, 3d sess., 1 (1875): 177–78, 186, 191–92, 273–79.

7. Alsace-Lorraine, Landesausschuss, *Verhandlungen,* 2d sess. (1876), 2:151.

8. See *Deutscher Universitäts-Kalender,* 1 (1872) et seq.

9. Between 1817 and 1900, 322 of 1,355 appointments to faculties of law, medicine, and theology in Germany were made without or against the recommendations of the faculties concerned; see Ringer, *German Mandarins,* p. 37.

10. Adolf Michaelis, "Die Kaiser Wilhelms-Universität Strassburg," pp. 30–31.

11. See Faculty of Philosophy (Section for Mathematics and the Natural Sciences) to Ledderhose, 13 July 1872, and Faculty of Philosophy to Bismarck, 15 July 1872, ADBR: AL 103, no. 241; and Spiegelberg, "Die orientalischen Studien," p. 47.

12. See Adolf Michaelis to Burckhardt, 14 Feb. 1874, and Burckhardt to Michaelis, 16 Feb. 1874, Burckhardt, *Briefe,* 5:410–11, 221–22.

13. Compiled from information in *Deutscher Universitäts-Kalender,* 2 (1872–73) et seq.

14. See Ludwig Dehio, "Die Kaiser-Wilhelms-Universität Strassburg," p. 4; Meinecke, "Drei Generationen," pp. 250–51; Schmoller, "Von der Strassburger Jubelfeier," pp. 204–6; Stieda, "Zur Erinnerung," pp. 226–27, 231–32; and "Zur Einführung," p. 8.

15. Hausmann, *Die Kaiser-Wilhelms-Universität Strassburg*, p. 36; Otto Mayer, *Die Kaiser-Wilhelms-Universität*, pp. 33–34.

16. Hausmann, *Die Kaiser-Wilhelms-Universität Strassburg*, p. 31; Sachse, *Friedrich Althoff*, p. 18.

17. The art historian Anton Springer was one of those against the idea and said so in his keynote speech at the university's inauguration; see Springer, "Festrede," pp. 22–23. Also see "Votum des Collegen Studemund gegen Trennung der philosophischen Fakultät in zwei Fakultäten" (a nine-page memorandum), 5 Feb. 1873, NPG: 6.

18. See minutes of the Academic Senate, 27 May, 8 and 29 July 1872, ADBR: AL 103, no. 73.

19. Hoseus, *Die Kaiser-Wilhelms-Universität zu Strassburg;* Adolf Michaelis, "Die Kaiser Wilhelms-Universität Strassburg"; Schmoller, *Bericht,* pp. 7–8. Also see Kluge, *Die Universitäts-Selbstverwaltung,* pp. 95–96.

20. "Denkschrift betreffend die für die Universität Strassburg in Aussicht genommenen Neubauten," Alsace-Lorraine, Landesausschuss, *Verhandlungen,* 3d sess. (1877), 1:1–2.

21. Germany, Reichstag, *Stenographische Berichte,* 3d leg. period, 1st sess., 2 (1877): 912. Also see minutes of the Academic Senate, 8 May 1875, ADBR: AL 103, no. 76; and Althoff to Ludwig von Cuny, 19 Apr. 1877, Althoff, *Aus Friedrich Althoffs Strassburger Zeit,* pp. 66–67.

22. Hermann Baumgarten to Ledderhose, 4 Jan. 1874, ADBR: AL 103, no. 898; minutes of the Academic Senate, 12 May 1875, ibid. no. 76.

23. Minutes of the Academic Senate, 16 Nov. 1874 and 8 May 1875, ADBR: AL 103, no. 76, and 8 May 1876, ibid., no. 77; "Denkschrift betreffend die für die Universität Strassburg in Aussicht genommenen Neubauten," Alsace-Lorraine, Landesausschuss, *Verhandlungen,* 3d sess. (1877), 1:2–12; Hammer-Schenk, "'Wer die Schule hat, hat das Land!'" pp. 128–33.

24. Alsace-Lorraine, Landesausschuss, *Verhandlungen,* 3d sess. (1877), 2:195–96; Otto Mayer, *Die Kaiser-Wilhelms-Universität,* pp. 52–53.

25. Althoff to Ludwig von Cuny, 25 Apr. 1877, Althoff, *Aus Friedrich Althoffs Strassburger Zeit,* p. 69. Also see minutes of the Academic Senate, 13 Mar. 1877, ADBR: AL 103, no. 78; and Hermann Baumgarten to Max Weber, 30 Mar. and 18 Apr. 1877, Wentzcke and Heyderhoff, *Deutscher Liberalismus,* 2:176–79.

26. The attempt to obtain an additional subsidy from the imperial government may well have influenced the faculty's decision to adopt this name; see minutes of the Academic Senate, 13 Mar. and 27 Apr. 1877, ADBR: AL 103, no. 78.

27. Alsace-Lorraine, Landesausschuss, *Verhandlungen,* 4th sess. (1877), 1:159–60, 2:89–95; Otto Mayer, *Die Kaiser-Wilhelms-Universität,* pp. 50–51.

28. Ludwig Dehio, "Die Kaiser-Wilhelms-Universität Strassburg," p. 16. On the architectural competition, see Hammer-Schenk, "'Wer die Schule hat, hat das Land!'" pp. 133–43. For Bismarck's preferences see Peter Reichensperger to H. von Poschinger, 29 Nov. 1893, Otto von Bismarck, *Die gesammelten Werke,* 8:661.

29. For the ceremonies, see University of Strasbourg, *Die Einweihung der Neubauten.* On the admiration of French observers for the university's facilities, see Berr, *Vie et science,* pp. 123–24; Hallays, "L'Université de Strasbourg," pp. 251–52; Lenel, *Die Universität Strassburg,* p. 17; and Muller, "Enseignement des sciences," pp. 737–40. For a general survey of the attitudes of French intellectuals to German scholarship and universities in this period, see Digeon, *La crise allemande de la pensée française.*

30. On the nonacademic attractions of some of the German universities and the concept of the *Modeuniversität,* see Goetz, *Historiker in meiner Zeit,* pp. 9–10; Henning, *Das westdeutsche Bürgertum,* pp. 375, 475; Holtzendorff, "Der Rückgang der berliner Uni-

versität," pp. 2–3; Laspeyres, "Die deutschen Universitäten," part 3, p. 119; and Robert Redslob, *Alma mater,* p. 43.

31. Emil Fischer, *Aus meinem Leben,* p. 54; Hoseus, *Die Kaiser-Wilhelms-Universität zu Strassburg,* pp. 46–47; Laband, *Lebenserinnerungen,* p. 76; "Die Universitäten Strassburg und Heidelberg."

32. Adolf Michaelis, "Die Kaiser Wilhelms-Universität Strassburg." Also see Gerlach, *Von Rechts nach Links,* p. 63; Eduard Schwartz, "Verlorenes Reich"; and Wiegand, "Elsässische Lebens-Erinnerungen," p. 94.

33. Schmoller, "Von der Strassburger Jubelfeier," p. 205. Also see Huisman, "Chronique strasbourgeoise," p. 72; Meinecke, *Strassburg/Freiburg/Berlin,* pp. 62–63; and Adolf Michaelis, "Die Kaiser Wilhelms-Universität Strassburg."

34. This phrase was used by, among others, the historian Erich Marcks, a student at the university in the 1870s; see Marcks, "Biographische Einleitung," p. ciii. Also see the philosopher Heinrich Rickert (a student at the university in the 1880s) as quoted in Glockner, *Heidelberger Bilderbuch,* p. 86.

35. On the reputations of the Faculties of Medicine and Law see, respectively, Bonner, *American Doctors and German Universities,* pp. 35, 111; and Lenel, "Otto Lenel," p. 145.

36. Braun-Vogelstein, *Heinrich Braun,* pp. 30–31; and Emil Fischer, "Erinnerungen," p. 15.

37. This is a conjecture based on data in Hausmann, *Die Kaiser-Wilhelms-Universität Strassburg,* pp. 57–59; and Adolf Michaelis, "Die Kaiser Wilhelms-Universität Strassburg," pp. 14–15. Also see Jost, "Zum hundertsten Geburtstag Anton de Barys," pp. 8–11.

38. Conrad, *Das Universitätsstudium in Deutschland,* table 1.

39. See ibid., pp. 43–48 and table 1.

40. Perry, *And Gladly Teach,* p. 102.

41. William H. Welch to his sister, 15 May 1876, quoted in Bonner, *American Doctors and German Universities,* p. 35.

42. Conrad, *Das Universitätsstudium in Deutschland,* pp. 30–33 and table 1; Hausmann, *Die Kaiser-Wilhelms-Universität Strassburg,* p. 46; Laspeyres, "Die deutschen Universitäten," part 3, pp. 119–25.

43. Hoche, *Strassburg und seine Universität,* pp. 62–64; Huisman, "Chronique strasbourgeoise," p. 72; Maisenbacher, *Ein Strassburger Bilderbuch,* pp. 34–35; Emil Müller, *Aus der engen Welt eines Dorfpfarrers,* p. 61; and, for the names of the fraternities and the dates they were established, *Strassburger Universitäts-Taschenbuch,* pp. 43–44.

44. On student life generally, see Paul Maria Baumgarten, *Römische und andere Erinnerungen,* p. 29; Duisberg, *Meine Lebenserinnerungen,* p. 27; Emil Fischer, *Aus meinem Leben,* p. 53; Lotz, "Erinnerungen an Lujo Brentano," p. 1; Lubarsch, *Ein bewegtes Gelehrtenleben,* pp. 27–28; Melle, *Jugenderinnerungen,* pp. 114–17; Emil Müller, *Aus der engen Welt eines Dorfpfarrers,* pp. 58–79; and Wiegand, "Elsässische Lebens-Erinnerungen," pp. 90–91. On the *Strassburger Kreis,* see Otto Baumgarten, *Meine Lebensgeschichte,* pp. 49–52; and Pauli, *Erinnerungen,* pp. 66–70.

45. Pascal David to Friedrich von Holstein, 10 May 1906, Holstein, *The Holstein Papers,* 4:422. Also see Hensel, "Lebenserinnerungen," pp. 400–401; Hoche, *Strassburg und seine Universität,* pp. 60–61; Igersheim, "Strasbourg, capitale du Reichsland," pp. 219–24; Kiehl, Rapp, and Nonn, "Strasbourg et le Reichsland," pp. 372–75; and Meinecke, *Strassburg/Freiburg/Berlin,* pp. 20, 144–46.

46. See Brandl, *Zwischen Inn und Themse,* pp. 234–35, 329; Brentano, *Elsässer Erinnerungen,* p. 9; Friedrich Curtius, *Deutsche Briefe und Elsässische Erinnerungen,* pp. 207–8; Ernsthausen, *Erinnerungen,* pp. 300, 308–9, 369–70; Heuss-Knapp, *Ausblick vom Münsterturm,* pp. 16–17; Hoche, *Jahresringe,* pp. 115–16; Lubarsch, *Ein bewegtes Gelehrtenleben,* pp. 27–28; Maisenbacher, *Ein Strassburger Bilderbuch,* p. 47; Marcks, "Biographische

Einleitung," p. xc; Naunyn, *Erinnerungen,* p. 479; Robert Redslob, *Entre la France et l'Allemagne,* pp. 118–19; and Waldeyer-Hartz, *Lebenserinnerungen,* p. 164.

47. Goetz, *Historiker in meiner Zeit,* p. 333; Groth, "Lebenserinnerungen," pp. 126–28; Heuss-Knapp, *Ausblick vom Münsterturm,* pp. 20, 49–50; Hoche, *Strassburg und seine Universität,* pp. 20, 22–23; Hutten-Czapski, *Sechzig Jahren,* 1:121; Naunyn, *Erinnerungen,* p. 477.

48. Nöldeke, *Jugend-Erinnerungen,* p. 41. Also see Otto Baumgarten, *Meine Lebensgeschichte,* p. 7.

49. Adolf Baeyer to Paul von Groth, 8 Jan. 1876, NPG: 10; Brentano, *Elsässer Erinnerungen,* p. 56; Hoche, *Strassburg und seine Universität,* pp. 57, 60; Laband, *Lebenserinnerungen,* p. 77; Gustav Schmoller as quoted in *Reden und Ansprachen,* p. 9; Gustav Schwartz, *Alles ist Übergang zur Heimat hin,* p. 10. On professorial subcultures in Germany as a whole, see McClelland, "The Wise Man's Burden," pp. 50–67.

50. Paul von Groth to ?, 17 May 1883, NPG: 9; Paul Hensel to Bernhard Roemer, 21 Nov. 1888, Hensel, *Sein Leben,* pp. 55–57; Naunyn, *Erinnerungen,* pp. 476–78; Sachse, *Friedrich Althoff,* p. 46.

51. Hensel, "Lebenserinnerungen," p. 424; Hoche, *Jahresringe,* p. 115; Meinecke, *Strassburg/Freiburg/Berlin,* pp. 144–45; Nöldeke, *Jugend-Erinnerungen,* pp. 146–47, 151.

52. Brentano, *Elsässer Erinnerungen,* pp. 56–57. Also see Hensel, "Lebenserinnerungen," pp. 416–17; Hoche, *Jahresringe,* pp. 120, 182; Leyden, *Lebenserinnerungen,* p. 131; Nöldeke, *Jugend-Erinnerungen,* pp. 41–43; and Waldeyer-Hartz, *Lebenserinnerungen,* p. 143. On the fancier salons, see Robert Redslob, *Alma mater,* p. 106.

53. See, for instance, Kraus, *Tagebücher,* p. 389.

54. Hensel, "Lebenserinnerungen," p. 409.

55. Bresslau, "Harry Bresslau," p. 46. Also see Eduard Schwartz, "Verlorenes Reich."

56. On the characteristics of an organizational saga, see Burton R. Clark, *The Distinctive College,* pp. 233–62.

57. On the difficult living conditions, see Roggenbach to Jakob Bernays, 7 Dec. 1872, Bernays, *Ein Lebensbild in Briefen,* pp. 145–46; Groth, "Lebenserinnerungen," p. 128; Laband, *Lebenserinnerungen,* pp. 72–73, 76; and Müller to his mother, 19 and 22 May 1872, Friedrich Max Müller, *Life and Letters,* 1:456–58. For complaints about the shortage of students, see Ludwig Aschoff to his family, 28 Oct. 1892, Aschoff, *Ein Gelehrtenleben,* p. 48; Eberhard Gothein to Friedrich von Weech, 24 Oct. 1884, Hermann Baier, ed., "Heidelberger Professorenbriefe," p. 194; Paul von Groth to ?, 17 May 1883, NPG: 9; Hermann von Holst to Friedrich Kapp, 28 Oct. 1872 and 9 Jan. 1873, HEHC: 8; and Erich Schmidt to Theodor Storm, [late Jan. 1879], Storm and Schmidt, *Briefwechsel,* 1:104–5.

58. See, for instance, Heuss-Knapp, *Ausblick vom Münsterturm,* p. 20; Marcks, "Biographische Einleitung," p. xci; and Nöldeke, *Jugend-Erinnerungen,* pp. 38–39.

59. Otto Mayer, *Die Kaiser-Wilhelms-Universität,* p. 28; Adolf Michaelis, "Die Kaiser Wilhelms-Universität Strassburg." Also see Baeyer, *Erinnerungen,* p. 22; Hoseus, *Die Kaiser-Wilhelms-Universität Strassburg,* p. 39; Leyden, *Lebenserinnerungen,* p. 150; Bismarck to Karl Ledderhose, 30 April and 18 June 1875, Wilhelm Scherer and Steinmeyer, *Briefwechsel,* pp. 319–20, 324; and Heinrich von Treitschke to Hermann Baumgarten, 1 Oct. 1872, Treitschke, "Briefe Treitschkes," pp. 1–2.

60. See, for instance, Brandl, *Zwischen Inn und Themse,* p. 231.

61. Heuss-Knapp, *Ausblick vom Münsterturm,* pp. 20, 54. Also see Hoche, *Strassburg und seine Universität,* pp. 85–86; Meinecke, *Strassburg/Freiburg/Berlin,* p. 24; Robert Redslob, *Alma mater,* pp. 31–32; and Heinrich Schneegans, "Gustav Gröber," pp. 128–30.

62. Brentano, "Über die deutschen Universitäten." Also see Meinecke, *Strassburg/Freiburg/Berlin,* p. 20.

63. On centers and peripheries, both generally and with reference to academic systems, see Ben-David, *The Scientist's Role;* Gizycki, "Centre and Periphery"; Shils, "Center and Periphery"; and Shils, "Metropolis and Provinces," pp. 355–71.

64. On ten Brink, see Brandl, *Zwischen Inn und Themse,* p. 240; on Scheffer-Boichorst, see Aloys Schulte to Ferdinand Güterbock, 13 May 1902, NPSB: 1. On discrimination against Catholics when nominating candidates for chairs, see Adolf Merkel to Ledderhose, 13 Nov. 1881, ADBR: AL 103, no. 244; and Groth, "Lebenserinnerungen," pp. 191–92.

65. Roggenbach to the Imperial Chancellery, 27 Feb. 1872, ADBR: AL 103, no. 241; Hauviller, *Franz Xaver Kraus,* pp. 23–24; Kraus, *Tagebücher,* pp. 334, 363–65; Adolf Michaelis, "Franz Xaver Kraus und die philosophische Fakultät"; and Adolf Michaelis, "Noch einmal F. X. Kraus und die philosophische Fakultät."

66. On Althoff, see Althoff, *Aus Friedrich Althoffs Strassburger Zeit,* p. 102; and Sachse, *Friedrich Althoff,* pp. 47, 125; on Geffcken, see Erich Foerster, *Adalbert Falk,* pp. 357, 541; on Sohm, see Paul Maria Baumgarten, *Römische und andere Erinnerungen,* pp. 28–29; and Valentini, *Kaiser und Kabinettschef,* p. 28.

67. Schmoller to Lujo Brentano, 25 Oct. 1878, Schmoller and Brentano, "Briefwechsel," pp. 197–98. Also see Erich Schmidt to Theodor Storm, 7 July 1878, Storm and Schmidt, *Briefwechsel,* 1:96.

68. See Eckart Kehr, "Das soziale System der Reaktion," pp. 71–72; and, on the appointment of professors as *Geheimräte,* Paulsen, *The German Universities,* p. 102.

69. On anti-Semitism at German universities, see Bleuel, *Deutschlands Bekenner,* pp. 34–38; and Paulsen, *The German Universities,* pp. 158–59. On the lack of anti-Semitism at the University of Strasbourg, see Breslauer, *Die Zurücksetzung der Juden,* pp. 9, 20; Huisman, "Chronique strasbourgeoise," p. 149; and Adolf Michaelis, "Die Kaiser Wilhelms-Universität Strassburg."

70. Hoche, *Jahresringe,* p. 116; Otto Mayer, *Die Kaiser-Wilhelms-Universität,* pp. 77–78; Adolf Michaelis, "Die Kaiser Wilhelms-Universität Strassburg"; Paulsen, *The German Universities,* p. 102; Robert Redslob, *Alma mater,* p. 88; Tompert, *Lebensformen und Denkweisen,* pp. 40–41.

71. See Meinecke, "Die deutschen Universitäten und der heutige Staat," p. 404; and Meinecke, "Drei Generationen," pp. 252, 262–63.

72. Meinecke, review of Alfred E. Hoche, *Jahresringe,* and Elly Heuss-Knapp, *Ausblick vom Münsterturm,* p. 597.

73. Humboldt, "Über die innere und äussere Organisation," p. 255.

74. See minutes of the Academic Senate, 21 Nov. 1881, ADBR: AL 103, no. 83; Brentano, *Elsässer Erinnerungen,* p. 53; and Winterer, "Le journal politique intime," p. 365.

75. See Bresslau, "Harry Bresslau," p. 49; and, on Althoff's interest in becoming a National Liberal candidate for election to the Reichstag in 1878 and again in 1882, Sachse, *Friedrich Althoff,* p. 35.

76. See Lujo Brentano to Gustav Schmoller, 15 Sept. 1881, NLB: 59; and Hermann Baumgarten to Otto Hartwig, 3 Aug. 1888, NOH: 323.

77. Hermann Baumgarten as quoted in Wentzcke, "Drei Darstellungen," p. 41.

78. Ibid., p. 42; Heuss-Knapp, *Ausblick vom Münsterturm,* p. 49.

79. Theodor Nöldeke to Lujo Brentano, 25 Nov. 1917, NLB: 2a, 44; Althoff, *Aus Friedrich Althoffs Strassburger Zeit,* pp. 20–22, 35–45; Friedrich Curtius, *Deutsche Briefe und Elsässische Erinnerungen,* pp. 197–200; Heuss-Knapp, *Ausblick vom Münsterturm,* pp. 49–50; Otto Mayer, *Die Kaiser-Wilhelms-Universität,* p. 73; Adolf Michaelis, "Die Kaiser Wilhelms-Universität Strassburg"; Sachse, *Friedrich Althoff,* pp. 12, 25–26, 28–31; Waldeyer-Hartz, *Lebenserinnerungen,* p. 167.

80. See, for example, Bismarck to Karl von Hofmann, 31 July 1880, Otto von Bismarck, *Die gesammelten Werke,* vol. 6, part 4, p. 192.

81. Ibid., p. 167, and 8:298–301; Marcks, "Bei Bismarck," pp. 67–68; Morsey, *Die oberste Reichsverwaltung*, pp. 176–85; Silverman, *Reluctant Union*, pp. 40–45; Wehler, "Elsass-Lothringen von 1870 bis 1918," pp. 151–56.

82. See Otto von Bismarck, *Die gesammelten Werke*, 8:381.

83. See, for instance, Weber to his father, 30 May 1884, Max Weber, *Jugendbriefe*, p. 117.

84. Otto Baumgarten, *Meine Lebensgeschichte*, pp. 35–36; Brentano, *Elsässer Erinnerungen*, pp. 13–14; Friedrich Curtius, *Deutsche Briefe und Elsässische Erinnerungen*, pp. 200–202; Morsey, *Die oberste Reichsverwaltung*, pp. 184–91; Schwander and Jaffé, "Die reichsländischen Regierungen und die Verfassung," pp. 30–44; Wehler, "Elsass-Lothringen von 1870 bis 1918," pp. 156–57.

85. Otto Baumgarten, *Meine Lebensgeschichte*, p. 36; Brentano, *Elsässer Erinnerungen*, p. 12; Ernsthausen, *Erinnerungen*, p. 365; Kapp, "Elsass-Lothringen und die Aera Hohenlohe-Schillingsfürst," p. 120; Sachse, "Die Kirchenpolitik," pp. 153–56; Stählin, *Geschichte Elsass-Lothringens*, p. 237; Max Weber, *Jugendbriefe*, pp. 84–85.

86. Theodor Nöldeke to Eduard Schwartz, 24 Nov. 1930, NES: 2,A; Brentano, *Elsässer Erinnerungen*, pp. 9–11; Ludwig Dehio, "Die Kaiser-Wilhelms-Universität Strassburg," p. 19; Otto Mayer, *Die Kaiser-Wilhelms-Universität*, pp. 75–76; Puttkamer, *Die Aera Manteuffel*, p. 59.

87. Hermann Baumgarten to Conrad Varrentrapp, 7 Feb. and 27 Mar. 1880, BCV: 1; Lujo Brentano to Gustav Schmoller, 20 June and 14 Aug. 1885, NLB: 59; Nöldeke, *Jugend-Erinnerungen*, pp. 30–31; Pauli, *Erinnerungen*, pp. 62–63, 71; Georg Gerland to Eifer, 2 Feb. 1880, Thoma and Gerland, *Briefwechsel*, p. 30; Waldeyer-Hartz, *Lebenserinnerungen*, pp. 168–70; Weber to his father, 30 Sept. 1884, Max Weber, *Jugendbriefe*, pp. 116–17.

88. See Manteuffel to Wilhelm von Bismarck, 8 Dec. 1881, Wilhelm von Bismarck, "Aus den Papieren," p. 175; Puttkamer, *Die Aera Manteuffel*, p. 114; G. Erwin Ritter, *Die elsass-lothringische Presse*, p. 146; and Seltz, "Edwin v. Manteuffel," p. 236.

89. Eduard Schwartz, "Die Kaiser-Wilhelms-Universität Strassburg," p. 12.

90. See Ludwig Dehio, "Die Kaiser-Wilhelms-Universität Strassburg," pp. 18–20.

91. See Althoff, *Aus Friedrich Althoffs Strassburger Zeit*, pp. 19, 25–28, 102–3; Hutten-Czapski, *Sechzig Jahren*, 1:120; Laband, *Lebenserinnerungen*, pp. 90–91, 102–6; D. R., "Heinrich Geffcken," p. 767; Sachse, "Die Kirchenpolitik," pp. 156–59; and Sachse, *Friedrich Althoff*, pp. 32–33.

92. For evidence of Manteuffel's desire to reward Althoff and Laband for their services with special honors, see Morsey, *Die oberste Reichsverwaltung*, pp. 188–89.

93. Althoff, *Aus Friedrich Althoffs Strassburger Zeit*, pp. 22, 109; Brentano, *Elsässer Erinnerungen*, p. 57; Brentano, *Mein Leben*, p. 120; Sachse, *Friedrich Althoff*, p. 47.

94. See Brentano, *Elsässer Erinnerungen*, p. 18; Friedrich Curtius, *Deutsche Briefe und Elsässische Erinnerungen*, p. 223; Holstein and Hohenlohe-Schillingsfürst, *Holstein und Hohenlohe*, pp. 239–45, 248–72; Morsey, *Die oberste Reichsverwaltung*, pp. 193–94; Nöldeke, *Jugend-Erinnerungen*, pp. 56–57; Pauli, *Erinnerungen*, pp. 62–63; and Seydler, *Hohenlohe-Schillingsfürst als Statthalter*, p. 173.

95. Karl von Hofmann to Lujo Brentano, 23 Mar. 1886, NLB: 25; Brentano, "Elsässer Erinnerungen," p. 18; Heuss-Knapp, *Ausblick vom Münsterturm*, pp. 49–50; Holstein to Hohenlohe, 10 Nov. 1886, Holstein and Hohenlohe-Schillingsfürst, *Holstein und Hohenlohe*, pp. 258–59; Otto Mayer, *Die Kaiser-Wilhelms-Universität*, pp. 74–75.

96. Ziekursch, *Politische Geschichte*, 2:394–97.

97. Schwarz, ed., *MdR: Biographisches Handbuch der Reichstage*, pp. 246–50.

98. Quoted in Nöldeke, *Jugend-Erinnerungen*, p. 68.

99. See Brentano, *Elsässer Erinnerungen*, p. 105; Holstein and Hohenlohe-Schillingsfürst, *Holstein und Hohenlohe*, pp. 273–301; and Silverman, *Reluctant Union*, pp. 51–53.

100. Silverman, *Reluctant Union*, pp. 52–54.

101. Brentano, *Elsässer Erinnerungen*, p. 61. Also see Holstein and Hohenlohe-Schillingsfürst, *Holstein und Hohenlohe*, p. 282; T. R., "Zukunftsverhältnisse"; Sachse, *Friedrich Althoff*, p. 35; Waldeyer-Hartz, *Lebenserinnerungen*, p. 172; Weber to Hermann Baumgarten, 29 June 1887, Max Weber, *Jugendbriefe*, p. 248.

102. *Strassburger Post*, 24 Mar. 1887.

103. Quoted in "Elsass-Lothringen." Also see Wentzcke, *Der deutschen Einheit Schicksalsland*, p. 136.

104. Hohenlohe to Puttkamer, 27 Mar. 1887, cited in Seydler, *Hohenlohe-Schillingsfürst als Staathalter*, p. 135.

105. Brentano, *Elsässer Erinnerungen*, p. 106; Brentano, *Mein Leben*, pp. 130–31; Hohenlohe-Schillingsfürst, *Memoirs*, 2:381–83; Otto Mayer, *Die Kaiser-Wilhelms-Universität*, p. 80.

106. See Bopp, "L'oeuvre de la haute bourgeoisie haut-rhinoise," pp. 387–402.

107. Herkner to Brentano, 9 Aug. and 7 Oct. 1886, NLB: 28; Martentin to Karl von Hofmann, 10 Aug. 1886 (two reports), and Seuster to Ministry of Alsace-Lorraine, 29 Dec. 1886, ADBR: AL 69, paq. 794, vol. 3.

108. Herkner, *Die oberelsässische Baumwollindustrie*, p. 410. Also see Dieter Lindenlaub, *Richtungskämpfe*, 1:163–64.

109. See Brentano, *Elsässer Erinnerungen*, pp. 86–102; Brentano, *Mein Leben*, pp. 125–29; and Herkner, "Lebenslauf," pp. 88–90.

110. Herkner to Brentano, 20 and 24 Apr. 1887, NLB: 28; Brentano, *Elsässer Erinnerungen*, pp. 111–13; Brentano, *Mein Leben*, pp. 132–34; *Frankfurter Zeitung*, 4 and 7 Apr. 1887; Herkner, *Eine Erwiderung*; and Holstein to Hohenlohe, 2 May 1887, Holstein and Hohenlohe-Schillingsfürst, *Holstein und Hohenlohe*, p. 339.

111. See Bismarck to Hohenlohe, 9 Aug. 1887, Otto von Bismarck, *Die gesammelten Werke*, vol. 6, part 4, pp. 363–64.

112. "Die Universität Strassburg" (*Die Post*).

113. Gustav Schmoller, review of Heinrich Herkner, *Die oberelsässische Baumwollindustrie und ihre Arbeiter*, p. 1339. Also see Schmoller to Brentano, 18 June 1887, quoted in Brentano, *Mein Leben*, p. 134; and Brentano to Heinrich von Treitschke, 12 Jan. 1888, quoted in Dieter Lindenlaub, *Richtungskämpfe*, 1:164n.

114. Brentano, *Elsässer Erinnerungen*, pp. 110–11, 113–14; Brentano, *Mein Leben*, pp. 134–35.

115. Brentano, *Elsässer Erinnerungen*, p. 115.

116. Hermann Baumgarten to Otto Hartwig, 27 Mar. 1888, NOH: 323.

117. Brentano, *Elsässer Erinnerungen*, pp. 64–65; Sachse, *Friedrich Althoff*, pp. 22–23.

118. Althoff, *Aus Friedrich Althoffs Berliner Zeit*, p. 69. Also see Wilamowitz-Möllendorff, *Erinnerungen*, p. 249; and Zahn-Harnack, *Adolf von Harnack*, p. 234.

119. See Brandl, *Zwischen Inn und Themse*, p. 219; Naunyn, *Erinnerungen*, pp. 64–66; and Sachse, *Friedrich Althoff*, pp. 169, 173, 176–81. For comprehensive discussions of Althoff's methods and policies, see Andernach, *Der Einfluss der Parteien*, pp. 110–84; Brocke, "Hochschul- und Wissenschaftspolitik"; McCormmach, *Night Thoughts of a Classical Physicist*, pp. 39–50; and Sachse, *Friedrich Althoff*, pp. 48–356.

120. See Althoff to Conrad Varrentrapp, 1 Dec. 1889, BCV: 4.

121. Brandl, *Zwischen Inn und Themse*, p. 218; Burchardt, "Wissenschaftspolitik und Reformdiskussion," p. 75; Max Lenz, *Geschichte der königlichen Friedrich-Wilhelms-Universität*, vol. 2, part 2, p. 371.

122. Hübinger, *Das historische Seminar*, pp. 175–78. Also see Sachse, *Friedrich Althoff*, pp. 174–75, 183.

123. Brentano, *Elsässer Erinnerungen*, p. 116; Schieder, *Das deutsche Kaiserreich von 1871 als Nationalstaat*, p. 63.

124. See minutes of the Faculty of Philosophy, 24 Oct. 1885, ADBR: AL 103, no. 119; and Althoff to Wilhelm Studemund, 3 Apr. 1884, quoted in Sachse, *Friedrich Althoff*, pp. 197–99.

125. Althoff to Wilhelm Studemund, 3 Apr. 1884, and Studemund to Althoff, 12 Aug. 1884, quoted in Sachse, *Friedrich Althoff*, pp. 197–99, 200.

126. On the opposition of the Strasbourg professors to Althoff's activities between 1882 and 1885, see Friedrich Kluge to Hermann Paul, n.d., NHP; Brentano, *Mein Leben*, p. 135; and Sachse, *Friedrich Althoff*, p. 197.

127. On the professors' high regard for Ledderhose, see Brentano, *Elsässer Erinnerungen*, pp. 109–10; Laband, *Lebenserinnerungen*, p. 93; and Otto Mayer, *Die Kaiser-Wilhelms-Universität*, p. 39.

128. Brentano, *Mein Leben*, pp. 131–32; Silverman, *Reluctant Union*, p. 84.

129. Hohenlohe to Richard Zöpffel, 14 Apr. 1887, Ledderhose to Zöpffel, 15 Apr. 1887, and Kaiser Wilhelm to Hohenlohe, n.d. [July 1887], ADBR: AL 103, no. 48.

130. See, for example, Hermann Baumgarten to Otto Hartwig, 7 Feb. 1888, NOH: 323; Ludwig Dehio, "Die Kaiser-Wilhelms-Universität Strassburg," pp. 18–22; and *Frankfurter Zeitung*, 4 Apr. 1887.

131. Hohenlohe to Gustav von Gossler, 4 May 1887, Hohenlohe to Heinrich Richter, 6 May 1887, and Richter to Hohenlohe, 20 May 1887, ADBR: AL 27, paq. 628.

132. "Von der Strassburger Universität" (*National-Zeitung*). Also see Lujo Brentano to Theodor Nöldeke, 2 Dec. 1917, BTN: A28.

133. Richter's remarks are quoted in Brentano, *Mein Leben*, p. 136. Also see ibid., pp. 137–39; and Naunyn, *Erinnerungen*, pp. 403–4.

134. Brentano, *Mein Leben*, pp. 135–37; Ludwig Dehio, "Die Kaiser-Wilhelms-Universität Strassburg," p. 20; Laband, *Lebenserinnerungen*, pp. 91–95; Otto Mayer, *Die Kaiser-Wilhelms-Universität*, p. 40; "Von der Strassburger Universität" (*National-Zeitung*).

135. See Brentano, *Mein Leben*, pp. 137–38; Brentano to Heinrich von Treitschke, 12 Jan. 1888, quoted in Dieter Lindenlaub, *Richtungskämpfe*, 1:161n; and Schreiber, *Deutschland und Österreich*, pp. 10–11.

136. See minutes of the Academic Senate, 18 May 1887, ADBR: AL 103, no. 88; Brentano, *Mein Leben*, p. 135; and "Zur Frage der Universität Strassburg."

137. See minutes of the Academic Senate, 28 July 1887, ADBR: AL 103, no. 88; Brentano, *Mein Leben*, p. 136; and Laband, *Lebenserinnerungen*, p. 94.

138. See Hohenlohe to Bismarck, 19 Aug. 1887, Hohenlohe-Schillingsfürst, *Memoirs*, 2:388.

139. Hohenlohe to Puttkamer, 31 July 1887, quoted in Seydler, *Hohenlohe-Schillingsfürst als Staathalter*, p. 135. Also see Brentano, *Mein Leben*, p. 136; Hausmann, *Die Kaiser-Wilhelms-Universität Strassburg*, pp. 63–64; Laband, *Lebenserinnerungen*, pp. 94–95; "Die Universität Strassburg und die Verwaltung der Reichslande"; and "Von der Strassburger Universität" (*National-Zeitung*).

140. Puttkamer to the Foreign Ministry of Prussia, 19 July 1887, ADBR: AL 103, no. 200; Puttkamer to Richter, 29 July 1887, ibid., no. 332; Seydler, *Hohenlohe-Schillingsfürst als Staathalter*, p. 135.

141. Brentano to Richter, 31 July 1887, ADBR: AL 103, no. 332; Brentano, *Mein Leben*, pp. 139–40.

142. See Hauschild to Manteuffel, 6 and 13 Nov. 1884, and Hauschild to Hohenlohe, 10 Nov. 1886, ADBR: AL 27, paq. 126.

143. Hohenlohe to Bismarck, 7 Nov. 1887, ADBR: AL 103, no. 59.

144. Bismarck as quoted in Hauschild to Hohenlohe, 21 Nov. 1887, ADBR: AL 103, no. 59.

145. Hauschild to Hohenlohe, 8 and 23 Feb. 1888, ADBR: AL 27, paq. 126; Germany, Reichstag, *Stenographische Berichte*, 7th leg. period, 2d sess., 2 (1888): 1080–84.

146. See minutes of the Academic Senate, 28 July and 31 Oct. 1887, ADBR: AL 103, no. 88; and Brentano, *Mein Leben*, pp. 140–41.

147. Hohenlohe to Holstein, 24 Dec. 1887, Holstein and Hohenlohe-Schillingsfürst, *Holstein und Hohenlohe*, pp. 305–6. Also see Holstein to Hohenlohe, 13 Oct. 1887, ibid., p. 302.

148. See minutes of the Academic Senate, 27 Jan. 1888, ADBR: AL 103, no. 48; and Hermann Baumgarten to Otto Hartwig, 7 Feb. 1888, NOH: 323.

149. Germany, Reichstag, *Stenographische Berichte*, 7th leg. period, 2d sess., 1 (1887): 156–57; and Brentano, *Mein Leben*, p. 141.

150. See Hermann Baumgarten to Otto Hartwig, 3 Aug. 1888, NOH: 323; and Bresslau, "Harry Bresslau," p. 49.

151. See Ludwig Dehio, "Die Kaiser-Wilhelms-Universität Strassburg," pp. 18–19.

152. "Die Universität Strassburg" (*Die Post*). Also see "Aus Elsass-Lothringen"; and "Deutschtum und Unterrichtswesen in Elsass-Lothringen."

153. Lujo Brentano to Theodor Nöldeke, 2 Dec. 1917, BTN: A28. Also see Brentano, "Über die deutschen Universitäten," p. 2; "Von der Strassburger Universität" (*National-Zeitung*); and "Zur Frage der Universität Strassburg."

154. See, for instance, Richard Zöpffel to Hohenlohe, 2 Nov. 1887, ADBR: AL 27, no. 693.

## Chapter 4

1. H. P., "L'Université de Strasbourg."

2. Hawkins, *Pioneer*, p. 33.

3. Grad, "La nouvelle Université de Strasbourg," p. 564.

4. Appell, *Souvenirs d'un alsacien*, pp. 130–31; Burger, "Vor sechzig Jahren," p. 261; Edmond Redslob, *D'un régime à un autre*, pp. 6–7; Roederer, "Cinq semestres à la Faculté de médecine de Strasbourg"; Schmoller, "Die Bedeutung der Strassburger Universität," p. 201.

5. Julius Klein and Edouard Goguel in Alsace-Lorraine, Landesausschuss, *Verhandlungen*, 3d sess. (1877), 2:183 and 190, respectively.

6. Baron Hugo Zorn von Bulach in ibid., p. 185.

7. August Schneegans in ibid., p. 186.

8. Baumgarten to Max Weber, 20 Mar. 1877, Wentzcke and Heyderhoff, eds., *Deutscher Liberalismus*, 2:177.

9. Baumgarten to Max Weber, 23 Dec. 1877, ibid., p. 190.

10. Brentano, *Elsässer Erinnerungen*, p. 26. For the proportion of the population in various communities and regions of the Reichsland who habitually spoke French, see Wolfram and Gley, eds., *Elsass-Lothringer Atlas*, maps 23b and 24.

11. Wahl, *L'option et l'émigration des alsaciens-lorrains*, pp. 153–92.

12. See Philippe Dollinger, "Bourgeoisies d'Alsace," p. 491; Imbs, "Notes sur la langue française," p. 311; and Waldeyer-Hartz, *Lebenserinnerungen*, p. 164.

13. Robert Redslob, *Alma mater*, p. 6.

14. See Herrenschmidt, *Mémoires pour la petite histoire*, p. 135; Robert Redslob, "La bourgeoisie alsacienne," pp. 446–47; and Veil, "Strassburgs medizinische Fakultät," p. 1853.

15. Friedrich Curtius, *Deutsche Briefe und Elsässische Erinnerungen*, p. 208; Heuss-Knapp, *Ausblick vom Münsterturm*, pp. 55–56; Hoche, *Jahresringe*, p. 113; Maisenbacher, *Ein Strassburger Bilderbuch*, pp. 52–53; Nöldeke, *Jugend-Erinnerungen*, p. 41; Edmond Redslob, *Chez nous*, pp. 46–47.

16. Althoff, *Aus Friedrich Althoffs Strassburger Zeit*, p. 22; Hensel, "Lebenserinnerungen," pp. 407–8; El. Lobstein and Ed. Lobstein, *Paul Lobstein*, pp. 80, 92, 100; Robert Redslob, *Alma mater*, pp. 102, 105, 108, 120–26; Ziegler, *Der deutsche Student*, p. 162.

17. See Emile Baas, "Notes pour une sociologie de la bourgeoisie alsacienne contemporaine"; Kapp, "Die Kaiser-Wilhelms-Universität Strassburg und das Elsässertum," pp. 264–66; and, in particular, Wittich, "Deutsche und französische Kultur im Elsass."

18. Johann Kiener in Alsace-Lorraine, Landesausschuss, *Verhandlungen,* 3d sess. (1877), 2:188. Also see Bruck, *Ich warte . . . ,* pp. 50, 52, 236, 369; Maisenbacher, *Ein Strassburger Bilderbuch,* pp. 16–17; and Wahl, *Confession et comportement,* pp. 422–45, 476–501.

19. Lienhard, *Jugendjahre,* pp. 146, 176. Also see petitions to Otto von Bismarck (signed, respectively, by thirty-five and seventy-five Alsatian pastors), 3 June and 5 Aug. 1874, ADBR: AL 103, no. 258; Otto Baumgarten, *Meine Lebensgeschichte,* pp. 16–17, 37; El. Lobstein and Ed. Lobstein, *Paul Lobstein,* pp. 68–69; and Will, "L'église protestante de Strasbourg," pp. 214, 216, 220–21.

20. See Berger, *Pascal David,* p. 109; Escherich, *Leben und Forschen,* pp. 47–48, 66; Hensel, "Lebenserinnerungen," p. 445; and, for the quotations, *Der Elsässer* (Strasbourg), 15 Feb. 1896; and Landolin Winterer in Germany, Reichstag, *Stenographische Berichte,* 2d leg. period, 2d sess., 1 (1874): 390, respectively.

21. See Ignace Simonis in Germany, Reichstag, *Stenographische Berichte,* 2d leg. period, 1st sess., 2 (1874): 1156–58; Landolin Winterer in ibid., 2d sess., 1 (1874): 390; and Joseph Guerber in ibid., 3d sess., 1 (1875): 186.

22. See Appell, *Souvenirs d'un alsacien,* pp. 130–31; Emile Baas, "Notes pour une sociologie de la bourgeoisie alsacienne contemporaine," p. 340; Brentano, *Elsässer Erinnerungen,* pp. 24, 53–54; Bresslau, "Harry Bresslau," pp. 47–49; Ludwig Dehio, "Die Kaiser-Wilhelms-Universität Strassburg," pp. 14, 18; Huck, "Les idées politiques, sociales et économiques d'un industriel bas-rhinois," p. 290; and Kapp, "Die Kaiser-Wilhelms-Universität Strassburg und das Elsässertum," pp. 264–65. For earlier proposals for the introduction of career-oriented programs, see the speech by Eduard Koechlin and "Denkschrift über die Errichtung von Lehrstühlen für Forstwissenschaft" in Alsace-Lorraine, Landesausschuss, *Verhandlungen,* 3d sess. (1877), 2:182 and 192–93, respectively.

23. See Hensel, "Lebenserinnerungen," pp. 406–8; Adolf Michaelis, "Die Kaiser Wilhelms-Universität Strassburg"; and Ropp, "Konrad Varrentrapp," p. 349.

24. See Hensel, "Lebenserinnerungen," p. 407; and Adolf Michaelis, "Die Kaiser Wilhelms-Universität Strassburg."

25. Paul Scheffer-Boichorst to Alfred Dove, June 1884, quoted in Güterbock, "Aus Scheffer-Boichorsts Leben," 1:51.

26. "Aufruf zum Beitritt zu dem am 17. Februar 1883 gegründeten Kunst-Verein zu Strassburg," NLB: 25; Paul Maria Baumgarten, *Römische und andere Erinnerungen,* pp. 36–38; Brandl, *Zwischen Inn und Themse,* p. 272; Brentano, *Elsässer Erinnerungen,* pp. 67–84; Ernsthausen, *Erinnerungen,* pp. 309, 317–18; Robert Redslob, *Alma mater,* p. 40; Springer, *Aus meinem Leben,* pp. 296–99; Volksbildungs-Verein zu Strassburg i. E., *Siebenter Jahresbericht,* pp. 19–26.

27. On the Protestant theological faculty, see Karl Ledderhose to Otto von Bismarck, 21 Mar. 1873, 12 Mar. and 19 Apr. 1876, Bismarck to Ledderhose, 9, 14, and 16 Apr. 1876, and Faculty of Protestant Theology to Ledderhose, 16 June 1876, ADBR: AL 103, no. 258; and Faculty of Protestant Theology to Ledderhose, 26 Feb. 1883, and Heinrich Richter to Faculty of Protestant Theology, 19 May 1887, ibid., no. 255.

28. Faculty of Medicine to Johann Friedrich Bruch, 12 July 1872, ibid., no. 241.

29. See Böhmer, "Strassburger Erlebnisse"; Gröber, *Wahrnehmungen and Gedanken,* pp. 33–34, 36; El. Lobstein and Ed. Lobstein, *Paul Lobstein,* p. 92; and Heinrich Schneegans, "Gustav Gröber," pp. 121, 125, 131.

30. On "cosmopolitans" and "locals" or "provincials," see Gouldner, "Cosmopolitans and Locals"; Lazarsfeld and Thielens, *The Academic Mind,* pp. 262–64; and Merton, "Patterns of Influence."

31. See Joseph Guerber to Carl Marbach, 3 Nov. 1870, n.d. [before 25 Dec. 1870], n.d. [before 1 Jan. 1871], and 16 Jan. 1871, and draft of memorandum by Marbach for Bishop Raess, Mar. 1871, [Guerber], "Briefe," pp. 430, 433–36, 440–43; reports of Civil Commissioner Kühlwetter, 15 Oct. and 14 Dec. 1870, quoted in Igersheim, "L'occupation allemande," pp. 294, 350–51; and L'Huillier, "L'attitude politique de Mgr Raess," pp. 249–51.

32. Hoseus, *Die Kaiser-Wilhelms-Universität zu Strassburg*, p. 45.

33. For Strasbourg, see ibid., pp. 48–49. In 1895–96, 25.5 percent of all Prussian students were attending universities outside Prussia, and many of the others were not at the university in their province of Prussia. In the same year 29.6 percent of all students from Baden were at universities outside Baden. See Prussia, Statistisches Landesamt, *Preussische Statistik*, 150:26; and Riese, *Die Hochschule auf dem Wege zum wissenschaftlichen Grossbetrieb*, pp. 343, 348.

34. France, Ministère de l'instruction publique et des beaux-arts, *Statistique de l'enseignement supérieur*, pp. 463, 501, 603; Roth, *La Lorraine annexée*, pp. 108–16, 168–69, 488–89.

35. Heitz, *Vues cavalières*, p. 188. Also see Roth, *La Lorraine annexée*, p. 169; and Wahl *L'option et l'émigration des alsaciens-lorrains*, pp. 74–78.

36. Robert Redslob, *Entre la France et l'Allemagne*, p. 67. Also see "Die politische Bedeutung der Strassburger Universität."

37. Hoseus, *Die Kaiser-Wilhelms-Universität zu Strassburg*, pp. 52–57. For student fees see Conrad, "Einige Ergebnisse," p. 489; and *Deutscher Universitäts-Kalender*, 1897–98, p. 204. At Prussian universities in the late 1890s about 29 percent of all German students received stipends of some kind; see Prussia, Statistisches Landesamt, *Preussische Statistik*, 167:153. The total expenses of the average student in 1900 were 1,200–1,500 marks per year; see Höroldt, "Zur wirtschaftlichen Bedeutung der Universitäten," pp. 32–37, 69.

38. Memorandum by Pierre Bucher enclosed with Bucher to Wittich, 20 Apr. 1900, PWW.

39. For patterns in France generally, see Harrigan, *Mobility, Elites, and Education in French Society*, pp. 13–55; and Ringer, *Education and Society in Modern Europe*, pp. 157–80.

40. This conclusion emerges from comparisons of selectivity indices and of indices of dissimilarity. For a discussion of these indices, see appendix A.

41. Alsace-Lorraine, Statistisches Bureau, *Statistisches Handbuch*, p. 468.

42. Wittmer, "Les Alsaciens à l'Université de Fribourg en Suisse."

43. To control for the confounding effects of regional differences within the Reichsland, the rates for religions after controlling for social origins are based on separate calculations for Strasbourg, the rest of Lower Alsace, Upper Alsace, and Lorraine. For the patterns if region is not controlled, see table 6, appendix B.

44. On primary and secondary education in the Reichsland, see Bruno Baier et al., "Das Unterrichtswesen in Elsass-Lothringen"; and Rossé et al., eds., *Das Elsass von 1870–1932*, 3:103–29.

45. Memorandum from Pierre Bucher enclosed with Bucher to Wittich, 20 Apr. 1900, PWW.

46. Robert Redslob, *Entre la France et l'Allemagne*, p. 127.

47. See Bonnet, *Sociologie politique et religieuse de la Lorraine*, pp. 18, 58; and Roth, *La Lorraine annexée*, pp. 677–78.

48. Robert Redslob, *Entre la France et l'Allemagne*, pp. 128–29.

49. At the University of Nancy in 1899 only five of the thirty-nine Alsatians studying medicine or pharmacy were from Lower Alsace. At the University of Fribourg in Switzerland, thirty-three of the fifty-six Alsatians matriculating in the 1890s were from Upper Alsace. See University of Nancy, *Séance de rentrée*, pp. 84, 176; and Wittmer, "Les Alsaciens à l'Université de Fribourg en Suisse."

50. On occupational socialization, see Brim, "Adult Socialization," pp. 196–205; Moore, "Occupational Socialization"; and Niemi and Sobieszek, "Political Socialization," pp. 225–29. On the allocating and legitimating roles of formal education and their relationship to socialization, see Meyer, "The Effects of Education as an Institution"; and Meyer and Rubinson, "Education and Political Development," pp. 141–44.

51. On anticipatory socialization, see Campbell, "Adolescent Socialization," pp. 823–27; Merton, *Social Theory and Social Structure,* pp. 265–71; Moore, "Occupational Socialization," pp. 871–73; and Wheeler, "The Structure of Formally Organized Socialization Settings," pp. 83–85.

52. For the general argument, see Barth, "Introduction"; and Barth, "Scale and Network," pp. 163–69. Also see Stinchcombe, "Social Structure and Politics," pp. 599–616; and, for an application to university students, Kaufert, "Situational Identity and Ethnicity."

53. See Georg Kaibel to Eduard Schwartz, 7 July 1897, NES: 2A; Brandl, *Zwischen Inn und Themse,* p. 233; Bresslau, "Harry Bresslau," pp. 48–49; Güterbock, "Aus Scheffer-Boichorsts Leben," p. 51; and Naumann, *Ernst Stadler,* pp. 9–10.

54. See Otto Michaelis, *Grenzlandkirche,* pp. 165–66; and "Strassburger Stadtnachrichten."

55. On these difficulties, see Juillard, *La vie rurale dans la plaine de Basse-Alsace,* pp. 276–78, 288–96, 308–30; and Michel Rochefort, *L'organisation urbaine de l'Alsace,* pp. 216–38.

56. For development of these points with reference to Germany as a whole and to the rest of Europe, see Craig, "Higher Education and Social Mobility"; and Craig and Spear, "Explaining Educational Expansion." On changes in the market for university graduates in Germany, see Conrad, "Einige Ergebnisse," pp. 452–74; and Huerkamp and Spree, "Arbeitsmarktstrategien der deutschen Ärzteschaft."

57. Hensel, "Lebenserinnerungen," p. 442. Also see Ludwig Dehio, "Die Kaiser-Wilhelms-Universität Strassburg," p. 18.

58. See Büchner, "Die Freiheit der Wissenschaft und die Universitäten"; Klose, *Freiheit schreibt auf eure Fahnen,* p. 173; Vierhaus, "Bildung," pp. 547–50; and Ziegler, *Der deutsche Student,* pp. 174–75, 179–80, 225.

59. Dahrendorf, *Society and Democracy in Germany,* p. 236.

60. Brentano, *Elsässer Erinnerungen,* p. 31; Ludwig Dehio, "Die Kaiser-Wilhelms-Universität Strassburg," p. 18; Flake, "Um 1900," p. 89; Adolf Michaelis, "Die Kaiser Wilhelms-Universität Strassburg."

61. Schwalb, "Das Rechts- und Gerichtswesen in Elsass-Lothringen," pp. 372, 379–80.

62. See Schweitzer, "Albert Schweitzer," pp. 207–9; and, for Schweitzer's experiences at the University of Strasbourg, Schweitzer, *Out of My Life and Thought,* pp. 16–162 passim.

63. See Moerlen and Bechelen, *La lutte de la jeunesse estudiantine,* p. 19; Edmond Redslob, *D'un régime à un autre,* p. 6; and Emil Clemens Scherer, "Der elsässische Student," p. 157.

64. Ludwig Dehio, "Die Kaiser-Wilhelms-Universität Strassburg," pp. 8–9; Otto Mayer, *Die Kaiser-Wilhelms-Universität,* pp. 57–58; Naunyn, *Erinnerungen,* pp. 193–95, 431–32, 469–73; Stein, "Aus der Geschichte der Strassburger Medizin," pp. 208–9; Waldeyer-Hartz, *Lebenserinnerungen,* pp. 162–63, 174–75.

65. See Lévy, *Histoire linguistique,* 2:458–61; Lion, "Das Elsass als Problem," pp. 339–40; and Rossé et al., eds., *Das Elsass von 1870–1932,* 2:20–21.

66. Barrès, "Les bastions de l'est," p. 28.

67. Georg Wolf as quoted in "Vergangenheit und Zukunft."

68. See minutes of the Academic Senate, 12 May 1875, ADBR: AL 103, no. 76; Franz Duncker in Germany, Reichstag, *Stenographische Berichte,* 2d leg. period, 3d sess., 1 (1875): 563; Richard Hirsch, *Strassburg: Ein Ruf,* pp. 7–9; "Die politische Bedeutung der Strassburger Universität"; and Ziegler, *Der deutsche Student,* pp. 104–5.

69. Heinrich Rickert quoted in Glockner, *Heidelberger Bilderbuch*, p. 86. On Alsatian students as more diligent than German students, see memorandum by Pierre Bucher enclosed with Bucher to Wittich, 20 Apr. 1900, PWW; Hensel, "Lebenserinnerungen," p. 442; and Gustav Schwartz, *Alles ist Übergang zur Heimat hin*, p. 32.

70. Emil Müller, *Aus der engen Welt eines Dorfpfarrers*, p. 58. Also see Emil Clemens Scherer, "Der elsässische Student," p. 160; and, on labeling and socialization, Feldman, "Some Theoretical Approaches," pp. 13–14.

71. See, for instance, Appell, *Souvenirs d'un alsacien*, pp. 130–31; Koessler, *Unser Elsass*, p. 9; d'Oux, "Der elsässische Student," pp. 252–54; and Wiegand, "Elsässische Lebens-Erinnerungen," pp. 90–91.

72. Gaster, "Strassburger Studentenleben," pp. 75–77; Müntzer, *Der elsässische Student*, pp. 21–22; Nöldeke, *Jugend-Erinnerungen*, pp. 53–55; Emil Clemens Scherer, "Der elsässische Student," pp. 158–59.

73. Jarausch, *Students, Society, and Politics*, pp. 264–65, 277–88; Klose, *Freiheit schreibt auf eure Fahnen*, pp. 179–95; Friedrich Schulze and Ssymank, *Das deutsche Studententum*, pp. 283–459 passim; Ziegler, *Der deutsche Student*, pp. 71–72, 125–26.

74. Otto Baumgarten, *Meine Lebensgeschichte*, pp. 48–54; Pauli, *Erinnerungen*, pp. 66–67.

75. See, for instance, Georg Wolfram as quoted in Die lose Vereinigung der ehemalige Strassburger Studenten und Dozenten, *Bericht über die erste Zusammenkunft*, p. 14.

76. Robert Will as quoted in "Vom 50. Stiftungsfeste der Wilhelmitana." Also see "Die Betheiligung der Elsässer"; Bronner, *1870/71 Elsass-Lothringen*, 2:363–64; Lienhard, *Jugendjahre*, pp. 116, 150; Moerlen and Bechelen, *La lutte de la jeunesse estudiantine*, pp. 7–9; and Strohl, *Le protestantisme en Alsace*, p. 441.

77. The observations concerning Wilhelmitana's members are based on the university's matriculation records (ADBR: AL 103, paqs. 1–9) and on the list of the club's surviving members in Wilhelmitana, *Die Wilhelmitana*, pp. 100–117. Also see Müntzer, *Der elsässische Student*, pp. 22–23.

78. Emil Müller, *Aus der engen Welt eines Dorfpfarrers*, p. 58; Emil Clemens Scherer, "Der elsässische Student," pp. 159–60.

79. Ritleng, *Souvenirs de jeunesse*, p. 15; Seltz, "40 Jahre Journalismus," pp. 104–6.

80. Moerlen and Bechelen, *La lutte de la jeunesse estudiantine*, pp. 13–14; M. R., "Kleine Chronik."

81. See, for example, Henry, *Témoignage pour les Alsaciens-Lorrains*, pp. 300–340; and Kühn, *Briefe von Elsass-Lothringen*, pp. 85–86.

82. "Die Betheiligung der Elsässer"; and Burger, "Vor sechzig Jahren," pp. 260–61.

83. On the emigration of students, see Wahl, *L'option et l'émigration des alsaciens-lorrains*, pp. 158–73 passim.

84. Moerlen and Bechelen, *La lutte de la jeunesse estudiantine*, p. 10; Pippo [pseud.], "La société d'étudiants alsaciens-lorrains Sundgovia-Erwinia," p. 243.

85. "Anzeige von der Gründung des 'Strassburger-Studenten Vereines' Sundgovia," 10 June 1881, ADBR: AL 103, no. 155.

86. E. Fidelis, "Quelques reflexions à propos du monôme," 20 Feb. 1885, included in the papers of the *Sauterelle* (the journal of the Sundgovia-Erwinia), BNUS: Ms 4846. Also see Bourson, "Monômes et 'banquets' des étudiants alsaciens," pp. 114–15; Haug, "Les étudiants alsaciens," p. 27; Moerlen and Bechelen, *La lutte de la jeunesse estudiantine*, pp. 10–11; and Pippo [pseud.], "La société d'étudiants alsaciens-lorrains Sundgovia-Erwinia," pp. 245–46.

87. The sample is based on a list of thirty-seven active and former members (undated but apparently from the winter semester of 1885–86) found in BNUS: Ms 4846. The distribution of Alsatian students generally in 1885–86 according to background and faculty is estimated

based on those enrolled in 1882–83 and in 1887–88. On the Sundgovia as the largest of the various student clubs, see *Journal d'Alsace* (Strasbourg), 13 Feb. 1883.

88. Maximilian von Puttkamer to Heinrich Richter, 2 Apr. 1887, ADBR: AL 103, no. 199.

89. Puttkamer to the Police Director of Strasbourg, 2 Apr. 1887, ibid., no. 198; and Puttkamer to Richter, 21 Apr. 1887, ibid., no. 199.

90. Poidevin, "Les élections de 1893 en Alsace-Lorraine," pp. 466–69, 474; Rossé et al., eds., *Das Elsass von 1870–1932*, 1:103–4, 4:66–72.

91. On the declining size and influence of the Francophile middle class, see Philippe Dollinger, "Bourgeoisies d'Alsace," pp. 491–92; Imbs, "Notes sur la langue française," p. 311; and Robert Redslob, "La bourgeoisie alsacienne," pp. 448–49.

92. On this incident, see Hoche, *Strassburg und seine Universität*, p. 64. On the Francophile students generally in this period, see ibid., pp. 64–65; Haug, "Les étudiants alsaciens," p. 28; and Kühn, *Briefe von Elsass-Lothringen*, pp. 85–86.

93. Moerlen and Bechelen, *La lutte de la jeunesse estudiantine*, pp. 19–20.

94. Pinner, "Western European Student Movements," p. 63. Also see Max Weber, *Gesammelte Aufsätze*, p. 390n.

95. Haug, "Les étudiants alsaciens," pp. 27–28; "Die politische Bedeutung der Strassburger Universität."

96. Fritsch, "Le monôme des étudiants alsaciens-lorrains," pp. 29–30; Haug, "Les étudiants alsaciens," p. 28; Moerlen and Bechelen, *La lutte de la jeunesse estudiantine*, p. 13.

97. Fritsch, "Le monôme des étudiants alsaciens-lorrains," p. 29; Haug, "Les étudiants alsaciens," p. 28; Robert Redslob, *Entre la France et l'Allemagne*, p. 24.

98. See, for instance, *The Scotsman* (Edinburgh) as quoted in *Academische Revue*, 1 (1895): 489; Ludwig Robert Müller, *Lebenserinnerungen*, p. 31; and *Schwäbischer Merkur* (Stuttgart), 14 Dec. 1896.

99. Johannes Höffel in Germany, Reichstag, *Stenographische Berichte*, 9th leg. period, 4th sess., 6 (1897): 4209; Otto Mayer, *Die Kaiser-Wilhelms-Universität*, p. 83; Moerlen and Bechelen, *La lutte de la jeunesse estudiantine*, p. 17; Edmond Redslob, *D'un régime à un autre*, pp. 7–8.

100. Otto Mayer, *Die Kaiser-Wilhelms-Universität*, pp. 83–84; *Schwäbischer Merkur* (Stuttgart), 14 Dec. 1896.

101. The petition was signed by thirty-five students of law, eighty students of medicine, twenty students of pharmacy, and nine students from the Faculties of Philosophy and the Sciences; see *Express* (Mulhouse), 23 Dec. 1896; and Adolf Michaelis, "Die Kaiser Wilhelms-Universität Strassburg." On the preparation of the petition, see Halley in Germany, Reichstag, *Stenographische Berichte*, 9th leg. period, 4th sess., 6 (1897): 4208; and Otto Mayer, *Die Kaiser-Wilhelms-Universität*, pp. 84–85.

102. Minutes of the Academic Senate, 16 and 19 Dec. 1896, ADBR: AL 103, no. 97; Otto Mayer, *Die Kaiser-Wilhelms-Universität*, p. 85.

103. Moerlen and Bechelen, *La lutte de la jeunesse estudiantine*, p. 18.

104. Quoted in Halley in Germany, Reichstag, *Stenographische Berichte*, 9th leg. period, 4th sess., 6 (1897): 4208.

105. Minutes of the Academic Senate, 8 Jan. 1897, ADBR: AL 103, no. 97; Otto Mayer, *Die Kaiser-Wilhelms-Universität*, pp. 86–87; Moerlen and Bechelen, *La lutte de la jeunesse estudiantine*, p. 19.

106. *Der Elsässer* (Strasbourg), 23 Dec. 1896, with quotation from *Express* (Mulhouse).

107. See Ernst Lieber in Germany, Reichstag, *Stenographische Berichte*, 9th leg. period, 4th sess., 6 (1897): 4207; and Moerlen and Bechelen, *La lutte de la jeunesse estudiantine*, p. 18.

108. *Soleil* (Paris) quoted in *L'Impartial de l'Est* (Nancy), 31. Dec. 1896.

109. *Deutsche Zeitung* (Heidelberg) quoted in *Strassburger Post*, 24 Dec. 1896.

110. Lieber in Germany, Reichstag, *Stenographische Berichte*, 9th leg. period, 4th sess., 6 (1897): 4207–8.

111. Halley in ibid., p. 4208.

112. Hamm in Alsace-Lorraine, Landesausschuss, *Verhandlungen*, 24th sess. (1897), 2:304.

113. The first public assertion that the establishment of the university had been a mistake apparently dates from the early 1890s; see Kühn, *Briefe von Elsass-Lothringen*, pp. 85–87. On the prevalence of this opinion among the university's German critics, see Ludwig Dehio, "Die Kaiser-Wilhelms-Universität Strassburg," p. 19; Hohenlohe, *Aus meinem Leben*, pp. 206–7; Nöldeke, *Jugend-Erinnerungen*, pp. 40–41; and W. R., "Das Deutschtum in Elsass-Lothringen," p. 3.

114. Alsace-Lorraine, Statistisches Bureau, *Statistisches Handbuch*, pp. 468–69.

115. Lieber in Germany, Reichstag, *Stenographische Berichte*, 9th leg. period, 4th sess., 6 (1897): 4210. Also see "Die politische Bedeutung der Strassburger Universität"; and Schmoller, "Die Bedeutung der Strassburger Universität," pp. 199–200.

116. *Münchener Neueste Nachrichten*, 31 Mar. 1897.

117. Schmoller, "Die Bedeutung der Strassburger Universität," p. 202. The article was published anonymously.

118. "Die politische Bedeutung der Strassburger Universität."

119. The Prussian minister of culture, Robert Bosse, was Althoff's immediate superior. Congratulatory messages also came from Bismarck and Roggenbach; see University of Strasbourg, *Das Stiftungsfest*, 1897, pp. 5–6, 43–44.

120. Prince Hermann zu Hohenlohe-Langenburg as quoted in ibid., pp. 3–4.

121. Windelband, "Rektoratsrede," pp. 48–49.

122. Ibid., pp. 46–47. Similar opinions were expressed by another Strasbourg professor in a two-part article published a few days before the ceremonies; see Adolf Michaelis, "Die Kaiser Wilhelms-Universität."

123. See Gustav Anrich, "Ehemalige Kaiser-Wilhelms-Universität Strassburg," p. 381; Ropp, "Konrad Varrentrapp," p. 349; and Eduard Schwartz, "Die Kaiser-Wilhelms-Universität Strassburg," pp. 11–12.

## Chapter 5

1. See Rossé et al., eds., *Das Elsass von 1870–1932*, 1:89–93, 103–22; and Schwander and Jaffé, "Die reichsländischen Regierungen und die Verfassung," pp. 51–56.

2. Ernst Matthias von Köller in interview with the *Lokalanzeiger* (Strasbourg), n.d. (late 1901), as quoted in Rossé et al., eds., *Das Elsass von 1870–1932*, 2:150. On the Statthalter's preoccupation with hunting, see Naunyn, *Erinnerungen*, p. 417.

3. Quoted by Eugène Muller in Alsace-Lorraine, Landtag: Zweite Kammer, *Verhandlungen*, 1st sess. (1911–13), 91:3835.

4. Ludwig Dehio, "Die Kaiser-Wilhelms-Universität Strassburg," p. 22; Favrot, *Le gouvernement allemand et le clergé catholique lorrain*, pp. 200, 203, 209; Hauviller, *Franz Xaver Kraus*, p. 61; Hohenlohe-Schillingsfürst, *Memoirs*, 2:391, 467; Rossé et al., eds., *Das Elsass von 1870–1932*, 3:450–52; Sachse, "Die Kirchenpolitik," p. 167.

5. Ludwig Dehio, "Die Kaiser-Wilhelms-Universität Strassburg," p. 22; Franz Xaver Kraus, "Denkschrift," quoted in Hauviller, *Franz Xaver Kraus*, p. 139; Heuss-Knapp, *Ausblick vom Münsterturm*, p. 54; Rossé et al., eds., *Das Elsass von 1870–1932*, 3:445–47. German did not replace French as the language of instruction at the seminary in Strasbourg until 1888, and never did at the seminary in Metz; see Zemb, *Témoin de son temps*, p. 41.

6. Jules Leyder to Albert Houtin, 22 Nov. 1899, PAH: 15717; Berger, *Pascal David*, p. 109; Brandl, *Zwischen Inn und Themse*, p. 233; Rossé et al., eds., *Das Elsass von 1870–1932*, 3:453; Zemb, *Témoin de son temps*, pp. 47–50.

7. Jules Leyder to Albert Houtin, 25 Mar. 1900, PAH: 15717. Also see Leyder to Houtin, 21 Nov. 1900, ibid.; "Einige Zustände in Elsass-Lothringen"; Favrot, *Le gouvernement*

*allemand et le clergé catholique lorrain,* pp. 200–209; and Rossé et al., eds., *Das Elsass von 1870–1932,* 3:453.

8. Hertling, *Erinnerungen,* 2:205; Sachse, *Friedrich Althoff,* pp. 131–32.

9. Bachem, *Zentrumspartei,* 3:304, 4:73–76, 240, 5:245; Hertling, *Erinnerungen,* 2:17–18, 151–52, 205–8; Horstmann, *Katholizismus und moderne Welt,* pp. 90–114; Sachse, *Friedrich Althoff,* pp. 125–27; Christoph Weber, *Der "Fall Spahn,"* pp. 41–54.

10. See Craig, "A Mission for German Learning," pp. 541–57; Favrot, *Le gouvernement allemand et le clergé catholique lorrain,* pp. 209–13; Hertling, *Erinnerungen,* 2:210–53; and Christoph Weber, *Der "Fall Spahn,"* pp. 62–70.

11. Below to Hohenlohe-Schillingsfürst, 16 Nov. 1898, and Rotenhan to Hohenlohe-Schillingsfürst, 14 Dec. 1899, MAE: 34/366–71, 647–50.

12. Hertling to Halley, 28 Nov. 1899; Hertling to Hohenlohe-Schillingsfürst, 9 Dec. 1899; and Rotenhan to Hohenlohe-Schillingsfürst, 29 Nov. and 11 and 14 Dec. 1899, MAE: 34/586–92, 637–38, 622, 639–41, and 647–50; and Hertling, *Erinnerungen,* 2:253.

13. *Arbeiterfreund* (Strasbourg), n.d., quoted in Hertling, *Erinnerungen,* 2:261.

14. *Elsässische Volksbote* (Strasbourg), 17 Jan. 1900, quoted in Hertling, *Erinnerungen,* 2:260.

15. Fritzen to Rampolla, 24 Jan. 1900, MAE: 34/764–67.

16. Quoted in Favrot, *Le gouvernement allemand et le clergé catholique lorrain,* p. 206. Also see Jules Leyder to Albert Houtin, 25 Mar. 1900, PAH: 15717; Hertling, *Erinnerungen,* 2:260–61; Rossé et al., eds., *Das Elsass von 1870–1932,* 3:452–53; and Sachse, *Friedrich Althoff,* p. 134.

17. On the defensiveness of Alsatian Protestants in the 1890s in the face of Catholic efforts to improve their position in Alsatian society generally and in the educational system particularly, see Rossé et al., eds., *Das Elsass von 1870–1932,* 3:109.

18. See Manegold, *Universität, Technische Hochschule und Industrie,* pp. 103–10.

19. "Memorandum über der Errichtung einer sechsten technischen Fakultät an der Kaiser Wilhelms-Universität zu Strassburg," Dec. 1899 and 16 Jan. 1900, ADBR: AL 103, no. 931. Also see Ferdinand Braun to Otto Back, 21 Mar. 1899, AACVS: B, 270/1489; Ziegler to Hohenlohe-Langenburg, 21 Jan. 1900, ADBR: AL 27, paq. 126; and Manegold, *Universität, Technische Hochschule und Industrie,* pp. 195–97. A copy of the revised version of the memorandum was sent to Felix Klein; see NFK: VI E. On Ziegler as a leader of the *Kulturkämpfer* on the Strasbourg faculty, see Paul Maria Baumgarten, *Römische und andere Erinnerungen,* p. 37.

20. "Memorandum über die Errichtung einer sechsten technischen Fakultät an der Kaiser Wilhelms-Universität zu Strassburg," Dec. 1899 and 16 Jan. 1900, ADBR: AL 103, no. 931.

21. Ibid.

22. Ibid.

23. Ibid.

24. Ibid.

25. Craig, "A Mission for German Learning," pp. 561–66; Favrot, *Le gouvernement allemand et le clergé catholique lorrain,* pp. 214–16; and Hertling, *Erinnerungen,* 2:262–69.

26. Craig, "A Mission for German Learning," pp. 566–73; Favrot, *Le gouvernement allemand et le clergé catholique lorrain,* pp. 217–18; and Hertling, *Erinnerungen,* 2:275–76.

27. For a copy of the letter sent to each of the thirty-three scholars, see MAE: 35/509.

28. See Prussian Foreign Office to Studt, 19 July 1901 and n.d.; and Studt to Bülow, 8 Aug. 1901, MAE: 35/495–507, 521; Bornhak, "Die Begründung der katholisch-theologischen Fakultät," p. 253; and Kraus, *Tagebücher,* p. 754.

29. See unsigned memorandum, 5 Sept. 1901, and Richthofen to Bülow, 6 Sept. 1901, MAE: 35/539–43 and 546–47.

30. Landolin Winterer in Alsace-Lorraine, Landesausschuss, *Verhandlungen*, 21st sess. (1894), 2:257–58, and 24th sess. (1897), 2:309; and Ignaz Spies in ibid., 23d sess. (1896), 2:148, and 25th sess. (1898), 2a:42.

31. See Puttkamer in ibid., 21st sess. (1894), 2:258, and 23d sess. (1896), 2:149; and Hamm in ibid., 23d sess. (1896), 2:151–52.

32. See Heinrich Finke to Aloys Schulte, 22 June 1899, in Braubach, "Zwei deutsche Historiker aus Westfalen," p. 31; and Martin Spahn to Friedrich Schneider, 8 Nov. 1898 and 22 July 1899, quoted in Georg May, "Die Errichtung von zwei mit Katholiken zu besetzenden Professuren," p. 276.

33. Studt to Hohenlohe-Schillingsfürst, 5 Feb. 1900, MAE: 34/752–60.

34. Hohenlohe-Langenburg to Bülow, 28 Feb. 1901, and Bülow to Hohenlohe-Langenburg, 9 Mar. 1901, MAE: 35/327–28, 347; Hohenlohe-Langenburg to the emperor, Mar. 1901, and the emperor to Hohenlohe-Langenburg, n.d., ADBR: AL 103, no. 863; Hohenlohe-Langenburg to the emperor, 28 Sept. 1901, Morsey, "Zwei Denkschriften," p. 247; Sachse, *Friedrich Althoff*, p. 136.

35. Althoff to Halley, 3 July 1901, ADBR: AL 103, no. 863; Hohenlohe-Langenburg to the emperor, 28 Sept. 1901, Morsey, "Zwei Denkschriften," pp. 248–49; Sachse, *Friedrich Althoff*, pp. 136–37.

36. Althoff to Halley, 3 July 1901, ADBR: AL 103, no. 863. The two potential candidates mentioned by Althoff were Erich Marcks, an *Ordinarius* at Heidelberg, and Otto Hintze, an *Extraordinarius* at Berlin.

37. Theodor Nöldeke to Hohenlohe-Langenburg, 13 July 1901, ADBR: AL 103, no. 863. Suspecting that Varrentrapp would accept the call to Marburg, the faculty had contacted at least one of its candidates, Marcks, as early as mid-June; see Marcks to Harry Bresslau, 17 June 1901, Paul Hirsch, ed., "Briefe namhafter Historiker," pp. 230–31.

38. See Karl J. Neumann to Meinecke, 18 Aug. 1901, NFM: 30; Harry Bresslau to Meinecke, 26 Aug. 1901, NFM: 5; Conrad Varrentrapp to Theodor Nöldeke, 28 Aug. 1901, and Neumann to Nöldeke, 4 Sept. 1901, BTN: A 284; and Bresslau, "Bericht über eine Unterredung mit dem Herrn Curator," 23 Nov. 1901, ADBR: AL 62, paq. 22. At least since mid-1899 the Strasbourg professors had suspected that the government might attempt to establish positions at their university for a Catholic historian and a Catholic philosopher; see Heinrich Finke to Aloys Schulte, 22 June 1899, in Braubach, "Zwei deutsche Historiker aus Westfalen," p. 31.

39. Hamm to Maximilian von Puttkamer, 19 July 1901, ADBR: AL 103, no. 863. Apparently this was not the first time Althoff had tried to find a university chair for Meinecke; see Meinecke, *Erlebtes 1862–1901*, p. 224.

40. Although Althoff's biographer claims otherwise (Sachse, *Friedrich Althoff*, p. 129), it is unlikely Althoff would have favored Spahn had it not been for his father's position and prominence; see Bornhak, "Die Begründung der katholisch-theologischen Fakultät," p. 251. As early as June 1898 Althoff had intentions of procuring a position in Strasbourg for Spahn (as an *Extraordinarius*); see Brocke, "Hochschul- und Wissenschaftspolitik," pp. 103–4.

41. Hamm to Puttkamer, 19 July 1901, ADBR: AL 103, no. 863. On Spahn's political opinions and activities, see Walter Ferber, "Der Weg Martin Spahns," pp. 218–29.

42. Hamm to Puttkamer, 19 July 1901, ADBR: AL 103, no. 863.

43. See Liebenstein to Puttkamer, 28 July 1901, and Hamm to Liebenstein, 29 July 1901, ibid.

44. See Hamm to Schaefer, 5 Aug. 1901; Schaefer to Hamm, 6 and 16 Aug. 1901; Hamm to the Faculty of Philosophy, 19 Aug. 1901; Hamm to Meinecke, 19 Aug. 1901; Hamm to Spahn, 19 Aug. 1901; Meinecke to Hamm, 22 Aug. 1901; and Spahn to Hamm, 24 Aug. 1901, ibid.; Schaefer to Harry Bresslau, 25 Aug. 1901, NHB: I; Braubach, "Aloys Schulte," pp. 98–99; and Schaefer, *Mein Leben*, p. 136. Spahn had long hoped for a position at the University of Strasbourg, thinking this would be a useful and exciting place for a "Ger-

manophile Catholic''; see Spahn to Friedrich Schneider, 8 Nov. 1898, quoted in Georg May, "Die Errichtung von zwei mit Katholiken zu besetzenden Professuren," p. 276.

45. Hamm to Puttkamer, 19 July 1901, ADBR: AL 103, no. 863.

46. Nöldeke to Hamm, 29 Aug. 1901, ibid.

47. Ibid.; Bresslau to Meinecke, 26 Aug. 1901, NFM: 5; Nöldeke to Theodor Mommsen, 26 Nov. 1901, BTN: A 284; Adolf Michaelis, "Das Verhalten der Strassburger philosophische Fakultät," pp. 225–31.

48. Bresslau to Nöldeke, 5 Sept. 1901, BTN: A 284; Nöldeke to Spahn, 9 Sept. 1901, ADBR: AL 62, paq. 22; petition of Faculty of Philosophy to the emperor, 9 Sept. 1901, ADBR: AL 103, no. 863; Bresslau to Meinecke, 10 Sept. 1901, NFM: 5; and Nöldeke to Theodor Mommsen, 26 Nov. 1901, BTN: A 284.

49. Hohenlohe-Langenburg to the emperor, 28 Sept. 1901, Morsey, "Zwei Denkschriften," p. 249. For the text of the full document, see ibid., pp. 246–49.

50. For the text of Althoff's memorandum, which was prepared for the Statthalter, see ibid., pp. 250–57. On Althoff's meeting with the emperor, see Sachse, *Friedrich Althoff*, p. 137.

51. Althoff to Hohenlohe-Langenburg, 15 Oct. 1901, Morsey, "Zwei Denkschriften," pp. 250–51.

52. Ibid., p. 251.

53. Ibid., p. 256.

54. See Sachse, *Friedrich Althoff*, p. 137; the emperor to Hohenlohe-Langenburg, 16 Oct. 1901, quoted in *Strassburger Correspondenz*, 17 Oct. 1901; and Christoph Weber, *Der "Fall Spahn*," pp. 126–27.

55. *Kölnische Volkszeitung*, 9 Sept. 1901. Also see *Schulthess' Europäischer Geschichts-kalender*, 42 (1901): 145.

56. *Allgemeine Zeitung* (Munich), 24 Sept. 1901.

57. See Christoph Weber, *Der "Fall Spahn*," pp. 7–21, 82–148.

58. *Germania* (Berlin), quoted in *Strassburger Post*, 21 Oct. 1901.

59. *Der Elsässer* (Strasbourg), 24 Oct. 1901.

60. See ibid., 16 Oct. 1901.

61. On the reaction of the Catholic press to the emperor's telegram, see *Schulthess' Europäischer Geschichtskalender*, 42 (1901): 146; *Schwäbischer Merkur* (Stuttgart), quoted in *Strassburger Post*, 21 Oct. 1901; and, with specific reference to the Reichsland's Catholic press, Berger, *Die Ursachen des Zusammenbruches*, p. 14.

62. At least one prominent liberal newspaper, the *Berliner Tageblatt*, supported Spahn's appointment; see *Strassburger Post*, 21 Oct. 1901. For the political orientations of the various newspapers considered here, see Koszyk, *Deutsche Presse im 19. Jahrhundert*, pp. 127–209.

63. See [Delbrück], "Die katholische Geschichts-Professur in Strassburg," pp. 384–87; *Geschichte der Frankfurter Zeitung*, p. 827; *Hamburger Nachrichten*, 10 Sept. 1901; Mommsen, "Universitätsunterricht und Konfession," pp. 28–29; Althoff to Hohenlohe-Langenburg, 15 Oct. 1901, Morsey, "Zwei Denkschriften," p. 256; and *Schwäbischer Merkur* (Stuttgart), quoted in *Strassburger Post*, 21 Oct. 1901.

64. Keyssner to Brentano, 24 Oct. 1901, Rossmann, *Wissenschaft, Ethik und Politik*, p. 142.

65. Brentano to Mommsen, 27 Oct. 1901, ibid., p. 23. Also see Brentano, *Mein Leben*, pp. 219–21.

66. Mommsen to Brentano, 30 Oct. 1901, Rossmann, *Wissenschaft, Ethik und Politik*, pp. 23–24.

67. See Mommsen to Brentano, 30 Oct., and 2, 6, 9, and 12 Nov. 1901, ibid., pp. 23–28.

68. Mommsen, "Universitätsunterricht und Konfession," pp. 28–29.

69. Ibid., pp. 29–30.

70. See, for example, Brentano to Paul von Groth, 12 Nov. 1901, NPG: X; Brentano to Paul Natorp, 10, 15, and 29 Nov. 1901, NPN; and Brentano to Hermann Paul, 13 Nov. 1901, NHP. The open letter from the professors of the University of Munich and Munich's Technische Hochschule first appeared, as the lead item, in *Münchener Neueste Nachrichten,* 17 Nov. 1901.

71. For the petitions and the names of those who signed, see *Frankfurter Zeitung,* 18 Nov.–18 Dec. 1901; *Tägliche Rundschau* (Berlin), 18 Nov.–18 Dec. 1901; and *Vossische Zeitung* (Berlin), 18 Nov.–18 Dec. 1901.

72. For the text, see "Die Universität Strassburg, Mommsen und Spahn," *Frankfurter Zeitung,* 3 Dec. 1901. Meinecke would have signed the petition had his appointment not been associated with Spahn's; see Meinecke to Harry Bresslau, 29 Aug. 1901, Paul Hirsch, ed., "Briefe namhafter Historiker," p. 236; and Meinecke to Georg von Below, 9 Dec. 1901, Meinecke, *Ausgewählter Briefwechsel,* p. 27.

73. Determined by comparing the names of those who signed with the names of all *Ordinarien* teaching at German universities in the winter semester of 1901–2. For the former, see note 71 above; for the latter, see *Minerva,* 9 (1901–2).

74. Mommsen to Brentano, 16 Nov. 1901, Rossmann, *Wissenschaft, Ethik und Politik,* pp. 37–38. Also see Mommsen to Brentano, 30 Oct., 6 and 12 Nov., and 1 Dec. 1901, ibid., pp. 23–28, 37, 40–41.

75. Mommsen to Brentano, 17 Dec. 1901, ibid., p. 44. Also see Mommsen to Brentano, 26 Nov. 1901, ibid., p. 38.

76. Paul Natorp to Brentano, 27 Nov. 1901, ibid., pp. 148–49. Also see Max Lenz to Paul Natorp, 16 Nov. 1901, NPN; and Franz Richarz to Halley, n.d., quoted in Sachse, *Friedrich Althoff,* p. 142.

77. Harnack to the editor, 28 Nov. 1901, *National-Zeitung* (Berlin), 29 Nov. 1901, in Rossmann, *Wissenschaft, Ethik und Politik,* p. 154. Also see Harnack to Gustav Krueger, 9 Dec. 1901, in Zahn-Harnack, *Adolf von Harnack,* pp. 303–5. Another Berlin professor, the historian Hans Delbrück, had argued similarly in an article published in October; see [Delbrück], "Die katholische Geschichts-Professur in Strassburg," pp. 385–86.

78. Harnack to the editor, 28 Nov. 1901, *National-Zeitung* (Berlin), 29 Nov. 1901, in Rossmann, *Wissenschaft, Ethik und Politik,* p. 154.

79. Adolf Michaelis, "Das Verhalten der Strassburger philosophische Fakultät," p. 225. On Michaelis's position of leadership in this faculty, see Keil, "Nachruf für der philosophische Fakultät," pp. 17–18; Meinecke to Siegfried Kaehler, 9 Jan. 1929, Meinecke, *Ausgewählter Briefwechsel,* p. 341; and Meinecke, *Strassburg/Freiburg/Berlin,* p. 36.

80. Adolf Michaelis, "Das Verhalten der Strassburger philosophischen Fakultät," pp. 227, 230–31. In a postscript Michaelis pointed out that Mommsen's manifesto had not come to his attention until after he had completed his article; ibid., p. 231.

81. Ibid., pp. 227–28.

82. Mommsen to Brentano, 23 Nov. 1901, in Rossmann, *Wissenschaft, Ethik und Politik,* p. 37. Also see Mommsen to Nöldeke, 24 Nov. 1901, BTN: A 284; and Mommsen to Althoff, 25 Nov. 1901, in Wickert, *Theodor Mommsen,* 4:304–5.

83. See Sachse, *Friedrich Althoff,* pp. 143–44; and Mommsen to Brentano, 26 and 29 Nov., and 1, 13, 14, and 17 Dec. 1901, and Natorp to Brentano, 27 Nov. 1901, in Rossmann, *Wissenschaft, Ethik und Politik,* pp. 37–41, 43–44, and 148–49.

84. Harnack to the editor, 28 Nov. 1901, *National-Zeitung* (Berlin), 29 Nov. 1901, in Rossmann, *Wissenschaft, Ethik und Politik,* pp. 154–55.

85. See Wilhelm Foerster, "Zur Anklage gegen die preussischen Universitätszustände," pp. 289–93; and Paul Kehr, "Zur Abwehr," pp. 321–26. For evidence that Althoff worked actively behind the scenes to promote this campaign in his own defense, see Althoff to Gustav Schmoller, 25, 26, and 27 Dec. 1901, GST: 45; Bornhak, "Die Begründung der

katholisch-theologischen Fakultät," pp. 251–52; and Mommsen to Althoff, 30 Dec. 1901, in Wickert, *Theodor Mommsen*, 4:306.

86. Schmoller, "Zwei Reden," p. 112. Also see Otto Hintze to Meinecke, 21 Jan. 1902, NFM: 15; and Sachse, *Friedrich Althoff*, pp. 144–47.

87. See Mommsen to Brentano, 26 Nov. and 1 Dec. 1901, and Natorp to Brentano, 27 Nov. 1901, in Rossmann, *Wissenschaft, Ethik und Politik*, pp. 37–38, 40–41, and 148–49.

88. Quoted in Althoff, *Aus Friedrich Althoffs Berliner Zeit*, p. 14. Also see Althoff to Richard Schröder, 15 Dec. 1901, in ibid., p. 35; Paul Ehrlich to Althoff, 5 Dec. 1901, and Althoff to Rudolf Virchow, 25 Dec. 1901, TFA: 1; and Bornhak, "Die Begründung der katholisch-theologischen Fakultät," pp. 51–52.

89. Minutes of the Academic Senate, 25 Nov. 1901, ADBR: AL 103, no. 100; Jules Leyder to Albert Houtin, 11 Jan. 1902, PAH: 15717; Eduard Schwartz to Harry Bresslau, 28 Jan. 1903, NHB: I; *Frankfurter Zeitung*, 3 Jan. 1902; *Hochschul-Nachrichten*, 12 (1901): 63–64; Meinecke to Conrad Varrentrapp, 21 Dec. 1901, Meinecke, *Ausgewählter Briefwechsel*, p. 27; "Politische Notizen: Strassburg." For evidence that the government intended to establish at least one of these chairs, the one for a Catholic philosopher, see Hamm to Hohenlohe-Langenburg, 26 Nov. 1901, ADBR: AL 103, no. 264; and Christoph Weber, *Der "Fall Spahn,"* pp. 124–25.

90. Unsigned note dated 8 Feb. 1902, MAE: 35/830–32. For an analysis of the arguments advanced by the canvassed scholars, see Conrad Bornhak, "Die Gutachten über der Plan der Errichtung einer katholisch-theologischen Fakultät an der Universität Strassburg," MAE: 35/784–828.

91. Craig, "A Mission for German Learning," pp. 635–39; and Hertling, *Erinnerungen*, 2:288–89.

92. Craig, "A Mission for German Learning," pp. 639–41; and Hertling, *Erinnerungen*, 2:294. On the anticlerical policies of the Waldeck-Rousseau and Combes ministries and their effects on the Vatican's relations with France, see Partin, *Waldeck-Rousseau, Combes, and the Church*. On the Vatican's generally favorable reaction to Spahn's appointment, see Rotenhan to Bülow, 24 Oct., 10 and 21 Nov., and 8 Dec. 1901, and Zorn von Bulach to Hohenlohe-Langenburg [?], 7 Nov. 1901, MAE: 35/703–7, 713–16, 731–37, 744–46, and 725–30; and Pastor, *Tagebücher-Briefe-Erinnerungen*, pp. 364–66.

93. "Note explicative," MAE: 36/545–49.

94. Prussian Foreign Office to Rotenhan, 26 Nov. 1902, and Rotenhan to the Prussian Foreign Office, 5 Dec. 1902, MAE: 36/560–62 and 574–75; and Hertling, *Erinnerungen*, 2:299–300, 303.

95. Hohenlohe-Langenburg to the Prussian Foreign Office, 19 Dec. 1902, MAE: 36/645–48. Before conferring with Bishop Fritzen the Statthalter had requested and received recommendations for appointments from Hertling and various government officials; see Hertling, *Erinnerungen*, 2:302–3; and Rossé et al., eds., *Das Elsass von 1870–1932*, 3:455.

96. On the eight theologians called in 1902–3, see Meinertz, *Begegnungen in meinem Leben*, pp. 17–25; Rossé et al., eds., *Das Elsass von 1870–1932*, 3:455–58; Vogel, "La faculté de théologie catholique," pp. 252–63; Zemb, *Témoin de son temps*, pp. 32–51; and, with specific reference to the controversial appointment of Ehrhard, Ehrhard to Eugène Muller, 19, 22, and 30 Nov. and 10, 11, 12, and 20 Dec. 1902, NAE; Dachs, "Albert Ehrhard," pp. 217–26; Dempf, *Albert Ehrhard*, pp. 111–27; and Pastor, *Tagebücher-Briefe-Erinnerungen*, pp. 396–99.

97. Hohenlohe-Langenburg to the Prussian Foreign Office, 19 Dec. 1902, MAE: 36/645–48; minutes of the Academic Senate, 19 Oct. 1903, ADBR: AL 103, no. 104; Otto Mayer, *Die Kaiser-Wilhelms-Universität*, p. 103; *Schulthess' Europäischer Geschichtskalender*, 44 (1903): 93; and Zemb, *Témoin de son temps*, p. 51.

98. Hertling to Bülow, 22 June 1902; Althoff to Bülow, 15 Sept. 1904; Bülow to Studt, n.d., MAE: 36/184–201, and 724–26; Jules Leyder to Albert Houtin, 25 Dec. 1902, PAH:

15717; Landolin Winterer in Alsace-Lorraine, Landesausschuss, *Verhandlungen*, 30th sess. (1903), 2:28–29; Favrot, *Le gouvernement allemand et le clergé catholique lorrain*, pp. 221–23; and Sachse, *Friedrich Althoff*, p. 141.

99. See Nicholas Delsor in Germany, Reichstag, *Stenographische Berichte*, 10th leg. period, 2d sess., 9 (1903): 8454. For claims that the faculty would contribute significantly to the Germanization of the Reichsland, see Halley in ibid., pp. 8444–45; and Schiemann, "Die katholisch-theologische Fakultät," pp. 738–39.

100. Schrader in Germany, Reichstag, *Stenographische Berichte*, 10th leg. period, 2d sess., 9 (1903): 8449.

101. See Heuss-Knapp, *Ausblick vom Münsterturm*, p. 55; Kapp, "Die Kaiser Wilhelms-Universität Strassburg: Ein Erinnerungswort," p. 34; Leumann, *Religion und Universität*, p. 27; Otto Mayer, *Die Kaiser-Wilhelms-Universität*, pp. 102–3; and Meinecke, *Strassburg/Freiburg/Berlin*, p. 11.

102. Speech by Harry Bresslau at a meeting of the Reichsland's Liberale Landespartei, 24 Jan. 1906, quoted by Adolf Goetz in Alsace-Lorraine, Landesausschuss, *Verhandlungen*, 33d sess. (1906), 2a:263.

103. See Ficker, *Die Kaiser-Wilhelms-Universität Strassburg*, pp. 14–15; Hoche, *Strassburg und seine Universität*, p. 76; Lenel, *Die Universität Strassburg*, pp. 18–19; "Die Universität Strassburg als Reichsinstitut"; and "Die Universität Strassburg im Landesausschuss."

104. Ficker, *Die Kaiser-Wilhelms-Universität Strassburg*, pp. 14–15; W. Sch., "Um die Reichsuniversität."

105. See Meinecke, review of Alfred E. Hoche, *Jahresringe*, and of Elly Heuss-Knapp, *Ausblick vom Münsterturm*, p. 597.

106. *Hochschul-Nachrichten*, 10 (1900): 42.

107. Naunyn, *Erinnerungen*, pp. 494–95. That the professors' concern was well-founded is evident from a comparison of the increase in the university's budget between 1883–84 and 1903–4 with the increases in the same period in the budgets of fourteen other German universities. (For the five remaining universities—Erlangen, Jena, Munich, Rostock, Würzburg—the relevant figures have not been found.) Even though the University of Strasbourg had added a faculty in the interim, its budget had grown at the slowest rate, while the average rate of increase at the fourteen other universities (85 percent) was more than three times the rate of increase at the Alsatian institution (27 percent). See Adolf Goetz in Alsace-Lorraine, Landesausschuss, *Verhandlungen*, 33d sess. (1906), 2a:264.

108. See Ernst Anrich, "Geschichte der deutschen Universität Strassburg," p. 135; Kapp, "Die Kaiser Wilhelms-Universität Strassburg: Ein Erinnerungswort," p. 33; Naunyn, *Erinnerungen*, pp. 473–75; and Eduard Schwartz, "Die Kaiser-Wilhelms-Universität Strassburg," pp. 11–12.

109. Wilamowitz-Möllendorff to Schwartz, 26 Nov. and 10 Dec. (two letters) 1901, and Schwartz to Wilamowitz-Möllendorff, 11 Dec. 1901, NES: IIA; Schwartz to Nöldeke (?), 24 Dec. 1901, ADBR: AL 62, paq. 22; Meinecke, *Strassburg/Freiburg/Berlin*, p. 35; and Gustav Schwartz, *Alles ist Übergang zur Heimat hin*, pp. 17–20.

110. See Hohenlohe-Langenburg to the emperor, 28 Sept. 1901, Morsey, "Zwei Denkschriften," pp. 247–48.

111. See Emile Wetterlé in Alsace-Lorraine, Landesausschuss, *Verhandlungen*, 29th sess. (1902), 2:21; Eugen Ricklin in ibid., p. 29; and Berger, *Die Ursachen des Zusammenbruches*, p. 14. The government was also praised in the Reichstag by a leader of the Center and by the anti-Semitic pastor Adolf Stoecker; see Carl Bachem in Germany, Reichstag, *Stenographische Berichte*, 10th leg. period, 2d sess., 4 (1902): 3297–3301, and Stoecker in ibid., p. 3335. Stoecker was not the only prominent anti-Semite to defend Spahn's appointment; see Chamberlain, "Der voraussetzungslose Mommsen."

112. See Ernst Matthias von Köller in Alsace-Lorraine, Landesausschuss, *Verhandlungen,* 29th sess. (1902), 2:21. Also see Friedrich Spitta (the rector) to the Academic Senate, 11 Nov. 1901, ADBR: AL 103, no. 237; and Köller in Germany, Reichstag, *Stenographische Berichte,* 10th leg. period, 2d sess., 4 (1902): 3297.

113. Meinecke to Conrad Varrentrapp, 21 Dec. 1901, Meinecke, *Ausgewählter Briefwechsel,* p. 27. Also see Wilhelm Windelband to Kuno Fischer, 2 Nov. 1901, NKF.

114. Wilhelm Windelband to Kuno Fischer, 30 Dec. 1902, NKF. Also see Hamm to Hohenlohe-Langenburg, 26 Nov. 1902, ADBR: AL 103, no. 264; terms of Baeumker's contract, ADBR: AL 103, no. 301; Eduard Schwartz to Harry Bresslau, 28 Jan. 1903, NHB: I; Baeumker, "Clemens Baeumker," pp. 14–15; Rickert, "Wilhelm Windelband," pp. 5–6, 25–26, 32–33; and "Strassburger Universitätsfragen."

115. Heuss-Knapp, *Ausblick vom Münsterturm,* p. 50.

116. Meinecke, *Strassburg/Freiburg/Berlin,* p. 56. Also see Meinecke to Harry Bresslau, 25 July and 22 Nov. 1906, NHB: I.

117. Meinecke to Walter Goetz, 16 Jan. 1906, NWG: 3.

118. Ibid.; Gustav Anrich, "Ehemalige Kaiser-Wilhelms-Universität Strassburg," p. 383; Ludwig Dehio, "Die Kaiser-Wilhelms-Universität Strassburg," p. 29; Heuss-Knapp, *Ausblick vom Münsterturm,* p. 50; Meinecke, *Strassburg/Freiburg/Berlin,* pp. 56–58; Meinecke, "Strassburger Erinnerungen," p. 285; Ruland, *Deutschtum und Franzosentum in Elsass-Lothringen,* p. 108.

119. *Hochschul-Nachrichten,* 13 (1903): 90.

120. "Die Universität Strassburg als Reichsinstitut."

121. *Norddeutsche Allgemeine Zeitung* (Berlin), n.d., as cited in *Hochschul-Nachrichten,* 16 (1906): 121.

## Chapter 6

1. The quotation is from Wedel to Wilhelm Rein, 18 Aug. 1911, Wedel, "Statthalter-Briefe," p. 303. Also see Schwander and Jaffé, "Die reichsländischen Regierungen und die Verfassung," pp. 67–76.

2. Schwander and Jaffé, "Die reichsländischen Regierungen und die Verfassung," pp. 76–79; Wehler, "Elsass-Lothringen von 1870 bis 1918," pp. 166–70; Zmarzlik, *Bethmann Hollweg,* pp. 92–103.

3. The quotation is from Wedel to Wilhelm Rein, 7 July 1912, Wedel, "Statthalter-Briefe," p. 459.

4. Rossé et al., eds., *Das Elsass von 1870–1932,* 1:133–35; Schwander and Jaffé, "Die reichsländischen Regierungen und die Verfassung," pp. 55–57, 67–79; Wehler, "Elsass-Lothringen von 1870 bis 1918," pp. 166–70; Zmarzlik, *Bethmann Hollweg,* pp. 92–103; and, for the text of the constitution, Huber, ed., *Dokumente zur deutschen Verfassungsgeschichte,* 2:355–58.

5. Wedel to Wilhelm Rein, 27 May 1912, Wedel, "Statthalter-Briefe," p. 305.

6. *Journal d'Alsace-Lorraine* (Strasbourg), 16 Jan. 1908.

7. Alsace-Lorraine, Landesausschuss, *Verhandlungen,* 35th sess. (1908), 1:148–51, and 2A:43, 224, 343, 357.

8. See *Minerva,* 17 (1907–8) and 23 (1913–14).

9. Eduard Schwartz, "Eduard Schwartz, wissenschaftlicher Lebenslauf," typescript dated 9 May 1932, Bayerische Staatsbibliothek (Munich), p. 8; Ludwig Dehio, "Die Kaiser-Wilhelms-Universität Strassburg," p. 29; Ficker, *Die Kaiser-Wilhelms-Universität Strassburg,* p. 15; Goetz, *Historiker in meiner Zeit,* p. 44; Otto Mayer, *Die Kaiser-Wilhelms-Universität,* pp. 105–6.

10. Legrand, "Zur elsässische Kulturfrage," p. 528.

11. Braun, "La littérature d'expression allemande et dialectale," pp. 377–78; Bronner, *Die Verfassungsbestrebungen des Landesausschusses,* pp. 207–8; Flake, "Elsässische Fragen," p. 1152.

12. Hallays, "Pierre Bucher," pp. 338–42; Herrenschmidt, *Mémoires pour la petite histoire,* pp. 94–97; Hilger, *Pierre Bucher;* Morrison, "The Intransigents"; Polaczek, "Eine elsässische Erinnerung"; [Wittich], "Pierre Bucher"; *Zehn Jahre Minenkrieg im Frieden,* pp. 20–28.

13. See Bresslau, "Harry Bresslau," p. 50; Mayeur, *Autonomie et politique en Alsace,* pp. 40–45; and Meinecke, *Strassburg/Freiburg/Berlin,* pp. 19–20.

14. Bronner, *Die Verfassungsbestrebungen des Landesausschusses,* pp. 108–9; Dallwitz, "Aus dem Nachlass," pp. 295–96; Rossé et al., eds., *Das Elsass von 1870–1932,* 1:129–31, 134, 144, 165, 172–73, and 3:62–65; Wehler, "Elsass-Lothringen von 1870 bis 1918," pp. 166–67; Zmarzlik, *Bethmann Hollweg,* pp. 91n, 97.

15. Joseph Pfleger in Alsace-Lorraine, Landtag: Zweite Kammer, *Verhandlungen,* 1st sess. (1911–13), 91:3827.

16. See Alsace-Lorraine, Landesausschuss, *Verhandlungen,* 36th sess. (1909), 3:302, and 38th sess. (1911), 2:334, 531; and Alsace-Lorraine, Landtag: Zweite Kammer, *Verhandlungen,* 1st sess. (1911–13), 91:3826–27, 3829–30, 3851, and 94:851.

17. See "Verzeichnis der in Elsass-Lothringen geborenen Dozenten der Universität (1911–12)," ADBR: AL 103, no. 140; and *Minerva,* 21 (1911–12): 1237–39.

18. Joseph Pfleger in Alsace-Lorraine, Landesausschuss, *Verhandlungen,* 38th sess. (1911), 2:328. Also see ibid., pp. 54, 331; and Alsace-Lorraine, Landtag: Zweite Kammer, *Verhandlungen,* 1st sess. (1911–13), 91:3287, and 94:852.

19. Alsace-Lorraine, Landesausschuss, *Verhandlungen,* 38th sess., (1911), 2:322–34.

20. Petition of the Academic Senate to the Statthalter, 27 May 1911, quoted in *Strassburger Correspondenz,* 9 June 1911 (emphasis in the original). Also see minutes of the Academic Senate, 3 May 1911, ADBR: AL 103, no. 112.

21. Wilhelm Nowack as quoted in Robert Redslob, *Alma mater,* p. 139. Also see Friedrich Spitta to Köller, 5 Mar. 1904, ADBR: AL 103, no. 257; and Strohl, *Le protestantisme en Alsace,* pp. 445, 449.

22. Robert Redslob, *Alma mater,* p. 108.

23. The faculty and ministry were particularly interested in Schneegans because, unlike most Alsatians teaching at German universities, he was openly Germanophile in sentiment. Schneegans turned down the position because he thought it would be extremely difficult for a Germanophile Alsatian to teach French literature in Strasbourg. Incidentally the Prussian authorities evidently shared the Alsatian ministry's belief that calling Schneegans to Strasbourg was desirable, for it made no attempt to keep him in Bonn. See Ernst Leumann to Stadler, 22 May 1909; Stadler to Ludwig Elster, 24 May 1909; Elster to Stadler, 1 and 23 June 1909; Stadler to Schneegans, 15 June 1909; and Schneegans to Stadler, 20 and 22 June 1909, ADBR: AL 103, no. 262; and Philipp August Becker, "Heinrich Schneegans," p. 613.

24. Petition of the Academic Senate to the Statthalter, 27 May 1911, quoted in *Strassburger Correspondenz,* 9 June 1911.

25. Harry Bresslau to ?, 8 May 1904, BNUS: Ms 4970. Also see Bresslau and Karl J. Neumann to Faculty of Philosophy, 7 Nov. 1901, and Theodor Nöldeke to Hohenlohe-Langenburg, 12 Nov. 1901, ADBR: AL 62, paq. 22; and Nöldeke to Hamm, 13 Nov. 1901 and 28 Jan. 1902; Hamm to Hohenlohe-Langenburg, 26 Nov. 1901 and 11 Sept. 1902; and Ernst Martin to Hohenlohe-Langenburg, 11 July 1902, ADBR: AL 103, no. 264.

26. See Jakob Preiss in Alsace-Lorraine, Landesausschuss, *Verhandlungen,* 38th sess. (1911), 2:331, 530–31; "Nationalistische Umtriebe"; and Robert Redslob, *Alma mater,* pp. 130–31.

27. Otto Back in Alsace-Lorraine, Landesausschuss, *Verhandlungen,* 38th sess. (1911), 2:334.

28. For evidence of the ministry's strong interest in bringing Schneegans to the university, see ibid., 37th sess. (1910), 3:161; and Stadler to Elster, 24 May 1909, ADBR: AL 103, no. 262.

29. Otto Back in Alsace-Lorraine, Landesausschuss, *Verhandlungen,* 38th sess. (1911), 2:333. Also see ibid., 3:197.

30. Otto Back in Alsace-Lorraine, Landtag: Zweite Kammer, *Verhandlungen,* 1st sess. (1911–13), 91:3843–44. Also see Stadler in Alsace-Lorraine, Landesausschuss, *Verhandlungen,* 36th sess. (1909), 2:162; and Kiener to Stadler, 11 May 1909, 11 Nov. 1909, and 3 July 1910, ADBR: AL 103, no. 487.

31. Otto Back as quoted in Robert Redslob, *Alma mater,* p. 147. Also see Redslob to Rudolf Schwander, 28 Oct. 1918, ADBR: AL 103, no. 254.

32. Wedel to Wilhelm Rein, 7 July 1912, Wedel, "Statthalter-Briefe," p. 459.

33. Ludwig Dehio, "Die Kaiser-Wilhelms-Universität Strassburg," pp. 27–28; Ficker, *Die Kaiser-Wilhelms-Universität Strassburg,* pp. 14–15; W. Sch., "Um die Reichsuniversität," p. 1; and, for representative assessments by students, Bergmann, *Rückschau,* pp. 95–98; Hal Downey to Henry C. Nachtrieb, 30 Oct. 1910, in Jones, "Hal Downey's Hematological Training," p. 181; Walter Flex to ?, n.d. [1908?], Flex, *Briefe,* pp. 21–22; and Isay, *Aus meinem Leben,* pp. 24–25.

34. See Hugo Haug to Henri Albert, 29 Mar. 1908, FHH: 13; Baensch, "Elsässisches Musikleben," pp. 399–400, 423; Flake, *Es wird Abend,* p. 68; Herrenschmidt, *Mémoires pour la petite histoire,* pp. 48–49, 119; Roth, *La Lorraine annexée,* pp. 448–49, 483–85; René Schickele to Hans Brandenburg, 9 Mar. 1903, and Schickele to Thomas Seltz, 25 June 1934, Schickele, *Werke,* 3:1140, 1200–1201; and Schmutz, *Alsace: Mythes et réalités,* pp. 24, 39.

35. Polizei-Präsident Dall to Hohenlohe-Langenburg, 14 Mar. 1900, ADBR: AL 27, no. 748; "Auszug aus dem Nachtwachtrapport," 16–17 Feb. 1905, ADBR: AL 103, no. 202; Kapp, "Die Kaiser Wilhelms-Universität Strassburg: Ein Erinnerungswort," p. 33; Emil Clemens Scherer, "Der elsässische Student," pp. 159–60.

36. See Polizei-Präsident Dall to Otto Pöhlmann, 23 May 1909, ADBR: AL 27, no. 748; *Echo du Cercle,* Mar. 1911, pp. 5–17; "Etudiants alsaciens-lorrains"; Moerlen and Bechelen, *La lutte de la jeunesse estudiantine,* pp. 23–32; J., "Bal," p. 14; and Morrison, "The Intransigents," pp. 222–27. On the Cercle's prominence as a stronghold of revanchism, see Bucher, "Discours," pp. 14–15.

37. Moerlen and Bechelen, *La lutte de la jeunesse estudiantine,* pp. 31–32.

38. See minutes of the Academic Senate, 15 Feb. 1909, ADBR: AL 103, no. 109; *Berliner Neueste Nachrichten,* 17 Jan. 1909; *Kölnische Zeitung,* 20 Jan. 1909; and *Journal d'Alsace-Lorraine* (Strasbourg), 21 Jan. 1909.

39. Hugo Haug to Henri Albert, 11 Mar. and 22 May 1906, FHH: 13; minutes of the Academic Senate, 26 Nov. 1906, ADBR: AL 103, no. 107; and Moerlen and Bechelen, *La lutte de la jeunesse estudiantine,* pp. 25–29.

40. [Munck], "Le bon sens commun," pp. 53–54.

41. Minutes of the Academic Senate, 23 May and 12 June 1911, ADBR: AL 103, no. 112; Henry, *Témoignage pour les alsaciens-lorrains,* p. 301; *Kölnische Zeitung,* 13 June 1911; Moerlen and Bechelen, *La lutte de la jeunesse estudiantine,* pp. 34–36; and *Strassburger Correspondenz,* 29 June 1911.

42. On the protests in France, see Henry, *Témoignage pour les alsaciens-lorrains,* pp. 304–40.

43. Pierre Bucher et al. to "Monsieur et cher camarade," June 1911, copy in ADBR: AL 105, no. 249; Moerlen and Bechelen, *La lutte de la jeunesse estudiantine,* p. 41; E. N., "Der Cercle und die Nationalisten," p. 12.

44. On the Club and its activities, see Chapellier to Comité du Cercle d'anciens étudiants alsaciens-lorrains, 10 Nov. 1911, FFD; Ch. Bouchholtz, "Der elsässische Student"; Liebert,

"Von der deutschen Universität Strassburg"; Moerlen and Bechelen, *La lutte de la jeunesse estudiantine*, pp. 41–43; Morrison, "The Intransigents," pp. 229–30 and 254n; d'Oux, "Der elsässische Student," pp. 257–58; and "Nationalistische Umtriebe." The maximum size of the Cercle and the Club has been determined from lists of members in ADBR: AL 105, no. 249.

45. "Noch einmal: Die Auflösung der Cercle." Also see "Nationalistische Strömungen in der Strassburger Studentenschaft."

46. For the suggestion that Alsatian students be forced to study at other German universities, see [Class], *Wenn ich der Kaiser war'*, p. 86; Liebert, "Von der deutschen Universität Strassburg"; and "Noch einmal: Die Auflösung der Cercle." On ending the imperial subsidy, see "Nationalistische Strömungen in der Strassburger Studentenschaft."

47. The remark about "patriotic duty" is from Heitz, *Souvenirs*, p. 68. Also see Ch. Bouchholtz, "Der elsässische Student," p. 2; Haug, "Les étudiants alsaciens," pp. 28–29; Heitz, *Vues cavalières*, pp. 180, 193; Herrenschmidt, *Mémoires pour la petite histoire*, p. 49; Moerlen and Bechelen, *La lutte de la jeunesse estudiantine*, pp. 52–53; Robert Redslob, *Alma mater*, pp. 102–3, 108, 130–31; Ulrich, "L'étudiant alsacien avant la guerre," pp. 34–39; and *Zehn Jahre Minenkrieg im Frieden*, pp. 28–30. In 1908–9 eighteen Alsatians matriculated at the university who had studied at French universities (twelve in Paris, two in Grenoble, and one each in Besançon, Bordeaux, Dijon, and Nancy); five years earlier the comparable figure was two (one each in Caen and Paris), and ten years earlier, one (in Paris). See the university's matriculation records, ADBR: AL 103, paqs. 1–6.

48. On the Association des étudiants alsaciens-lorrains, see Haug, "Les étudiants alsaciens," p. 28; Müntzer, *Der elsässische Student*, p. 18; Specklin, "Les étudiants de Strasbourg," p. 27; and, for the differences of one of its presidents with the Francophile purists, Paul Casper to Ferdinand Dollinger, 3 Feb. 1912, FFD; and *Echo du Cercle*, Mar. 1911, p. 16.

49. On Gustav Schickele as an *ancien* active in the affairs of the Cercle, see "Ausgeräuchert!"; and *Echo de Cercle*, Mar. 1911, pp. 10, 27. Others known to have participated actively in Bucher's movement are Kiener, Redslob, and the venerable Protestant theologian Paul Lobstein. On Lobstein, see El. Lobstein and Ed. Lobstein, *Paul Lobstein*, pp. 117–18; and Strohl, *Le protestantisme en Alsace*, p. 448.

50. For the number in the monômes see the police reports dated 16–17 Feb. 1905, 19–20 Feb. 1908, and 17 Feb. 1912, ADBR: AL 103, no. 202.

51. On the anticlericalism of the Cercle, see E. N., "Der Cercle und die Nationalisten," pp. 17–18; and M. R., "Kleine Chronik"; On anticlericalism as a characteristic of French student life, see "Réquisitoire d'un étudiant contre l'organisation des études supérieures," PEL: 25171(1).

52. Hugo Haug to Henri Albert, 27 Oct. 1907, FHH: 13. Also see Haug to Albert, 27 Oct. 1908, ibid. On the social origins of the members of the Cercle and the Club, see Müntzer, *Der elsässische Student*, pp. 17–18; "Pierre Bucher"; and *L'est républicain* (Nancy), 20 June 1911, quoted in *Rheinisch-Westfälische Zeitung* (Essen), 21 June 1911.

53. Robert Redslob, *Entre la France et l'Allemagne*, p. 66. Also see Ernst Robert Curtius, *Maurice Barrès*, p. 177; and Müntzer, *Der elsässische Student*, pp. 16–17.

54. Unless otherwise noted, all figures, percentages, and indices in this section are based on the sources and estimating procedures outlined in appendix A.

55. See Rossé et al., eds., *Das Elsass von 1870–1932*, 2:28–29; and Zemb, *Témoin de son temps*, pp. 44–50.

56. See "Liste des membres," pp. 25–29.

57. The estimate of the number of Alsatian students in Corps, Burschenschaften, and Protestant confessional fraternities is based on "Lettre de Strasbourg: L'étudiant alsacien"; and Rossé et al., eds., *Das Elsass von 1870–1932*, 4:212. On students as German nationalists, also see Grucker, "Protestantismus und Deutschtum im Elsass," p. 15; Kapp, "Die Kaiser

Wilhelms-Universität Strassburg: Ein Erinnerungswort," pp. 32–33; Müntzer, *Der elsässische Student,* pp. 21–22, 32; Rossé et al., eds., *Das Elsass von 1870–1932,* 3:28–29; and "Die Wilhelmitana im S. B.," pp. 41, 54–55, 58.

58. Jarausch, *Students, Society, and Politics,* pp. 296–97; "Lettre de Strasbourg: L'étudiant alsacien"; and Rossé et al., eds., *Das Elsass von 1870–1932,* 4:212. Also see *Der Elsässer* (Strasbourg), 12 Dec. 1905; d'Oux, "Der elsässische Student," pp. 254–57; Emil Clemens Scherer, *Eckart,* pp. 14–93; and Emil Clemens Scherer, "Der elsässische Student," pp. 158–60.

59. Fleischhack, *Helene Schweitzer,* pp. 11–13; Heuss, *Erinnerungen,* p. 124; Heuss-Knapp, *Ausblick vom Münsterturm,* pp. 62–64, 71; Meinecke, *Strassburg/Freiburg/Berlin,* p. 53; Robert Redslob, *Alma mater,* p. 51; Rossé et al., eds., *Das Elsass von 1870–1932,* 1:151; Emil Clemens Scherer, *Eckart,* pp. 82–85.

60. See Dominicus, *Strassburgs deutsche Bürgermeister,* pp. 22–23; Müntzer, *Der elsässische Student,* pp. 22–23; Rossé et al., eds., *Das Elsass von 1870–1932,* 3:29; and Stadler, *Jugendschicksale,* pp. 41–44, 59, 120–21.

61. Rolland to Guerrieri-Gonzaga, [late spring 1905], Rolland, *Chère Sofia,* p. 225.

62. On the origins of the movement, see Flake, "Um 1900," p. 93; Ritleng, *Souvenirs de jeunesse,* pp. 16, 18; Schickele, "In memoriam: Zur Einführung," pp. 2–3; and Wendel, *Jugenderinnerungen eines Metzers,* p. 200. On the movement's ideology, see Fichter, *René Schickele et l'Alsace,* pp. 37–62; Martens, "Stürmer in Rosen"; and Schultz, "Das literarische Leben in Elsass-Lothringen," pp. 192–95.

63. René Schickele in *Der Stürmer,* 15 Sept. 1902, quoted in Rossé et al., eds., *Das Elsass von 1870–1932,* 3:265–66.

64. Wendel, "Die Stürmer," part 2, p. 6.

65. Flake, *Freitagskind,* p. 38. On Flake and Youngest Alsace, see Flake, *Es wird Abend,* pp. 70–86; and Flake, "Das Junge Elsass," pp. 1051–57.

66. Bentmann, ed., *René Schickele,* pp. 15–36; Gier, *Die Entstehung des deutschen Expressionismus,* pp. 35–82; Rauscher, "Nachruf für einen Gefallenen"; Rossé et al., eds., *Das Elsass von 1870–1932,* 3:264–67; Schultz, "Das literarische Leben in Elsass-Lothringen," pp. 192–94.

67. Among them were Otto Baensch, Fritz van Calker, Ernst Polaczek, Georg Simmel, Ernst Stadler, and Werner Wittich. On Baensch, a philosopher, see Ernst Robert Curtius to Friedrich Gundolf, 24 Aug. 1909, Gundolf, *Briefwechsel,* p. 135; and Lion, "Das Elsass als Problem," p. 349. On van Calker, a jurist, see Berger, *Pascal David,* p. 123; and Léon Boll, "Par où commencer?" On Polaczek, Simmel, Stadler, and Wittich, see below. For evidence of the popularity of these ideas among other members of the faculty, see Wilfried von Seidlitz to Richard von Mises, 20 Oct. 1910, RMP: 4574.5; and Jean de Pange, *Journal,* 2:172.

68. For the quotation see Dallwitz, "Aus dem Nachlass," p. 293. Also see Rolland to Bloch, 15 Apr. 1912, Jean-Richard Bloch and Rolland, *Deux hommes se rencontrent,* p. 114; Ernst Robert Curtius, *Französischer Geist,* pp. 514–23; Edschmid, *Lebendiger Expressionismus,* p. 90; and Maisenbacher, *Ein Strassburger Bilderbuch,* pp. 52–53.

69. Wittich, "Deutsche und französische Kultur im Elsass"; and Wittich, "Kultur- und Nationalbewusstsein im Elsass." The first of these articles encouraged Bucher to shift the orientation of his Francophile movement from nostalgia for France as the home of liberty and human rights to admiration for France as the home of refined culture; see Kiener, "Werner Wittich und das Elsass," p. 92. For Bucher's initial reaction to this article, see Bucher to Wittich, 20 Apr. 1900, PWW.

70. See Dirk Forster, "Erinnerungen an Ernst Stadler," pp. 316–17; Schneider, "Das Leben"; and, for a list of Stadler's contributions, Stadler, *Dichtungen,* 2:379–86.

71. See Hugo Haug to Henri Albert, 23 July 1905, 29 Oct. 1905, and 23 Nov. 1907, FHH: 13; Katharina Dehio, "Die Geschichte einer elsässischen Industrie"; Heitz, *Souvenirs,*

pp. 80–81; Heuss-Knapp, *Ausblick vom Münsterturm,* pp. 46–47, 82, 94; and Singer, "Die Wende."

72. Stadler to Schickele, late July 1914, quoted in Schickele, *Werke,* 3:604–5. Also see Bk, "Georg Simmel, Goethe und das Elsass," p. 225; and Weisbach, *"Und Alles ist zerstorben,"* p. 384.

73. Kapp, "Eduard Schwartz," p. 430.

74. Schultz, "Die Strassburger Universität," pp. 190–91.

75. Richard von Mises to his mother, 4 Nov. 1911, RMP: 4574.5.2.

76. "Elsass-Lothringische Chronik," p. 229; Umfrid, "Mobilmachung der Kirchen"; and, more generally, Rüdiger vom Bruch, *Wissenschaft, Politik und öffentliche Meinung,* pp. 66–92, 229–49; Chickering, *Imperial Germany and a World without War,* pp. 148–62; and Ringer, *German Mandarins,* pp. 139–41.

77. Paul Laband, "Die Verfassung Elsass-Lothringens," p. 558.

78. Rossé et al., eds., *Das Elsass von 1870–1932,* 2:68; Winterberg, "Die politische Entwicklung Elsass-Lothringens," pp. 158–59.

79. Ziegler, "Die deutsche Erbsünde des Partikularismus." Also see "L'autonomie de l'Alsace-Lorraine et le professeur Ziegler."

80. Goetz, *Historiker in meiner Zeit,* p. 335; Hoche, *Strassburg und seine Universität,* pp. 75–76; Meinecke, *Strassburg/Freiburg/Berlin,* p. 11; and, for the quotation, Meinecke to Conrad Varrentrapp, 13 Mar. 1905, Meinecke, *Ausgewählter Briefwechsel,* p. 29.

81. See Richard von Mises to his mother, 19 Feb. 1911, RMP: 4574.5.2; and Trippen, *Theologie und Lehramt im Konflikt,* pp. 146–50.

82. See minutes of the Faculty of Philosophy, 30 Nov. 1912, 11 Jan., 25 Jan., and 8 Feb. 1913, ADBR: AL 103, no. 120; Enno Littmann to Wedel, 9 June 1913, ibid., no. 266; Paul Hensel to Hugo Münsterberg, 31 Nov. 1913, HMP; Alsaticus [pseud.], "Die katholische Philosophieprofessur"; "Eine konfessionelle Professur in Strassburg"; and "Der Strassburger Betrug."

83. On the university's fêtes, see Richard von Mises to his mother, 19 Jan. and 1 May 1911, RMP: 4574.5.2. On the honorary degrees for Lienhard and Pfitzner, see, respectively, Edschmid, *Lebendiger Expressionismus,* p. 280; and Abendroth, *Hans Pfitzner,* p. 180. On the election of Wiegand and his identification with the "chauvinists," see Richard von Mises to his mother, 4 Nov. 1911, RMP: 4574.5.2; Rossé et al., eds., *Das Elsass von 1870–1932,* 4:76; and Schenck, *Der Fall Zabern,* pp. 82–84.

84. See Richard von Mises to his mother, 8 and 15–16 Nov. 1909 and 17 Oct. 1910, RMP: 4574.5.2; Ficker, *Die Kaiser-Wilhelms-Universität Strassburg,* pp. 14–15; Hoche, *Strassburg und seine Universität,* pp. 76–77; Otto Mayer, *Die Kaiser-Wilhelms-Universität,* p. 109; Schultz, "Die Strassburger Universität," p. 190; and Wollenberg, *Erinnerungen eines alten Psychiaters,* pp. 111, 113.

85. See Walter Goetz to Karl Brandi, 19 Jan. 1913, BAK: Kl. Erw. Nr. 357; Brandi to Goetz, 21 Jan. 1913, NWG: 32; Eduard Schwartz to Goetz, 29 Jan. 1914, NWG: 40; Gustav Anrich, "Zu Herrn Poincaré's Strassburger Universitätsrede," p. 159; Lapp, "Studien aus dem Elsass: III"; and W. Sch., "Um die Reichsuniversität."

86. On Spahn, see Spahn, "Selbstbiographie," p. 485; and Stadler, *Jugendschicksale,* pp. 42–43, 120–23, 148–49, 188. On faculty members and the Naumann movement, see Rossé et al., eds., *Das Elsass von 1870–1932,* 1:62–64; and Theodor [pseud.], "Zum Abschied," p. 402. On the influence of Naumann and his movement among German professors generally, see Rüdiger vom Bruch, *Wissenschaft, Politik und öffentliche Meinung,* pp. 235–36, 278–84.

87. On research on Alsatian topics, see Rossé et al., eds., *Das Elsass von 1870–1932,* 3:177–88. On public courses, see [Cercle des anciens étudiants], *L'avenir de l'Université de Strasbourg,* p. 34; Heitz, *Souvenirs,* pp. 80–81; and Robert Redslob, *Alma mater,* p. 39. On the two scholarly societies, see Rossé et al., eds., *Das Elsass von 1870–1932,* 3:179–

80; Wolfram, "Die wissenschaftliche Vereine," p. 128; and Ziegler, "Nachruf," pp. 14–15. On the professors of theology, see Ludwig Dehio, "Die Kaiser-Wilhelms-Universität Strassburg," p. 28; Ficker, *Die Kaiser-Wilhelms-Universität Strassburg,* p. 30; and Emil Walter Mayer, "Emil Walter Mayer," p. 140. On the Strassburger studentische Wanderbühne, see Fritz Bouchholtz, "Ernst Stadler und die Strassburger studentische Wanderbühne"; Fritz Bouchholtz, "Die Strassburger studentische Wanderbühne"; and Naumann, *Ernst Stadler,* pp. 19–20.

88. On the general disaffection and emerging class consciousness of the *Privatdozenten* (fostered by their economic uncertainties, their declining autonomy, and their limited prospects for promotion) see Hoche, *Strassburg und seine Universität,* pp. 77–78; Naunyn, *Erinnerungen,* pp. 421–22; and, more generally, Busch, *Privatdozenten,* pp. 106–35; Eulenburg, *Der "Akademische Nachwuchs";* and Riese, *Die Hochschule auf dem Wege zum wissenschaftlichen Grossbetrieb,* pp. 153–92. On the "clerical party," see Meinecke to Walter Goetz, 12 Jan. 1913, NWG: 3.

89. On Goetz, see Goetz to his parents, 19 Feb. 1914, and to his mother, 12 Mar. 1914, NWG: 138; Friedrich Curtius to Goetz, 25 May 1914, NWG: 15; Goetz, *Historiker in meiner Zeit,* pp. 44–45, 333–34; Goetz, "Partikularismus und Einheitsstreben"; "Unsere Vorträge"; and, for the quotation, Goetz to Karl Brandi, 19 Jan. 1913, BAK: Kl. Erw. Nr. 357.

90. On Schwartz, see Schwartz to Goetz, 29 Jan. 1914, NWG: 40; Schwartz to Albert Ehrhard, 2 Feb. 1914, NAE; and Gustav Schwartz, *Alles ist Übergang zur Heimat hin,* p. 13.

91. For the quotation, see Enno Littmann to Wedel, 8 Dec. 1913, ADBR: AL 103, no. 266. On Simmel's impact, see Bk., "Georg Simmel, Goethe und das Elsass," p. 225; and Hauter, "Strassburger Erinnerungen," p. 252.

92. Albert Thumb et al. to Wedel, 12 Dec. 1913, ADBR: AL 103, no. 266; Joseph Pfleger in Alsace-Lorraine, Landtag: Zweite Kammer, *Verhandlungen,* 2d sess. (1913–14), 94:850, 1329; and Simmel, "Auszüge aus den Lebenserinnerungen," pp. 264–66.

93. See Goetz to Wilhelm Busch and his wife, 14 Nov. 1913, NWG: 149; Henri Albert to Hugo Haug, 24 Jan. 1914, FHH; and Schenk, *Der Fall Zabern,* pp. 122–24.

94. Goetz, *Historiker in meiner Zeit,* p. 45. Also see Goetz to Wilhelm Busch, 3 May 1914, NWG: 149; and Goetz to Meinecke, 7 May 1914, NFM: 3.

95. See Harry Bresslau to Goetz, 29 Mar. 1915, NWG: 151; Spahn to Goetz, 17 July 1915, NWG: 40; and, for the quotation, Kiener to Goetz, 3 Oct. 1915, NWG: 151. For examples of other "moderates" popular with their Alsatian students, see Robert Redslob, *Alma mater,* pp. 25, 30–31, 35–37.

96. Schultz, "Die Strassburger Universität," p. 188.

97. Naumann, *Ernst Stadler,* p. 13.

## Chapter 7

1. Lenel, *Die Universität Strassburg,* p. 21.

2. Friedrich Curtius, *Deutsche Briefe und elsässische Erinnerungen,* p. 243; Lion, "Das Elsass als Problem," p. 343; Rossé et al., eds., *Das Elsass von 1870–1932,* 1:228; Schmutz, *Alsace: Mythes et réalités,* pp. 48–49.

3. Wolfram, "Wissenschaft, Kunst und Literatur," p. 86.

4. Friedrich Curtius, *Deutsche Briefe und elsässische Erinnerungen,* pp. 243–45; Lenel, *Die Universität Strassburg,* pp. 22–23; Spindler, *L'Alsace pendant la guerre,* pp. 276–78; Wollenberg, *Erinnerungen eines alten Psychiaters,* pp. 137–38.

5. Johann von Dallwitz to Friedrich von Payer, 28 Feb. 1918, Schmidt, ed., *Die geheimen Pläne,* p. 240. On the climate of opinion in the Reichsland during the war, see Rossé et al., eds., *Das Elsass von 1870–1932,* 1:179–421; Roth, *La Lorraine annexée,* pp. 593–615; and Spindler, *L'Alsace pendant la guerre.*

6. Lion, "Das Elsass als Problem," p. 343. Also see Jean de Pange, "Le Conseil national d'Alsace et de Lorraine," pp. 912, 914; and Spindler, *L'Alsace pendant la guerre,* pp. 278, 535.

7. Schwabe, *Wissenschaft und Kriegsmoral,* pp. 22–25; "To the Civilized World."

8. *Erklärung der Hochschullehrer des Deutschen Reiches,* p. 1. Only two of the Strasbourg professors who signed, the Protestant theologian Gustav Anrich and the oriental philologist Josef Karst, were Alsatians; see ibid., pp. 25–26.

9. Eduard Schwartz, "Eduard Schwartz, wissenschaftlicher Lebenslauf," typescript dated 9 May 1932, Bayerische Staatsbibliothek (Munich), p. 9; Ficker, *Die Kaiser-Wilhelms-Universität Strassburg,* p. 31; and, on the program of "enlightening speeches," the memorandum by Ludwig Jost, 15 Jan. 1917, ADBR: AL 103, no. 47.

10. Schwabe, *Wissenschaft und Kriegsmoral,* pp. 54–56, 169–70; Spahn, "An den Pforten des Weltkriegs"; Spahn, "Selbstbiographie," p. 486.

11. Schwabe, *Wissenschaft und Kriegsmoral,* pp. 151–55.

12. See memorandum by Ludwig Jost, 15 Jan. 1917, ADBR: AL 103, no. 47; Gothein, *Eberhard Gothein,* p. 276; Elly Heuss-Knapp to Georg Friedrich Knapp, 16 Oct. 1914, Heuss-Knapp, *Bürgerin zweier Welten,* p. 152; Spindler, *L'Alsace pendant la guerre,* p. 472; and, for the quotation, Alfred Dove to Friedrich Meinecke, 31 Dec. 1914, Dove, *Ausgewählte Aufsätze und Briefe,* 2:299.

13. Siegfried von Rödern (?) to Otto Back, 13 Aug. 1915, and ? to Rödern, 17 Aug. 1915, ADBR: AL 27, no. 24. Also see Simmel, "Auszüge aus den Lebenserinnerungen," pp. 266–67.

14. See, for example, Hallays, "L'Université de Strasbourg," p. 254; Pfister, "L'Université de Strasbourg," pp. 252–54; and Rossé et al., eds., *Das Elsass von 1870–1932,* 1:367.

15. See Robert Redslob to Rudolf Schwander, 28 Oct. 1918, ADBR: AL 103, no. 254; and Robert Redslob, *Alma mater,* p. 277.

16. Ludwig Jost to Otto Back, 5 Feb. 1917, ADBR: AL 103, no. 71; Emil Walter Mayer, "Emil Walter Mayer," pp. 148–49; Rossé et al., eds., *Das Elsass von 1870–1932,* 1:364–67, 3:460–61; Spindler, *L'Alsace pendant la guerre,* p. 427; Zemb, *Témoin de son temps,* p. 57.

17. Alsace-Lorraine, Landtag: Zweite Kammer, *Vertrauliche Verhandlungen der Budgetkommission,* cols. 281–87, 300; Baechler, "L'Alsace entre la guerre et la paix," pp. 230–35; and Rossé et al., eds., *Das Elsass von 1870–1932,* 1:366–67.

18. See Fritz Kiener to Walter Goetz, 4 Mar. 1915, NWG: 234; and Goetz to Karl Stählin, 3 May 1917, NWG: 46.

19. Friedrich Brie to Otto Pöhlmann, 20 July 1917, ADBR: AL 103, no. 266. Also see Johannes Haller to Pöhlmann, 11 July 1917, ibid.; and Friedrich Schur to Richard von Mises, 21 Apr. 1918, RMP: 4574.5.

20. Robert Schuman quoted in Robert Rochefort, *Robert Schuman,* p. 39 (the remark was made in 1916). Also see Gothein, *Eberhard Gothein,* p. 213; and Robert Redslob, *Alma mater,* p. 36.

21. On the low morale of the faculty see Georg Simmel to Margarete Bendemann-Susman, 25 June 1917, GSP; Hugo Bücking to Paul Groth, 4 May 1918, NPG: X; and Gustav Schwartz, *Alles ist Übergang zur Heimat hin,* p. 47.

22. Albert Ehrhard, "Die Zukunft des Reichslandes: Gutachten über den Vortrag von Professor Dr. E. Schwarz: Gegenwort um Zukunft des Elsass," n.d., copy in NAE; Erzberger, *Erlebnisse im Weltkrieg,* p. 162.

23. Clemens Baeumker to Albert Ehrhard, 30 Mar. 1915, NAE; Janssen, *Macht und Verblendung,* pp. 238–39: Matthias and Morsey, eds., *Der Interfraktionelle Ausschuss 1917/18,* part 1, p. 9.

24. Janssen, *Macht und Verblendung,* p. 93; Schmidt, ed., *Die geheimen Pläne,* p. 207.

25. Brentano, *Elsässer Erinnerungen,* p. 149.

26. Harry Bresslau to Walter Goetz, 24 Jan. 1915, NWG: 33; Theodor Nöldeke to Lujo Brentano, 25 Nov. 1917, NLB: 44; Clemens Baeumker to Albert Ehrhard, 30 Mar. 1915, NAE; Otto Lenel to Meinecke, 11 May 1915, NFM: 22; Eduard Schwartz, "Il futuro statale dei 'Reichslande'"; Gustav Schwartz, *Alles ist Übergang zur Heimat hin*, p. 48.

27. El. Lobstein and Ed. Lobstein, *Paul Lobstein*, pp. 183–84; Jean de Pange, "Le Conseil national d'Alsace et de Lorraine," p. 912; Spindler, *L'Alsace pendant la guerre*, pp. 276–77, 436, 535, 600, 607.

28. Matthias and Morsey, eds., *Der Interfraktionelle Ausschuss 1917/18*, part 1, p. 9; Reiss, ed., *Von Bassermann zu Stresemann*, pp. 351–59.

29. Quoted in Spindler, *L'Alsace pendant la guerre*, p. 472.

30. Werner Wittich to Lujo Brentano, 29 Feb. 1916 and 13 Nov. 1917, NLB: 65; Brentano to Maximilian Harden, 20 May, 26 May, and 8 June 1917, NMH: 21; Werner Wittich, "Die elsass-lothringische Frage" (memorandum written in 1917 for the German General Staff), copy in PWW; Brentano, *Mein Leben*, pp. 153–57; Spindler, *L'Alsace pendant la guerre*, p. 501.

31. Matthias and Morsey, eds., *Der Interfraktionelle Ausschuss 1917/18*, part 1, pp. 109, 334–40, 359; Reiss, ed., *Von Bassermann zu Stresemann*, p. 355.

32. The memorandum apparently was written by Albert Ehrhard; see the draft copy dated 6 Aug. 1917, NAE; and minutes of the Prussian Council of Ministers, 1 Oct. 1917, André Scherer and Grunewald, eds., *L'Allemagne et les problèmes de la paix*, 2:476–77.

33. See Georg Dehio to Johannes Haller, 9, 10, 11, and 26 Aug. 1917, NJH: 5; Haller to ?, 14 Oct. 1917, and copy of untitled memorandum, NJH: 5; and Schwabe, *Wissenschaft und Kriegsmoral*, pp. 160–61, 265n.

34. Harry Bresslau to Walter Goetz, 24 Jan. 1915, NWG: 33.

35. See an untitled memorandum from the Faculty of the Sciences, 6 June 1917, ADBR: AL 103, no. 1425; and the minutes of the Academic Senate, 16 June 1917, ibid., no. 118.

36. Johann von Dallwitz, "Denkschrift über die zukünftige staatsrechtliche Gestaltung von Elsass-Lothringen," 19 Dec. 1917, Schmidt, ed., *Die geheimen Pläne*, pp. 154–55. Also see Emil Walter Mayer to the Academic Senate, 25 July 1917, ADBR: AL 103, no. 72.

37. See Emil Walter Mayer to Max Wallraf, 16 Jan. 1918, ADBR: AL 103, no. 1431; Klostermann, "Strassburgs Hochschule," p. 216; minutes of the Prussian Council of Ministers, 1 Oct. 1917, André Scherer and Grunewald, eds., *L'Allemagne et les problèmes de la paix*, 2:468; memorandum of Max Wallraf, 29 Dec. 1917, Schmidt, ed., *Die geheimen Pläne*, p. 187; and, for the quotation, the memorandum by Friedrich Rose, 6 June 1917, ADBR: AL 103, no. 1425.

38. Matthias and Morsey, eds., *Der Interfraktionelle Ausschuss 1917/18*, part 2, pp. 281–83, 710–17; and Gerhard Ritter, *Staatskunst und Kriegshandwerk*, 4:179–82.

39. See minutes of the Prussian Council of Ministers, 1 Oct. 1917, André Scherer and Grunewald, eds., *L'Allemagne et les problèmes de la paix*, 2:476–77; and Schmidt, ed., *Die geheimen Pläne*, pp. 115–17, 207, 211.

40. Baechler, "L'Alsace entre la guerre et la paix," pp. 320–21, 344, 347; Bresslau, "Harry Bresslau," p. 72; El. Lobstein and Ed. Lobstein, *Paul Lobstein*, pp. 194–95; Spahn, "Die letzten Tage des Zusammenbruchs," pp. 224, 226.

41. Bresslau, "Harry Bresslau," p. 72; Matthias and Morsey, eds., *Die Regierung des Prinzen Max von Baden*, pp. 109–10, 178, 213–14, 294, 312, 419; Prince Max von Baden, *Erinnerungen und Dokumente*, p. 337; Eduard Schwartz, "Das Ende der Strassburger Universität," p. 259.

42. Matthias and Morsey, eds., *Die Regierung des Prinzen Max von Baden*, pp. 424, 467–68; Nelson, *Land and Power*, pp. 60–61, 86, 111–12, 116; Jean de Pange, "Le Conseil national d'Alsace et de Lorraine," pp. 915–17.

43. See Jean-Jacques Becker, *1914*, pp. 53–62, 330–32; Stevenson, *French War Aims*, pp. 11–12, 17–19, 78–79; and Renouvin, "Les buts de guerre du gouvernement français."

44. Andler, *Vie de Lucien Herr*, pp. 260–64; Eccard, *Le livre de ma vie*, pp. 68–71; Henri Lichtenberger and André Lichtenberger, *La question d'Alsace-Lorraine*, pp. 83–92, 108–22.

45. France, Ministère des affaires étrangères, *Procès-verbaux de la Conférence d'Alsace-Lorraine*, 1:67.

46. Ibid., 1:59–66.

47. That the author may have been Gillot is suggested by internal evidence, particularly the report's comments about courses and exams in French literature at the German university, and by a later reference to Gillot's contributions to the planning of the French institution; see Christian Pfister to Sebastien Charléty, 13 Nov. 1920, AN: F[17] 13085.

48. "L'Université de Strasbourg," *Bulletin alsacien-lorrain du S. R. de Belfort*, Aug.–Sept. 1915, copy in FAT: 210.

49. Ibid.

50. Ibid. In 1913 there were 2,248 students enrolled at the University of Nancy, as compared with 2,071 at the University of Strasbourg; see *Minerva*, 23 (1913–14): 977, 1377.

51. "L'Université de Strasbourg," *Bulletin alsacien-lorrain du S. R. de Belfort*, Aug.–Sept. 1915, copy in FAT: 210.

52. Ibid.

53. France, Ministère de la guerre, Service d'Alsace-Lorraine, Section d'études de l'instruction publique: Sous-commission de l'enseignement supérieur, Procès-verbal, 13 Sept. 1917, copy in FAT: 209.

54. Ibid., Sous-commission de l'enseignement supérieur, Procès-verbaux, 13, 20, 28 Sept., 4, 11, 25 Oct., and 30 Nov. 1917, and 21 Feb. 1918, copies in FAT: 209; France, Ministère des affaires étrangères, *Procès-verbaux de la Conférence d'Alsace-Lorraine*, 2:185–89; Pfister, "La première année," p. 321. On Pfister, see Marc Bloch, "Christian Pfister"; Madelin, "Christian Pfister"; and Salomon, "Christian Pfister."

55. For the quotations see [Pfister], "Rapport sur l'Université de Strasbourg," BNUS: Ms 4850, pp. 96, 73, and 93, respectively. This version of the report, a draft in Pfister's hand, is ninety-nine pages in length. Almost three-quarters of the report traces the history of higher education in Strasbourg, with particular attention to the period since the Franco-Prussian War. The last twenty-seven pages present and discuss the subcommittee's recommendations.

56. [Pfister], "Rapport sur l'Université de Strasbourg," BNUS: Ms 4850, pp. 73, 82–83, 93–94, 98; for the quotation, see ibid., p. 94.

57. France, Ministère de la guerre, Service d'Alsace-Lorraine, Section d'études de l'instruction publique: Sous-commission de l'enseignement supérieur, Procès-verbal, 13 Sept. 1917, copy in FAT: 209.

58. On the chair of sociology, see Craig, "France's First Chair of Sociology," pp. 8–12.

59. Henri Lichtenberger and André Lichtenberger, *La question d'Alsace-Lorraine*, p. 115.

60. [Pfister], "Rapport sur l'Université de Strasbourg," BNUS: Ms 4850, pp. 77, 82–85, 92; for the quotation, see ibid., p. 82.

61. Ibid., pp. 78–79, 97–98; and, for the quotation, France, Ministère de la guerre, Service d'Alsace-Lorraine, Section d'études de l'instruction publique: Sous-commission de l'enseignement supérieur, Procès-verbal, 20 Sept. 1917, copy in FAT: 209.

62. France, Ministère de la guerre, Service d'Alsace-Lorraine, Section d'études de l'instruction publique: Sous-commission de l'enseignement supérieur, Procès-verbaux, 4, 11, and 25 Oct. 1917, copies in FAT: 209; and [Pfister], "Rapport sur l'Université de Strasbourg," BNUS: Ms 4850, pp. 86, 99.

63. [Pfister], "Rapport sur l'Université de Strasbourg," BNUS: Ms 4850, pp. 87–89.

64. Ibid., pp. 91–93; for the quotation, see ibid., p. 92.

65. On the role and composition of the advisory councils (*conseils consultatifs*), see Amestoy, *Les universités françaises*, pp. 361–65.

66. [Pfister], "Rapport sur l'Université de Strasbourg," BNUS: Ms 4850, pp. 81–82, 99.

67. Ibid., p. 95.

68. Karl Stählin to Walter Goetz, 17 Nov. 1918, NWG: 109; Andreas von Tuhr (the rector) to all members of the faculty, 20 Nov. 1918, RMP: 4574.5; Eduard Schwartz to Franz Boll, 20 Nov. 1918, NFB: 2108; Gustav Anrich to Albert Ehrhard, 28 Dec. 1918, NAE; Albert Ehrhard to Karl von Amira, 1 Dec. 1925, NKA: 1; Bresslau, "Harry Bresslau," pp. 72–73; Klostermann, *Die Rückkehr der Strassburger Dozenten*, p. 4; Eduard Schwartz, "Das Ende der Strassburger Universität," p. 259; Spahn, "Die letzten Tage des Zusammenbruchs," pp. 226–31; Wollenberg, *Erinnerungen eines alten Psychiaters*, p. 147.

69. Memorandum by Jules Coulet, 3 Dec. 1918, ADBR: AL 103, no. 53; Eugène Muller to Strasbourg faculty, 2 Dec. 1918, quoted in Klostermann, *Die Rückkehr der Strassburger Dozenten*, pp. 21–22n.

70. Richard von Mises to his mother, 12 Dec. 1918, RMP: 4574.5.3; Claudius von Schwerin to Karl von Amira, 4 Jan. 1919, NKA: 1; Albert Ehrhard to Eugène Muller, 7 Apr. 1920, NAE; Bresslau, "Harry Bresslau," pp. 50, 72–73; Chevrillon, "Aux pays d'Alsace et de Lorraine," pp. 466–67; Ficker, *Die Kaiser-Wilhelms-Universität Strassburg*, pp. 31–32; Heuss-Knapp, *Ausblick vom Münsterturm*, p. 65; Klostermann, *Die Rückkehr der Strassburger Dozenten*, pp. 5, 7, 22n; Georg Friedrich Knapp to Friedrich Bendixen, 10 Apr. and 2 Oct. 1919, Knapp and Bendixen, *Zur staatlichen Theorie des Geldes*, pp. 199, 202; Emil Walter Mayer, "Emil Walter Mayer," pp. 149–52; Nöldeke, *Jugend-Erinnerungen*, pp. 39–40; Robert Redslob, *Entre la France et l'Allemagne*, p. 121; Spindler, *L'Alsace pendant la guerre*, pp. 749–50, 752, 762–63.

71. Richard von Mises to his mother, 11 and 20 Nov. 1918, RMP: 4574.5.2; Jules Leyder to Albert Houtin, 19 Mar. 1919, PAH: 15717; Baechler, "L'Alsace entre la guerre et la paix," pp. 386–87, 392, 404; Spindler, *L'Alsace pendant la guerre*, pp. 731–42; Wahl, *Confession et comportement*, pp. 1126–31.

72. Baechler, "L'Alsace entre la guerre et la paix," pp. 404–10; Spindler, *L'Alsace pendant la guerre*, pp. 749–50.

73. "Université de Strasbourg: Rapport de la Commission," (ADBR: UStr), p. 48.

74. Ibid., pp. 27–33 (the quotation is from p. 32).

75. Ibid., p. 2.

76. Ibid., p. 86.

77. Ibid., p. 76.

78. Ibid., p. 89.

79. Ibid., p. 2; Lanson, "La renaissance," pp. 323–24; Pfister, "La première année," pp. 324–26.

80. Hallays, "L'Université de Strasbourg," pp. 243–45; Lanson, "La renaissance," pp. 326–30; Pfister, "La première année," pp. 326–34; Rossé et al., eds., *Das Elsass von 1870–1932*, 3:139.

81. Canet to Millerand, 10 Apr. 1919, FM: 46, III (9); Pfister to Coulet, 10 Apr. 1919, ADBR: UStr; Dreyfus, *La vie politique en Alsace*, pp. 33–35; Poincaré, *A la recherche de la paix*, pp. 140–42, 198–99, 205–6, 208–10, 243, 247, 257; Roussel, "L'Université de Strasbourg," p. 501.

82. [Albert Thomas], "Note sur l'Université de Strasbourg," 13 Mar. 1919, FAT: 211 (for the concluding quotation); Jules Leyder to Albert Houtin, 19 Mar. 1919, PAH: 15717; [Canet], "Le personnel enseignant de l'Université de Strasbourg en 1914, en avril 1918, en mai 1919," FM: 46, III (8) (for the rumored remark by the official at the ministry); Appell, *Souvenirs d'un alsacien*, pp. 309–10; Hallays, "L'Université de Strasbourg," p. 245; Lanson, "La renaissance," pp. 330–31; Poincaré, *A la recherche de la paix*, pp. 140–41, 265, 271; "Universitätsfragen."

83. Cercle des anciens étudiants alsaciens et lorrains to Millerand, 19 May 1919, FM: 46, III (8); [Albert Thomas], "Note sur la conversation avec M. Bucher," 5 Aug. 1919, FAT:

212; "Une crise à Strasbourg"; Garcin, "L'activité du Cercle depuis l'armistice," pp. 4–5; Moerlen and Bechelen, *La lutte de la jeunesse estudiantine*, p. 47; Pfister, "La première année," pp. 338–39.

84. Dreyfus, *La vie politique en Alsace*, pp. 42–43; Poincaré, *A la recherche de la paix*, pp. 257–60, 262–65; Roussel, "L'Université de Strasbourg," p. 502.

85. Lanson, "La renaissance," p. 336; Millerand, *Le retour de l'Alsace-Lorraine*, pp. 9, 87; "M. Millerand à l'Université"; Pfister, "La première année," p. 338; Poincaré, *A la recherche de la paix*, p. 271. On Bucher's role in Millerand's administration, see Baldensperger, *Une vie parmi d'autres*, pp. 318–19; and Hallays, "Pierre Bucher," pp. 349–52. On Millerand's administration generally, see Millerand, *Le retour de l'Alsace-Lorraine*, pp. 5–113; and Rossé et al., eds., *Das Elsass von 1870–1932*, 1:563–68.

86. Gustav Anrich to Albert Ehrhard, 28 Dec. 1918, NAE; "Notes autographes concernant Paul Sabatier," PAH: 15748; Paul Sabatier to Alfred Loisy, 10 Mar. 1919, PAL: 15661; Jules Leyder to Albert Houtin, 25 Mar. and 15 Nov. 1919, PAH: 15717; Canet to Millerand, 10 and 12 Apr. 1919, FM: 46, III (9); Hallays, "L'Université de Strasbourg," p. 261; Rossé et al., eds., *Das Elsass von 1870–1932*, 3:462–64; Zemb, *Témoin de son temps*, pp. 58–59.

87. Rossé et al., eds., *Das Elsass von 1870–1932*, 3:464–65; Zemb, *Témoin de son temps*, p. 59.

88. See Les compagnons de l'université nouvelle, *L'université nouvelle*, vol. 1; "Une réponse d'un groupe d'universitaires"; and Simoni, "La vie intellectuelle de la France."

89. [Cercle des anciens étudiants], *L'avenir de l'Université de Strasbourg*, p. 6. Also see Cercle des anciens étudiants, "Résolution," 19 May 1919, FM: 46, III (8); and "Die Zukunft der Strassburger Universität."

90. [Cercle des anciens étudiants], *L'avenir de l'Université de Strasbourg*, p. 39.

91. Ibid., pp. 10–14.

92. Ibid., pp. 17–19 (the quotation is from p. 18); and Cercle des anciens étudiants, "Résolution," 19 May 1919, FM: 46, III (8).

93. [Canet], "Du futur régime de l'Université de Strasbourg," FM: 46, III (8). For the identity of the author, see Pierre Weiss (?) to Millerand, 26 May 1919, ibid.

94. For Lot's ideas concerning university reform, see Perrin, *Un historien français*, pp. 41–42, 45–47.

95. On Andler's proposals, see Alsace-Lorraine, Conseil supérieur, *Procès-verbaux*, session of Aug. 1919, pp. 23–26, 34–36; and Tonnelat, *Charles Andler*, pp. 196–97, 249–52. For examples of other reform proposals, see Lucien Herr to Albert Houtin, 29 Oct. 1919, PAH: 15710; Alsace-Lorraine, Conseil supérieur, *Procès-verbaux*, session of June 1919, p. 23; and Lanson, "La renaissance," pp. 334–35.

96. Notes on Coulet's meeting with the provisional deans, 12 May 1919, FM: 46, III (8); Coulet to Millerand, 23 May 1919, ADBR: UStr; and, for the law of 10 July 1896, its antecedents, and its critics, Prost, *Histoire de l'enseignement en France*, pp. 235–40.

97. See minutes of the Faculties of Law (13 May 1919), Medicine (18 May), Science (19 May), and Letters (20 May), and Christian Pfister (on behalf of the acting deans), "Note au sujet du statut de l'Université," 20 May 1919, ADBR: UStr.

98. Coulet to Millerand, 23 May 1919, ADBR: UStr.

99. Alfaric, *De la foi à la raison*, p. 274; Pfister, "L'Université de Strasbourg," p. 255. For the final recommendations, see the notes on the meetings of the *conseils consultatifs* on 5 and 6 June 1919, FM: 46, III (8); and the minutes of the Section permanent du Conseil supérieur de l'instruction publique, 13 June 1919, AN: F$^{17}$ 13667.

100. [Albert Thomas], "Note sur l'Université de Strasbourg," 13 Mar. 1919, FAT: 211; Albert Thomas to Millerand, 8 May 1919, FAT: 408; interviews with Jean Gaudemet, 28 June 1976, and A. G. Weiss, 1 July 1976; Pfister, "Georges Pariset," p. xiii; Poincaré, *A la recherche de la paix*, pp. 140, 271. For Pfister's recommendations, see Pfister to Coulet, 7

Mar. 1919, "Rapport de M. Pfister sur l'organisation future de la Faculté des lettres de l'Université de Strasbourg," 19 Mar. 1919, and Pfister to Coulet, 22 May 1919, ADBR: UStr.

101. Interview with Jean Gaudemet, 28 June 1976. Also see Canet to Coulet, 15 Feb. 1919, ADBR: UStr; and Eccard, *Le livre de ma vie*, p. 106.

102. Pfister, "La première année," pp. 325–53. The officials' generosity did not extend to offering a position to Werner Wittich, the one German professor permitted to remain in Alsace, despite urging from Bucher, Charles Rist, and others; see de Quirielle, "Werner Wittich"; and Rist, "Werner Wittich," pp. 1456–57.

103. On the role of patrons in French academic life, see Terry Nichols Clark, *Prophets and Patrons*, pp. 67–74.

104. Cohen, *Ceux que j'ai connus*, p. 94.

105. Ibid., p. 143.

106. Lanson to Cohen, 3 Apr. 1919, PGC: 1; Cohen to Johannes Tielrooy, 9 July 1919, LJT: 15009; Cohen, *Ceux que j'ai connus*, pp. 143–44.

107. Alfaric, *De la foi à la raison*, pp. 271–72. On the solicitude of many university officials and patrons for defrocked priests, see Guirand, "Notes et Notices."

108. Alfaric to Albert Houtin, 27 Apr. 1919, PAH: 15688.

109. For the quotation, ibid. On the French academic community's attitudes concerning centralization and anticlericalism, see Andler, *Vie de Lucien Herr*, pp. 276–77; and Prost, *Histoire de l'enseignement en France*, pp. 339–40, 367–68.

110. Alfaric to Albert Houtin, 12 June and 31 July 1919, PAH: 15688; Alfaric, *De la foi à la raison*, pp. 272–73; and, on the Ligue républicaine d'Alsace et de Lorraine, Andler, *Vie de Lucien Herr*, p. 261; and Tonnelat, *Charles Andler*, pp. 189–95. Lavisse also had a major impact on other decisions affecting the curriculum and staffing of the new university; see Pfister to Coulet, 2 May 1919, and Lavisse to Alfred Coville, 4 June 1919, ADBR: UStr; and notes on the meeting of the Conseil consultatif (Lettres), 6 June 1919, FM: 46, III (8).

111. For the quotations see, respectively, Alfaric to Albert Houtin, 7 July 1919, PAH: 15688, and Alfaric, *De la foi à la raison*, p. 274. Also see Alfaric to Houtin, 1 July and 9 Nov. 1919, PAH: 15688; Christian Pfister, "Observations particulières," n.d. [1920], Alfaric's dossier, AN: F$^{17}$ 25093; and Alfaric, *De la foi à la raison*, pp. 273–74.

112. Alfaric, *De la foi à la raison*, pp. 275–76; and, for the quotations from Lévy-Bruhl's memorandum, ibid., p. 275.

113. Alfaric to Albert Houtin, 10 and 31 July 1919, PAH: 15688; and Alfaric, *De la foi à la raison*, p. 275.

114. See Charles Hauter to Eugène Ehrhardt (?), n.d., ADBR: AL 103, no. 900; [Albert Houtin], "Notes autographes concernant Paul Sabatier," PAH: 15748; Paul Lobstein to Coulet, 5 May 1919, ADBR: UStr; Canet, "La Faculté de théologie protestante," 10 July 1919, FM: 46, III (8); and Pfister, "La première année," p. 345.

115. Mgr Charles Ruch to Vicar-Capitular Jost, n.d. [Sept. 1919], Le Léannac, "L'enseignement supérieur," p. 304.

116. Canet to Vicar-Capitular Jost, 27 Sept. 1919, ibid.

117. Cardinal Pietro Gasparri to Mgr Charles Ruch, 13 Nov. 1919, ibid., pp. 304–5.

118. Coulet to Millerand, 4 June 1919, [Canet], "Sur une note de M. le Recteur (4 juin 1919) sur la Faculté de théologie catholique," 6 June 1919, and Canet to Sébastien Charléty (?), 30 June 1919, FM: 46, III (8); Mollat, "Les débuts de la faculté française," pp. 270–71; Pfister, "Rapport général," p. 4; Rossé et al., eds., *Das Elsass von 1870–1932*, 3:465; Zemb, *Témoin de son temps*, pp. 59–60.

119. Pfister, "Rapport général," pp. 3–4.

120. Interview with A. G. Weiss, 1 July 1976; and Robert Redslob, "Raymond Carré de Malberg," pp. 15–16. Also see Edouard Spenlé to André Fontaine (?), 16 Dec. 1918, and Millerand to Coulet, 26 Apr. 1919, ADBR: UStr.

121. Febvre to Albert Thomas, n.d., quoted in Thomas to Millerand, 8 May 1919, FAT: 408. Also see Jean Monnier to Coulet (?), 13 Dec. 1918, ADBR: UStr; Baldensperger, "A travers les universités: Strasbourg," p. 17; Febvre, "Marc Bloch et Strasbourg," p. 391; and Vermeil, "La mission européenne de Strasbourg," p. 128.

122. "Rapport de M. Pfister sur l'organisation future de la Faculté des lettres de l'Université de Strasbourg," 19 Mar. 1919, ADBR: UStr; minutes of the Faculty of Protestant Theology, 12 and 26 May 1919, BFT; "Résolutions adoptées à la réunion plenière des membres du corps enseignant de l'Université de Strasbourg," 4 Nov. 1920, ADBR: AL 98, paq. 367; Aaron[Georges Delahache, pseud.], "Strasbourg 1918–1920," pp. 501–2; Millerand in Alsace-Lorraine, Conseil supérieur, Procès-verbaux, session of Oct. 1919, p. 60.

123. Millerand to Clemenceau, 27 July 1919, FM: 46, III (8); "Rapport fait au nom de la Commission des finances . . . ," France, Journal officiel, Chambre des députés, 12th leg., 1920 (ord. sess.), Documents parlementaires, 1:761.

124. Charléty, "Rapport sur les projets relatifs à l'Université de Strasbourg" [Aug. 1919], copy in FAT: 211.

125. Charléty to Albert Thomas, 9 Aug. 1919, FAT: 211; Charléty to Thomas, 27 Aug. 1919, and Thomas to Charléty, 25 and 31 Aug. 1919, FAT: 411; Millerand, Le retour de l'Alsace-Lorraine, p. 102; and Pfister, "Rapport général," p. 14.

126. Millerand, Le retour de l'Alsace-Lorraine, pp. 19–20, 25.

127. See Albert Thomas's notes on his copy of Charléty, "Rapport sur les projets relatifs à l'Université de Strasbourg" [Aug. 1919], FAT: 211; and, on the powers and composition of the Conseils généraux, Nast, Le malaise alsacien-lorrain, pp. 21–22; and Rossé et al., eds., Das Elsass von 1870–1932, 4:108, 110.

128. See [Pfister], "Rapport sur l'Université de Strasbourg," p. 74, BNUS: Ms 4850; Ferdinand Dollinger, "La Société des amis," p. 930; Hallays, "Discours," p. 23; Hallays, "L'Université de Strasbourg," pp. 264–65; Labadens, "La Société des amis," pp. 407–8; and Pfister, "André Hallays et l'Université de Strasbourg," p. 347. On French precedents, see Weisz, "The French Universities and Education for the New Professions," pp. 98–128.

129. Charléty to Albert Thomas, 27 Aug. 1919, FAT: 411; [Cercle des anciens étudiants], L'avenir de l'Université de Strasbourg, pp. 12–14; Eccard, Le livre de ma vie, pp. 108–9; Labadens, "La Société des amis," p. 408.

130. Charléty, "Rapport sur les projets relatifs à l'Université de Strasbourg" [Aug. 1919], copy in FAT: 211; minutes of the Faculty of Protestant Theology, 15 Oct., 23 Oct., and 13 Nov. 1919, BFT; minutes of the University Council, 24 Oct. 1919, ADBR: AL 98, paq. 367; Alfaric to Albert Houtin, 9 Nov. 1919, PAH: 15688; Febvre, "Marc Bloch et Strasbourg," p. 391.

131. For the quotations see, respectively, Pfister, "L'Université de Strasbourg," p. 255; Millerand to Albert Thomas, 24 Nov. 1919, FAT: 408; and Millerand, "Souvenirs d'Alsace et de Lorraine," p. 15.

132. See speeches by Pfister, Bucher, and Poincaré, University of Strasbourg, Université de Strasbourg: Fêtes d'inauguration, pp. 13–19, 26–29.

133. Ibid., pp. 32 and 21, respectively.

134. Unidentified speaker quoted in "La cérémonie d'inauguration du 22 novembre 1919," p. 450.

135. University of Strasbourg, Université de Strasbourg: Fêtes d'inauguration, pp. 13–14.

136. See Lucien Herr to Albert Houtin, 29 Oct. 1919, PAH: 15710; Henri Albert as quoted in Kapp, "Die Kaiser Wilhelms-Universität Strassburg: Ein Erinnerungswort," p. 29; Zind, Elsass-Lothringen, pp. 179, 280, 287; and, for the quotation, Garcin, "L'activité du Cercle depuis l'armistice," p. 6.

## Chapter 8

1. See "Résolutions adoptées à la réunion plenière des membres du corps enseignant de l'Université de Strasbourg," 4 Nov. 1920, ADBR: AL 98, paq. 367; and Grenier, "Les publications de la Faculté des lettres de Strasbourg," p. 932.

2. See Berr, "L'esprit de synthèse dans l'enseignement supérieur."

3. Geiger, "Reform and Restraint in Higher Education," pp. 40–84; Prost, *Histoire de l'enseignement en France*, pp. 230–40; Shinn, *Savoir scientifique et pouvoir social*, pp. 70–75; Weisz, *The Emergence of Modern Universities in France*, pp. 81–161.

4. Ferdinand Lot to Ernest Lavisse, 7 Dec. 1912, BN: FNA 25168 (III). Also see Lot, "Où en est la Faculté des lettres de Paris?"; Geiger, "Reform and Restraint in Higher Education," pp. 76–84; and Weisz, *The Emergence of Modern Universities in France*, pp. 319–28.

5. Baldensperger, "Quarante mois après," p. 391.

6. See Paul Sabatier to Alfred Loisy, 19 Apr. 1926, BN: NAF 15661; Berr, "L'esprit de synthèse dans l'enseignement supérieur," part 1, pp. 6–8; Paul Lobstein, "Rapport," pp. 21–22; Pfister, "La première année," pp. 345–52; and Weiss, "Rapport," pp. 49–53.

7. Berr, "L'esprit de synthèse dans l'enseignement supérieur," part 1, p. 8. Also see Marc Bloch, "Christian Pfister," pp. 568–69; and Marc Bloch and Lucien Febvre, "Le problème de l'agrégation," pp. 123–24.

8. The term "environment for learning" has been adapted from Gaff, Crombag, and Chang, "Environments for Learning in a Dutch University." Also see Blau, *The Organization of Academic Work*, pp. 109–19.

9. See [Pfister], "Rapport sur l'Université de Strasbourg," BNUS: Ms 4850, pp. 59–60; Baldensperger, "Quarante mois après," p. 391; Berr, "L'esprit de synthèse dans l'enseignement supérieur," part 1, pp. 1–7; Weiss, "Rapport," p. 53.

10. Les compagnons de l'université nouvelle, *L'université nouvelle*, 1:40–48; Ringer, *German Mandarins*, pp. 280–82, 384–403.

11. Minutes of the Faculty of Letters (Assemblée), 10 May and 11 July 1919, ADBR: AL 154, no. 2; Commission universitaire nommée pour l'étude d'un projet d'Institut du travail, "Résumé des travaux de la Commission à ce jour," PFS: 1963; Baldensperger, "L'Université de Strasbourg," p. 928; Baulig, "Lucien Febvre à Strasbourg," pp. 179–80; Berr, "L'esprit de synthèse dans l'enseignement supérieur," part 1, pp. 6–13; "Chronique: I—Réunions du samedi."

12. Quoted in Berr, "L'esprit de synthèse dans l'enseignement supérieur," part 1, p. 11. Also see Febvre, "L'Université de Nancy," p. 178.

13. Craig, "Maurice Halbwachs à Strasbourg," pp. 281–83; Febvre, "Marc Bloch et Strasbourg," pp. 398–99; Leuilliot, "Aux origines des 'Annales,'" pp. 317–24.

14. For the birthdates of most faculty members, see "Tableaux de classement du personnel enseignant des Facultés de droit, de médecine, des sciences et des lettres," ADBR: AL 98, paq. 362. For the ministry's preference for the appointment of relatively young scholars, see Ernest Lavisse to Alfred Coville, 4 June 1919, ibid., UStr.

15. Hughes, *Consciousness and Society*, pp. 33–66.

16. On the background, see Bénéton, "La génération de 1912–14."

17. Interview with François-Georges Pariset, 24 July 1976; Callot, "Les études médicales et pharmaceutiques," p. 129; Weiss, "Rapport," pp. 50–51.

18. Ferdinand Lot to Ernest Lavisse, 7 Dec. 1912, BN: FNA 25168 (III).

19. See Baldensperger, "Quarante mois après," pp. 391–92; Cohen, "Souvenir universitaire"; Fréchet, "Les mathématiques à l'Université de Strasbourg," pp. 338–43; and, on the background, Karady, "Stratégies de réussite et modes de faire-valoir," pp. 71–73; and de Tarde and Massis [Agathon], *L'esprit de la nouvelle Sorbonne*.

20. Interview with Henri Cartan, 30 June 1976.

21. Jean Bon in France, *Journal officiel*, Chambre des députés, 11th leg., 1919, *Débats parlementaires*, p. 3061.

22. University of Strasbourg, *Université de Strasbourg: Fêtes d'inauguration*, p. 38.

23. Sebastien Charléty quoted in Victor Prevel, "Rapport fait au nom de la Commission du budget du Conseil supérieur d'Alsace et de Lorraine pour l'exercice 1920," Feb. 1920, copy in FAT: 211.

24. "Projet de loi relatif au statut de l'Université de Strasbourg" [1921], and Gabriel Alapetite to Théodore Tissier, 26 Aug. 1921, ADBR: AL 98, paq. 359. Also see Weiss, "L'Alsace et l'Université de Strasbourg," pp. 467–68.

25. See Commissaire général du gouvernement français aux Etats-Unis pour l'Exposition de Saint-Louis to the Ministry of Public Instruction, 14 Mar. 1904, AN: F$^{17}$ 2760; Baldensperger, *Une vie parmi d'autres*, pp. 134–39, 230–37; Düwell, *Deutschlands auswärtige Kulturpolitik*, pp. 38–47; Luchaire, *Confession d'un français moyen*, 1:152–69; McMurry and Lee, *The Cultural Approach*, pp. 9–15; Weisz, *The Emergence of Modern Universities in France*, pp. 252–68.

26. See Baldensperger, *Une vie parmi d'autres*, pp. 268–75, 362–63; Cohen, *Ceux que j'ai connus*, p. 76; Emile Durkheim to Georges Davy, 16 July 1916, Davy, *L'homme, le fait social et le fait politique*, pp. 311–12; Luchaire, *Confession d'un français moyen*, 2:24–44; and, more generally, Kleinert, "Von der Science allemande zur deutschen Physik"; Paul, *The Sorcerer's Apprentice*, pp. 29–76; and Schroeder-Gudehus, *Les scientifiques et la paix*, pp. 63–97.

27. See Abelein, *Die Kulturpolitik*, pp. 24–27; Kohler, "Le rayonnement de l'université française"; McMurry and Lee, *The Cultural Approach*, pp. 15–21; and Schroeder-Gudehus, *Les scientifiques et la paix*, pp. 101–60.

28. Edouard Herriot, "Rapport fait au nom de la commission des finances . . . ," France, *Journal officiel*, Chambre des députés, 12th leg. 1920 (ord. sess.), *Documents parlementaires*, 1:755.

29. André Hallays to Raymond Poincaré, 13 May 1922, PRP: 16003; minutes of the Faculty of Protestant Theology, 7 Dec. 1922 and 6 July 1923, BFT; Pfister, "Rapport sommaire sur les universités des villes visitées," pp. 827–29.

30. Minutes of the University Council, 11 Nov. 1919, ADBR: AL 101 (3); minutes of the Faculty of Letters, 12 Dec. 1919, ADBR: AL 154, no. 2; "Rapport de M. Sylvain Lévi pour l'organisation des langues orientales pendant l'année scolaire 1920–1921," AN: F$^{17}$ 13090; interview with Marcel Simon, 31 Aug. 1976.

31. Sebastien Charléty to Albert Thomas, 9 Aug. 1919, FAT: 211; minutes of the University Council, 20 Feb. 1920, 14 Dec. 1920, 25 June 1921, 23 Dec. 1922, ADBR: AL 101 (3); André Hallays to Raymond Poincaré, 15 Jan. 1923, PRP: 16003; minutes of the Faculty of Letters, 20 Nov. 1924, ADBR: AL 154, no. 2; Beudant, "Le Grand-Duché de Luxembourg et l'Université de Strasbourg."

32. Minutes of the Faculty of Protestant Theology, 13 Nov. 1919, 7 Dec. 1922, and 6 July 1923, BFT; Fernand Baldensperger to Jean de Pange, 8 Feb. 1920, 29 Mar. 1920, and 9 Feb. 1921, AFDP; minutes of the University Council, 8 Mar. 1920, ADBR: AL 101 (3); Paul Sabatier to Ferdinand Dollinger, 5 Jan. 1923, FFD; and Ehrhardt, "Rapport général," pp. 16–19. For one result of these efforts to publicize the university, see "The New Strasbourg University."

33. France, Statistique générale de la France, *Annuaire statistique*, 39 (1923): 40; and ibid., 46 (1930): 38.

34. See Sebastien Charléty to Albert Thomas, 9 Aug. 1919, FAT: 211; Fernand Baldensperger to Jean de Pange, 6 Jan. 1920, 29 Mar. 1920, and 9 Feb. 1921, AFDP; Pierre Bucher to Raymond Poincaré, 23 July 1920, PRP: 15955; and Gabriel Moy to Jacques Peirotes, 20 Nov. 1928, AACVS: B. 286/1579.

35. For the number of foreign students at the university according to national origin, see France, Statistique générale de la France, *Annuaire statistique,* 39 (1923): 40 et seq.

36. "L'Université de Strasbourg," *Bulletin alsacien-lorrain du S. R. de Belfort,* Aug.–Sept. 1915, copy in FAT: 210.

37. Thomas in Alsace-Lorraine, Conseil supérieur, *Procès-verbaux,* session of Aug. 1919, p. 36.

38. Pierre Bucher to Raymond Poincaré, 6 June 1920, PRP: 15995; Barrès, *Le génie du Rhin.*

39. See, for instance, Gustave Cohen to Johannes Tielrooy, 14 Feb. 1920, LJT: 15009; and Marc Bloch, *Strange Defeat,* p. 155.

40. See Berr, "L'esprit de synthèse dans l'enseignement supérieur," part 1, pp. 10n, 13; Minder, "Panorama des études germaniques en France," pp. 219–20, 229; and Vermeil, "L'Institut germanique," p. 944.

41. Minutes of the University Council, 20 May 1920, ADBR: AL 101 (3); minutes of the Faculty of Letters (Assemblée), 8 July 1921 and n.d. [Nov. 1921], ADBR: AL 154, no. 2; Jean-Edouard Spenlé (?) to Directeur de l'enseignement supérieur, 2 Oct. 1929, PRP: 16012; Vézian, "Le Centre d'études germaniques."

42. Schlagdenhauffen, "Le Centre d'études germaniques de Strasbourg"; Vézian, "Le Centre d'études germaniques."

43. Vermeil to Albert Thomas, 17 May 1923, FAT: 386; Lang, "Rapport général," p. 6; Vermeil, "L'Information allemande à Strasbourg."

44. Vermeil, "L'Institut germanique," p. 944.

45. Ibid., pp. 943–44; Vermeil to Albert Thomas, n.d. [Oct. 1925], FAT: 386; K. R. Guerrier to Wilhelm Kapp, 31 May 1930, NWK; interview with Robert Minder, 15 July 1976; Ernst Robert Curtius, *Französischer Geist,* pp. 242–54; and Minder, "Panorama des études germaniques," pp. 214–30.

46. See Zeldin, *France, 1848–1945,* 2:324–25; and, for the government's allocations to universities in representative years, France, *Journal officiel,* Chambre des députés, *Documents parlementaires,* 12th leg., 1920 (ord. sess.), 1:754–62; 12th leg., 1922 (ord. sess.), 2:1900, 2154–60; 12th leg., 1924 (ord. sess.), 2:1606, 1812–13; 13th leg., 1926 (ord. sess.), 2:1271, 1550–52; and 14th leg., 1929 (extraord. sess.), 1:393–94.

47. See "Enseignement supérieur public: Université de Strasbourg, situation financière," ADBR: UStr; Gabriel Alapetite to Louis Barthou, 4 May 1922, ADBR: AL 98, paq. 359; and Riedinger, "Cinquante ans d'histoire," pp. 413–14.

48. "Projet de loi relatif au statut de l'Université de Strasbourg," n.d. [July 1921], ADBR: AL 98, paq. 359. Also see Robert Beudant to Théodore Tissier, 13 July 1921, and Gabriel Alapetite to Tissier, 26 Aug. 1921, ibid.

49. "Association des membres du personnel enseignant de l'Université de Strasbourg: Ordre du jour," n.d. [1922], ADBR: AL 98, paq. 367.

50. "Note sur le statut spécial de l'Université de Strasbourg," n.d., ADBR: AL 98, paq. 359.

51. Association du personnel enseignant de l'Université de Strasbourg to deputies and senators from Alsace-Lorraine, 3 Mar. 1923, copy in ibid.; and "Loi relative au statut des fonctionnaires d'Alsace et de Lorraine," France, *Journal officiel, Lois et décrets,* 28 July 1923, p. 7362.

52. "Loi portant ouverture et annulation de credits . . . ," art. 28, France, *Journal officiel, Lois et décrets,* 1 Apr. 1926, p. 3980.

53. See ibid., 6 Mar. 1926, pp. 2948–49; 31 Mar. 1926, pp. 3924–25; and 15 Jan. 1927, pp. 609–10.

54. Minutes of the Faculty of Protestant Theology, 19 Feb. 1927, BFT. Also see Paul Collomp to Gustave Cohen, 20 Dec. 1927, and Albert Grenier to Cohen, 23 Feb. 1928, PGC: 4. Grumbling over the favored treatment given Parisian professors was not confined to

Strasbourg or to the interwar years; see, for instance, Nye, "The Scientific Periphery in France," pp. 382–83.

55. Febvre, "L'Université de Nancy," p. 183.

56. Audollent, "Y a-t-il lieu de 'spécialiser' et de 'moderniser' nos universités provinciales?" pp. 129–30; and Zeldin, *France, 1848–1945*, 2:325–26.

57. See minutes of the Faculty of Letters (Conseil), 3 Nov. 1925 and 9 Feb. 1929, ADBR: AL 154, no. 3.

58. Minutes of the Section permanente du Conseil supérieur of the Ministry of Public Instruction, 4 Apr. 1924, AN: F$^{17}$ 13668. Also see minutes of the Faculty of Letters (Conseil), 12 May 1923 and 8 Mar. 1924, ADBR: AL 154, no. 3.

59. Minutes of the Section permanente du Conseil supérieur of the Ministry of Public Instruction, 4 Apr. 1924, AN: F$^{17}$ 13668. Also see Adolphe Terracher to Gustave Cohen, 23 Aug. 1924, PGC: 3.

60. See Baldensperger, "Quarante mois après," p. 391; Baldensperger, "L'Université de Strasbourg," p. 928; and Mary, "Les succès de la Faculté des Lettres." The observations concerning patterns of student migration are based on the lists of students receiving diplomas in 1924; the lists are in AN: F$^{17}$* 3399, 3420, 3442, 3470, and 3472.

61. Albert Grenier to Gustave Cohen, 18 Aug. 1925, PGC: 3; Lucien Febvre to Henri Pirenne, 13 Jan. 1926, PHP; Jean Pommier to Gustave Cohen, n.d. [30 Apr. 1927], PGC: 4; and interviews with Philippe Dollinger, 23 June 1976; Paul Leuilliot, 23 July 1976; Pierre Marthelot, 1 July 1976; and Robert Minder, 15 July 1976.

62. See "Résolutions adoptées à la réunion plénière des membres du corps enseignant de l'Université de Strasbourg," 4 Nov. 1920, and "Associations des membres du personnel enseignant de l'Université de Strasbourg: Ordre du jour," n.d. [1922], ADBR: AL 98, paq. 67; and Gabriel Alapetite to Louis Barthou, 4 May 1922, ibid., paq. 359.

63. Albert Grenier to Gustave Cohen, 26 Apr. 1927, PGC: 4. Also see Raymond Bloch, "Bio-bibliographie d'Albert Grenier," pp. 6–7.

64. Ernest Hoepffner to Gustave Cohen, 2 Feb. 1926, PGC: 4. Also see Paul Collomp to Cohen, 20 Dec. 1927, and Albert Grenier to Cohen, 30 May 1928, ibid.; and Imbs, "Ernest Hoepffner," p. 148.

65. "Zehn Jahre französische Universität in Strassburg," p. 68.

66. See Albert Grenier to Gustave Cohen, 23 Feb. 1928, PGC: 4; Jean Pommier to Cohen, 29 Oct. 1931, PGC: 6; and Febvre, "Marc Bloch et Strasbourg," p. 401.

67. See André Mazon to Gustave Cohen, 16 Dec. 1923, PGC: 2; Febvre, "Un psychologue: Charles Blondel," p. 374; and, on the professors' disillusionment with trends in French higher education, Marc Bloch, "Sur la réforme de l'enseignement," pp. 249–55; and Febvre, "L'enseignement supérieur," pp. 15'08.12–15'10.3.

68. Christian Pfister to Gustave Cohen, 20 Sept. 1925, PGC: 3.

69. Untitled memorandum, 20 Nov. 1932, ADBR: AL 98, paq. 367; Baldensperger, "L'Université de Strasbourg," p. 928; Mary, "Les succès de la Faculté des lettres"; Pfister, "La rentrée de l'université."

## Chapter 9

1. France, Statistique générale, *Annuaire statistique,* 37 (1921), et seq.; Germany, Statistisches Reichsamt, *Statistisches Jahrbuch für das Deutsche Reich,* 33 (1912): 306–7.

2. France, Statistique générale, *Annuaire statistique,* 36 (1919–20), et seq.

3. Ibid., 37 (1921), et seq.

4. Ibid., 20 (1900)–33 (1913); Germany, Statistisches Reichsamt, *Statistisches Jahrbuch,* 31 (1910)–34 (1913).

5. See "Université de Strasbourg: Relève des étudiants par faculté," ADBR: UStr; Adolphe Terracher to Bureau universitaire de statistique, 26 Apr. 1939, ibid.; Alsace-Lorraine, Conseil consultatif, *Procès-verbaux,* Jan. 1921 sess., p. 169; and tables 1 and 11, appendix B.

6. The relevant "Répertoires des diplômes" are in AN: F¹⁷* 3399, 3420, 3442, 3470, and 3472.

7. See table 3, appendix B.

8. "Faculté des lettres: Registre d'immatriculations des étudiants, 1923–24," ADBR: UStr; "Faculté des lettres: Statistique" (1932), ADBR: AL 154, no. 6; Verax [pseud.], "Die Frequenz der Strassburger Universität," pp. 270–71.

9. "Dix ans d'université française"; Verax [pseud.], "Die Frequenz der Strassburger Universität," pp. 268–69.

10. Minutes of the University Council, 12 Jan. 1920, ADBR: AL 101 (3); "Dix ans d'université française"; interview with Henri Cartan, 30 June 1976.

11. See the file headed STA* 13: Origine sociale at the Département de la documentation, Ministère de l'éducation, Vanves; and Ministère de l'éducation nationale to Adolphe Terracher, 14 Jan. 1939, ADBR: UStr.

12. See Prost, *Histoire de l'enseignement en France*, pp. 415–17; and Worms, "The French Student Movement," p. 268.

13. Adolphe Terracher to Bureau universitaire de statistique, 26 Apr. 1939, ADBR: UStr.

14. Evidence from *Who's Who in France*, 11 (1973–74), suggests that the families of 8 or 9 percent of all French students at the University of Strasbourg in the mid- and late 1930s had migrated to Alsace-Lorraine from the interior in or after 1919. Specifically, about a third of the entries born in the interior who studied in Strasbourg in the mid- or late 1930s had also attended lycées or collèges in Alsace-Lorraine.

15. See the file headed STA* 13: Origine sociale at the Département de la documentation, Ministère de l'éducation, Vanves.

16. Estimated from data in Adolphe Terracher to Bureau universitaire de statistique, 26 Apr. 1939, ADBR: UStr.

17. It could be argued, however, that declining opportunities for employment in these sectors would have increased the incentives for youths of these backgrounds to invest in education. (For developments of this argument, see Craig, "The Expansion of Education"; and Craig and Spear, "Explaining Educational Expansion.") In fact during the 1950s the proportion of all French university students from these declining occupational categories increased greatly, from 11.1 percent to 18.2 percent (see France, Institut pédagogique national, *Informations statistiques*, no. 22 [1960]: 300). This was not the case in Strasbourg between the wars, but it should be noted that the only underrepresented occupational category for which the selectivity index did not fall sharply between 1913–14 and 1938–39, the peasantry, was the only one declining in size both relatively and absolutely.

18. France, Statistique générale, *Annuaire statistique*, 43 (1927): 35–44; interviews with Paul Buck, 6 July 1976, and René Metz, 8 July 1976.

19. See Amestoy, *Les universités françaises*, pp. 109–16; Febvre, "L'enseignement supérieur," p. 15'08.16; Goblot, *La barrière et le niveau*, pp. 77–87; Suleiman, *Elites in French Society*, pp. 24–56; and Weisz, *The Emergence of Modern Universities in France*, pp. 107–17.

20. Robert Beudant to Jean de Pange, 21 Aug. 1924, AFDP; Baldensperger, "A travers les universités: Strasbourg," pp. 16–17; Febvre, "Marc Bloch et Strasbourg," p. 391; Vermeil, "L'opinion allemande et le problème alsacien."

21. Cohen, "Souvenir universitaire."

22. Fernand Baldensperger in minutes of the Faculty of Letters (Conseil), 16 Oct. 1919, ADBR: AL 154, no. 3.

23. See minutes of the University Council, 26 Mar. 1920, ADBR: UStr; Cohen, "Souvenir universitaire," p. 892; and Minder, "Edmond Vermeil," pp. i–ii.

24. Baldensperger, "Quarante mois après," p. 391.

25. Baldensperger, "L'Université de Strasbourg," pp. 927–28; interviews with Emile Baas, 27 Aug. 1976, and Robert Minder, 15 July 1976.

26. Minutes of the Faculty of Protestant Theology, 23 Oct. 1919, BFT; Paul Lobstein, "Rapport," pp. 20–21; Pfister, "Rapport général," pp. 7–8.

27. Minutes of the Faculty of Letters (Assemblée), 7 July 1934, ADBR: AL 154, no. 2; Nast, "Le redressement nécessaire"; interviews with Emile Baas, 27 Aug. 1976; Philippe Dollinger, 23 June 1976; and Jean P. Rothé, 9 July 1976. For the quotation see Paul Valot, "Statut du personnel de l'Université de Strasbourg," n.d. [1922?], ADBR: AL 98, paq. 359.

28. See Henri Albert to Hugo Haug, 21 Apr. 1920, FHH; "Méthodes universitaires françaises en Alsace," trans. from *Neue Badische Landeszeitung* (Mannheim), 24 Sept. 1925, ADBR: UStr; Baldensperger, "Quarante mois après," p. 391; Perrin, "L'enseignement secondaire en Alsace et Lorraine," p. 326; "Universitätsfragen."

29. Minutes of the University Council, 26 Mar. 1920, ADBR: UStr; Jean Pommier to Gustave Cohen, 1 Mar. 1924, PGC: 3; Baldensperger, "L'Université de Strasbourg," pp. 927–28; Lörcher, "Die Universität Strassburg und die Franzosen," p. 233.

30. "Méthodes universitaires françaises en Alsace," trans. from *Neue Badische Landeszeitung* (Mannheim), 24 Sept. 1925, ADBR: UStr.

31. Bergner, "Quelques silhouettes universitaires," p. 477; Craig, "Maurice Halbwachs à Strasbourg," pp. 287–89; Juillard, "Henri Baulig," p. 167; L'Huillier, "Georges Lefebvre à Strasbourg," pp. 371–72.

32. Philippe Dollinger, "Marc Bloch et Lucien Febvre," pp. 172–73; interview with Emile Baas, 27 Aug. 1976; Jacques Schwartz to the author, 25 Nov. 1977.

33. Gustave Cohen to Christian Pfister, 21 Oct. 1925, ADBR: UStr; K. R. Guerrier to Wilhelm Kapp, 31 May 1930, NWK; Baldensperger, "Quarante mois après," p. 391; A. M., "Alma mater im Flüchtlingsstrom"; *Lothringer Volkszeitung* as quoted in "Zehn Jahre französische Universität in Strassburg," p. 69.

34. Lucien Febvre to Henri Pirenne, 31 Jan. 1926, PHP; Paul Sabatier to Alfred Loisy, 19 Apr. 1926, PAL: 15661; Jean Pommier to Gustave Cohen, [30 Apr. 1927] and 8 Jan. 1930, PGC: 4, 5; interview with Jean Gaudemet, 28 June 1976.

35. Minutes of the Faculty of Letters (Assemblée), 10 Jan. 1920, ADBR: AL 154, no. 2.

36. France, Statistique générale, *Annuaire statistique,* 45 (1929): 43.

37. See "Origine des candidats aux diverses agrégations en 1925, 1926, 1927," ADBR: AL 154, no. 4.

38. Cohen, "Souvenir universitaire," p. 891. Also see Paul Sabatier to Alfred Loisy, 19 Apr. 1926, PAL: 15661; and Pfister, "Rapport général," pp. 7–8.

39. Most of the literature on higher education and socialization is specifically concerned with American higher education. For a comprehensive introduction, see Feldman and Newcomb, *The Impact of College on Students.*

40. Minutes of the Faculty of Letters (Assemblée), 26 June 1919, ADBR: AL 154, no. 2; minutes of the Faculty of Protestant Theology, 15 Apr. 1926, BFT; André Hallays to Ferdinand Dollinger, [25 Apr. 1921], FFD; André Hallays to Raymond Poincaré, 13 May 1922 and n.d. (2), PRP: 16003.

41. Brion, "Les étudiants alsaciens et lorrains à Paris," p. 330. Also see Betz, "Chez les étudiants alsaciens de Paris."

42. Brion, "Les étudiants alsaciens et lorrains à Paris," p. 330.

43. Spieser, *Tausend Brücken,* pp. 68–72; interviews with Paul Leuilliot, 23 July 1976; François-Georges Pariset, 4 Aug. 1976; and Ernest Schneegans, 24 June 1976.

44. Minutes of the Faculty of Protestant Theology, 15 Apr. 1926, BFT. Also see Lucien Herr to Albert Houtin, [29 Oct. 1919], PAH: 15710; and Pfister, "La première année," pp. 354–55.

45. Minutes of the Faculty of Letters (Assemblée), 25 Nov. 1922, ADBR: AL 154, no. 2.

46. France, Ministère de la guerre, Service d'Alsace-Lorraine, Sous-commission de l'enseignement supérieur, 28 Sept. 1917, FAT: 209; minutes of the Faculty of Letters (Assemblée), 13 Mar. 1920, ADBR: AL 154, no. 2.

47. Baldensperger, "L'Université de Strasbourg," p. 928; Mary, "Les succès de la Faculté des lettres," p. 966.

48. "Ein Kulturproblem."

49. "Statistique des étudiants arrêté au 31 juillet 1929," ADBR: UStr.

50. Robert Beudant to Sebastien Charléty, 9 Nov. 1919, ADBR: UStr.

51. Robert Beudant to Sebastien Charléty, 11 Nov. 1921, ADBR: UStr. Also see minutes of the University Council, 8 Jan. 1920, ADBR: UStr; and Hallays, "L'Université de Strasbourg," pp. 262–64.

52. Haut-commissariat de la République française dans les provinces du Rhin: Procès-verbal, 14 Dec. 1919, ADBR: UStr; minutes of the University Council, 8 Jan. 1920, ibid.; minutes of the Faculty of Protestant Theology, 15 Jan. 1920, BFT. Also see Louis Canet, "La Faculté de théologie catholique de l'Université de Strasbourg et les intérêts français," 11 Apr. 1919; and Anon., "Note sur la Faculté de théologie catholique de Strasbourg," 5 June 1919, FM: 46, III (9).

53. Eugène Bataillon to Sebastien Charléty, 6 Jan. 1920, ADBR: UStr. Also see [Kohler], "Die Strassburger Universität."

54. Minutes of the University Council, 8 Jan. 1920, ADBR: UStr.

55. France, Statistique générale, *Annuaire statistique,* 37 (1921)–45 (1929), passim.

56. Sebastien Charléty to Albert Thomas, 9 Aug. 1919, FAT: 211.

57. Minutes of the University Council, 20 Feb. and 8 Mar. 1920, ADBR: UStr; Jadin, "Rapport général," p. 5; Pfister, "Rapport général," pp. 12–13.

58. Fernand Baldensperger to Jean de Pange, 29 Mar. 1920, AFDP; "Méthodes universitaires françaises en Alsace," trans. from *Neue Badische Landeszeitung* (Mannheim), 24 Sept. 1925, ADBR: UStr; Pfister, "La Faculté des lettres de Strasbourg," p. 3.

59. [Cercle des anciens étudiants], "L'avenir de l'Université de Strasbourg"; Specklin, "Les étudiants de Strasbourg," p. 28.

60. P. Deteix to Henri Borromée, 5 June 1923, ADBR: D 286, paq. 77, no. 28; A. B. G., "15 années de vie corporative estudiantine," p. 4.

61. Quoted from a speech by A. Autrand (prefect of the Seine), "Le voyage à Paris du Cercle E. S.," p. 22.

62. Cercle des étudiants de Strasbourg, *Fêtes universitaires,* p. 110.

63. University of Strasbourg, *Université de Strasbourg: Fêtes d'inauguration,* pp. 40–42. For general surveys of the Cercle's activities in the year preceding the opening of the university, see Garcin, "L'activité du Cercle depuis l'armistice," pp. 4–7; and Moerlen and Bechelen, *La lutte de la jeunesse estudiantine,* pp. 46–49.

64. Sebastien Charléty to Paul Valot, 28 July 1926, ADBR: AL 98, paq. 362, no. 66.

65. Ibid.; Garcin, "L'activité du Cercle depuis l'armistice," p. 6.

66. See "Liste des membres actifs du Cercle des étudiants," FHH: 7.

67. "Eine elsässische Studentin für viele" to Albert Ehrhard, 1 Dec. 1918, NAE. Also see A. B. G., "15 années de vie corporative estudiantine," p. 4.

68. "Méthodes universitaires françaises en Alsace," trans. from *Neue Badische Landeszeitung* (Mannheim), 24 Sept. 1925, ADBR: UStr. Also see A. Barthelmé, "Zusammenhänge," p. 15; "Nos enquêtes: Strasbourg-Universitaire"; and Rossé et al., eds., *Das Elsass von 1870–1932,* 3:140.

69. On Wilhelmitana, see Wilhelmitana, *Die Wilhelmitana,* pp. 70–73, 76–80.

70. Duquesne, *Le catholicisme et la jeunesse universitaire en Alsace,* pp. 1–2 (for the quotation), 14; *Der Elsässer,* 7 Mar. 1922.

71. On the Cercle Ozanam, see A. B. G., "15 années de vie corporative estudiantine," p. 4; and Platon [pseud.], "Le cachet spécifique de notre cercle," p. 13.

72. Wilhelmitana, *Die Wilhelmitana,* p. 76. Also see Zind, *Elsass-Lothringen,* pp. 179, 280, 287.

73. Quoted in "Studentenstreiche."

74. Untitled and undated manifesto from "Vindex," copy in ADBR: AL 140, no. 46; "Anniversaire," pp. 1–2; "Studentenstreiche"; interview with René Sartory, 24 Aug. 1976.

75. Services de police de Strasbourg to [?], 21 and 23 Apr. 1921, ADBR: AL 140, no. 46; "Studentenstreiche."

76. Vermeil, "La mission européenne de Strasbourg," p. 128; interviews with Philippe Dollinger, 23 June 1976, and Pierre Marthelot, 1 July 1976.

77. "A propos de la manifestation estudiantine"; "Studentenstreiche."

78. "Les étudiants alsaciens et lorrains et leurs camarades d'outre-Vosges." Also see "Comité des étudiants organisés de Strasbourg"; "Les étudiants réclament"; Pagny, "Aidons les étudiants de notre université"; and Ricklin, "Les débuts de l'A. F. G.," p. 5.

79. A. B. G., "15 années de vie corporative estudiantine," p. 4; "Histoire de l'A. G. en 1924," pp. 4–5.

80. "Anniversaire," pp. 1–2; Bobtcheff, "Activité de l'A. G. en 1923," pp. 5–7; Curvale, "Le S. E. C.," p. 22; A. B. G., "15 années de vie corporative estudiantine," p. 4; "Histoire de l'A. G. en 1924," pp. 2–6; "Le journal de l'A. G.," p. 1; "Nos amicales"; Ricklin, "Les débuts de l'A. F. G.," p. 5; "Strassburger Studentenleben."

81. Fernand Baldensperger to Jean de Pange, 29 Mar. 1920, AFDP; minutes of the University Council, 4 Nov. 1920, 1 July and 3 Nov. 1923, and 2 May 1925, ADBR: UStr.

82. Minutes of the University Council, 21 Feb. 1923, ADBR: UStr.

83. Sebastien Charléty to F. Deteix, 12 June 1923, ADBR: D 286, paq. 77, no. 28. Also see Henri Borromée to F. Deteix, 14 June 1923, ibid.

84. Beudant, "La Faculté de droit et des sciences politiques," pp. 52–53; Ehrhardt, "Rapport général," pp. 22–23.

85. Gustave Cohen to Christian Pfister, 21 Oct. 1925, ADBR: UStr.

86. Durkheim, "Rôle des universités dans l'éducation sociale du pays," p. 185. Also see Weisz, *The Emergence of Modern Universities in France*, pp. 303–7.

87. Minutes of the University Council, 1 July 1923, ADBR: UStr. Also see Fernand Baldensperger to Jean de Pange, 29 Mar. 1920, AFDP.

88. Memorandum by Unterstaatssekretär Lewald, 16 Oct. 1918, reprinted in Schwander and Jaffé, "Die reichsländischen Regierungen und die Verfassung," pp. 128–29.

89. Jules Leyder to Albert Houtin, 19 Mar. 1919, PAH: 15717.

90. Quoted in Rothenberger, *Die elsass-lothringische Heimat- und Autonomiebewegung*, p. 46. Also see Lion, *Das Elsass als Problem*, p. 355.

91. Price, "Strasbourg in Alsace," p. 200. Also see Jules Leyder to Albert Houtin, 13 Jan., 29 Mar., and 22 Nov. 1920, and 10 Oct. 1921, PAH: 15717.

92. See Baechler, "L'Alsace entre la guerre et la paix," pp. 404–10.

93. Rothenberger, *Die elsass-lothringische Heimat- und Autonomiebewegung*, pp. 44–45, 51–53.

94. Ibid., pp. 53–56; Jules Leyder to Albert Houtin, 25 Mar. 1919, PAH: 15717; Sebastien Charléty to Ernest Lavisse, 10 Mar. 1921, PEL: 25172; Dreyfus, *La vie politique en Alsace*, pp. 36–50.

95. France, *Journal officiel*, Chambre des députés, 12th leg., 1921 (ord. sess.), *Documents parlementaires*, 1:379.

96. Jules Leyder to Albert Houtin, 19 Mar. and 17 Oct. 1919, PAH: 15717; Sebastien Charléty to Ernest Lavisse, 9 and 14 Feb. [1921], PEL: 25172; Boulanger to Ernest Lavisse, 9 Mar. 1921, PEL: 25172; Rothenberger, *Die elsass-lothringische Heimat- und Autonomiebewegung*, pp. 49, 52; Wahl, *Confession et comportement*, pp. 814–22.

97. Direction de police de Strasbourg to Ministère de l'Intérieur, 1 May 1920, AN: F[7] 13377; Jules Leyder to Albert Houtin, 29 Apr. 1922, PAH: 15717; André Hallays to Ferdinand Dollinger, [Mar. 1926], FFD; Rothenberger, *Die elsass-lothringische Heimat- und Autonomiebewegung*, pp. 46–47.

98. Albert Thomas, "Note sur la conversation avec M. Bucher," 5 Aug. 1919, FAT: 212; Jules Leyder to Albert Houtin, 13 Jan., 29 Mar., and 31 May 1920, and 10 Oct. 1921, PAH: 15717; M. Jourdan to Ernest Lavisse, 14 Mar. 1921, PEL: 25172; Fritz Kiener to Jean de Pange, 22 June 1928, AFDP; Rothenberger, *Die elsass-lothringische Heimat- und Autonomiebewegung,* pp. 48–50.

99. Direction de police de Strasbourg to Ministère de l'Intérieur, 1 May 1920, AN: F⁷ 13377; Antoni, *Grenzlandschicksal-Grenzlandtragik,* pp. 28–29; Herber, *Elsässisches Lust- und Leidbuch,* p. 124; "Les 'Herren Doktoren'"; Rothenberger, *Die elsass-lothringische Heimat- und Autonomiebewegung,* pp. 38–39, 48–50, 56–58; Strohl, *Le protestantisme en Alsace,* pp. 458–59.

100. Direction de police de Strasbourg to Ministère de l'Intérieur, 1 May 1920 and 3 Mar. 1921, AN: F⁷ 13377; Henri Borromée to Aristide Briand, 15 Dec. 1925, ADBR: AL 98, paq. 1283; Dreyfus, *La vie politique en Alsace,* pp. 69–71; Rothenberger, *Die elsass-lothringische Heimat- und Autonomiebewegung,* pp. 58–71.

101. Dreyfus, *La vie politique en Alsace,* pp. 52–56.

102. Interviews with Henri Cartan, 30 June 1976; Jean Gaudemet, 28 June 1976; and Jean Gagé, 3 July 1976.

103. Albert Grenier to Louis Havet, 4 May 1919, BN: NAF 24495 (2); Marc Bloch, *Strange Defeat,* pp. 155–72; Halbwachs, "Notre politique en Alsace-Lorraine"; Levinas, "Emmanuel Levinas," p. 325; Sée, *Histoire de la Ligue des droits de l'homme,* pp. 179, 183–85; interviews with Philippe Dollinger, 23 June 1976; Fernand L'Huillier, 22 June 1976; and François-Georges Pariset, 4 Aug. 1976. For the French academic community generally see Blanchard, *Je découvre l'université,* pp. 90–91; Bourgin, *De Jaurès à Léon Blum,* pp. 111–13, 400–402, 449–51, 485–87; Debray, *Teachers, Writers, Celebrities,* pp. 49–59; Gerbod, *Les enseignants et la politique,* pp. 9–15, 23–29, 32–39, 42–55; L'Huillier, *Dialogues franco-allemands,* p. 29; Smith, *The Ecole Normale Supérieure,* pp. 86–103; and Thibaudet, *La république des professeurs,* pp. 14, 18, 23, 56–63.

104. Interviews with Georges Cerf, 2 Sept. 1976; Jean Gaudemet, 28 June 1976; Robert Minder, 15 July 1976; François-Georges Pariset, 4 Aug. 1976; and A. G. Weiss, 1 July 1976.

105. Interviews with Henri Cartan, 30 June 1976; Jean Gaudemet, 28 June 1976; René Sartory, 24 Aug. 1976; Jacques Schwartz, 30 Aug. 1976; Alex Weill, 25 Aug. 1976; and A. G. Weiss, 1 July 1976. For the French academic community generally, see Blanchard, *Je découvre l'université,* pp. 89–90; Bourgin, *De Jaurès à Léon Blum,* p. 276; Gerbod, *Les enseignants et la politique,* pp. 15–22, 29–32, 39–42, 55–57; and Thibaudet, *La république des professeurs,* pp. 120–22.

106. Fernand Baldensperger to Jean de Pange, 7 Aug. 1922, AFDP; Baldensperger, *Une vie parmi d'autres,* pp. 319–20; Nast, *Le malaise alsacien-lorrain,* pp. 48–50.

107. Two from the interior who may have been in this group were the jurists Raymond Carré de Malberg, a revenant, and Joseph Duquesne; see Fritz Kiener to Jean de Pange, 21 Nov. 1928, AFDP; and de Pange, *Journal,* 1:141–42.

108. Maurice Halbwachs to Albert Thomas, 21 Nov. 1919 and 6 Jan. 1924, FAT: 211 and 381; Cerf, "Edmond Rothé, citoyen."

109. Delpech, "Centralisation et régionalisme"; Dreyfus, *La vie politique en Alsace,* pp. 72–73; Gerbod, *Les enseignants et la politique,* p. 41; Nast, *Was hinter der elsass-lothringischen Frage steckt!* pp. 29–33; "Notre enquête sur le régionalisme"; Sigmann, "La bourgeoisie et l'opinion politique du Bas-Rhin," pp. 460, 474, 477; Vedel, "Paul Gemaehling," p. 445.

110. Rossé et al., eds., *Das Elsass von 1870–1932,* 4:97, 108–9.

111. Bloch, *Strange Defeat,* pp. 171–73; Bourgin, *De Jaurès à Léon Blum,* pp. 411–12, 425; Prélot, "Introduction."

112. Robert Beudant to Jean de Pange, 21 Aug. 1924, AFDP. Also: Leriche, *Souvenirs de ma vie morte,* p. 76; and interviews with Emile Baas, 27 Aug. 1976; Jean Gaudemet, 28 June 1976; Robert Minder, 15 July 1976; and Jacques Schwartz, 30 Aug. 1976.

113. See Amestoy, *Les universités françaises,* pp. 111–12; Audollent, "Y a-t-il lieu de 'spécialiser' et de 'moderniser' nos universités provinciales?" p. 133; Durkheim, "Rôle des universités dans l'éducation sociale du pays," pp. 181–82; and Prost, *Histoire de l'enseignement en France,* pp. 227–28, 230, 234.

114. Minutes of the Faculty of Letters (Assemblée), 15 Oct. 1919, ADBR: AL 154, no. 2; minutes of the Faculty of Protestant Theology, 13 Dec. 1919, BFT; Pfister, "Rapport de M. Chr. Pfister," p. 128; Pfister, "Rapport général," p. 8.

115. Minutes of the University Council, 31 Oct. 1919, ADBR: UStr. Also see [Pfister], "Rapport sur l'Université de Strasbourg," BNUS: Ms 4850, p. 77.

116. Minutes of the University Council, 8 Jan. 1920, ADBR: UStr; minutes of the Faculty of Letters (Assemblée), 12 Dec. 1919 and 23 Jan. 1920, ADBR: AL 154, no. 2.

117. Minutes of the University Council, 14 Dec. 1920, ADBR: UStr; minutes of the Faculty of Letters (Assemblée), 28 May 1921, ADBR: AL 154, no. 2; Lang, "Rapport général," pp. 10–11; Robert Redslob, "Huit années d'extension universitaire."

118. Ehrhardt, "Rapport général," p. 18; Pfister, "Rapport de M. Chr. Pfister," p. 133.

119. P. Muller to Sebastien Charléty, 28 Nov. 1921, AN: F[17] 13085; "Ecole de formation sociale"; Ehrhardt, "Rapport général," p. 18; Koch, "L'Université de Strasbourg et ses rapports avec l'économie régionale," p. 942.

120. Gabriel Maugain to [?], 4 Feb. 1928, ADBR: AL 154, no. 4; Ehrhardt, "Rapport général," p. 18; Terracher, "Les cours populaires de langue française," p. 1175.

121. Gabriel Maugain to [?], 4 Feb. 1928, ADBR: AL 154, no. 4; Ehrhardt, "Rapport général," p. 18.

122. Paul Perdrizet to Jean de Pange, 24 Oct. 1923, AFDP.

123. Jean Gentzbourger to Albert Thomas, 10 Nov. 1919, FAT: 211; Jean Gentzbourger to M. Berninger, 24 Jan. 1920, ADBR: AL 74, vol. 20.

124. Sebastien Charléty's reports in the dossier of Christian Pfister, AN: F[17] 24214; Gabriel Maugain's and Christian Pfister's reports in the dossier of Georges Lefebvre, ADBR: UStr; L'Huillier, "Georges Lefebvre à Strasbourg," pp. 371–72; Pommier, *Le spectacle intérieur,* pp. 329–30, 349.

125. Bergner, "Quelques silhouettes universitaires," p. 479. Also see ibid., pp. 477–80; Gabriel Maugain to [?], 4 Feb. 1928, ADBR: AL 154, no. 4; and Pfister, "Rapport de M. Chr. Pfister," p. 126.

126. Baldeck, "Elsässer Brief," p. 488; Bergner, "Quelques silhouettes universitaires," pp. 479–80; Lang, "Rapport général," pp. 10–11; Lange, "L'enseignement populaire du français en Alsace," pp. 631–32; Robert Redslob, "Huit années d'extension universitaire," pp. 161–62; interviews with Emile Baas, 27 Aug. 1976; Paul Leuilliot, 29 June and 23 July 1976; François-Georges Pariset, 24 July and 4 Aug. 1976; and Jean Rothé, 9 July 1976.

127. Nast, "Le redressement nécessaire"; interviews with Paul Leuilliot, 29 June 1976; Pierre Marthelot, 1 July 1976; and Henri Maresquelle, 22 June 1976.

128. Jean Gentzbourger to Albert Thomas, 10 Nov. 1919, FAT: 211; Jean Gentzbourger to M. Berninger, 24 Jan. 1920, ADBR: AL 74, vol. 20.

129. Minutes of the University Council, 1 Dec. 1919, ADBR: UStr; "Note sur le Ruskin College Oxford," "Note sur la 'London School of Economics and Political Science' (Université de Londres)," "Université du Travail 'Charleroi,'" and Institut du Travail: Compte rendu des travaux, PFS: 1963.

130. Charles Andler, "Aperçus sur un Institut du Travail pour l'Université de Strasbourg," ibid.

131. See minutes of the University Council, 26 Mar. 1920, ADBR: UStr; Charles Brouilhet to François Simiand, 17 Apr. 1920, PFS: 1963; and M. Vidal to Gabriel Alapetite, 20 Jan. 1921, AACVS: B. 270/1490.

132. Jules Leyder to Albert Houtin, 15 May 1926, PAH: 15717.

133. Charles Hauter to Eugène Ehrhardt, n.d. [ca. 1921], 22 and 29 May 1925, ADBR: AL 103, no. 900; Ligue des amis de la Confession d'Augsbourg en Alsace et Lorraine to Eugène Ehrhardt, 17 Apr. 1922, and Eugène Ehrhardt to Ligue des amis . . . , 29 Apr. 1922, ibid.; minutes of the Faculty of Protestant Theology, 12 May 1921, BFT; interviews with François G. Dreyfus, 5 July 1976, and Pierre Marthelot, 1 July 1976.

134. Minutes of the University Council, 27 Jan. 1923, ADBR: UStr. Later in 1923 the Vatican, at the urging of France's Ministry of Foreign Affairs, agreed to recognize the continued applicability of the accord concluded in 1902 by Hertling and Rampolla, thus ending the lingering uncertainty over the status of the Catholic theological faculty; for the relevant documents, see Le Léannac, "L'enseignement supérieur," pp. 305–9.

135. Interviews with Jean Gaudemet, 28 June 1976, and Pierre Marthelot, 1 July 1976.

136. See, for instance, "Studentenstreiche."

137. Joseph Pfleger in Alsace-Lorraine, Conseil consultatif, *Procès-verbaux,* Jan. 1921 sess., p. 171.

138. L. L., "Die Strassburger Universität."

139. See Abbé Hackspill in Alsace-Lorraine, Conseil supérieur, *Procès-verbaux,* Mar. 1920 sess., pp. 24–25; and Eugène Muller in Alsace-Lorraine, Conseil consultatif, *Procès-verbaux,* Jan. 1921 sess., pp. 171–72.

140. See Albert Helmer in Alsace-Lorraine, Conseil supérieur, *Procès-verbaux,* Aug. 1919 sess., p. 33; and Eugène Muller in Alsace-Lorraine, Conseil consultatif, *Procès-verbaux,* Jan. 1921 sess., pp. 171–72.

141. See Xavier Haegy in Alsace-Lorraine, Conseil consultatif, *Procès-verbaux,* Jan. 1921 sess., pp. 169–70.

142. Baldensperger, *Une vie parmi d'autres,* p. 320.

143. Jules Leyder to Albert Houtin, 10 Oct. 1921, PAH: 15717; Joseph Pfleger in Alsace-Lorraine, Conseil consultatif, *Procès-verbaux,* Jan. 1921 sess., pp. 170–71. Also see Pfister to Charléty, 13 Nov. 1920 and 16 Dec. 1923, AN: F[17] 13085 and 13086.

144. Y., "Universität und Kulturpolitik." Also see Eugène Muller in the University Council, 26 Mar. 1920, ADBR: UStr; Xavier Haegy in Alsace-Lorraine, Conseil consultatif, *Procès-verbaux,* Jan. 1921 sess., pp. 169–70; L. L., "Die Strassburger Universität"; and "Universitätsfragen."

145. See, for instance, Daigle, *La culture en partage,* pp. 109–11.

146. See [Hugo Haug], "Appel des partis bourgeois, réunis en cartel de l'ordre," n.d. [1919?], FHH: 11.

147. Alexandre Millerand, "Arrête relatif à la constitution d'une Commission consultative chargée de l'étude du projet de création d'une Ecole technique supérieure en Alsace et Lorraine," 10 Feb. 1920; M. Vidal to Gabriel Alapetite, 20 Jan. 1921; and "Aide-mémoire concernant l'Ecole nationale technique et l'ancien projet d'une nouvelle Ecole d'arts et métiers," 24 Nov. 1935, AACVS: B. 270/1490; Alsace-Lorraine, Conseil supérieur, *Procès-verbaux,* Dec. 1919 sess., pp. 28–29, 50–61, and Feb. 1920 sess., pp. 25–29; Koch, "L'Université de Strasbourg et ses rapports avec l'économie régionale," p. 942; Weiller, "L'Université de Strasbourg."

148. Henri Albert quoted in "Die Strassburger Universität," p. 282. Also see Henri Lichtenberger and André Lichtenberger, *La question d'Alsace-Lorraine,* pp. 114–15.

149. [Kohler], "Die Strassburger Universität." Also see Baldensperger, "Quarante mois après," p. 391; and Baldensperger, "L'Université de Strasbourg," p. 928.

150. Pfister to Charléty, 4 Mar. 1922, ADBR: UStr.

151. Vermeil, "Le cinquantenaire de l'Université Kaiser Wilhelm," p. 370.

152. Georges Weiss to Charléty, 12 Nov. 1920, AN: F[17] 13084.

153. Pfister to Charléty, 13 Nov. 1920, AN: F[17] 13085. Also see Pfister to Charléty [?], 29 Jan. 1921, ADBR: UStr; and Pfister to Charléty, 16 Dec. 1923, AN: F[17] 13086.

154. Minutes of the Faculty of Letters (Conseil), 5 Feb. 1920, ADBR: AL 154, no. 3; minutes of the Faculty of Protestant Theology, 12 May 1921, BFT; Charles Hauter to Eugène Ehrhardt, n.d. [ca. 1921], ADBR: AL 103, no. 900; interviews with Ernest Schneegans, 8 July 1976, and A. G. Weiss, 1 July 1976.

155. See, for instance, Jean Pommier to Gustave Cohen, 1 Mar. 1924, PGC: 3.

156. Fernand Baldensperger to Jean de Pange, 8 May 1920, AFDP; Pierre Bucher to Raymond Poincaré, 14 Dec. 1920 and 10 Jan. 1921, PRP: 15995; André Hallays to Raymond Poincaré, 13 May 1922, PRP: 16003; Ferdinand Dollinger, "La Société des amis," pp. 930–31; Pfister, "Rapport général," pp. 13–14.

157. Baldensperger, Une vie parmi d'autres, p. 321.

158. On the regionalists' special interest in Alsace-Lorraine after World War I, see Andler, Vie de Lucien Herr, pp. 276–77; Dreyfus, La vie politique en Alsace, pp. 51–52; and Millerand, Le retour de l'Alsace-Lorraine, pp. 218–19.

159. Minutes of the Faculty of Letters (Assemblée), 13 Mar. 1920, ADBR: AL 154, no. 2. Also see Baldensperger, "Maurice Barrès et la Rhénanie"; and Baldensperger, Une vie parmi d'autres, pp. 322–26.

160. Minutes of the Faculty of Letters (Assemblée), 13 Mar. 1920, ADBR: AL 154, no. 2; Maurice Halbwachs to Albert Thomas, 21 Oct. 1920, FAT: 381; interview with François-Georges Pariset, 4 Aug. 1976.

161. Jean de Pange, "Discours" on Maurice Barrès, n.d.[Nov. 1920], AFDP; Baldensperger, "Les grands jours strasbourgeois de Maurice Barrès," pp. 965–66; "Le génie français sur le Rhin."

162. Baldensperger, Une vie parmi d'autres, p. 322; Bloch, Strange Defeat, p. 155; interview with François-Georges Pariset, 4 Aug. 1976.

163. Direction de police de Strasbourg to Ministére de l'Intérieur, 6 Dec. 1920, AN: F[7] 13377; Baldensperger, "Les grands jours strasbourgeois de Maurice Barrès," pp. 965–66; Lörcher, "Die Universität Strassburg und die Franzosen," p. 234; interview with Robert Heitz, 22 June 1976. For the text of the lectures, see Barrès, Le génie du Rhin.

164. See, for instance, minutes of the Faculty of Letters (Assemblée), 23 Oct. 1920, ADBR: AL 154, no. 2.

165. André Hallays to Ferdinand Dollinger, n.d. [autumn 1922], FFD: 13. Also see Pierre Bucher to Raymond Poincaré, 10 Jan. 1921, PRP: 15995.

166. André Hallays to Ferdinand Dollinger, 9 Dec. 1922, FFD: 13.

167. On the municipal hospital and the medical faculty, see Alsace-Lorraine, Conseil consultatif, Procès-verbaux, Jan. 1921 sess., p. 170.

168. Aaron [Georges Delahache, pseud.], Strasbourg, pp. 89–90; interviews with François G. Dreyfus, 5 July 1976; Fernand L'Huillier, 22 June 1976; Alex Weill, 25 Aug. 1976; and A. G. Weiss, 1 July 1976.

169. Maurice Halbwachs to Albert Thomas, 21 Nov. 1919, FAT: 211; Vermeil, "La mission européenne de Strasbourg," pp. 126–27; J. L. Koszul to the author, 18 May and 15 June 1976.

170. Henri Strohl, "Paul Sabatier (1858–1928)," copy in ADBR: AL 103, no. 900; Minder, "Introduction," pp. 18–19; Robert Redslob, "Raymond Carré de Malberg," pp. 17–18; interviews with Henri Cartan, 30 June 1976; Jean Gaudemet, 28 June 1976; Robert Minder, 15 July 1976; and François-Georges Pariset, 24 July 1976.

171. Lucien Febvre to Henri Pirenne, 13 Jan. 1926, PHP; interviews with Henri Cartan, 30 June 1976; Jean Gaudemet, 28 June 1976; and Jean Rothé, 9 July 1976.

172. Jean de Pange, *Journal*, 4:147; interviews with Emile Baas, 27 Aug. 1976; Henri Cartan, 30 June 1976; and Jean Gaudemet, 28 June 1976.

## Chapter 10

1. Ehrhardt, "Rapport général," p. 3.
2. Edouard Herriot in France, *Journal officiel*, Chamber of Deputies, 13th leg., 1924 (ord. sess.), *Débats*, p. 2306.
3. Robert Schuman in ibid., p. 2347.
4. Geneviève Baas, *Le malaise alsacien*, pp. 122–31; Bonnefous, *Histoire politique de la Troisième République*, 4:40–42; Dreyfus, *La vie politique en Alsace*, pp. 81–89; Rossé et al., eds., *Das Elsass von 1870–1932*, 1:663–75; Rothenberger, *Die elsass-lothringische Heimat- und Autonomiebewegung*, pp. 82–88.
5. Paul Painlevé in France, *Journal officiel*, Chamber of Deputies, 13th leg., 1925 (ord. sess.), *Débats*, pp. 2215.
6. Bonnefous, *Histoire politique de la troisième république*, 4:42; Dreyfus, *La vie politique en Alsace*, p. 89; Rossé et al., eds., *Das Elsass von 1870–1932*, 1:675–88; Rothenberger, *Die elsass-lothringische Heimat- und Autonomiebewegung*, pp. 86–88.
7. Eugen Jacobi to Wilhelm Kapp, 7 Jan. 1926, and Karl Roos to Kapp, 12 Oct. 1926, NWK: 1.
8. "Zum Geleit!"
9. Services généraux de polices d'Alsace et de Lorraine to Sûreté générale (Paris), 9 Jan. 1926, ADBR: AL 98, paq. 1283; Baldeck, "Elsässer Brief," p. 488.
10. For the text of the manifesto see Rossé et al., eds., *Das Elsass von 1870–1932*, 4:498–501. On the background see ibid., 1:697–704, 708–13; Antoni, *Grenzlandschicksal-Grenzlandtragik*, pp. 124–26; Dreyfus, *La vie politique en Alsace*, pp. 90–102; Rothenberger, *Die elsass-lothringische Heimat- und Autonomiebewegung*, pp. 89–113; Zind, *Elsass-Lothringen*, pp. 153–282.
11. Henri Borromée to ?, 15 Dec. 1925, and Borromée to Pierre Laval, 2 June 1926, ADBR: AL 98, paq. 1283; Berstein, "Une greffe politique manquée," pp. 91–99; Dreyfus, *La vie politique en Alsace*, pp. 102–17; "Die Gründung der autonomistischen Partei"; Reimeringer, "Un communisme régionaliste?" pp. 370–77; Rossé et al., eds., *Das Elsass von 1870–1932*, 1:704–8, 724–28; Rothenberger, *Die elsass-lothringische Heimat- und Autonomiebewegung*, pp. 123–37.
12. Henri Borromée to Louis Malvy, 17 Mar. 1926, ADBR: AL 98, paq. 1283.
13. Henri Borromée to Pierre Laval, 1 June 1926, and Borromée to Aristide Briand, 29 July and 9 Sept. 1926, ibid.; Antoni, *Grenzlandschicksal-Grenzlandtragik*, pp. 132–43; Gras, "La presse française et l'autonomisme alsacien en 1926," pp. 359–60; Maugué, *Le particularisme alsacien*, pp. 81–84; Rossé et al., eds., *Das Elsass von 1870–1932*, 1:713–24; Rothenberger, *Die elsass-lothringische Heimat- und Autonomiebewegung*, pp. 113–23, 137–38.
14. Friedrich König to Wilhelm Kapp, 22 Dec. 1928, NWK: 1.
15. Henri Borromée to Paul Valot, 14 Nov. 1928 and 16 Aug. 1929, ADBR: AL 98, paq. 1278; Valot to Raymond Poincaré, 19 May 1931, PRP: 16018; Dreyfus, *La vie politique en Alsace*, pp. 133–207; Maugué, *Le particularisme alsacien*, pp. 85–98; Rossé et al., eds., *Das Elsass von 1870–1932*, 1:752–84; Rothenberger, *Die elsass-lothringische Heimat- und Autonomiebewegung*, pp. 165–212.
16. "Die Gründung der Autonomistischen Partei"; "Strassburger Studentenleben"; "Die studierende Jugend Elsass-Lothringens," p. 3; "Universität, Landesbibliothek und höhere Schulen unter Charléty," p. 5; "Von der Strassburger Universität" (*Die Zukunft*), p. 3.
17. Rossé et al., eds., *Das Elsass von 1870–1932*, 4:498.
18. Herber, *Elsässisches Lust- und Leidbuch*, pp. 72, 109.
19. Rossé et al., eds., *Das Elsass von 1870–1932*, 4:500.

424     Notes to Pages 295–299

20. Wolf, *Das elsässische Problem*, pp. 94, 96–97. Also see ibid., p. 112.

21. "Programme du 'Landespartei,'" p. 191.

22. Rossé et al., eds., *Das Elsass von 1870–1932*, 3:195–97.

23. Ibid., pp. 191–92, 195–97; Fritz Kiener to Jean de Pange, 28 Feb. 1932, AFDP; Spieser, *Kampfbriefe aus dem Elsass*, pp. 125–27.

24. Bickler, "Studenten im elsässischen Volkstumskampf," p. 188; Wilhelmitana, *Die Wilhelmitana*, pp. 70, 80, 83–85; interview with François-Georges Pariset, 4 Aug. 1976.

25. René Paira and Gabriel Moy to André Helmer, 7 Apr. 1926, and Rapport sur l'Association fédérative générale et sur les étudiants de Strasbourg, 5 Aug. 1926, ADBR: AL 98, paq. 362; Wilhelmitana, *Die Wilhelmitana*, pp. 87–89, 92–94.

26. "Alsatia et Argentina"; Bickler, *Ein besonderes Land*, pp. 93–94, 132–35; Kissel, "Alsatia-Strasbourg," pp. 18–19; "Liste des anciens"; Platon [pseud.], "Rückblick auf das Gründungsjahr," p. 16–17; Wach, "De Alsatia," p. 10; Zind, *Elsass-Lothringen*, pp. 609–10.

27. Brauner, "Der interkorporative Vertreterausschuss," p. 28.

28. Ibid.; Wilhelmitana, *Die Wilhelmitana*, pp. 89–90, 94–95; Zind, *Elsass-Lothringen*, pp. 608–9.

29. Fritz Spieser to Wilhelm Kapp, 13 Jan. 1926, NWK: 1; Christian Pfister, "Rapport sur le fonctionnement du service de l'enseignement supérieur en Alsace et en Lorraine du 30 juin 1928 au 1er août 1929," ADBR: AL 98, paq. 335; Hecker, "Um die Meisterlockerdebatte."

30. Emile Baas, *Situation de l'Alsace*, p. 58; Delage, "La vie des étudiants: Strasbourg"; Lucas, "Un mouvement autonomiste à l'Université de Strasbourg," pp. 15–16; de Pange, *Journal*, 1:54; L. S., "Protest."

31. Dreyfus, *La vie politique en Alsace*, p. 105; interviews with Philippe Dollinger, 23 June 1976; René Mehl, 26 Aug. 1976; René Metz, 8 July 1976; and Ernest Schneegans, 24 June 1976.

32. Christian, "Korporationsprinzip und studentische Verhältnisse in Strassburg," p. 32. Also see Bennrath, "Quatre étudiants allemands en Alsace."

33. A. Ricklin to Raymond Poincaré, 14 Oct. 1926, ADBR: AL 98, paq. 363. On these leagues and French student politics in the 1920s, see Soucy, "Centrist Fascism"; and Eugen Weber, *Action Française*, pp. 155, 157–59, 180–81, 210–11.

34. Rapport sur l'Association fédérative générale et sur les étudiants de Strasbourg, 5 Aug. 1926, ADBR: AL 98, paq. 362; "Von der Strassburger Universität" (*Die Zukunft*), p. 3.

35. A. Ricklin to Raymond Poincaré, 14 Oct. 1926, ADBR: AL 98, paq. 362; Bennrath, "Quatre étudiants allemands en Alsace," p. 152; [Heitz], *Petite histoire de l'autonomisme*, pp. 80–81; "Sin d'Stüdente, wo stüdiere!"; "Die Studenten sind wieder da"; interview with Jean Rothé, 9 July 1976.

36. René Paira and Gabriel Moy to André Helmer, 7 Apr. 1926, and Paira to Paul Valot, 27 Apr. 1926, ADBR: AL 98, paq. 362; "Die studierende Jugend Elsass-Lothringens," p. 3.

37. Rapport sur l'Association fédérative générale et sur les étudiants de Strasbourg, 5 Aug. 1926, ADBR: AL 98, paq. 362. Also: A. Ricklin to Raymond Poincaré, 28 Aug. 1926, ADBR: AL 98, paq. 362; A. B. G., "15 années de vie corporative estudiantine," p. 4; and interview with A. Ricklin, 3 Sept. 1976.

38. René Paira and Gabriel Moy to André Helmer, 7 Apr. 1926, ADBR: AL 98, paq. 362.

39. Rapport sur l'Association fédérative générale et sur les étudiants de Strasbourg, 5 Aug. 1926, ADBR: AL 98, paq. 362.

40. René Paira and Gabriel Moy to André Helmer, 7 Apr. 1926, ADBR: AL 98, paq. 362. Also see René Paira to Paul Valot, 27 Apr. 1926, and A. Ricklin to Raymond Poincaré, 14 Oct. 1926, ibid.

41. Paul Valot to Raymond Poincaré, 8 Oct. 1926, and A. Ricklin to Poincaré, 14 Oct. 1926, ibid.; minutes of the University Council, 17 Apr. 1928, ADBR: UStr; "Anniversaire"; "Maison de la Jeune Alsace"; Rennwald, "A.F.G.E.S. 1935/36," p. 19; "La résurrection du Cercle des étudiants."

42. Keller, "La Gallia, restaurant de l' A.F.G."

43. Gabriel Moy to Paul Valot, 29 Jan. 1929, ADBR: AL 98, paq. 353. Also see Moy to Raymond Poincaré, 17 Jan. 1929, ibid.; A. Ricklin to Poincaré, 28 July 1926, ibid., paq. 363; "Anniversaire"; Deck, "Le Strasbourg-Etudiant-Club"; Moy, "Deux ans à l'A.F.G.," pp. 6–8; "L'oeuvre des étudiants de Strasbourg"; Rennwald, "A.F.G.E.S. 1935/36," p. 21.

44. Gabriel Moy to Christian Pfister, 1 Feb. 1928, ADBR: AL 98, paq. 363. Also see Moy to Paul Valot, 29 Jan. 1929, ibid., paq. 353.

45. Gabriel Moy to Raymond Poincaré, 28 Jan. 1929, ibid., paq. 353.

46. Gabriel Moy to Raymond Poincaré, 17 Jan. 1929, ibid.

47. Christian Pfister to Paul Valot, n.d. [Nov. 1928], Raymond Poincaré to Paul Painlevé, 14 Feb. 1929, A. Petenot and Emile Aron, "Plan d'organisation en vue de la construction d'une cité universitaire," n.d.[ca. Jan. 1930], and M. Heraud (?) to Poincaré, 21 Jan. 1930, ibid.; Pfister to Poincaré, 22 Feb. 1930, PRP: 16012; Moy, "Deux ans à l'A.F.G.," p. 7; Rennwald, "A.F.G.E.S. 1935/36," p. 21.

48. Gabriel Moy to Jacques Peirotes, 20 Nov. 1928, AACVS: B. 286/1579; Allonas, "L'activité de l'A.F.G."; Petenot, "Lettre d'un ancien président," p. 9; Rennwald, "A.F.G.E.S. 1935/36," p. 19.

49. Les amis des étudiants, *Association 'Les amis des étudiants de Strasbourg': Statuts*, pp. 3–8; Petenot, "Chez nos amis," p. 1; deWitt-Guizot, "La Société des amis des étudiants," p. 26.

50. "A propos des élections à l'A.F.G."; "Après la faillité de l'A.F.G."; "Editorial," p. 1; "Nos enquêtes: Strasbourg-Universitaire"; "Quelques perles du dernier 'Strasbourg-Etudiant'"; interview with Jacques Schwartz, 30 Aug. 1976.

51. "Eine skandalöse Sitzung im Strassburger Gemeinderat"; Kissel, "Alsatia-Strasbourg," pp. 24–27; "Nos enquêtes: Strasbourg-Universitaire"; "La presse alsacienne et lorraine," p. 1027; Wilhelmitana, *Die Wilhelmitana*, pp. 95–97.

52. Baul (?) to Pierre Roland-Marcel, 14 Dec. 1931, and Roland-Marcel to Paul Marchandeau, 7 July 1932, ADBR: AL 98, paq. 360; Christian Hallier to Wilhelm Kapp, 21 Dec. 1932, NWK: 1; Bickler, *Ein besonderes Land*, pp. 95–98, 149–52; Kissel, "Alsatia-Strasbourg," pp. 25–27; interviews with François-Georges Pariset, 4 Aug. 1976, and Jacques Schwartz, 30 Aug. 1976.

53. K. R. Guerrier to Wilhelm Kapp, 29 Dec. 1928 and 12 Mar. 1929, NWK: 1; minutes of the University Council, 23 May 1933, ADBR: UStr; "Alsatia et Argentina."

54. Paul Valot to Joseph Dresch, 24 Feb. 1932, and Henri Strohl to Dresch, 29 Feb. 1932, ADBR: AL 98, paq. 360; Bickler, *Ein besonderes Land*, pp. 142–44; Spieser, *Tausend Brücken*, pp. 328–30, 366; Zind, *Elsass-Lothringen*, pp. 597–608.

55. Henri Strohl to Joseph Dresch, 16 Jan. 1932 and 2 Mar. 1932, ADBR: AL 98, paq. 360; *Der Wanderfalke*, no. 1 (July 1931) et seq.; Zind, *Elsass-Lothringen*, pp. 606–7.

56. [Elsass-Lothringische Jungmannschaft], *Elsass-Lothringische Jungmannschaft*, pp. 1, 7, 15.

57. Bickler, "Studenten im elsässischen Volkstumskampf," p. 188. Also see Wilhelm Kapp to ?, 22 Dec. 1935, NWK; Bickler, *Ein besonderes Land*, pp. 219–48; Bickler, *Widerstand*, pp. 15–17; "Nos enquêtes: Strasbourg-Universitaire"; and Zind, *Elsass-Lothringen*, pp. 618–30.

58. Quoted in "A propos d'un monôme."

59. "A propos d'un monôme"; "La Faculté de Médecine proteste"; "Nos enquêtes: Strasbourg-Universitaire"; Vézian, "La vie universitaire: Le communisme à l'université"; interview with René Mehl, 26 Aug. 1976.

60. Bieber, "Unsere Universität."

61. "An die elsass-lothringischen Studenten!" reprinted in Bickler, *Ein besonderes Land,* pp. 258–59.

62. Joseph Dresch to Paul Valot, 3 Dec. 1931, and press summaries dated 26 Nov., 30 Nov., and 3 Dec. 1931, ADBR: AL 98, paq. 366; Delage, "La vie des étudiants: Strasbourg"; Lucas, "Un mouvement autonomiste à l'Université de Strasbourg," pp. 15–16.

63. Albert Grenier to Gustave Cohen, 28 Sept. 1931, PGC: 6; Christian Pfister to Raymond Poincaré, 12 Sept. 1930, PRP: 16012.

64. Christian Pfister to Raymond Poincaré, 17 Dec. 1929, 27 Feb. 1930, and 14 Oct. 1930, PRP: 16012; "Aus dem Strassburger Gemeinderat."

65. Nast, "Où allons-nous?" Also see Fritz Kiener to Jean de Pange, 15 Apr. 1932, AFDP; de Pange, *Journal,* 2:108, 118; Price, "Strasbourg in Alsace," pp. 206–7; "Les projets d'extension"; and Rossé et al., eds., *Das Elsass von 1870–1932,* 3:309–12.

66. The deans to Joseph Dresch, 14 Nov. 1932, ADBR: AL 154, no. 6; Dreyfus, *La vie politique en Alsace,* pp. 99–100; Kiener, "L'Alsace après le verdict de Colmar," pp. 51–57; Wolf, *Das elsässische Problem,* pp. 126–27; interview with A. G. Weiss, 1 July 1976.

67. "A propos de l'étudiante alsacienne"; "Le problème alsacien vu par un français de l'intérieur"; interviews with Paul Leuilliot, 23 July 1978, and Jean Gaudemet, 28 June 1976.

68. Merklen, "Georges Weiss," p. 182; "Strassburger Gemeinderat: Sturm im Gemeindeparlament?"

69. Dreyfus, *La vie politique en Alsace,* pp. 99–103.

70. Henri Borromée to Pierre Laval, 4 June 1926, and Borromée to Paul Valot, 20 Oct. 1926, ADBR: AL 98, paq. 1283; Alfaric, *De la foi à la raison,* pp. 284–85; Rossé et al., eds., *Das Elsass von 1870–1932,* 1:703; interviews with Georges Cerf, 2 Sept. 1976, and François-Georges Pariset, 24 July and 4 Aug. 1976.

71. For the deposition, see de Pange, *Journal,* 1:369–70.

72. "Les conséquences du procès de Colmar." Also see "La place de M. de Pange n'est plus parmi les Amis."

73. Georges Weiss to Gabriel Maugain, 9 May 1928, ADBR: AL 154, no. 4; Ferdinand Dollinger to Jean de Pange, 13 May 1928, AFDP.

74. de Pange to Ferdinand Dollinger, 10 May 1928, de Pange, *Journal,* 1:371.

75. de Pange to Peter Wust, 15 May 1928, Wust, *Gesammelte Werke,* 9:112–15.

76. Quoted in "Actions et réactions."

77. Quoted in Perrin, "Fritz Kiener," p. 114. Also see Kiener to de Pange, 27 May, 28 May, 31 May, and 22 June 1928, 25 Dec. 1929, and 4 June 1938, AFDP; Kiener, "L'Alsace après le verdict de Colmar," pp. 49–70; and de Pange, *Journal,* 1:47–56.

78. Kiener to de Pange, 27 May and 21 Nov. 1928, and Robert Minder to de Pange, 30 May and 3 July 1928, AFDP; Perrin, "Fritz Kiener," pp. 114–15.

79. Kiener to de Pange, 1 June 1928, AFDP. Also see Kiener to de Pange, 21 Nov. 1928, ibid.; and de Pange, *Journal,* 1:217–18.

80. Kiener to de Pange, 8 Aug. 1930, AFDP. Also: Bergner, "Quelques silhouettes universitaires," pp. 475–76; Hervé, "Tradition alsacienne et enseignement officiel," pp. 11–12; interviews with André Burg, 25 June 1976; Philippe Dollinger, 23 June 1976; Paul Leuilliot, 23 July 1976; Fernand L'Huillier, 22 June 1976; and Ernest Schneegans, 24 June 1976.

81. Minutes of the University Council, 26 Oct. 1928, 8 Feb. 1930, 12 Nov. 1931, and 24 Nov. 1932, ADBR: UStr; resolution of the Faculty of Law, 28 Nov. 1929, ibid.; minutes of the Faculty of Letters (Assemblée), 30 Nov. 1929, ADBR: AL 154, no. 2; "Der 22. November in Strassburg."

82. Joseph Dresch to Paul Valot, 4 Mar. 1932, ADBR: AL 98, paq. 360. Also see Henri Strohl to Joseph Dresch, 29 Feb. and 2 Mar. 1932, ibid.; and minutes of the Faculty of Protestant Theology, 15 Apr. 1931, BFT.

83. Christian Pfister to Raymond Poincaré, 21 and 29 Oct. 1930, PRP: 16012.

84. Quoted in "Nos morticules, ferments d'autonomisme," p. 2.

85. Ibid.; "A la Faculté de médecine"; "Aufruf!"; "Protest"; "Der Skandal an der medizinischen Fakultät"; interviews with René Mehl, 26 Aug. 1976; Ernest Schneegans, 8 July 1976; A. G. Weiss, 1 July 1976.

86. Joseph Dresch to Guy La Chambre, 23 Feb. 1933, ADBR: AL 98, paq. 360.

87. Joseph Dresch to Paul Valot, 2 Feb. 1933, ibid.

88. Joseph Dresch to Paul Valot, 3 Feb. 1933, ibid.

89. Ibid. Also see minutes of the University Council, 10 Feb. 1933, ADBR: UStr.

90. "M. Poincaré préside le banquet d'ouverture du Congrès national des étudiants." Also see Johann Smend to Gerhard Köpke, 15 Dec. 1927, Germany, Auswärtiges Amt, *Akten zur deutschen auswärtigen Politik*, series B, 7:528.

91. On the pressure for a chair in the history of Alsatian literature, see "Lehrstuhl für elsass-lothringische Literatur gefordert."

92. Interview with Ernest Schneegans, 8 July 1976. Also see Callot, "Les études médicales et pharmaceutiques," pp. 129–30.

93. Minutes of the Faculty of Protestant Theology, 16 June 1928, BFT.

94. See Gabriel Maugain to Christian Pfister, 24 Nov. 1927, ADBR: UStr; and, more generally, "L'aspect intellectuel du problème provincial," p. 476.

95. France, Statistique générale, *Annuaire statistique*, 40 (1924)–45 (1929). Also see Laitenberger, *Akademischer Austausch und auswärtige Kulturpolitik*, pp. 11–35, 173–81, 278–90.

96. Christian Pfister to Paul Valot, 16 Mar. 1928, ADBR: AL 98, paq. 360.

97. Raymond Poincaré to Christian Pfister, 18 Apr. 1928, ibid.; France, Statistique générale, *Annuaire statistique*, 40 (1924)–55 (1939).

98. Germany, Statistisches Reichsamt, *Vierteljahrshefte zur Statistik*, 37 (1928)–39 (1930).

99. In 1923–24, for instance, there were nine Alsatians at the University of Basel, and in 1933 there were five; see University of Basel, *Personal Verzeichnis*, winter semester 1923–24 and summer semester 1933.

100. Wilhelm Kapp to G. Asal, 4 Oct. 1928, NWK: 1; interviews with Philippe Dollinger, 23 June 1976; Robert Minder, 15 July 1976; and A. Ricklin, 3 Sept. 1976.

101. Craig, "Maurice Halbwachs à Strasbourg," pp. 284–85; Driesch, "Davoser Hochschulkurse 1928"; L'Huillier, *Dialogues franco-allemands*, pp. 73, 91, 103; Maugain, "Rapport," pp. 31–32.

102. Minutes of the Faculty of Letters (Conseil), 24 Nov. 1928, ADBR: AL 154, no. 3; Christian Pfister to Paul Valot, 7 Dec. 1928, ADBR: AL 98, paq. 360.

103. Raymond Poincaré to Edouard Herriot, 26 Feb. 1929, ADBR: AL 98, paq. 360; minutes of the University Council, 9 Mar. 1929, ADBR: UStr.

104. "La conférence de M. Witkopf [sic] sur Mann"; interview with Robert Minder, 15 July 1976.

105. Direction de la Sûreté générale (Affaires d'Alsace et de Lorraine) to Paul Valot, 6 Nov. 1933, ADBR: AL 98, paq. 366; "Ein Nazi-Lektor an der Universität Strassburg?"

106. Minutes of the Faculty of Letters (Conseil), 24 Nov. 1928, ADBR: AL 154, no. 3.

107. Fritz Kiener to Jean de Pange, 19 Jan. and 8 Aug. 1930, AFDP.

108. Minutes of the University Council, 10 Feb. 1933, ADBR: UStr. Also see minutes of the Faculty of Letters (Conseil), 12 Mar. 1928, ADBR: AL 154, no. 3; Gabriel Maugain's reports on Georges Lefebvre, 12 July 1931 and 21 Feb. 1934, ADBR: UStr; and minutes of the University Council, 17 Dec. 1932, ADBR: UStr.

109. Jean Pommier to Gustave Cohen, 17 Nov. 1930, PGC: 5.

110. Minutes of the Faculty of Letters (Conseil), 19 May 1928, ADBR: AL 154, no. 3.

111. Christian Pfister to Paul Valot, 5 June 1928, ADBR: AL 98, paq. 361; Raymond Poincaré to Edouard Herriot, 28 June 1928, ibid.; minutes of the Faculty of Letters (Assemblée), 11 July 1928, ibid., AL 154, no. 2; Marc Bloch to Gabriel Maugain, 12 July 1928,

ibid., AL 154, no. 4; minutes of the Faculty of Letters (Conseil), 24 Nov. 1928 and 21 June 1930, ibid., AL 154, no. 3; Maugain to Valot, 8 June 1939, ibid., AL 98, paq. 357.

112. Christian Pfister to Paul Valot, 11 Feb. 1929, ibid., AL 98, paq. 353; minutes of the Faculty of Letters (Conseil), 9 Feb. 1929, ibid., AL 154, no. 3; minutes of the Faculty of Letters (Assemblée), 30 Apr. and 30 Nov. 1929, 8 Nov. 1930, 1 Mar. 1932, ibid., AL 154, no. 2; minutes of the University Council, 28 Oct. 1930, ibid., UStr; S. E., "Le bal des étudiants à la préfecture."

113. Henri Borromée to Paul Valot, 20 Oct. 1926 and n.d. [ca. 28 May 1928], ADBR: AL 98, paq. 1283; Borromée to Valot, 14 Nov. 1928, ibid., paq. 1278; minutes of the Faculty of Letters (Assemblée), 5 Apr. 1930, ibid., AL 154, no. 2; Jean Pommier to Gustave Cohen, 17 Nov. 1930, PGC: 5.

114. M. Motz to Jacques Peirotes, 16 May 1928, "Création d'une Université populaire à Strasbourg," n.d. [May 1928], and Peirotes to Christian Pfister, 11 June 1928, AACVS: B. 263/1.

115. See Bourgin, *De Jaurès à Léon Blum,* pp. 62–69, 213–15; Dintzer, "Le mouvement des universités populaires"; and Weisz, *The Emergence of Modern Universities in France,* pp. 311–14.

116. M. Motz to Jacques Peirotes, 16 May 1928, AACVS: B. 263/1; "Université populaire: Réunion du 6 juillet 1928," ibid., 263/3; minutes of the University Council, 16 Nov. 1928, ADBR: UStr.

117. Christian Pfister to Paul Valot, 14 Mar. 1930, ADBR: AL 98, paq. 365.

118. Hubert Gillot to Jacques Peirotes, 20 Mar. 1929, AACVS: B. 263/1.

119. Hubert Gillot to ?, n.d. [Jan. 1929], and to Jacques Peirotes, 20 Mar. 1929, and posters listing courses of the Université populaire for 1929–30 and 1930–31, ibid.

120. "Compte rendu sur l'activité de l'Université populaire . . . ," 25 Mar. 1931, ibid., 263/2; poster listing courses of the Université populaire for 1932–33, ibid., 263/—; "Von der Université populaire," ibid., 264/7; "Statistique de la fréquentation des conférences organisées par l'Université populaire," ibid., 265/1468.

121. "Statistiques des auditeurs de l'Université populaire . . . 1931/32," ibid., 265/1468.

122. Dintzer, "Le mouvement des universités populaires," pp. 7–8.

123. Minutes of the Comité d'action de l'Université populaire, 3 Nov. 1936, AACVS: B. 263/2; E. S., "Eine Stunde in der Volkshochschule."

124. E. S., "Eine Stunde in der Volkshochschule." Also see minutes of the Comité d'action de l'Université populaire, 15 Nov. 1933, AACVS: B. 263/2.

125. Dreyfus, *La vie politique en Alsace,* pp. 159, 171, 234–39; Rothenberger, *Die elsass-lothringische Heimat- und Autonomiebewegung,* pp. 221–22.

126. Ludwig Hallier to Wilhelm Kapp, 20 Sept. 1933, NWK: 1; Charles Wolf to René Schickele, 4 Mar. 1934, NRS; Dreyfus, *La vie politique en Alsace,* pp. 171, 195–247; Fuchs, Nonn, and Rapp, "L'entre-deux-guerres, l'occupation nazie, et la Libération," pp. 432–37; Rothenberger, *Die elsass-lothringische Heimat- und Autonomiebewegung,* pp. 188, 198, 201–12, 217.

127. Fuchs, Nonn, and Rapp, "L'entre-deux-guerres, l'occupation nazie, et la Libération," pp. 437–39; Lestra, *Le conflit religieux et scolaire;* Mayeur, "Une bataille scolaire"; de Pange, *Journal,* 3:435, 4:50; Rothenberger, *Die elsass-lothringische Heimat- und Autonomiebewegung,* pp. 200, 214–16, 221–34, 249.

128. "La fête nationale du 14 juillet"; Mary, "La vie politique"; Naegelen, *Avant que meure le dernier . . . ,* pp. 70–71; de Pange, *Journal,* 4:221; Rothenberger, *Die elsass-lothringische Heimat- und Autonomiebewegung,* pp. 222, 233–41.

129. R. W., "De juris studiorum utilitate."

130. Ibid.; Marc Bloch, "Sur la réforme de l'enseignement," pp. 250–55; A. M., "La jeunesse devant les portes fermées"; "Nos enquêtes: Strasbourg-Universitaire"; Strohl, "Rapport général," pp. 23–25. On the market for university graduates in France as a whole,

see Gerbod, "Associations et syndicalismes universitaires de 1929 à 1937," pp. 79–82; and Legaret, "La crise et l'avenir de la jeunesse universitaire," pp. 462–75.

131. "Editorial"; A. M., "La jeunesse devant les portes fermées"; "Nos enquêtes: Strasbourg-Universitaire."

132. On trends in France generally, see Andreu, "Les idées politiques de la jeunesse intellectuelle de 1927 à la guerre."

133. "A la Faculté de médecine," p. 180; "L'action de l'Union fédérale des étudiants contre la P.M.S. obligatoire"; "Après la faillité de l'A.F.G.," pp. 1–2; Hervé, "Tradition alsacienne et enseignement officiel," pp. 11–12.

134. "Nos enquêtes: Strasbourg-Universitaire"; Vézian, "La vie universitaire: Le communisme à l'université."

135. Direction de la Sûreté générale (Commissariat spécial) to Pierre Roland-Marcel, 16 Feb. 1932, M. Monnard to Emile Roblot, 4 May 1935, and A. Geis to Paul Valot, 28 Feb. 1937, ADBR: AL 98, paq. 360.

136. "Après les incidents au théâtre municipal," pp. 5–7; "Protestation des étudiants contre la propagande théâtrale allemande," pp. 1, 9.

137. M. Monnard to Paul Valot, 25 Feb. 1937, and Emile Roblot to Valot, 25 Feb. 1937, ADBR: AL 98, paq. 360; "Brunschwicq-Aria"; Lestra, *Le conflit religieux et scolaire*, pp. 89–90.

138. J. E. Lobstein to Joseph Dresch, 4 Apr. 1935, Lobstein to Paul Valot, 6 Apr. 1935, and M. Monnard to Emile Roblot, 4 May 1935, ADBR: AL 98, paq. 360; Holtzmann, "Après la grève," p. 3.

139. Georges Rennwald to Joseph Dresch, 19 Mar. 1937, and Dresch to François de Tessan, 19 Mar. 1937, ADBR: AL 98, paq. 360.

140. "Protest."

141. Emile Roblot to Paul Valot, 16 Aug. 1935, and Henri Strohl to Joseph Dresch, 13 Jan. 1938, ADBR: AL 98, paq. 360; "Alsatia am 8. Februar 1936," pp. 37–38.

142. Friedrich König to Wilhelm Kapp, 27 Dec. 1936, NWK: 1; E., "Einige Gedanken über den elsass-lothringischen Akademiker," pp. 8–10; interview with Emile Baas, 27 Aug. 1976.

143. M. Monnard to Emile Roblot, 21 Mar. 1936, Henri Strohl to Joseph Dresch, 13 Jan. 1938, and Paul Valot to Edouard Daladier, 9 Feb. 1938, ADBR: AL 98, paq. 360; Bickler, "Studenten im elsässischen Volkstumskampf," p. 188; Spieser, *Kampfbriefe aus dem Elsass*, p. 168.

144. Charles Altorffer to Paul Valot, 31 Dec. 1935, ADBR: AL 98, paq. 360; Kissel, "Alsatia-Strasbourg," pp. 26–27.

145. Henri Strohl to Joseph Dresch, 13 Jan. 1938, ADBR: AL 98, paq. 360. Also: Oscar Cullman to author, 21 June 1976.

146. See Henri Strohl to Joseph Dresch, 26 June 1934, and Dresch to Paul Valot, 13 July 1934, ADBR: AL 98, paq. 360; minutes of the University Council, 10 July 1934, ibid., UStr; Spieser, *Kampfbriefe aus dem Elsass*, p. 142.

147. Fritz Kiener to Jean de Pange, 12 Apr. 1929 and 14 June 1936, AFDP; Friedrich König to Wilhelm Kapp, 27 Dec. 1936, NWK: 1; Lucas, "Un mouvement autonomiste à l'Université de Strasbourg," pp. 15–16; interview with François-Georges Pariset, 24 July 1976.

148. Press reports of 26 Nov. and 13 Dec. 1931, ADBR: AL 98, paq. 366; E., "Einige Gedanken über den elsass-lothringischen Akademiker," pp. 8–10; de Pange, *Journal*, 3:84.

149. "Après les incidents au théâtre municipale," pp. 5–7; Hervé, "Tradition alsacienne et enseignement officiel," pp. 11–12; "Öffentliche Versammlung der Union fédérale des étudiants," p. 11.

150. Minutes of the University Council, 24 Nov. 1932, ADBR: UStr.

151. Martial Guéroult to Gabriel Maugain, 12 Nov. 1932, ADBR: AL 154, no. 6.

152. "Note sur l'indemnité de fonction de l'Université de Strasbourg," ibid., AL 98, paq. 367.

153. Martial Guéroult to Gabriel Maugain, 12 Nov. 1932, ibid., AL 154, no. 6. Also see the deans of the faculties to Joseph Dresch, 14 Nov. 1932, ibid.; and Joseph Duquesne (?) to ?, 21 Nov. 1932, ibid., AL 98, paq. 367.

154. Resolution of the University Council, 24 Nov. 1932, ibid., AL 98, paq. 364.

155. Ibid.

156. "Note sur l'indemnité de fonction de l'Université de Strasbourg," ibid., paq. 367. Also see Joseph Dresch to Paul Valot, 25 Nov. 1932, ibid.; and Gabriel Maugain to Edouard Herriot, 16 Nov. 1932, ibid., AL 154, no. 6.

157. "Note sur l'indemnité de fonction de l'Université de Strasbourg," Nov. 1935, ibid., AL 98, paq. 359. Also see the deans of the faculties to Joseph Dresch, 22 June and 18 Dec. 1936, Emile Terroine to Paul Valot, 22 June 1936, the deans of the faculties to Valot, n.d. [Nov. 1937], and "Note relative à l'indemnité de fonction des membres du personnel enseignant et scientifique de l'Université de Strasbourg," ibid.

158. M. Cabouat to M. Ramadier, n.d. [Aug. 1936], ibid.

159. See Joseph Dresch to Paul Valot, 23 Sept. 1933, ibid., paq. 364; Dresch to Georges Mandel, 26 May 1936, ibid., paq. 365; Dresch to Valot, 23 Oct. 1936, ibid., paq. 352; and, more generally, Weil, "Science française?"

160. Georges Mandel to Joseph Dresch, 29 May 1936, ibid., paq. 365; "Note pour Monsieur le Ministre chargé des affaires d'Alsace et de Lorraine" (1936), ibid., paq. 352.

161. Minutes of the Faculty of Letters (Assemblée), 8 Dec. 1936 and 16 Mar. 1937, ibid., AL 154, no. 2.

162. Jean Cavaillès to his parents (?), 11 Nov. 1938, Gabrielle Ferrières, Jean Cavaillès, p. 131. Also: Godechot, "Georges Lefebvre," pp. 23–24; Mary, "Attaques contre l'Université de Strasbourg"; Mary, "Revendications autonomistes"; and interview with Henri Maresquelle, 22 June 1976.

163. "L'Université populaire" (undated four-page report) and "Université populaire: Statistique des inscriptions du semestre d'hiver 1938," AACVS: B. 265/1468.

164. Interviews with Emile Baas, 27 Aug. 1976, and Jean Gaudemet, 28 June 1976.

165. Joseph Dresch to François de Tessan, 19 Mar. 1937, ADBR: AL 98, paq. 360.

166. Cerf, "Edmond Rothé, citoyen"; "Echos," p. 17; Gruffat, "Les écrits de doctrine de René Capitant," pp. 24, 48; M. R., "Notre action," p. 1; interviews with Georges Cerf, 2 Sept. 1976; Henri Maresquelle, 22 June 1976; François-Georges Pariset, 24 July and 4 Aug. 1976; and Jean P. Rothé, 9 July 1976.

167. Interviews with Jean Gaudemet, 28 June 1976; Jacques Schwartz, 30 Aug. 1976; and A. G. Weiss, 1 July 1976.

168. Alfaric, De la foi à la raison, pp. 286–88. Also: "Sport scolaire et politique"; and interviews with Jean Gaudemet, 28 June 1976; A. Ricklin, 3 Sept. 1976; and Marcel Simon, 31 Aug. 1976.

169. Minutes of the University Council, 15 Feb. 1935, ADBR: UStr; Ferdinand Dollinger to Henri Laufenburger, 21 Feb. 1935, FFD; interview with François-Georges Pariset, 24 July 1976.

170. Minutes of the University Council, 8 Feb. and 3 Mar. 1939, ADBR: UStr.

171. Cerf, "Edmond Rothé, citoyen."

172. Albert Fuchs to Mme Jean de Pange, 26 May and 12 June 1938, and Fritz Kiener to Jean de Pange, 29 Mar. 1939, AFDP; Marc Bloch, Strange Defeat, p. 6; interviews with Henri Cartan, 30 June 1976; Pierre Marthelot, 1 July 1976; René Metz, 8 July 1976; Jean P. Rothé, 9 July 1976.

173. "Une adresse de 128 professeurs de Strasbourg"; interviews with Georges Cerf, 2 Sept. 1976, and François-Georges Pariset, 24 July 1976. Also see Dupeux, "La revue L'Al-

*lemagne Contemporaine* 1936–1939,'' pp. 167–69, 174–77; and Dupeux, ''René Capitant et l'analyse idéologique du Nazisme,'' pp. 627–37.

174. Maurice Halbwachs to Albert Thomas, 3 Dec. 1930, FAT: 381.

175. Jean Pommier to Gustave Cohen, 29 Oct. 1931, PGC: 6.

176. Godechot, ''Georges Lefebvre,'' pp. 23–24; interview with Philippe Dollinger, 23 June 1976.

177. Minutes of the Faculty of Protestant Theology, 29 Apr. 1938, BFT. Also see Cullmann, ''Autobiographische Skizze,'' pp. 685–86.

178. See ''Note relative à l'indemnité de fonction des membres du personnel enseignant et scientifique de l'Université de Strasbourg,'' ADBR: AL 98, paq. 359.

179. Minutes of the Faculty of Letters (Assemblée), 3 Nov. 1934, ibid., AL 154, no. 2; interview with Jean Gaudemet, 28 June 1976.

180. ''M. Terracher, recteur de l'Académie de Strasbourg''; ''Der neue Rektor des Strassburger Universität.''

181. Paul Valot to Emile Terroine, 19 Nov. 1938, ADBR: AL 98, paq. 359; France, *Journal officiel, Lois et décrets,* 15 Nov. 1938, p. 12966.

182. Terracher to Paul Valot, 7 Oct. 1938, ADBR: AL 98, paq. 367. Also see Th. Rosset to Valot, 28 Nov. 1938, ibid.; and Leriche, *Souvenirs de ma vie morte,* p. 82.

183. ''La séance solennelle de rentrée,'' p. 57.

184. Ibid.; Mary, ''Un exposé de M. Camille Chautemps,'' p. 76.

185. See L'Huillier, ''Georges Lefebvre à Strasbourg,'' pp. 373–75; and Livet, ''L'Institut et la chaire d'histoire moderne,'' pp. 204–6.

186. ''La séance solennelle de rentrée,'' p. 54.

187. Ibid., p. 55. Also see minutes of the University Council, 3 Mar. 1939, ADBR: UStr.

188. See Christian Hallier to Wilhelm Kapp, 18 May 1937 and 10 Jan. 1939, NWK: 1. On the origins and activities of the Frankfurt Institute, see Hallier, ''Das Wissenschaftliche Institut der Elsass-Lothringer im Reich''; and Kluke, *Die Stiftungsuniversität Frankfurt am Main,* pp. 413–22, 548–49.

189. Minutes of the University Council, 8 Feb., 3 March, and 16 June 1939, ADBR: UStr.

## Postscript

1. Officials had selected Clermont as a potential refuge back in 1934, but the professors and students did not learn of this decision until the eve of the war; see Direction de l'instruction publique à Strasbourg, ''Plan de mobilisation, 1934,'' ADBR: UStr.; and Mollat, ''Les débuts de la faculté française,'' p. 271.

2. Minutes of the Faculty of Letters (Assemblée), 18 Nov. 1939, ADBR: AL 154, no. 2; France, Statistique générale, *Annuaire statistique,* 56 (1940–45): 56; Plagnieux, ''Chronique de la faculté repliée,'' pp. 289–90; ''L'Université en chiffres,'' pp. 537–38.

3. On the evacuation and return, see Kettenacker, *Nationalsozialistische Volkstumspolitik im Elsass,* pp. 131–33, 136–38, 318n, 320n.

4. The quotations are from, respectively, *Strassburger Neueste Nachrichten,* 31 Dec. 1940, and Ernst Anrich to Robert Ernst, 23 May 1941, as quoted in Kettenacker, *Nationalsozialistische Volkstumspolitik im Elsass,* pp. 186, 187. Also see Ernst Anrich, ''Von der Bedeutung der Strassburger Universität,'' pp. 78–79; and Scherberger, ''Universität Strassburg—Vermächtnis und Aufgabe,'' pp. 7–11.

5. Friedrich König to Wilhelm Kapp, 3 June 1941, NWK: 1; Ernst, *Rechenschaftsbericht eines Elsässers,* pp. 322–24; Kettenacker, *Nationalsozialistische Volkstumspolitik im Elsass,* pp. 184–92.

6. Johannes Ficker, Wilhelm Kapp, and Otto Michaelis, ''Entwurf eines Rundschreibens,'' Aug. 1940, NWK: 1; Bopp, *L'Alsace sous l'occupation allemande,* pp. 165–66; Kettenacker, *Nationalsozialistische Volkstumspolitik im Elsass,* p. 187; Schmutz, *Alsace: Mythes et réalités,* p. 127.

7. Kettenacker, *Nationalsozialistische Volkstumspolitik im Elsass*, p. 193.

8. Quoted in Lassus, *Souvenirs d'un cobaye*, p. 79.

9. France, Bureau universitaire de statistique, *Receuil de statistiques scolaires et professionnelles*, p. 137; France, Statistique générale, *Annuaire statistique*, 56 (1940–45): 56; Halls, *The Youth of Vichy France*, p. 259; Scherberger, "Die studentische Aufbauarbeit im deutschen Elsass," p. 189.

10. André Forster, "L'Université repliée," p. 34; Freund, "Chapelet de souvenirs," p. 10; A. M. "Alma mater im Flüchtlingsstrom," pp. 755–59; Maugain, "La vie de la Faculté des lettres," pp. 14–15, 46–47; Plagnieux, "Chronique de la faculté repliée," p. 286.

11. André Forster, "L'Université repliée," pp. 32–33; Kettenacker, *Nationalsozialistische Volkstumspolitik im Elsass*, pp. 192–93; Maugain, "La vie de la Faculté des lettres," pp. 17–26.

12. On the university community and the resistance see: Canguilhem, "Jean Cavaillès," pp. 147–48; Ferrières, *Jean Cavaillès*, pp. 163–64; Grell, *Têtes carrées*, pp. 20–22; Lassus, *Souvenirs d'un cobaye*, pp. 56–64, 80–81, 205; Lassus, "L'Université captive," pp. 39–43; and Luchaire, *Confession d'un français moyen*, 2:273–83.

13. Halls, *The Youth of Vichy France*, pp. 257, 259–60; Lassus, *Souvenirs d'un cobaye*, pp. 68–69; interviews with Georges Cerf, 2 Sept. 1976; Albert Fuchs, 1 Sept. 1976; A. Ricklin, 3 Sept. 1976; and Jacques Schwartz, 30 Aug. 1976.

14. André Forster, "L'Université repliée," p. 33; Lassus, *Souvenirs d'un cobaye*, pp. 101–7; Maugain, "La vie de la Faculté des lettres," pp. 27–43; Plagnieux, "Chronique de la faculté repliée," pp. 287–88; Prélot, "Allocution du recteur," pp. 10–11. On those deported to Germany and their fates, see University of Strasbourg, Faculty of Letters, *De l'université aux camps de concentration*.

15. Maugain, "La vie de la Faculté des lettres," pp. 47–49; Prélot, "Allocution du recteur," p. 9; Prélot, "L'université libérée," pp. 46–49.

16. Prélot, "L'université libérée," p. 45. Also: ibid., pp. 49–53; and interviews with Emile Baas, 27 Aug. 1976; Pierre Marthelot, 1 July 1976; François-Georges Pariset, 4 Aug. 1976; and Marcel Simon, 31 Aug. 1976.

17. Prélot, "Allocution du recteur," p. 13.

18. Ibid., pp. 12–13; interviews with Emile Baas, 27 Aug. 1976; Pierre Marthelot, 1 July 1976; Alex Weill, 25 and 30 Aug. 1976.

19. Minutes of the Faculty of Letters (Assemblée), 13 Nov. 1945, ADBR: AL 154, no. 2; interviews with Emile Baas, 27 Aug. 1976, and Pierre Marthelot, 1 July 1976.

20. *Le Monde* (Paris), 19 Mar. 1949, quoted in Schaeffer, *L'Alsace et l'Allemagne de 1945 à 1949*, p. 375n.

21. Schaeffer, *L'Alsace et l'Allemagne de 1945 à 1949*, pp. 346–48.

22. Minutes of the Faculty of Letters (Conseil), 6 Apr. 1949, ADBR: AL 154, no. 3.

23. Minutes of the Faculty of Letters (Conseil), 8 Jan. 1949, ibid.; minutes of the Faculty of Letters (Assemblée), 13 Nov. 1945, 17 May 1946, and 22 June 1949, ibid., no. 2; Ponteil, "La vie pathétique de l'Université de Strasbourg," p. 116; Simon, "Situation de l'université," pp. 120–27; interviews with Georges Cerf, 2 Sept. 1976; Jean Gagé, 3 July 1976; Pierre Marthelot, 1 July 1976; Jean P. Rothé, 9 July 1976; and Jacques Schwartz, 30 Aug. 1976.

24. Minutes of the Faculty of Letters (Conseil), 6 Apr. 1949, ADBR: AL 154, no. 3.

25. "Contre une université européenne à Strasbourg," *Dernières Nouvelles d'Alsace* (Strasbourg), 12 Apr. 1949, reprinted in Schaeffer, *L'Alsace et l'Allemagne de 1945 à 1949*, pp. 375–76.

26. Quoted in Schaeffer, *L'Alsace et l'Allemagne de 1945 à 1949*, p. 48. Also see Hoffet, *Psychanalyse de l'Alsace*, pp. 16–17.

27. Schaeffer, *L'Alsace et l'Allemagne de 1945 à 1949*, p. 48.

28. Minutes of the Faculty of Letters (Assemblée), 3 June 1949, ADBR: AL 154, no. 2; Council of Europe, Consultative Assembly, *Reports,* 1st sess., part 4, pp. 1056, 1080–86.

29. Minutes of the Faculty of Letters (Assemblée), 3 June 1949, 28 Jan. 1950, and 4 Feb. 1950, ADBR: AL 154, no. 2.

30. Minutes of the Faculty of Letters (Assemblée), 4 Feb., 11 Feb., 22 Apr., and 1 July 1950, ibid.; minutes of the Faculty of Protestant Theology, 25 Mar. 1950, BFT; Emile Baas, *Situation de l'Alsace,* pp. 190–91, 199; Council of Europe, Consultative Assembly, *Documents,* ord. sess. 1950, part 3, pp. 881–82, 1018; Hubert, "Discours," pp. 26–28; Robert Redslob, "Eine europäische Universität im Elsass," p. 42; interviews with Emile Baas, 27 Aug. 1976; René Metz, 8 July 1976; Paul Ricoeur, 28 Jan. and 17 Mar. 1982; and J. P. Staub, 27 Aug. 1976.

31. Minutes of the Faculty of Protestant Theology, 24 Feb. 1945, BFT; Schaeffer, *L'Alsace et l'Allemagne de 1945 à 1949,* pp. 102–5; interview with Alex Weill, 25 Aug. 1976.

32. On the effect of the war on the Alsatian question, see Baas, *Situation de l'Alsace;* Hoffet, *Psychanalyse de l'Alsace;* and Schaeffer, *L'Alsace et l'Allemagne de 1945 à 1949,* pp. 83, 137, 154, 351–52.

## Conclusion

1. The quotation is from Kapp, "Die Kaiser Wilhelms-Universität Strassburg: Ein Erinnerungswort," p. 35.

2. Kapp, "Die Kaiser Wilhelms-Universität Strassburg und das Elsässertum," p. 266.

3. Rossé et al., eds., *Das Elsass von 1870–1932,* 3:29.

4. See, for instance, R. Fachot to Ernest Lavisse, 11 Mar. 1921, PEL: 25172; and the deans to Joseph Dresch, 14 Nov. 1932, ADBR: AL 154, no. 6.

5. Brentano, *Elsässer Erinnerungen,* p. 54.

6. See, for instance, Bennrath, "Quatre étudiants allemands en Alsace," p. 152; and E., "Einige Gedanken über den elsass-lothringischen Akademiker," pp. 8–10.

7. André Danjon as quoted in Jean de Pange, *Journal,* 4:147.

8. For this suggestion see Eugène Muller in Alsace-Lorraine, Landtag: Zweite Kammer, *Verhandlungen,* 1st sess. (1911–13), 91:3833–34.

9. Febvre, "Politique royale ou civilisation française?" pp. 49–50.

10. For references to Strasbourg's German and French universities as Potemkin villages see, respectively, "Die Universität Strassburg"; and Verax [pseud.], "Die Frequenz der Strassburger Universität," p. 269.

# Bibliography

**1. Manuscript Sources**

Bergheim (Haut-Rhin). Langenschloessel (residence of Mlle Georgine Wittich).
    Papers of Werner Wittich.
Berlin (E.). Deutsche Staatsbibliothek zu Berlin.
    Teilnachlass Friedrich Althoff.
Berlin (W.). Deutsches Archäologisches Institut.
    Teilnachlass Adolf Michaelis.
————. Preussischer Kulturbesitz, Geheimes Staatsarchiv.
    Nachlass Friedrich Meinecke.
    Briefe aus dem Nachlass des Professors Dr. Conrad Varrentrapp.
————. Staatsbibliothek Preussischer Kulturbesitz, früher Preussische Staatsbibliothek.
    Nachlass Harry Bresslau.
    Nachlass Anton de Bary.
    Nachlass Bernhard Naunyn.
    Nachlass Paul Scheffer-Boichorst.
Bonn. Universitätsbibliothek.
    Nachlass Karl Lamprecht.
Boston. Boston Public Library.
    Hugo Münsterberg Papers.
Cambridge, Mass. Harvard University Archives.
    Richard von Mises Papers.
Chicago. University of Chicago Library.
    Hermann Eduard von Holst Collection.
Freiburg im Breisgau. Universitätsbibliothek.
    Nachlass von Wilhelm Kapp.
Göttingen. Niedersächsische Staats- und Universitätsbibliothek.
    Nachlass Wilhelm Dilthey.
    Nachlass von Felix Klein.
Heidelberg. Universitätsbibliothek.
    Nachlass von Franz Boll.
    Nachlass von Kuno Fischer.
    Nachlass von Alfred Stern.

Hierges (Ardennes). Chateau of the Pirenne family.
    Papers of Henri Pirenne (transcriptions in the possession of Ms. Hilah
        F. Thomas, New York City).
Kiel. Schleswig-Holsteinische Landesbibliothek.
    Nachlass von Ferdinand Tönnies.
Koblenz. Bundesarchiv.
    Nachlass Lujo Brentano.
    Nachlass Hans Delbrück.
    Nachlass Walter Goetz.
    Professor Walter Goetz an Professor Karl Brandi, 1892–1917. (Kl. Erw.
        Nr. 357)
    Nachlass Johannes Haller.
    Nachlass Maximilian Harden.
    Familienarchiv Knapp.
Marbach am Neckar. Schiller Nationalmuseum. Deutsches Literaturarchiv.
    Nachlass von René Schickele.
Marburg. Universitäts-Bibliothek.
    Nachlass von Paul Natorp.
Munich. Bayerische Staatsbibliothek.
    Nachlass von Karl von Amira.
    Nachlass von Paul von Groth.
    Nachlass von Eduard Schwartz.
    Schwartz, Eduard. "Eduard Schwartz, wissenschaftlicher Lebens-
        lauf." Typescript dated 9 May 1932.
    ———. Universitätsbibliothek.
    Nachlass von Hermann Paul.
New York City. Leo Baeck Institute.
    Georg Simmel Papers.
Oldenburg. Niedersächsisches Staatsarchiv.
    Nachlass Hermann Oncken.
Paris. Archives Nationales.
    Archives imprimées: Instruction publique. (AD XIX H)
    Instruction publique. (F$^{17}$)
    Instruction publique: Registres. (F$^{17*}$)
    Police générale. (F$^7$)
    Papiers Gustave Cohen. (59 AP)
    Papiers du Comité pour le cent-cinquantenaire de la Révolution fran-
        çaise. (AB XIX 3054–3056$^B$)
    Papiers de l'historien Philippe Sagnac. (AB XIX 3525–3534)
    Papiers de François Simiand. (AB XIX 1962–1966)
    Fonds Albert Thomas. (94 AP)
    Papiers Henri Wallon. (360 AP)
    ———. Bibliothèque Nationale.
    Correspondance et papiers de Louis Havet.

Papiers d'Albert Houtin.
Papiers Ernest Lavisse.
Papiers d'Alfred Loisy.
Fonds Millerand.
Papiers Raymond Poincaré.
Correspondance et papiers de Joseph Reinach.
Lettres adressées à Johannes Tielrooy.
———. Ministère des Affaires Etrangères.
Germany. Auswärtiges Amt. Abtheilung IA. Elsass-Lothr. 3. Nr. 1 *secr.*
    Die Universität in Strassburg. Vols. 1–9. 28 Apr. 1894–Feb. 1920.
    (Filmed documents; serial numbers MAE 34/344–37/42)
Scheyern (Oberbayern). Abtrei Scheyern. Byzantinisches Institut.
Nachlass Albert Ehrhard.
Strasbourg. Archives Départementales du Bas-Rhin.
Commissariat général de la République à Strasbourg et de la Haute-
    commission interalliée des territoires rhénanes. (AL 140)
Commissariat général: Direction de l'intérieur. (AL 69)
Dossiers réunis à la date du 29 juin 1926. (AL 74)
Ministère d'Alsace-Lorraine: Direction de l'intérieur. (AL 87)
Ministère de l'instruction publique. (AL 12)
Einlieferung Oberschulrat 25 Juin 1942. (AL 105)
Archives de l'ancien bureau du Statthalter. (AL 27)
Extraits de presse allemands provenant du bureau du Statthalter. (AL
    132)
Akten der Sûreté von Strassburg und Mülhausen. (AL 102)
Archives de l'Université de Strasbourg, 1872–1919. (AL 103)
Archives of the University of Strasbourg, 1919–1970. (Uncataloged;
    cited as UStr)
Université de Strasbourg, 1920–1929. (D 286 [77])
Délibérations du Conseil de l'Université. (AL 101 [3])
Université de Strasbourg: Décanat (Faculté de philosophie). (AL 62)
Université de Strasbourg. Faculté des lettres: Administration univer-
    sitaire et correspondance du doyen. (AL 154)
Université: Rectorat. (AL 20)
Valot-Akten. (AL 98)
———. Archives Municipales.
Archives de Henri Albert.
Fonds Ferdinand Dollinger.
Fonds Hugo Haug.
Archives Sénateur Muller.
Archives de la famille Redslob.
Archives administratives et contemporaines de la ville de Strasbourg.
———. Bibliothèque des Facultés de théologie.
Procès-verbaux des séances de la Faculté de théologie protestante.

————. Bibliothèque Municipale.
　Correspondance Rodolphe Reuss–Chr. Pfister. (Ms 430)
————. Bibliothèque Nationale et Universitaire.
　Alsatia: Cercle universitaire catholique, Strasbourg. (MR 10062)
　Autographes. (Ms 4970)
　Fonds Adolphe Michaelis.
　[Pfister, Christian]. Rapport sur l'Université de Strasbourg. (Ms 4850)
　Sundgovia-Erwinia. (Ms 4846)
————. Residence of M. Victor de Pange.
　Archives de la famille de Pange.
Tübingen. Universitätsbibliothek.
　Julius Euting in memoriam. (Md. 676 d)
　Briefe an Karl Johannes Fuchs.
　Robert von Mohl: Briefwechsel.
　Briefwechsel Theodor Nöldekes.
　Gustav von Schmoller: Teilnachlass.
　Briefwechsel Eduard Zellers.
Vanves (Hauts-de-Seine). Ministère de l'Education. Département de la
　Documentation et de la Diffusion de l'Information Statistique.
　Origine sociale. (STA* 13; file in the office of the director of the de-
　partment, M. R. Naudin)
Washington, D. C. Library of Congress.
　Collection of Correspondence of Friedrich Kapp, 1842–1884.
Wiesbaden. Hessische Landesbibliothek.
　Nachlass Otto Hartwig.


## 2. Interviews

Baas, Emile. Strasbourg, 27 Aug. 1976.
Brunschwig, Henri. Chicago, 13 Apr. 1976.
Buck, Paul. Strasbourg, 6 July 1976.
Burg, André. Haguenau (Bas-Rhin), 25 June 1976.
Cartan, Henri. Paris, 30 June 1976.
Cerf, Georges. Strasbourg, 2 Sept. 1976.
Cullmann, Oscar. Basel, 26 June 1976.
Dollinger, Philippe. Strasbourg, 23 June 1976.
Dreyfus, François-G. Strasbourg, 5 July and 7 Sept. 1976.
Fontaine, René. Strasbourg, 18 June 1976.
Fuchs, Albert. Strasbourg, 1 Sept. 1976.
Gagé, Jean. Paris, 3 July 1976.
Gaudemet, Jean. Paris, 28 June 1976.
Hauter, Charles. Strasbourg, 27 Aug. 1978.
Heitz, Robert. Strasbourg, 22 June 1976.

Himly, François-J. Strasbourg, 28 Aug. 1978.
Leuilliot, Paul. Paris, 29 June and 23 July 1976.
L'Huillier, Fernand. Strasbourg, 22 June 1976.
Livet, Georges. Strasbourg, 6 July and 23 Aug. 1978.
Maresquelle, Henri. Strasbourg, 22 June 1976.
Marthelot, Pierre. Paris, 1 July 1976.
Mehl, René. Strasbourg, 26 Aug. 1976.
Metz, René. Strasbourg, 8 July 1976.
Minder, Robert. Gunsbach (Haut-Rhin), 15 July 1976.
Pariset, François-Georges. Paris, 24 July and 4 Aug. 1976.
Ricklin, A. Strasbourg, 3 Sept. 1976.
Ricoeur, Paul. Chicago, 28 Jan. and 17 Mar. 1982.
Ritter, G. Erwin. Strasbourg, 26 Aug. 1976.
Rothé, Jean P. Strasbourg, 9 July 1976.
Sartory, René. Strasbourg, 24 Aug., 26 Aug., and 6 Sept. 1976.
Schlagdenhauffen, Alfred. Strasbourg, 18 June 1976.
Schneegans, Ernest. Strasbourg, 24 June and 8 July 1976.
Schwartz, Jacques. Strasbourg, 30 Aug. 1976.
Simon, Marcel. Thann (Haut-Rhin), 31 Aug. 1976.
Staub, J. P. Strasbourg, 27 Aug. 1976.
Weill, Alex. Strasbourg, 25 Aug. and 30 Aug. 1976.
Weiss, A. G. Paris, 1 July 1976.
Wittich, Georgine. Bergheim (Haut-Rhin), 12 July 1976.

## 3. Works Cited

"A la Faculté de médecine." *L'Alsace Française* 13 (26 Feb. 1933): 179–
    80.
"A propos d'un monôme." *Journal d'Alsace et de Lorraine* (Strasbourg),
    4 Dec. 1928.
"A propos de l'étudiante alsacienne." *L'Alsace Française* 9 (31 Jan. 1929):
    1.
"A propos de la manifestation estudiantine." *Dernières Nouvelles de
    Strasbourg,* 23 Apr. 1921.
"A propos des élections à l'A. F. G." *Les Etudiants d'Avant-Garde,* no.
    2 (Dec. 1932): 7–10.
Aaron, Lucien [Georges Delahache, pseud.]. *Strasbourg.* 3d ed. Paris,
    1949.
————. "Strasbourg 1918–1920." *La Revue de Paris* 27 (1 Aug. 1920):
    487–513.
Abelein, Manfred. *Die Kulturpolitik des Deutschen Reiches und der Bun-
    desrepublik Deutschland.* Cologne, 1968.
Abendroth, Walter. *Hans Pfitzner.* Munich, 1935.

*Academische Revue* (Munich), 1894–97.

"L'action de l'Union fédérale des étudiants contre la P. M. S. obligatoire." *Les Etudiants d'Avant-Garde,* no. 2 (Dec. 1932): 2–3.

"Actions et réactions." *L'Alsace Française* 8 (1 July 1928): 543.

"Une adresse de 128 professeurs de Strasbourg au président de la république." *Le Temps* (Paris), 30 Jan. 1939.

Alfaric, Prosper. *De la foi à la raison: Scènes vécues.* Paris 1955.

*Allgemeine Zeitung* (Augsburg; Munich), 1871–1901.

Allonas, Paul-L. "L'activité de l'A. F. G." *L'Echo de Paris,* 25 Nov. 1932.

Almond, Gabriel A., and G. Bingham Powell, Jr. *Comparative Politics: A Developmental Approach.* Boston, 1966.

Alsace-Lorraine. Conseil consultatif d'Alsace et de Lorraine. *Procès-verbaux annuels des sessions.* Strasbourg, 1920–24.

——. Conseil supérieur d'Alsace et de Lorraine. *Procès-verbaux.* Strasbourg, 1919–20.

——. Landesausschuss. *Verhandlungen des Landesausschusses für Elsass-Lothringen.* Strasbourg, 1875–1911.

——. Landtag: Erste Kammer. *Verhandlungen der Ersten Kammer des Landtags für Elsass-Lothringen.* Strasbourg, 1911–18.

——. Landtag: Zweite Kammer. *Verhandlungen der Zweiten Kammer des Landtags für Elsass-Lothringen.* Strasbourg, 1911–18.

——. Landtag: Zweite Kammer. *Vertrauliche Verhandlungen der Budgetkommission der zweiten Kammer des Landtags für Elsass-Lothringen in den Kriegsjahren 1916, 1917 und 1918.* Strasbourg, 1919.

——. Statistisches Bureau. *Statistisches Handbuch für Elsass-Lothringen.* Strasbourg, 1902.

——. Statistisches Bureau. *Statistisches Jahrbuch für Elsass-Lothringen.* 7 vols. Strasbourg, 1907–14.

"Alsatia am 8. Februar 1936." *Cercle Universitaire Catholique Alsatia: Bulletin,* 1935–36, no. 7: 37–38.

"Alsatia et Argentina." *Journal d'Alsace et de Lorraine* (Strasbourg), 27 Feb. 1929.

Alsaticus [pseud.]. "Die katholische Philosophieprofessur an der Universität Strassburg." *Allgemeine Zeitung* (Munich), 19 July 1913.

Althoff, Friedrich. *Aus Friedrich Althoffs Berliner Zeit: Erinnerungen für seine Freunde.* Ed. Marie Althoff. Jena, 1918.

——. *Aus Friedrich Althoffs Strassburger Zeit: Erinnerungen für seine Freunde.* Ed. Marie Althoff. Jena, 1914.

Amestoy, Georges. *Les universités françaises.* Special number of *Education et Gestion.* N.p. 1968.

Les amis des étudiants de Strasbourg. *Association 'Les amis des étudiants de Strasbourg': Statuts.* Strasbourg, 1930.

Andernach, Norbert. *Der Einfluss der Parteien auf das Hochschulwesen in Preussen 1848–1918.* Göttingen, 1972.

Andler, Charles. *Vie de Lucien Herr (1864–1926)*. Paris, 1932.

Andreu, Pierre. "Les idées politiques de la jeunesse intellectuelle de 1927 à la guerre." *Revue des Travaux de l'Académie des Sciences Morales et Politiques* 110 (1957, 2d semester): 17–30.

"Anniversaire." *Strasbourg-Etudiant* 2 (Jan. 1931): 1–3.

Anrich, Ernst. "Geschichte der deutschen Universität Strassburg." In *Zur Geschichte der deutschen Universität Strassburg*, 7–148. Strasbourg, [1941].

――――. "Von der Bedeutung der Strassburger Universität." *Strassburger Monatshefte* 4 (Aug.–Sept. 1940): 71–79.

Anrich, Ernst, ed. *Die Idee der deutschen Universität und die Reform der deutschen Universitäten*. Darmstadt, 1960.

Anrich, Gustav. "Ehemalige Kaiser-Wilhelms-Universität Strassburg." In *Das akademische Deutschland*, vol. 1, ed. Michael Doeberl et al., pp. 373–84. Berlin, 1930.

――――. "Die Universität Strassburg von 16. Jahrhundert bis 1918." In *Studien der Erwin von Steinbach-Stiftung*, vol. 3, 183–246. Frankfurt am Main, 1971.

――――. "Zu Herrn Poincaré's Strassburger Universitätsrede." *Elsass-Lothringische Mitteilungen* 4 (18 Mar. 1922): 157–59.

Antoni, Victor. *Grenzlandschicksal—Grenzlandtragik: Lebenserinnerungen und menschliche Betrachtungen eines Lothringers zu den politischen Irrungen und Wirrungen seiner Zeit*. Saarbrücken, 1957.

Appell, Paul. *Souvenirs d'un alsacien*. Paris, 1923.

"Après la faillite de l'A. F. G." *Les Etudiants d'Avant-Garde*, no. 3 (Jan. 1933): 1–2.

"Après les incidents au théâtre municipal." *Les Etudiants d'Avant-Garde*, no. 5 (May 1933): 5–7.

Aschoff, Ludwig. *Ein Gelehrtenleben in Briefen an die Familie*. Freiburg im Breisgau, 1966.

"L'aspect intellectuel du problème provincial." *L'Alsace Française* 10 (15 June 1930): 473–79.

Audollent, Auguste. "Y a-t-il lieu de 'spécialiser' et de 'moderniser' nos universités provinciales?" *Revue Internationale de l'Enseignement* 80 (1926): 129–36.

Auerbach, Berthold. *Berthold Auerbach: Briefe an seinen Freund Jakob Auerbach*. 2 vols. Frankfurt am Main, 1884.

――――. *Wieder unser: Gedenkblätter zur Geschichte dieser Tage*. Stuttgart, 1871.

"Aufruf!" *E. L. Z.* (Strasbourg), 3 Feb. 1933.

Aulard, Alphonse. *Napoléon I<sup>er</sup> et le monopole universitaire*. Paris, 1911.

"Aus dem Deutschen Reichstag." *Allgemeine Zeitung* (Augsburg), 27 May 1871.

"Aus dem Strassburger Gemeinderat." *Der Elsässer* (Strasbourg), 26 Nov. 1929.

"Aus Elsass-Lothringen." *National-Zeitung* (Berlin), 30 Mar. 1887.

"Ausgeräuchert!" *Rheinisch-Westfälische Zeitung* (Essen), 17 June 1911.

"L'autonomie de l'Alsace-Lorraine et le professeur Ziegler." *Chronique d'Alsace-Lorraine* 13, no. 2 (1911): 17–18.

B., M. "Zur Geschichte des elsässischen Studentenwesens: Aus Anlass einer neuen Veröffentlichung." *Elsass-Lothringen: Heimatstimmen* 17 (1939): 209–14.

Baas, Emile. "Notes pour une sociologie de la bourgeoisie alsacienne contemporaine." In *La bourgeoisie alsacienne: Etudes d'histoire sociale,* 333–41. Strasbourg, 1954.

———. *Situation de l'Alsace.* 2d ed. Colmar, 1973.

Baas, Geneviève. *Le malaise alsacien 1919–1924.* Strasbourg, 1972.

Bachem, Karl. *Vorgeschichte, Geschichte und Politik der deutschen Zentrumspartei.* 9 vols. Cologne, 1927–32.

Baden. Statistisches Landesamt. *Statistisches Jahrbuch für das Grossherzogtum Baden.* 44 vols. Karlsruhe, 1869–1938.

Baechler, Christian. "L'Alsace entre la guerre et la paix: Recherches sur l'opinion publique (1917–1918)." Thèse pour le doctorat de troisième cycle, University of Strasbourg, 1969.

Baensch, Otto. "Elsässisches Musikleben von 1871–1918." In *Wissenschaft, Kunst und Literatur in Elsass-Lothringen 1871–1918,* ed. Georg Wolfram, 377–473. Frankfurt am Main, 1934.

Baeumker, Clemens. "Clemens Baeumker." In *Die Philosophie der Gegenwart in Selbstdarstellungen,* vol. 2, ed. Raymund Schmidt, 1–30. Leipzig, 1923.

Baeyer, Adolf. *Erinnerungen aus meinem Leben.* Braunschweig, 1935.

Baier, Bruno, et al. "Das Unterrichtswesen in Elsass-Lothringen." In *Verfassung und Verwaltung von Elsass-Lothringen 1871–1918,* part 2, ed. Georg Wolfram, 1–230. Berlin, 1937.

Baier, Hermann, ed. "Heidelberger Professorenbriefe." *Zeitschrift für die Geschichte des Oberrheins* 89 (1937): 170–206.

Baldeck, P. E. "Elsässer Brief." *Die Literatur* 28 (1925–26): 487–89.

Baldensperger, Fernand. "A travers les universités: Strasbourg." *La Vie Universitaire* 2 (Dec. 1920): 16–17.

———. "Les grands jours strasbourgeois de Maurice Barrès." *L'Alsace Française* 4 (11 Oct. 1924): 965–66.

———. "Maurice Barrès et la Rhénanie." *Journal d'Alsace et de Lorraine* (Strasbourg), 14 Nov. 1920.

———. "Quarante mois après: Notes d'un professeur de l'Université de Strasbourg." *L'Alsace Française* 3 (28 Apr. 1923): 391–92.

———. "L'Université de Strasbourg et la vie universitaire française." *L'Alsace Française* 7 (19 Nov. 1927): 927–28.

————. *Une vie parmi d'autres.* Paris, 1940.

Bamberger, Ludwig. *Bismarcks grosses Spiel: Die geheimen Tagebücher Ludwig Bambergers.* Ed. Ernst Feder. Frankfurt am Main, 1932.

"Le banquet des anciens étudiants de l'Université de Strasbourg." *Journal d'Alsace et de Lorraine* (Strasbourg), 27 Nov. 1928.

Barrès, Maurice. "Les bastions de l'est." *Revue des Deux Mondes,* 5th ser., 24 (1 Nov. 1904): 5–51.

————. *Le génie du Rhin.* Paris, 1921.

Barth, Fredrik. "Introduction." In *Ethnic Groups and Boundaries: The Social Organization of Cultural Difference,* ed. Fredrik Barth, 9–38. Boston, 1969.

————. "Scale and Network in Urban Western Society." In *Scale and Social Organization,* ed. Fredrik Barth, 163–83. Oslo, 1978.

Barthelmé, A. "Zusammenhänge." *Alsatia Academica* 1, no. 3 (1927): 14–16.

Barthelmé, G. "Etudiants alsaciens et étudiants allemands en 1867." *L'Alsace Française* 11 (20 Dec. 1931): 1021–24.

Baulig, Henri. "Lucien Febvre à Strasbourg." *Bulletin de la Faculté des Lettres de Strasbourg* 36 (1957–58): 175–84.

Baum, Mathilde. *Johann Wilhelm Baum: Ein protestantischen Charakterbild aus dem Elsass, 1809–1878.* Bremen, 1880.

Baumgarten, Otto. *Meine Lebensgeschichte.* Tübingen, 1928.

Baumgarten, Paul Maria. *Römische und andere Erinnerungen.* Düsseldorf, 1927.

Becker, Jean-Jacques *1914: Comment les Français sont entrés dans la guerre.* Paris, 1977.

Becker, Josef. "Baden, Bismarck und die Annexion von Elsass und Lothringen." *Zeitschrift für die Geschichte des Oberrheins* 115 (1967): 167–204.

Becker, Philipp August. "Heinrich Schneegans 1863–1914." *Germanisch-Romanische Monatsschrift* 6 (1914): 609–15.

Ben-David, Joseph. *The Scientist's Role in Society: A Comparative Study.* Englewood Cliffs, N.J., 1971.

Bénéton, Philippe. "La génération de 1912–14: Image, mythe et réalité?" *Revue Française de Science Politique* 21 (1971): 981–1009.

Bennrath, Frédéric. "Quatre étudiants allemands en Alsace." *L'Alsace Française* 13 (19 Feb. 1933): 151–53.

Bentmann, Friedrich, ed. *René Schickele: Leben und Werk in Dokumenten.* Nuremberg, 1974.

Berger, Martin. *Pascal David und die politische Entwicklung Elsass-Lothringens 1882–1907.* Munich, 1910.

————. *Die Ursachen des Zusammenbruches des Deutschtums in Elsass-Lothringen.* Freiburg im Breisgau, 1919.

Bergmann, Gustav von. *Rückschau: Geschehen und Erleben auf meiner Lebensbühne*. Munich, 1953.

Bergner, Georges. "Quelques silhouettes universitaires." *L'Alsace Française* 12 (5 June 1932): 469–91.

*Berliner Neueste Nachrichten*, 1909.

Bernays, Jakob. *Jakob Bernays: Ein Lebensbild in Briefen*. Ed. Michael Fränkel. Breslau, 1932.

Berr, Henri. "L'esprit de synthèse dans l'enseignement supérieur: L'Université de Strasbourg," parts 1, 2. *Revue de Synthèse Historique* 32 (1921): 1–13; 34 (1922): 1–6.

————. *Vie et science: Lettres d'un vieux philosophe strasbourgeois et d'un étudiant parisien*. Paris, 1894.

Berstein, Serge. "Une greffe politique manquée: Le radicalisme alsacien de 1919 à 1939." *Revue d'Histoire Moderne et Contemporaine* 17 (1970): 78–103.

"Die Betheiligung der Elsässer bei der Einweihung der Strassburger Universität." *Allgemeine Zeitung* (Augsburg), 8 May 1872.

Betz, Maurice. "Chez les étudiants alsaciens de Paris." *L'Alsace Française* 5 (28 Feb. 1925): 204–5.

Beudant, Robert. "La Faculté de droit et des sciences politiques de l'Université de Strasbourg pendant l'année scolaire 1922–23." *Revue Internationale de l'Enseignement* 78 (1924): 46–54.

————. "Le Grand-Duché de Luxembourg et l'Université de Strasbourg." *L'Alsace Française* 1 (30 July 1921): 494–95.

Bezold, Friedrich von. *Geschichte der Rheinischen Friedrich-Wilhelms-Universität von der Gründung bis zum Jahr 1870*. 2 vols. Bonn, 1920–33.

Bickler, Hermann. *Ein besonderes Land: Erinnerungen und Betrachtungen eines Lothringers*. Lindhorst, Federal Republic of Germany, 1978.

————. "Studenten im elsässischen Volkstumskampf." *Der Altherrenbund* 3 (1941): 187–88.

————. *Widerstand: Zehn Jahre Volkstumskampf der Elsass-Lothringischen Jungmannschaft*. Strasbourg, [1943].

Bieber, P. "Unsere Universität." *E. L. Z.* (Strasbourg), 21 Mar. 1931.

Bismarck, Otto von. *Die gesammelten Werke*. 15 vols. in 19. Berlin, 1924–35.

Bismarck, Wilhelm von. "Aus den Papieren des Grafen Wilhelm Bismarck: Bismarck und Edwin von Manteuffel." Ed. Hans Goldschmidt. *Elsass-Lothringisches Jahrbuch* 15 (1936): 133–82.

Bk. "Georg Simmel, Goethe und das Elsass." *Elsass-Lothringen: Heimatstimmen* 10 (1932): 225–29.

Blanchard, Raoul. *Je découvre l'université: Douai, Lille, Grenoble*. Paris, 1963.

Blau, Peter M. *The Organization of Academic Work.* New York, 1973.

Bleek, Wilhelm. *Von der Kameralausbildung zum Juristenprivileg: Studium, Prüfung und Ausbildung der höheren Beamten des allgemeinen Verwaltungsdienstes in Deutschland im 18. und 19. Jahrhundert.* Berlin (W.), 1972.

Bleuel, Hans Peter. *Deutschlands Bekenner: Professoren zwischen Kaiserreich und Diktatur.* Bern, 1968.

Bloch, Jean-Richard, and Romain Rolland. *Deux hommes se rencontrent: Correspondance entre Jean-Richard Bloch et Romain Rolland (1910–1918).* Paris, 1964.

Bloch, Marc. "Christian Pfister: II.—Les oeuvres." *Revue Historique* 172 (1933): 563–70.

———. *Strange Defeat.* Trans. Gerard Hopkins. London, 1949.

———. "Sur la réforme de l'enseignement." In *L'étrange défaite,* 2d ed., 246–62. Paris, 1957.

Bloch, Marc, and Lucien Febvre. "Le problème de l'agrégation." *Annales d'Histoire Economique et Sociale* 9 (1937): 115–29.

Bloch, Raymond. "Bio-bibliographie d'Albert Grenier." In *Hommage à Albert Grenier,* vol. 1, ed. Marcel Renard, 1–12. Brussels-Berchem, 1962.

Bobtcheff, Sava K. "Activité de l'A. G. en 1923." *Strasbourg Universitaire* 1, no. 2 (1924): 4–7.

Boeckel, Ernst. *Hermann Köchly: Ein Bild seines Lebens und seiner Persönlichkeit.* Heidelberg, 1904.

Böhmer, Eduard. "Strassburger Erlebnisse." *Romanische Studien* 4 (1879–80): 649–52.

Boll, Léon. "Par où commencer pour résoudre la question d'Alsace-Lorraine?" *Journal d'Alsace-Lorraine* (Strasbourg), 9, 11, 12, and 14 May 1907.

Bonjour, Edgar. *Die Universität Basel von den Anfängen bis zur Gegenwart.* Basel, 1960.

Bonnefous, Edouard. *Histoire politique de la Troisième République.* 7 vols. Paris, 1956–67.

Bonner, Thomas Neville. *American Doctors and German Universities: A Chapter in International Intellectual Relations, 1870–1914.* Lincoln, Neb., 1963.

Bonnet, Serge. *Sociologie politique et religieuse de la Lorraine.* Paris, 1972.

Bopp, Marie-Joseph. *L'Alsace sous l'occupation allemande 1940–1945.* Le Puy, 1945.

———. *Die evangelischen Geistlichen und Theologen in Elsass und Lothringen von der Reformation bis zur Gegenwart.* Neustadt an der Aisch, Federal Republic of Germany, 1959.

————. "L'oeuvre de la haute bourgeoisie haut-rhinoise au XIX$^e$ siècle." In *La bourgeoisie alsacienne: Etudes d'histoire sociale,* 387–402. Strasbourg, 1954.

————. "Strassburger Studentenleben bis 1850: Ein Beitrag zur Geschichte der Strassburger Studentenverbindungen." *Annuaire de la Société Historique, Littéraire et Scientifique du Club Vosgien,* n. s. 2 (1934): 172–259.

Bordmann, Joseph, and Otto Imgart. "Strassburger Studentenleben zur Zeit des ersten Kaiserreiches." *Quellen und Darstellungen zur Geschichte der Burschenschaft und der Deutschen Einheitsbewegung* 15 (1938): 217–61.

Bornhak, Conrad. "Die Begründung der katholisch-theologischen Fakultät in Strassburg." *Elsass-Lothringisches Jahrbuch* 12 (1933): 249–69.

Borries, Emil von. *Geschichte der Stadt Strassburg.* Strasbourg, 1909.

Borscheid, Peter. *Naturwissenschaft, Staat und Industrie in Baden (1848–1914).* Stuttgart, 1976.

Bouchholtz, Ch. "Der elsässische Student." *Vossische Zeitung* (Berlin), 2 May 1914.

Bouchholtz, Fritz. "Ernst Stadler und die Strassburger studentische Wanderbühne." *Elsass-Lothringen: Heimatstimmen* 4 (1926): 643–45.

————. "Die Strassburger studentische Wanderbühne." In *Wissenschaft, Kunst und Literatur in Elsass-Lothringen 1871–1918,* ed. Georg Wolfram, 355–59. Frankfurt am Main, 1934.

Bourgin, Hubert. *De Jaurès à Léon Blum.* Paris, 1938.

Bourson, Paul. "Monômes et 'banquets' des étudiants alsaciens." *La Vie en Alsace* 10 (1932): 108–15.

Brandl, Alois. *Zwischen Inn und Themse: Lebensbeobachtungen eines Anglisten.* Berlin, 1936.

Braubach, Max. "Aloys Schulte—Kämpfe und Ziele." *Historisches Jahrbuch* 78 (1959): 82–109.

————. "Zwei deutsche Historiker aus Westfalen: Briefe Heinrich Finkes an Aloys Schulte." *Westfälische Zeitschrift* 118 (1968): 9–113.

Braun, Jean. "La littérature alsacienne d'expression allemande et dialectale de 1870 à 1918." In *Les lettres en Alsace,* 369–83. Strasbourg, 1962.

Braun-Vogelstein, Julie. *Heinrich Braun: Ein Leben für den Sozialismus.* Stuttgart, 1967.

Brauner, [?]. "Der interkorporative Vertreterausschuss." *Alsatia Academica* 1, no. 1 (1927): 28.

Brentano, Lujo. *Elsässer Erinnerungen.* Berlin, 1917.

————. *Mein Leben im Kampf um die soziale Entwicklung Deutschlands.* Jena, 1931.

————. "Über die deutschen Universitäten." *Die Zeit* (Vienna), 25 Dec. 1906.

Breslauer, Bernhard. *Die Zurücksetzung der Juden an den Universitäten Deutschlands.* Berlin, 1911.

Bresslau, Harry. "Harry Bresslau." In *Die Geschichtswissenschaft der Gegenwart in Selbstdarstellungen,* vol. 2, ed. Sigfrid Steinberg, 29–83. Leipzig, 1926.

Brim, Orville G., Jr. "Adult Socialization." In *Socializaton and Society,* ed. John A. Clausen, 182–226. Boston, [1968].

Brion, Jacques. "Les étudiants alsaciens et lorrains à Paris." *L'Alsace Française* 8 (22 Apr. 1928): 330–31.

Brocke, Bernhard vom. "Hochschul- und Wissenschaftspolitik in Preussen und im Deutschen Kaiserreich 1882–1907: Das 'System Althoff.'" In *Bildungspolitik in Preussen zur Zeit des Kaiserreichs,* ed. Peter Baumgart, 9–118. Stuttgart, 1980.

Bronner, Fritz. *1870–71 Elsass-Lothringen: Zeitgenössische Stimmen für und wider der Eingliederung in das Deutsche Reich.* 2 vols. Frankfurt am Main, 1970.

————. *Die Verfassungsbestrebungen des Landesausschusses für Elsass-Lothringen (1875–1911).* Heidelberg, 1926.

Bruch, Johann Friedrich. *Johann Friedrich Bruch: Seine Wirksamkeit in Schule und Kirche 1821–1872.* Ed. Th. G. Strasbourg, 1890.

Bruch, Rüdiger vom. *Wissenschaft, Politik und öffentliche Meinung: Gelehrtenpolitik im Wilhelminischen Deutschland (1890–1914).* Husum, 1980.

Bruck, Niklaus. *Ich warte . . . Ein Strassburger Roman.* Stuttgart, 1918.

"Brunschwicq-Aria ou la rosette de Gemaehling." *L'Appel: Tribune de L'Etudiant Français de Strasbourg* 5, no. 2 (1937): 3.

Brunschwig, Henri. "L'assimilation d'une famille mulhousienne à la France au XIXᵉ siècle." *L'Alsace Française* 9 (29 Dec. 1929): 1104–6.

Bucher, Pierre. "Discours prononcé par M. le docteur Bucher à l'inauguration de l'Université de Strasbourg le 22 novembre 1919." In University of Strasbourg, *Université de Strasbourg: Fêtes d'inauguration,* 14–19. Strasbourg, 1920.

Büchner, Ludwig. "Die Freiheit der Wissenschaft und die Universitäten." *Die Gegenwart* 53 (1898): 161–63.

Buchner, Rudolf. "Die elsässische Frage und das deutsch-französische Verhältnis im 19. Jahrhundert." In *Ein Leben aus freier Mitte: Festschrift für Professor Dr. Ulrich Noack,* 57–109. Göttingen, 1961.

Burchardt, Lothar. "Wissenschaftspolitik und Reformdiskussion im Wilhelminischen Deutschland." *Konstanzer Blätter für Hochschulfragen* 8 (1975): 71–84.

Burckhardt, Jakob. *Briefe.* 9 vols. Ed. Max Burckhardt. Basel, 1949–80.

Burger, Emil. "Vor sechzig Jahren auf der Universität." *Evangelisch-protestantischer Kirchenbote für Elsass und Lothringen* 61 (1932): 236–38, 244–45, 260–61, 275–77.

Busch, Alexander. *Die Geschichte der Privatdozenten.* Stuttgart, 1959.

Busch, Moritz. *Tagebuchblätter.* 3 vols. Leipzig, 1899.

*Cahiers Alsaciens / Elsässer Hefte* (Strasbourg), 1912–14.

Callot, Jacques. "Les études médicales et pharmaceutiques." *Saisons d'Alsace,* no. 2 (1951): 129–32.

Campbell, Ernest Q. "Adolescent Socialization." In *Handbook of Socialization Theory and Research,* ed. David A. Goslin, 821–59. Chicago, 1969.

Canguilhem, Georges. "Jean Cavaillès (1903–1945)." In University of Strasbourg, Faculty of Letters, *Mémorial des années 1939–1945,* 141–58. Paris, 1947.

Canivez, André. *Jules Lagneau, professeur de philosophie: Essai sur la condition du professeur de philosophie jusqu'à la fin du XIX$^e$ siècle.* 2 vols. Paris, 1965.

[Cercle des anciens étudiants]. *L'avenir de l'Université de Strasbourg.* N.p. 1919.

Cercle des étudiants de Strasbourg. *Fêtes universitaires à l'occasion du VIII$^{me}$ Congrès national et interallié de l'Union national des associations d'étudiants.* Strasbourg, 1920.

"La cérémonie d'inauguration du 22 novembre 1919." *Saisons d'Alsace,* n. s., no. 36 (1970): 449–50.

Cerf, Georges. "Edmond Rothé, citoyen." In *Edmond Rothé, professeur à l'Université de Strasbourg (1873–1942).* Strasbourg, 1968.

Chamberlain, Houston Stewart. "Der voraussetzungslose Mommsen." *Die Fackel,* no. 87 (7 Dec. 1901): 1–13.

Châtellier, Louis. *Tradition chrétienne et renouveau catholique dans le cadre de l'ancien diocèse de Strasbourg (1650–1770).* Paris, 1981.

Châtellier, Louis, Bernard Vogler, and Marcel Thomann. "Cultures, religions, société: L'esprit européen." In *Histoire de Strasbourg des origines à nos jours,* vol. 3, ed. Georges Livet and Francis Rapp, 377–454. Strasbourg, 1981.

Chevrillon, André. "Aux pays d'Alsace et de Lorraine (décembre 1918)." *La Revue de Paris* 26 (1919): 449–76, 811–46.

Chickering, Roger. *Imperial Germany and a World without War: The Peace Movement and German Society, 1892–1914.* Princeton, 1975.

Christian, G. "Korporationsprinzip und studentische Verhältnisse in Strassburg." *Cercle Universitaire Catholique Alsatia: Bulletin,* 1935–36, no. 7: 29–34.

"Chronique: I.—Réunions du samedi." *Bulletin de la Faculté des Lettres de Strasbourg* 1 (1922–23): 106–9.

Clark, Burton R. *The Distinctive College: Antioch, Reed & Swarthmore.* Chicago, 1970.

Clark, Terry Nichols. *Prophets and Patrons: The French University and the Emergence of the Social Sciences.* Cambridge, Mass., 1973.

Class Heinrich [Daniel Frymann, pseud.]. *Wenn ich der Kaiser war'.* 5th ed. Leipzig, 1914.

Cohen, Gustave. *Ceux que j'ai connus.* Montreal, 1946.

————. "Souvenir universitaire." *L'Alsace Française* 13 (19–26 Nov. 1933): 891–92.

"Comité des étudiants organisés de Strasbourg." *Journal d'Alsace et de Lorraine* (Strasbourg), 7 June 1919.

Les compagnons de l'université nouvelle. *L'université nouvelle.* 2 vols. Paris, 1918–19.

"La conférence de M. Witkopf [sic] sur Mann." *Journal d'Alsace et de Lorraine* (Strasbourg), 26 May 1928.

Conrad, Johannes. "Einige Ergebnisse der deutschen Universitätsstatistik." *Jahrbücher für Nationalökonomie und Statistik* 87 (1906): 433–92.

————. *Das Universitätsstudium in Deutschland während der letzten 50 Jahren.* Jena, 1884.

"Les conséquences du procès de Colmar." *Le Temps* (Paris), 10 May 1928.

Council of Europe. Consultative Assembly. *Documents.* 26 sessions. Strasbourg, 1949–74.

————. *Reports.* 2 sessions. Strasbourg, 1949–50.

Craig, John E. "The Expansion of Education." *Review of Research in Education* 9 (1981): 151–213.

————. "France's First Chair of Sociology: A Note on the Origins." *Etudes Durkheimiennes,* no. 4 (Dec. 1979): 8–13.

————. "Higher Education and Social Mobility in Germany." In *The Transformation of Higher Learning, 1860–1930: Expansion, Diversification, Social Opening, and Professionalization in England, Germany, Russia, and the United States,* ed. Konrad H. Jarausch, 219–44. Chicago, 1983.

————. "Maurice Halbwachs à Strasbourg." *Revue Française de Sociologie* 20 (1979): 273–92.

————. "A Mission for German Learning: The University of Strasbourg and Alsatian Society, 1870–1918." Ph.D. diss., Stanford University, 1973.

Craig, John E., and Norman Spear. "Explaining Educational Expansion." In *The Sociology of Educational Expansion: Take-Off, Growth and Inflation in Educational Systems,* ed. Margaret S. Archer, 133–57. London, 1982.

*Création d'une université à Nancy.* Nancy, 1890.

"Une crise à Strasbourg." *Journal d'Alsace et de Lorraine* (Strasbourg), 22 Jan. 1919.

Cron, Ludwig "Der Zugang der Badener zu den badischen Universitäten und zur Technische Hochschule Karlsruhe in den Jahren 1869 bis 1893." Doctoral diss., University of Heidelberg, 1897.

Cullmann, Oscar. "Autobiographische Skizze." In Oscar Cullmann, *Vorträge und Aufsätze 1925–1962*, 683–87. Tübingen, 1966.

Curtius, Ernst Robert. *Französischer Geist im neuen Europa*. Stuttgart, [1925].

———. *Französischer Geist im zwanzigsten Jahrhundert*. 2d ed. Bern, 1952.

———. "Gustav Gröber und die romanische Philologie." In Ernst Robert Curtius, *Gesammelte Aufsätze zur romanischen Philologie*, 428–55. Bern, 1960.

———. *Maurice Barrès und die geistigen Grundlagen des französischen Nationalismus*. Bonn, 1921.

Curtius, Friedrich. *Deutsche Briefe und Elsässische Erinnerungen*. Frauenfeld, 1920.

Curvale, J. "Le S. E. C." *Strasbourg Universitaire* 1, no. 3 (1924): 22–24.

Dachs, Herbert. "Albert Ehrhard—Vermittler oder Verräter?" In *Der Modernismus: Beiträge zu seiner Erforschung*, ed. Erika Weinzierl, 213–33. Graz, 1974.

Dahn, Felix. "Die deutsche Provinz 'Elsass-Lothringen.'" *Allgemeine Zeitung* (Augsburg), 31 Oct. 1870.

Dahrendorf, Ralf. *Society and Democracy in Germany*. Garden City, N.Y., 1967.

Daigle, Jean-Guy. *La culture en partage: Grenoble et son élite au milieu du 19ᵉ siècle*. Ottawa, 1977.

Dallwitz, Hans von. "Aus dem Nachlass des ehemaligen kaiserlichen Statthalters von Elsass-Lothringen, früheren preussischen Ministers des Innern von Dallwitz." Ed. Albert von Mutius. *Preussische Jahrbücher* 214 (1928): 1–22, 147–66, 290–303.

Davy, Georges. *L'homme, le fait social et le fait politique*. Paris, 1973.

Debray, Régis. *Teachers, Writers, Celebrities: The Intellectuals of Modern France*. Trans. David Macey. London, 1981.

Deck, Jean. "Le Strasbourg-Etudiant-Club." *Strasbourg-Etudiant* 1 (Nov. 1930): 6–7.

Dehio, Katharina. "Die Geschichte einer elsässischen Industrie." *Cahiers Alsaciens* 1 (1912): 294–303.

Dehio, Ludwig. "Die Kaiser-Wilhelms-Universität Strassburg." In *Wissenschaft, Kunst und Literatur in Elsass-Lothringen 1871–1918*, ed. Georg Wolfram, 1–30. Frankfurt am Main, 1934.

Delage, Jean. "La vie des étudiants: Strasbourg." *L'Echo de Paris,* 25 Nov. 1932.

[Delbrück, Hans]. "Politische Korrespondenz: Die katholische Geschichts-Professur in Strassburg." *Preussische Jahrbücher* 106 (1901): 384–87.

Delpech, Joseph. "Centralisation et régionalisme." *Journal d'Alsace et de Lorraine* (Strasbourg), 5 July, 17 July, 26 Aug., 6 Sept. 1920.

Dempf, Alois. *Albert Ehrhard: Der Mann und sein Werk in der Geistesgeschichte um die Jahrhundertwende.* Colmar, [194-].

*Deutsche Hochschulstatistik,* vol. 7. Ed. Hochschulverwaltungen. Berlin, 1931.

"Die deutschen Universitäten und die neue Universität in Strassburg." *Die Grenzboten* 30 (1871): 601–8.

*Deutscher Universitäts-Kalender.* Ed. Ferdinand Ascherson et al. 101 vols. Leipzig, 1872–1927.

"Deutschtum und Unterrichtswesen in Elsass-Lothringen." *Strassburger Post* (quoted in *National-Zeitung* [Berlin], 17 May 1887).

deWitt-Guizot, F. "La Société des amis des étudiants." *Strasbourg-Université* 7 (Apr. 1936): 25–26.

Dickerhof, Harald. "Bildung und Ausbildung im Programm der bayerischen Universitäten im 19. Jahrhundert." *Historisches Jahrbuch* 95, part 1 (1975): 142–69.

Dietzel, Carl. *Strassburg als deutsche Reichsuniversität und die Neugestaltung des juristischen und staatswissenschaftlichen Studiums.* Frankfurt am Main, 1871.

Digeon, Claude. *La crise allemande de la pensée française (1870–1914).* Paris, 1959.

Dillmann, A. "Ewald: Georg Heinrich August E." In *Allgemeine Deutsche Biographie,* vol. 6, 438–42. Leipzig, 1877.

Dilthey, Wilhelm. "Entwurf zu einem Gutachten über die Gründung der Universität Strassburg." *Die Erziehung* 16 (1941): 81–85.

Dintzer, Lucien. "Le mouvement des universités populaires." *Le Mouvement Social,* no. 36 (1961): 3–29.

"Dix ans d'université française." *La Libre Lorraine* (Metz), 1 Dec. 1928.

Dollinger, Ferdinand. "La Société des amis de l'Université de Strasbourg." *L'Alsace Française* 7 (19 Nov. 1927): 930–32.

Dollinger, Philippe. "Bourgeoisies d'Alsace." In *La bourgeoisie alsacienne: Etudes d'histoire sociale,* 485–92. Strasbourg, 1954.

———. "Marc Bloch et Lucien Febvre: Quelques souvenirs et réflexions d'une de leurs élèves." In Philippe Dollinger, *Pages d'histoire: France et Allemagne médiévales, Alsace,* 171–73. Paris, 1977.

Dominicus, Alexander. *Strassburgs deutsche Bürgermeister Back und Schwander, 1873–1918.* Frankfurt am Main, 1939.

Dorpalen, Andreas. *Heinrich von Treitschke.* New Haven, 1957.

Dove, Alfred. *Ausgewählte Aufsätze und Briefe*. Ed. Friedrich Meinecke and Oswald Dammann. 2 vols. Munich, 1925.

———. "Der Strassburger Hochschule zum Grusse." *Im Neuen Reich* 2 (1872): 673–78.

Dreyfus, François-G. "L'Université protestante de Strasbourg dans la seconde moitié du XVIIIᵉ siècle." *Revue d'Allemagne* 3 (1971): 84–97.

———. *La vie politique en Alsace 1919–1936*. Paris, 1969.

Driesch, Margarete. "Davoser Hochschulkurse 1928." *Nord und Süd* 51 (1928): 455–59.

Duisberg, Carl. *Meine Lebenserinnerungen*. Leipzig, 1933.

Dupeux, Louis. "René Capitant et l'analyse idéologique du Nazisme (1934–1939)." *Francia* 5 (1977): 627–37.

———. "La revue *L'Allemagne Contemporaine* 1936–1939." In *Les relations franco-allemands 1933–1939*, 167–77. Paris, 1976.

Duquesne, Joseph. *Le catholicisme et la jeunesse universitaire en Alsace*. Strasbourg, 1923.

Durkheim, Emile. "Rôle des universités dans l'éducation sociale du pays." *Revue Française de Sociologie* 17 (1976): 181–89.

Düwell, Kurt. *Deutschlands auswärtige Kulturpolitik 1918–1932: Grundlinien und Dokumente*. Cologne, 1976.

E. "Einige Gedanken über den elsass-lothringischen Akademiker." *Der Wanderfalke* 4, no. 3 (1935): 8–10.

E., S. "Le bal des étudiants à la préfecture." *Strasbourg-Etudiant* 3 (Feb. 1932): 2.

Eccard, Frédéric. *Le livre de ma vie*. Paris, 1951.

*Echo du Cercle* (Strasbourg), Mar. 1911.

"Echos." *Strasbourg-Université* 6 (May 1935): 17.

"Ecole de formation sociale." *Journal d'Alsace et de Lorraine* (Strasbourg), 18 Oct. 1928.

"Editorial." *L'Etudiant Libre* (Strasbourg), 1 (Jan. 1936): 1.

Edschmid, Kasimir. *Lebendiger Expressionismus: Auseinandersetzungen, Gestalten, Erinnerungen*. Vienna, 1961.

Ehrhardt, Eugène. "Rapport général sur la situation et les travaux de l'Université de Strasbourg pendant l'année scolaire 1922–1923." In University of Strasbourg, *Travaux de l'Université de Strasbourg pendant l'année scolaire 1922–1923*, 3–23. Strasbourg, 1924.

Ehrismann, H. "Julius (Friedrich Emil) Rathgeber: Lebensbild eines elsässischen evangelischen Geistlichen und Gelehrten." *Jahrbuch für Geschichte, Sprache und Litteratur Elsass-Lothringens* 10 (1894): 110–64.

"Einige Zustände in Elsass-Lothringen." *Allgemeine Zeitung* (Munich), Beilage, 19 Mar. 1887.

Elias, Otto-Heinrich. "Die Bedeutung der Universitäten im politschen Leben der südwestdeutschen Universitätsstädte im 19. Jahrhundert." In *Stadt und Hochschule im 19. und 20. Jahrhundert,* ed. Erich Maschke and Jürgen Sydow, 147–77. Sigmaringen, 1979.

*Der Elsässer* (Strasbourg), 1896–1922.

"Elsässische Wünsche in Bezug auf die Übergangszeit in Elsass-Lothringen." *Allgemeine Zeitung* (Augsburg), 20 Apr. 1871.

"Elsass-Lothringen." *National-Zeitung* (Berlin), 23 Mar. 1887.

"Elsass-Lothringische Chronik." *Elsässische Kulturfragen* 2 (1911–12): 229–32.

[Elsass-Lothringische Jungmannschaft]. *Elsass-Lothringische Jungmannschaft.* Strasbourg, n.d.

Engel, Josef. "Die deutschen Universitäten und die Geschichtswissenschaft." *Historische Zeitschrift* 189 (1959): 223–378.

Engelhardt, Wolf Freiherr von, and Hansmartin Decker-Hauff, eds. *Quellen zur Gründungsgeschichte der Naturwissenschaftlichen Fakultät in Tübingen, 1859–1963.* Tübingen, 1963.

*Erklärung der Hochschullehrer des Deutschen Reiches.* Berlin, 1914.

Ermarth, Michael. *Wilhelm Dilthey: The Critique of Historical Reason.* Chicago, 1978.

Ernst, Robert. *Rechenschaftsbericht eines Elsässers.* 2d ed. Berlin (W.), 1955.

Ernsthausen, A. Ernst von. *Erinnerungen eines Preussischen Beamten.* Bielefeld, 1894.

"Die Eröffnung der Universität Strassburg." *Allgemeine Zeitung* (Augsburg), 4, 5, 6 May 1872.

Erzberger, Matthias. *Erlebnisse im Weltkrieg.* Stuttgart, 1920.

Escherich, Karl. *Leben und Forschen, Kampf um eine Wissenschaft.* Berlin, 1944.

"Les étudiants alsaciens et lorrains et leurs camarades d'outre-Vosges." *Journal d'Alsace et de Lorraine* (Strasbourg), 14 Feb. 1920.

"Etudiants alsaciens-lorrains." *Nouvelliste d'Alsace-Lorraine* (Colmar), 14 Mar. 1910.

"Les étudiants réclament." *Journal d'Alsace et de Lorraine* (Strasbourg), 21 Nov. 1920.

Eulenburg, Franz. *Der 'Akademische Nachwuchs': Eine Untersuchung über die Lage und die Aufgaben der Extraordinarien und Privatdozenten.* Leipzig, 1908.

———. *Die Frequenz der deutschen Universitäten von ihrer Gründung bis zur Gegenwart.* Leipzig, 1904.

*Express* (Mulhouse), 23 Dec. 1896.

Faber, Karl-Georg. *Die nationalpolitische Publizistik Deutschlands von 1866 bis 1871: Eine kritische Bibliographie.* 2 vols. Düsseldorf, 1963.

"La Faculté de médecine proteste." *La République* (Strasbourg), 4 Feb. 1933.

Favrot, Brigitte. *Le gouvernement allemand et le clergé catholique lorrain de 1890 à 1914.* Metz, 1980.

Febvre, Lucien. "L'enseignement supérieur." In *Encyclopédie française,* vol. 15, ed. Célestin Bouglé, 15'08.5–15'10.3. Paris, 1939.

———. "Marc Bloch et Strasbourg." In Lucien Febvre, *Combats pour l'histoire,* 391–407. Paris, 1953.

———. "Politique royale ou civilisation française? Remarques sur un problème d'histoire linguistique." *Revue de Synthèse Historique* 38 (Dec. 1924): 37–53.

———. "Un psychologue: Charles Blondel." In Lucien Febvre, *Combats pour l'histoire,* 370–75. Paris, 1953.

———. "L'Université de Nancy de 1890 à 1900: Souvenirs et leçons." *Annales de L'Est,* 5th series, 5, no. 3 (1954): 175–85.

Feldman, Kenneth A. "Some Theoretical Approaches to the Study of Change and Stability in College Students." *Review of Educational Research* 42 (1972): 1–26.

Feldman, Kenneth A., and Theodore M. Newcomb. *The Impact of College on Students.* 2 vols. San Francisco, 1969.

Fenske, Hans. "Das Elsass in der deutschen öffentlichen Meinung von 1820 bis 1866." *Zeitschrift für die Geschichte des Oberrheins* 119 (1971): 233–80.

Ferber, Christian von. *Die Entwicklung des Lehrkörpers der deutschen Universitäten und Hochschulen 1864–1954.* Göttingen, 1956.

Ferber, Walter. "Der Weg Martin Spahns: Zur Ideengeschichte des politischen Rechtskatholizismus." *Hochland* 62 (1970): 218–29.

Ferrières, Gabrielle. *Jean Cavaillès: Philosophe et combattant, 1903–1944.* Paris, 1950.

"La fête nationale du 14 juillet." *L'Alsace Française* 19 (Aug. 1939): 228.

Fichter, Charles. *René Schickele et l'Alsace jusqu'en 1914.* Obernai, France, 1978.

Ficker, Johannes. "Eines elsässische Denkschrift für die Neuerrichtung der Strassburger Universität 1871." *Archiv für Reformations-Geschichte* 37 (1940): 305–20.

———. *Die Kaiser-Wilhelms-Universität Strassburg und ihre Tätigkeit.* Halle, 1922.

Fischer, Emil. *Aus meinem Leben.* Berlin, 1922.

———. "Erinnerungen aus der Strassburger Studienzeit, 1872 bis 1875." In Adolf Baeyer, *Erinnerungen aus meinem Leben,* 15–21. Braunschweig, 1905.

Fischer, Fritz, "Der deutsche Protestantismus und die Politik im 19. Jahrhundert." *Historische Zeitschrift* 171 (1951): 473–518.

Flake, Otto. "Elsässiche Fragen." *Die Neue Rundschau* 23, part 2 (1912): 1146–56.

———. *Es wird Abend: Bericht aus einem langen Leben.* Gütersloh, 1960.

———. *Freitagskind.* 1913. Reprint. Berlin, [1925].

———. "Das Junge Elsass: Aus meinen Erinnerungen." *Deutsche Rundschau* 81 (1955): 1051–57.

———. "Um 1900." *Merian* 9 (1956), no. 12: 89–93.

Fleischhack, Marianne. *Helene Schweitzer: Stationen ihres Lebens.* 6th ed. Berlin (W.), n.d.

Flex, Walter. *Briefe von Walter Flex.* Ed. Walther Eggert-Windegg. Munich, [1927].

Foerster, Erich. *Adalbert Falk: Sein Leben und Wirken als Preussischer Kultusminister.* Gotha, 1927.

Foerster, Wilhelm. "Zur Anklage gegen die preussischen Universitätszustände." *Der Lotse* 2 (1901): 289–93.

Foessel, Georges. "Le règne des notables: Strasbourg et la Monarchie constitutionnelle (1815–1848)." In *Histoire de Strasbourg des origines à nos jours,* vol. 4, ed. Georges Livet and Francis Rapp, 1–88. Strasbourg, 1982.

———. "La vie quotidienne à Strasbourg à la veille de la guerre de 1870." In *L'Alsace en 1870–1871,* ed. Fernand L'Huillier, 11–42. Gap, 1971.

Foessel, Georges, and Roland Oberlé. "Le règne des notables: La Deuxième République et le Second Empire (1848–1870)." In *Histoire de Strasbourg des origines à nos jours,* vol. 4, ed. Georges Livet and Francis Rapp, 89–194. Strasbourg, 1982.

Ford, Franklin L. *Strasbourg in Transition, 1648–1789.* Cambridge, Mass., 1958.

Forster, André. "L'Université repliée." In University of Strasbourg, *Université de Strasbourg: 1945,* 31–37. N.p., n.d.

Forster, Dirk. "Erinnerungen an Ernst Stadler." *Literaturwissenschaftliches Jahrbuch,* n. s. 8 (1967): 311–19.

Fox, Robert, and George Weisz. "The Institutional Basis of French Science in the Nineteenth Century." In *The Organization of Science and Technology in France 1808–1914,* ed. Robert Fox and George Weisz, 1–28. Cambridge, 1980.

France. Assemblée nationale. *Annales de l'Assemblée nationale.* 45 vols. Paris, 1871–76.

———. Bureau universitaire de statistique. *Receuil de statistiques scolaires et professionnelles: 1949–1950–1951.* Paris, n.d.

———. Institut pédagogique national. *Informations statistiques,* no. 22. Paris, 1960.

———. *Journal officiel de la république française.* Paris, 1870–.

———. Ministère de l'instruction publique et des beaux-arts. *Statistique de l'enseignement supérieur, 1878–1888.* Paris, 1889.

————. Ministère des affaires étrangères. *Procès-verbaux de la Conférence d'Alsace-Lorraine.* 2 vols. Paris, 1917–19.

————. Statistique générale. *Annuaire statistique de la France.* 56 vols. Paris, 1878–1945.

————. Statistique générale. *Recensement général de la population effectué le 10 mars 1946.* Vol. 7. Paris, 1950.

————. Statistique générale. *Résultats statistiques du recensement général de la population effectué le 6 mars 1921.* 3 vols. in 2. Paris, 1923–28.

————. Statistique générale. *Résultats statistiques du recensement général de la population effectué le 7 mars 1926.* 4 vols. in 5. Paris, 1928–32.

————. Statistique générale. *Résultats statistiques du recensement général de la population effectué le 8 mars 1936.* 3 vols. in 2. Paris, 1938–44.

————. Statistique générale. *Statistique des familles en 1926.* Paris, 1932.

*Frankfurter Zeitung,* 1887–1901.

Fréchet, Maurice. "Les mathématiques à l'Université de Strasbourg." *La Revue du Mois* 15 (10 Apr. 1920): 337–62.

Freund, Julien. "Chapelet de souvenirs." *Bulletin de la Faculté des Lettres de Strasbourg* 47 (1968–69): 9–20.

Friedrich I, Grossherzog von Baden. *Grossherzog Friedrich I. von Baden und die deutsche Politik von 1854–1871.* Ed. Hermann Oncken. 2 vols. Stuttgart, 1927.

————. *Grossherzog Friedrich I. von Baden und die Reichspolitik 1871–1907,* vol. 1. Ed. Walther Peter Fuchs. Stuttgart, 1968.

Friedrich III, Kaiser. *Das Kriegstagebuch von 1870–71.* Ed. Heinrich Otto Meisner. Berlin, 1926.

Frijhoff, Willem. "Surplus ou déficit? Hypothèses sur le nombre réel des étudiants en Allemagne à l'époque moderne (1576–1815)." *Francia* 7 (1979): 173–218.

Fritsch, Gustave. "Le monôme des étudiants alsaciens-lorrains." *Echo du Cercle* (Strasbourg), 22 Nov. 1919, 29–32.

Fuchs, René, Henri Nonn, and Francis Rapp. "L'entre-deux-guerres, l'occupation nazie, et la Libération (1919–1945)." In *Histoire de Strasbourg des origines à nos jours,* vol. 4, ed. Georges Livet and Francis Rapp, 409–502. Strasbourg, 1982.

"Für die deutsche Universität zu Strassburg." *Allgemeine Zeitung* (Augsburg), 8 July 1871.

G., A. B. "15 années de vie corporative estudiantine (1918–1933)." *L'Appel: Tribune de l'Etudiant Français de Strasbourg* 1 (6 Apr. 1933): 4.

Gaff, J. G., H. F. M. Crombag, and T. M. Chang. "Environments for Learning in a Dutch University." *Higher Education* 5 (1976): 285–99.

Gain, André. "L'enseignement supérieur à Nancy de 1789 à 1896." *Annales de l'Est*, 4th ser., 1 (1933): 199–232; 2 (1934): 43–92.

Gall, Lothar. *Der Liberalismus als regierende Partei: Das Grossherzogtum Baden zwischen Restauration und Reichsgründung.* Wiesbaden, 1968.

———. "Die partei- und sozialgeschichtliche Problematik des badischen Kulturkampfes." *Zeitschrift für die Geschichte des Oberrheins* 113 (1965): 151–96.

Garcin, R. "L'activité du Cercle depuis l'armistice." *Echo du Cercle,* 22 Nov. 1919, 4–7.

Gaster, B. "Strassburger Studentenleben in deutscher Zeit." *Das Auslandsdeutsche* 14 (1931): 75–78.

Geiger, Roger L. "Prelude to Reform: The Faculties of Letters in the 1860s." In *The Making of Frenchmen: Current Directions in the History of Education in France, 1679–1979,* ed. Donald N. Baker and Patrick J. Harrigan, 337–61. Waterloo, Ont., 1980.

———. "Reform and Restraint in Higher Education: The French Experience, 1865–1914." Working Paper of the Institution for Social and Policy Studies, Yale University, New Haven, 1975.

Genevray, Pierre. "Professeurs protestants dans l'enseignement supérieur pendant la Restauration." *Bulletin Historique et Littéraire de la Société de l'Histoire du Protestantisme Français* 89 (1940): 22–39, 164–81, 288–304.

"Le génie français sur le Rhin." *Journal d'Alsace et de Lorraine* (Strasbourg), 16 Nov. 1920.

Gerbod, Paul. "Associations et syndicalismes universitaires de 1929 à 1937 dans l'enseignement secondaire public." *Le Mouvement Social,* no. 73 (Oct.–Dec. 1970): 79–110.

———. *La condition universitaire en France au XIX<sup>e</sup> siècle.* Paris, 1965.

———. *Les enseignants et la politique.* Paris, 1976.

Gerlach, Hellmut von. *Von Rechts nach Links.* Ed. Emil Ludwig. Zurich, 1937.

Germany. Auswärtiges Amt. *Akten zur deutschen auswärtigen Politik 1918–1945.* Series B (1925–1933), vol. 7. Göttingen, 1974.

———. Bundesrath. *Protokolle und Drucksache des Bundesraths des Deutschen Reichs.* Berlin, 1871–1918.

———. Reichstag. *Stenographische Berichte über die Verhandlungen des Deutschen Reichstages.* Berlin, 1871–1938.

———. Statistisches Reichsamt. *Statistik des Deutschen Reichs.* 1st ser. 63 vols. Berlin, 1873–83. N. s. 601 vols. Berlin, 1884–1944.

————. Statistisches Reichsamt. *Statistisches Jahrbuch für das Deutsche Reich.* 59 vols. Berlin, 1880–1942.

————. Statistisches Reichsamt. *Vierteljahrshefte zur Statistik des Deutschen Reichs.* 51 vols. Berlin, 1892–1942.

Gérold, Charles Théodore. *La Faculté de théologie et le Séminaire protestant de Strasbourg (1803–1872).* Strasbourg, 1923.

*Geschichte der Frankfurter Zeitung.* Volksausgabe. Frankfurt am Main, 1911.

Gier, Helmut. *Die Entstehung des deutschen Expressionismus und die antisymbolistische Reaktion in Frankreich: Die literarische Entwicklung Ernst Stadlers.* Munich, 1977.

Gizycki, Rainald von. "Centre and Periphery in the International Scientific Community: Germany, France and Great Britain in the 19th Century." *Minerva* 11 (1973): 474–94.

Glockner, Hermann. *Heidelberger Bilderbuch.* Bonn, 1969.

Goblot, Edmond. *La barrière et le niveau: Etude sociologique sur la bourgeoisie française moderne.* New ed. Paris, 1967.

Godechot, Jacques. "Georges Lefebvre, historien du Directoire, du Consulat et de l'Empire." In *Hommage à Georges Lefebvre (1874–1959),* 21–31. Nancy, 1960.

Goetz, Walter. *Historiker in meiner Zeit: Gesammelte Aufsätze.* Cologne, 1957.

————. "Partikularismus und Einheitsstreben in der deutschen Geschichte." *Elsass-Lothringische Kulturfragen* 4 (1914): 1–13.

Gothein, Marie Luise. *Eberhard Gothein: Ein Lebensbild.* Stuttgart, 1931.

Gouldner, Alvin W. "Cosmopolitans and Locals: Toward an Analysis of Latent Social Roles." *Administrative Science Quarterly* 2 (1957–58): 281–306, 444–80.

Grad, Charles. "La nouvelle Université de Strasbourg." *Revue Internationale de l'Enseignement* 8 (1884): 564–72.

Gras, Solange. "La presse française et l'autonomisme alsacien en 1926." In *Régions et régionalisme en France du XVIIIᵉ siècle à nos jours,* ed. Christian Gras and Georges Livet, 337–60. Paris, 1977.

Grell, Ernest. *Têtes carrées.* Strasbourg, [1955].

Grenier, Albert. "Les publications de la Faculté des lettres de Strasbourg." *L'Alsace Française* 7 (19 Nov. 1927): 932–36.

Gröber, Gustav. *Wahrnehmungen und Gedanken (1875–1910).* Strasbourg, [1910].

Groth, Paul von. "Lebenserinnerungen eines Naturforschers." Typescript in Nachlass von Paul von Groth, Bayerische Staatsbibliothek, Munich.

Grucker, E. "Protestantismus und Deutschtum im Elsass." *Daheim* 43 (3 Nov. 1906): 13–15.

Gruffat, Jean-Claude. "Les écrits de doctrine de René Capitant." *Politique*, no. 49–52 (1970): 9–112.

"Die Gründung der Autonomistischen Partei." *Die Zukunft* 3 (28 Sept. 1927): 1–4.

[Guerber, Joseph]. "Briefe von Joseph Guerber an den jungen Carl Marbach, den späteren Weihbischof von Strassburg, aus den Jahren 1859 bis 1871." Ed. Joseph Brauner. *Archiv für elsässische Kirchengeschichte* 8 (1933): 371–448.

Guirand, Jean. "Notes et notices." *La Croix* (Paris), 30–31 May 1926.

Guiraud, Paul. "Fustel de Coulanges." *Biographisches Jahrbuch für Alterthumskunde,* ed. Iwan von Müller, 12 (1889): 138–49.

Gundolf, Friedrich. *Friedrich Gundolf: Briefwechsel mit Herbert Steiner und Ernst Robert Curtius.* Ed. Lothar Helbring and Claus Victor Bock. Amsterdam, 1963.

Güterbock, Ferdinand. "Aus Scheffer-Boichorsts Leben." In Paul Scheffer-Boichorst, *Gesammelte Schriften,* vol. 1, 1–62. Berlin, 1903.

Halbwachs, Maurice. "Notre politique en Alsace-Lorraine." *Cahiers des Droits de l'Homme* 20 (20 Dec. 1920): 3–8.

Hallays, André. "Discours de M. André Hallays." In *Pierre Bucher 1869–1921,* 22–24. Paris, 1922.

———. "Pierre Bucher: Notes et souvenirs." *Revue des Deux Mondes,* 6th ser., 62 (1921): 337–54.

———. "L'Université de Strasbourg—Sa renaissance et son avenir." *Revue des Deux Mondes,* 6th ser., 53 (1919): 241–69.

Hallier, Christian. "Das Wissenschaftliche Institut der Elsass-Lothringer im Reich an der Universität Frankfurt a. M. 1920–1945: Eine Rückschau." In *Studien der Erwin von Steinbach-Stiftung,* vol. 1, ed. Christian Hallier, 133–44. Frankfurt am Main, 1965.

Halls, W. D. *The Youth of Vichy France.* Oxford, 1981.

*Hamburger Nachrichten,* 1901.

Hammer-Schenk, Harold. "'Wer die Schule hat, hat das Land!' Gründung und Ausbau der Universität Strassburg nach 1870." In *Kunstverwaltung, Bau- und Denkmal-Politik in Kaiserreich,* ed. Ekkehard Mai and Stephan Waetzoldt, 121–45. Berlin (W.), 1981.

Hammerstein, Notker. *Jus und Historie: Ein Beitrag zur Geschichte des historischen Denkens an deutschen Universitäten im späten 17. und im 18. Jahrhundert.* Göttingen, 1972.

Harrigan, Patrick J. *Mobility, Elites, and Education in French Society of the Second Empire.* Waterloo, Ont., 1980.

Hart, James Morgan. *German Universities.* New York, 1874.

Haug, Hugo. "Les étudiants alsaciens de l'Université de Strasbourg sous le régime allemand." *Strasbourg-Université* 7 (Apr. 1936): 27–29.

Hausmann, Sebastian. *Die Kaiser-Wilhelms-Universität Strassburg: Ihre Entwicklung und ihre Bauten.* Strasbourg, 1897.

Hauter, Charles. "Strassburger Erinnerungen." In *Buch des Dankes an Georg Simmel,* ed. Kurt Gassen and Michael Landmann, 251–57. Berlin (W.), 1958.

Hauviller, Ernst. *Franz Xaver Kraus: Ein Lebensbild aus der Zeit des Reformkatholizismus.* Colmar, 1904.

————. "Un prélat germanisateur dans l'Alsace française: Mgr Raess, évêque de Strasbourg." *Revue Historique* 179 (1937): 98–121.

Hawkins, Hugh. *Pioneer: A History of the Johns Hopkins University, 1874–1889.* Ithaca, 1960.

Hecker, Fritz. "Um die Meiselockerdebatte." *La République* (Strasbourg), 27 Nov. 1929.

[Heitz, Robert]. *Petite histoire de l'autonomisme.* N.p. 1928.

Heitz, Robert. *Souvenirs de jadis et de naguère.* Woerth, 1964.

————. *Vues cavalières: Réflexions et souvenirs.* Strasbourg, 1972.

Henning, Hansjoachim. *Das westdeutsche Bürgertum in der Epoche der Hochindustrialisierung 1860–1914: Soziales Verhalten und soziale Strukturen,* part 1 (*Das Bildungsbürgertum in den preussischen Westprovinzen*). Wiesbaden, 1972.

Henry, René. *Témoignage pour les alsaciens-lorrains.* Paris, 1925.

Hensel, Paul. "Lebenserinnerungen—In Strassburg als Privatdozent." In Paul Hensel, *Sein Leben in seinen Briefen,* ed. Elisabeth Hensel, 399–499. Frankfurt am Main, [1938].

————. *Sein Leben in seinen Briefen.* Ed. Elisabeth Hensel. Frankfurt am Main, [1938].

Herber, Edmond. *Elsässisches Lust- und Leidbuch: Erinnerungen und Eindrücke seit 1918.* Haguenau, 1926.

Herkner, Heinrich. "Der Lebenslauf eines 'Kathedersozialisten.'" In *Die Volkswirtschaftslehre der Gegenwart in Selbstdarstellungen,* vol. 1, ed. Felix Meiner, 77–116. Leipzig, 1924.

————. *Die oberelsässische Baumwollindustrie und die deutsche Gewerbeordnung: Eine Erwiderung an meine Gegner.* Strasbourg, 1887.

————. *Die oberelsässiche Baumwollindustrie und ihre Arbeiter.* Strasbourg, 1887.

"Les 'Herren Doktoren.'" *Journal d'Alsace et de Lorraine* (Strasbourg), 11 Feb. 1920.

Herrenschmidt, Suzanne. *Mémoires pour la petite histoire: Souvenirs d'une Strasbourgeoise.* Strasbourg, 1973.

Herrmann, Ulrich. *Die Pädagogik Wilhelm Diltheys.* Göttingen, 1971.

Hertling, Georg von. *Erinnerungen aus meinen Leben.* Ed. Karl von Hertling. 2 vols. Kempten, 1920.

Hervé, [?]. "Tradition alsacienne et enseignement officiel." *L'Etudiant Libre* 1 (Nov. 1935): 11–12.

Hess, R. "Zur forstlichen Unterrichtsfrage in Elsass-Lothringen." *Allgemeine Zeitung* (Augsburg), Beilage, 4 Apr. 1871.

Heuss, Theodor. *Erinnerungen: 1905–1933.* Tübingen, 1963.

Heuss-Knapp, Elly. *Ausblick vom Münsterturm.* 3d ed. Tübingen, 1953.

———. *Bürgerin zweier Welten.* Tübingen, 1961.

Heyderhoff, Julius, ed. *Im Ring der Gegner Bismarcks: Denkschriften und politischer Briefwechsel Franz v. Roggenbachs mit Kaiserin Augusta und Albrecht v. Stosch 1865–1896.* 2d ed. Leipzig, 1943.

Hilger, Gustav. *Pierre Bucher: Der 'Apostel' französischer Propaganda im deutschen Elsass, 1897–1918.* Freiburg im Breisgau, 1926.

Hirsch, Paul, ed. "Briefe namhafter Historiker an Harry Bresslau." *Die Welt als Geschichte* 14 (1954): 223–41.

Hirsch, Richard. *Strassburg: Ein Ruf an die Deutsche Studentenschaft.* Leipzig, 1887.

"Histoire de l'A.G. en 1924." *Strasbourg Universitaire* 1, no. 2 (1924): 2–6.

Hoche, Alfred E. *Jahresringe: Innenansicht eines Menschenlebens.* Munich, 1950.

———. *Strassburg und seine Universität: Ein Buch der Erinnerung.* Munich, 1939.

*Hochschul-Nachrichten* (Munich). 29 vols. 1890–1919.

Höfele, Karl Heinrich. "Sendungsglaube und Epochenbewusstsein in Deutschland 1870–71." *Zeitschrift für Religions- und Geistesgeschichte* 15 (1963): 265–76.

Hoffet, Frédéric. *Psychanalyse de l'Alsace.* 2d ed. Colmar, 1973.

Hofmann, August Wilhelm. *Die Frage der Theilung der philosophischen Facultät.* Berlin, 1880.

Hohenlohe[-Schillingsfürst], Alexander von. *Aus meinem Leben.* Frankfurt am Main, 1925.

Hohenlohe-Schillingsfürst, Chlodwig zu. *Memoirs of Prince Chlodwig of Hohenlohe Schillingsfürst.* Ed. Friedrich Curtius. Trans. George W. Chrystal. 2 vols. London, 1907.

Holborn, Hajo. "Der deutsche Idealismus in sozialgeschichtlicher Beleuchtung." *Historische Zeitschrift* 174 (1952): 359–84.

Holstein, Friedrich von. *The Holstein Papers.* Ed. Norman Rich and M. H. Fisher. 4 vols. Cambridge, 1955–63.

Holstein, Friedrich von, and Chlodwig zu Hohenlohe-Schillingsfürst. *Holstein und Hohenlohe: Neue Beiträge zu Friedrich von Holsteins Tätigkeit als Mitarbeiter Bismarcks und als Ratgeber Hohenlohes.* Ed. Helmuth Rogge. Stuttgart, 1957.

Holtzendorff, F. von. "Der Rückgang der berliner Universität." *Die Gegenwart* 4, no. 27 (5 July 1873): 1–4; no. 28 (12 July 1873): 19–22.

Holtzmann, Pierre. "Après la grève." *Strasbourg-Université* 6 (May 1935): 3.

Höroldt, Dietrich. "Zur wirtschaftlichen Bedeutung der Universitäten für ihre Städte." In *Stadt und Hochschule im 19. und 20. Jahrhundert,* ed. Erich Maschke and Jürgen Sydow, 25–76. Sigmaringen, 1979.

Horstmann, Johannes. *Katholizismus und moderne Welt: Katholikentage, Wirtschaft, Wissenschaft—1848 bis 1914.* Munich, 1976.

Hoseus, Heinrich. *Die Kaiser-Wilhelms-Universität zu Strassburg, ihr Recht und ihre Verwaltung.* Strasbourg, 1897.

Huber, Ernst Rudolf, ed. *Dokumente zur deutschen Verfassungsgeschichte.* 3 vols. Stuttgart, 1961–66.

Hubert, René. "Discours." In University of Strasbourg, *Université de Strasbourg: 1950,* 25–28. N.p., n.d.

Hübinger, Paul Egon. *Das historische Seminar der Rheinischen Friedrich-Wilhelms-Universität zu Bonn.* Bonn, 1963.

Huck, Joseph-Louis. "Les idées politiques, sociales et économiques d'un industriel bas-rhinois vers le milieu du XIX<sup>e</sup> siècle, G. Goldenberg." In *La bourgeoisie alsacienne: Etudes d'histoire sociale,* 285–95. Strasbourg, 1954.

Huerkamp, Claudia, and Reinhard Spree. "Arbeitsmarktstrategien der deutschen Ärzteschaft im späten 19. und frühen 20. Jahrhundert." In *Historische Arbeitsmarktforschung: Entstehung, Entwicklung und Probleme der Vermarktung von Arbeitskraft,* ed. Toni Pierenkemper and Richard Tilly, 77–116. Göttingen, 1982.

Hughes, H. Stuart. *Consciousness and Society.* New York, 1958.

Huisman, Michel. "Chronique strasbourgeoise." *Revue de l'Université de Bruxelles* 4 (1898–99): 68–72, 149–53, 230–35.

Humboldt, Wilhelm von. "Über die innere und äussere Organisation der höheren wissenschaftlichen Anstalten in Berlin." In Wilhelm von Humboldt, *Wilhelm von Humboldts politische Denkschriften,* vol. 1, ed. Bruno Gebhardt, 250–60. Berlin, 1903.

Hutten-Czapski, Bogdan Graf von. *Sechzig Jahren Politik und Gesellschaft.* 2 vols. Berlin, 1936.

Igersheim, François. "L'occupation allemande en Alsace et en Lorraine: Le Commissariat civil du gouvernement général d'Alsace et de Lorraine d'août 1870 à février 1871: Un aperçu." In *L'Alsace en 1870–1871,* ed. Fernand L'Huillier, 249–367. Gap, 1971.

———. "Strasbourg, capitale du Reichsland: Le gouvernement de la cité et la politique municipale." In *Histoire de Strasbourg des origines à nos jours,* vol. 4, ed. Georges Livet and Francis Rapp, 195–266. Strasbourg, 1982.

Ihering, Rudolf von. *Rudolph von Ihering in Briefen an seine Freunde.* Ed. Helene Ehrenberg. Leipzig, 1913.

Imbs, Paul. "Ernest Hoepffner (1879–1956)." *Bulletin de la Faculté des Lettres de Strasbourg* 35 (1956–57): 147–50.

————. "Notes sur la langue française dans la bourgeoisie alsacienne." In *La bourgeoisie alsacienne: Etudes d'histoire sociale*, 307–27. Strasbourg, 1954.

*L'Impartial de l'Est* (Nancy), 1896.

Isay, Rudolf. *Aus meinem Leben*. Weinheim (Bergstrasse), 1960.

J. "Bal." *Echo du Cercle*, Mar. 1911, 13–14.

Jadin, F. "Rapport général sur la situation et les travaux de l'Université de Strasbourg." In University of Strasbourg, *Travaux de l'Université de Strasbourg pendant l'année scolaire 1927–1928*, 3–7. Strasbourg, n.d.

Jaffé, Fritz, ed. *Elsässische Studenten an deutschen Hochschulen (1648–1870), mit besonderer Berücksichtigung des 18. Jahrhunderts*. Frankfurt am Main, 1932.

Janssen, Karl-Heinz. *Macht und Verblendung: Kriegszielpolitik der deutschen Bundesstaaten 1914–1918*. Göttingen, 1963.

Jarausch, Konrad H. *Students, Society, and Politics in Imperial Germany: The Rise of Academic Illiberalism*. Princeton, 1982.

Jeismann, Karl-Ernst. *Das preussische Gymnasium in Staat und Gesellschaft*. Stuttgart, 1974.

Jones, Oliver P. "Hal Downey's Hematological Training in Germany, 1910–11." *Journal of the History of Medicine and Allied Sciences* 27 (1972): 173–86.

Jost, Ludwig. "Zum hundertsten Geburtstag Anton de Barys." *Zeitschrift für Botanik* 24 (1930): 1–74.

*Journal d'Alsace* (Strasbourg), 1883.

*Journal d'Alsace-Lorraine* (Strasbourg), 1908–9.

"Le journal de l'A.G." *Strasbourg Universitaire* 1 (Mar. 1924): 1.

Juillard, Etienne. "Henri Baulig (1877–1962): Le savant—le professeur—l'homme." *Bulletin de la Faculté des Lettres de Strasbourg* 41 (1962–63): 165–69.

————. *La vie rurale dans la plaine de Basse-Alsace: Essai de géographie sociale*. Paris, 1953.

Kapp, Wilhelm. "Eduard Schwartz." *Elsass-Lothringen: Heimatstimmen* 11 (1933): 429–30.

————. "Elsass-Lothringen und die Aera Hohenlohe-Schillingsfürst." *Elsass-Lothringen: Heimatstimmen* 3 (1925): 114–21.

————. "Die Kaiser Wilhelms-Universität Strassburg: Ein Erinnerungswort zum Geburtstag der Gründung." *Preussische Jahrbücher* 189 (1922): 29–36.

————. "Die Kaiser-Wilhelms-Universität Strassburg und das Elsässertum." *Elsass-Lothringen: Heimatstimmen* 4 (1926): 262–68.

————. "Politische Hochspannung im letzten Jahrzehnt." *Süddeutsche Monatshefte* 29 (Dec. 1931): 218–24.

Karady, Victor. "Stratégies de réussite et modes de faire-valoir de la sociologie chez les durkheimiennes." *Revue Française de Sociologie* 20 (1979): 49–82.

Kaufert, Joseph M. "Situational Identity and Ethnicity among Ghanaian University Students." *Journal of Modern African Studies* 15 (1977): 126–35.

Kehr, Eckart. "Das soziale System der Reaktion in Preussen unter dem Ministerium Puttkamer." In Eckart Kehr, *Der Primat der Innenpolitik,* ed. Hans-Ulrich Wehler, 64–86. Berlin (W.), 1965.

Kehr, Paul. "Zur Abwehr." *Der Lotse* 2 (1901): 321–26.

Keil, Bruno. "Nachruf für die philosophische Fakultät der Kaiser-Wilhelms-Universität zu Strassburg und für die Strassburger Graeca." In *Adolph Michaelis: Zum Gedächtnis,* ed. Wissenschaftliche Gesellschaft in Strassburg, 17–23. Strasbourg, 1913.

Keller, Emile. "La Gallia, restaurant de l'A. F. G." *Strasbourg-Université* 7 (Apr. 1936): 10.

Kettenacker, Lothar. *Nationalsozialistische Volkstumspolitik im Elsass.* Stuttgart, 1973.

Kiehl, Roger, Francis Rapp, and Henri Nonn. "Strasbourg et le Reichsland: Pouvoirs—Cultures—Sociétés." In *Histoire de Strasbourg des origines à nos jours,* vol. 4, ed. Georges Livet and Francis Rapp, 341–408. Strasbourg, 1982.

Kiener, Fritz. "L'Alsace après le verdict de Colmar." *Revue des Vivants* 2 (1928): 49–70.

———. "Werner Wittich und das Elsass." *Strassburger Monatshefte* 2 (Feb. 1938): 90–94.

Kissel, Louis. "Alsatia-Strasbourg: Ein Rückblick 1926–1936." *Cercle Universitaire Catholique Alsatia: Bulletin,* 1935–36, no. 7 (8 Feb. 1936): 18–28.

Klein, Marc. "La Faculté de médecine de Strasbourg au temps de Goethe." *Revue d'Allemagne* 3 (1971): 98–122.

———. "La Faculté de médecine de Strasbourg sous le Second Empire." In *L'Alsace en 1870–1871,* ed. Fernand L'Huillier, 73–96. Gap, 1971.

Kleinert, Andreas. "Von der science allemande zur deutschen Physik: Nationalismus und moderne Naturwissenschaft in Frankreich und Deutschland zwischen 1914 und 1940." *Francia* 6 (1978): 509–25.

Klose, Werner. *Freiheit schreibt auf eure Fahnen: 800 Jahre deutsche Studenten.* Oldenburg, 1967.

Klostermann, Erich. *Die Rückkehr der Strassburger Dozenten 1918–19 und ihre Aufnahme.* Halle, 1932.

———. "Strassburgs Hochschule im Wechsel der Zeiten." *Die evangelische Diaspora* 22 (Nov. 1940): 211–16.

Kluge, Alexander. *Die Universitäts-Selbstverwaltung: Ihre Geschichte und gegenwärtige Rechtsform.* Frankfurt am Main, [1958].

Kluke, Paul. *Die Stiftungsuniversität Frankfurt am Main 1914–1932,* Frankfurt am Main, 1972.

Knapp, Georg Friedrich, and Friedrich Bendixen. *Zur staatlichen Theorie des Geldes: Ein Briefwechsel, 1905–1920.* Ed. Kurt Singer. Basel, 1958.

Koch, Marcel. "L'Université de Strasbourg et ses rapports avec l'économie régionale." *L'Alsace Française* 7 (19 Nov. 1927): 940–43.

Koessler, Alfred. *Unser Elsass: Aus meinem Tagebuch.* Strasbourg, 1928.

Kohler, Eugène. "Le rayonnement de l'université française." *L'Alsace Française* 4 (14 June 1924): 560–62.

[Kohler, Eugène]. "Die Strassburger Universität." *Strassburger Neue Zeitung,* 1 Mar. 1922.

*Kölnische Volkszeitung,* 1901.

*Kölnische Zeitung,* 1909, 1911.

"Eine konfessionelle Professur in Strassburg." *Kölnische Zeitung,* 27 Dec. 1912.

König, René. *Vom Wesen der deutschen Universität.* 2d ed. Darmstadt, 1970.

Koprio, Georg. *Basel und die eidgenössische Universität.* Basel, 1963.

Koszyk, Kurt. *Deutsche Presse im 19. Jahrhundert.* Berlin (W.), 1966.

Kraus, Franz Xaver. *Tagebücher.* Ed. Hubert Schiel. Cologne, 1957.

Krieger, Leonard. *The German Idea of Freedom: History of a Political Tradition.* Boston, 1957.

Kühn, Emil. *Briefe von Elsass-Lothringen.* Leipzig, 1892.

"Ein Kulturproblem." *Der Elsässer* (Strasbourg), 23 Feb. 1922.

L. L. "Die Strassburger Universität." *Der Elsässer* (Strasbourg), 3 Mar. 1922.

Labadens, Guillaume. "La Société des amis de l'Université de Strasbourg à cinquante ans." *Saisons d'Alsace,* n. s., no. 36 (1970): 407–11.

Laband, Paul. *Lebenserinnerungen.* Ed. Wilhelm Bruck. Berlin, 1918.

———. "Die Verfassung Elsass-Lothringens." *Morgen* 1 (1907): 549–58.

Laissus, Joseph. "Wilhelm-Philippe Schimper (1808–1880)." In *Comptes rendus du 92ᵉ Congrès national des sociétés savantes: Section des sciences,* vol. 1, 189–205. Paris, 1969.

Laissus, Yves. "L'Université de Strasbourg il y a cent ans d'après les papiers d'Adolphe Brongniart." In *Comptes rendus du 92ᵉ Congrès national des sociétés savantes: Section des sciences,* vol. 1, 177–88. Paris, 1969.

Laitenberger, Volkhard. *Akademischer Austausch und auswärtige Kulturpolitik: Der Deutsche Akademische Austauschdienst (DAAD) 1923–1945.* Göttingen, 1976.

Lang, Albert. "Rapport général sur la situation et les travaux de l'Université de Strasbourg pendant l'année scolaire 1921–1922." In University of Strasbourg, *Travaux de l'Université de Strasbourg pendant l'année scolaire 1921–1922,* 3–13. Strasbourg, 1923.

Lange, Maurice. "L'enseignement populaire du français en Alsace." *La Revue de France* 5 (1921): 412–16, 630–37.

Lanson, Gustave. "La renaissance de l'université française de Strasbourg." *Revue Universitaire* 28 (1919): 323–36.

Lapp, Adolf. "Studien aus dem Elsass: III." *Vossische Zeitung* (Berlin), 3 Mar. 1914.

Laspeyres, E. "Die deutschen Universitäten." *Deutsche Revue* 8 (1883), pt. 1: 100–119, 252–62; pt. 2: 93–113; pt. 3: 108–27, 239–48.

Lassus, Jean. *Souvenirs d'un cobaye.* Colmar, 1973.

———. "L'Université captive." In University of Strasbourg, *Université de Strasbourg: 1945,* 39–44. N.p., n.d.

Latourette, Kenneth Scott. *Christianity in a Revolutionary Age: A History of Christianity in the Nineteenth and Twentieth Centuries.* 5 vols. New York, 1958–62.

Lavisse, Ernest. "Université de Bonn et facultés de Strasbourg." Manuscript in FNA 25171 (1), Bibliothèque nationale, Paris.

Lazarsfeld, Paul F., and Wagner Thielens, Jr. *The Academic Mind: Social Scientists in a Time of Crisis.* Glencoe, Ill., 1958.

Le Léannac, Bernard. "L'enseignement supérieur." In *Eglises et état en Alsace et en Moselle: Changement ou fixité?* ed. Jean Schlick, 301–16. Strasbourg, 1979.

Lees, Andrew. *Revolution and Reflection: Intellectual Change in Germany during the 1850's.* The Hague, 1974.

Lefftz, Joseph. *Die gelehrten und literarischen Gesellschaften im Elsass vor 1870.* Heidelberg, 1931.

Legaret, Gustave. "La crise et l'avenir de la jeunesse universitaire." *Journal des Economistes* 192 (1935): 462–75.

Legrand, A. "Zur elsässische Kulturfrage: Eine persönliche Aussprache." *Hochland* 7 (Feb. 1901): 524–40.

"Lehrstuhl für elsass-lothringische Literatur gefordert." *Elsass-Lothringische Mitteilungen* 14 (1932): 390.

Lenel, Otto. "Otto Lenel." In *Die Rechtswissenschaft der Gegenwart in Selbstdarstellungen,* vol. 1, ed. Hans Planitz, 133–52. Leipzig, 1924.

———. *Die Universität Strassburg: 1621–1921.* Freiburg im Breisgau, 1921.

Lenz, Gustav. *Die alten Reichslande Elsass und Lothringen und ihre Stellung zum neuen Reich: Eine Skizze.* Greifswald, 1870.

Lenz, Max. *Geschichte der königlichen Friedrich-Wilhelms-Universität zu Berlin.* 4 vols. in 5. Halle, 1910–18.

Leriche, René. *Souvenirs de ma vie morte.* Paris, 1956.

Lestra, Antoine. *Le conflit religieux et scolaire en Alsace et en Lorraine (1936–1937).* Paris, [1938].

"Lettre de Strasbourg: L'étudiant alsacien." *Le Nouvelliste d'Alsace-Lorraine* (Colmar), 21 Nov. 1910.

Leuilliot, Paul. *L'Alsace au début du XIXᵉ siècle.* 3 vols. Paris, 1959–60.

———. "Aux origines des 'Annales d'histoire économique et sociale' (1928): Contribution à l'historiographie française." In *Mélanges en l'honneur de Fernand Braudel,* vol. 2, 317–24. Toulouse, 1973.

Leumann, Ernst. *Religion und Universität: Zum Fall Spahn.* Frankfurt am Main, 1902.

Levinas, Emmanuel. "Emmanuel Levinas." In *Les philosophes français d'aujourd'hui par eux-mêmes,* ed. Gérard Deledalle and Denis Huisman, 325–28. N.p. 1961.

Lévy, Paul. *Histoire linguistique d'Alsace et de Lorraine.* 2 vols. Paris, 1929.

Lexis, Wilhelm, ed. *Die deutschen Universitäten.* 2 vols. Berlin, 1893.

Leyden, Ernst von. *Lebenserinnerungen.* Ed. Clarissa Lohde-Bötticher. Stuttgart, 1910.

L'Huillier, Fernand. "L'attitude politique de Mgr Raess entre 1859 et 1879." In *Etudes alsaciennes,* 245–62. Strasbourg, 1947.

———. *Dialogues franco-allemands 1925–1933.* Paris, 1971.

———. "L'enseignement primaire en Alsace à la fin du Second Empire." In *L'Alsace en 1870–1871,* ed. Fernand L'Huillier, 43–56. Gap, 1971.

———. "Georges Lefebvre à Strasbourg." *Bulletin de la Faculté des Lettres de Strasbourg* 38 (1959–60): 371–76.

———. *Recherches sur l'Alsace napoléonienne de Brumaire à l'invasion (1799–1813).* Strasbourg, [1945].

Liard, Louis, *L'enseignement supérieur en France, 1789–1889.* 2 vols. Paris, 1888–94.

Lichtenberger, Frédéric. "La Faculté de théologie de Strasbourg." *Revue Chrétienne* 22 (Jan. 1875): 1–24.

Lichtenberger, Henri, and André Lichtenberger. *La question d'Alsace-Lorraine.* 2d ed. Paris, 1915.

Liebert, E. von. "Von der deutschen Universität Strassburg." *Schwäbischer Merkur* (Stuttgart), 31 Jan. 1913.

Lienhard, Friedrich. *Jugendjahre.* 11th ed. Stuttgart, 1920.

Lindenlaub, Dieter. *Richtungskämpfe im Verein für Sozialpolitik.* 2 vols. Wiesbaden, 1967.

Lindenlaub, Th. "Université de Strasbourg." In *Société pour l'étude des questions d'enseignement supérieur, Etudes de 1879,* 411–69. Paris, 1879.

Lion, Ferdinand. "Das Elsass als Problem." *Die Neue Rundschau* 32, part 1 (1921): 337–61.

"Liste des anciens du Cercle universitaire catholique 'Alsatia,' Strasbourg." Undated typescript in MR 10062, Bibliothèque nationale et universitaire, Strasbourg.

"Liste des membres." *Echo du Cercle,* Mar. 1911, 25–29.

Livet, Georges. "L'Institut et la chaire d'histoire moderne de la Faculté des lettres de Strasbourg de 1919 à 1955." *Bulletin de la Faculté des Lettres de Strasbourg* 36 (1957–58): 197–213.

Lobstein, El., and Ed. Lobstein. *Paul Lobstein: Un Alsacien idéal.* Strasbourg, 1926.

Lobstein, Paul. "Rapport de M. Lobstein, doyen de la Faculté de théologie protestante." In University of Strasbourg, *Travaux de l'Université de Strasbourg pendant l'année scolaire 1919–1920,* 20–23. Strasbourg, 1921.

Loening, Edgar. "Die katholische Kirche im Elsass und in Preussen." *Preussische Jahrbücher* 27 (1871): 716–39.

[Loening, Edgar]. "Die Neuschöpfung der Strassburger Universität." *Im Neuen Reich* 1 (1871): 345–53, 381–400.

Löher, Franz von. *Aus Natur und Geschichte von Elsass-Lothringen.* Leipzig, 1871.

Lörcher, Ulrich. "Die Universität Strassburg und die Franzosen." *Das Neue Deutschland* 9 (May 1922): 233–34.

Die lose Vereinigung der ehemalige Strassburger Studenten und Dozenten. *Bericht über die erste Zusammenkunft.* Frankfurt am Main, 1928.

Lot, Ferdinand. "Où en est la Faculté des lettres de Paris?" *La Grande Revue* 75 (1912): 369–84, 641–61.

Lotz, Walther. "Erinnerungen an Lujo Brentano." *Schmollers Jahrbuch* 56 (1932): 1–6.

Lubarsch, Otto. *Ein bewegtes Gelehrtenleben: Erinnerungen und Erlebnisse, Kämpfe und Gedanken.* Berlin, 1931.

Lucas, Georges. "Un mouvement autonomiste à l'Université de Strasbourg." *Notre Temps* 6 (31 Jan. 1932): 15–16.

Luchaire, Julien. *Confession d'un français moyen.* 2 vols. Florence, [1965].

"Ludw. Spach und die künftige oberrheinische Universität." *Magazin für die Literatur des Auslandes* 40 (24 June 1871): 363.

Ludwig, Hermann. *Strassburg vor hundert Jahren: Ein Beitrag zur Kulturgeschichte.* Stuttgart, 1888.

"M. Millerand à l'Université." *Journal d'Alsace et de Lorraine* (Strasbourg), 8 Apr. 1919.

"M. Poincaré préside le banquet d'ouverture du Congrès national des étudiants." *Journal d'Alsace et de Lorraine* (Strasbourg), 21 Apr. 1927.

"M. Terracher, recteur de l'Académie de Strasbourg." *Journal d'Alsace et de Lorraine* (Strasbourg), 30 July 1938.

M., A. "Alma mater im Flüchtlingsstrom." *Strassburger Monatshefte* 5 (1941): 755–59.

M., A. "La jeunesse devant les portes fermées: I. Celle de l'enseignement." *Strasbourg-Université* 5 (Apr. 1934): 4.

McClelland, Charles E. *State, Society, and University in Germany 1700–1914*. Cambridge, 1980.

———. "The Wise Man's Burden: The Role of Academicians in Imperial German Culture." In *Essays on Culture and Society in Modern Germany*, ed. Gary D. Stark and Bede Karl Lackner, 45–69. College Station, Tex., 1982.

McCormmach, Russell. *Night Thoughts of a Classical Physicist*. Cambridge, Mass., 1982.

McMurray, Ruth Emily, and Muna Lee. *The Cultural Approach: Another Way in International Relations*. Chapel Hill, 1947.

Madelin, Louis, "Christian Pfister." *Annales de l'Est,* 4th ser., 2, no. 3 (1934): 131–52.

Maisenbacher, Fritz. *Ein Strassburger Bilderbuch: Erinnerungen aus den Jahren 1870–1918*. Strasbourg, 1931.

"Maison de la Jeune Alsace." *Journal d'Alsace et de Lorraine* (Strasbourg), 24 Feb. 1928.

Manegold, Karl-Heinz. *Universität, Technische Hochschule und Industrie*. Berlin (W.), 1970.

Marcks, Erich. "Bei Bismarck am 14. März 1893." In Erich Marcks, *Männer und Zeiten,* 5th ed., vol. 2, 53–73. Leipzig, [1918].

———. "Biographische Einleitung." In Hermann Baumgarten, *Historische und politische Aufsätze und Reden,* v–cxxxiv. Strasbourg, 1894.

Martens, Gunter. "Stürmer in Rosen: Zum Kunstprogramm einer Strassburger Dichtergruppe der Jahrhundertwende." In *Fin de Siècle: Zu Literatur und Kunst der Jahrhundertwende,* ed. Roger Bauer et al., 481–507. Frankfurt am Main, 1977.

Martin, Ernst. *Karl August Barack: Lebensumriss*. Strasbourg, 1901.

Martin, Ged. "The Cambridge Lectureship of 1866: A False Start in American Studies." *Journal of American Studies* 7 (1973): 17–29.

Marx, Roland. *La révolution et les classes sociales en Basse-Alsace: Structures agraires et vente des biens nationaux*. Paris, 1974.

Mary, Gustave. "Attaques contre l'Université de Strasbourg." *L'Alsace Française* 19 (Mar. 1939): 77.

———. "Un exposé de M. Camille Chautemps devant la Commission d'Alsace et de Lorraine." *L'Alsace Française* 19 (Mar. 1939): 75–77.

———. "Revendications autonomistes." *L'Alsace Française* 18 (Dec. 1938): 302.

———. "Les succès de la Faculté des lettres." *L'Alsace Française* 12 (27 Nov. 1932): 966.

———. "La vie politique." *L'Alsace Française* 18 (Feb. 1938): 45–46.

Matthias, Erich, and Rudolf Morsey, eds. *Der Interfraktionelle Ausschuss 1917–18*. 2 parts. Düsseldorf, 1959.

———. *Die Regierung des Prinzen Max von Baden*. Düsseldorf, 1962.

Maugain, Gabriel. "Rapport de M. Maugain, doyen de la Faculté des lettres." In University of Strasbourg, *Travaux de l'Université de Strasbourg pendant l'année scolaire 1927–1928*, 27–33. Strasbourg, n.d.

————. "La vie de la Faculté des lettres de Strasbourg de 1939 à 1945." In University of Strasbourg, Faculty of Letters, *Mémorial des années 1939–1945*, 3–50. Paris, 1947.

Maugué, Pierre. *Le particularisme alsacien 1918–1967.* Paris, 1970.

Maurenbrecher, Wilhelm. *Elsass—eine deutsche Provinz.* Berlin, 1870.

Max von Baden, Prince. *Erinnerungen und Dokumente.* Ed. Golo Mann and Andreas Burckhardt. Stuttgart, 1968.

May, Gaston, *La lutte pour le français en Lorraine avant 1870.* Nancy, 1919.

May, Georg. "Die Errichtung von zwei mit Katholiken zu besetzenden Professuren in der philosophischen Fakultät der Universität Strassburg im Jahre 1902–03." In *Speculum Iuris et Ecclesiarum: Festschrift für Willibald M. Plöchl zum 60. Geburtstag,* ed. Hans Lentze and Inge Gampl, 245–81. Vienna, 1967.

Mayer, Emil Walter. "Emil Walter Mayer." In *Die Religionswissenschaft der Gegenwart in Selbstdarstellungen,* vol. 5, ed. D. Erich Stange, 123–58. Leipzig, 1929.

Mayer, Otto. *Die Kaiser-Wilhelms-Universität: Ihre Entstehung und Entwicklung.* Berlin, 1922.

Mayeur, Jean-Marie. *Autonomie et politique en Alsace: La constitution de 1911.* Paris, 1970.

————. "Une bataille scolaire: Les catholiques alsaciens et la politique scolaire du gouvernement de front populaire." *Cahiers d'Association Interuniversitaire de l'Est* 4 (1962): 85–101.

Meinecke, Friedrich. *Ausgewählter Briefwechsel.* Ed. Ludwig Dehio and Peter Classen. Stuttgart, 1962.

————. "Die deutschen Universitäten und der heutige Staat." In Friedrich Meinecke, *Politische Schiften und Reden,* ed. Georg Kotowski, 402–13. Munich, 1958.

————. "Drei Generationen deutscher Gelehrtenpolitik." *Historische Zeitschrift* 125 (1922): 248–83.

————. *Erlebtes 1862–1901.* Leipzig, 1941.

————. Review of *Jahresringe,* by Alfred E. Hoche, and *Ausblick vom Münsterturm,* by Elly Heuss-Knapp. *Historische Zeitschrift* 151 (1935): 596–99.

————. *Strassburg/Freiburg/Berlin 1901–1919.* Stuttgart, [1949].

————. "Strassburger Erinnerungen." *Die Erziehung* 15 (Sept. 1940): 281–88.

Meinertz, Max. *Begegnungen in meinem Leben,* Münster, 1956.

Melle, Werner von. *Jugenderinnerungen.* Hamburg, [1928].

Menze, Clemens. *Die Bildungsreform Wilhelm von Humboldts.* Hannover, 1975.

Merklen, Prosper. "Georges Weiss (1859–1931)." *L'Alsace Française* 11 (8 Mar. 1931): 181–83.

Merton, Robert K. "Patterns of Influence." In *Communications Research 1948–49,* ed. Paul F. Lazarsfeld and Frank N. Stanton, 180–219. New York, 1949.

———. *Social Theory and Social Structure.* Rev. ed. Glencoe, Ill., 1957.

Metz, René. "La Faculté de théologie de l'ancienne université catholique." *Revue des Sciences Religieuses* 43 (1969): 201–24.

Meyer, John W. "The Effects of Education as an Institution." *American Journal of Sociology* 83 (1977): 55–77.

Meyer, John W., and Richard Rubinson. "Education and Political Development." *Review of Research in Education* 3 (1975): 134–62.

Michaelis, Adolf. "Franz Xaver Kraus und die philosophische Fakultät der Kaiser Wilhelms-Universität." *Strassburger Post,* 1904, no. 480.

———. "Die Kaiser Wilhelms-Universität Strassburg." *Allgemeine Zeitung* (Munich), Beilage, 24 Apr., 26 Apr., 1897.

———. "Noch einmal F. X. Kraus und die philosophische Fakultät." *Strassburger Post,* 1904, no. 554.

———. "Das Verhalten der Strassburger philosophische Fakultät im Falle Spahn." *Der Lotse* 2 (1901): 225–31.

Michaelis, Otto. *Grenzlandkirche: Eine evangelische Kirchengeschichte Elsass-Lothringens 1870–1918.* Essen, 1934.

Millerand, Alexandre. *Le retour de l'Alsace-Lorraine à la France.* Paris, 1923.

———. "Souvenirs d'Alsace et de Lorraine." *La Revue Hebdomadaire* 34 (Feb. 1925): 5–21.

Minder, Robert, "Edmond Vermeil (1878–1964)." *Etudes Germaniques* 19, no. 2 (1964): i–iv.

———. "Introduction." In *La musique en Alsace hier et aujourd'hui,* 11–20. Strasbourg, 1970.

———. "Panorama des études germaniques en France." *Annales. Economies—Sociétés—Civilisations* 13 (1958): 214–30.

*Minerva: Jahrbuch der gelehrten Welt* (Strasbourg et al.), 1891– .

Moerlen, Ivan, and Lucien Bechelen. *La lutte de la jeunesse estudiantine alsacienne et lorraine contre l'emprise allemande de 1871 à 1918.* Strasbourg-Cronenbourg, 1957.

Mohl, Robert von. *Lebenserinnerungen.* 2 vols. Stuttgart, 1902.

Mollat, Guillaume. "Les débuts de la faculté française." *Revue des Sciences Religieuses* 43 (1969): 269–72.

Mommsen, Theodor. "Universitätsunterricht und Konfession." In Kurt Rossmann, *Wissenschaft, Ethik und Politik: Erörterung des Grund-*

*satzes der Voraussetzungslosigkeit in der Forschung,* 28–30. Heidelberg, 1949.

Moore, Wilbert E. "Occupational Socialization." In *Handbook of Socialization Theory and Research,* ed. David A. Goslin, 861–83. Chicago, 1969.

Morrison, Jack G. "The Intransigents: Alsace-Lorrainers against the Annexation, 1900–1914." Ph.D. diss., University of Iowa, 1970.

Morsey, Rudolf. *Die oberste Reichsverwaltung unter Bismarck 1867–1890.* Münster, 1957.

————. "Zwei Denkschriften zum 'Fall Martin Spahn' (1901): Ein Beitrag zur preussisch-deutschen Wissenschaftspolitik." *Archiv für Kulturgeschichte* 38 (1956): 244–57.

Moy, Gabriel. "Deux ans à l'A. F. G." *Strasbourg-Université* 7 (Apr. 1936): 6–8.

Müllenhoff, Karl, and Wilhelm Scherer. *Briefwechsel zwischen Karl Müllenhoff und Wilhelm Scherer.* Ed. Albert Leitzmann. Berlin, 1937.

Müller, Emil [E. Montanus, pseud.]. *Aus der engen Welt eines Dorfpfarrers: Erinnerungen.* Kaiserslautern, 1903.

Müller, Friedrich Max. *The Life and Letters of the Right Honourable Friedrich Max Müller.* Ed. his wife. 2 vols. London, 1902.

Müller, Ludwig Robert. *Lebenserinnerungen.* Munich, 1957.

Muller, Paul. "Enseignement des sciences: L'Université de Strasbourg." *Revue Scientifique* 31 (1883): 737–40.

*Münchener Neueste Nachrichten,* 1897–1901.

Munck, Etienne [Polemicus Vosgemont, pseud.]. "Le bon sens commun: Pérégrinations philosophiques à travers ronces et broussailles: Pamphlet du jour." *Echo du Cercle,* Mar. 1911, 30–55.

Müntzer, Désiré. *Der elsässische Student und das Deutschtum.* Strasbourg, [1910].

N., E. "Der Cercle und die Nationalisten." *Elsässische Kulturfragen* 2 (July 1911): 12–18.

"Ein Nachwort zu den Universitätsfesten dieses Jahres." *Die Gegenwart* 2 (28 Sept. 1872): 196–97.

Naegelen, Marcel-Edmond. *Avant que meure le dernier . . . .* Paris, 1958.

Nast, Marcel. *Le malaise alsacien-lorrain.* Paris, 1920.

————. "Où allons-nous?" *Journal d'Alsace et de Lorraine* (Strasbourg), 19 June 1928.

————. "Le redressement nécessaire." Part 6. *Journal d'Alsace et de Lorraine* (Strasbourg), 9 Mar. 1928.

————. *Was hinter der elsass-lothringischen Frage steckt!* Strasbourg, 1923.

"Nationalistische Strömungen in der Strassburger Studentenschaft." *Schwäbischer Merkur* (Stuttgart), 22 June 1914.

"Nationalistische Umtriebe an der Strassburger Universität." *Schwäbischer Merkur* (Stuttgart), 27 Mar. 1913.

Naumann, Hans. *Ernst Stadler: Worte zu seinem Gedächtnis.* Berlin-Wilmersdorf, 1920.

Naunyn, Bernhard. *Erinnerungen, Gedanken und Meinungen.* Munich, 1925.

"Ein Nazi-Lektor an der Universität Strassburg?" *La République* (Strasbourg), 15 Oct. 1933.

Nelson, Harold I. *Land and Power: British and Allied Policy on Germany's Frontiers, 1916–19.* London, 1963.

"Der neue Rektor der Strassburger Universität." *La République* (Strasbourg), 30 July 1938.

"The New Strasbourg University." *The Athenaeum,* no. 4681 (16 Jan. 1920): 82.

Niemi, Richard G., and Barbara I. Sobieszek. "Political Socialization." *Annual Review of Sociology* 3 (1977): 209–33.

Nietzsche, Friedrich. *Nietzsche Briefwechsel.* Part 2 (1869–1879). Ed. Giorgio Colli and Mazzino Montinari. 6 vols. in 7. Berlin (W.), 1977–80.

"Noch einmal: Die Auflösung der Cercle." *Strassburger Post,* 18 June 1911.

Nöldeke, Arnold. *Jugend-Erinnerungen aus dem Deutschen Elsass.* Hamburg, 1934.

"Nos amicales." *Strasbourg-Université* 7 (Apr. 1936): 14–17.

"Nos enquêtes: Strasbourg-Universitaire." *La France de l'Est* (Mulhouse), 7 June, 8 June 1933.

"Nos morticules, ferments d'autonomisme: L'explication des professeurs." *La Province d'Alsace* 4 (28 Jan. 1933): 2.

"Notre enquête sur le régionalisme." *Journal d'Alsace et de Lorraine* (Strasbourg), 12 Feb. 1921.

Nye, Mary Jo. "The Scientific Periphery in France: The Faculty of Sciences at Toulouse (1880–1930)." *Minerva* 13 (1975): 374–403.

Oberlé, Raymond. *L'enseignement à Mulhouse de 1798 à 1870.* Paris, 1961.

O'Boyle, Lenore. "Klassische Bildung und soziale Struktur in Deutschland zwischen 1800 und 1848." *Historische Zeitschrift* 207 (1968): 584–608.

"L'oeuvre des étudiants de Strasbourg." *Journal d'Alsace et de Lorraine* (Strasbourg), 20 June, 27 June 1928.

"Öffentliche Versammlung der Union fédérale des étudiants." *Les Etudiants d'Avant-Garde,* no. 3 (Jan. 1933): 11.

Oncken, Hermann. "Aus dem Lager der deutschen Whigs: I. Freiherr von Roggenbach." In Hermann Oncken, *Historisch-politische Aufsätze und Reden,* vol. 2, 265–73. Munich, 1914.

d'Oux, Louis. "Der elsässische Student." *Cahiers Alsaciens* 3 (1914): 250–59.

P., H. "L'Université de Strasbourg." *Revue de l'Instruction Publique en Belgique* 20 (1872), part 2: 132–34.

Pagny, Jean. "Aidons les étudiants de notre université." *Journal d'Alsace et de Lorraine* (Strasbourg), 15 June 1920.

Pange, Jean de. "Le Conseil national d'Alsace et de Lorraine." *Revue des Deux Mondes,* 6th ser., 51 (1919): 907–26.

———. *Journal.* 4 vols. Paris, 1964–75.

Pariset, Georges. "La Revue Germanique de Dollfus et Nefftzer." *Revue Germanique* 1 (1905): 617–40; 2 (1906): 28–62.

Partin, Malcolm O. *Waldeck-Rousseau, Combes, and the Church: The Politics of Anti-Clericalism, 1899–1905.* Durham, N.C., 1969.

Pasteur, Louis. *Correspondance 1840–1895.* Ed. Pasteur Vallery-Radot. 4 vols. Paris, 1940–51.

Pastor, Ludwig Freiherr von. *Tagebücher—Briefe—Erinnerungen.* Ed. Wilhelm Wühr. Heidelberg, 1950.

Paul, Harry W. *The Sorcerer's Apprentice: The French Scientist's Image of German Science 1840–1919.* Gainesville, Fla., 1972.

Pauli, Gustav. *Erinnerungen aus sieben Jahrzehnten.* Leipzig, 1936.

Paulsen, Friedrich. *The German Universities and University Study.* Trans. Frank Thilly and William W. Elwang. New York, 1906.

———. *Geschichte des gelehrten Unterrichts.* 2d ed. 2 vols. Leipzig, 1896–97.

Perrin, Charles-Edmond. "L'enseignement secondaire en Alsace et Lorraine." *La Revue de Paris* 28 (15 Jan. 1921): 309–29.

———. "Fritz Kiener (1874–1942)." In University of Strasbourg, Faculty of Letters, *Mémorial des années 1939–1945,* 99–117. Paris, 1947.

———. *Un historien français: Ferdinand Lot 1866–1952.* Geneva, 1968.

Perry, Bliss. *And Gladly Teach: Reminiscences.* Boston, 1935.

Petenot, [André?]. "Chez nos amis." *L'Escholier d'Alsace,* no. 4 (Mar. 1930): 1.

Petenot, André. "Lettre d'un ancien président." *Strasbourg-Université* 7 (Apr. 1936): 9.

Pfetsch, Frank R. *Zur Entwicklung der Wissenschaftspolitik in Deutschland 1750–1914.* Berlin (W.), 1974.

Pfister, Christian. "André Hallays et l'Université de Strasbourg." *L'Alsace Française* 10 (4 May 1930): 347.

———. "Un épisode de l'histoire de la Faculté des lettres de Strasbourg: L'affaire Ferrari." *Revue Internationale de l'Enseignement* 80 (1926): 334–55.

———. "La Faculté des lettres de Strasbourg." *Bulletin de la Faculté des Lettres de Strasbourg* 1 (1922–23): 2–6.

————. "Fustel de Coulanges à la Faculté des lettres de Strasbourg." *L'Alsace Française* 10 (16 Mar. 1930): 204–6.

————. "Georges Pariset, 1865–1927." In Georges Pariset, *Etudes d'histoire révolutionnaire et contemporaine*, v–xiv. Paris, 1929.

————. "La première année de la nouvelle Université de Strasbourg (1918–1919)." *Revue Internationale de l'Enseignement* 68 (1919): 313–55.

————. "Rapport de M. Chr. Pfister, doyen de la Faculté des lettres." In University of Strasbourg, *Travaux de l'Université de Strasbourg pendant l'année scolaire 1921–1922*, 121–45. Strasbourg, 1923.

————. "Rapport général sur la situation et les travaux de l'Université de Strasbourg pendant l'année scolaire 1919–1920." In University of Strasbourg, *Travaux de l'Université de Strasbourg pendant l'année scolaire 1919–1920*, 3–16. Strasbourg, 1921.

————. "Rapport sommaire sur les universités des villes visitées par la mission du Comité alsacien d'études et d'informations (10 septembre–7 octobre 1924)." *L'Alsace Française* 13 (29 Oct. 1933): 827–32.

————. "La rentrée de l'université." *L'Alsace Française* 8 (25 Nov. 1928): 985–86.

————. "L'Université de Strasbourg." In Christian Pfister, *Pages alsaciennes*, 229–56. Paris, 1927.

"Pierre Bucher." *Freie Presse* (Strasbourg), 23 Feb. 1921.

Pinner, Frank W. "Western European Student Movements through Changing Times." In *Students in Revolt*, ed. Seymour Martin Lipset and Philip G. Altbach, 60–95. Boston, 1969.

Pippo [pseud.]. "La société d'étudiants alsaciens-lorrains Sundgovia-Erwinia: A propos du 25ᵉ anniversaire de la dissolution, souvenirs d'un ancien." In *Almanach pour les étudiants et pour la jeunesse d'Alsace-Lorraine—1913*, 243–47. Strasbourg, 1913.

"La place de M. de Pange n'est plus parmi les Amis de l'Université de Strasbourg." *Journal d'Alsace et de Lorraine* (Strasbourg), 9 May 1928.

Plagnieux, Jean. "Chronique de la faculté repliée à Clermont-Ferrand (1939–1945)." *Revue des Sciences Religieuses* 43 (1969): 280–94.

Platon [pseud.]. "Le cachet spécifique de notre cercle." *Alsatia Academica* 1, no. 1 (1927): 12–15.

————. "Rückblick auf das Gründungsjahr." *Alsatia Academica* 1, no. 1 (1927): 16–17.

Poidevin, Raymond. "Les élections de 1893 en Alsace-Lorraine." *Bulletin de la Faculté des Lettres de Strasbourg* 44 (1965–66): 465–79.

Poincaré, Raymond. *A la recherche de la paix 1919*. Paris, 1974.

Polaczek, Ernst. "Eine elsässische Erinnerung: Zum Tode Pierre Buchers." *Frankfurter Zeitung*, 8 Mar. 1921.

"Die politische Bedeutung der Strassburger Universität." *National-Zeitung* (Berlin). 10 Jan. 1897.

"Politische Notizen: Strassburg." *Die Zeit,* no. 14 (2 Jan. 1902): 417.

Pommier, Jean. *Renan et Strasbourg.* Paris, 1926.

———. *Le spectacle intérieur.* Paris, 1970.

Ponteil, Félix. "La vie pathétique de l'Université de Strasbourg." *Saisons d'Alsace,* no. 2 (1951): 108–16.

"Portraits universitaires." *Dernières Nouvelles de Strasbourg,* 17 June 1932.

Prélot, Marcel. "Allocution du recteur de l'Académie de Strasbourg." In University of Strasbourg, *Université de Strasbourg: 1945,* 9–14. N.p., n.d.

———. Introduction to "Troisième séance de travail." In *Relation des journées d'études en l'honneur de Carré de Malberg, 1861–1935,* 121–25. Paris, 1966.

———. "L'université libérée." In University of Strasbourg, *Université de Strasbourg: 1945,* 45–53. N.p., n.d.

"La presse alsacienne et lorraine." *L'Alsace Française* 9 (1 Dec. 1929): 1027–28.

Preuss, Ulrich K. "Bildung und Bürokratie: Sozialhistorische Bedingungen in der ersten Hälfte des 19. Jahrhunderts." *Der Staat* 14 (1975): 371–96.

Price, Lawrence M. "Strasbourg in Alsace." *University of California Chronicle* 25 (1923): 195–211.

"Le problème alsacien vu par un français de l'intérieur." *Journal d'Alsace et de Lorraine* (Strasbourg), 31 May 1930.

"Programme du 'Landespartei' (parti national) indépendent d'Alsace-Lorraine." *Notre Droit Régional* 2 (1928): 185–92.

"Les projets d'extension de la Faculté des sciences." *Journal d'Alsace et de Lorraine* (Strasbourg), 24 June 1930.

Prost, Antoine. *Histoire de l'enseignement en France 1800–1967.* Paris, 1968.

"Protest." *E. L. Z.* (Strasbourg), 3 Feb. 1933.

"Protestation des étudiants contre la propagande théâtrale allemande." *L'Appel: Tribune de l'Etudiant Français de Strasbourg* 1 (6 Apr. 1933): 1–2, 9.

Prussia. Statistisches Landesamt. *Preussische Statistik.* 305 vols. Berlin, 1861–1935.

———. Statistisches Landesamt. *Statistisches Handbuch für den Preussischen Staat.* 4 vols. Berlin, 1888–1903.

———. Statistisches Landesamt. *Statistisches Jahrbuch für den Preussischen Staat.* 30 vols. Berlin, 1904–34.

Puttkamer, Alberta von. *Die Aera Manteuffel: Federzeichnungen aus Elsass-Lothringen.* Stuttgart, [1904].

"Quelques perles du dernier 'Strasbourg-Etudiant.'" *Les Etudiants d'Avant-Garde,* no. 4 (Mar. 1933): 5–7.

Quirielle, Pierre de. "Werner Wittich." *Journal des Débats* (Paris), 7 Sept. 1937.

R., D. "Heinrich Geffcken." In *Allgemeine Deutsche Biographie,* vol. 55, 763–70. Leipzig, 1910.

R., M. "Kleine Chronik: Vom Bankett der elsass-lothringischen Studenten . . . " *Der Elsässer* (Strasbourg), 22 Feb. 1919.

R., M. "Notre action." *Les Etudiants Nouveaux* 1, no. 1 (1928): 1.

R., T. "Zukunftsverhältnisse in Elsass-Lothringen." *Allgemeine Zeitung* (Munich), 15 Apr. 1887.

R., W. "Das Deutschtum in Elsass-Lothringen." *Die Grenzboten* 61, part 2 (1902): 1–11.

Rauscher, Ulrich. "Nachruf für einen Gefallenen." *Frankfurter Zeitung,* 10 Nov. 1914.

*Reden und Ansprachen gehalten am 24. Juni bei der Feier von Gustav Schmollers 70. Geburtstag.* [Altenburg], 1908.

Redslob, Edmond. *Chez nous: Hier et aujourd'hui.* Paris, n.d.

———. *D'un régime à un autre: Ce que j'ai vécu.* Paris, n.d.

Redslob, Robert. *Alma mater: Mes souvenirs des universités allemandes.* Paris, 1958.

———. "La bourgeoisie alsacienne sous le régime allemand." In *La bourgeoisie alsacienne: Etudes d'histoire sociale,* 443–52. Strasbourg, 1954.

———. *Entre la France et l'Allemagne: Souvenirs d'un Alsacien.* Paris, 1934.

———. "Eine europäische Universität im Elsass." *Honneur et Patrie* 14 (28 Aug. 1959): 7.

———. "Huit années d'extension universitaire." *L'Alsace Française* 8 (26 Feb. 1929): 161–63.

———. "Raymond Carré de Malberg, la personnalité." In *Relation des journées d'études en l'honneur de Carré de Malberg, 1861–1935,* 15–19. Paris, 1966.

Régamey, Jeanne, and Frédéric Régamey. *L'Alsace au lendemain de la conquête.* 5th ed. Paris, 1912.

Reimeringer, Bernard. "Un communisme régionaliste? Le communisme alsacien." In *Régions et régionalisme en France du XVIIIᵉ siècle à nos jours,* ed. Christian Gras and Georges Livet, 361–92. Paris, 1977.

Reiss, Karl-Peter, ed. *Von Bassermann zu Stresemann: Die Sitzungen des nationalliberalen Zentralvorstandes 1912–1917.* Düsseldorf, [1967].

Rennwald, Georges. "A. F. G. E. S. 1935–36." *Strasbourg-Université* 7 (Apr. 1936): 18–21.

Renouvin, Pierre. "Les buts de guerre du gouvernement français, 1914–1918." *Revue Historique* 235 (1966): 1–38.

"Une réponse d'un groupe d'universitaires mobilisés aux doyens de faculté." *Excelsior* (Paris), 13 May 1918.

"La résurrection du Cercle des étudiants." *Journal d'Alsace et de Lorraine* (Strasbourg), 2 Feb. 1927.

Reuss, Eduard. *Eduard Reuss' Briefwechsel mit seinem Schüler und Freunde Karl Heinrich Graf.* Ed. Karl Budde and Heinrich J. Holtzmann. Giessen, 1904.

Reuss, Rodolphe. *Histoire de Strasbourg depuis ses origines jusqu'à nos jours.* Paris, 1922.

*Rheinisch-Westfälische Zeitung* (Essen), 1911.

Rickert, Heinrich. *Wilhelm Windelband.* 2d ed. Tübingen, 1929.

Ricklin, A. "Les débuts de l'A. F. G." *Strasbourg-Université* 7 (Apr. 1936): 5.

Riedinger, André. "Cinquante ans d'histoire: Chronique de la Société des amis de l'Université de Strasbourg, 1920–1970." *Saisons d'Alsace,* n. s., no. 36 (1970): 412–20.

Rienhardt, Albert. "Das Universitätsstudium der Württemberger seit der Reichsgründung." *Württembergische Jahrbücher für Statistik und Landeskunde,* Jahrgang 1916: 160–282.

Riese, Reinhard. *Die Hochschule auf dem Wege zum wissenschaftlichen Grossbetrieb: Die Universität Heidelberg und das badischen Hochschulwesen 1860–1914.* Stuttgart, 1977.

Ringer, Fritz K. *The Decline of the German Mandarins.* Cambridge, Mass., 1969.

————. *Education and Society in Modern Europe.* Bloomington, Ind., 1979.

Rist, Charles. "Werner Wittich." *Revue d'Economie Politique* 51 (1931): 1455–58.

Ritleng, Georges. *Souvenirs de jeunesse d'un vieux strasbourgeois 1875–1905.* Strasbourg, 1964.

Ritschl, Otto. *Albrecht Ritschls Leben.* 2 vols. Freiburg im Breisgau, 1896.

Ritter, G. Erwin. *Die elsass-lothringische Presse im letzten Drittel des 19. Jahrhunderts.* Heidelberg, 1934.

Ritter, Gerhard. *Staatskunst und Kriegshandwerk: Das Problem des 'Militarismus' in Deutschland.* 4 vols. Munich, 1954–69.

Rochefort, Michel. *L'organisation urbaine de l'Alsace.* Paris, 1960.

Rochefort, Robert. *Robert Schuman.* Paris, 1968.

Roederer, Jean. "Cinq semestres à la Faculté de médecine de Strasbourg: Souvenirs d'un étudiant alsacien." *Annuaire de la Société des Amis du Vieux-Strasbourg* 1 (1970): 48–51.

Roggenbach, Franz von. "Zwei Briefe Franz von Roggenbachs." Ed. Ernst Traumann. *Süddeutsche Monatshefte* 4 (Sept. 1907): 316–21.

Rohr, Jean. *Victor Duruy, ministre de Napoléon III.* Paris, 1967.

Rokkan, Stein. "Dimensions of State Formation and Nation-Building: A Possible Paradigm for Research on Variations within Europe." In *The*

*Formation of National States in Western Europe,* ed. Charles Tilly, 562–600. Princeton, 1975.

Rolland, Romain. *Chère Sofia: Choix de lettres de Romain Rolland à Sofia Bertolini Guerrieri-Gonzaga (1901–1908).* Paris, 1959.

Ropp, Goswin Freiherr von der. "Konrad Varrentrapp." *Historische Zeitschrift* 107 (1911): 345–50.

Rosenberg, Hans. *Grosse Depression und Bismarckzeit.* Berlin (W.), 1967.

Rossé, Joseph, Marcel Stürmel, Albert Bleicher, F. Deiber, and Jean Keppi, eds., *Das Elsass von 1870–1932.* 4 vols. Colmar, [1936]–38.

Rossmann, Kurt. *Wissenschaft, Ethik und Politik: Erörterung des Grundsatzes der Voraussetzungslosigkeit in der Forschung.* Heidelberg, 1949.

Roth, François. *La Lorraine annexée: Etude sur la présidence de Lorraine dans l'Empire allemand (1870–1918).* Sainte-Ruffine, France, 1976.

Rothenberger, Karl-Heinz. *Die elsass-lothringische Heimat- und Autonomiebewegung zwischen den beiden Weltkriegen.* Bern, 1975.

Roussel, Pierre. "L'Université de Strasbourg." *Le Flambeau* 2, vol. 2 (1919): 486–505.

Ruland, Heinrich. *Deutschtum und Franzosentum in Elsass-Lothringen: Eine Kulturfrage.* 2d ed. Strasbourg, 1909.

S., E. "Eine Stunde in der Volkshochschule." *E. L. Z.* (Strasbourg), 11 Jan. 1933.

S., L. "Protest." *E. L. Z.* (Strasbourg), 3 Feb. 1933.

Sachse, Arnold. *Friedrich Althoff und sein Werk.* Berlin, 1928.

————. "Die Kirchenpolitik des Statthalters Freiherrn von Manteuffel." *Elsass-Lothringisches Jahrbuch* 5 (1926): 146–71.

Salomon, Henri. "Christian Pfister: I.—La vie." *Revue Historique* 172 (1933): 548–63.

Samwer, Karl. *Zur Erinnerung an Franz v. Roggenbach.* Wiesbaden, 1909.

Sch., W. "Um die Reichsuniversität." *Neue Zürcher Zeitung,* 7 Feb. 1913.

Schaefer, Dietrich. *Mein Leben.* Berlin, 1926.

Schaeffer, Patrick J. *L'Alsace et l'Allemagne de 1945 à 1949.* Metz, 1976.

Scheidhauer, Marcel. "La création de la Faculté de théologie protestante de Paris (1877)." *Revue d'Histoire et de Philosophie Religieuses* 57 (1977): 291–325.

Schelsky, Helmut. *Einsamkeit und Freiheit.* 2d ed. Düsseldorf, 1971.

Schenk, Erwin. *Der Fall Zabern.* Stuttgart, 1927.

Scherberger, Richard. "Die studentische Aufbauarbeit im deutschen Elsass." *Der Altherrenbund* 3 (1941): 188–90.

————. "Universität Strassburg—Vermächtnis und Aufgabe." In University of Strasbourg, *Hochschulführer der Reichsuniversität Strassburg,* 7–11. Strasbourg, 1942.

Scherer, André, and Jacques Grunewald, eds. *L'Allemagne et les problèmes de la paix pendant la première guerre mondiale.* 4 vols. Paris, 1962–78.

Scherer, Emil Clemens. *Eckart: Die Geschichte einer Verbindung katholischer deutscher Studenten an den Universitäten Strassburg und Köln von 1905 bis 1930.* Cologne, 1930.

————. "Der elsässiche Student und die Universität Strassburg." *Elsass-Lothringen: Heimatstimmen* 10 (1932): 155–60.

Scherer, Wilhelm, and Elias von Steinmeyer. *Briefwechsel 1872–1886.* Ed. Horst Brunner and Joachim Helbig. Göppingen, 1982.

Schickele, René. "In memoriam: Zur Einführung." *Der Stürmer,* no. 1 (July 1902): 2–3.

————. *Werke in drei Bänden.* Ed. Hermann Kesten and Anna Schickele. 3 vols. Cologne, 1959.

Schieder, Theodor. *Das Deutsche Kaiserreich von 1871 als Nationalstaat.* Cologne, 1961.

Schiemann, Theodor. "Die katholisch-theologische Fakultät an der Universität Strassburg." *Deutsche Monatsschrift für das gesamte Leben der Gegenwart* 2 (1903): 736–39.

Schindling, Anton. *Humanistische Hochschule und freie Reichsstadt: Gymnasium und Akademie in Strassburg 1538–1621.* Wiesbaden, 1977.

Schlagdenhauffen, Alfred. "Le Centre d'études germaniques de Strasbourg 1921–1961." *Bulletin de la Faculté des Lettres de Strasbourg* 40 (1961–62): 467–76.

Schmidt, Charles, ed. *Die geheimen Pläne der deutschen Politik in Elsass-Lothringen (1915–1918).* Paris, 1923.

Schmidt, Charles. "Georges Pariset." *L'Alsace Française* 7 (19 Nov. 1927): 929.

Schmoller, Gustav. "Die Bedeutung der Strassburger Universität." In Gustav Schmoller, *Zwanzig Jahre Deutscher Politik (1897–1917): Aufsätze und Vorträge,* 197–202. Munich, 1920.

————. *Berichte über die Zeit vom 1. Oktober 1874 bis 1. April 1876.* Strasbourg, n.d.

————. Review of *Die oberelsässische Baumwollindustrie und ihre Arbeiter,* by Heinrich Herkner, *Jahrbuch für Gesetzgebung, Verwaltung und Volkswirtschaft im Deutschen Reich (Schmollers Jahrbuch)* 11 (1887): 1338–41.

————. "Von der Strassburger Jubelfeier." In Gustav Schmoller, *Zwanzig Jahre Deutscher Politik (1897–1917): Aufsätze und Vorträge,* 203–6. Munich, 1920.

————. "Zwei Reden über Ministerialdirektor Friedrich Althoff." In Gustav Schmoller, *Charakterbilder,* 112–20. Munich, 1913.

Schmoller, Gustav, and Lujo Brentano. "Der Briefwechsel Gustav Schmollers mit Lujo Brentano." Ed. Walter Goetz. *Archiv für Kul-*

*turgeschichte* 28 (1938): 316–54; 29 (1939): 147–83, 331–47; 30 (1949): 142–207.

Schmutz, Théo. *Alsace: Mythes et réalités, 1850–1950.* N.p., [1967].

Schnabel, Franz. *Deutsche Geschichte im neunzehnten Jahrhundert.* 4 vols. Freiburg im Breisgau, 1929–36.

Schneegans, August. *Memoiren: Ein Beitrag zur Geschichte des Elsasses in der Übergangszeit.* Ed. Heinrich Schneegans. Berlin, 1904.

Schneegans, Heinrich. "Gustav Gröber." *Zeitschrift für französische Sprache und Litteratur* 39 (1912): 119–31.

Schneider, Karl Ludwig. "Das Leben." In Ernst Stadler, *Dichtungen: Gedichte und Übertragungen mit einer Auswahl der kleinen kritischen Schriften und Briefen,* comp. Karl Ludwig Schneider, vol. 1, 9–52. Hamburg, [1954].

Schreiber, Georg. *Deutschland und Österreich: Deutsche Begegnungen mit Österreichs Wissenschaft und Kultur.* Cologne, 1956.

Schroeder-Gudehus, Brigitte. *Les scientifiques et la paix: La communauté scientifique internationale au cours des années 20.* Montreal, 1978.

*Schulthess' Europäischer Geschichtskalender,* ed. Heinrich Schulthess et al. 81 vols. Nördlingen, Maunich, 1861–1942.

Schultz, Franz. "Das literarische Leben in Elsass-Lothringen von 1871–1918." In *Wissenschaft, Kunst und Literatur in Elsass-Lothringen 1871–1918,* ed. Georg Wolfram, 139–206. Frankfurt am Main, 1934.

———. "Die Strassburger Universität." *Süddeutsche Monatshefte* 29 (Dec. 1931): 185–91.

Schulze, Arthur. *Die örtliche und soziale Herkunft der Strassburger Studenten 1621–1793.* Heidelberg, 1926.

Schulze, Friedrich, and Paul Ssymank. *Das Deutsche Studententum von den ältesten Zeiten bis zur Gegenwart.* Leipzig, 1910.

Schützenberger, Charles. *De la réforme de l'enseignement supérieur et des libertés universitaires.* Strasbourg, 1870.

———. "De la réorganisation de l'Université de Strasbourg." Manuscript in ADBR: AL 12, paq. 7, Strasbourg.

Schwabe, Klaus. *Wissenschaft und Kriegsmoral.* Göttingen, [1969].

*Schwäbischer Merkur* (Stuttgart), 1896.

Schwalb, Maximilian. "Das Rechts- und Gerichtswesen in Elsass-Lothringen." In *Verfassung und Verwaltung von Elsass-Lothringen 1871–1918,* ed. Georg Wolfram, 367–436. Berlin, 1936.

Schwander, Rudolf, and Fritz Jaffé. "Die reichsländischen Regierungen und die Verfassung." In *Verfassung und Verwaltung von Elsass-Lothringen 1871–1918,* ed. Georg Wolfram, 1–139. Berlin, 1936.

Schwartz, Eduard. "Das Ende der Strassburger Universität." In Eduard Schwartz, *Gesammelte Schriften,* vol. 1, 259–65. Berlin, 1938.

———. "Il futuro statale dei 'Reichslande.'" Trans. Andrea Favuzzi. *Quaderni di storia* 6 (1977): 173–77.

―――. "Die Kaiser-Wilhelms-Universität Strassburg und ihre Bedeutung für Deutschland." In *Die lose Vereinigung der ehemalige Strassburger Studenten und Dozenten, Bericht über die zweite Zusammenkunft,* 9–17. Frankfurt am Main, 1929.

―――. "Verlorenes Reich . . . : Erinnerungen an die Strassburger Kaiser-Wilhelms-Universität." *Münchner Neueste Nachrichten,* 16 July 1930.

Schwartz, Gustav. *Alles ist Übergang zur Heimat hin: Mein Elternhaus: Eduard Schwartz und die seinen in ihrer Zeit 1897–1941.* Munich, 1964.

Schwartz, Max, ed. *MdR: Biographisches Handbuch der Reichstage.* Hannover, [1965].

Schweitzer, Albert. "Albert Schweitzer." In *Die Philosophie der Gegenwart in Selbstdarstellungen,* vol 7, ed. Raymund Schmidt, 205–48. Leipzig, 1929.

―――. *Out of My Life and Thought: An Autobiography.* Trans. C. T. Campion. New York, 1933.

"La séance solennelle de rentrée de l'Université de Strasbourg (22 novembre 1938)." *Revue Internationale de l'Enseignement* 93 (1939): 46–57.

Sée, Henri. *Histoire de la Ligue des droits de l'homme (1898–1926).* Paris, 1927.

Seltz, Thomas. "Edwin v. Manteuffel, der erste Statthalter von Elsass-Lothringen (1879–1885): Elsässische Erinnerungen." *Die Heimat* 15 (1935): 235–37.

―――. "40 Jahre Journalismus: Jugend-Erinnerungen." *Die Heimat* 15 (1935): 104–7.

Seydler, Wilhelm. *Fürst Chlodwig zu Hohenlohe-Schillingsfürst als Statthalter im Reichslande Elsass-Lothringen 1885–1894.* Frankfurt am Main, 1929.

Shils. Edward. "Center and Periphery." In Edward Shils, *Center and Periphery: Essays in Macrosociology,* 3–16. Chicago, 1975.

―――. "Metropolis and Provinces in the Intellectual Community." In Edward Shils, *The Intellectuals and the Powers and Other Essays,* 355–71. Chicago, 1972.

Shinn, Terry. "The French Science Faculty System, 1808–1914: Institutional Change and Research Potential in Mathematics and the Physical Sciences." *Historical Studies in the Physical Sciences* 10 (1979): 271–332.

―――. *Savoir scientifique et pouvoir social: L'Ecole polytechnique 1794–1914.* Paris, 1980.

Sieber, Eberhard. "Der politische Professor um die Mitte des 19. Jahrhunderts." In *Beiträge zur Geschichte der Universität Tübingen 1477–1977,* ed. Hansmartin Decker-Hauff, Gerhard Fichtner, and Klaus Schreiner, 285–306. Tübingen, 1977.

Sigmann, Jean. "La bourgeoisie et l'opinion politique de Bas-Rhin entre 1919 et 1924." In *La bourgeoisie alsacienne: Etudes d'histoire sociale,* 453–79. Strasbourg, 1954.

Silverman, Dan P. *Reluctant Union: Alsace-Lorraine and Imperial Germany, 1871–1918.* University Park, Pa., 1972.

Simmel, Hans. "Auszüge aus den Lebenserinnerungen." In *Ästhetik und Soziologie um die Jahrhundertwende: Georg Simmel,* ed. Hannes Böhringer and Karlfried Gründer, 247–68. Frankfurt am Main, 1976.

Simon, Marcel. "Situation de l'université." *Saisons d'Alsace,* no. 2 (1951): 117–28.

Simoni, Henri. "La vie intellectuelle de la France." *Excelsior* (Paris), 26 Apr.–3 May 1918.

"Sin d'Stüdente, wo stüdiere!" *Elsass-Lothringische Mitteilungen* 11 (1929): 8–9.

Singer, Kurt. "Die Wende des deutschen und des französischen Geistes." *Cahiers Alsaciens* 1 (1912): 119–25.

"Ein Skandal an der medizinischen Fakultät." *E. L. Z.* (Strasbourg), 1 Feb. 1933.

"Der Skandal an der medizinischen Faklutät." *E. L. Z.* (Strasbourg), 2 Feb., 7 Feb., 8 Feb., and 9 Feb. 1933.

"Eine skandalöse Sitzung im Strassburger Gemeinderat." *La République* (Strasbourg), 26 Nov. 1929.

Smith, Robert J. *The Ecole Normale Supérieure and the Third Republic.* Albany, N.Y., 1982.

Soucy, Robert. "Centrist Fascism: The Jeunesses Patriotes." *Journal of Contemporary History* 16 (1981): 349–68.

Spach, Louis. "La ville et l'université de Strasbourg en 1770." In Louis Spach, *Oeuvres choisies,* vol. 3, 421–46. Paris, 1867.

Spahn, Martin. "An den Pforten des Weltkriegs." *Hochland* 12 (Oct. 1914): 14–29.

———. "Die letzten Tage des Zusammenbruchs." *Süddeutsche Monatshefte* 29 (Dec. 1931): 224–31.

———. "Selbstbiographie." In *Deutscher Aufstieg,* ed. Hans von Arnim and Georg von Below, 479–88. Berlin, [1925].

Specklin, Paul. "Les étudiants de Strasbourg." *Echo du Cercle,* 22 Nov. 1919, 24–28.

Spiegelberg, Wilhelm. "Die orientalischen Studien an der deutschen Universität Strassburg." *Deutsches Vaterland* 4 (Jan.–Feb. 1922): 47–49.

Spieser, Friedrich. *Kampfbriefe aus dem Elsass.* Berlin, 1941.

———. *Tausend Brücken: Eine Erzählung aus dem Schicksal eines Landes.* Ed. Agnes Gräfin Dohna. Stuttgart, 1956.

Spindler, Charles. *L'Alsace pendant la guerre.* Strasbourg, 1925.

"Sport scolaire et politique." *L'Alsace Française* 18 (July 1938): 183–84.

Springer, Anton. *Aus meinem Leben*. Berlin, 1892.

————. "Festrede Anton Springers gehalten am 1. Mai 1872." In *Alte Strassburger Universitätsreden*, ed. Vorstand der losen Vereinigung ehemaligen Strassburger Dozenten und Studenten, 15–24. Frankfurt am Main, 1932.

Stadler, Ernst. *Dichtungen: Gedichte und Übertragungen mit einer Auswahl der kleinen kritischen Schriften und Briefen*. 2 vols. Comp. Karl Ludwig Schneider. Hamburg, [1954].

Stadtler, Eduard. *Jugendschicksale 1886–1914*. Düsseldorf, 1935.

Stählin, Karl. *Geschichte Elsass-Lothringens*. Munich, 1920.

Stein, Johannes. "Aus der Geschichte der Strassburger Medizin." In *Zur Geschichte der deutschen Universität Strassburg*, 149–211. Strasbourg, [1941].

Stevenson, D. *French War Aims against Germany 1914–1919*. Oxford, 1982.

Stieda, Wilhelm. "Zur Erinnerung an Gustav Schmoller und seine Strassburger Zeit." *Schmollers Jahrbuch* 45, no. 4 (1921): 219–57.

Stinchcombe, Arthur L. "Social Structure and Politics." In *Handbook of Political Science*, vol. 3, ed. Fred I. Greenstein and Nelson W. Polsby, 557–622. Reading, Mass., 1975.

Storm, Theodor, and Erich Schmidt. *Theodor Storm–Erich Schmidt Briefwechsel*, vols. 1 and 2, ed. Karl Ernst Laage. Berlin (W.), 1972–76.

"Der Strassburger Betrug." *Tägliche Rundschau* (Berlin), 22 Jan. 1913.

*Strassburger Correspondenz*, 1901–11.

"Die Strassburger Festtage." *Allgemeine Zeitung* (Augsburg), Beilage, 8 May 1872.

"Strassburger Gemeinderat: Sturm im Gemeindeparlament?" *E. L. Z.* (Strasbourg), 4 Feb. 1930.

*Strassburger Post*, 1887–1901.

"Strassburger Nachrichten." *Strassburger Post*, 30 Oct. 1901.

"Strassburger Studentenleben." *Die Zukunft* 1 (25 July 1925), Beilage.

"Die Strassburger Universität." *Schweizerische Monatshefte für Politik und Kultur* 1 (Sept. 1921): 282.

*Strassburger Universitäts-Taschenbuch: Sommer-Semester 1893*. Strasbourg, n.d.

"Strassburger Universitätsfragen." *Allgemeine Zeitung* (Munich), 22 Nov. 1922.

Strauss, David Friedrich. *Ausgewählte Briefe*. Ed. Eduard Zeller. Bonn, 1895.

Streitberger, Ingeborg. *Der königliche Prätor von Strassburg 1685–1789: Freie Stadt im absoluten Staat*. Wiesbaden, 1961.

Strohl, Henri. *Le protestantisme en Alsace*. Strasbourg, 1950.

————. "Rapport général sur la situation et les travaux de l'Université de Strasbourg." In University of Strasbourg, *Université de Strasbourg: 1937*, 9–29. N.p., n.d.

"Die Studenten sind wider da." *E. L. Z.* (Strasbourg), 23 Nov. 1931.

"Studentenstreiche." *La République* (Strasbourg), 23 Apr. 1921.

"Die studierende Jugend Elsass-Lothringens in den Strömungen der Zeit." *Die Zukunft* 2 (30 Jan. 1926): 3.

Suleiman, Ezra N. *Elites in French Society: The Politics of Survival.* Princeton, 1978.

*Tägliche Rundschau* (Berlin), 1901.

Tarde, Guillaume de, and Henri Massis [Agathon, pseud.]. *L'esprit de la nouvelle Sorbonne.* 2d ed. Paris, 1911.

Taufflieb, Emile Adolphe. *Souvenirs d'un enfant de l'Alsace 1870–1914.* Strasbourg, 1934.

Terracher, Adolphe. "Les cours populaires de langue française." *L'Alsace Française* 4 (13 Dec. 1924): 1175.

Theodor, Ernst [pseud.]. "Zum Abschied." *Das neue Elsass* 1 (1911): 401–2.

Thibaudet, Albert. *La république des professeurs.* Paris, 1927.

Thoma, Hans, and Georg Gerland. *Briefwechsel Hans Thoma und Georg Gerland: Ein Beitrag zur oberrheinischen Kultur am Ende des XIX. Jahrhunderts.* Ed. Joseph August Beringer. Karlsruhe, 1938.

"To the Civilized World." *Current History* 1 (1914–15): 185–87.

Tompert, Helene. *Lebensformen und Denkweisen der akademischen Welt Heidelbergs im Wilhelminischen Zeitalter.* Lübeck, 1969.

Tonnelat, Ernest. *Charles Andler: Sa vie et son oeuvre.* Paris, 1937.

Tönnies, Ferdinand. "Ferdinand Tönnies—Lebenserinnerungen aus dem Jahre 1935 an Kindheit, Schulzeit, Studium und erste Dozententätigkeit (1855–1894)." Ed. Rainer Polley. *Zeitschrift der Gesellschaft für Schleswig-Holsteinische Geschichte* 105 (1980): 187–227.

Treitschke, Heinrich von. "Briefe Treitschkes an Historiker und Politiker vom Oberrhein." Ed. Willy Andreas. *Preussische Jahrbücher* 237 (1934): 207–26; 238 (1934): 1–17, 97–105.

————. *Heinrich von Treitschkes Briefe.* Ed. Max Cornicelius. 3 vols. Leipzig, 1913–20.

————. "Was fordern wir von Frankreich?" *Preussische Jahrbücher* 26 (1870): 367–409.

Trippen, Norbert. *Theologie und Lehramt im Konflikt: Die kirchlichen Massnahmen gegen den Modernismus im Jahre 1907 und ihre Auswirkungen in Deutschland.* Freiburg im Breisgau, 1977.

Turner, R. Steven. "The *Bildungsbürgertum* and the Learned Professions in Prussia, 1770–1830: The Origins of a Class." *Histoire Sociale* 13 (1980): 105–35.

―――. "The Growth of Professorial Research in Prussia, 1818–1848—Causes and Context." *Historical Studies in the Physical Sciences* 3 (1971): 137–82.

―――. "The Prussian Universities and the Research Imperative, 1806–1848." Ph.D. diss., Princeton University, 1973.

―――. "University Reformers and Professorial Scholarship in Germany, 1760–1806." In *The University in Society,* vol. 2, ed. Lawrence Stone, 495–531. Princeton, 1974.

Ulrich, Paul. "L'étudiant alsacien avant la guerre, l'un des principaux obstacles à la germanisation." *Echo du Cercle,* 22 Nov. 1919, 32–39.

Umfrid, Otto. "Mobilmachung der Kirchen gegen den Krieg." *Die Friedens-Warte* 15 (June 1913): 208–11.

"Universität, Landesbibliothek und höhere Schulen unter Charléty." *Die Zukunft* 3 (19 Mar. 1927): 5.

"Die Universität Strassburg." *Allgemeine Zeitung* (Augsburg), 13 Sept. 1871.

"Die Universität Strassburg." *Die Post* (Berlin), 15 May 1887.

"Die Universität Strassburg als Reichsinstitut." *Strassburger Post,* 6 Feb. 1906.

"Die Universität Strassburg im Landesausschuss." *Frankfurter Zeitung,* 9 Mar. 1906.

"Die Universität Strassburg in neuer Zeit." *Magazin für die Literatur des Auslandes* 40 (13 May 1871): 1.

"Die Universität Strassburg, Mommsen und Spahn." *Frankfurter Zeitung,* 3 Dec. 1901.

"Die Universität Strassburg und die Verwaltung der Reichslande." *Allgemeine Zeitung* (Munich), 16 June 1887.

"Die Universitäten Strassburg und Heidelberg." *Allgemeine Zeitung* (Augsburg), 27 Apr. 1872.

"Die Universitäts- und die Festungsfrage." *Allgemeine Zeitung* (Augsburg), 7 June 1871.

"Universitätscommission." *Allgemeine Zeitung* (Augsburg), 29 Dec. 1871.

"Universitätsfragen." *Der Elsässer* (Strasbourg), 24 May 1919.

"L'Université en chiffres." *Saisons d'Alsace,* n. s., no. 36 (1970): 537–41.

University of Basel. *Personal Verzeichnis der Universität Basel.* Basel, 1880–.

University of Nancy. *Séance de rentrée de l'Université de Nancy, 9 nov. 1899.* Nancy, 1900.

University of Strasbourg. *Amtliches Verzeichniss des Personals und der Studenten der Kaiser-Wilhelms-Universität Strassburg.* Strasbourg, 1875–1912.

―――. *Amtliches Verzeichniss des Personals und der Studenten der Universität Strassburg.* Strasbourg, 1872–75.

————. *Die Einweihung der Neubauten der Kaiser-Wilhelms-Universität Strassburg, 26–28 October 1884: Officieller Festbericht,* Strasbourg, 1884.

————. *Die Einweihung der Strassburger Universität am 1. Mai 1872: Officieller Festbericht.* Strasbourg, 1872.

————. *Kaiser Wilhelms-Universität Strassburg: Personalverzeichnis.* Strasbourg, 1912–18.

————. *Das Stiftungsfest der Kaiser-Wilhelms-Universität Strassburg.* Strasbourg, 1890–1918.

————. *Travaux de l'Université de Strasbourg pendant l'année scolaire.* Strasbourg, 1920–36.

————. *Université de Strasbourg: Fêtes d'inauguration.* Strasbourg, 1920.

————. Faculty of Letters. *De l'université aux camps de concentration: Témoignages strasbourgeois.* 2d ed. Paris, 1954.

"Unsere Vorträge." *Elsass-Lothringische Kulturfragen* 3 (1913): 394–400.

Valentini, Rudolf von. *Kaiser und Kabinettschef.* Oldenburg, 1931.

Varrentrapp, Conrad. "Die Strassburger Universität in der Zeit der französischen Revolution." *Zeitschrift für die Geschichte des Oberrheins* 52 (1898): 448–81.

Vedel, Georges. "Paul Gemaehling (1883–1962)." *Annales de l'Université de Paris* 33 (1963): 445–46.

Veil, Wolfgang H. "Strassburgs medizinische Fakultät um die Jahrhundertwende." *Deutsche Medizinische Wochenschrift* 63 (1937): 1812–15, 1850–53.

Verax [pseud.]. "Die Frequenz der Strassburger Universität." *Die Heimat* 15 (1935): 217–23, 268–72.

"Vergangenheit und Zukunft." *Strassburger Post,* 25 Jan. 1893.

Vermeil, Edmond. "Le cinquantenaire de l'Université Kaiser Wilhelm." *L'Alsace Française* 2 (13 May 1922): 369–70.

————. "L'Information allemande à Strasbourg." *Revue de Genève* 11 (1925): 917–26.

————. "L'Institut germanique de l'Université de Strasbourg." *L'Alsace Française* 7 (19 Nov. 1927): 943–44.

————. "La mission européenne de Strasbourg." In *Etudes strasbourgeoises,* 125–32. Strasbourg, 1953.

————. "L'opinion allemande et le problème alsacien." *Journal d'Alsace et de Lorraine* (Strasbourg), 10 Oct. 1920.

Vézian, Etienne. "Le Centre d'études germaniques." *L'Alsace Française* 10 (9 Nov. 1930): 389–90.

————. "La vie universitaire: Le communisme à l'université." *La France de l'Est* (Mulhouse), 14 May, 15 May 1933.

Vierhaus, Rudolf. "Bildung." In *Geschichtliche Grundbegriffe,* vol. 1, ed. Otto Brunner, Werner Conze, and Reinhart Koselleck, 502–51. Stuttgart, 1972.

Vogel, Cyrille. "La Faculté de théologie catholique de 1902 à 1918." *Revue des Sciences Religieuses* 43 (1969): 225–63.

Volger, Franz. *Elsass, Lothringen und unsere Friedensbedingungen: Eine politische Studie.* 4th ed. Anklam, 1870.

Volksbildungs-Verein zu Strassburg in Elsass. *Siebenter Jahresbericht des Volksbildungs-Vereins (Cours d'adultes) zu Strassburg i. E. über das Vereinsjahr vom 1. April 1882–83.* Strasbourg, 1883.

"Vom 50. Stiftungsfeste der Wilhelmitana." *Strassburger Post,* 29 July 1905.

"Von der Strassburger Universität." *National-Zeitung* (Berlin), 21 June 1887.

"Von der Strassburger Universität." *Die Zukunft* 3 (7 May 1927): 3.

Voss, Jürgen. *Universität, Geschichtswissenschaft und Diplomatie im Zeitalter der Aufklärung: Johann Daniel Schöpflin (1694–1771).* Munich, 1979.

*Vossische Zeitung* (Berlin), 1901.

Vossler, Otto. "Humboldts Idee der Universität." *Historische Zeitschrift* 178 (1954): 251–68.

"Le voyage à Paris du Cercle E. S." *Echo du Cercle,* 22 Nov. 1919, 14–24.

W., R. "De juris studiorum utilitate." *Strasbourg-Université* 6 (Apr. 1935): 5.

Wach, Paul. "De Alsatia." *Alsatia Academica* 1, no. 1 (1927): 10–12.

Wahl, Alfred. *Confession et comportement dans les campagnes d'Alsace et de Bade 1871–1939.* 2 vols. N.p. 1980.

———. *L'option et l'émigration des alsaciens-lorrains (1871–1872).* Paris, 1974.

———. "La question des courants annexionnistes en Allemagne et 'l'Alsace-Lorraine.'" In *L'Alsace en 1870–1871,* ed. Fernand L'Huillier, 185–210. Gap, 1971.

Waldeyer-Hartz, Wilhelm von. *Lebenserinnerungen.* Bonn, 1920.

*Der Wanderfalke* (Strasbourg), 1931–36.

Weber, Christoph. *Der "Fall Spahn" (1901): Ein Beitrag zur Wissenschafts-und Kulturdiskussion im ausgehenden 19. Jahrhundert.* Rome, 1980.

[Weber, Emil Alfred]. *Aegri Somnia: Aphorismen und Fragmente.* Strasbourg, 1900.

———. *Von der Schulbank zum Lehrstuhl: Tagebuchnotizen eines Alt-Elsassers.* Strasbourg, 1893.

Weber, Eugen. *Action Française.* Stanford, 1962.

Weber, Max. *Gesammelte Aufsätze zur Soziologie und Sozialpolitik.* Tübingen, 1924.

———. *Jugendbriefe.* Tübingen, [1936].

Wedel, Karl von. "Statthalter-Briefe aus Elsass-Lothringen: Unveröffentlichte Briefe des Grafen von Wedel an einen deutschen Professor." Ed. Friedrich Leinhard. *Der Türmer* 26 (1924): 302–6, 458–63, 533–40.

Wehler, Hans-Ulrich. "Elsass-Lothringen von 1870 bis 1918: Das 'Reichsland' als politisch-staatsrechtliche Problem des zweiten deutschen Kaiserreichs." *Zeitschrift für die Geschichte des Oberrheins* 109 (1961): 133–99.

Weil, André. "Science française?" *Nouvelle Revue Française,* 2d. ser., 3 (1955): 97–109.

Weiller, Lazare. "L'Université de Strasbourg." *Journal d'Alsace et de Lorraine* (Strasbourg), 23 June 1919.

Weisbach, Werner. *"Und Alles ist zerstorben": Erinnerungen aus der Jahrhundertwende.* Vienna, 1937.

Weiss, Georges. "L'Alsace et l'Université de Strasbourg." *Revue Scientifique* 58 (14 Aug. 1920): 466–68.

———. "Rapport de M. Weiss, doyen de la Faculté de médecine." In University of Strasbourg, *Travaux de l'Université de Strasbourg pendant l'année scolaire 1921–1922,* 49–99. Strasbourg, 1923.

Weisz, George. *The Emergence of Modern Universities in France, 1863–1914.* Princeton, 1983.

———. "The French Universities and Education for the New Professions, 1885–1914: An Episode in French University Reform." *Minerva* 17 (1979): 98–128.

———. "Reform and Conflict in French Medical Education, 1870–1914." In *The Organization of Science and Technology in France 1808–1914,* ed. Robert Fox and George Weisz, 61–94. Cambridge, 1980.

Weizsäcker, Julius. "Eine Denkschrift Julius Weizsäckers über Elsass-Lothringen vom August 1870." Ed. Gustav Anrich. *Elsass-Lothringisches Jahrbuch* 8 (1929): 285–96.

Wendel, Hermann. *Jugenderinnerungen eines Metzers.* Strasbourg, 1934.

———. "Die Stürmer: Erinnerungen aus literarische Elsass vor 30 Jahren." *Elsässisches Literatur-Blatt* 2 (3 June 1931): 4 (1 July 1931): 6.

Wentzcke, Paul. *Der deutschen Einheit Schicksalsland.* Munich, 1921.

———. "Drei Darstellungen elsass-lothringischer Geschichte." *Historische Zeitschrift* 125 (1922): 19–44.

———. "Zur Entstehungsgeschichte des Reichslandes Elsass-Lothringen." *Süddeutsche Monatshefte* 8 (May 1911): 607–26.

Wentzcke, Paul, and Julius Heyderhoff, eds. *Deutscher Liberalismus im Zeitalter Bismarcks.* 2 vols. Bonn, 1925–26.

Wheeler, Stanton. "The Structure of Formally Organized Socialization Settings." In Orville J. Brim, Jr., and Stanton Wheeler, *Socialization after Childhood: Two Essays,* 51–116. New York, 1966.

*Who's Who in France.* 11th ed., 13th ed. Paris, 1973, 1977.

Wickert, Lothar. *Theodor Mommsen: Eine Biographie.* 4 vols. Frankfurt am Main, 1959–80.

Wiegand, Wilhelm. "Elsässische Lebens-Erinnerungen." *Zeitschrift für die Geschichte des Oberrheins* 39 (1926): 84–117.

Wieger, Friedrich. *Geschichte der Medicin und ihrer Lehranstalten in Strassburg.* Strasbourg, 1885.

Wilamowitz-Möllendorff, Ulrich von. *Erinnerungen, 1848–1914.* Leipzig, [1928].

Wilhelmitana. *Die Wilhelmitana an ihrem 75. Stiftungsfest.* Strasbourg, n.d.

"Die Wilhelmitana im S. B." In Wilhelmitana, *Die Wilhelmitana an ihrem 75. Stiftungsfest,* 40–63. Strasbourg, n.d.

Will, Robert. "L'église protestante de Strasbourg: Eglise et culture, 1870–1914." *Revue d'Histoire et de Philosophie Religieuses* 32 (1952): 212–23.

———. "Les églises protestantes de Strasbourg sous le Second Empire." *Revue d'Histoire et de Philosophie Religieuses* 27 (1947): 64–90.

Windelband, Wilhelm. "Rektoratsrede Wilhelm Windelbands am 1. Mai 1897 beim 25 jährigen Jubiläum der Universität." In *Alte Strassburger Universitätsreden,* ed. Vorstand der losen Vereinigung ehemaligen Strassburger Dozenten und Studenten, 42–50. Frankfurt am Main, 1932.

Winterberg, Max. "Die politische Entwicklung Elsass-Lothringens seit Einführung der neuen Verfassung." *Die Grenzboten* 71 (23 Oct. 1912): 149–59.

Winterer, Landolin. "Le journal politique intime de Mgr Winterer." Ed. J. Wagner. *Revue Catholique d'Alsace,* n. s., 46 (1931): 15–22, 74–83, 278–89, 359–72, 444–53, 491–99, 569–84; 47 (1932): 21–38, 85–97, 157–70, 249–54.

Wittich, Werner. "Deutsche und französische Kultur im Elsass." *Revue Alsacienne Illustrée* 2 (1900): 71–92, 113–40, 177–216.

———. "Kultur- und Nationalbewusstsein im Elsass." *Revue Alsacienne Illustrée* 11 (1909): 27–36.

[Wittich, Werner]. "Pierre Bucher: Ein Erinnerungsblatt aus Freundeshand." *Neue Zeitung* (Strasbourg), 18 Feb. 1921.

Wittmer, Charles. "Les Alsaciens à l'Université de Fribourg en Suisse, 1889–1930." In *L'Alsace et la Suisse à travers les siècles,* 397–410. Strasbourg, 1952.

Wittrock, Gerhard. *Die Kathedersozialisten bis zur Eisenacher Versammlung 1872.* Berlin, 1939.

Wolf, Georges. *Das elsässische Problem.* Strasbourg, 1926.

Wolfram, Georg. "Die Bibliotheken." In *Wissenschaft, Kunst und Literatur in Elsass-Lothringen 1871–1918,* ed. Georg Wolfram, 31–58. Frankfurt am Main, 1934.

———. "Wissenschaft, Kunst und Literatur." In *Elsass-Lothringen: 1871–1918—Eine Vortragsfolge,* 75–103. Frankfurt am Main, 1938.

———. "Die wissenschaftliche Vereine in Elsass-Lothringen von 1871–1918." In *Wissenschaft, Kunst und Literatur in Elsass-Lothringen 1871–1918,* ed. Georg Wolfram, 113–38. Frankfurt am Main, 1934.

Wolfram, Georg, and Werner Gley, eds. *Elsass-Lothringer Atlas.* Frankfurt am Main, 1931.

Wollenberg, Robert. *Erinnerungen eines alten Psychiaters.* Stuttgart, 1931.

Worms, Jean-Pierre. "The French Student Movement." In *Student Politics,* ed. Seymour Martin Lipset, 267–79. New York, 1967.

Wrotnowska, Denise. "Pasteur, professeur à Strasbourg (1849–1854)." In *Comptes rendus du 92ᵉ Congrès national des sociétés savantes: Section des sciences,* vol. 1, 135–44. Paris, 1969.

Wunder, Bernd. *Privilegierung und Disziplinierung: Die Entstehung des Berufsbeamtentums in Bayern und Württemberg (1780–1825).* Munich, 1978.

Württemberg. Statistisches Landesamt. *Statistisches Handbuch für das Königreich Württemberg.* 24 vols. Stuttgart, 1886–1928.

———. Statistisches Landesamt. *Württembergische Jahrbücher für Statistik und Landeskunde.* 111 vols. Stuttgart, 1818–1938.

Wust, Peter. *Gesammelte Werke.* Ed. Wilhelm Vernekohl. 10 vols. Münster, 1963–69.

Y. "Universität und Kulturpolitik." *Der Elsässer* (Strasbourg), 21 June 1920.

Zahn-Harnack, Agnes von. *Adolf von Harnack.* Berlin, 1951.

"Zehn Jahre französische Universität in Strassburg." *Elsass-Lothringische Mitteilungen* 12 (1930): 68–69.

*Zehn Jahre Minenkrieg im Frieden: Ein neues Schuldbuch.* Bern, 1918.

Zeldin, Theodore. *France, 1848–1945.* 2 vols. Oxford, 1973–77.

Zemb, Joseph. *Témoin de son temps: Le chanoine Eugène Muller.* Paris, 1961.

Ziegler, Theobald. "Die deutsche Erbsünde des Partikularismus und das Elsass." *Schwäbischer Merkur* (Stuttgart), 10 Jan. 1911.

———. *Der deutsche Student am Ende des 19. Jahrhunderts.* Stuttgart, 1895.

———. "Nachruf für die Wissenschaftliche Gesellschaft in Strassburg." In *Adolf Michaelis: Zum Gedächtnis,* ed. Wissenschaftliche Gesellschaft in Strassburg, 14–16. Strasbourg, 1913.

Ziekursch, Johannes. *Politische Geschichte des neuen deutschen Kaiserreiches.* 3 vols. Frankfurt am Main, 1925–30.

Zind, Pierre. *Elsass-Lothringen, Alsace-Lorraine: Une nation interdite, 1870–1940*. Paris, 1979.

Zmarzlik, Hans-Günter. *Bethmann Hollweg als Reichskanzler 1909–1914*. Düsseldorf, [1957].

"Die Zukunft der Strassburger Universität." *Der Elsässer* (Strasbourg), 21 May 1919.

"Zum Geleit!" *Die Brücke* 1 (24 Apr. 1926): 1.

"Zur Einführung." In *Alte Strassburger Universitätsreden,* ed. Vorstand der losen Vereinigung ehemaligen Strassburger Dozenten und Studenten, 7–10. Frankfurt am Main, 1932.

"Zur Frage der Universität Strassburg." *Die Post* (Berlin), 21 May 1887.

"Zwanglose Briefe über deutsche Universitäten: I. Die Neugründung in Strassburg." *Allgemeine Zeitung* (Augsburg), 3 Mar. 1872, Beilage.

"Der 22. November in Strassburg." *E. L. Z.* (Strasbourg), 24 Nov. 1933, Beilage.

# Index